MERCEDES COUPES/SEDANS/WAGONS 1974-84 REPAIR MANUAL

President	Dean F. Morgantini, S.A.E.
Vice President–Finance	Barry L. Beck
Vice President–Sales	Glenn D. Potere
Executive Editor	Kevin M. G. Maher
Production Manager	Ben Greisler, S.A.E.
Project Managers	Michael Abraham, George B. Heinrich III, Will Kessler, A.S.E., Richard Schwartz
Editor	Thomas A. Mellon, S.A.E.

CHILTON™ *Automotive Books*

PUBLISHED BY **W. G. NICHOLS, INC.**

Manufactured in USA
© 1997 W. G. Nichols
1020 Andrew Drive
West Chester, PA 19380
ISBN 0-8019-9076-9
Library of Congress Catalog Card No. 97-67986
1234567890 6543210987

Contents

Contents

DRIVE TRAIN   **7**

SUSPENSION AND STEERING   **8**

BRAKES   **9**

BODY   **10**

GLOSSARY

MASTER INDEX

SAFETY NOTICE

Proper service and repair procedures are vital to the safe, reliable operation of all motor vehicles, as well as the personal safety of those performing repairs. This manual outlines procedures for servicing and repairing vehicles using safe, effective methods. The procedures contain many NOTES, CAUTIONS and WARNINGS which should be followed along with standard procedures to eliminate the possibility of personal injury or improper service which could damage the vehicle or compromise its safety.

It is important to note that the repair procedures and techniques, tools and parts for servicing motor vehicles, as well as the skill and experience of the individual performing the work vary widely. It is not possible to anticipate all of the conceivable ways or conditions under which vehicles may be serviced, or to provide cautions as to all of the possible hazards that may result. Standard and accepted safety precautions and equipment should be used when handling toxic or flammable fluids, and safety goggles or other protection should be used during cutting, grinding, chiseling, prying, or any other process that can cause material removal or projectiles.

Some procedures require the use of tools specially designed for a specific purpose. Before substituting another tool or procedure, you must be completely satisfied that neither your personal safety, nor the performance of the vehicle will be endangered.

Although information in this manual is based on industry sources and is complete as possible at the time of publication, the possibility exists that some vehicle manufacturers made later changes which could not be included here. While striving for total accuracy, W. G. Nichols, Inc. cannot assume responsibility for any errors, changes or omissions that may occur in the compilation of this data.

PART NUMBERS

Part numbers listed in this reference are not recommendations by Chilton for any product by brand name. They are references that can be used with interchange manuals and aftermarket supplier catalogs to locate each brand supplier's discrete part number.

SPECIAL TOOLS

Special tools are recommended by the vehicle manufacturer to perform their specific job. Use has been kept to a minimum, but where absolutely necessary, they are referred to in the text by the part number of the tool manufacturer. These tools can be purchased, under the appropriate part number, from your local dealer or regional distributor, or an equivalent tool can be purchased locally from a tool supplier or parts outlet. Before substituting any tool for the one recommended, read the SAFETY NOTICE at the top of this page.

ACKNOWLEDGMENTS

W. G. Nichols, Inc. expresses appreciation to Mercedes-Benz of North America, Inc., for their generous assistance.

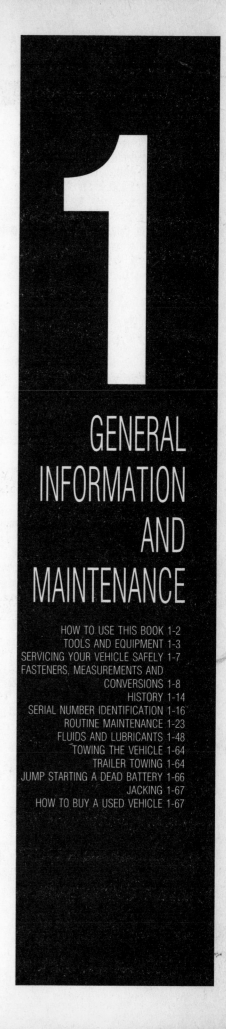

1

GENERAL INFORMATION AND MAINTENANCE

HOW TO USE THIS BOOK

Chilton's Total Car Care manual is intended to help you learn more about the inner workings of your vehicle while saving you money on its upkeep and operation.

The beginning of the book will likely be referred to the most, since that is where you will find information for maintenance and tune-up. The other sections deal with the more complex systems of your vehicle. Operating systems from engine through brakes are covered to the extent that the average do-it-yourselfer becomes mechanically involved. This book will not explain such things as rebuilding a differential for the simple reason that the expertise required and the investment in special tools make this task uneconomical. It will, however, give you detailed instructions to help you change your own brake pads and shoes, replace spark plugs, and perform many more jobs that can save you money, give you personal satisfaction and help you avoid expensive problems.

A secondary purpose of this book is a reference for owners who want to understand their vehicle and/or their mechanics better. In this case, no tools at all are required.

Where to Begin

Before removing any bolts, read through the entire procedure. This will give you the overall view of what tools and supplies will be required. There is nothing more frustrating than having to walk to the bus stop on Monday morning because you were short one bolt on Sunday afternoon. So read ahead and plan ahead. Each operation should be approached logically and all procedures thoroughly understood before attempting any work.

All sections contain adjustments, maintenance, removal and installation procedures, and in some cases, repair or overhaul procedures. When repair is not considered practical, we tell you how to remove the part and then how to install the new or rebuilt replacement. In this way, you at least save the labor costs. Backyard repair of some components is just not practical.

Avoiding Trouble

Many procedures in this book require you to "label and disconnect . . ." a group of lines, hoses or wires. Don't be lulled into thinking you can remember where everything goes—you won't. If you hook up vacuum or fuel lines incorrectly, the vehicle will run poorly, if at all. If you hook up electrical wiring incorrectly, you may instantly learn a very expensive lesson.

You don't need to know the official or engineering name for each hose or line. A piece of masking tape on the hose and a piece on its fitting will allow you to assign your own label such as the letter A or a short name. As long as you remember your own code, the lines can be reconnected by matching similar letters or names. Do remember that tape will dissolve in gasoline or other fluids; if a component is to be washed or cleaned, use another method of identification. A permanent felt-tipped marker can be very handy for marking metal parts. Remove any tape or paper labels after assembly.

Maintenance or Repair?

It's necessary to mention the difference between maintenance and repair. Maintenance includes routine inspections, adjustments, and replacement of parts which show signs of normal wear. Maintenance compensates for wear or deterioration. Repair implies that something has broken or is not working. A need for repair is often caused by lack of maintenance. Example: draining and refilling the automatic transmission fluid is maintenance recommended by the manufacturer at specific mileage intervals. Failure to do this can ruin the transmission/transaxle, requiring very expensive repairs. While no maintenance program can prevent items from breaking or wearing out, a general rule can be stated: MAINTENANCE IS CHEAPER THAN REPAIR.

Two basic mechanic's rules should be mentioned here. First, whenever the left side of the vehicle or engine is referred to, it is meant to specify the driver's side. Conversely, the right side of the vehicle means the passenger's side. Second, most screws and bolts are removed by turning counterclockwise, and tightened by turning clockwise.

Safety is always the most important rule. Constantly be aware of the dangers involved in working on an automobile and take the proper precautions. See the information in this section regarding SERVICING YOUR VEHICLE SAFELY and the SAFETY NOTICE on the acknowledgment page.

Avoiding the Most Common Mistakes

Pay attention to the instructions provided. There are 3 common mistakes in mechanical work:

1. **Incorrect order of assembly, disassembly or adjustment.** When taking something apart or putting it together, performing steps in the wrong order usually just costs you extra time; however, it CAN break something. Read the entire procedure before beginning disassembly. Perform everything in the order in which the instructions say you should, even if you can't immediately see a reason for it. When you're taking apart something that is very intricate, you might want to draw a picture of how it looks when assembled at one point in order to make sure you get everything back in its proper position. We will supply exploded views whenever possible. When making adjustments, perform them in the proper order; often, one adjustment affects another, and you cannot expect even satisfactory results unless each adjustment is made only when it cannot be changed by any other.

2. **Overtorquing (or undertorquing).** While it is more common for overtorquing to cause damage, undertorquing may allow a fastener to vibrate loose causing serious damage. Especially when dealing with aluminum parts, pay attention to torque specifications and utilize a torque wrench in assembly. If a torque figure is not available, remember that if you are using the right tool to perform the job, you will probably not have to strain yourself to get a fastener tight enough. The pitch of most threads is so slight that the tension you put on the wrench will be multiplied many times in actual force on what you are tightening. A good example of how critical torque is can be seen in the case of spark plug in-

stallation, especially where you are putting the plug into an aluminum cylinder head. Too little torque can fail to crush the gasket, causing leakage of combustion gases and consequent overheating of the plug and engine parts. Too much torque can damage the threads or distort the plug, changing the spark gap.

There are many commercial products available for ensuring that fasteners won't come loose, even if they are not torqued just right (a very common brand is Loctite®). If you're worried about getting something together tight enough to hold, but loose enough to avoid mechanical damage during assembly, one of these products might offer substantial insurance. Before choosing a threadlocking compound, read the label on the package and make sure the product is compatible with the materials, fluids, etc. involved.

3. **Crossthreading.** This occurs when a part such as a bolt is screwed into a nut or casting at the wrong angle and forced. Crossthreading is more likely to occur if access is difficult. It helps to clean and lubricate fasteners, then to start threading with the part to be installed positioned straight in. Then, start the bolt, spark plug, etc. with your fingers. If you encounter resistance, unscrew the part and start over again at a different angle until it can be inserted and turned several times without much effort. Keep in mind that many parts, especially spark plugs, have tapered threads, so that gentle turning will automatically bring the part you're threading to the proper angle, but only if you don't force it or resist a change in angle. Don't put a wrench on the part until it's been tightened a couple of turns by hand. If you suddenly encounter resistance, and the part has not seated fully, don't force it. Pull it back out to make sure it's clean and threading properly.

Always take your time and be patient; once you have some experience, working on your vehicle may well become an enjoyable hobby.

TOOLS AND EQUIPMENT

Naturally, without the proper tools and equipment it is impossible to properly service your vehicle. It would also be virtually impossible to catalog every tool that you would need to perform all of the operations in this book. Of course, It would be unwise for the amateur to rush out and buy an expensive set of tools on the theory that he/she may need one or more of them at some time.

The best approach is to proceed slowly, gathering a good quality set of those tools that are used most frequently. Don't be misled by the low cost of bargain tools. It is far better to spend a little more for better quality. Forged wrenches, 6 or 12-point sockets and fine tooth ratchets are by far preferable to their less expensive counterparts. As any good mechanic can tell you, there are few worse experiences than trying to work on a vehicle with bad tools. Your monetary savings will be far outweighed by frustration and mangled knuckles.

Begin accumulating those tools that are used most frequently: those associated with routine maintenance and tune-up. In addition to the normal assortment of screwdrivers and pliers, you should have the following tools:

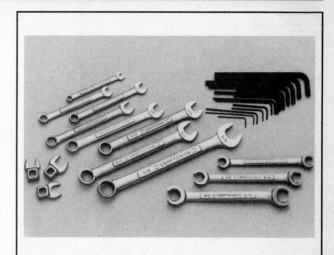

In addition to ratchets, a good set of wrenches and hex keys will be necessary

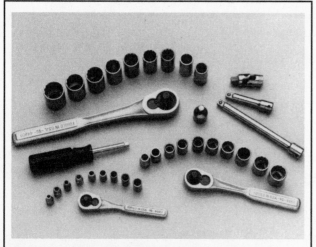

All but the most basic procedures will require an assortment of ratchets and sockets

A hydraulic floor jack and a set of jackstands are essential for lifting and supporting the vehicle

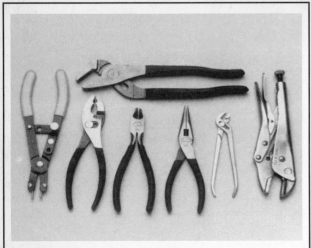

An assortment of pliers, grippers and cutters will be handy for old rusted parts and stripped bolt heads

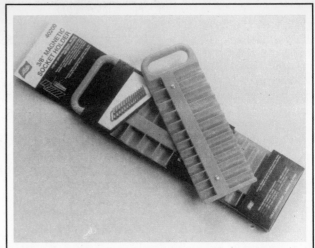

Tools from specialty manufacturers such as Lisle® are designed to make your job easier . . .

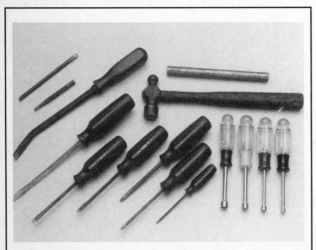

Various drivers, chisels and prybars are great tools to have in your toolbox

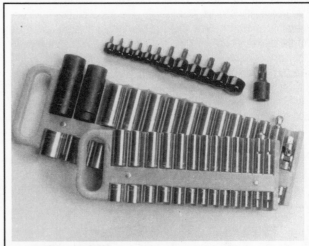

. . . these Torx® drivers and magnetic socket holders are just 2 examples of their handy products

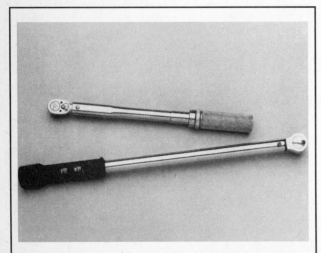

Many repairs will require the use of a torque wrench to assure the components are properly fastened

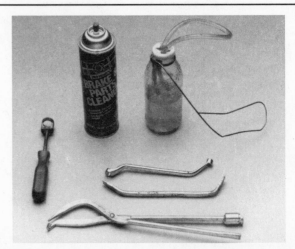

Although not always necessary, using specialized brake tools will save time

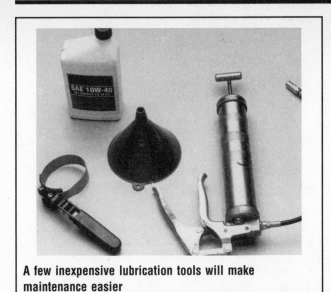

A few inexpensive lubrication tools will make maintenance easier

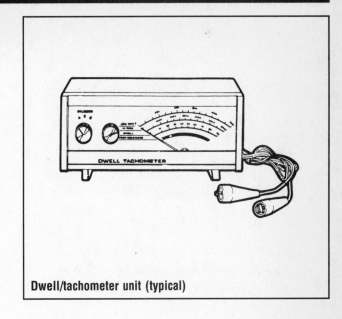

Dwell/tachometer unit (typical)

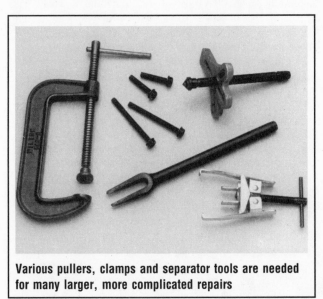

Various pullers, clamps and separator tools are needed for many larger, more complicated repairs

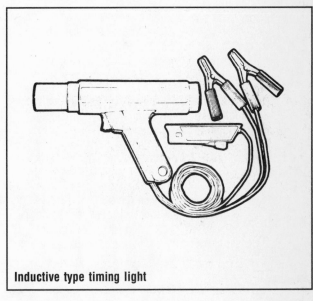

Inductive type timing light

A variety of tools and gauges should be used for spark plug gapping and installation

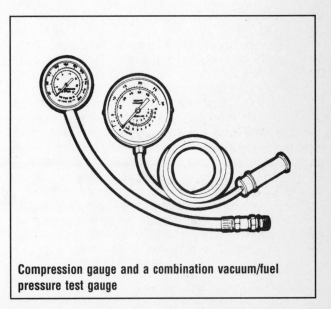

Compression gauge and a combination vacuum/fuel pressure test gauge

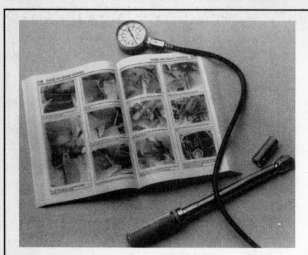

Proper information is vital, so always have a Chilton Total Car Care manual handy

• Wrenches/sockets and combination open end/box end wrenches in sizes from ⅛–¾ in. or 3mm–19mm (depending on whether your vehicle uses standard or metric fasteners) and a ¹³⁄₁₆ in. or ⅝ in. spark plug socket (depending on plug type).

➡**If possible, buy various length socket drive extensions. Universal-joint and wobble extensions can be extremely useful, but be careful when using them, as they can change the amount of torque applied to the socket.**

• Jackstands for support.
• Oil filter wrench.
• Spout or funnel for pouring fluids.
• Grease gun for chassis lubrication (unless your vehicle is not equipped with any grease fittings—for details, please refer to information on Fluids and Lubricants found later in this section).
• Hydrometer for checking the battery (unless equipped with a sealed, maintenance-free battery).
• A container for draining oil and other fluids.
• Rags for wiping up the inevitable mess.

In addition to the above items there are several others that are not absolutely necessary, but handy to have around. These include Oil Dry® (or an equivalent oil absorbent gravel—such as cat litter) and the usual supply of lubricants, antifreeze and fluids, although these can be purchased as needed. This is a basic list for routine maintenance, but only your personal needs and desire can accurately determine your list of tools.

After performing a few projects on the vehicle, you'll be amazed at the other tools and non-tools on your workbench. Some useful household items are: a large turkey baster or siphon, empty coffee cans and ice trays (to store parts), ball of twine, electrical tape for wiring, small rolls of colored tape for tagging lines or hoses, markers and pens, a note pad, golf tees (for plugging vacuum lines), metal coat hangers or a roll of mechanics's wire (to hold things out of the way), dental pick or similar long, pointed probe, a strong magnet, and a small mirror (to see into recesses and under manifolds).

A more advanced set of tools, suitable for tune-up work, can be drawn up easily. While the tools are slightly more sophisticated, they need not be outrageously expensive. There are several inexpensive tach/dwell meters on the market that are every bit as good for the average mechanic as a professional model. Just be sure that it goes to a least 1200–1500 rpm on the tach scale and that it works on 4, 6 and 8-cylinder engines. (If you own one or more vehicles with a diesel engine, a special tachometer is required since diesels don't use spark plug ignition systems). The key to these purchases is to make them with an eye towards adaptability and wide range. A basic list of tune-up tools could include:

• Tach/dwell meter.
• Spark plug wrench and gapping tool.
• Feeler gauges for valve or point adjustment. (Even if your vehicle does not use points or require valve adjustments, a feeler gauge is helpful for many repair/overhaul procedures).

A tachometer/dwell meter will ensure accurate tune-up work on vehicles without electronic ignition. The choice of a timing light should be made carefully. A light which works on the DC current supplied by the vehicle's battery is the best choice; it should have a xenon tube for brightness. On any vehicle with an electronic ignition system, a timing light with an inductive pickup that clamps around the No. 1 spark plug cable is preferred.

In addition to these basic tools, there are several other tools and gauges you may find useful. These include:

• Compression gauge. The screw-in type is slower to use, but eliminates the possibility of a faulty reading due to escaping pressure.
• Manifold vacuum gauge.
• 12V test light.
• A combination volt/ohmmeter
• Induction Ammeter. This is used for determining whether or not there is current in a wire. These are handy for use if a wire is broken somewhere in a wiring harness.

As a final note, you will probably find a torque wrench necessary for all but the most basic work. The beam type models are perfectly adequate, although the newer click types (breakaway) are easier to use. The click type torque wrenches tend to be more expensive. Also keep in mind that all types of torque wrenches should be periodically checked and/or recalibrated. You will have to decide for yourself which better fits your purpose.

Special Tools

Normally, the use of special factory tools is avoided for repair procedures, since these are not readily available for the do-it-yourself mechanic. When it is possible to perform the job with more commonly available tools, it will be pointed out, but occasionally, a special tool was designed to perform a specific function and should be used. Before substituting another tool, you should be convinced that neither your safety nor the performance of the vehicle will be compromised.

Special tools can usually be purchased from an automotive parts store or from your dealer. In some cases special tools may be available directly from the tool manufacturer.

SERVICING YOUR VEHICLE SAFELY

It is virtually impossible to anticipate all of the hazards involved with automotive maintenance and service, but care and common sense will prevent most accidents.

The rules of safety for mechanics range from "don't smoke around gasoline," to "use the proper tool(s) for the job." The trick to avoiding injuries is to develop safe work habits and to take every possible precaution.

Do's

• Do keep a fire extinguisher and first aid kit handy.
• Do wear safety glasses or goggles when cutting, drilling, grinding or prying, even if you have 20–20 vision. If you wear glasses for the sake of vision, wear safety goggles over your regular glasses.
• Do shield your eyes whenever you work around the battery. Batteries contain sulfuric acid. In case of contact with the eyes or

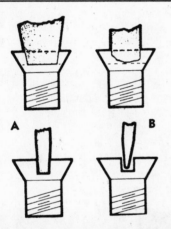

Screwdrivers should be kept in good condition to prevent injury or damage which could result if the blade slips from the screw

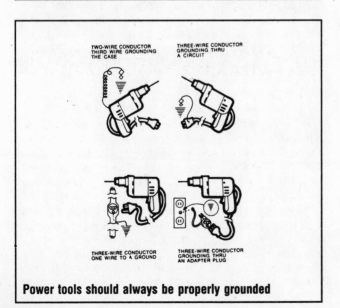

Power tools should always be properly grounded

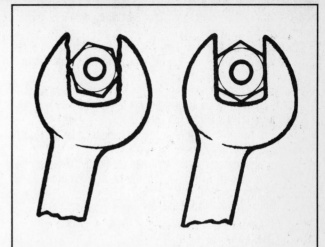

Using the correct size wrench will help prevent the possibility of rounding off a nut

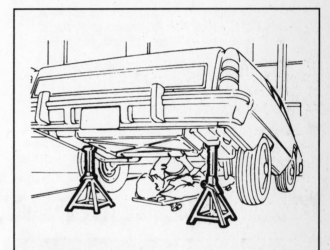

NEVER work under a vehicle unless it is supported using safety stands (jackstands)

skin, flush the area with water or a mixture of water and baking soda, then seek immediate medical attention.
• Do use safety stands (jackstands) for any undervehicle service. Jacks are for raising vehicles; jackstands are for making sure the vehicle stays raised until you want it to come down. Whenever the vehicle is raised, block the wheels remaining on the ground and set the parking brake.
• Do use adequate ventilation when working with any chemicals or hazardous materials. Like carbon monoxide, the asbestos dust resulting from some brake lining wear can be hazardous in sufficient quantities.
• Do disconnect the negative battery cable when working on the electrical system. The secondary ignition system contains EXTREMELY HIGH VOLTAGE. In some cases it can even exceed 50,000 volts.
• Do follow manufacturer's directions whenever working with potentially hazardous materials. Most chemicals and fluids are poisonous if taken internally.

• Do properly maintain your tools. Loose hammerheads, mushroomed punches and chisels, frayed or poorly grounded electrical cords, excessively worn screwdrivers, spread wrenches (open end), cracked sockets, slipping ratchets, or faulty droplight sockets can cause accidents.

• Likewise, keep your tools clean; a greasy wrench can slip off a bolt head, ruining the bolt and often harming your knuckles in the process.

• Do use the proper size and type of tool for the job at hand. Do select a wrench or socket that fits the nut or bolt. The wrench or socket should sit straight, not cocked.

• Do, when possible, pull on a wrench handle rather than push on it, and adjust your stance to prevent a fall.

• Do be sure that adjustable wrenches are tightly closed on the nut or bolt and pulled so that the force is on the side of the fixed jaw.

• Do strike squarely with a hammer; avoid glancing blows.

• Do set the parking brake and block the drive wheels if the work requires a running engine.

Don'ts

• Don't run the engine in a garage or anywhere else without proper ventilation—EVER! Carbon monoxide is poisonous; it takes a long time to leave the human body and you can build up a deadly supply of it in your system by simply breathing in a little every day. You may not realize you are slowly poisoning yourself. Always use power vents, windows, fans and/or open the garage door.

• Don't work around moving parts while wearing loose clothing. Short sleeves are much safer than long, loose sleeves. Hard-toed shoes with neoprene soles protect your toes and give a better grip on slippery surfaces. Jewelry such as watches, fancy belt buckles, beads or body adornment of any kind is not safe working around a vehicle. Long hair should be tied back under a hat or cap.

• Don't use pockets for toolboxes. A fall or bump can drive a screwdriver deep into your body. Even a rag hanging from your back pocket can wrap around a spinning shaft or fan.

• Don't smoke when working around gasoline, cleaning solvent or other flammable material.

• Don't smoke when working around the battery. When the battery is being charged, it gives off explosive hydrogen gas.

• Don't use gasoline to wash your hands; there are excellent soaps available. Gasoline contains dangerous additives which can enter the body through a cut or through your pores. Gasoline also removes all the natural oils from the skin so that bone dry hands will suck up oil and grease.

• Don't service the air conditioning system unless you are equipped with the necessary tools and training. When liquid or compressed gas refrigerant is released to atmospheric pressure it will absorb heat from whatever it contacts. This will chill or freeze anything it touches. Although refrigerant is normally non-toxic, R-12 becomes a deadly poisonous gas in the presence of an open flame. One good whiff of the vapors from burning refrigerant can be fatal.

• Don't use screwdrivers for anything other than driving screws! A screwdriver used as an prying tool can snap when you least expect it, causing injuries. At the very least, you'll ruin a good screwdriver.

• Don't use a bumper or emergency jack (that little ratchet, scissors, or pantograph jack supplied with the vehicle) for anything other than changing a flat! These jacks are only intended for emergency use out on the road; they are NOT designed as a maintenance tool. If you are serious about maintaining your vehicle yourself, invest in a hydraulic floor jack of at least a 1½ ton capacity, and at least two sturdy jackstands.

FASTENERS, MEASUREMENTS AND CONVERSIONS

Bolts, Nuts and Other Threaded Retainers

Although there are a great variety of fasteners found in the modern car or truck, the most commonly used retainer is the threaded fastener (nuts, bolts, screws, studs, etc). Most threaded retainers may be reused, provided that they are not damaged in use or during the repair. Some retainers (such as stretch bolts or torque prevailing nuts) are designed to deform when tightened or in use and should not be reinstalled.

Whenever possible, we will note any special retainers which should be replaced during a procedure. But you should always inspect the condition of a retainer when it is removed and replace any that show signs of damage. Check all threads for rust or corrosion which can increase the torque necessary to achieve the desired clamp load for which that fastener was originally selected. Additionally, be sure that the driver surface of the fastener has not been compromised by rounding or other damage. In some cases a driver surface may become only partially rounded, allowing the driver to catch in only one direction. In many of these occurrences, a fastener may be installed and tightened, but the driver would not be able to grip and loosen the fastener again. (This could lead to frustration down the line should that component ever need to be disassembled again).

If you must replace a fastener, whether due to design or damage, you must ALWAYS be sure to use the proper replacement. In all cases, a retainer of the same design, material and strength should be used. Markings on the heads of most bolts will help determine the proper strength of the fastener. The same material, thread and pitch must be selected to assure proper installation and safe operation of the vehicle afterwards.

Thread gauges are available to help measure a bolt or stud's thread. Most automotive and hardware stores keep gauges available to help you select the proper size. In a pinch, you can use another nut or bolt for a thread gauge. If the bolt you are replacing is not too badly damaged, you can select a match by finding another bolt which will thread in its place. If you find a nut which threads properly onto the damaged bolt, then use that nut to help select the replacement bolt. If however, the bolt you are replacing is so badly damaged (broken or drilled out) that its threads cannot be used as a gauge, you might start by looking for another bolt (from the same assembly or a similar location on your vehicle) which will thread into the damaged bolt's mounting. If so, the other bolt can be used to select a nut; the nut can then be used to select the replacement bolt.

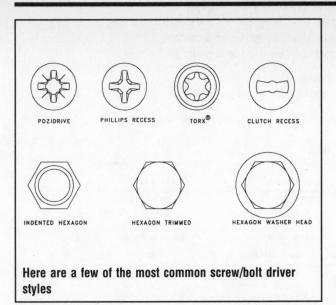

Here are a few of the most common screw/bolt driver styles

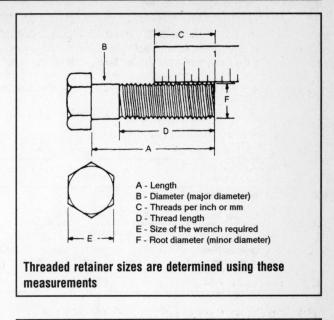

Threaded retainer sizes are determined using these measurements

A - Length
B - Diameter (major diameter)
C - Threads per inch or mm
D - Thread length
E - Size of the wrench required
F - Root diameter (minor diameter)

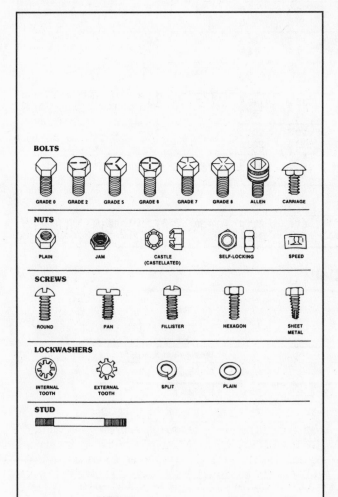

There are many different types of threaded retainers found on vehicles

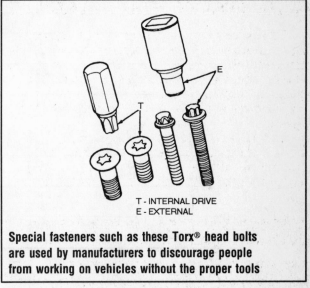

T - INTERNAL DRIVE
E - EXTERNAL

Special fasteners such as these Torx® head bolts are used by manufacturers to discourage people from working on vehicles without the proper tools

In all cases, be absolutely sure you have selected the proper replacement. Don't be shy, you can always ask the store clerk for help.

❋❋ WARNING

Be aware that when you find a bolt with damaged threads, you may also find the nut or drilled hole it was threaded into has also been damaged. If this is the case, you may have to drill and tap the hole, replace the nut or otherwise repair the threads. NEVER try to force a replacement bolt to fit into the damaged threads.

Torque

Torque is defined as the measurement of resistance to turning or rotating. It tends to twist a body about an axis of rotation. A common example of this would be tightening a threaded retainer such as a nut, bolt or screw. Measuring torque is one of the most

Standard Torque Specifications and Fastener Markings

In the absence of specific torques, the following chart can be used as a guide to the maximum safe torque of a particular size/grade of fastener.
- There is no torque difference for fine or coarse threads.
- Torque values are based on clean, dry threads. Reduce the value by 10% if threads are oiled prior to assembly.
- The torque required for aluminum components or fasteners is considerably less.

U.S. Bolts

SAE Grade Number	1 or 2			5			6 or 7		
Number of lines always 2 less than the grade number.									
Bolt Size (Inches)—(Thread)	Maximum Torque			Maximum Torque			Maximum Torque		
	Ft./Lbs.	Kgm	Nm	Ft./Lbs.	Kgm	Nm	Ft./Lbs.	Kgm	Nm
¼ — 20	5	0.7	6.8	8	1.1	10.8	10	1.4	13.5
— 28	6	0.8	8.1	10	1.4	13.6			
⁵/₁₆ — 18	11	1.5	14.9	17	2.3	23.0	19	2.6	25.8
— 24	13	1.8	17.6	19	2.6	25.7			
⅜ — 16	18	2.5	24.4	31	4.3	42.0	34	4.7	46.0
— 24	20	2.75	27.1	35	4.8	47.5			
⁷/₁₆ — 14	28	3.8	37.0	49	6.8	66.4	55	7.6	74.5
— 20	30	4.2	40.7	55	7.6	74.5			
½ — 13	39	5.4	52.8	75	10.4	101.7	85	11.75	115.2
— 20	41	5.7	55.6	85	11.7	115.2			
⁹/₁₆ — 12	51	7.0	69.2	110	15.2	149.1	120	16.6	162.7
— 18	55	7.6	74.5	120	16.6	162.7			
⅝ — 11	83	11.5	112.5	150	20.7	203.3	167	23.0	226.5
— 18	95	13.1	128.8	170	23.5	230.5			
¾ — 10	105	14.5	142.3	270	37.3	366.0	280	38.7	379.6
— 16	115	15.9	155.9	295	40.8	400.0			
⅞ — 9	160	22.1	216.9	395	54.6	535.5	440	60.9	596.5
— 14	175	24.2	237.2	435	60.1	589.7			
1 — 8	236	32.5	318.6	590	81.6	799.9	660	91.3	894.8
— 14	250	34.6	338.9	660	91.3	849.8			

Metric Bolts

Relative Strength Marking	4.6, 4.8			8.8		
Bolt Markings						
Bolt Size Thread Size x Pitch (mm)	Maximum Torque			Maximum Torque		
	Ft./Lbs.	Kgm	Nm	Ft./Lbs.	Kgm	Nm
6 x 1.0	2–3	.2–.4	3–4	3–6	.4–.8	5–8
8 x 1.25	6–8	.8–1	8–12	9–14	1.2–1.9	13–19
10 x 1.25	12–17	1.5–2.3	16–23	20–29	2.7–4.0	27–39
12 x 1.25	21–32	2.9–4.4	29–43	35–53	4.8–7.3	47–72
14 x 1.5	35–52	4.8–7.1	48–70	57–85	7.8–11.7	77–110
16 x 1.5	51–77	7.0–10.6	67–100	90–120	12.4–16.5	130–160
18 x 1.5	74–110	10.2–15.1	100–150	130–170	17.9–23.4	180–230
20 x 1.5	110–140	15.1–19.3	150–190	190–240	26.2–46.9	160–320
22 x 1.5	150–190	22.0–26.2	200–260	250–320	34.5–44.1	340–430
24 x 1.5	190–240	26.2–46.9	260–320	310–410	42.7–56.5	420–550

Standard and metric bolt torque specifications based on bolt strengths—WARNING: use only as a guide

common ways to help assure that a threaded retainer has been properly fastened.

When tightening a threaded fastener, torque is applied in three distinct areas, the head, the bearing surface and the clamp load. About 50 percent of the measured torque is used in overcoming bearing friction. This is the friction between the bearing surface of the bolt head, screw head or nut face and the base material or washer (the surface on which the fastener is rotating). Approximately 40 percent of the applied torque is used in overcoming thread friction. This leaves only about 10 percent of the applied torque to develop a useful clamp load (the force which holds a joint together). This means that friction can account for as much as 90 percent of the applied torque on a fastener.

TORQUE WRENCHES

In most applications, a torque wrench can be used to assure proper installation of a fastener. Torque wrenches come in various designs and most automotive supply stores will carry a variety to suit your needs. A torque wrench should be used any time we supply a specific torque value for a fastener. A torque wrench can also be used if you are following the general guidelines in the accompanying charts. Keep in mind that because there is no worldwide standardization of fasteners, the charts are a general guideline and should be used with caution. Again, the general rule of "if you are using the right tool for the job, you should not have to strain to tighten a fastener" applies here.

Beam Type

The beam type torque wrench is one of the most popular types. It consists of a pointer attached to the head that runs the length of the flexible beam (shaft) to a scale located near the handle. As the wrench is pulled, the beam bends and the pointer indicates the torque using the scale.

Click (Breakaway) Type

Another popular design of torque wrench is the click type. To use the click type wrench you pre-adjust it to a torque setting. Once the torque is reached, the wrench has a reflex signalling fea-

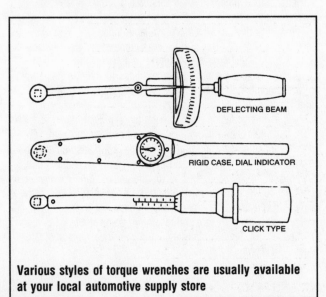

Various styles of torque wrenches are usually available at your local automotive supply store

(labels within image: DEFLECTING BEAM, RIGID CASE, DIAL INDICATOR, CLICK TYPE)

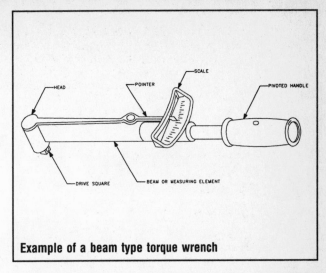

Example of a beam type torque wrench

(labels within image: HEAD, POINTER, SCALE, PIVOTED HANDLE, DRIVE SQUARE, BEAM OR MEASURING ELEMENT)

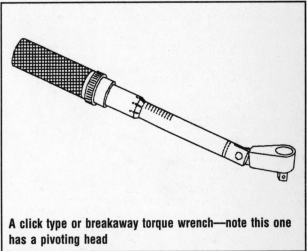

A click type or breakaway torque wrench—note this one has a pivoting head

ture that causes a momentary breakaway of the torque wrench body, sending an impulse to the operator's hand.

Pivot Head Type

Some torque wrenches (usually of the click type) may be equipped with a pivot head which can allow it to be used in areas of limited access. BUT, it must be used properly. To hold a pivot head wrench, grasp the handle lightly, and as you pull on the handle, it should be floated on the pivot point. If the handle comes in contact with the yoke extension during the process of pulling, there is a very good chance the torque readings will be inaccurate because this could alter the wrench loading point. The design of the handle is usually such as to make it inconvenient to deliberately misuse the wrench.

➡️**It should be mentioned that the use of any U-joint, wobble or extension will have an effect on the torque readings, no matter what type of wrench you are using. For the most accurate readings, install the socket directly on the wrench driver. If necessary, straight extensions (which hold a socket directly under the wrench driver) will have the least effect on the torque reading. Avoid any extension that alters the length of the wrench from the handle to the head/driving point (such as a crow's foot). U-joint or Wobble extensions can greatly affect the readings; avoid their use at all times.**

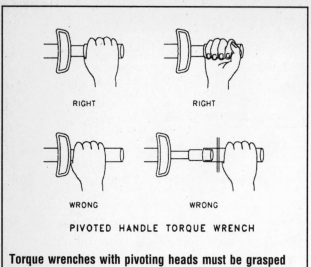

Torque wrenches with pivoting heads must be grasped and used properly to prevent an incorrect reading

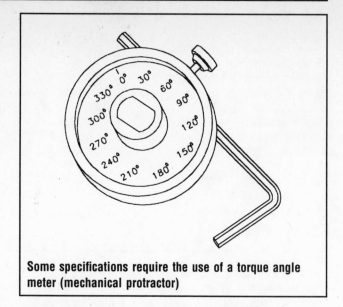

Some specifications require the use of a torque angle meter (mechanical protractor)

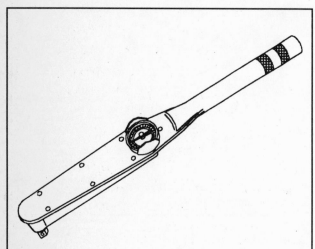

The rigid case (direct reading) torque wrench uses a dial indicator to show torque

Rigid Case (Direct Reading)

A rigid case or direct reading torque wrench is equipped with a dial indicator to show torque values. One advantage of these wrenches is that they can be held at any position on the wrench without affecting accuracy. These wrenches are often preferred because they tend to be compact, easy to read and have a great degree of accuracy.

TORQUE ANGLE METERS

Because the frictional characteristics of each fastener or threaded hole will vary, clamp loads which are based strictly on torque will vary as well. In most applications, this variance is not significant enough to cause worry. But, in certain applications, a manufacturer's engineers may determine that more precise clamp loads are necessary (such is the case with many aluminum cylinder heads). In these cases, a torque angle method of installation would be specified. When installing fasteners which are torque angle tightened, a predetermined seating torque and standard torque wrench are usually used first to remove any compliance from the joint. The fastener is then tightened the specified additional portion of a turn measured in degrees. A torque angle gauge (mechanical protractor) is used for these applications.

Standard and Metric Measurements

Throughout this manual, specifications are given to help you determine the condition of various components on your vehicle, or to assist you in their installation. Some of the most common measurements include length (in. or cm/mm), torque (ft. lbs., inch lbs. or Nm) and pressure (psi, in. Hg, kPa or mm Hg). In most cases, we strive to provide the proper measurement as determined by the manufacturer's engineers.

Though, in some cases, that value may not be conveniently measured with what is available in your toolbox. Luckily, many of the measuring devices which are available today will have two scales so the Standard or Metric measurements may easily be taken. If any of the various measuring tools which are available to you do not contain the same scale as listed in the specifications, use the accompanying conversion factors to determine the proper value.

The conversion factor chart is used by taking the given specification and multiplying it by the necessary conversion factor. For instance, looking at the first line, if you have a measurement in inches such as "free-play should be 2 in." but your ruler reads only in millimeters, multiply 2 in. by the conversion factor of 25.4 to get the metric equivalent of 50.8mm. Likewise, if the specification was given only in a Metric measurement, for example in Newton Meters (Nm), then look at the center column first. If the measurement is 100 Nm, multiply it by the conversion factor of 0.738 to get 73.8 ft. lbs.

CONVERSION FACTORS

LENGTH–DISTANCE

Inches (in.)	x 25.4	= Millimeters (mm)	x .0394	= Inches
Feet (ft.)	x .305	= Meters (m)	x 3.281	= Feet
Miles	x 1.609	= Kilometers (km)	x .0621	= Miles

VOLUME

Cubic Inches (in3)	x 16.387	= Cubic Centimeters	x .061	= in3
IMP Pints (IMP pt.)	x .568	= Liters (L)	x 1.76	= IMP pt.
IMP Quarts (IMP qt.)	x 1.137	= Liters (L)	x .88	= IMP qt.
IMP Gallons (IMP gal.)	x 4.546	= Liters (L)	x .22	= IMP gal.
IMP Quarts (IMP qt.)	x 1.201	= US Quarts (US qt.)	x .833	= IMP qt
IMP Gallons (IMP gal.)	x 1.201	= US Gallons (US gal.)	x .833	= IMP gal.
Fl. Ounces	x 29.573	= Milliliters	x .034	= Ounces
US Pints (US pt.)	x .473	= Liters (L)	x 2.113	= Pints
US Quarts (US qt.)	x .946	= Liters (L)	x 1.057	= Quarts
US Gallons (US gal.)	x 3.785	= Liters (L)	x .264	= Gallons

MASS–WEIGHT

Ounces (oz.)	x 28.35	= Grams (g)	x .035	= Ounces
Pounds (lb.)	x .454	= Kilograms (kg)	x 2.205	= Pounds

PRESSURE

Pounds Per Sq. In. (psi)	x 6.895	= Kilopascals (kPa)	x .145	= psi
Inches of Mercury (Hg)	x .4912	= psi	x 2.036	= Hg
Inches of Mercury (Hg)	x 3.377	= Kilopascals (kPa)	x .2961	= Hg
Inches of Water (H_2O)	x .07355	= Inches of Mercury	x 13.783	= H_2O
Inches of Water (H_2O)	x .03613	= psi	x 27.684	= H_2O
Inches of Water (H_2O)	x .248	= Kilopascals (kPa)	x 4.026	= H_2O

TORQUE

Pounds–Force Inches (in–lb)	x .113	= Newton Meters (N·m)	x 8.85	= in–lb
Pounds–Force Feet (ft–lb)	x 1.356	= Newton Meters (N·m)	x .738	= ft–lb

VELOCITY

Miles Per Hour (MPH)	x 1.609	= Kilometers Per Hour (KPH)	x .621	= MPH

POWER

Horsepower (Hp)	x .745	= Kilowatts	x 1.34	= Horsepower

FUEL CONSUMPTION*

Miles Per Gallon IMP (MPG)	x .354	= Kilometers Per Liter (Km/L)
Kilometers Per Liter (Km/L)	x 2.352	= IMP MPG
Miles Per Gallon US (MPG)	x .425	= Kilometers Per Liter (Km/L)
Kilometers Per Liter (Km/L)	x 2.352	= US MPG

*It is common to covert from miles per gallon (mpg) to liters/100 kilometers (1/100 km), where mpg (IMP) x 1/100 km = 282 and mpg (US) x 1/100 km = 235.

TEMPERATURE

Degree Fahrenheit (°F)	= (°C x 1.8) + 32
Degree Celsius (°C)	= (°F – 32) x .56

Standard and metric conversion factors chart

HISTORY

The history of Mercedes-Benz cars is steeped in a tradition of engineering excellence and performance. Mercedes-Benz cars have no peer for quality, craftsmanship engineering safety and performance.

While the name Mercedes-Benz is familiar to most Americans, few are aware that the firm is the world's oldest automobile manufacturer. Two mechanical engineers, Gottlieb Daimeler and Karl Benz, share the credit for simultaneously inventing the automobile. It was 1886, 22 years before Henry Ford's Model T, when they brought their revolutionary machines to life.

The name Mercedes was adopted in 1901, when a wealthy businessman Emil Jellinek, agreed to buy one entire year's production, on the condition that the car be named after his daughter, Mercedes. In 1906, a license to reproduce Mercedes automobiles in the United States was granted to the Daimler Manufacturing Company, operating at the site of the Steinway Piano Company, 939 Steinway Avenue, Long Island City, New York. The idea was to duplicate the 45 horsepower, 1906 Mercedes in the United States. Since the royalty paid for this privilege would have been less than the import duty to buy a European Mercedes, the American Mercedes became a bargain at $7500, almost $3000 less than the "Foreign" Mercedes. Unfortunately, shortly after production began, a fire destroyed the factory and the dreams of an American Mercedes.

In 1926, the firms of Daimler and Benz merged and the familiar Mercedes-Benz emblem was created from the 3-pointed star of Mercedes and the circular symbol of Benz.

To this day, Daimler-Benz has remained a company ruled by engineers, who follow the basic rule that "form is determined by function." Over 90 years of engineering "firsts" attest to their reputation for engineering excellence.

1886—Karl Benz is granted patent number 37435 for the "Patent Motorcar" on January 29. The public introduction took place on July 3, 1886.

1894—The first automobile race in the world is won by a car with a Daimler engine.

1895—The first automobile race in the U.S. is won by Benz.

1931—Mercedes-Benz pioneers the use of 4-wheel independent suspension.

1936—The first diesel engine production car is introduced (260D).

1954—Fuel injection is pioneered on the 300SL Gullwing.

1975—World's first 5-cylinder diesel passenger car (300D)

1978—World's first turbocharged 5-cylinder passenger car (300SD)

The firm's two concessions to tradition are the upright, honeycomb design radiator grille, used since 1901 on every sedan bearing the name "Mercedes," and the use of numbers (and sometimes letters) in place of names. It has been more than 40 years since Daimler-Benz made a car designated by a name instead of numbers. In their ultralogical, though sometimes confusing system, the number refers to the engine displacement in liters. Thus, the engine in the 450SEL displaces 4.5 liters; the engine in the 300D displaces 3.0 liters, and so forth. The exception to this is when a larger engine is installed in the same body at a later date. The most recent example of this was in 1978, when the 6.9 liter V8 was made available in the 450SEL. The number 6.9 (designating the engine displacement in liters) is simply tacked on the end,

making it a 450SEL 6.9, though it is called simply, the "6.9." The letters, if any, usually apply to the chassis and can be deciphered as follows:

- S—Sports Model
- E—Einspritz (German for fuel injection)
- L—Long (when used on sedans)
- SL—Super Leicht (German for Super Light) when used on sports cars
- D—Diesel
- T—Station wagon (Touring and transport)
- C—Coupe

In addition to pioneering such technical advances as fuel injected engines and the first diesel powered car, Mercedes-Benz has played a prominent role in racing. No other car manufacturer can match Mercedes' record of over 4400 competition victories—a long string stretching back to history's first auto race from Paris to Rouen in 1894. In the pursuit of land speed records, Mercedes-Benz has been equally successful. The legendary Blitzen Benz was the world's fastest automobile from 1911 to 1924, and a 1938 Mercedes-Benz record of 271.5 mph still stands as the highest speed ever recorded on a highway.

More recently, in April of 1978, a Mercedes-Benz C-111/III established 9 world speed marks while averaging 195.398 mph/14.7 mpg for 12 hours, on a test track in Italy. The most amazing part of the record, however, is that it was set by a car powered by a turbocharged, 5-cylinder diesel, similar to the engine in the 300SD, but with about twice the horsepower.

In 1968, Mercedes-Benz introduced the "New Generation" of Mercedes-Benz cars. These new sedans, the 220D/8, 220/8, 230/8 and the 250/8, share the same new body style and represent a nine year advance in automotive design (the preceding models were first introduced in 1959). The new bodies featured a sharply sloping hood with decreased frontal area, to insure a smoother flow of air over the car, greater glass area and a squared off rear deck. These new features combine to give the cars a look that is clean and simple, and at the same time, classic. The smaller sedans were followed by the 280 series and the 300 series, all the way up to the 300SEL 6.3 in 1970. All bodies share the same basic concept of clean and timeless styling.

The 350 SLC (450SLC in 1973) marked an important change in the coupe design philosophy of Mercedes-Benz. Previous coupe designs had been derived from the contemporary sedan models but the 350 and 450SLC models are based on the new "wedge" body, resulting in a vehicle which combines sports car performance with luxurious looks and comfort. The 350 and 450SLC replace the coupe and convertible sedan models which were built until 1971. The introduction of the 350 and 450SL and SLC models was followed by the introduction of the 450SE and 450SEL in 1973. These cars share the wedge body design with the newer SL and SLC series. The 450SE and 450SEL use the 4.5 liter DOHC V-8 used in the 450SL and 450SLC. The front axle is a modified design taken from the rotary engined test vehicle, the C-111.

1974 Mercedes-Benz models remained basically unchanged from those in 1973. The next new car to come along was the 280S, introduced in 1975. Basically, the 280S combined the chassis of the 450SE and SEL with the DOHC, 6-cylinder engine from the 280 and 280C models. Best described as an economical luxury car, it filled a gap between the smaller coupes and larger sedans.

In 1977, the 280S became the 280SE and the 280 became the 280E, both cars using a fuel injected version of the twin cam 6-cylinder. In addition, the first completely new Mercedes intermediate sedans since 1968 were introduced. The 240D, 300D, 230 and 280E received a scaled down version of the W123 "wedge" body used by the 450 sedans and sports cars. Also incorporated on the new intermediate sedans was the "zero-offset" front end from the larger sedans.

Late in 1977, the 6.9, successor to the 300SEL 6.3 was introduced. In all, less than 1000 of these high performance sedans were made and the entire production was bought before they were even made. Technically these were 1978 models, but to those who coughed up more than $44,000 for what may be the world's finest (certainly, the fastest) sedan, it wouldn't have mattered if they were 1977 models.

For years, the use of diesel engines was confined to large trucks. Even today, that remains the popular image of the diesel—a smoke belching, rumbling monster that didn't go very fast, but would last forever. This image of the diesel was bolstered by the occasional glimpse of a stately Mercedes diesel laboring away from a stop light. These glimpses only reinforced our view of the diesel as reliable, but slow (and ignored the fact that owners of these types of cars *habitually* drove as though they were on a journey to somewhere disagreeable). Today, the diesel has suddenly emerged as a possible alternative to the conventional spark-ignition engine.

1978 also saw the introduction of the 300CD, the coupe version of the 5-cylinder 300D introduced in 1975. This also shared the W123 chassis and body of the other intermediate sedans. But the introduction of the 300SD far overshadowed it. The 300SD is the world's first turbocharged diesel sedan, a full size car capable of more than 100 mph with an average fuel consumption of better than 26 miles per gallon. Mercedes-Benz has long been a leader in the field of diesel technology and the 300SD joins the 240D, 300D and 300SD, representing more than half of the Mercedes-Benz sales in the United States. Clearly the reputation of the diesel car is changing from one of a smoke-belching monster to that of an engine capable of powering a full-size car with good performance and economy.

The 1979 300TD marks another milestone in Mercedes-Benz history. "Estate cars" and "shooting brakes" based on various Mercedes models have been assembled by numerous custom body builders, but this is the first station wagon actually produced by Mercedes-Benz. The modern station wagon evolved from the original "shooting brake," a large open vehicle intended to carry members of hunting parties around the grand estates of Europe. In truth, Karl Benz (one of the founders of Daimler-Benz, the parent company) produced an 8-seater "shooting brake" in 1894, but it has not been until recently that there has been any interest in a Mercedes wagon. The result is the 300TD, a full-size station wagon powered by the 5-cylinder diesel engine from the 300D, combining the added load capacity and functionalism of a wagon with the handling, comfort and fuel economy of a sedan. The EPA estimates that the 300TD will deliver 23 mpg (city) and 28 mpg (highway).

The 1980 model line-up continued virtually unchanged from 1979. The only significant event was the passing from the line of the 6.9, one of the fastest and best handling sedans in the world,

a victim of limited sales and its less than tolerable effect on CAFE (Corporate Average Fuel Economy).

In 1981, the 380SL/380SLC and 380SEL replaced the 450SL and 450SEL respectively. The 380SL and SLC models were basically the same vehicle with a new 3.8 liter V-8 engine. But, the 380SEL, along with the 300SD, were built on the newly redesigned W126 chassis. The new chassis and bodywork retained the classic Mercedes-Benz styling and comfort, while further reducing fuel consumption through reduced vehicle weight and improved aerodynamics. At the same time, the normally-aspirated 5 cylinder diesel engine in the 300TD was replaced by the turbocharged version, and the designation changed to the 300TD Turbo-diesel.

The following year, 1982, was a year of refining the model line-up. The 280E and 280CE were dropped from the model line, but the major change was the installation of the turbocharged diesel engine in all diesel models except for the 240D. This brought the number of turbocharged Mercedes-Benz diesel models to four, at a time when diesel sales in the U.S. were reaching a peak, and not coincidentally, diesels were accounting for nearly ⅔ of all Mercedes-Benz U.S. sales. The 3.0 liter, 5 cylinder oil-burner had established itself, not only as a clean, efficient and tractable powerplant for even large sedans, but also as one of the best diesel engines in the world. It still accounts for nearly half of all Mercedes-Benz' U.S. sales at a time when the bottom has fallen out of the U.S. diesel market. The year 1982 also saw the introduction of the 380SEC, which was to replace the 380SLC. Mechanically identical to the 380SEL, the big coupe was marked by the flowing, graceful lines that have been a hallmark of Mercedes-Benz coupes for 20 years. Not since the days of the 280SE coupe and convertible, had the company been able to lay claim to one of the world's most beautifully sculpted cars.

The model line remained intact, with only minor mechanical changes, until 1984, when four new models were introduced.

The 240D was dropped entirely, and its place taken by an entirely new series, the first all-new Mercedes-Benz cars in 10 years. The 190 cars represent a new era of Mercedes-Benz passenger cars, offering a smaller than traditional model, with lower fuel consumption than any existing Mercedes-Benz model, along with ride and handling comparable to that of the S-class cars. The path to fuel economy was through the power train, aerodynamics, and reduced weight. The 190E 2.3 uses an all new 4 cylinder gasoline engine and the 190D 2.2 uses an all new 4 cylinder, normally aspirated diesel engine. Both models are available with 5 speed manual transmissions or 4 speed automatic transmissions. Both cars have a low drag coefficient (cd) of .35 and weigh more than 600 pounds less than the 240D.

Roadholding is excellent and traditional Mercedes-Benz design parameters—the chassis must be capable of holding the road at any speed the engine can produce—are upheld. In short, it is left to the forthcoming 16-valve Cosworth head, installed on the 190E in Europe to allow the car to live up to its potential.

The 380SEL was dropped, but the 380SE remains as a gasoline powered alternative to the 300SD. The 500SEL and 500SEC take their place at the top of the Mercedes-Benz line. Since the introduction of the 5.0 liter gasoline V8 in Europe, these cars have been finding their way to the U.S. even in U.S. emissions trim. The 5.0 liter gasoline engine makes the sedan and coupe significantly faster than their 3.8 liter cousins and fills a niche for a high-priced, high-performance car for those accustomed to serious motoring.

SERIAL NUMBER IDENTIFICATION

Since Mercedes-Benz design is a continuous process of evolution and development, the newest developments are put into production as soon as they are available, rather than waiting for a new model year. While arbitrary cut-off chassis numbers are chosen each year to designate the onset of a "new" model year, it does not necessarily mean that a 1974 car, for example, is radically different from a 1976 car. Especially it does not mean that an "old" 1974 car is obsolete.

All this is great for the owner, but it presents a problem when ordering parts. The solution is found in the comprehensive Daimler-Benz identification plates, found in various places, but usually under the hood and on the door posts. Consulting the illustration pertaining to your model, find the location of the chassis number plate, type plate and engine number. With these numbers, plus other sub-system numbers, you'll have all the information you need to identify your car.

When ordering parts, give the complete chassis or engine number, plus the number of the concerned area. The engine and chassis numbers are quite complicated, but each is a 6-digit number divided by a decimal point. The 3 digits to the left of the decimal point identify the basic chassis or engine, and the 3 digits to the right identify specific modifications. This is the reason you have to give the entire identifying number when ordering parts. The Model/Engine identification chart gives a picture of the model/engine/chassis combinations that have been imported to the U.S. that are covered by this book. Some models, of course began production before 1974 (the first year this book covers). For space reasons, these models are covered in another book, *CHILTON'S Mercedes-Benz 1968–73 Repair & Tune-Up Guide.*

➡ **Be careful with the model designations. Just because the same number is used to identify a car, it does not mean components are necessarily the same. For example, the 300CD and 300SD do not share the same chassis design, nor do the 280CE and 280SE.**

Chassis Numbers

◗ **See Figures 1 thru 7 (p. 16–20)**

Refer to the accompanying illustrations for the location of all important data concerning your car. The chassis number will usually appear something like this:

• 107.044-12-00001

By referring to the engine/vehicle identification chart, the 107.044 identifies the car as a 450SL or 450SLC. The middle number will always be either a "10" or "12". A 10 indicates a manual transmission (240D only since 1974 until the introduction of the 5 speed 190 in 1984) and a 12 indicates an automatic transmission. The rest of the numbers are a sequential serial number. Various other numbers are located throughout the vehicle, but the most important are the transmission number and the emission control plate.

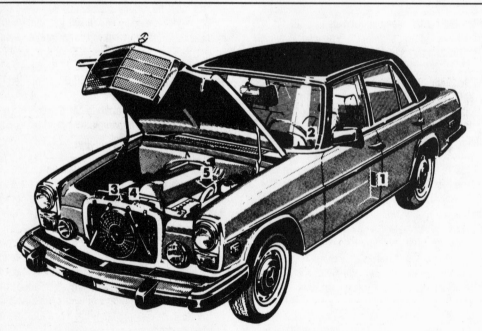

1. Certification tag (left door pillar)
2. Identification tag (left window post)
3. Chassis no.
4. Body no. and paintwork no.
5. Engine no.

Fig. 1 Locations of the identification data—1974–76 230, 240D, 280, 280C and 300D models

Engine/Vehicle Identification

Model	Chassis Type	Engine Type	No. of Cyls	Engine Description Fuel, Fuel Delivery, Valve Gear, Displacement	Production Years
190D	201.122	601.921	4	Diesel, Fuel Inj., DHC, 2197 cc	1984
190E	201.024	102.961	4	Gas, Fuel Inj., OHC, 2299 cc	1984
230	115.017	115.951	4	Gas, Carb., OHC, 2307 cc	1974–76
	123.023	115.954	4	Gas, Carb., OHC, 2307 cc	1977–78
240D	115.117	616.916	4	Diesel, Fuel Inj., OHC, 2404 cc	1974–76
	123.123	616.912	4	Diesel, Fuel Inj., OHC, 2404 cc	1977–83
280	114.060	110.921	6	Gas, Carb., DOHC, 2746 cc	1973–76
280C	114.073	110.921	6	Gas, Carb., DOHC, 2746 cc	1973–76
280E	123.033	110.984 ①	6	Gas, Fuel Inj., DOHC, 2746 cc	1977–81
280CE	123.053	110.984 ①	6	Gas, Fuel Inj., DOHC, 2746 cc	1978–81
280S	116.020	110.922	6	Gas, Carb., DOHC, 2746 cc	1975–76
280SE	116.024	110.985 ①	6	Gas, Fuel Inj., DOHC, 2746 cc	1977–80
300D	115.114	617.910	5	Diesel, Fuel Inj., OHC, 3005 cc	1975–76
	123.130	617.912	5	Diesel, Fuel Inj., OHC, 2998 cc ②	1977–81
	123.133	617.952	5	Diesel, Turbo., Fuel Inj., OHC, 2998 cc	1982–84
300CD	123.150	617.912	5	Diesel, Fuel Inj., OHC, 2998 cc ②	1978–81
	123.153	617.952	5	Diesel, Turbo., Fuel Inj., OHC, 2998 cc	1982–84
300SD	116.120	617.950	5	Diesel, Turbocharged, Fuel Inj., 2998 cc	1978–80
	126.120	617.951	5	Diesel, Turbocharged, Fuel Inj., 2998 cc	1981–84
300TD	123.190	617.912	5	Diesel, Fuel Inj., OHC, 2998 cc	1979–80
	123.190	617.953	5	Diesel, Turbocharged, Fuel Inj., 2998 cc	1981–84
380SE	126.032	116.963	8	Gas, Fuel Inj., OHC, 3839 cc	1984
380SEL	126.033	116.961	8	Gas, Fuel Inj., OHC, 3839 cc	1981–83
380SL	107.045	116.960	8	Gas, Fuel Inj., OHC, 3839 cc	1981–84
380SLC	107.025	116.960	8	Gas, Fuel Inj., OHC, 3839 cc	1981–82
380SEC	126.043	116.963	8	Gas, Fuel Inj., OHC, 3839 cc	1982–83
450SE	116.032	117.983	8	Gas, Fuel Inj., DOHC, 4520 cc	1973–75
	116.032	117.986 ①	8	Gas, Fuel Inj., DOHC, 4520 cc	1976
450SEL	116.033	117.983	8	Gas, Fuel Inj., DOHC, 4520 cc	1973–75
	116.033	117.986 ①	8	Gas, Fuel Inj. DOHC, 4520 cc	1976–80
450SL	107.044	117.982	8	Gas, Fuel Inj., DOHC, 4520 cc	1973–75
	107.044	117.985 ①	8	Gas, Fuel Inj., DOHC, 4520 cc	1976–80
450SLC	107.024	117.982	8	Gas, Fuel Inj., DOHC, 4520 cc	1973–75
	107.024	117.985 ①	8	Gas, Fuel Inj., DOHC, 4520 cc	1976–80
500SEC	126.044	117.963	8	Gas, Fuel Inj., OHC, 4973 cc	1984
500SEL	126.037	117.963	8	Gas, Fuel Inj., OHC, 4973 cc	1984
6.9	116.036	100.985 ①	8	Gas, Fuel Inj., DOHC, 6836 cc	1978–79

NOTE: *Production years given since inception, but only 1974–79 models are covered.*
Engine designations are as follows: C = 1982, D = 1983, E = 1984
  DMB 2.4D6-J501-2.4 liter Diesel   DMB 3.8V6-FSE8-3.8 liter V8 (380SEL/SEC)
  DMB 3.0D9-J508-3.0 liter Turbodiesel   DMB 3.8V6-FSL6-3.8 liter V8 (380 SEL)
① Air flow controlled fuel injection (Bosch K-Jetronic®)
② 1977–78: 3005 cc

1. Catalyst and certification tag (left door pillar)
2. Identification tag (left window post)
3. Chassis no.
4. Body no. and paintwork no.
5. Engine no. on rear engine block
6. Emission control information

Fig. 2 Locations of the identification data—1977–84 models except 190D and 190E; 300SD and 300TD; 380SE and 380SL; 450SL and 450SLC; 500SEC and 500SEL

1. Catalyst and certification tag (left door pillar)
2. Identification tag (left window post)
3. Chassis no.
4. Body no. and paintwork no.
5. Engine no. on rear engine block
6. Emission control information

Fig. 3 Locations of the identification data—380SL, 450SL and 450SLC models

1	Certification Tag (left door pillar)	3	Chassis No.	
2	Identification Tag (left window post)	4	Engine No.	
		5	Body No. and Paintwork No.	

6 Emission Control Tag

7 Information Tag
California version
Vacuum line routing for emission
control system

8 Emission Control Tag
Catalyst Information

Fig. 4 Locations of the identification data—380SE, 500SEC and 500SEL models

1 Certification Tag
(left door pillar)

2 Identification Tag
(left window post)

3 Chassis No.

4 Engine No.

5 Body No. and Paintwork No.

6 Information Tag
California version
Vacuum line routing
for emission control system

7 Emission Control Tag

8 Emission Control Tag
Catalyst Information

Fig. 5 Locations of the identification data—300TD models

1   Certification Tag
    (left door pillar)
2   Identification Tag
    (left window post)
3   Chassis No.
4   Engine No.
5   Body No. and Paintwork No.

6   Information Tag
    California version
    Vacuum line routing
    for emission control system
7   Emission Control Tag
8   Emission Control Tag
    Catalyst Information

Fig. 6 Locations of the identification data—190D and 190E models

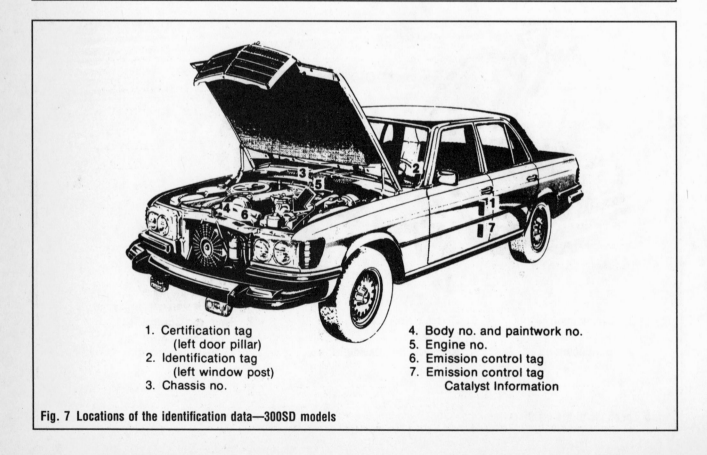

1. Certification tag
   (left door pillar)
2. Identification tag
   (left window post)
3. Chassis no.

4. Body no. and paintwork no.
5. Engine no.
6. Emission control tag
7. Emission control tag
   Catalyst Information

Fig. 7 Locations of the identification data—300SD models

The Vehicle Identification Number (VIN) can be found on the inside of the door

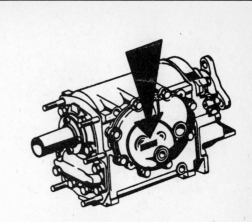

Fig. 8 The manual transmission serial numbers can be found on a pad on the left side of the transmission

Transmission Number Location

▶ **See Figure 8**

Manual transmission serial numbers are located on a pad on the left side of the transmission. Only two models covered in this book use a manual transmission, the 240D and the new 190 series. Automatic transmission serial numbers are located on a plate attached to the driver's side of the transmission.

Emission Control Label Location

▶ **See Figures 9 and 10**

The type of emission control system, model year and important tune-up data can be found on the Emission Control Information Plate, which is attached to the crossmember above the radiator. Beginning with 1977 models, there is also a plate attached to the drivers side door pillar, which tells whether the vehicle is equipped with a catalytic converter. The type of emission system can also be identified by the color coding of the plate.

Transmission Applications

Model	Automatic Transmission	Manual Transmission
190D	W4A 020	GL68/20A-5
190E	W4A 020	GL68/20B-5
230	W4B 025	—
240D (thru '80)	W4B 025	G-76/18C(4-spd.)
240D ('81 and later)	W4B 025	GL68/20A(4-spd.)
280, 280C, 280E, 280CE	W4B 025	—
280S, 280SE	W4B 025	—
300D, 300CD, 300TD	W4B 025	—
300D Turbo, 300CD Turbo	W4A 040	—
300TD Turbo 1981–83	W4A 040	—
300SD 1978–80	W4B 025	—
300SD 1981–83	W4A 040	—
380SL, 380SLC, 380SEL, 380SEC, 380SE	W4A 040	—
450SE, 450SEL, 450SL, 450SLC	W3A 040	—
500SEL, 500SEC	W4A 040	—
6.9	W3B 050	—

Fig. 9 Location of the emission control information plate (1) and catalyst plate (2)

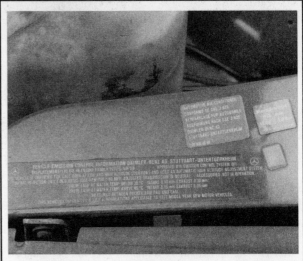

The emission control label is located under the hood

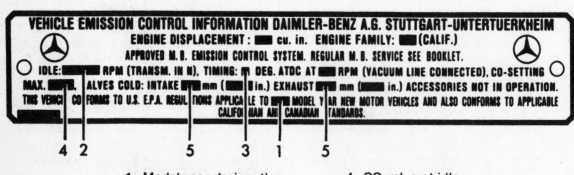

1. Model year designation
2. Idle speed
3. Idle ignition timing at rpm.
4. CO value at idle
5. Valve clearance

Fig. 10 A common emission control label contains the emission system, model year and tune-up information

ROUTINE MAINTENANCE

UNDERHOOD MAINTENANCE COMPONENT LOCATIONS—300D SHOWN

1. Battery
2. Battery cable
3. Air filter housing
4. Automatic transmission dipstick
5. Oil filter housing
6. Fuse panel
7. Brake master cylinder reservoir
8. Fuel filter
9. Power steering pump
10. Windshield washer reservoir
11. Upper radiator hose
12. Radiator
13. Radiator cap
14. Drive belt
15. Engine oil dipstick
16. Oil filler cap
17. Glow plug
18. PCV valve

Routine maintenance is the self-explanatory term used to describe the sort of periodic work necessary to keep a car in safe and reliable working order. A regular program aimed at monitoring essential systems ensures that the car's components are functioning correctly (and will continue to do so until the next inspection, one hopes), and can prevent small problems from developing into major headaches. Routine maintenance also pays off big dividends in keeping major repair costs at a minimum, extending the life of the car, and enhancing resale value, should you ever desire to part with your Mercedes.

A very definite maintenance schedule is provided by Mercedes-Benz, and must be followed, not only to keep the new car working properly. The "Maintenance Intervals" chart in this section outlines the routine maintenance which must be performed according to intervals based on accumulated mileage. Your car also came with a maintenance schedule provided by Mercedes-Benz. Adherence to these schedules will result in a longer life for your car, and will, over the long run, save you money and time.

The checks and adjustments in the following sections generally require only a few minutes of attention every few weeks; the services to be performed can be easily accomplished in a morning. The most important part of any maintenance program is regularity. The few minutes or occasional morning spent on these seemingly trivial tasks will forestall or eliminate major problems later.

Special Lubricants

AUTOMATIC LEVEL CONTROL

Mercedes-Benz recommends that only the following fluids be used in the automatic level control unit:
- Aral 1010 (must be used on 6.9)
- Gasolin 1010
- Shell Tellus T 17
- Shell Aero Fluid 4

RECOMMENDED ENGINE OILS (INCLUDING DIESEL)

There are many high quality engine oils available, but the following are particularly recommended for Mercedes-Benz engines, providing the greatest engine life and the best service. Only multi-viscosity oils are listed, and the appropriate viscosity should be chosen according to anticipated ambient temperatures. All oils are available in the U.S. unless otherwise noted:
- Castrol GTX 2 (Canada only)
- Mobiloil Special
- Mobiloil Super
- Mobil Delvac Special
- Quaker State Super Blend
- Quaker State Deluxe
- Pennzoil Z-7 Multi-Vis
- Sum Motor Oil 3800-X Series
- Texaco Havoline
- Valvoline All Climate HD
- Valvoline XLD

Air Cleaner

An air cleaner is used to keep air-borne dirt and dust out of the air flowing through the engine. Proper maintenance is vital, as a clogged element will undesirably richen the fuel mixture, restrict air flow and power, and allow excessive contamination of the oil with abrasives.

All models covered in this book are equipped with a disposable, paper cartridge air cleaner element. The filter should be checked at every tune-up (sooner if the car is operated in a dusty area). Loose dust can sometimes be removed by striking the filter against a hard surface several times or by blowing through it with compressed air (never more than 70 psi).

REMOVAL & INSTALLATION

Unscrew the nut(s) (if so equipped), lift off the housing cover and remove the filter element. Many models may also have three

To remove the air filter element, unscrew the housing cover retainer . . .

. . . then unsnap the cover retaining clips

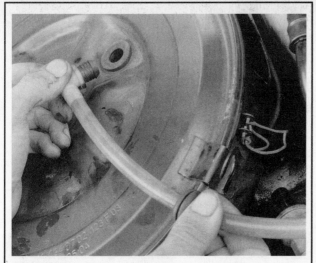

If applicable, disconnect and tag all the hoses

Remove the air filter housing cover . . .

. . . then remove the filter element from the housing

or four thumb latches which will also have to be released before removing the housing cover. Before installing the original or the replacement filter, wipe out the inside of the housing with a clean lint-free rag or paper towel soaked in kerosene. Install the paper air cleaner filter, seat the top cover on the bottom housing and tighten the nut(s). Clip on the thumb latches if so equipped.

Flame Guard Element

1974 gasoline engine models use a flame guard element in the crankcase ventilation system. On V-8's and 4-cylinder engines, the element is located in the rocker cover; on 6-cylinder engines it is located in the air filter housing.

REMOVAL & INSTALLATION

1. On V8's and 4-cylinder engines remove the crankcase breather hose from the air cleaner housing or rocker arm cover.
2. Remove the flame guard element with pliers.
3. Clean the element with gasoline and allow it to thoroughly air dry.
4. Reinstall the element with the long wire element facing inward, toward the air cleaner housing or engine.

Battery

GENERAL MAINTENANCE

All batteries, regardless of type, should be carefully secured by a battery hold-down device. If this is not done, the battery terminals or casing may crack from stress applied to the battery during vehicle operation. A battery which is not secured may allow acid to leak out, making it discharge faster; such leaking corrosive acid can also eat away components under the hood. A battery that is not sealed must be checked periodically for electrolyte level. You cannot add water to a sealed maintenance-free battery (though not all maintenance-free batteries are sealed), but a sealed battery must also be checked for proper electrolyte level as indicated by the color of the built-in hydrometer "eye."

Keep the top of the battery clean, as a film of dirt can help completely discharge a battery that is not used for long periods. A solution of baking soda and water may be used for cleaning, but be careful to flush this off with clear water. DO NOT let any of the solution into the filler holes. Baking soda neutralizes battery acid and will de-activate a battery cell.

✳✳ CAUTION

Always use caution when working on or near the battery. Never allow a tool to bridge the gap between the negative and positive battery terminals. Also, be careful not to allow a tool to provide a ground between the positive cable/terminal and any metal component on the vehicle. Either of these conditions will cause a short circuit leading to sparks and possible personal injury.

Batteries in vehicles which are not operated on a regular basis can fall victim to parasitic loads (small current drains which are

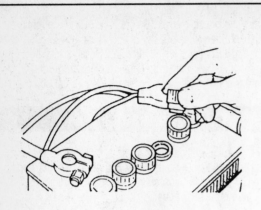

On non-maintenance free batteries, the level can be checked through the case on translucent batteries; the cell caps must be removed on other models

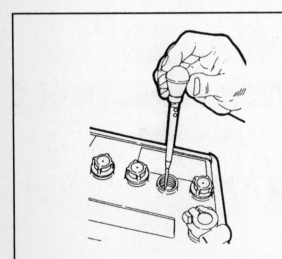

Check the specific gravity of the battery's electrolyte with a hydrometer

constantly drawing current from the battery). Normal parasitic loads may drain a battery on a vehicle that is in storage and not used for 6–8 weeks. Vehicles that have additional accessories such as a cellular phone, an alarm system or other devices that increase parasitic load may discharge a battery sooner. If the vehicle is to be stored for 6–8 weeks in a secure area and the alarm system, if present, is not necessary, the negative battery cable should be disconnected at the onset of storage to protect the battery charge.

Remember that constantly discharging and recharging will shorten battery life. Take care not to allow a battery to be needlessly discharged.

BATTERY FLUID

✳✳ CAUTION

Battery electrolyte contains sulfuric acid. If you should splash any on your skin or in your eyes, flush the affected area with plenty of clear water. If it lands in your eyes, get medical help immediately.

The fluid (sulfuric acid solution) contained in the battery cells will tell you many things about the condition of the battery. Because the cell plates must be kept submerged below the fluid level in order to operate, maintaining the fluid level is extremely important. And, because the specific gravity of the acid is an indication of electrical charge, testing the fluid can be an aid in determining if the battery must be replaced. A battery in a vehicle with a properly operating charging system should require little maintenance, but careful, periodic inspection should reveal problems before they leave you stranded.

Fluid Level

Check the battery electrolyte level at least once a month, or more often in hot weather or during periods of extended vehicle operation. On non-sealed batteries, the level can be checked either through the case on translucent batteries or by removing the cell caps on opaque-cased types. The electrolyte level in each cell

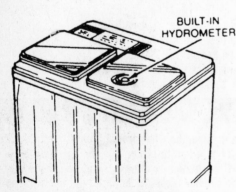

Location of indicator on sealed battery

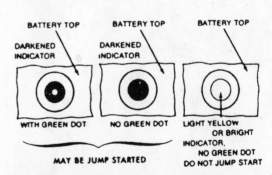

Check the appearance of the charge indicator on top of the battery before attempting a jump start; if it's not green or dark, do not jump start the car

A typical sealed (maintenance-free) battery with a built-in hydrometer—NOTE that the hydrometer eye may vary between battery manufacturers; always refer to the battery's label

should be kept filled to the split ring inside each cell, or the line marked on the outside of the case.

If the level is low, add only distilled water through the opening until the level is correct. Each cell is separate from the others, so each must be checked and filled individually. Distilled water should be used, because the chemicals and minerals found in most drinking water are harmful to the battery and could significantly shorten its life.

If water is added in freezing weather, the vehicle should be driven several miles to allow the water to mix with the electrolyte. Otherwise, the battery could freeze.

Although some maintenance-free batteries have removable cell caps for access to the electrolyte, the electrolyte condition and level on all sealed maintenance-free batteries must be checked using the built-in hydrometer "eye." The exact type of eye varies between battery manufacturers, but most apply a sticker to the battery itself explaining the possible readings. When in doubt, refer to the battery manufacturer's instructions to interpret battery condition using the built-in hydrometer.

➡ **Although the readings from built-in hydrometers found in sealed batteries may vary, a green eye usually indicates a properly charged battery with sufficient fluid level. A dark eye is normally an indicator of a battery with sufficient fluid, but one which may be low in charge. And a light or yellow eye is usually an indication that electrolyte supply has dropped below the necessary level for battery (and hydrometer) operation. In this last case, sealed batteries with an insufficient electrolyte level must usually be discarded.**

Specific Gravity

As stated earlier, the specific gravity of a battery's electrolyte level can be used as an indication of battery charge. At least once a year, check the specific gravity of the battery. It should be between 1.20 and 1.26 on the gravity scale. Most auto supply stores carry a variety of inexpensive battery testing hydrometers. These can be used on any non-sealed battery to test the specific gravity in each cell.

The battery testing hydrometer has a squeeze bulb at one end and a nozzle at the other. Battery electrolyte is sucked into the hydrometer until the float is lifted from its seat. The specific gravity is then read by noting the position of the float. If gravity is low in one or more cells, the battery should be slowly charged and checked again to see if the gravity has come up. Generally, if after charging, the specific gravity between any two cells varies more than 50 points (0.50), the battery should be replaced as it can no longer produce sufficient voltage to guarantee proper operation.

On sealed batteries, the built-in hydrometer is the only way of checking specific gravity. Again, check with your battery's manufacturer for proper interpretation of its built-in hydrometer readings.

CABLES

Once a year (or as necessary), the battery terminals and the cable clamps should be cleaned. Loosen the clamps and remove the cables, negative cable first. On batteries with posts on top, the use of a puller specially made for this purpose is recommended.

Maintenance is performed with household items and with special tools like this post cleaner

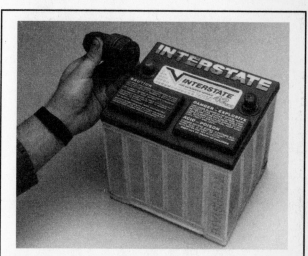

The underside of this special battery tool has a wire brush to clean post terminals

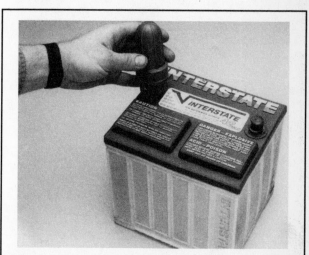

Place the tool over the terminals and twist to clean the post

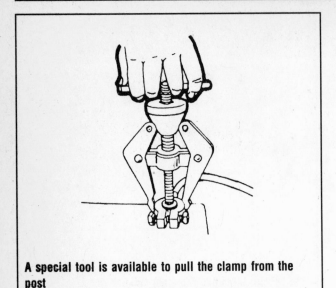

A special tool is available to pull the clamp from the post

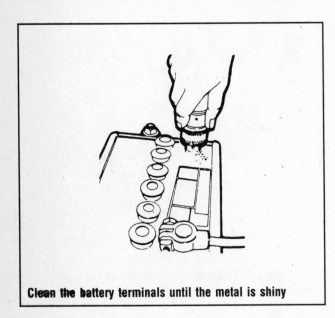

Clean the battery terminals until the metal is shiny

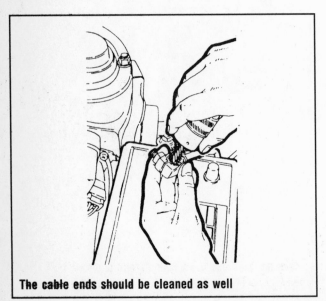

The cable ends should be cleaned as well

These are inexpensive and available in most auto parts stores. Side terminal battery cables are secured with a small bolt.

Clean the cable clamps and the battery terminal with a wire brush, until all corrosion, grease, etc., is removed and the metal is shiny. It is especially important to clean the inside of the clamp (an old knife is useful here) thoroughly, since a small deposit of foreign material or oxidation there will prevent a sound electrical connection and inhibit either starting or charging. Special tools are available for cleaning these parts, one type for conventional top post batteries and another type for side terminal batteries.

Before installing the cables, loosen the battery hold-down clamp or strap, remove the battery and check the battery tray. Clear it of any debris, and check it for soundness (the battery tray can be cleaned with a baking soda and water solution). Rust should be wire brushed away, and the metal given a couple coats of anti-rust paint. Install the battery and tighten the hold-down clamp or strap securely. Do not overtighten, as this can crack the battery case.

After the clamps and terminals are clean, reinstall the cables, negative cable last; DO NOT hammer the clamps onto post batteries. Tighten the clamps securely, but do not distort them. Give the clamps and terminals a thin external coating of grease after installation, to retard corrosion.

Check the cables at the same time that the terminals are cleaned. If the cable insulation is cracked or broken, or if the ends are frayed, the cable should be replaced with a new cable of the same length and gauge.

CHARGING

✳✳ CAUTION

The chemical reaction which takes place in all batteries generates explosive hydrogen gas. A spark can cause the battery to explode and splash acid. To avoid serious personal injury, be sure there is proper ventilation and take appropriate fire safety precautions when connecting, disconnecting, or charging a battery and when using jumper cables.

A battery should be charged at a slow rate to keep the plates inside from getting too hot. However, if some maintenance-free batteries are allowed to discharge until they are almost "dead," they may have to be charged at a high rate to bring them back to "life." Always follow the charger manufacturer's instructions on charging the battery.

REPLACEMENT

When it becomes necessary to replace the battery, select one with a rating equal to or greater than the battery originally installed. Deterioration and just plain aging of the battery cables, starter motor, and associated wires makes the battery's job harder in successive years. The slow increase in electrical resistance over time makes it prudent to install a new battery with a greater capacity than the old.

Belts

INSPECTION

Inspect the belts for signs of glazing or cracking. A glazed belt will be perfectly smooth from slippage, while a good belt will have a slight texture of fabric visible. Cracks will usually start at the inner edge of the belt and run outward. All worn or damaged drive belts should be replaced immediately. It is best to replace all drive belts at one time, as a preventive maintenance measure, during this service operation.

Under a pressure of approximately 15 lbs. (strong thumb pressure), the deflection at the middle of the longest span should be as listed in the accompanying chart.

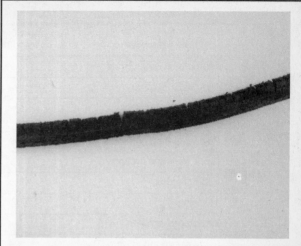

Deep cracks in this belt will cause flex, building up heat that will eventually lead to belt failure

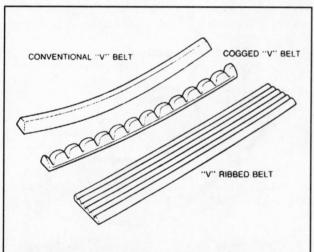

There are typically 3 types of accessory drive belts found on vehicles today

The cover of this belt is worn, exposing the critical reinforcing cords to excessive wear

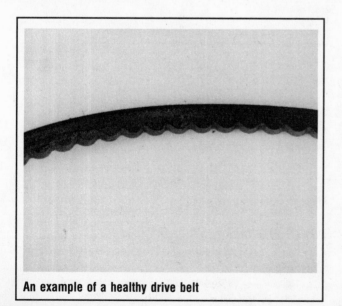

An example of a healthy drive belt

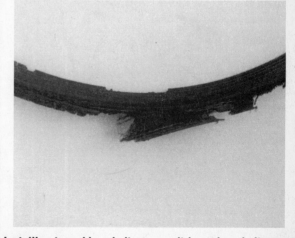

Installing too wide a belt can result in serious belt wear and/or breakage

Drive Belt Deflection (in.)

Driven Components	Diesel Engines 4 and 5 Cylinder	Gasoline Engines 4 and 6 Cylinder	Gasoline Engine 8 Cylinder
Alternator & water pump	½	½	—
Alternator	—	—	½
Water pump & power steering pump	—	—	½
Power steering pump	½	¼	—
Refrigerant compressor	½	½	¼
Vacuum pump	½	½	—
Air pump	½	½	½
Air compressor	—	—	½
Comfort hydraulic pump	—	—	¼

ADJUSTMENT

Diesel Engines

♦ **See Figures 11 and 12**

➡Unlike other diesel engines, the 190D uses only one extra-wide V-belt which drives all necessary devices. An automatic tensioner eliminates the need for any routine adjustment.

ALTERNATOR/WATER PUMP

1. Loosen the pivot bolt and adjusting bolt.
2. Adjust the belt by turning the adjusting bolt along the toothed rack.
3. Tighten the nut on the adjusting bolt and the nut on the pivot bolt. Check the belt tension.

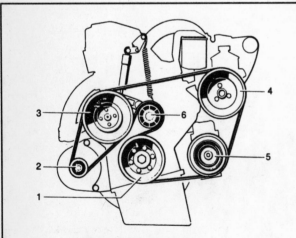

1. Crankshaft pulley
2. Alternator pulley
3. Coolant pump pulley
4. Power steering pump pulley
5. Air conditioning compressor pulley
6. Tensioning pulley

Fig. 11 Serpentine belt routing—190D models

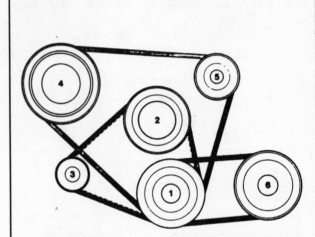

1. Crankshaft	4. Refrigerant compressor
2. Water pump	5. Tensioning roller
3. Alternator	6. Power steering pump

Fig. 12 Drive belt routing—diesel engines

A/C COMPRESSOR

The air conditioning compressor belt is adjusted with a tensioning roller. Loosen the mounting nut and swivel the roller. Tighten the attaching bolt and check the belt tension.

POWER STEERING PUMP—1974–76 MODELS

1. Loosen the bolts at the front and rear of the pump.
2. Pry the pump outward to tighten the belt. Do not pry on the pump housing.
3. Tighten the screws and check the belt tension.

POWER STEERING PUMP—1977–84 MODELS

1. Loosen the nut on the mounting stud and the nuts on the adjusting bolts.
2. Tighten the belt tension using the adjusting screw. Check the tension and tighten the pivot and mounting bolts.

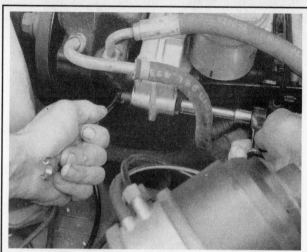

To adjust the power steering pump drive belt tension, loosen the nut on the mounting stud . . .

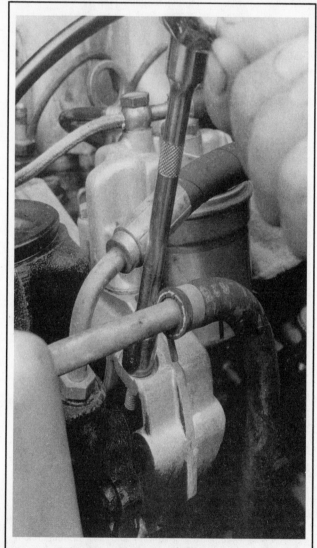

. . . then tighten or loosen the adjusting screw until the proper belt tension is reached

V8 Engines

WATER PUMP/POWER STEERING PUMP

♦ See Figures 13 and 14

1. Loosen the 3 attaching screws.
2. Loosen the pivot bolt slightly.
3. Adjust the belt tension by pushing the power steering pump outwards. Starting in 1975, adjust the belt by turning the hex headed toothed lockwasher.
4. Tighten the pivot and attaching bolts. Check the belt tension. If the belt is still in good shape but cannot be adjusted, the attaching bolt (2) can be removed and reinstalled in another hole. If you do this, be sure you replace the bolt in the original hole when you replace the belt.

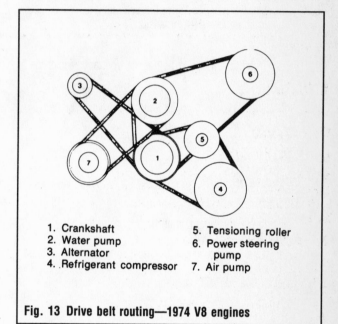

1. Crankshaft
2. Water pump
3. Alternator
4. Refrigerant compressor
5. Tensioning roller
6. Power steering pump
7. Air pump

Fig. 13 Drive belt routing—1974 V8 engines

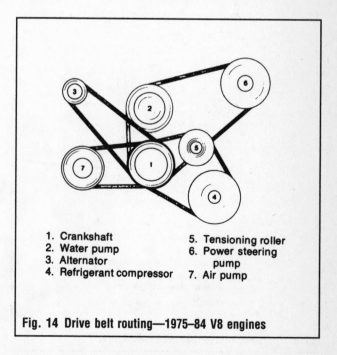

1. Crankshaft
2. Water pump
3. Alternator
4. Refrigerant compressor
5. Tensioning roller
6. Power steering pump
7. Air pump

Fig. 14 Drive belt routing—1975–84 V8 engines

ALTERNATOR

There are 2 types of adjustments on the alternator. Early types use a threaded rod and later models use a hex-headed, toothed washer.

1. On early models, loosen the 2 pivot bolts and the lockwasher. Turn the adjusting nut on the threaded rod to adjust the belt tension. Check the tension and tighten the locknut and pivot bolts.

2. On later models, loosen the pivot and attaching bolts. Adjust the tension by turning the hex-headed, toothed washer. Check the belt tension and tighten the mounting and adjusting bolts.

A/C COMPRESSOR

The air conditioning compressor belt is adjusted by means of a tensioning roller (idler pulley). Loosen the idler pulley mounting bolt and swivel the roller to adjust the belt tension. Tighten the mounting nut and check the belt tension.

AIR PUMP

1. Loosen the top mounting bolt at the front and rear of the air pump.

2. Slightly loosen the pivot bolt at the bottom of the air pump. Push the pump outwards by hand, until the belt tension is correct. Do not pry on the pump housing.

3. Tighten the mounting and pivot bolts.

230 Models

▶ **See Figure 15**

ALTERNATOR

1. Loosen the attaching bolt at the bottom of the alternator. Loosen the adjusting bolt at the top.

2. Adjust the belt tension by turning the hex-headed, toothed washer.

3. Tighten the adjusting bolt and pivot bolt. Check the belt tension.

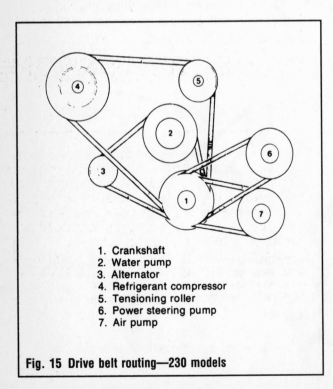

1. Crankshaft
2. Water pump
3. Alternator
4. Refrigerant compressor
5. Tensioning roller
6. Power steering pump
7. Air pump

Fig. 15 Drive belt routing—230 models

A/C COMPRESSOR

1. Loosen the attaching screw behind the idler pulley.

2. Swivel the idler pulley to adjust the belt and tighten the mounting bolt.

3. Recheck the belt tension.

POWER STEERING PUMP—1974 MODELS

1. Loosen the 2 mounting bolts and lever the pump outwards to tighten the belt. Do not pry on the pump housing.

2. Tighten the attaching bolts and check the belt tension.

POWER STEERING PUMP—1975–76 MODELS

On 1975 models, you'll have to swing the evaporative canister aside and remove the battery and tray to allow access.

1. Loosen the mounting bolts at the top and bottom.

2. Locate the adjusting nut at the rear of the power steering pump carrier. Loosen the locknut on the adjusting bolt.

3. Turn the adjusting bolt to adjust the belt tension and tighten the locknut and mounting nuts.

4. Check the belt tension and be sure there is sufficient clearance for the power steering pump supply line.

POWER STEERING PUMP—1977–78 MODELS

1. Loosen the mounting nut and bolt on the face of the pump.

2. To adjust the belt, loosen the hex-headed, toothed adjusting nut and bolt and turn the bolt.

3. Tighten the adjusting bolt/nut and the mounting nut and bolt. Check the belt tension.

VACUUM PUMP

1. Loosen the attaching bolts at the top and bottom.

2. Adjust the belt by swivelling the vacuum pump outward.

3. Tighten the attaching screws and check the belt tension.

AIR PUMP—1975–76 MODELS

1. To allow access to the air pump adjustment on 1975 models, pull the evaporative canister aside and remove the battery and tray.

2. Loosen the mounting nuts and adjust the belt tension with the threaded adjusting rod. Tighten the attaching screws and check the belt tension.

3. Replace the battery, battery tray and evaporative canister.

AIR PUMP—1977–78 MODELS

1. Loosen the mounting bolts and the nut on the rear of the hex-headed adjusting bolt.

2. To adjust the belt tension, turn the hex-headed, toothed lockwasher.

3. Check the belt tension and tighten the mounting nuts and nut on the rear of the adjusting bolt.

6-Cylinder Engine

▶ **See Figure 16**

ALTERNATOR

1. Loosen the upper (adjusting) bolt and the lower (pivot) bolts.

2. Models through 1976, and 1977 and later air conditioned models can be adjusted at either end of the upper bolt. One end is a hex-headed, toothed washer and the other end is 6 mm square. All other models are adjusted with the hex-headed toothed washer.

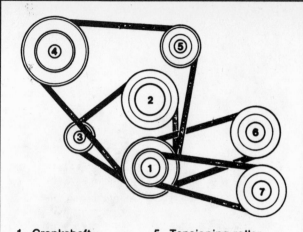

1. Crankshaft
2. Water pump
3. Alternator
4. Refrigerant compressor
5. Tensioning roller
6. Power steering pump
7. Air pump

Fig. 16 Drive belt routing—6-cyl. engines. On 1974–76 models, the air pump is below the power steering pump

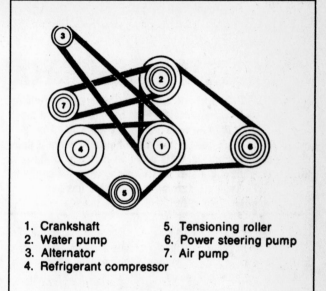

1. Crankshaft
2. Water pump
3. Alternator
4. Refrigerant compressor
5. Tensioning roller
6. Power steering pump
7. Air pump

Fig. 17 Drive belt routing—6.9 models

3. Tighten the upper and lower nuts/bolts and check the belt tension.

POWER STEERING PUMP—1974–76 MODELS

Loosen the adjusting (lower) bolt and pry the power steering pump outward to tighten the belt. Tighten the adjusting bolt and check the belt tension.

POWER STEERING PUMP—1977–81 MODELS

1. Loosen the attaching (pivot) bolt on the face of the pump.
2. Loosen the nut behind the toothed adjusting bolt.
3. Turn the hex-headed toothed lockwasher to adjust the belt.
4. Tighten the nut and pivot bolt and check the belt tension.

A/C COMPRESSOR

The air conditioning compressor is adjusted at the idler pulley. Loosen the center screw of the idler pulley and adjust the belt tension with the adjusting screw. Tighten the center screw to 12 ft. lbs.

AIR PUMP

Loosen the adjusting bolt and adjust the belt tension by prying the air pump outward. Do not pry on the air pump housing. Tighten the adjusting bolt and check the belt tension.

6.9 Models

▶ See Figure 17

POWER STEERING PUMP

1. Loosen the attaching bolts and nuts.
2. Loosen the nut behind the toothed adjuster.
3. Adjust the belt tension by turning the hex-headed, toothed washer. Tighten the adjusting nut and mounting bolts.
4. Check the belt tension.

AIR PUMP

Loosen the attaching bolt and adjust the belt tension with the adjusting screw. Tighten the attaching bolt and check the belt tension.

A/C COMPRESSOR

Loosen the pivot bolt and the bolt in front of the toothed adjuster. Turn the hex-headed toothed adjuster to adjust belt tension. Tighten the adjusting bolt and attaching bolt. Check the belt tension.

ALTERNATOR

Loosen the upper and lower nuts on the adjusting and pivot bolts. Tighten the belt by turning the toothed washer and retighten the nuts. Check the belt tension.

Hoses

INSPECTION

Upper and lower radiator hoses along with the heater hoses should be checked for deterioration, leaks and loose hose clamps at least every 15,000 miles (24,000 km). It is also wise to check the hoses periodically in early spring and at the beginning of the fall or winter when you are performing other maintenance. A quick visual inspection could discover a weakened hose which might have left you stranded if it had remained unrepaired.

Whenever you are checking the hoses, make sure the engine and cooling system are cold. Visually inspect for cracking, rotting or collapsed hoses, and replace as necessary. Run your hand along the length of the hose. If a weak or swollen spot is noted when squeezing the hose wall, the hose should be replaced.

REMOVAL & INSTALLATION

1. Remove the radiator pressure cap.

2. Position a clean container under the radiator and/or engine draincock or plug, then open the drain and allow the cooling system to drain to an appropriate level. For some upper hoses, only a little coolant must be drained. To remove hoses positioned

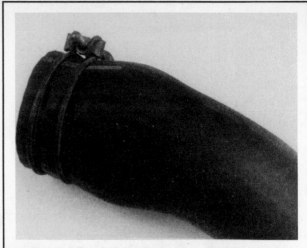

A soft spongy hose (identifiable by the swollen section) will eventually burst and should be replaced

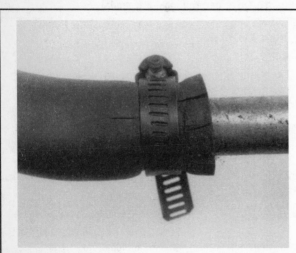

The cracks developing along this hose are a result of age-related hardening

Hoses are likely to deteriorate from the inside if the cooling system is not periodically flushed

A hose clamp that is too tight can cause older hoses to separate and tear on either side of the clamp

lower on the engine, such as a lower radiator hose, the entire cooling system must be emptied.

3. Loosen the hose clamps at each end of the hose requiring replacement. Clamps are usually either of the spring tension type (which require pliers to squeeze the tabs and loosen) or of the screw tension type (which require screw or hex drivers to loosen). Pull the clamps back on the hose away from the connection.

4. Twist, pull and slide the hose off the fitting, taking care

not to damage the neck of the component from which the hose is being removed.

➡**If the hose is stuck at the connection, do not try to insert a screwdriver or other sharp tool under the hose end in an effort to free it, as the connection and/or hose may become damaged. Heater connections especially may be easily damaged by such a procedure. If the hose is to be replaced, use a single-edged razor blade to make a slice along the portion of the hose which is stuck on the connection, perpendicular to the end of the hose. Do not cut deep so as to prevent damaging the connection. The hose can then be peeled from the connection and discarded.**

5. Clean both hose mounting connections. Inspect the condition of the hose clamps and replace them, if necessary.

To install:

6. Dip the ends of the new hose into clean engine coolant to ease installation.

7. Slide the clamps over the replacement hose, then slide the hose ends over the connections into position.

8. Position and secure the clamps at least ¼ in. (6.35mm) from the ends of the hose. Make sure they are located beyond the raised bead of the connector.

9. Close the radiator or engine drains and properly refill the cooling system with the clean drained engine coolant or a suitable mixture of ethylene glycol coolant and water.

10. If available, install a pressure tester and check for leaks. If a pressure tester is not available, run the engine until normal operating temperature is reached (allowing the system to naturally pressurize), then check for leaks.

✳✳ CAUTION

If you are checking for leaks with the system at normal operating temperature, BE EXTREMELY CAREFUL not to touch any moving or hot engine parts. Once temperature has been reached, shut the engine OFF, and check for leaks around the hose fittings and connections which were removed earlier.

Air Conditioning

➡**Be sure to consult the laws in your area before servicing the air conditioning system. In most areas, it is illegal to perform repairs involving refrigerant unless the work is done by a certified technician. Also, it is quite likely that you will not be able to purchase refrigerant without proof of certification.**

SAFETY PRECAUTIONS

There are two major hazards associated with air conditioning systems and they both relate to the refrigerant gas. First, the refrigerant gas (R-12) is an extremely cold substance. When exposed to air, it will instantly freeze any surface it comes in contact with, including your eyes. The other hazard relates to fire. Although normally non-toxic, the R-12 gas becomes highly poisonous in the presence of an open flame. One good whiff of the vapor formed by burning R-12 can be fatal. Keep all forms of fire (including cigarettes) well clear of the air conditioning system.

Because of the inherent dangers involved with working on air conditioning systems and R-12 refrigerant, these safety precautions must be strictly followed.

• Avoid contact with a charged refrigeration system, even when working on another part of the air conditioning system or vehicle. If a heavy tool comes into contact with a section of tubing or a heat exchanger, it can easily cause the relatively soft material to rupture.

• When it is necessary to apply force to a fitting which contains refrigerant, as when checking that all system couplings are securely tightened, use a wrench on both parts of the fitting involved, if possible. This will avoid putting torque on refrigerant tubing. (It is also advisable to use tube or line wrenches when tightening these flare nut fittings.)

➡**R-12 refrigerant is a chlorofluorocarbon which, when released into the atmosphere, can contribute to the depletion of the ozone layer in the upper atmosphere. Ozone filters out harmful radiation from the sun.**

• Do not attempt to discharge the system without the proper tools. Precise control is possible only when using the service gauges and a proper A/C refrigerant recovery station. Wear protective gloves when connecting or disconnecting service gauge hoses.

• Discharge the system only in a well ventilated area, as high concentrations of the gas which might accidentally escape can exclude oxygen and act as an anesthetic. When leak testing or soldering, this is particularly important, as toxic gas is formed when R-12 contacts any flame.

• Never start a system without first verifying that both service valves are properly installed, and that all fittings throughout the system are snugly connected.

• Avoid applying heat to any refrigerant line or storage vessel. Charging may be aided by using water heated to less than 125°F (50°C) to warm the refrigerant container. Never allow a refrigerant storage container to sit out in the sun, or near any other source of heat, such as a radiator or heater.

• Always wear goggles to protect your eyes when working on a system. If refrigerant contacts the eyes, it is advisable in all cases to consult a physician immediately.

• Frostbite from liquid refrigerant should be treated by first gradually warming the area with cool water, and then gently applying petroleum jelly. A physician should be consulted.

• Always keep refrigerant drum fittings capped when not in use. If the container is equipped with a safety cap to protect the valve, make sure the cap is in place when the can is not being used. Avoid sudden shock to the drum, which might occur from dropping it, or from banging a heavy tool against it. Never carry a drum in the passenger compartment of a vehicle.

• Always completely discharge the system into a suitable recovery unit before painting the vehicle (if the paint is to be baked on), or before welding anywhere near refrigerant lines.

• When servicing the system, minimize the time that any refrigerant line or fitting is open to the air in order to prevent moisture or dirt from entering the system. Contaminants such as moisture or dirt can damage internal system components. Always replace O-rings on lines or fittings which are disconnected. Prior to installation coat, but do not soak, replacement O-rings with suitable compressor oil.

GENERAL SERVICING PROCEDURES

➡**It is recommended, and possibly required by law, that a qualified technician perform the following services.**

The most important aspect of air conditioning service is the maintenance of a pure and adequate charge of refrigerant in the system. A refrigeration system cannot function properly if a significant percentage of the charge is lost. Leaks are common because the severe vibration encountered underhood in an automobile can easily cause a sufficient cracking or loosening of the air conditioning fittings; allowing, the extreme operating pressures of the system to force refrigerant out.

The problem can be understood by considering what happens to the system as it is operated with a continuous leak. Because the expansion valve regulates the flow of refrigerant to the evaporator, the level of refrigerant there is fairly constant. The receiver/drier stores any excess refrigerant, and so a loss will first appear there as a reduction in the level of liquid. As this level nears the bottom of the vessel, some refrigerant vapor bubbles will begin to appear in the stream of liquid supplied to the expansion valve. This vapor decreases the capacity of the expansion valve very little as the valve opens to compensate for its presence. As the quantity of liquid in the condenser decreases, the operating pressure will drop there and throughout the high side of the system. As the R-12 continues to be expelled, the pressure available to force the liquid through the expansion valve will continue to decrease, and, eventually, the valve's orifice will prove to be too much of a restriction for adequate flow even with the needle fully withdrawn.

At this point, low side pressure will start to drop, and a severe reduction in cooling capacity, marked by freeze-up of the evaporator coil, will result. Eventually, the operating pressure of the evaporator will be lower than the pressure of the atmosphere surrounding it, and air will be drawn into the system wherever there are leaks in the low side.

Because all atmospheric air contains at least some moisture, water will enter the system and mix with the R-12 and the oil. Trace amounts of moisture will cause sludging of the oil, and corrosion of the system. Saturation and clogging of the filter/drier, and freezing of the expansion valve orifice will eventually result. As air fills the system to a greater and greater extent, it will interfere more and more with the normal flows of refrigerant and heat.

From this description, it should be obvious that much of the repairman's focus in on detecting leaks, repairing them, and then restoring the purity and quantity of the refrigerant charge. A list of general rules should be followed in addition to all safety precautions:

- Keep all tools as clean and dry as possible.
- Thoroughly purge the service gauges/hoses of air and moisture before connecting them to the system. Keep them capped when not in use.
- Thoroughly clean any refrigerant fitting before disconnecting it, in order to minimize the entrance of dirt into the system.
- Plan any operation that requires opening the system beforehand, in order to minimize the length of time it will be exposed to open air. Cap or seal the open ends to minimize the entrance of foreign material.
- When adding oil, pour it through an extremely clean and dry

tube or funnel. Keep the oil capped whenever possible. Do not use oil that has not been kept tightly sealed.
- Use only R-12 refrigerant. Purchase refrigerant intended for use only in automatic air conditioning systems.
- Completely evacuate any system that has been opened for service, or that has leaked sufficiently to draw in moisture and air. This requires evacuating air and moisture with a good vacuum pump for at least one hour. If a system has been open for a considerable length of time it may be advisable to evacuate the system for up to 12 hours (overnight).
- Use a wrench on both halves of a fitting that is to be disconnected, so as to avoid placing torque on any of the refrigerant lines.
- When overhauling a compressor, pour some of the oil into a clean glass and inspect it. If there is evidence of dirt, metal particles, or both, flush all refrigerant components with clean refrigerant before evacuating and recharging the system. In addition, if metal particles are present, the compressor should be replaced.
- Schrader valves may leak only when under full operating pressure. Therefore, if leakage is suspected but cannot be located, operate the system with a full charge of refrigerant and look for leaks from all Schrader valves. Replace any faulty valves.

Additional Preventive Maintenance

USING THE SYSTEM

The easiest and most important preventive maintenance for your A/C system is to be sure that it is used on a regular basis. Running the system for five minutes each month (no matter what the season) will help assure that the seals and all internal components remain lubricated.

ANTIFREEZE

In order to prevent heater core freeze-up during A/C operation, it is necessary to maintain a proper antifreeze protection. Use a hand-held antifreeze tester (hydrometer) to periodically check the condition of the antifreeze in your engine's cooling system.

➡**Antifreeze should not be used longer than the manufacturer specifies.**

RADIATOR CAP

For efficient operation of an air conditioned vehicle's cooling system, the radiator cap should have a holding pressure which meets manufacturer's specifications. A cap which fails to hold these pressures should be replaced.

CONDENSER

Any obstruction of or damage to the condenser configuration will restrict the air flow which is essential to its efficient operation. It is therefore a good rule to keep this unit clean and in proper physical shape.

➡**Bug screens which are mounted in front of the condenser, (unless they are original equipment), are regarded as obstructions.**

CONDENSATION DRAIN TUBE

This single molded drain tube expels the condensation, which accumulates on the bottom of the evaporator housing, into the engine compartment. If this tube is obstructed, the air conditioning performance can be restricted and condensation buildup can spill over onto the vehicle's floor.

SYSTEM INSPECTION

➡ **R-12 refrigerant is a chlorofluorocarbon which, when released into the atmosphere, can contribute to the depletion of the ozone layer in the upper atmosphere. Ozone filters out harmful radiation from the sun.**

The easiest and often most important check for the air conditioning system consists of a visual inspection of the system components. Visually inspect the air conditioning system for refrigerant leaks, damaged compressor clutch, compressor drive belt tension and condition, plugged evaporator drain tube, blocked condenser fins, disconnected or broken wires, blown fuses, corroded connections and poor insulation.

An antifreeze tester can be used to determine the freezing and boiling levels of the coolant

A refrigerant leak will usually appear as an oily residue at the leakage point in the system. The oily residue soon picks up dust or dirt particles from the surrounding air and appears greasy. Through time, this will build up and appear to be a heavy dirt impregnated grease. Most leaks are caused by damaged or missing O-ring seals at the component connections, damaged charging valve cores or missing service gauge port caps.

For a thorough visual and operational inspection, check the following:

1. Check the surface of the radiator and condenser for dirt, leaves or other material which might block air flow.

2. Check for kinks in hoses and lines. Check the system for leaks.

3. Make sure the drive belt is under the proper tension. When the air conditioning is operating, make sure the drive belt is free of noise or slippage.

4. Make sure the blower motor operates at all appropriate positions, then check for distribution of the air from all outlets with the blower on **HIGH**.

➡ **Keep in mind that under conditions of high humidity, air discharged from the A/C vents may not feel as cold as expected, even if the system is working properly. This is because the vaporized moisture in humid air retains heat more effectively than does dry air, making the humid air more difficult to cool.**

Make sure the air passage selection lever is operating correctly. Start the engine and warm it to normal operating temperature, then make sure the hot/cold selection lever is operating correctly.

DISCHARGING, EVACUATING & CHARGING

Discharging, evacuating and charging the air conditioning system must be performed by a properly trained and certified mechanic in a facility equipped with refrigerant recovery/recycling equipment that meets SAE standards for the type of system to be serviced.

If you don't have access to the necessary equipment, we recommend that you take your vehicle to a reputable service station to have the work done. If you still wish to perform repairs on the vehicle, have them discharge the system, then take your vehicle home and perform the necessary work. When you are finished, return the vehicle to the station for evacuation and charging. Just be sure to cap ALL A/C system fittings immediately after opening them and keep them protected until the system is recharged.

Tires and Wheels

Common sense and good driving habits will afford maximum tire life. Fast starts, sudden stops and hard cornering are hard on tires and will shorten their useful life span. Make sure that you don't overload the vehicle or run with incorrect pressure in the tires. Both of these practices will increase tread wear.

➡ **For optimum tire life, keep the tires properly inflated, rotate them often and have the wheel alignment checked periodically.**

Inspect your tires frequently. Be especially careful to watch for bubbles in the tread or sidewall, deep cuts or underinflation. Replace any tires with bubbles in the sidewall. If cuts are so deep that they penetrate to the cords, discard the tire. Any cut in the sidewall of a radial tire renders it unsafe. Also look for uneven tread wear patterns that may indicate the front end is out of alignment or that the tires are out of balance.

TIRE ROTATION

Tires must be rotated periodically to equalize wear patterns that vary with a tire's position on the vehicle. Tires will also wear in an uneven way as the front steering/suspension system wears to the point where the alignment should be reset.

Rotating the tires will ensure maximum life for the tires as a set, so you will not have to discard a tire early due to wear on only part of the tread. Regular rotation is required to equalize wear.

When rotating "unidirectional tires," make sure that they always roll in the same direction. This means that a tire used on the left side of the vehicle must not be switched to the right side and vice-versa. Such tires should only be rotated front-to-rear or rear-to-front, while always remaining on the same side of the vehicle. These tires are marked on the sidewall as to the direction of rotation; observe the marks when reinstalling the tire(s).

Some styled or "mag" wheels may have different offsets front to rear. In these cases, the rear wheels must not be used up front

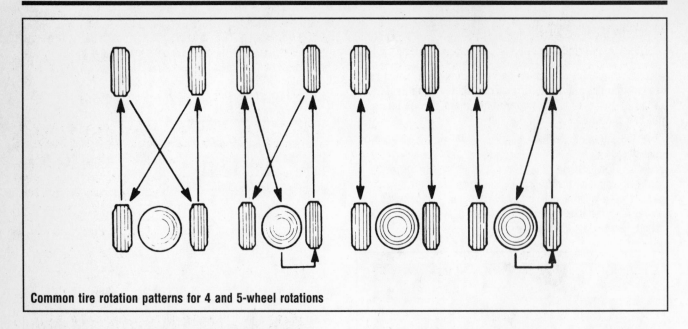

Common tire rotation patterns for 4 and 5-wheel rotations

Unidirectional tires are identifiable by sidewall arrows and/or the word "rotation"

and vice-versa. Furthermore, if these wheels are equipped with unidirectional tires, they cannot be rotated unless the tire is remounted for the proper direction of rotation.

➡**The compact or space-saver spare is strictly for emergency use. It must never be included in the tire rotation or placed on the vehicle for everyday use.**

TIRE DESIGN

For maximum satisfaction, tires should be used in sets of four. Mixing of different types (radial, bias-belted, fiberglass belted) must be avoided. In most cases, the vehicle manufacturer has designated a type of tire on which the vehicle will perform best. Your first choice when replacing tires should be to use the same type of tire that the manufacturer recommends.

When radial tires are used, tire sizes and wheel diameters should be selected to maintain ground clearance and tire load capacity equivalent to the original specified tire. Radial tires should always be used in sets of four.

✳✳ CAUTION

Radial tires should never be used on only the front axle.

When selecting tires, pay attention to the original size as marked on the tire. Most tires are described using an industry size code sometimes referred to as P-Metric. This allows the exact identification of the tire specifications, regardless of the manufacturer. If selecting a different tire size or brand, remember to check the installed tire for any sign of interference with the body or suspension while the vehicle is stopping, turning sharply or heavily loaded.

Snow Tires

Good radial tires can produce a big advantage in slippery weather, but in snow, a street radial tire does not have sufficient

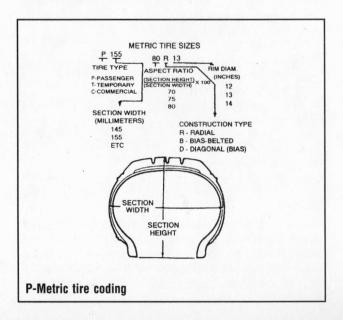

P-Metric tire coding

tread to provide traction and control. The small grooves of a street tire quickly pack with snow and the tire behaves like a billiard ball on a marble floor. The more open, chunky tread of a snow tire will self-clean as the tire turns, providing much better grip on snowy surfaces.

To satisfy municipalities requiring snow tires during weather emergencies, most snow tires carry either an M + S designation after the tire size stamped on the sidewall, or the designation "all-season." In general, no change in tire size is necessary when buying snow tires.

Most manufacturers strongly recommend the use of 4 snow tires on their vehicles for reasons of stability. If snow tires are fitted only to the drive wheels, the opposite end of the vehicle may become very unstable when braking or turning on slippery surfaces. This instability can lead to unpleasant endings if the driver can't counteract the slide in time.

Note that snow tires, whether 2 or 4, will affect vehicle handling in all non-snow situations. The stiffer, heavier snow tires will noticeably change the turning and braking characteristics of the vehicle. Once the snow tires are installed, you must re-learn the behavior of the vehicle and drive accordingly.

➡**Consider buying extra wheels on which to mount the snow tires. Once done, the "snow wheels" can be installed and removed as needed. This eliminates the potential damage to tires or wheels from seasonal removal and installation. Even if your vehicle has styled wheels, see if inexpensive steel wheels are available. Although the look of the vehicle will change, the expensive wheels will be protected from salt, curb hits and pothole damage.**

TIRE STORAGE

If they are mounted on wheels, store the tires at proper inflation pressure. All tires should be kept in a cool, dry place. If they are stored in the garage or basement, do not let them stand on a concrete floor; set them on strips of wood, a mat or a large stack of newspaper. Keeping them away from direct moisture is of paramount importance. Tires should not be stored upright, but in a flat position.

INFLATION & INSPECTION

The importance of proper tire inflation cannot be overemphasized. A tire employs air as part of its structure. It is designed around the supporting strength of the air at a specified pressure. For this reason, improper inflation drastically reduces the tires's ability to perform as intended. A tire will lose some air in day-to-day use; having to add a few pounds of air periodically is not necessarily a sign of a leaking tire.

Two items should be a permanent fixture in every glove compartment: an accurate tire pressure gauge and a tread depth gauge. Check the tire pressure (including the spare) regularly with a pocket type gauge. Too often, the gauge on the end of the air hose at your corner garage is not accurate because it suffers too much abuse. Always check tire pressure when the tires are cold, as pressure increases with temperature. If you must move the vehicle to check the tire inflation, do not drive more than a mile before checking. A cold tire is generally one that has not been driven for more than three hours.

A plate or sticker is normally provided somewhere in the vehicle (door post, hood, tailgate or trunk lid) which shows the proper pressure for the tires. Never counteract excessive pressure build-up by bleeding off air pressure (letting some air out). This will cause the tire to run hotter and wear quicker.

✷✷ CAUTION

Never exceed the maximum tire pressure embossed on the tire! This is the pressure to be used when the tire is at maximum loading, but it is rarely the correct pressure for everyday driving. Consult the owner's manual or the tire pressure sticker for the correct tire pressure.

Once you've maintained the correct tire pressures for several weeks, you'll be familiar with the vehicle's braking and handling

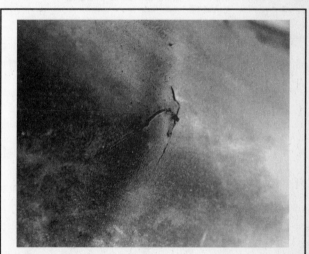

Tires should be checked frequently for any sign of puncture or damage

Tires with deep cuts, or cuts which show bulging should be replaced immediately

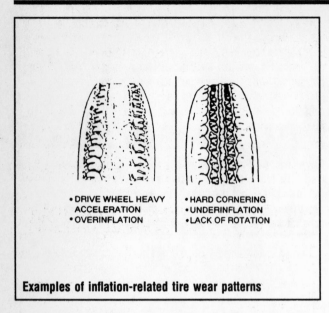

- DRIVE WHEEL HEAVY ACCELERATION
- OVERINFLATION

- HARD CORNERING
- UNDERINFLATION
- LACK OF ROTATION

Examples of inflation-related tire wear patterns

PROPERLY INFLATED · IMPROPERLY INFLATED

RADIAL TIRE

Radial tires have a characteristic sidewall bulge; don't try to measure pressure by looking at the tire. Use a quality air pressure gauge

personality. Slight adjustments in tire pressures can fine-tune these characteristics, but never change the cold pressure specification by more than 2 psi. A slightly softer tire pressure will give a softer ride but also yield lower fuel mileage. A slightly harder tire will give crisper dry road handling but can cause skidding on wet surfaces. Unless you're fully attuned to the vehicle, stick to the recommended inflation pressures.

All tires made since 1968 have built-in tread wear indicator bars that show up as ½ in. (13mm) wide smooth bands across the tire when 1/16 in. (1.5mm) of tread remains. The appearance of tread wear indicators means that the tires should be replaced. In fact, many states have laws prohibiting the use of tires with less than this amount of tread.

You can check your own tread depth with an inexpensive gauge or by using a Lincoln head penny. Slip the Lincoln penny (with Lincoln's head upside-down) into several tread grooves. If you can see the top of Lincoln's head in 2 adjacent grooves, the tire has less than 1/16 in. (1.5mm) tread left and should be replaced. You can measure snow tires in the same manner by using the "tails" side of the Lincoln penny. If you can see the top of the Lincoln memorial, it's time to replace the snow tire(s).

CARE OF SPECIAL WHEELS

If you have invested money in magnesium, aluminum alloy or sport wheels, special precautions should be taken to make sure your investment is not wasted and that your special wheels look good for the life of the vehicle.

Special wheels are easily damaged and/or scratched. Occasionally check the rims for cracking, impact damage or air leaks. If any of these are found, replace the wheel. But in order to prevent this type of damage and the costly replacement of a special wheel, observe the following precautions:

- Use extra care not to damage the wheels during removal, installation, balancing, etc. After removal of the wheels from the vehicle, place them on a mat or other protective surface. If they are to be stored for any length of time, support them on strips of wood. Never store tires and wheels upright; the tread may develop flat spots.

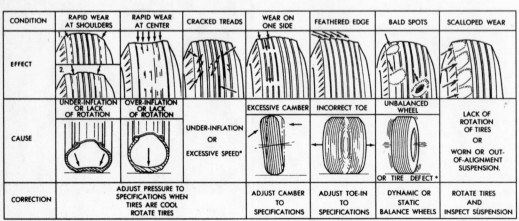

CONDITION	RAPID WEAR AT SHOULDERS	RAPID WEAR AT CENTER	CRACKED TREADS	WEAR ON ONE SIDE	FEATHERED EDGE	BALD SPOTS	SCALLOPED WEAR
EFFECT							
CAUSE	UNDER-INFLATION OR LACK OF ROTATION	OVER-INFLATION OR LACK OF ROTATION	UNDER-INFLATION OR EXCESSIVE SPEED*	EXCESSIVE CAMBER	INCORRECT TOE	UNBALANCED WHEEL OR TIRE DEFECT *	LACK OF ROTATION OF TIRES OR WORN OR OUT-OF-ALIGNMENT SUSPENSION.
CORRECTION	ADJUST PRESSURE TO SPECIFICATIONS WHEN TIRES ARE COOL ROTATE TIRES			ADJUST CAMBER TO SPECIFICATIONS	ADJUST TOE-IN TO SPECIFICATIONS	DYNAMIC OR STATIC BALANCE WHEELS	ROTATE TIRES AND INSPECT SUSPENSION

*HAVE TIRE INSPECTED FOR FURTHER USE.

Common tire wear patterns and causes

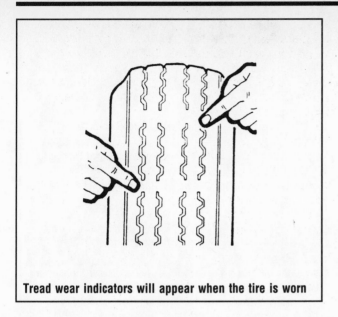

Tread wear indicators will appear when the tire is worn

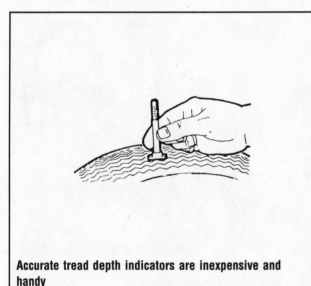

Accurate tread depth indicators are inexpensive and handy

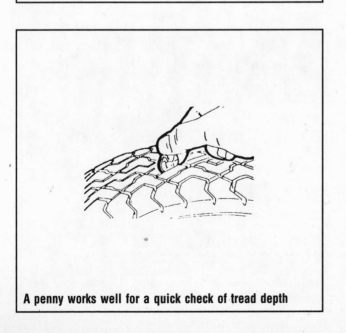

A penny works well for a quick check of tread depth

• When driving, watch for hazards; it doesn't take much to crack a wheel.

• When washing, use a mild soap or non-abrasive dish detergent (keeping in mind that detergent tends to remove wax). Avoid cleansers with abrasives or the use of hard brushes. There are many cleaners and polishes for special wheels.

• If possible, remove the wheels during the winter. Salt and sand used for snow removal can severely damage the finish of a wheel.

• Make certain the recommended lug nut torque is never exceeded or the wheel may crack. Never use snow chains on special wheels; severe scratching will occur.

Fuel Filter

REMOVAL & INSTALLATION

Gasoline Engines

4-CYLINDER CARBURETED ENGINE

1. Loosen the hose clips.
2. Remove the fuel filter.
3. Install a new filter in the direction of flow (arrow) along with new fuel hoses.
4. Replace the hose clips.
5. Check for proper sealing.

6-CYLINDER CARBURETED ENGINES

The fuel filter is located in the carburetor housing. Put some rags under the fuel return valve to absorb the inevitable gasoline spillage.

1. Unscrew the fuel return valve and plug it at the carburetor.
2. Remove the fuel filter.
3. Renew the gasket at the seal plug.
4. Install a new filter. Check for leaks.

FUEL INJECTED ENGINES—ALL MODELS

Two types of filter are used, one on the electronically controlled fuel injection and the other on the CIS fuel injection. Both are located between the rear axle and the fuel tank.

1. Unscrew the cover box.
2. Remove the pressure hoses.
3. Loosen the attaching screws and remove the filter. Remove the connecting plug from the old filter and install it on a new filter using a new gasket.
4. Install a new filter in the direction of flow.
5. Replace the attaching screws.
6. Install the pressure hoses.
7. On 1976 and later models, install the fuel filter in the holder by positioning it in the center of the transparent holder.
8. Replace the cover box and check for proper sealing.

Diesel Engines

MAIN FUEL FILTER–1974–76 240D AND 300D MODELS

▶ **See Figure 18**

1. Drain the fuel from the housing.
2. Remove the center bolt and remove the filter housing and filter.

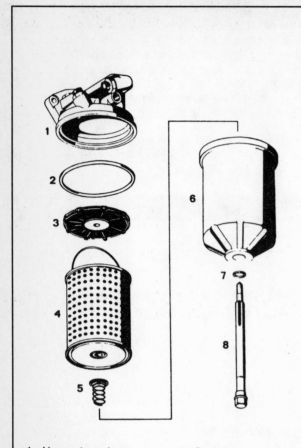

1. Upper housing
2. Rubber sealing ring
3. Filter screen
4. Filter element
5. Spring
6. Lower filter housing
7. Washer
8. Bolt

Fig. 18 View of the diesel engine fuel filter—1974–76 models. Later models use an upright filter

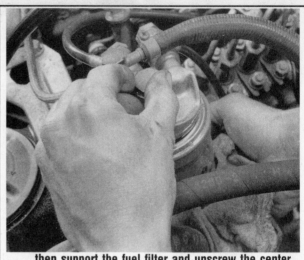

. . . then support the fuel filter and unscrew the center bolt

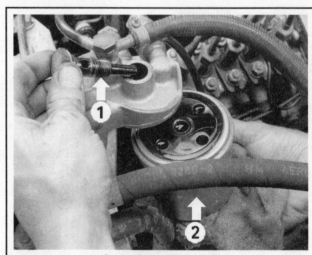

1. Center Bolt   2. Fuel Filter

Remove the filter and the center bolt

To remove the fuel filter, loosen the filter's center bolt . . .

To bleed the injection pump on 5-cyl. engines, open the bleed screw atop the filter housing . . .

. . . then operate the hand pump until the fuel emerges free of air bubbles

3. Wash the filter housing in clean diesel fuel and install a new filter element.

4. Use a new gasket in the filter cap and reassemble the filter and housing.

5. Bleed the injection pump. On 5-cylinder engines, loosen the bleed bolt on the fuel filter housing and release the manually operated delivery pump. Operate the delivery pump until the fuel emerges free of bubbles at the bleed screw. Close the bleed bolt and operate the pump until the overflow valve on the injection pump opens (a buzzing noise will be heard). Close the manual pump before starting the engine. To bleed the injection pump on 4-cylinder diesels, loosen the bleed screw on the injection pump and keep pumping the hand pump until fuel emerges free of bubbles.

➡**The 190D uses a self-bleeding fuel pump, therefore the hand pump has been eliminated. No bleeding is necessary.**

MAIN FUEL FILTER—1977–84 MODELS

Loosen the center attaching bolt and remove the filter cartridge downward. Lubricate the new filter gasket with clean diesel fuel and install a new filter cartridge.

To bleed the fuel filter, see Step 5 of the previous procedure.

DIESEL PREFILTER

Diesel engines use a prefilter in addition to the main fuel filter, since even the most minute particle of dirt will clog the injection system. The prefilter is located in the line just before it enters the injection pump.

Unscrew the clamps on each end and remove the old filter. Install a new filter and bleed the system (see Main Fuel Filter).

Fuel Pump Strainer

REMOVAL & INSTALLATION

Carbureted Engines

Plunger type fuel pumps on carbureted engines use a strainer located behind the cover.

1. Disconnect and plug the fuel line at the pump.

2. Remove the center screw and remove the cover. A small amount of fuel will run out.

3. Replace the strainer, gasket, screw and aluminum washer, all of which are part of the replacement kit.

4. Replace the cover. There are assembly marks on the cover and fuel pump body.

5. Reconnect the fuel line. Start the engine and check for leaks.

Windshield Wipers

ELEMENT (REFILL) CARE & REPLACEMENT

For maximum effectiveness and longest element life, the windshield and wiper blades should be kept clean. Dirt, tree sap, road tar and so on will cause streaking, smearing and blade deterioration if left on the glass. It is advisable to wash the windshield carefully with a commercial glass cleaner at least once a month. Wipe off the rubber blades with the wet rag afterwards. Do not attempt to move wipers across the windshield by hand; damage to the motor and drive mechanism will result.

To inspect and/or replace the wiper blade elements, place the wiper switch in the **LOW** speed position and the ignition switch in the **ACC** position. When the wiper blades are approximately vertical on the windshield, turn the ignition switch to **OFF.**

Examine the wiper blade elements. If they are found to be cracked, broken or torn, they should be replaced immediately. Replacement intervals will vary with usage, although ozone deterioration usually limits element life to about one year. If the wiper pattern is smeared or streaked, or if the blade chatters across the glass, the elements should be replaced. It is easiest and most sensible to replace the elements in pairs.

If your vehicle is equipped with aftermarket blades, there are several different types of refills and your vehicle might have any kind. Aftermarket blades and arms rarely use the exact same type blade or refill as the original equipment. Here are some typical aftermarket blades; not all may be available for your vehicle:

The Anco® type uses a release button that is pushed down to allow the refill to slide out of the yoke jaws. The new refill slides back into the frame and locks in place.

Some Trico® refills are removed by locating where the metal backing strip or the refill is wider. Insert a small screwdriver blade between the frame and metal backing strip. Press down to release the refill from the retaining tab.

Other types of Trico® refills have two metal tabs which are un-

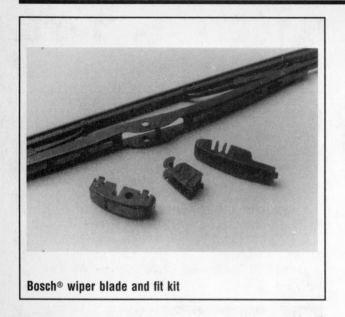

Bosch® wiper blade and fit kit

Trico® wiper blade and fit kit

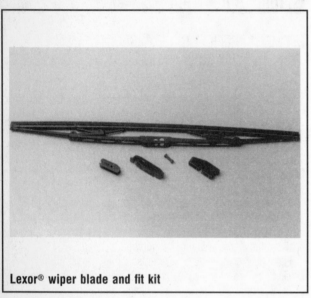

Lexor® wiper blade and fit kit

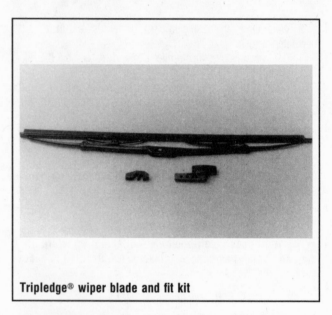

Tripledge® wiper blade and fit kit

Pylon® wiper blade and adaptor

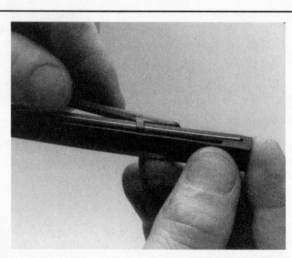

To remove and install a **Lexor®** wiper blade refill, slip out the old insert and slide in a new one

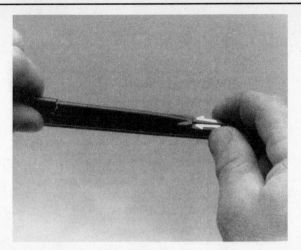

On Pylon® inserts, the clip at the end has to be removed prior to sliding the insert off

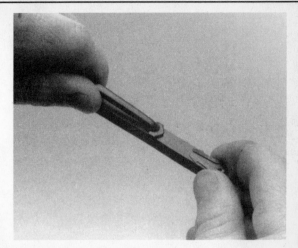

The Tripledge® wiper blade insert is removed and installed using a securing clip

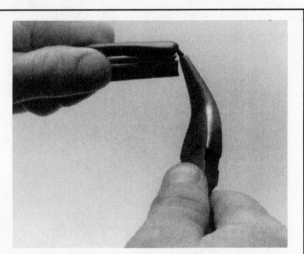

On Trico® wiper blades, the tab at the end of the blade must be turned up . . .

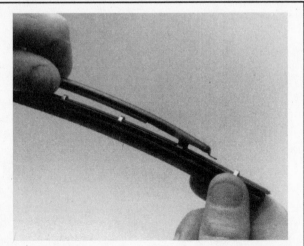

. . . then the insert can be removed. After installing the replacement insert, bend the tab back

locked by squeezing them together. The rubber filler can then be withdrawn from the frame jaws. A new refill is installed by inserting the refill into the front frame jaws and sliding it rearward to engage the remaining frame jaws. There are usually four jaws; be certain when installing that the refill is engaged in all of them. At the end of its travel, the tabs will lock into place on the front jaws of the wiper blade frame.

Another type of refill is made from polycarbonate. The refill has a simple locking device at one end which flexes downward out of the groove into which the jaws of the holder fit, allowing easy release. By sliding the new refill through all the jaws and pushing through the slight resistance when it reaches the end of its travel, the refill will lock into position.

To replace the Tridon® refill, it is necessary to remove the wiper blade. This refill has a plastic backing strip with a notch about 1 in. (25mm) from the end. Hold the blade (frame) on a hard surface so that the frame is tightly bowed. Grip the tip of the backing strip and pull up while twisting counterclockwise. The backing strip will snap out of the retaining tab. Do this for the remaining tabs until the refill is free of the blade. The length of these refills is molded into the end and they should be replaced with identical types.

Regardless of the type of refill used, be sure to follow the part manufacturer's instructions closely. Make sure that all of the frame jaws are engaged as the refill is pushed into place and locked. If the metal blade holder and frame are allowed to touch the glass during wiper operation, the glass will be scratched.

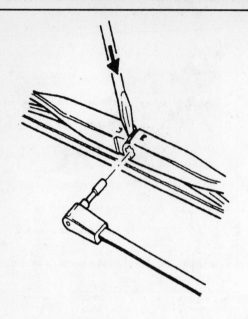

BLADE REPLACEMENT

1. CYCLE ARM AND BLADE ASSEMBLY TO UP POSITION-ON THE WINDSHIELD WHERE REMOVAL OF BLADE ASSEMBLY CAN BE PERFORMED WITHOUT DIFFICULTY. TURN IGNITION KEY OFF AT DESIRED POSITION.

2. TO REMOVE BLADE ASSEMBLY, INSERT SCREWDRIVER IN SLOT, PUSH DOWN ON SPRING LOCK AND PULL BLADE ASSEMBLY FROM PIN (VIEW A)

3. TO INSTALL, PUSH THE BLADE ASSEMBLY ON THE PIN SO THAT THE SPRING LOCK ENGAGES THE PIN (VIEW A). BE SURE THE BLADE ASSEMBLY IS SECURELY ATTACHED TO PIN

VIEW A

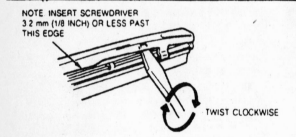

NOTE INSERT SCREWDRIVER 3 2 mm (1/8 INCH) OR LESS PAST THIS EDGE

TWIST CLOCKWISE

ELEMENT REPLACEMENT

1 INSERT SCREWDRIVER BETWEEN THE EDGE OF THE SUPER STRUCTURE AND THE BLADE BACKING DRIP (VIEW B) TWIST SCREWDRIVER SLOWLY UNTIL ELEMENT CLEARS ONE SIDE OF THE SUPER STRUC-TURE CLAW

2 SLIDE THE ELEMENT INTO THE SUPER STRUCTURE CLAWS

VIEW B

4 INSERT ELEMENT INTO ONE SIDE OF THE END CLAWS (VIEW D) AND WITH A ROCKING MOTION PUSH ELEMENT UPWARD UNTIL IT SNAPS IN (VIEW E)

VIEW D

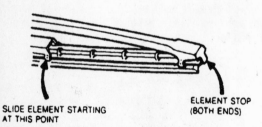

SLIDE ELEMENT STARTING AT THIS POINT

ELEMENT STOP (BOTH ENDS)

3. SLIDE THE ELEMENT INTO THE SUPER STRUCTURE CLAWS, STARTING WITH SECOND SET FROM EITHER END (VIEW C) AND CONTINUE TO SLIDE THE BLADE ELEMENT INTO ALL THE SUPER STRUCTURE CLAWS TO THE ELEMENT STOP (VIEW C)

VIEW C

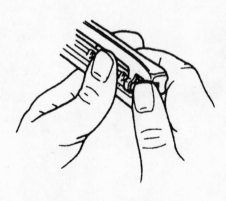

VIEW E

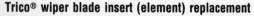

Trico® wiper blade insert (element) replacement

BLADE REPLACEMENT

1. Cycle arm and blade assembly to a position on the windshield where removal of blade assembly can be performed without difficulty. Turn ignition key off at desired position.
2. To remove blade assembly from wiper arm, pull up on spring lock and pull blade assembly from pin (View A). Be sure spring lock is not pulled excessively or it will become distorted.
3. To install, push the blade assembly onto the pin so that the spring lock engages the pin (View A). Be sure the blade assembly is securely attached to pin.

ELEMENT REPLACEMENT

1. In the plastic backing strip which is part of the rubber blade assembly, there is an 11.11mm (7/16 inch) long notch located approximately one inch from either end. Locate either notch.
2. Place the frame of the wiper blade assembly on a firm surface with either notched end of the backing strip visible.
3. Grasp the frame portion of the wiper blade assembly and push down until the blade assembly is tightly bowed.
4. With the blade assembly in the bowed position, grasp the tip of the backing strip firmly, pulling up and twisting C.C.W. at the same time. The backing strip will then snap out of the retaining tab on the end of the frame.
5. Lift the wiper blade assembly from the surface and slide the backing strip down the frame until the notch lines up with the next retaining tab, twist slightly, and the backing strip will snap out. Continue this operation with the remaining tabs until the blade element is completely detached from the frame.
6. To install blade element, reverse the above procedure, making sure all six (6) tabs are locked to the backing strip before installing blade to wiper arm.

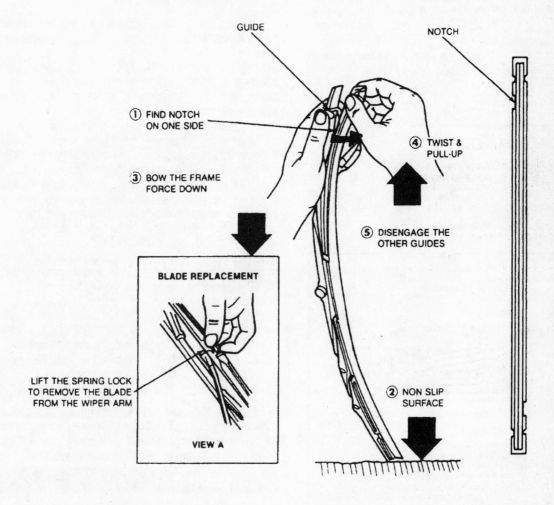

Tridon® wiper blade insert (element) replacement

FLUIDS AND LUBRICANTS

Fluid Disposal

Used fluids such as engine oil, transmission fluid, antifreeze and brake fluid are hazardous wastes and must be disposed of properly. Before draining any fluids, consult with your local authorities; in many areas waste oil, etc. is being accepted as a part of recycling programs. A number of service stations and auto parts stores are also accepting waste fluids for recycling.

Be sure of the recycling center's policies before draining any fluids, as many will not accept different fluids that have been mixed together.

Oil and Fuel Recommendations

Mercedes-Benz is constantly testing and analyzing fuels and lubricants in an effort to determine which lubricants and fuels are suitable and provide the best service in their vehicles. The recommended fluids and their applications are published by Mercedes-Benz under the title "Specifications for Service Products". It is impossible to detail, in this book, those materials which are suitable at any given time, since the publication is constantly revised and updated by Mercedes-Benz.

In general, most any high quality material is suitable for the particular application, with the exceptions noted below.

OIL

♦ See Figures 19 and 19a

The Society of Automotive Engineers (SAE) grade number indicates the viscosity of the engine oil and thus its ability to lubricate at a given temperature. The lower the SAE grade number, the lighter the oil; the lower the viscosity, the easier it is to crank the engine in cold weather.

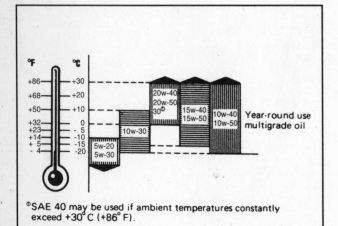

*SAE 40 may be used if ambient temperatures constantly exceed +30° C (+86° F).

Fig. 19 Oil viscosity chart—gasoline engines

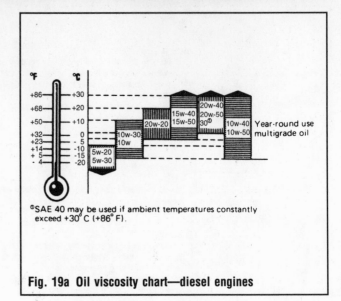

*SAE 40 may be used if ambient temperatures constantly exceed +30° C (+86° F)

Fig. 19a Oil viscosity chart—diesel engines

Oil viscosities should be chosen from those oils recommended for the lowest anticipated temperatures during the oil change interval.

Multi-viscosity oils (10W-30, 20W-50 etc.) offer the important advantage of being adaptable to temperature extremes. They allow easy starting at low temperatures, yet they give good protection at high speeds and engine temperature. This is a decided advantage in changeable climates or in long distance touring.

The American Petroleum Institute (API) designation indicates the classification of engine oil used under certain given operating conditions. Only oils designated for use "Service SE" should be used. Oils of the SE type perform a variety of functions inside the engine in addition to their basic function as a lubricant. Through a balanced system of metallic detergents and polymeric dispersants, the oil prevents the formation of high and low temperature deposits and also keeps sludge and particles of dirt in suspension. Acids, particularly sulfuric acid, as well as other byproducts of combustion, are neutralized. Both the SAE grade number and the API designation can be found on top of the oil can.

Diesel engines also require SE engine oil. In addition, the oil must qualify for a CC rating. The API has a number of different diesel engine ratings, including CB, CC and CD. Any of these other oils are fine as long as the designation CC appears on the can along with them. Do not use oil labeled only SE or only CC. Both designations must always appear together.

For recommended oil viscosities, refer to the chart.

➡ **As of late 1980, the API has come out with a new designation of motor oil, SF. Oils designated for use "Service SF" are equally acceptable in your pre-'80 car and should be used exclusively in 1981 and later models.**

✳✳ WARNING

Non-detergent or straight mineral oils should not be used in your car.

SYNTHETIC OIL

There are many excellent synthetic and fuel-efficient oils currently available that can provide better gas mileage, longer service life, and in some cases better engine protection. These benefits do not come without a few hitches, however—the main one being the price of synthetic oils, which is three or four times the price per quart of conventional oil.

Synthetic oil is not for every car and every type of driving, so you should consider your engine's condition and your type of driving. Also, check your car's warranty conditions regarding the use of synthetic oils.

Both brand new engines and older, high mileage engines are the wrong candidates for synthetic oil. The synthetic oils are so slippery that they can prevent the proper break-in of new engines; most manufacturers recommend that you wait until the engine is properly broken in (5,000 miles) until using synthetic oil. Older engines with wear have a different problem with synthetics: they "use" (consume during operation) more oil as they age. Slippery synthetic oils get past these worn parts easily—if your engine is "using" conventional oil, it will use synthetics much faster. Also, if your car is leaking oil past old seals you'll have a much greater leak problems with synthetics.

Consider your type of driving. If most of your accumulated mileage is high speed, highway type driving, the more expensive synthetic oils may be of benefit. Extended highway driving gives the engine a chance to warm up, accumulating less acids in the oil and putting less stress on the engine over the long run. Under these conditions, the oil change interval can be extended (as long as your oil filter can last the extended life of the oil) up to the advertised mileage claims of the synthetics. Cars with synthetic oils may show increased fuel economy in highway driving, due to less internal friction. However, many automotive experts agree that 50,000 miles is too long to keep any oil in your engine.

Cars used under harder circumstances, such as stop-and-go, city type driving, short trips, or extended idling, should be serviced more frequently. For the engines in these cars, the much greater cost of synthetic or fuel-efficient oils may not be worth the investment. Internal wear increases much quicker on these cars, causing greater oil consumption and leakage.

➡**The mixing of conventional and synthetic oils is not recommended. If you are using synthetic oil, it might be wise to carry two or three quarts with you no matter where you drive, as not all service stations carry this type of lubricant.**

FUEL

Gasoline

The fuel requirement (octane rating) for your vehicle is listed in the owner's manual or available from any Mercedes-Benz dealer. In general, since 1974, Mercedes-Benz engines are designed to run on regular gasoline or regular unleaded gasoline if a converter is used. In the event that a fuel of the proper octane rating is not available, the timing can be retarded but this is as an emergency measure only. The proper fuel should be obtained as quickly as possible and the timing should be reset to specifications as soon as possible.

➡**If the timing has been retarded because of low octane fuel, the car should not be driven at high speeds.**

Diesel

◗ **See Figure 20**

Use only commercially available No. 2 or No. 1 diesel fuel. Mercedes-Benz does not recommend the use of marine diesel fuel or heating oil.

At very low temperatures, the viscosity of No. 2 summer diesel fuel may become insufficient (the fuel will not adequately flow); winter diesel fuel should be unaffected as low as approximately 0°F.

If summer diesel fuel clogs at low winter temperatures, a specified percentage of kerosene can be mixed with No. 2 summer diesel fuel to improve its viscosity.

Add kerosene according to the following table, but keep the percentage of kerosene to a minimum since a loss of engine power will likely result. At no time should the % of kerosene exceed 50%. Regular gasoline can be substituted for kerosene, but the amount should not exceed 30%, and it is not recommended to dilute No. 1 diesel fuel.

Ambient Temperature (°F)	% No. 2 Summer Diesel Fuel	% Kerosene
+32 to +14	70	30
+14 to +5	50	50

Fig. 20 Diesel engine fuel mixture requirements

AUTOMATIC TRANSMISSION FLUID

Since 1974, all Mercedes-Benz automatic transmissions have been of the torque converter type. All use DEXRON® B, Type B fluid, of which there are many high quality brands available.

REAR AXLE LUBRICANT

There are many high quality gear lubricants available for use with standard type differentials. Just be sure that the lubricant is specified SAE 90 viscosity for hypoid gears.

Vehicles equipped with a limited slip (positive traction) type differential should use only special lubricant available at Mercedes-Benz dealers. It has special additives for use with limited slip rear axles.

HYDROPNEUMATIC SUSPENSION OIL

A list of approved lubricants for the hydropneumatic suspension can be found earlier in this section. The 6.9 can use only Aral 1010, available from dealerships.

ENGINE COOLANT

A 50/50 mixture of water and anti-freeze serves as coolant for Mercedes-Benz engines. Generally tap water meets the requirements for water. It is important that you do not use sea water, brackish water, brine, or industrial waste waters. Also, lime-free water, completely distilled water, rain water, or desalinated water should not be used, as this will only hasten the corrosion process.

In addition, an emulsifying corrosion inhibitor should be used (add a can of corrosion inhibitor every time you change the coolant). This is to combat the effects of rust, scale, and other deposits which tend to reduce the cooling properties of the coolant due to poor heat conductivity.

Engine

OIL LEVEL CHECK

Every time you stop for fuel, check the engine oil as follows:
1. Park the car on level ground.

✳✳ CAUTION

The EPA warns that prolonged contact with used engine oil may cause a number of skin disorders, including cancer! You should make every effort to minimize your exposure to used engine oil. Protective gloves should be worn when changing the oil. Wash your hands and any other exposed skin areas as soon as possible after exposure to used engine oil. Soap and water, or waterless hand cleaner should be used.

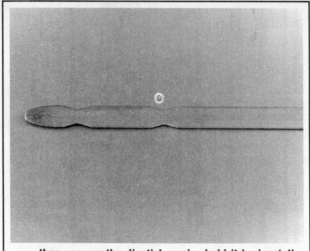

. . . then remove the dipstick again, hold it horizontally and read the oil level

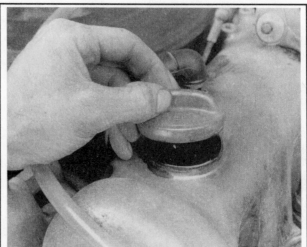

If oil has to be added, remove the oil filler cap from the valve cover . . .

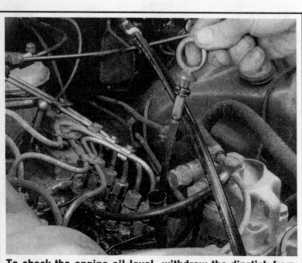

To check the engine oil level, withdraw the dipstick from the tube, wipe it clean and reinsert it . . .

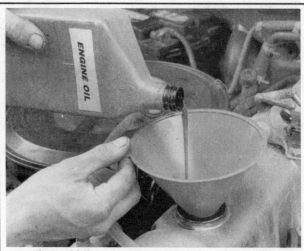

. . . then add the correct amount and grade of oil to the crankcase

2. When checking the oil level it is best for the engine to be at operating temperature, although checking the oil immediately after stopping will lead to a false reading. Wait a few minutes after turning off the engine to allow the oil to drain back into the crankcase.

3. Open the hood and remove the dipstick from the engine. Generally, the dipstick is located on the front of the engine near the distributor (230 and 6-cylinder engines), on the right side of the engine, near the exhaust manifold (190E), on the front of the engine near the battery (V-8's) or at the front on the right-hand side (diesel engines).

4. Pull the dipstick out again and, holding it horizontally, read the oil level. The oil should be between the "upper (maximum)" and "lower (minimum)" marks on the dipstick. If the oil is below the "lower" mark, add oil of the proper viscosity through the capped opening on the top of the cylinder head cover (on the 6.9, add oil through the oil supply tank opening). See the "Oil and Fuel Recommendations" chart in this section for the proper viscosity and rating of oil to use.

5. Replace the dipstick and check the oil level again after adding any oil. Be careful not to overfill the crankcase. Approximately one quart of oil will raise the level from the "lower" to the "upper." Excess oil will generally be consumed at an accelerated rate.

OIL & FILTER CHANGE

The oil should be changed approximately every 6,000 miles.

The oil drain plug is located on the bottom of the oil pan (bottom of the engine, underneath the car).

The mileage figures given here and in the chart are the Mercedes-Benz recommended intervals assuming normal driving and conditions. If your car is being used under dusty, polluted or off-road conditions, change the oil and filter more frequently than specified. The same goes for cars driven in stop-and-go traffic or only for short distances. Always drain the oil after the engine has been running long enough to bring it to normal operating temperature. Hot oil will flow easier and more contaminents will be removed along with the oil than if it were drained cold. To change the oil and filter:

Gasoline Engines—Except 190E

◆ **See Figures 21, 22, 23 and 24**

✳✳ CAUTION

The EPA warns that prolonged contact with used engine oil may cause a number of skin disorders, including cancer! You should make every effort to minimize your exposure to used engine oil. Protective gloves should be worn when changing the oil. Wash your hands and any other exposed skin areas as soon as possible after exposure to used engine oil. Soap and water, or waterless hand cleaner should be used.

1. Run the engine until it reaches normal operating temperature.

2. Jack up the front of the car and support it on safety stands.

3. From under the car, loosen but do not remove the oil

drain plug. The drain plug may be a conventional hex head plug or an allen head type.

4. Position a pan, sufficient to hold all of the oil, under the drain hole.

5. Slowly unscrew the drain plug with your fingers and at the

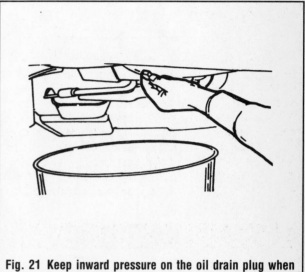

Fig. 21 Keep inward pressure on the oil drain plug when removing it to prevent being burned by hot oil

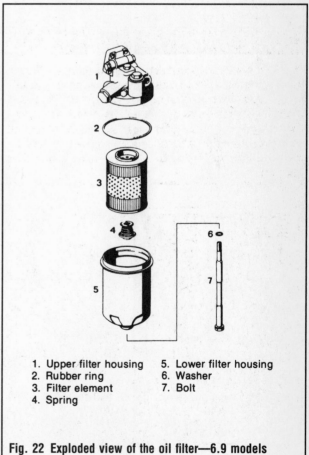

1. Upper filter housing
2. Rubber ring
3. Filter element
4. Spring
5. Lower filter housing
6. Washer
7. Bolt

Fig. 22 Exploded view of the oil filter—6.9 models

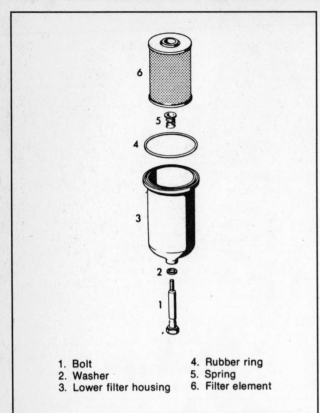

1. Bolt
2. Washer
3. Lower filter housing
4. Rubber ring
5. Spring
6. Filter element

Fig. 23 Exploded view of the oil filter—overhead cam 6-cyl. engines

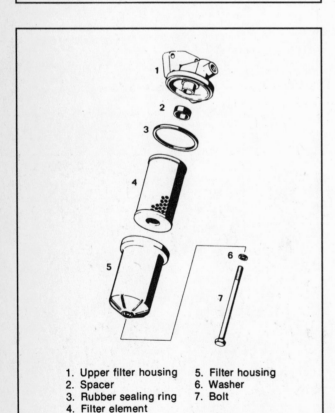

1. Upper filter housing
2. Spacer
3. Rubber sealing ring
4. Filter element
5. Filter housing
6. Washer
7. Bolt

Fig. 24 Exploded view of the oil filter—4-cyl. engines (except 190E)

same time push the drain plug threads against the threads in the drain hole. This will prevent hot oil from leaking past the threads while the plug is being removed. The 6.9 has an oil supply tank; opening the cap will speed the draining process.

✳✳ CAUTION

The engine oil will be very hot. Be careful to stay out of the way as the oil drains out of the engine.

6. As the drain plug comes to the end of the threads, quickly remove it from the hole allowing the oil to escape. By using this method you can also avoid having to reach into a pan full of warm, dirty oil, to retrieve the drain plug.

7. If so equipped, drain the oil from the oil cooler in the same manner.

8. Carefully unscrew the oil filter bowl. This is done by holding the filter bowl and unscrewing the long bolt which holds it. *Be careful, since there will still be oil in the filter bowl.*

9. Empty the filter bowl, wash it out, and blow it dry.

10. Throw the old filter element away.

11. Check the condition of the sealing ring and renew it if necessary.

12. Note the position of the pressure spring. This must be installed properly when the filter is assembled.

13. Renew the large rubber sealing ring around the top of the filter bowl.

14. Insert a new filter element into the filter bowl and install the filter bowl.

15. Install new sealing rings on all drain plugs and reinstall the plugs.

16. Refill the engine with the proper amount of oil.

17. Remove the jackstands and position the car on a level surface again.

18. Run the engine and check for leaks.

✳✳ WARNING

Do not run the engine above idle speed until it has built up oil pressure, indicated when the oil light goes out.

19. Turn off the engine, wait several minutes for the oil to drain into the crankcase, and check the oil level.

➡All new Mercedes-Benz automobiles are equipped with a special finepore filter element for break-in purposes. This should be replaced at the first service inspection. If the engine is rebuilt, it is necessary to use this type filter again, but under no circumstances should it be used for other than break-in.

190E and All Diesel Engines

✳✳ CAUTION

The EPA warns that prolonged contact with used engine oil may cause a number of skin disorders, including cancer! You should make every effort to minimize your exposure to used engine oil. Protective gloves should be worn when changing the oil. Wash your hands and any other exposed skin areas as soon as possible after exposure to used engine oil. Soap and water, or waterless hand cleaner should be used.

1. Run the engine until it reaches normal operating temperature.

2. Jack up the front of the car and support it on safety stands.

3. From under the car, loosen but do not remove the oil drain plug.

4. Position a pan, sufficient size to hold all of the oil, under the drain hole.

5. Beginning with 1977 models, 2 versions of an upright oil filter are used. On the first (earlier) type, oil from the filter flows back into the engine when the center bolt is removed about 2 in. On the 2nd (later) version, the oil will run back when the cover is removed. On these later versions, the cover is attached by 2 bolts instead of a center bolt (except the 190E which has only 1 center bolt).

In either case the oil should be allowed to drain into the engine before removing the drain plug.

6. Slowly unscrew the drain plug with your fingers and at the same time push the drain plug threads against the threads in the drain hole. This will prevent hot oil from leaking past the threads while the plug is being removed.

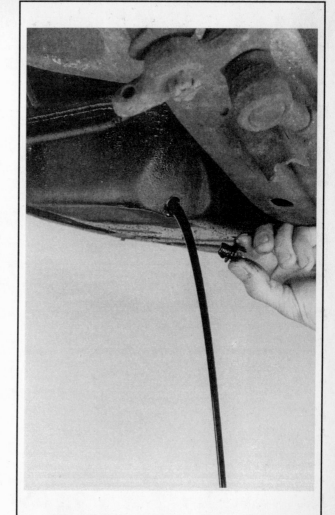

. . . then remove the plug and drain the oil into a suitable container

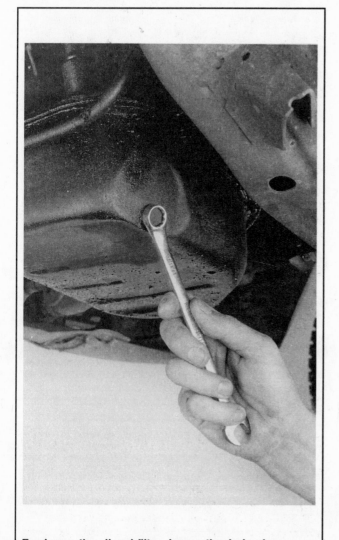

To change the oil and filter, loosen the drain plug . . .

1. Oil filter housing cover

Loosen the oil filter housing cover retainers . . .

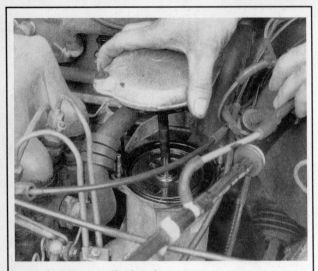

. . . then remove the housing cover

Grasp the wire handle of the oil filter element . . .

1. Wire handle   2. Oil filter element
. . . then lift the filter element up and out of the housing

✳✳ CAUTION

The engine oil will be very hot. Be careful to stay out of the way as the oil drains out of the engine.

7. As the drain plug comes to the end of the threads, quickly remove it from the hole allowing the oil to escape. By using this method you can also avoid having to reach into a pan full of warm, dirty oil to retrieve the drain plug.

8. If so equipped, drain the oil from the oil cooler in the same manner.

9. On 1976 and earlier models carefully unscrew the oil filter bowl. This is done by holding the filter bowl and unscrewing the long bolt which holds it. Be careful, since there is still oil in the filter bowl.

10. On 1977 and later models, remove the cover, and lift out the filter element using the wire handle.

11. On 1976 and earlier models, empty the filter bowl, wash it out, and blow it dry.

12. Throw the old element away.

13. Check the condition of the sealing ring and renew if necessary.

14. Note the position of the pressure spring. This must be installed properly when the filter is assembled. *The upright filter with 2 attaching nuts (1 on the 190E) uses no pressure spring.*

15. Using pliers, wash out the fine mesh filter element in gasoline and blow it dry with low air pressure. 1977 and later models use no fine mesh filter.

16. Renew the large rubber sealing ring.

17. Install a new filter cartridge and the fine mesh filter (if so equipped). It is important that the filter be installed as shown. 1977 and later models use no fine mesh filter. Install the top to the housing.

➡ **At the first prescribed maintenance job (200–600 miles) the break-in filter is to be replaced with the service filter and the full flow fine mesh filter supplied.**

18. Renew the drain plug sealing rings and tighten the drain plugs.

19. Fill the engine with the proper amount of oil.

20. Remove the car from the jackstands and position the car on a level surface.

21. Run the engine and check for leaks.

✳✳ WARNING

Do not run the engine above idle speed until it has built up oil pressure, indicated when the oil light goes out.

22. Turn the engine off and wait several minutes for the oil to drain into the crankcase. Check the oil level.

Manual Transmission

FLUID LEVEL CHECK

◆ See Figure 25

The transmission oil level should be checked at the recommended intervals or sooner. Since there is no dipstick, the level

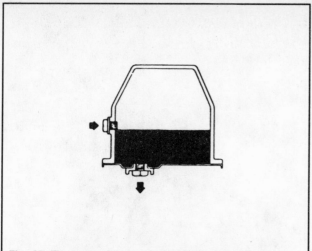

Fig. 25 The manual transmission fluid should be level with the bottom of the filler (upper) plug hole

is checked at the filler and drain plugs. In the event that a major loss of oil is found, the problem should be found and corrected immediately.

Check the level when the fluid is hot. You'll need a 14 mm Allen socket to remove the plug. If fluid is needed use Type A Automatic Transmission Fluid (ATF) with Suffix A, or its equivalent.

1. With the car parked on a level surface, remove the filler plug (upper arrow in illustration) from the side of the transmission housing.

2. If the lubricant begins to trickle out of the hole, there is enough. Otherwise, carefully insert your finger (watch out for sharp threads) and check to see if the oil is up to the edge of the hole.

✳✳ CAUTION

The EPA warns that prolonged contact with used engine oil may cause a number of skin disorders, including cancer! You should make every effort to minimize your exposure to used engine oil. Protective gloves should be worn when changing the oil. Wash your hands and any other exposed skin areas as soon as possible after exposure to used engine oil. Soap and water, or waterless hand cleaner should be used.

3. If not, add oil through the hole until the level is at the edge of the hole. Most gear lubricants come in a plastic squeeze bottle with a nozzle, making additions simple. You can also use a common everyday kitchen baster.

4. Replace the filler plug, run the engine and check for leaks.

DRAIN & REFILL

Manual Transmission

The manual transmission oil should be changed at least every 25,000–30,000 miles. To change, proceed as follows:

1. The oil must be hot before it is drained. If the car is driven until the engine is at normal operating temperature, the oil should be hot enough.

2. Remove the filler plug to provide a vent.

3. The drain plug is on the bottom of the transmission. Place a large container underneath the transmission and remove the plug.

4. Allow the oil to drain completely. Clean off the plug and replace it using a new washer. Tighten it until it is just snug.

5. Fill the transmission with the proper lubricant. Use a plastic squeeze bottle with a long nozzle; or you can use a squeeze bulb or a kitchen baster to squirt the oil in. Refer to the "Capacities" chart for the proper amount of oil to put in. The oil level should come up to the top of the filler hole.

6. Replace the filler plug, drive the car for a few minutes, then stop, and check for any leaks.

Automatic Transmission

FLUID LEVEL CHECK

♦ See Figures 26 and 27

Too little or too much fluid will impair the proper operation of the automatic transmission. The fluid level should be checked regularly (see "Maintenance Intervals") by using the transmission dipstick, which is accessible through the engine compartment. During this check, the car should be on a level surface and the engine and transmission should be at normal operating temperature.

1. Apply the parking brake.

2. Move the selector lever into the Park position.

3. Run the engine at normal operating temperature.

4. Remove the dipstick and wipe it with a clean, lint-free rag.

➡**Some automatic transmissions have a clamp lock that must be released; others do not.**

5. Insert the dipstick, remove it again, and read the fluid level.

6. With a correct fluid level and a warm transmission, the fluid level should be at the upper marking or at least between the two marks.

The fluid level will change with temperature. The "min" and "max" marks on the dipstick apply when the fluid is hot, after 5

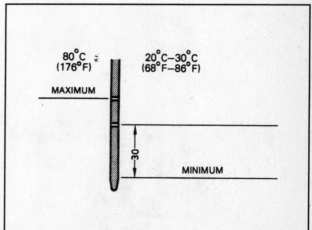

Fig. 26 The fluid level of the automatic transmission should not fall more than 30mm below the dipstick's lower mark

Fig. 27 Add automatic transmission fluid through the dipstick tube using a funnel

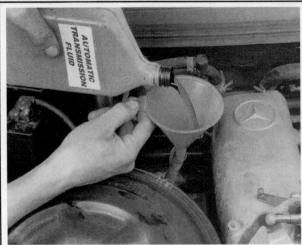

Use a funnel to add the correct amount and grade of transmission fluid through the dipstick tube

To check the automatic transmission fluid level, withdraw the dipstick from the tube and wipe clean . . .

minutes driving. When the fluid is cold, the fluid level will be approximately 1 in. below the minimum mark.

7. Additional oil (use only Dexron B) can be added through the dipstick guide (engine running) by using a funnel. Be careful not to add too much fluid. As a rough guide, there is approximately 0.3 quart between the maximum and minimum dipstick markings.

DRAIN & REFILL

Before attempting to drain the transmission fluid, be sure that the vehicle is on level ground and that the transmission is at normal operating temperature. The engine should be shut off.

1. Drain the fluid from the transmission either by removing the filler pipe under the transmission or by removing the drain plug.

2. Observe the same safety precautions as are listed for "Engine Oil Changes," regarding hot oil and safety.

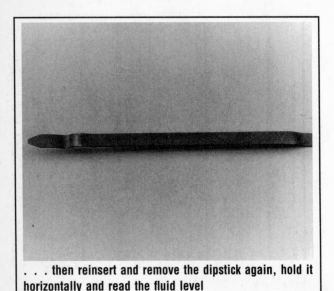

. . . then reinsert and remove the dipstick again, hold it horizontally and read the fluid level

To change the transmission oil and filter, loosen the pan's drain plug . . .

. . . then let the transmission fluid drain into a suitable container

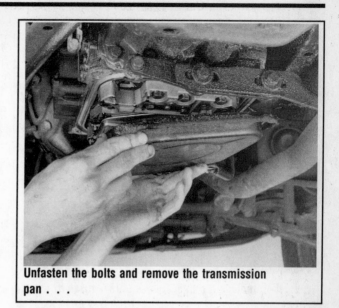

Unfasten the bolts and remove the transmission pan . . .

. . . then remove the old gasket from the pan

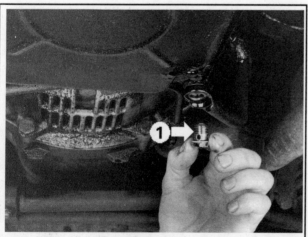

1. Transmission drain plug

Remove the drain plug from the pan after all the fluid has drained

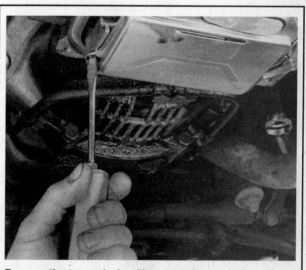

Remove the transmission filter retaining screws

. . . then remove the filter from the transmission

To check the differential housing fluid level, use an Allen wrench to loosen the filler plug . . .

3. When all the fluid is drained, remove the transmission oil pan. Be sure the filler pipe is disconnected.

4. Replace the oil filter, making sure that all bolts are tightened. The oil filter should not be cleaned, but replaced with a new one.

✷✷ CAUTION

The filter may have oil remaining in it.

5. Clean the inside of the pan with a clean lint-free rag.

6. Install the oil pan.

7. Install the filler pipe or drain plug using new washers or gaskets in each case.

8. Insert a funnel with a fine mesh strainer into the dipstick tube and add a large portion (not all) of the transmission oil capacity. This should be done with the engine stopped.

9. Start the engine and run it at idle speed with the selector lever in Park. Gradually add the remaining fluid. Do not overfill the transmission.

10. Check the oil level with the transmission at operating temperature.

11. Be sure to remove any excess fluid.

Rear Axle

FLUID LEVEL CHECK

The rear axle lubricant should be checked at the interval specified in the chart, or sooner.

1. Before checking the rear axle lubricant level, be sure that the vehicle is on level ground.

2. Slowly unscrew the drain plug from the oil filler hole (upper hole). You will need a 14mm hex allen wrench. If the lubricant level is satisfactory, lubricant will begin to seep past the threads of the plug. If lubricant does not seep past the threads, remove the plug entirely. The lubricant level should be up to the bottom of the filler hole. If not, lubricant can be added through the filler hole by using a pressure gun. Add only enough lubricant to bring the level to the bottom edge of the filler hole.

. . . then remove the filler plug from the housing

If the lubricant is not level with the bottom of the filler hole, add fluid to the proper level

➡Rear axles without limited slip may use any high quality SAE 90 hypoid gear oil. The limited slip differential can be filled only with special Limited Slip Special lubricant available at Mercedes-Benz dealers. Identification of this type differential is by a plate attached to the rear axle housing, reading "Achtung Spezial—Öl Sperr-differential." (Caution! Special oil—limited slip differential.)

3. Replace the oil filler plug.

DRAIN & REFILL

The rear axle need not be drained regularly, but if desired, the car must be on a level surface with the weight on the wheels or with the axle tubes supported by jackstands. This is necessary to prevent oil from entering the axle tubes.

1. Remove the bottom drain plug and loosen the top drain plug.
2. After the fluid has drained, replace the bottom drain plug using a new washer.

3. Refill the unit with the specified lubricant. Be sure that the proper lubricant is used. Consult the "Oil and Fuel Recommendations" section.

4. Replace the top plug using a new washer. The fluid level should be at the top of the oil filler opening.

Coolant

LEVEL CHECK

Dealing with the cooling system can be a dangerous matter unless the proper precautions are observed. It is best to check the coolant level in the radiator when the engine is cold. This is done by removing the radiator cap and seeing that the coolant reaches the mark on the bottom of the filler neck. On later models, the cooling system has, as one of its components, an expansion tank. As long as the coolant is visible above the "Low" mark on the

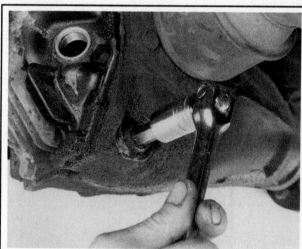

To drain the fluid from the differential, use an Allen wrench to loosen the drain plug . . .

To check the coolant level, remove the radiator cap and observe the fluid level . . .

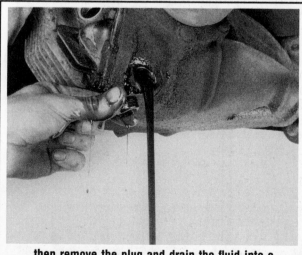

. . . then remove the plug and drain the fluid into a suitable container

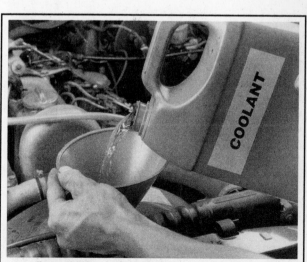

. . . then add the correct amount of coolant and water to the system

tank, the level is satisfactory. Always be certain that the filler caps on both the radiator and the reservoir are tightly closed.

In the event that the coolant level must be checked when the engine is warm on engines without the expansion tank, place a thick rag over the radiator cap and slowly turn the cap counterclockwise until it reaches the first detent. Allow all the hot steam to escape. This will allow the pressure in the system to drop gradually, preventing an explosion of hot coolant. When the hissing noise stops, remove the cap the rest of the way.

If the coolant level is low, add equal amounts of ethylene glycol-based antifreeze and clean water. On models without an expansion tank, add coolant through the radiator filler neck. Fill the expansion tank to the "Full" level on cars with that system.

✳✳ WARNING

Never add cold coolant to a hot engine unless the engine is running, to avoid cracking the engine block.

If the coolant level is chronically low or rusty, refer to Chapter 10 for diagnosis of the problem.

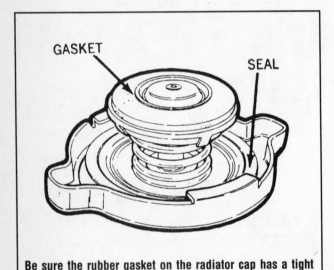

GASKET

SEAL

Be sure the rubber gasket on the radiator cap has a tight seal

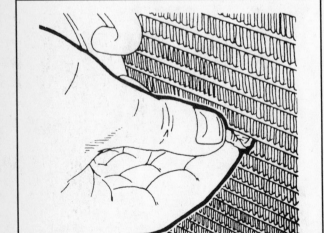

Periodically remove all debris from the radiator fins

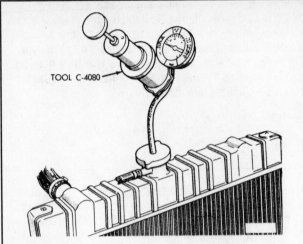

TOOL C-4080

Cooling systems should be pressure tested for leaks periodically

The radiator hoses and clamps and the radiator cap should be checked at the same time as the coolant level. Hoses which are brittle, cracked, or swollen should be replaced. Clamps should be checked for tightness (screwdriver tight only—do not allow the clamp to cut into the hose or crush the fitting). The radiator cap gasket should be checked for any obvious tears, cracks, or swelling, or any signs of incorrect seating in the radiator neck.

Check the freezing protection rating at least once a year, preferably just before the winter sets in. This can be done with an antifreeze tester (most service stations will have one on hand and will probably check it for you, if not, they are available at an auto parts store). Maintain a protection rating of at least −20°F (−29°C) to prevent engine damage as a result of freezing and to assure the proper engine operating temperature.

DRAIN SYSTEM, FLUSH & REFILL

✳✳ CAUTION

When draining engine coolant, keep in mind that cats and dogs are attracted to ethylene glycol antifreeze and could drink any that is left in an uncovered container or in puddles on the ground. This will prove fatal in sufficient quantity. Always drain coolant into a sealable container. Coolant should be reused unless it is contaminated or is several years old.

The cooling system should be drained, thoroughly flushed and then refilled at least every 25,000–30,000 miles. This should be done with the engine cold.

1. Remove the radiator cap and the expansion tank cap (if so equipped).

2. With the caps removed, run the engine until the upper radiator hose is hot. This means that the thermostat is open and the coolant is flowing through the system.

3. With the engine stopped, position a suitable drain pan (or pans), then open the radiator draincock located at the bottom of the radiator. To speed draining, also open the engine block drain on the right-hand side. Before opening the radiator drain, it is a

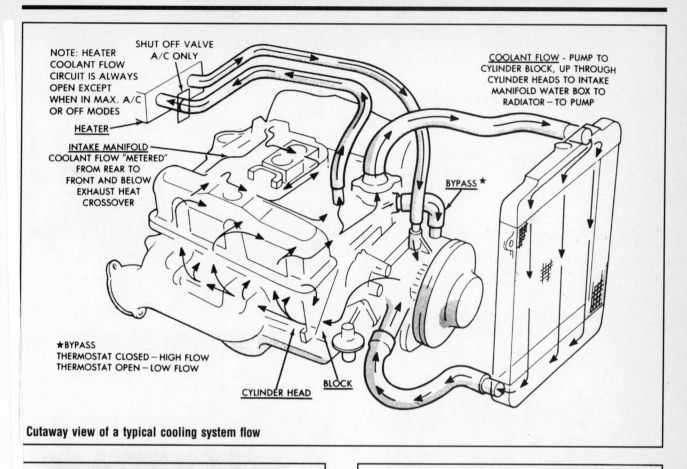

NOTE: HEATER COOLANT FLOW CIRCUIT IS ALWAYS OPEN EXCEPT WHEN IN MAX. A/C OR OFF MODES

SHUT OFF VALVE A/C ONLY

HEATER

INTAKE MANIFOLD COOLANT FLOW "METERED" FROM REAR TO FRONT AND BELOW EXHAUST HEAT CROSSOVER

COOLANT FLOW - PUMP TO CYLINDER BLOCK, UP THROUGH CYLINDER HEADS TO INTAKE MANIFOLD WATER BOX TO RADIATOR - TO PUMP

BYPASS ★

★BYPASS
THERMOSTAT CLOSED – HIGH FLOW
THERMOSTAT OPEN – LOW FLOW

CYLINDER HEAD

BLOCK

Cutaway view of a typical cooling system flow

To drain the cooling system, unscrew the radiator drain plug . . .

. . . then drain the coolant into a suitable container

good idea to soak it for a few minutes with penetrating oil to loosen it. The radiator can also be emptied by siphoning, using the type of siphon used for gasoline, or coolant can be drained by removing the lower radiator hose.

➡**Do not attempt to siphon coolant by sucking on the end of a hose. The coolant is poisonous and can cause death or serious illness if swallowed.**

4. Completely drain the coolant, and close the draincocks. Add clean water until the system is filled.
5. Repeat Steps 3 and 4 several times until the drained liquid is nearly colorless.
6. Tighten the drain valve and then fill the radiator with a 50/50 mixture of ethylene glycol or other suitable antifreeze and water.
7. With the radiator cap still removed, run the engine until the upper radiator hose is hot. Add coolant if necessary, replace the caps and check for any leaks.

Brake Master Cylinder

FLUID LEVEL CHECK

The brake master cylinder is attached to the brake booster which is located on the firewall (driver's side). To check the fluid level, proceed as follows.
1. Clean the area around the cap since even minute particles of dirt can cause a malfunction of the system.
2. Remove the top from the reservoir and check to see that the fluid is up to the marks stamped in the reservoir.
3. Add fluid, if necessary, to bring the level up to the marks.

➡**Use only a high quality brake fluid. Mercedes-Benz recommends ATE Blue Original brake fluid. In countries where this is difficult to obtain, use only fluid which meets or exceeds SAE J 1703B standards. This will be marked on the container.**

. . . then add fluid until the level marked on the side of the reservoir is reached. Replace the cap

✳✳ WARNING

Do not allow brake fluid to contact the vehicle's paint because brake fluid acts as a solvent.

4. Replace the reservoir cap, making sure that the ventilation bore in the top is not blocked.

Power Steering Pump

FLUID LEVEL CHECK

Check the level of the fluid in the power steering reservoir at the interval specified in the chart.
1. Position the car on a level surface and center the steering gear.

To add fluid to the brake master cylinder, unscrew the cap . . .

To check the power steering fluid level, remove the wing nut from the reservoir cover . . .

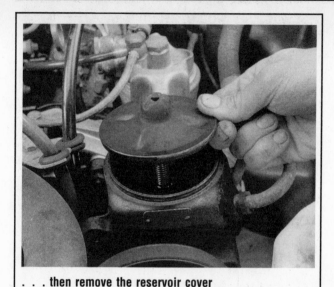

. . . then remove the reservoir cover

Check the mark stamped on the inside of the reservoir; add fluid if necessary

2. Loosen the wing nut or knurled nut and remove the reservoir cover.

3. With the fluid at operating temperature, the fluid should reach to the mark stamped in the reservoir. If not, add sufficient automatic transmission fluid (ATF) to bring the level up to the mark.

4. Replace the cover and be sure that the cover and paper gasket are seated correctly.

5. Tighten the wing or knurled nut.

Manual Steering Gear

FLUID LEVEL CHECK

1974–76 230, 240D, 300D and 280 Models

Check the fluid level of the manual steering gear at the interval specified.

1. Position the car on a level surface with the steering gear in the central position.

2. Remove the plug from the threaded hole.

3. The oil level should reach to the lower edge of the threaded hole.

4. If not, add enough SAE 90 hypoid transmission oil to bring the level up to the lower edge of the hole.

5. Replace the plug.

Hydro-Pneumatic Suspension Reservoir

FLUID LEVEL CHECK

450 Series Sedans, 300TD and 6.9 Models

The hydro-pneumatic suspension uses a special oil. See the list of approved oils in the beginning of this chapter.

The car should be level and the engine warm.

1. Remove the cover from the oil reservoir. The reservoir is located at the driver's side front corner of the engine compartment.

2. Remove the dipstick and wipe it clean.

3. Reinsert the dipstick and read the oil level. It should be between the maximum and minimum marks on the dipstick. There is about 2 pts between the "max" and "min" levels.

Clutch Master Cylinder

FLUID LEVEL CHECK

Some models use a separate clutch master cylinder, located next to the brake master cylinder. Other models, use the brake master cylinder as a reservoir and have a separate line leading to the clutch master cylinder.

If your car has a common reservoir, refer to the section on checking the fluid level in the brake master cylinder, in this chapter. If your car has a separate reservoir, the level should be maintained at the mark on the plastic reservoir.

Regardless of which type you have, clean the ventilation bore in the cap.

Carburetor Damper Reservoir

FLUID LEVEL CHECK

230 Models

Up to 1976 models, use ATF in the carburetor damper. Beginning with 1977 models, use ATF in the winter and engine oil in the summer.

Some carburetor models use an oil reservoir and some do not. If no reservoir is used, unscrew and remove the damper. The oil level should be at the upper edge of the piston pin. If a reservoir is used, the oil level should be as specified (see illustration).

Injection Pump

FLUID LEVEL CHECK

Diesel Engines

1. Screw out the check screw.
2. If there is too much oil, allow the oil to drain as far as the check bore.
3. If no oil flows from the check bore, unscrew the filter and add engine oil up to the check bore.

Chassis Greasing

It is not necessary to lubricate the chassis of models covered in this book. Development and use of long term lubricants has made this unnecessary.

Body Lubrication

The following points should be lubricated with multipurpose, lithium base chassis grease. The door hinges require the use of a grease gun; at other points, lubricant can be applied on the end of your finger.

Other points on the body should be lubricated with engine oil.

Wheel Bearings

Refer to Section 9 for wheel bearing service, adjustment and re-packing.

TOWING THE VEHICLE

For towing, the vehicle has a tow ring at the front of the chassis side member. A similar ring is provided at the rear for attaching a tow rope. It goes without saying that these two rings are for emergency use and for short distances only. A strong, flexible, woven fabric strap should be used. Never use a steel cable or rope.

✳✳ CAUTION

Whenever a vehicle is towed, for any reason, great care should be used.

Vehicles equipped with manual transmissions should be towed in Neutral and vehicles with automatic transmissions should be towed with the selector level in Neutral. The towing speed should never exceed 30 miles per hour.

✳✳ CAUTION

On vehicles with a damaged front end, the driveshaft must be disconnected to ensure that cooling water does not enter the transmission fluid or that the transmission is no longer lubricated due to an interrupted oil circuit.

TRAILER TOWING

General Recommendations

Your vehicle was primarily designed to carry passengers and cargo. It is important to remember that towing a trailer will place additional loads on your vehicles engine, drivetrain, steering, braking and other systems. However, if you decide to tow a trailer, using the prior equipment is a must.

Local laws may require specific equipment such as trailer brakes or fender mounted mirrors. Check your local laws.

Trailer Weight

The weight of the trailer is the most important factor. A good weight-to-horsepower ratio is about 35:1, 35 lbs. of Gross Combined Weight (GCW) for every horsepower your engine develops. Multiply the engine's rated horsepower by 35 and subtract the weight of the vehicle passengers and luggage. The number re-

maining is the approximate ideal maximum weight you should tow, although a numerically higher axle ratio can help compensate for heavier weight.

Hitch (Tongue) Weight

Calculate the hitch weight in order to select a proper hitch. The weight of the hitch is usually 9–11% of the trailer gross weight and should be measured with the trailer loaded. Hitches fall into various categories: those that mount on the frame and rear bumper, the bolt-on type, or the weld-on distribution type used for larger trailers. Axle mounted or clamp-on bumper hitches should never be used.

Check the gross weight rating of your trailer. Tongue weight is usually figured as 10% of gross trailer weight. Therefore, a trailer with a maximum gross weight of 2000 lbs. will have a maximum tongue weight of 200 lbs. Class I trailers fall into this category. Class II trailers are those with a gross weight rating of 2000–

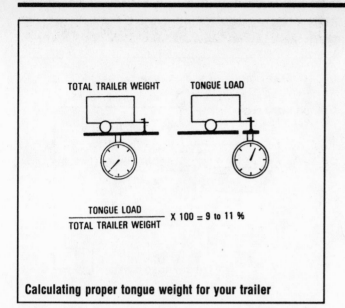

TOTAL TRAILER WEIGHT   TONGUE LOAD

$$\frac{\text{TONGUE LOAD}}{\text{TOTAL TRAILER WEIGHT}} \times 100 = 9 \text{ to } 11 \%$$

Calculating proper tongue weight for your trailer

3000 lbs., while Class III trailers fall into the 3500–6000 lbs. category. Class IV trailers are those over 6000 lbs. and are for use with fifth wheel trucks, only.

When you've determined the hitch that you'll need, follow the manufacturer's installation instructions, exactly, especially when it comes to fastener torques. The hitch will subjected to a lot of stress and good hitches come with hardened bolts. Never substitute an inferior bolt for a hardened bolt.

Cooling

ENGINE

Overflow Tank

One of the most common, if not THE most common, problems associated with trailer towing is engine overheating. If you have a cooling system without an expansion tank, you'll definitely need to get an aftermarket expansion tank kit, preferably one with at least a 2 quart capacity. These kits are easily installed on the radiator's overflow hose, and come with a pressure cap designed for expansion tanks.

Flex Fan

Another helpful accessory for vehicles using a belt-driven radiator fan is a flex fan. These fans are large diameter units designed to provide more airflow at low speeds, by using fan blades that have deeply cupped surfaces. The blades then flex, or flatten out, at high speed, when less cooling air is needed. These fans are far lighter in weight than stock fans, requiring less horsepower to drive them. Also, they are far quieter than stock fans. If you do de-

cide to replace your stock fan with a flex fan, note that if your vehicle has a fan clutch, a spacer will be needed between the flex fan and water pump hub.

Oil Cooler

Aftermarket engine oil coolers are helpful for prolonging engine oil life and reducing overall engine temperatures. Both of these factors increase engine life. While not absolutely necessary in towing Class I and some Class II trailers, they are recommended for heavier Class II and all Class III towing. Engine oil cooler systems usually consist of an adapter, screwed on in place of the oil filter, a remote filter mounting and a multi-tube, finned heat exchanger, which is mounted in front of the radiator or air conditioning condenser.

TRANSMISSION

An automatic transmission is usually recommended for trailer towing. Modern automatics have proven reliable and, of course, easy to operate, in trailer towing. The increased load of a trailer, however, causes an increase in the temperature of the automatic transmission fluid. Heat is the worst enemy of an automatic transmission. As the temperature of the fluid increases, the life of the fluid decreases.

It is essential, therefore, that you install an automatic transmission cooler. The cooler, which consists of a multi-tube, finned heat exchanger, is usually installed in front of the radiator or air conditioning compressor, and hooked in-line with the transmission cooler tank inlet line. Follow the cooler manufacturer's installation instructions.

Select a cooler of at least adequate capacity, based upon the combined gross weights of the vehicle and trailer.

Cooler manufacturers recommend that you use an aftermarket cooler in addition to, and not instead of, the present cooling tank in your radiator. If you do want to use it in place of the radiator cooling tank, get a cooler at least two sizes larger than normally necessary.

➡**A transmission cooler can, sometimes, cause slow or harsh shifting in the transmission during cold weather, until the fluid has a chance to come up to normal operating temperature. Some coolers can be purchased with or retrofitted with a temperature bypass valve which will allow fluid flow through the cooler only when the fluid has reached above a certain operating temperature.**

Handling A Trailer

Towing a trailer with ease and safety requires a certain amount of experience. It's a good idea to learn the feel of a trailer by practicing turning, stopping and backing in an open area such as an empty parking lot.

JUMP STARTING A DEAD BATTERY

Whenever a vehicle is jump started, precautions must be followed in order to prevent the possibility of personal injury. Remember that batteries contain a small amount of explosive hydrogen gas which is a by-product of battery charging. Sparks should always be avoided when working around batteries, especially when attaching jumper cables. To minimize the possibility of accidental sparks, follow the procedure carefully.

✳✳ CAUTION

NEVER hook the batteries up in a series circuit or the entire electrical system will go up in smoke, including the starter!

Vehicles equipped with a diesel engine may utilize two 12 volt batteries. If so, the batteries are connected in a parallel circuit (positive terminal to positive terminal, negative terminal to negative terminal). Hooking the batteries up in parallel circuit increases battery cranking power without increasing total battery voltage output. Output remains at 12 volts. On the other hand, hooking two 12 volt batteries up in a series circuit (positive terminal to negative terminal, positive terminal to negative terminal) increases total battery output to 24 volts (12 volts plus 12 volts).

Jump Starting Precautions

- Be sure that both batteries are of the same voltage. Vehicles covered by this manual and most vehicles on the road today utilize a 12 volt charging system.
- Be sure that both batteries are of the same polarity (have the same terminal, in most cases NEGATIVE grounded).
- Be sure that the vehicles are not touching or a short could occur.
- On serviceable batteries, be sure the vent cap holes are not obstructed.
- Do not smoke or allow sparks anywhere near the batteries.
- In cold weather, make sure the battery electrolyte is not frozen. This can occur more readily in a battery that has been in a state of discharge.
- Do not allow electrolyte to contact your skin or clothing.

Jump Starting Procedure

1. Make sure that the voltages of the 2 batteries are the same. Most batteries and charging systems are of the 12 volt variety.
2. Pull the jumping vehicle (with the good battery) into a position so the jumper cables can reach the dead battery and that vehicle's engine. Make sure that the vehicles do NOT touch.
3. Place the transmissions/transaxles of both vehicles in **Neutral** (MT) or **P** (AT), as applicable, then firmly set their parking brakes.

➡**If necessary for safety reasons, the hazard lights on both vehicles may be operated throughout the entire procedure without significantly increasing the difficulty of jumping the dead battery.**

4. Turn all lights and accessories OFF on both vehicles. Make sure the ignition switches on both vehicles are turned to the **OFF** position.

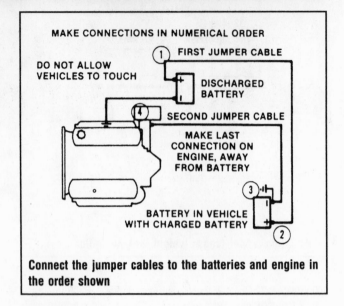

MAKE CONNECTIONS IN NUMERICAL ORDER

DO NOT ALLOW VEHICLES TO TOUCH

① FIRST JUMPER CABLE

DISCHARGED BATTERY

SECOND JUMPER CABLE

MAKE LAST CONNECTION ON ENGINE, AWAY FROM BATTERY

③

BATTERY IN VEHICLE WITH CHARGED BATTERY

②

Connect the jumper cables to the batteries and engine in the order shown

5. Cover the battery cell caps with a rag, but do not cover the terminals.
6. Make sure the terminals on both batteries are clean and free of corrosion or proper electrical connection will be impeded. If necessary, clean the battery terminals before proceeding.
7. Identify the positive (+) and negative (−) terminals on both batteries.
8. Connect the first jumper cable to the positive (+) terminal of the dead battery, then connect the other end of that cable to the positive (+) terminal of the booster (good) battery.
9. Connect one end of the other jumper cable to the negative (−) terminal on the booster battery and the final cable clamp to an engine bolt head, alternator bracket or other solid, metallic point on the engine with the dead battery. Try to pick a ground on the engine that is positioned away from the battery in order to minimize the possibility of the 2 clamps touching should one loosen during the procedure. DO NOT connect this clamp to the negative (−) terminal of the bad battery.

✳✳ CAUTION

Be very careful to keep the jumper cables away from moving parts (cooling fan, belts, etc.) on both engines.

10. Check to make sure that the cables are routed away from any moving parts, then start the donor vehicle's engine. Run the engine at moderate speed for several minutes to allow the dead battery a chance to receive some initial charge.
11. With the donor vehicle's engine still running slightly above idle, try to start the vehicle with the dead battery. Crank the engine for no more than 10 seconds at a time and let the starter cool for at least 20 seconds between tries. If the vehicle does not start in 3 tries, it is likely that something else is also wrong or that the battery needs additional time to charge.
12. Once the vehicle is started, allow it to run at idle for a few seconds to make sure that it is operating properly.
13. Turn ON the headlights, heater blower and, if equipped, the rear defroster of both vehicles in order to reduce the severity

of voltage spikes and subsequent risk of damage to the vehicles' electrical systems when the cables are disconnected. This step is especially important to any vehicle equipped with computer control modules.

14. Carefully disconnect the cables in the reverse order of connection. Start with the negative cable that is attached to the engine ground, then the negative cable on the donor battery. Disconnect the positive cable from the donor battery and finally, disconnect the positive cable from the formerly dead battery. Be careful when disconnecting the cables from the positive terminals not to allow the alligator clips to touch any metal on either vehicle or a short and sparks will occur.

JACKING

Your vehicle was supplied with a jack for emergency road repairs. This jack is fine for changing a flat tire or other short term procedures not requiring you to go beneath the vehicle. If it is used in an emergency situation, carefully follow the instructions provided either with the jack or in your owner's manual. Do not attempt to use the jack on any portions of the vehicle other than specified by the vehicle manufacturer. Always block the diagonally opposite wheel when using a jack.

A more convenient way of jacking is the use of a garage or floor jack.

Never place the jack under the radiator, engine or transmission components. Severe and expensive damage will result when the jack is raised. Additionally, never jack under the floorpan or bodywork; the metal will deform.

Whenever you plan to work under the vehicle, you must support it on jackstands or ramps. Never use cinder blocks or stacks of wood to support the vehicle, even if you're only going to be under it for a few minutes. Never crawl under the vehicle when it is supported only by the tire-changing jack or other floor jack.

➡**Always position a block of wood or small rubber pad on top of the jack or jackstand to protect the lifting point's finish when lifting or supporting the vehicle.**

Small hydraulic, screw, or scissors jacks are satisfactory for raising the vehicle. Drive-on trestles or ramps are also a handy and safe way to both raise and support the vehicle. Be careful though, some ramps may be too steep to drive your vehicle onto without scraping the front bottom panels. Never support the vehicle on any suspension member (unless specifically instructed to do so by a repair manual) or by an underbody panel.

Jacking Precautions

The following safety points cannot be overemphasized:
• Always block the opposite wheel or wheels to keep the vehicle from rolling off the jack.
• When raising the front of the vehicle, firmly apply the parking brake.
• When the drive wheels are to remain on the ground, leave the vehicle in gear to help prevent it from rolling.
• Always use jackstands to support the vehicle when you are working underneath. Place the stands beneath the vehicle's jacking brackets. Before climbing underneath, rock the vehicle a bit to make sure it is firmly supported.

HOW TO BUY A USED VEHICLE

Many people believe that a two or three year old used car or truck is a better buy than a new vehicle. This may be true as most new vehicles suffer the heaviest depreciation in the first two years and, at three years old, a vehicle is usually not old enough to present a lot of costly repair problems. But keep in mind, when buying a non-warranted automobile, there are no guarantees. Whatever the age of the used vehicle you might want to purchase, this section and a little patience should increase your chances of selecting one that is safe and dependable.

Tips

1. First decide what model you want, and how much you want to spend.

2. Check the used car lots and your local newspaper ads. Privately owned vehicles are usually less expensive, however, you may not get a warranty that, in many cases, comes with a used vehicle purchased from a lot. Of course, some aftermarket warranties may not be worth the extra money, so this is a point you will have to debate and consider based on your priorities.

3. Never shop at night. The glare of the lights make it easy to miss faults on the body caused by accident or rust repair.

4. Try to get the name and phone number of the previous owner. Contact him/her and ask about the vehicle. If the owner

of a lot refuses this information, look for a vehicle somewhere else.

A private seller can tell you about the vehicle and maintenance. But remember, there's no law requiring honesty from private citizens selling used vehicles. There is a law that forbids tampering with or turning back the odometer mileage. This includes both the private citizen and the lot owner. The law also requires that the seller or anyone transferring ownership of the vehicle must provide the buyer with a signed statement indicating the mileage on the odometer at the time of transfer.

5. You may wish to contact the National Highway Traffic Safety Administration (NHTSA) to find out if the vehicle has ever been included in a manufacturer's recall. Write down the year, model and serial number before you buy the vehicle, then contact NHTSA (there should be a 1-800 number that your phone company's information line can supply). If the vehicle was listed for a recall, make sure the needed repairs were made.

6. Refer to the Used Vehicle Checklist in this section and check all the items on the vehicle you are considering. Some items are more important than others. Only you know how much money you can afford for repairs, and depending on the price of the vehicle, may consider performing any needed work yourself. Beware, however, of trouble in areas that will affect operation, safety or emission. Problems in the Used Vehicle Checklist break down as follows:

• Numbers 1–8: Two or more problems in these areas indicate a lack of maintenance. You should beware.

• Numbers 9–13: Problems here tend to indicate a lack of proper care, however, these can usually be corrected with a tune-up or relatively simple parts replacement.

• Numbers 14–17: Problems in the engine or transmission can be very expensive. Unless you are looking for a project, walk away from any vehicle with problems in 2 or more of these areas.

7. If you are satisfied with the apparent condition of the vehicle, take it to an independent diagnostic center or mechanic for a complete check. If you have a state inspection program, have it inspected immediately before purchase, or specify on the bill of sale that the sale is conditional on passing state inspection.

8. Road test the vehicle—refer to the Road Test Checklist in this section. If your original evaluation and the road test agree—the rest is up to you.

USED VEHICLE CHECKLIST

➡ **The numbers on the illustrations refer to the numbers on this checklist.**

1. Mileage: Average mileage is about 12,000–15,000 miles per year. More than average mileage may indicate hard usage or could indicate many highway miles (which could be less detrimental than half as many tough around town miles).

2. Paint: Check around the tailpipe, molding and windows for overspray indicating that the vehicle has been repainted.

3. Rust: Check fenders, doors, rocker panels, window moldings, wheelwells, floorboards, under floormats, and in the trunk for signs of rust. Any rust at all will be a problem. There is no way to permanently stop the spread of rust, except to replace the part or panel.

➡ **If rust repair is suspected, try using a magnet to check for body filler. A magnet should stick to the sheet metal parts of the body, but will not adhere to areas with large amounts of filler.**

4. Body appearance: Check the moldings, bumpers, grille, vinyl roof, glass, doors, trunk lid and body panels for general over-

all condition. Check for misalignment, loose hold-down clips, ripples, scratches in glass, welding in the trunk, severe misalignment of body panels or ripples, any of which may indicate crash work.

5. Leaks: Get down and look under the vehicle. There are no normal leaks, other than water from the air conditioner evaporator.

6. Tires: Check the tire air pressure. One old trick is to pump the tire pressure up to make the vehicle roll easier. Check the tread wear, then open the trunk and check the spare too. Uneven wear is a clue that the front end may need an alignment.

7. Shock absorbers: Check the shock absorbers by forcing downward sharply on each corner of the vehicle. Good shocks will not allow the vehicle to bounce more than once after you let go.

8. Interior: Check the entire interior. You're looking for an interior condition that agrees with the overall condition of the vehicle. Reasonable wear is expected, but be suspicious of new seat covers on sagging seats, new pedal pads, and worn armrests. These indicate an attempt to cover up hard use. Pull back the carpets and look for evidence of water leaks or flooding. Look for missing hardware, door handles, control knobs, etc. Check lights and signal operations. Make sure all accessories (air conditioner, heater, radio, etc.) work. Check windshield wiper operation.

9. Belts and Hoses: Open the hood, then check all belts and hoses for wear, cracks or weak spots.

10. Battery: Low electrolyte level, corroded terminals and/or cracked case indicate a lack of maintenance.

11. Radiator: Look for corrosion or rust in the coolant indicating a lack of maintenance.

12. Air filter: A severely dirty air filter would indicate a lack of maintenance.

13. Ignition wires: Check the ignition wires for cracks, burned spots, or wear. Worn wires will have to be replaced.

14. Oil level: If the oil level is low, chances are the engine uses oil or leaks. Beware of water in the oil (there is probably a cracked block or bad head gasket), excessively thick oil (which is often used to quiet a noisy engine), or thin, dirty oil with a distinct gasoline smell (this may indicate internal engine problems).

15. Automatic Transmission: Pull the transmission dipstick out when the engine is running. The level should read FULL, and the fluid should be clear or bright red. Dark brown or black fluid that

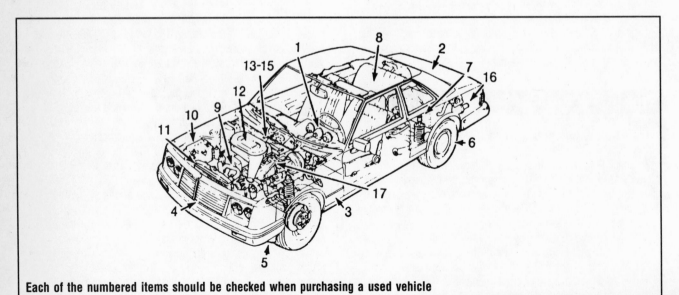

Each of the numbered items should be checked when purchasing a used vehicle

has distinct burnt odor, indicates a transmission in need of repair or overhaul.

16. Exhaust: Check the color of the exhaust smoke. Blue smoke indicates, among other problems, worn rings. Black smoke can indicate burnt valves or carburetor problems. Check the exhaust system for leaks; it can be expensive to replace.

17. Spark Plugs: Remove one or all of the spark plugs (the most accessible will do, though all are preferable). An engine in good condition will show plugs with a light tan or gray deposit on the firing tip.

ROAD TEST CHECKLIST

1. Engine Performance: The vehicle should be peppy whether cold or warm, with adequate power and good pickup. It should respond smoothly through the gears.

2. Brakes: They should provide quick, firm stops with no noise, pulling or brake fade.

3. Steering: Sure control with no binding harshness, or looseness and no shimmy in the wheel should be expected. Noise or vibration from the steering wheel when turning the vehicle means trouble.

4. Clutch (Manual Transmission/Transaxle): Clutch action should give quick, smooth response with easy shifting. The clutch pedal should have free-play before it disengages the clutch. Start the engine, set the parking brake, put the transmission in first gear and slowly release the clutch pedal. The engine should begin to stall when the pedal is ½–¾ of the way up.

5. Automatic Transmission/Transaxle: The transmission should shift rapidly and smoothly, with no noise, hesitation, or slipping.

6. Differential: No noise or thumps should be present. Differentials have no normal leaks.

7. Driveshaft/Universal Joints: Vibration and noise could mean driveshaft problems. Clicking at low speed or coast conditions means worn U-joints.

8. Suspension: Try hitting bumps at different speeds. A vehicle that bounces excessively has weak shock absorbers or struts. Clunks mean worn bushings or ball joints.

9. Frame/Body: Wet the tires and drive in a straight line. Tracks should show two straight lines, not four. Four tire tracks indicate a frame/body bent by collision damage. If the tires can't be wet for this purpose, have a friend drive along behind you and see if the vehicle appears to be traveling in a straight line.

Maintenance Intervals (All Figures in Thousands of Miles)

Model(s)	Automatic Trans Fluid		Engine Oil		Oil Filter Change	Coolant		Paper Element Air Filter		Inj Pump Oil Check	Clutch Master Cylinder Fluid Check	Manual Trans Oil Check
	Check & Refill	Change	Check* & Refill	** Change		Check Level	Renew	Clean	Change			
1974												
230	10	30	1	5	5	5	24	10	①	—	10	10
240D	10	30	1	3	3	5	24	10	①	10	—	—
280, 280C	10	30	1	5	5	5	24	10	①	—	—	—
450SE, 450SEL, 450SL, 450SLC	10	30	1	5	5	5	24	10	①	—	—	—
1975--76												
230	6	25	1	6	6	5	24	12.5	①	—	—	—
240D, 300D	6	25	1	3	3	5	24	12.5	①	3	6	12.5
All others	6	25	1	6	6	5	24	12.5	①	—	—	—
1977 and later												
190D, 240D, 300D, 300CD, 300SD, 300TD	6	30	1	5	5	5	24	12.5	①	12.5	3	15
230, 280E, 280CE	6	30	1	6	6	5	24	12.5	①	—	—	—
6.9	6	30	1	12.5	12.5	5	24	12.5	①	—	—	—
All others	6	30	1	7.5	7.5	5	24	12.5	①	—	—	15

Maintenance Intervals (All Figures in Thousands of Miles) (cont.)

Model(s)	Power Steering Fluid Check	Manual Steering Oil Check	Rear Axle Oil Check	Level Control Fluid Check	Brake Fluid Level Check	Fuel Filter		Carburetor Damper Fluid Check	Flame Guard Element Clean	Drive Belts Check/ Adjust	Body Lubrication
						Element	Fuel Pump Strainer				
1974											
230	10	10	10	—	10	—	30	10	10	10	10
240D	10	10	10	—	10	30	30	—	—	10	10
280, 280C	10	10	10	—	10	30	30	—	10	10	10
450SE, 450SEL, 450SL, 450SLC	10	—	10	—	10	30	—	—	10	10	10
1975–76											
230	6	—	12.5	—	6	—	25	6	—	12.5	12.5
240D, 300D	6	—	12.5	—	6	25	25	—	—	12.5	12.5
All others	6	—	12.5	12.5	6	25	—	—	—	12.5	12.5
1977 and Later											
240D, 300D, 300CD, 300TD	—	—	6	6	6	30	30	—	—	12.5	12.5
230, 280E, 280CE	6	—	6	—	6	37.5	37.5	6	—	12.5	12.5
6.9	6	—	6	6	6	37.5	—	—	—	12.5	12.5
All others	6	—	6	6	6	30	—	—	—	12.5	12.5

① Replace as necessary   — Not Applicable

Capacities

Year	Model	Cooling System (qts)	Crankcase Engine (qts)▲		Transmission (pts)		Drive Axle (pts)	Steering Gear (pts)		Level Control (qts)
			With Filter	Without Filter	Manual	Automatic		Pwr	Man	
1984	190E	9.0	4.8	4.3	3.2	11.6	1.5	1.0	—	—
1984	190D	9.0	6.3	5.8	3.2	11.6	1.5	1.0	—	—
1974–78	230	10.5	5.8	5.3	—	11.5	②	3.0	⅝	—
1974–76	240D	10.5	6.3	5.3	3.4	11.5	②	3.0	⅝	—
1977–83	240D	10.5	6.3	5.3	3.4	11.5	②	3.0	⅝	—
1973–76	280, 280C	11.5	6.3	5.8	—	12.3	②	3.0	—	—
1977–81	280E, 280CE	11.5	6.3	5.8	—	12.3	2.1	3.0	—	—
1975–76	280S	11.5	6.3	5.8	—	12.3	2.1	3.0	—	—
1977–80	280SE	11.5	6.3	5.8	—	12.3	2.1	3.0	—	—
1975–76	300D	11.7	6.8	5.8	—	11.5	③	3.0	—	—
1977–81	300D, 300CD	11.7	6.8	5.3	—	11.5	2.1	3.0	—	—
1982–84	300D, 300CD	13.2	8.0	6.3	—	13.2	2.2	3.0	—	—
1978–80	300SD, 300TD	12.7	6.8	5.3	—	11.5	2.1	3.0	—	6.2④
1981–84	300SD, 300TD	13.2	8.0	6.3	—	13.2	2.2	3.0	—	3.7
1981	380SL, SLC, SEL	13.7	8.5	8.0	—	13.0	2.7	⑤	—	—
1982–84	380SL, 380SE	13.2	8.5	8.0	—	16.2	2.7	3.0	—	—
1982–83	380SEL, 380SEC	13.2	8.5	8.0	—	13.0	2.7	2.5	—	—
1974–80	450SE, 450SEL, 450SL, 450SLC	16.0	8.5	8.0	—	16.5	①	3.0	—	6.2④
1984	500SEC, 500SEL	13.7	8.5	8.0	—	16.2	2.8	2.6	—	—
1978–79	6.9	16.0	11.5	10.5	—	16.5	2.7	3.0	—	6.2④

▲ Add approximately ½ quart if equipped with additional oil cooler
— Not Applicable
① 450SL, 450SLC—2.7 pts
  450SE 450SEL—3.0 pts
② See text: 1st version—2.4 pts
    2nd version—2.1 pts
③ 1975–76—1st version—2.4 pts ⎫ See Text
    2nd version—2.1 pts ⎭
④ Approximately 1 qt between dipstick maximum and minimum marks
⑤ 380SEL—2.5
  380SL, 380SLC—3.0

ENGLISH TO METRIC CONVERSION: MASS (WEIGHT)

Current **mass** measurement is expressed in pounds and ounces (lbs. & ozs.). The metric unit of mass (or weight) is the kilogram (kg). Even although this table does not show conversion of masses (weights) larger than 15 lbs, it is easy to calculate larger units by following the data immediately below.

To convert ounces (oz.) to grams (g): multiply th number of ozs. by 28
To convert grams (g) to ounces (oz.): multiply the number of grams by .035

To convert pounds (lbs.) to kilograms (kg): multiply the number of lbs. by .45
To convert kilograms (kg) to pounds (lbs.): multiply the number of kilograms by 2.2

lbs	kg	lbs	kg	oz	kg	oz	kg
0.1	0.04	0.9	0.41	0.1	0.003	0.9	0.024
0.2	0.09	1	0.4	0.2	0.005	1	0.03
0.3	0.14	2	0.9	0.3	0.008	2	0.06
0.4	0.18	3	1.4	0.4	0.011	3	0.08
0.5	0.23	4	1.8	0.5	0.014	4	0.11
0.6	0.27	5	2.3	0.6	0.017	5	0.14
0.7	0.32	10	4.5	0.7	0.020	10	0.28
0.8	0.36	15	6.8	0.8	0.023	15	0.42

ENGLISH TO METRIC CONVERSION: TEMPERATURE

To convert Fahrenheit (°F) to Celsius (°C): take number of °F and subtract 32; multiply result by 5; divide result by 9

To convert Celsius (°C) to Fahrenheit (°F): take number of °C and multiply by 9; divide result by 5; add 32 to total

Fahrenheit (F)		Celsius (C)		Fahrenheit (F)		Celsius (C)		Fahrenheit (F)		Celsius (C)	
°F	°C	°C	°F	°F	°C	°C	°F	°F	°C	°C	°F
−40	−40	−38	−36.4	80	26.7	18	64.4	215	101.7	80	176
−35	−37.2	−36	−32.8	85	29.4	20	68	220	104.4	85	185
−30	−34.4	−34	−29.2	90	32.2	22	71.6	225	107.2	90	194
−25	−31.7	−32	−25.6	95	35.0	24	75.2	230	110.0	95	202
−20	−28.9	−30	−22	100	37.8	26	78.8	235	112.8	100	212
−15	−26.1	−28	−18.4	105	40.6	28	82.4	240	115.6	105	221
−10	−23.3	−26	−14.8	110	43.3	30	86	245	118.3	110	230
−5	−20.6	−24	−11.2	115	46.1	32	89.6	250	121.1	115	239
0	−17.8	−22	−7.6	120	48.9	34	93.2	255	123.9	120	248
1	−17.2	−20	−4	125	51.7	36	96.8	260	126.6	125	257
2	−16.7	−18	−0.4	130	54.4	38	100.4	265	129.4	130	266
3	−16.1	−16	3.2	135	57.2	40	104	270	132.2	135	275
4	−15.6	−14	6.8	140	60.0	42	107.6	275	135.0	140	284
5	−15.0	−12	10.4	145	62.8	44	112.2	280	137.8	145	293
10	−12.2	−10	14	150	65.6	46	114.8	285	140.6	150	302
15	−9.4	−8	17.6	155	68.3	48	118.4	290	143.3	155	311
20	−6.7	−6	21.2	160	71.1	50	122	295	146.1	160	320
25	−3.9	−4	24.8	165	73.9	52	125.6	300	148.9	165	329
30	−1.1	−2	28.4	170	76.7	54	129.2	305	151.7	170	338
35	1.7	0	32	175	79.4	56	132.8	310	154.4	175	347
40	4.4	2	35.6	180	82.2	58	136.4	315	157.2	180	356
45	7.2	4	39.2	185	85.0	60	140	320	160.0	185	365
50	10.0	6	42.8	190	87.8	62	143.6	325	162.8	190	374
55	12.8	8	46.4	195	90.6	64	147.2	330	165.6	195	383
60	15.6	10	50	200	93.3	66	150.8	335	168.3	200	392
65	18.3	12	53.6	205	96.1	68	154.4	340	171.1	205	401
70	21.1	14	57.2	210	98.9	70	158	345	173.9	210	410
75	23.9	16	60.8	212	100.0	75	167	350	176.7	215	414

ENGLISH TO METRIC CONVERSION: LENGTH

To convert inches (ins.) to millimeters (mm): multiply number of inches by 25.4

To convert millimeters (mm) to inches (ins.): multiply number of millimeters by .04

Inches	Decimals	Milli-meters	Inches to millimeters inches	mm	Inches	Decimals	Milli-meters	Inches to millimeters inches	mm
1/64	0.051625	0.3969	0.0001	0.00254	33/64	0.515625	13.0969	0.6	15.24
1/32	0.03125	0.7937	0.0002	0.00508	17/32	0.53125	13.4937	0.7	17.78
3/64	0.046875	1.1906	0.0003	0.00762	35/64	0.546875	13.8906	0.8	20.32
1/16	0.0625	1.5875	0.0004	0.01016	9/16	0.5625	14.2875	0.9	22.86
5/64	0.078125	1.9844	0.0005	0.01270	37/64	0.578125	14.6844	1	25.4
3/32	0.09375	2.3812	0.0006	0.01524	19/32	0.59375	15.0812	2	50.8
7/64	0.109375	2.7781	0.0007	0.01778	39/64	0.609375	15.4781	3	76.2
1/8	0.125	3.1750	0.0008	0.02032	5/8	0.625	15.8750	4	101.6
9/64	0.140625	3.5719	0.0009	0.02286	41/64	0.640625	16.2719	5	127.0
5/32	0.15625	3.9687	0.001	0.0254	21/32	0.65625	16.6687	6	152.4
11/64	0.171875	4.3656	0.002	0.0508	43/64	0.671875	17.0656	7	177.8
3/16	0.1875	4.7625	0.003	0.0762	11/16	0.6875	17.4625	8	203.2
13/64	0.203125	5.1594	0.004	0.1016	45/64	0.703125	17.8594	9	228.6
7/32	0.21875	5.5562	0.005	0.1270	23/32	0.71875	18.2562	10	254.0
15/64	0.234375	5.9531	0.006	0.1524	47/64	0.734375	18.6531	11	279.4
1/4	0.25	6.3500	0.007	0.1778	3/4	0.75	19.0500	12	304.8
17/64	0.265625	6.7469	0.008	0.2032	49/64	0.765625	19.4469	13	330.2
9/32	0.28125	7.1437	0.009	0.2286	25/32	0.78125	19.8437	14	355.6
19/64	0.296875	7.5406	0.01	0.254	51/64	0.796875	20.2406	15	381.0
5/16	0.3125	7.9375	0.02	0.508	13/16	0.8125	20.6375	16	406.4
21/64	0.328125	8.3344	0.03	0.762	53/64	0.828125	21.0344	17	431.8
11/32	0.34375	8.7312	0.04	1.016	27/32	0.84375	21.4312	18	457.2
23/64	0.359375	9.1281	0.05	1.270	55/64	0.859375	21.8281	19	482.6
3/8	0.375	9.5250	0.06	1.524	7/8	0.875	22.2250	20	508.0
25/64	0.390625	9.9219	0.07	1.778	57/64	0.890625	22.6219	21	533.4
13/32	0.40625	10.3187	0.08	2.032	29/32	0.90625	23.0187	22	558.8
27/64	0.421875	10.7156	0.09	2.286	59/64	0.921875	23.4156	23	584.2
7/16	0.4375	11.1125	0.1	2.54	15/16	0.9375	23.8125	24	609.6
29/64	0.453125	11.5094	0.2	5.08	61/64	0.953125	24.2094	25	635.0
15/32	0.46875	11.9062	0.3	7.62	31/32	0.96875	24.6062	26	660.4
31/64	0.484375	12.3031	0.4	10.16	63/64	0.984375	25.0031	27	690.6
1/2	0.5	12.7000	0.5	12.70					

ENGLISH TO METRIC CONVERSION: TORQUE

To convert foot-pounds (ft. lbs.) to Newton-meters: multiply the number of ft. lbs. by 1.3

To convert inch-pounds (in. lbs.) to Newton-meters: multiply the number of in. lbs. by .11

in lbs	N-m	in lbs	N-m	in lbs	N-m	in lbs	N-m	in lbs	N-m
0.1	0.01	1	0.11	10	1.13	19	2.15	28	3.16
0.2	0.02	2	0.23	11	1.24	20	2.26	29	3.28
0.3	0.03	3	0.34	12	1.36	21	2.37	30	3.39
0.4	0.04	4	0.45	13	1.47	22	2.49	31	3.50
0.5	0.06	5	0.56	14	1.58	23	2.60	32	3.62
0.6	0.07	6	0.68	15	1.70	24	2.71	33	3.73
0.7	0.08	7	0.78	16	1.81	25	2.82	34	3.84
0.8	0.09	8	0.90	17	1.92	26	2.94	35	3.95
0.9	0.10	9	1.02	18	2.03	27	3.05	36	4.0

ENGLISH TO METRIC CONVERSION: TORQUE

Torque is now expressed as either foot-pounds (ft./lbs.) or inch-pounds (in./lbs.). The metric measurement unit for torque is the Newton-meter (Nm). This unit—the Nm—will be used for all SI metric torque references, both the present ft./lbs. and in./lbs.

ft lbs	N-m	ft lbs	N-m	ft lbs	N-m	ft lbs	N-m
0.1	0.1	33	44.7	74	100.3	115	155.9
0.2	0.3	34	46.1	75	101.7	116	157.3
0.3	0.4	35	47.4	76	103.0	117	158.6
0.4	0.5	36	48.8	77	104.4	118	160.0
0.5	0.7	37	50.7	78	105.8	119	161.3
0.6	0.8	38	51.5	79	107.1	120	162.7
0.7	1.0	39	52.9	80	108.5	121	164.0
0.8	1.1	40	54.2	81	109.8	122	165.4
0.9	1.2	41	55.6	82	111.2	123	166.8
1	1.3	42	56.9	83	112.5	124	168.1
2	2.7	43	58.3	84	113.9	125	169.5
3	4.1	44	59.7	85	115.2	126	170.8
4	5.4	45	61.0	86	116.6	127	172.2
5	6.8	46	62.4	87	118.0	128	173.5
6	8.1	47	63.7	88	119.3	129	174.9
7	9.5	48	65.1	89	120.7	130	176.2
8	10.8	49	66.4	90	122.0	131	177.6
9	12.2	50	67.8	91	123.4	132	179.0
10	13.6	51	69.2	92	124.7	133	180.3
11	14.9	52	70.5	93	126.1	134	181.7
12	16.3	53	71.9	94	127.4	135	183.0
13	17.6	54	73.2	95	128.8	136	184.4
14	18.9	55	74.6	96	130.2	137	185.7
15	20.3	56	75.9	97	131.5	138	187.1
16	21.7	57	77.3	98	132.9	139	188.5
17	23.0	58	78.6	99	134.2	140	189.8
18	24.4	59	80.0	100	135.6	141	191.2
19	25.8	60	81.4	101	136.9	142	192.5
20	27.1	61	82.7	102	138.3	143	193.9
21	28.5	62	84.1	103	139.6	144	195.2
22	29.8	63	85.4	104	141.0	145	196.6
23	31.2	64	86.8	105	142.4	146	198.0
24	32.5	65	88.1	106	143.7	147	199.3
25	33.9	66	89.5	107	145.1	148	200.7
26	35.2	67	90.8	108	146.4	149	202.0
27	36.6	68	92.2	109	147.8	150	203.4
28	38.0	69	93.6	110	149.1	151	204.7
29	39.3	70	94.9	111	150.5	152	206.1
30	40.7	71	96.3	112	151.8	153	207.4
31	42.0	72	97.6	113	153.2	154	208.8
32	43.4	73	99.0	114	154.6	155	210.2

ENGLISH TO METRIC CONVERSION: FORCE

Force is presently measured in pounds (lbs.). This type of measurement is used to measure spring pressure, specifically how many pounds it takes to compress a spring. Our present force unit (the pound) will be replaced in SI metric measurements by the Newton (N). This term will eventually see use in specifications for electric motor brush spring pressures, valve spring pressures, etc.

To convert pounds (lbs.) to Newton (N): multiply the number of lbs. by 4.45

lbs	N	lbs	N	lbs	N	oz	N
0.01	0.04	21	93.4	59	262.4	1	0.3
0.02	0.09	22	97.9	60	266.9	2	0.6
0.03	0.13	23	102.3	61	271.3	3	0.8
0.04	0.18	24	106.8	62	275.8	4	1.1
0.05	0.22	25	111.2	63	280.2	5	1.4
0.06	0.27	26	115.6	64	284.6	6	1.7
0.07	0.31	27	120.1	65	289.1	7	2.0
0.08	0.36	28	124.6	66	293.6	8	2.2
0.09	0.40	29	129.0	67	298.0	9	2.5
0.1	0.4	30	133.4	68	302.5	10	2.8
0.2	0.9	31	137.9	69	306.9	11	3.1
0.3	1.3	32	142.3	70	311.4	12	3.3
0.4	1.8	33	146.8	71	315.8	13	3.6
0.5	2.2	34	151.2	72	320.3	14	3.9
0.6	2.7	35	155.7	73	324.7	15	4.2
0.7	3.1	36	160.1	74	329.2	16	4.4
0.8	3.6	37	164.6	75	333.6	17	4.7
0.9	4.0	38	169.0	76	338.1	18	5.0
1	4.4	39	173.5	77	342.5	19	5.3
2	8.9	40	177.9	78	347.0	20	5.6
3	13.4	41	182.4	79	351.4	21	5.8
4	17.8	42	186.8	80	355.9	22	6.1
5	22.2	43	191.3	81	360.3	23	6.4
6	26.7	44	195.7	82	364.8	24	6.7
7	31.1	45	200.2	83	369.2	25	7.0
8	35.6	46	204.6	84	373.6	26	7.2
9	40.0	47	209.1	85	378.1	27	7.5
10	44.5	48	213.5	86	382.6	28	7.8
11	48.9	49	218.0	87	387.0	29	8.1
12	53.4	50	224.4	88	391.4	30	8.3
13	57.8	51	226.9	89	395.9	31	8.6
14	62.3	52	231.3	90	400.3	32	8.9
15	66.7	53	235.8	91	404.8	33	9.2
16	71.2	54	240.2	92	409.2	34	9.4
17	75.6	55	244.6	93	413.7	35	9.7
18	80.1	56	249.1	94	418.1	36	10.0
19	84.5	57	253.6	95	422.6	37	10.3
20	89.0	58	258.0	96	427.0	38	10.6

ENGLISH TO METRIC CONVERSION: LIQUID CAPACITY

Liquid or fluid capacity is presently expressed as pints, quarts or gallons, or a combination of all of these. In the metric system the liter (l) will become the basic unit. Fractions of a liter would be expressed as deciliters, centiliters, or most frequently (and commonly) as milliliters.

To convert pints (pts.) to liters (l): multiply the number of pints by .47
To convert liters (l) to pints (pts.): multiply the number of liters by 2.1
To convert quarts (qts.) to liters (l): multiply the number of quarts by .95

To convert liters (l) to quarts (qts.): multiply the number of liters by 1.06
To convert gallons (gals.) to liters (l): multiply the number of gallons by 3.8
To convert liters (l) to gallons (gals.): multiply the number of liters by .26

gals	liters	qts	liters	pts	liters
0.1	0.38	0.1	0.10	0.1	0.05
0.2	0.76	0.2	0.19	0.2	0.10
0.3	1.1	0.3	0.28	0.3	0.14
0.4	1.5	0.4	0.38	0.4	0.19
0.5	1.9	0.5	0.47	0.5	0.24
0.6	2.3	0.6	0.57	0.6	0.28
0.7	2.6	0.7	0.66	0.7	0.33
0.8	3.0	0.8	0.76	0.8	0.38
0.9	3.4	0.9	0.85	0.9	0.43
1	3.8	1	1.0	1	0.5
2	7.6	2	1.9	2	1.0
3	11.4	3	2.8	3	1.4
4	15.1	4	3.8	4	1.9
5	18.9	5	4.7	5	2.4
6	22.7	6	5.7	6	2.8
7	26.5	7	6.6	7	3.3
8	30.3	8	7.6	8	3.8
9	34.1	9	8.5	9	4.3
10	37.8	10	9.5	10	4.7
11	41.6	11	10.4	11	5.2
12	45.4	12	11.4	12	5.7
13	49.2	13	12.3	13	6.2
14	53.0	14	13.2	14	6.6
15	56.8	15	14.2	15	7.1
16	60.6	16	15.1	16	7.6
17	64.3	17	16.1	17	8.0
18	68.1	18	17.0	18	8.5
19	71.9	19	18.0	19	9.0
20	75.7	20	18.9	20	9.5
21	79.5	21	19.9	21	9.9
22	83.2	22	20.8	22	10.4
23	87.0	23	21.8	23	10.9
24	90.8	24	22.7	24	11.4
25	94.6	25	23.6	25	11.8
26	98.4	26	24.6	26	12.3
27	102.2	27	25.5	27	12.8
28	106.0	28	26.5	28	13.2
29	110.0	29	27.4	29	13.7
30	113.5	30	28.4	30	14.2

ENGLISH TO METRIC CONVERSION: PRESSURE

The basic unit of pressure measurement used today is expressed as pounds per square inch (psi). The metric unit for psi will be the kilopascal (kPa). This will apply to either fluid pressure or air pressure, and will be frequently seen in tire pressure readings, oil pressure specifications, fuel pump pressure, etc.

To convert pounds per square inch (psi) to kilopascals (kPa): multiply the number of psi by 6.89

Psi	kPa	Psi	kPa	Psi	kPa	Psi	kPa
0.1	0.7	37	255.1	82	565.4	127	875.6
0.2	1.4	38	262.0	83	572.3	128	882.5
0.3	2.1	39	268.9	84	579.2	129	889.4
0.4	2.8	40	275.8	85	586.0	130	896.3
0.5	3.4	41	282.7	86	592.9	131	903.2
0.6	4.1	42	289.6	87	599.8	132	910.1
0.7	4.8	43	296.5	88	606.7	133	917.0
0.8	5.5	44	303.4	89	613.6	134	923.9
0.9	6.2	45	310.3	90	620.5	135	930.8
1	6.9	46	317.2	91	627.4	136	937.7
2	13.8	47	324.0	92	634.3	137	944.6
3	20.7	48	331.0	93	641.2	138	951.5
4	27.6	49	337.8	94	648.1	139	958.4
5	34.5	50	344.7	95	655.0	140	965.2
6	41.4	51	351.6	96	661.9	141	972.2
7	48.3	52	358.5	97	668.8	142	979.0
8	55.2	53	365.4	98	675.7	143	985.9
9	62.1	54	372.3	99	682.6	144	992.8
10	69.0	55	379.2	100	689.5	145	999.7
11	75.8	56	386.1	101	696.4	146	1006.6
12	82.7	57	393.0	102	703.3	147	1013.5
13	89.6	58	399.9	103	710.2	148	1020.4
14	96.5	59	406.8	104	717.0	149	1027.3
15	103.4	60	413.7	105	723.9	150	1034.2
16	110.3	61	420.6	106	730.8	151	1041.1
17	117.2	62	427.5	107	737.7	152	1048.0
18	124.1	63	434.4	108	744.6	153	1054.9
19	131.0	64	441.3	109	751.5	154	1061.8
20	137.9	65	448.2	110	758.4	155	1068.7
21	144.8	66	455.0	111	765.3	156	1075.6
22	151.7	67	461.9	112	772.2	157	1082.5
23	158.6	68	468.8	113	779.1	158	1089.4
24	165.5	69	475.7	114	786.0	159	1096.3
25	172.4	70	482.6	115	792.9	160	1103.2
26	179.3	71	489.5	116	799.8	161	1110.0
27	186.2	72	496.4	117	806.7	162	1116.9
28	193.0	73	503.3	118	813.6	163	1123.8
29	200.0	74	510.2	119	820.5	164	1130.7
30	206.8	75	517.1	120	827.4	165	1137.6
31	213.7	76	524.0	121	834.3	166	1144.5
32	220.6	77	530.9	122	841.2	167	1151.4
33	227.5	78	537.8	123	848.0	168	1158.3
34	234.4	79	544.7	124	854.9	169	1165.2
35	241.3	80	551.6	125	861.8	170	1172.1
36	248.2	81	558.5	126	868.7	171	1179.0

ENGLISH TO METRIC CONVERSION: PRESSURE

The basic unit of pressure measurement used today is expressed as pounds per square inch (psi). The metric unit for psi will be the kilopascal (kPa). This will apply to either fluid pressure or air pressure, and will be frequently seen in tire pressure readings, oil pressure specifications, fuel pump pressure, etc.

To convert pounds per square inch (psi) to kilopascals (kPa): multiply the number of psi by 6.89

Psi	kPa	Psi	kPa	Psi	kPa	Psi	kPa
172	1185.9	216	1489.3	260	1792.6	304	2096.0
173	1192.8	217	1496.2	261	1799.5	305	2102.9
174	1199.7	218	1503.1	262	1806.4	306	2109.8
175	1206.6	219	1510.0	263	1813.3	307	2116.7
176	1213.5	220	1516.8	264	1820.2	308	2123.6
177	1220.4	221	1523.7	265	1827.1	309	2130.5
178	1227.3	222	1530.6	266	1834.0	310	2137.4
179	1234.2	223	1537.5	267	1840.9	311	2144.3
180	1241.0	224	1544.4	268	1847.8	312	2151.2
181	1247.9	225	1551.3	269	1854.7	313	2158.1
182	1254.8	226	1558.2	270	1861.6	314	2164.9
183	1261.7	227	1565.1	271	1868.5	315	2171.8
184	1268.6	228	1572.0	272	1875.4	316	2178.7
185	1275.5	229	1578.9	273	1882.3	317	2185.6
186	1282.4	230	1585.8	274	1889.2	318	2192.5
187	1289.3	231	1592.7	275	1896.1	319	2199.4
188	1296.2	232	1599.6	276	1903.0	320	2206.3
189	1303.1	233	1606.5	277	1909.8	321	2213.2
190	1310.0	234	1613.4	278	1916.7	322	2220.1
191	1316.9	235	1620.3	279	1923.6	323	2227.0
192	1323.8	236	1627.2	280	1930.5	324	2233.9
193	1330.7	237	1634.1	281	1937.4	325	2240.8
194	1337.6	238	1641.0	282	1944.3	326	2247.7
195	1344.5	239	1647.8	283	1951.2	327	2254.6
196	1351.4	240	1654.7	284	1958.1	328	2261.5
197	1358.3	241	1661.6	285	1965.0	329	2268.4
198	1365.2	242	1668.5	286	1971.9	330	2275.3
199	1372.0	243	1675.4	287	1978.8	331	2282.2
200	1378.9	244	1682.3	288	1985.7	332	2289.1
201	1385.8	245	1689.2	289	1992.6	333	2295.9
202	1392.7	246	1696.1	290	1999.5	334	2302.8
203	1399.6	247	1703.0	291	2006.4	335	2309.7
204	1406.5	248	1709.9	292	2013.3	336	2316.6
205	1413.4	249	1716.8	293	2020.2	337	2323.5
206	1420.3	250	1723.7	294	2027.1	338	2330.4
207	1427.2	251	1730.6	295	2034.0	339	2337.3
208	1434.1	252	1737.5	296	2040.8	240	2344.2
209	1441.0	253	1744.4	297	2047.7	341	2351.1
210	1447.9	254	1751.3	298	2054.6	342	2358.0
211	1454.8	255	1758.2	299	2061.5	343	2364.9
212	1461.7	256	1765.1	300	2068.4	344	2371.8
213	1468.7	257	1772.0	301	2075.3	345	2378.7
214	1475.5	258	1778.8	302	2082.2	346	2385.6
215	1482.4	259	1785.7	303	2089.1	347	2392.5

2

ENGINE PERFORMANCE AND TUNE-UP

SPARK PLUGS AND WIRES

In order to extract the full measure of performance and economy from your engine it is essential that it be properly tuned at regular intervals. A regular tune-up will keep your Mercedes' engine running smoothly and will prevent the annoying minor breakdowns and poor performance associated with an untuned engine.

A complete tune-up should be performed every 15,000 miles or twelve months, whichever comes first. This interval should be halved if the car is operated under severe conditions, such as trailer towing, prolonged idling, continual stop and start driving, or if starting or running problems are noticed. It is assumed that

Gasoline Engine Tune-Up Specifications

When analyzing compression test results, look for uniformity among cylinders, rather than specific pressures.

Year	Model	Spark Plugs Type	Spark Plugs Gap (in.)	Distributor Point Dwell (deg)	Ignition Timing (deg) ①	Intake Valve Opens (deg) ⊕	Fuel Pump Pressure (psi)	▲ Idle Speed (rpm)	Valve Clear* (Cold) (in.) In	Valve Clear* (Cold) (in.) Ex
1974	230	N9Y	0.024	47–53	10B w/vacuum	14B	2–3	800–900	0.004	0.008
	280, 280C	N9Y	0.024	34–40	4A w/vacuum	②	3.5–5.0	④	0.004	0.010
	450SE, 450SEL	N9Y	0.024	30–34	5A w/vacuum	4B	30③	700–800	0.004	0.008
	450SL, 450SLC	N9Y	0.024	30–34	5A w/vacuum	4B	30③	700–800	0.004	0.008
1975	230	N9Y	0.024	47–53	10B w/o vacuum	14B	2–3	800–900	0.004	0.008
	280, 280C, 280S	N9Y	0.024	34–40	7B w/vacuum	7B	3.5–5.0	800–900	0.004	0.010
	450SE, 450SEL	N9Y	0.024	30–34	TDC w/vacuum	⑤	30③	700–800	0.004	0.008
	450SL, 450SLC	N9Y	0.024	30–34	TDC w/vacuum	⑤	30③	700–800	0.004	0.008
1976	230	N9Y	0.024	47–53	10B w/o vacuum	14B	2–3	800–900	0.004	0.008
	280, 280C, 280S	N9Y	0.024	34–40	7B w/vacuum	7B	3.5–5.0	800–900	0.004	0.010
	450SE, 450SEL	N9Y	0.024	Elec.	TDC w/vacuum	⑥	75–84③	700–800	Hyd.	Hyd.
	450SL, 450SLC	N9Y	0.024	Elec.	TDC w/vacuum	⑥	75–84③	700–800	Hyd.	Hyd.
1977	230	N10Y	0.028	46–53	10B w/vacuum	14B	2–3	850	0.004	0.008
	280E	N10Y	0.028	Elec.	TDC w/vacuum	7B	75–84③	800	0.004	0.010
	280SE	N10Y	0.028	Elec.	TDC w/vacuum	7B	75–84③	800	0.004	0.010
	450SE, 450SEL	N10Y	0.028	Elec.	TDC w/vacuum	⑥	75–84③	750	Hyd.	Hyd.
	450SL, 450SLC	N10Y	0.028	Elec.	TDC w/vacuum	⑥	75–84③	750	Hyd.	Hyd.
1978–79	230	N10Y	0.032	Elec.	10B w/vacuum	14B	2–3	850	0.004	0.008
	280E, 280CE, 280SE	N10Y	0.032	Elec.	TDC w/vacuum	7B	75–84③	800	0.004	0.010
	450SEL	N10Y	0.032	Elec.	TDC w/vacuum	⑥	75–84③	750	Hyd.	Hyd.
	450SL, 450SLC	N10Y	0.032	Elec.	TDC w/vacuum	⑥	75–84③	750	Hyd.	Hyd.
	6.9	N10Y	0.032	Elec.	TDC w/vacuum	⑦	75–84③	600	Hyd.	Hyd.

the routine maintenance described in Section 1 has been kept up, as this will have a decided effect on the results of a tune-up. All of the applicable steps of a tune-up should be followed in order, as the result is a cumulative one.

If the specifications on the tune-up sticker in the engine com-partment of your Mercedes-Benz disagree with the "Tune-Up Spec-ifications" chart in this section, the figures on the sticker must be used. The sticker often reflects changes made during the produc-tion run.

Gasoline Engine Tune-Up Specifications (cont.)

When analyzing compression test results, look for uniformity among cylinders, rather than specific pressures.

Year	Model	Spark Plugs Type	Gap (in.)	Distributor Point Dwell (deg)	Ignition Timing (deg) ①	Intake Valve Opens (deg) ●	Fuel Pump Pressure (psi)	▲ Idle Speed (rpm)	Valve Clear* (Cold) (in.) In	Ex
1980	280E, 280CE, 280SE	N10Y	0.032	Elec.	10B	7B	⑨	700–800	0.004	0.010
	450SEL	N10Y	0.032	Elec.	5B	⑩	⑨	600–700	Hyd.	Hyd.
	450SL, 450SLC	N10Y	0.032	Elec.	5B	⑩	⑨	600–700	Hyd.	Hyd.
1981	280E, 280CE	N10Y	0.032	Elec.	10B	7B	⑨	700–800	0.004	0.010
	380SEL	N10Y	0.032	Elec.	5B	24A	⑨	500	Hyd.	Hyd.
	380SL, 380SLC	N10Y	0.032	Elec.	5B	24A	⑨	500	Hyd.	Hyd.
1982	380SL	N10Y	0.032	Elec.	5B	24A	⑨	500–600	Hyd.	Hyd.
	380SEL	N10Y	0.032	Elec.	5B	24A	⑨	500–600	Hyd.	Hyd.
	380SEC	N10Y	0.032	Elec.	5B	24A	⑨	500–600	Hyd.	Hyd.
1983–84	190E	S12YC	0.032	Elec.	5B	⑧	77–80	700–800	Hyd.	Hyd.
	380SE	N10Y	0.032	Elec.	TDC w/o vacuum	24A	⑨	500–600	Hyd.	Hyd.
	380SL	N10Y	0.032	Elec.	TDC w/o vacuum	24A	⑨	500–600	Hyd.	Hyd.
	380SEL	N10Y	0.032	Elec.	TDC w/o vacuum	24A	⑨	500–600	Hyd.	Hyd.
	380SLC	N10Y	0.032	Elec.	TDC w/o vacuum	24A	⑨	500–600	Hyd.	Hyd.
	500SEC	N10Y	0.032	Elec.	TDC w/o vacuum	⑩	⑨	600–700	Hyd.	Hyd.
	500SEL	N10Y	0.032	Elec.	TDC w/o vacuum	⑩	⑨	600–700	Hyd.	Hyd.

CAUTION: *If the specifications listed above differ from those on the tune-up decal in the engine compartment, use those listed on the tune-up decal.*

NOTES: 1. On transistor ignitions, only a transistorized dwell meter can be used. Transistor ignitions are recognizable by the "Blue" ignition coil, 2 series resistors and the transistor switchgear.
2. To counteract wear of the fiber contact block, adjust the dwell to the lover end of the range.

A After Top Dead Center
B Before Top Dead Center
w/vacuum—vacuum advance connected
w/o vacuum—advance disconnected
* Below 0°F; increase valve clearance by 0.002 in.
—Not Available
▲ In Drive
● Timing for test measurements @ 2mm valve lift

① —At idle
② —11B—Federal; 6B—California
③ —Injection pump pressure
④ 750–900 Federal; 700–900 California
⑤ Right-side camshift—3° BTDC
　 Left-side camshaft—5° BTDC
⑥ Right-side camshaft—4.5° BTDC
　 Left-side camshaft—6.5° BTDC

⑦ Right-side camshaft—12° BTDC
　 Left-side camshaft—10° BTDC
⑧ New timing chain: 17A
　 Used timing chain (12,000 miles): 18A
⑨ Approx. 1 quart in 30 seconds
⑩ Right-side camshaft—20° ATDC
　 Left-side camshaft—22° ATDC

% CO at Idle (With or Without Air Injection)
(Gasoline Engines Only)

Model	1974	1975	1976	1977	1978–79
230	0.4–1.5 without	0.4–1.5 without	0.4–1.5 without	0.4–2.0 with	0.4–2.0 with
280 280C, 280S	max. 1.5 with	max. 1.0 without	max. 1.0 without	—	—
280E, 280CE, 280SE	—	—	—	0.4–2.0 without	0.4–2.0 without
450SE, 450SEL, 450SL, 450SLC	0.5–2.0 max. 1.0 with (Calif.)	max. 1.5 without	0.2–1.5 without	①	①
6.9	—	—	—	—	②

—Not Applicable
① California 0.2–2.0 without
   Federal 0.2–2.0 with
   Federal high altitude 0.2–2.0 with
② Federal and California 0.2–2.0 without
   Federal high altitude 0.2–1.2 without

Diesel Engine Tune-Up Specifications

Model	Valve Clearance (cold) ①		Intake Valve Opens (deg)	Injection Pump Setting (deg)	Injection Nozzle Pressure (psi)		Idle Speed (rpm) ②	Cranking Compression Pressure (psi)
	Intake (in.)	Exhaust (in.)			New	Used		
190D	Hyd.	Hyd.	⑤	15A	1564–1706	1422–1706	700–800	284–327
240D (4-cylinder) '74–'81	0.004	0.016	13.5B	24B	1564–1706	1422–1706	750–800	284–327
240D 4-cylinder '82–'83	0.004	0.016	13.5B	24B	1564–1706	1422–1706	700–800	284–327
300D, 300CD, 300TD (5-cylinder, non-turbo)	0.004	0.012	13.5B	24B ④	1635–1750 ③	1422	700–800	284–327
300SD, 300TD (5-cylinder, turbo) '77–'81	0.004	0.014	13.5B	24B ④	1958–2074	1740	650–850–	284–327
300D 300CD 300SD 300TD (5-cylinder, turbo) '82–'84	0.004	0.014	13.5B	24B ④⑦	1958–2074	1740	650–850 ⑥	284–327

B Before Top Dead Center
① In cold weather (below 5°F.), increase valve clearance 0.002 in.
② Manual transmission in Neutral; Automatic in Drive.
③ Difference in opening pressure on injection nozzles should not exceed 71 psi.
④ The injection pump is in start of delivery position when the mark on the pump camshaft is aligned with the mark on the injection pump flange.
⑤ New timing chain—11A
   Used timing chain (12,000 miles)— 12A
⑥ 1984—700–800
⑦ 1984—15A

Spark Plugs

A typical spark plug consists of a metal shell surrounding a ceramic insulator. A metal electrode extends downward through the center of the insulator and protrudes a small distance. Located at the end of the plug and attached to the side of the outer metal shell is the side electrode. The side electrode bends in at a 90° angle so that its tip is just past and parallel to the tip of the center electrode. The distance between these two electrodes (measured in thousandths of an inch or hundredths of a millimeter) is called the spark plug gap.

The spark plug does not produce a spark but instead provides a gap across which the current can arc. The coil produces anywhere from 20,000 to 50,000 volts (depending on the type and application) which travels through the wires to the spark plugs. The current passes along the center electrode and jumps the gap to the side electrode, and in doing so, ignites the air/fuel mixture in the combustion chamber.

SPARK PLUG HEAT RANGE

Spark plug heat range is the ability of the plug to dissipate heat. The longer the insulator (or the farther it extends into the engine), the hotter the plug will operate; the shorter the insulator (the closer the electrode is to the block's cooling passages) the cooler it will operate. A plug that absorbs little heat and remains too cool will quickly accumulate deposits of oil and carbon since it is not hot enough to burn them off. This leads to plug fouling and consequently to misfiring. A plug that absorbs too much heat will have no deposits but, due to the excessive heat, the electrodes will burn away quickly and might possibly lead to preignition or other ignition problems. Preignition takes place when plug tips get so hot that they glow sufficiently to ignite the air/fuel mixture before the actual spark occurs. This early ignition will usually cause a pinging during low speeds and heavy loads.

The general rule of thumb for choosing the correct heat range when picking a spark plug is: if most of your driving is long distance, high speed travel, use a colder plug; if most of your driving is stop and go, use a hotter plug. Original equipment plugs

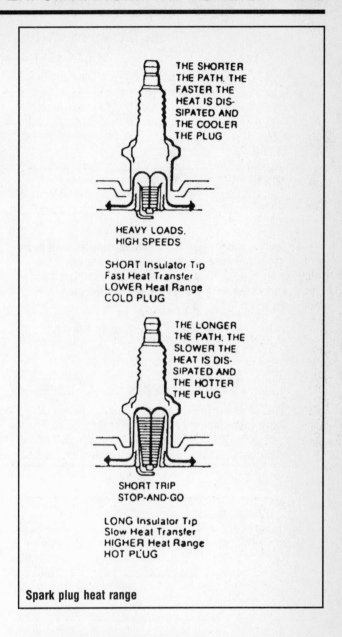

THE SHORTER THE PATH, THE FASTER THE HEAT IS DISSIPATED AND THE COOLER THE PLUG

HEAVY LOADS.
HIGH SPEEDS

SHORT Insulator Tip
Fast Heat Transfer
LOWER Heat Range
COLD PLUG

THE LONGER THE PATH, THE SLOWER THE HEAT IS DISSIPATED AND THE HOTTER THE PLUG

SHORT TRIP
STOP-AND-GO

LONG Insulator Tip
Slow Heat Transfer
HIGHER Heat Range
HOT PLUG

Spark plug heat range

are generally a good compromise between the 2 styles and most people never have the need to change their plugs from the factory-recommended heat range.

REMOVAL & INSTALLATION

A set of spark plugs usually requires replacement after about 20,000–30,000 miles (32,000–48,000 km), depending on your style of driving. In normal operation plug gap increases about 0.001 in. (0.025mm) for every 2500 miles (4000 km). As the gap increases, the plug's voltage requirement also increases. It requires a greater voltage to jump the wider gap and about two to three times as much voltage to fire the plug at high speeds than at idle. The improved air/fuel ratio control of modern fuel injection combined with the higher voltage output of modern ignition systems will often allow an engine to run significantly longer on a set of standard spark plugs, but keep in mind that efficiency will drop as the gap widens (along with fuel economy and power).

When you're removing spark plugs, work on one at a time.

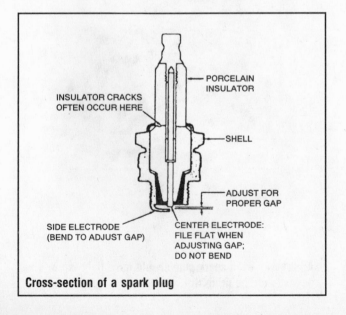

PORCELAIN INSULATOR

INSULATOR CRACKS OFTEN OCCUR HERE

SHELL

ADJUST FOR PROPER GAP

SIDE ELECTRODE
(BEND TO ADJUST GAP)

CENTER ELECTRODE:
FILE FLAT WHEN ADJUSTING GAP;
DO NOT BEND

Cross-section of a spark plug

Don't start by removing the plug wires all at once, because, unless you number them, they may become mixed up. Take a minute before you begin and number the wires with tape.

1. Disconnect the negative battery cable, and if the vehicle has been run recently, allow the engine to thoroughly cool.

2. Carefully twist the spark plug wire boot to loosen it, then pull upward and remove the boot from the plug. Be sure to pull on the boot and not on the wire, otherwise the connector located inside the boot may become separated.

3. Using compressed air, blow any water or debris from the spark plug well to assure that no harmful contaminants are allowed to enter the combustion chamber when the spark plug is removed. If compressed air is not available, use a rag or a brush to clean the area.

➡**Remove the spark plugs when the engine is cold, if possible, to prevent damage to the threads. If removal of the plugs is difficult, apply a few drops of penetrating oil or silicone spray to the area around the base of the plug, and allow it a few minutes to work.**

4. Using a spark plug socket that is equipped with a rubber insert to properly hold the plug, turn the spark plug counterclockwise to loosen and remove the spark plug from the bore.

✳✳ WARNING

Be sure not to use a flexible extension on the socket. Use of a flexible extension may allow a shear force to be applied to the plug. A shear force could break the plug off in the cylinder head, leading to costly and frustrating repairs.

To install:

5. Inspect the spark plug boot for tears or damage. If a damaged boot is found, the spark plug wire must be replaced.

6. Using a wire feeler gauge, check and adjust the spark plug gap. When using a gauge, the proper size should pass between the electrodes with a slight drag. The next larger size should not be able to pass while the next smaller size should pass freely.

7. Carefully thread the plug into the bore by hand. If resistance is felt before the plug is almost completely threaded, back the plug out and begin threading again. In small, hard to reach areas, an old spark plug wire and boot could be used as a threading tool. The boot will hold the plug while you twist the end of the wire and the wire is supple enough to twist before it would allow the plug to crossthread.

✳✳ WARNING

Do not use the spark plug socket to thread the plugs. Always carefully thread the plug by hand or using an old plug wire to prevent the possibility of crossthreading and damaging the cylinder head bore.

8. Carefully tighten the spark plug. If the plug you are installing is equipped with a crush washer, seat the plug, then tighten about ¼ turn to crush the washer. If you are installing a tapered seat plug, tighten the plug to specifications provided by the vehicle or plug manufacturer.

9. Apply a small amount of silicone dielectric compound to the end of the spark plug lead or inside the spark plug boot to prevent sticking, then install the boot to the spark plug and push un-

til it clicks into place. The click may be felt or heard, then gently pull back on the boot to assure proper contact.

INSPECTION & GAPPING

Check the plugs for deposits and wear. If they are not going to be replaced, clean the plugs thoroughly. Remember that any kind of deposit will decrease the efficiency of the plug. Plugs can be cleaned on a spark plug cleaning machine, which can sometimes be found in service stations, or you can do an acceptable job of cleaning with a stiff brush. If the plugs are cleaned, the electrodes must be filed flat. Use an ignition points file, not an emery board or the like, which will leave deposits. The electrodes must be filed perfectly flat with sharp edges; rounded edges reduce the spark plug voltage by as much as 50%.

Check spark plug gap before installation. The ground electrode (the L-shaped one connected to the body of the plug) must be parallel to the center electrode and the specified size wire gauge (please refer to the Tune-Up Specifications chart for details) must pass between the electrodes with a slight drag.

A normally worn spark plug should have light tan or gray deposits on the firing tip

A carbon fouled plug, identified by soft, sooty, black deposits, may indicate an improperly tuned vehicle. Check the air cleaner, ignition components and engine control system

A physically damaged spark plug may be evidence of severe detonation in that cylinder. Watch that cylinder carefully between services, as a continued detonation will not only damage the plug, but could also damage the engine

A variety of tools and gauges are needed for spark plug service

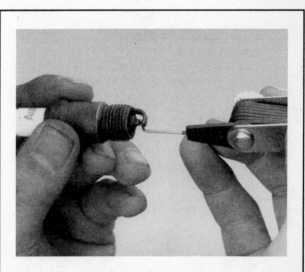

Checking the spark plug gap with a feeler gauge

An oil fouled spark plug indicates an engine with worn piston rings and/or bad valve seals allowing excessive oil to enter the chamber

This spark plug has been left in the engine too long, as evidenced by the extreme gap—Plugs with such an extreme gap can cause misfiring and stumbling accompanied by a noticeable lack of power

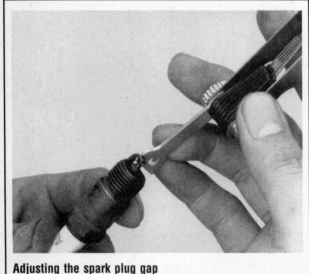

Adjusting the spark plug gap

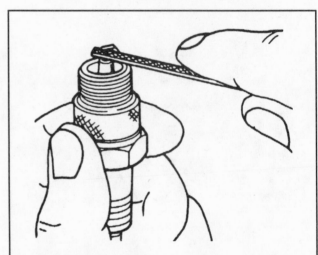

If the standard plug is in good condition, the electrode may be filed flat—CAUTION: do not file platinum plugs

A bridged or almost bridged spark plug, identified by a build-up between the electrodes caused by excessive carbon or oil build-up on the plug

➡NEVER adjust the gap on a used platinum type spark plug.

Always check the gap on new plugs as they are not always set correctly at the factory. Do not use a flat feeler gauge when measuring the gap on a used plug, because the reading may be inaccurate. A round-wire type gapping tool is the best way to check the gap. The correct gauge should pass through the electrode gap with a slight drag. If you're in doubt, try one size smaller and one larger. The smaller gauge should go through easily, while the larger one shouldn't go through at all. Wire gapping tools usually have a bending tool attached. Use that to adjust the side electrode until the proper distance is obtained. Absolutely never attempt to bend the center electrode. Also, be careful not to bend the side electrode too far or too often as it may weaken and break off within the engine, requiring removal of the cylinder head to retrieve it.

Spark Plug Wires

TESTING & REPLACING

At every tune-up, visually inspect the spark plug cables for burns, cuts, or breaks in the insulation. Check the boots and the nipples on the distributor cap and coil. Replace any damaged wiring.

Every 36,000 miles or so, the resistance of the wires should be checked with an ohmmeter. Wires with excessive resistance will cause misfiring, and may make the engine difficult to start in damp weather. Generally the useful life of the cables is 36,000–50,000 miles.

To check resistance, remove the distributor cap, leaving the

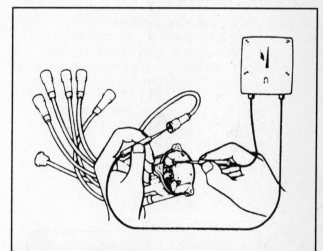

Checking plug wire resistance through the distributor cap with an ohmmeter

Checking individual plug wire resistance with a digital ohmmeter

wires attached. Connect one lead of an ohmmeter to an electrode within the cap; connect the other lead to the corresponding spark plug terminal (remove it from the plug for this test). Replace any wire which shows a resistance over 25,000 ohms. Test the high tension lead from the coil by connecting the ohmmeter between the center contact in the distributor cap and either of the primary terminals of the coil. If resistance is more than 25,000 ohms, remove the cable from the coil and check the resistance of the cable alone. Anything over 15,000 ohms is cause for replacement. It should be remembered that resistance is also a function of length; the longer the cable, the greater the resistance. Thus, if the cables on your car are longer than the factory originals, resistance will be higher, quite possibly outside these limits.

When installing new cables, replace them one at a time to avoid mixups. Start by replacing the longest one first. Install the boot firmly over the spark plug. Route the wire over the same path as the original. Insert the nipple firmly into the tower on the cap or the coil.

FIRING ORDERS

♦ **See Figures 1, 2 and 3**

➡**To avoid confusion, remove and tag the spark plug wires one at a time, for replacement.**

If a distributor is not keyed for installation with only one orientation, it could have been removed previously and rewired. The resultant wiring would hold the correct firing order, but could change the relative placement of the plug towers in relation to the engine. For this reason it is imperative that you label all wires before disconnecting any of them. Also, before removal, compare the current wiring with the accompanying illustrations. If the current wiring does not match, make notes in your book to reflect how your engine is wired.

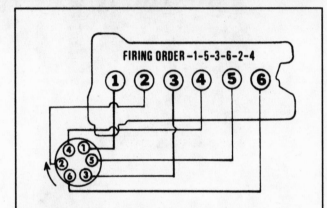

Fig. 2 Six cylinder gasoline engines
Firing order: 1–5–3–6–2–4
Distributor rotation: Clockwise

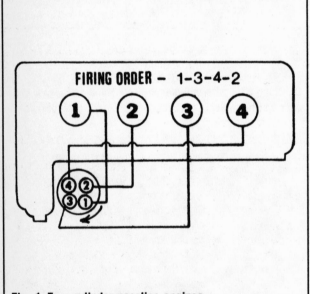

Fig. 1 Four cylinder gasoline engines
Firing order: 1–3–4–2
Distributor rotation: Clockwise

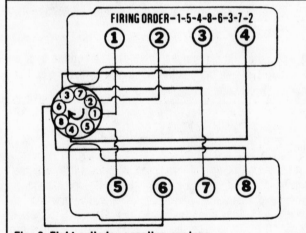

Fig. 3 Eight cylinder gasoline engines
Firing order: 1–5–4–8–6–3–7–2
Distributor rotation: Clockwise

POINT TYPE IGNITION

Breaker Points and Condenser

➡ The diesel engine has no distributor so there are no breaker points or condensers to replace. Also, 1976 and later V-8's, 1977 and later 6-cylinder engines and 1977 and later 4-cylinder engines use a breakerless, electronic ignition which has no breaker points.

The points function as a circuit breaker for the primary circuit of the ignition system. The ignition coil must boost the 12 volts of electrical pressure supplied by the battery to as much as 25,000 volts in order to fire the plugs. To do this, the coil depends on the points and the condenser to make a clean break in the primary circuit.

The coil has both primary and secondary circuits. When the ignition is turned on, the battery supplies voltage through the coil and onto the points. The points are connected to ground, completing the primary circuit. As the current passes through the coil, a magnetic field is created in the iron center core of the coil. When the cam in the distributor turns, the points open, breaking the primary circuit. The magnetic field in the primary circuit of the coil then collapses and cuts through the secondary circuit windings around the iron core. Because of the physical principle called "electromagnetic induction," the battery voltage is increased to a level sufficient to fire the spark plugs.

When the points open, the electrical charge in the primary circuit tries to jump the gap created between the two open contacts of the points. If this electrical charge were not transferred elsewhere, the metal contacts of the points would start to change rapidly.

The function of the condenser is to absorb excessive voltage from the points when they open and thus prevent the points from becoming pitted or burned.

If you have ever wondered why it is necessary to tune-up your engine occasionally, consider the fact that the ignition system must complete the above cycle each time a spark plug fires. On a four-cylinder, four-cycle engine, two of the four plugs must fire once for every engine revolution. If the idle speed of your engine is 800 revolutions per minute (800 rpm), the breaker points open and close two times for each revolution. For every minute your engine idles, your points open and close 1600 times ($2 \times 800 = 1600$). And that is just at idle. What about at 60 mph?

There are two ways to check breaker point gap: with a feeler gauge or with a dwell meter. Either way you set the points, you are adjusting the amount of time (in degrees of distributor rotation) that the points will remain open. If you adjust the points with a feeler gauge, you are setting the maximum amount the points will open when the rubbing block on the points is on a high point of the distributor cam. When you adjust the points with a dwell meter, you are measuring the number of degrees (of distributor cam rotation) that the points will remain closed before they start to open as a high point of the distributor cam approaches the rubbing block of the points.

If you still do not understand how the points function, take a friend, go outside, and remove the distributor cap from your engine. Have your friend operate the starter (make sure that the transmission is not in gear) as you look at the exposed parts of the distributor.

There are two rules that should always be followed when adjusting or replacing points. *The points and condenser are a matched set; never replace one without replacing the other. If you change the point gap or dwell of the engine, you also change the ignition timing. Therefore, if you adjust the points, you must also adjust the timing.*

IGNITION SYSTEM PRECAUTIONS

Mercedes-Benz has determined that some transistorized switching units have been damaged due to improper handling during service and maintenance work. The following precautions should be observed when working with transistorized switching units.

1. Do not shut off a running engine by shorting terminal 15 of the ignition coil to ground or the transistorized switching unit will be destroyed.

2. Do not steam clean or apply water pressure to transistorized switching units, fuel injection control units, or ignition components, since water may enter these and short them.

3. Do not assume that transistor switching units are defective without checking the plug terminals. The plug terminals are frequently corroded because the rubber boot was not properly seated. In addition, the terminals can become corroded even if the rubber boot is properly seated. Mercedes-Benz recommends that all contacts be cleaned before assuming that a transistorized switching unit is defective.

INSPECTION & CLEANING

The breaker points should be inspected and cleaned at 6000 mile intervals. To do so, perform the following steps:

1. Disconnect the high-tension lead from the coil.

2. Unsnap the two distributor cap retaining clips and lift the cap straight up. Leave the leads connected to the cap and position it out of the way.

3. Remove the rotor and dust cover by pulling them straight up.

4. Place a screwdriver against the breaker points and pry them open. Examine their condition. If they are excessively worn, burned, or pitted, they should be replaced.

5. Clean the distributor cap and rotor with alcohol. Inspect the cap terminals for looseness and corrosion. Check the rotor tip for excessive burning. Inspect both cap and rotor for cracks. Replace either if they show any of the above signs of wear or damage.

6. Check the operation of the centrifugal advance mechanism by turning the rotor clockwise. Release the rotor; it should return to its original position. If it doesn't, check for binding parts.

7. If the points do not require replacement, proceed with the adjustment section below. Otherwise perform the point and condenser replacement procedures.

REMOVAL & INSTALLATION

◆ See Figure 4

1. Raise the hood and locate the distributor. Remove the rubber or plastic cover (if equipped).

2. Release the clips on the side of the distributor cap and remove the cap. Lay it aside.

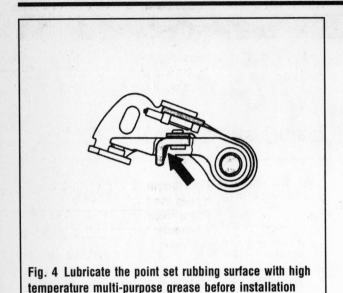

Fig. 4 Lubricate the point set rubbing surface with high temperature multi-purpose grease before installation

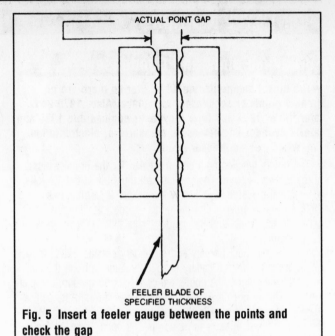

Fig. 5 Insert a feeler gauge between the points and check the gap

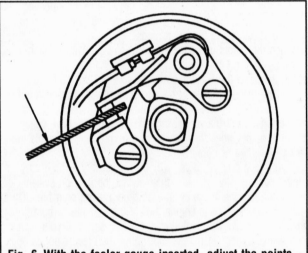

Fig. 6 With the feeler gauge inserted, adjust the points until a slight drag is felt

3. Remove the rotor and dust shield from the distributor shaft. The rotor only fits one way.

4. Some distributors have a protective cover installed over the points, which must be removed.

5. Remove the distributor contact holder by removing the screw or screws. Some models also have a snapring on the bearing contact lever, which must also be removed. Pry the wire from the connecting terminal or loosen the screw at the terminal and remove the wire from the connecting terminal.

6. Disconnect the condenser wire and remove the condenser from its bracket. The condenser screw is located on the outside of the distributor.

To install:

7. Before installing new points, clean the contact surfaces by squeezing them against a clean matchbook cover. This will remove any film or grease. Also be sure the point contact faces are aligned. If not, bend the fixed contact arm so that the points align and close squarely.

8. Lightly coat the rubbing arm of the contact breaker with high temperature multipurpose grease. It is no longer necessary to lubricate the felt pad.

9. Install a new condenser and connect the wire.

10. Install a new contact set or sets into the distributor.

11. Install the hold-down screw(s) or the snaprings on the bearing pins of the contact plate.

12. Connect the wire to the terminal and tighten the nut, if necessary.

13. If equipped, install the cover over the breaker points. Be sure it does not interfere with the distributor cam.

14. Install the plate and rotor on the shaft.

15. Install the cap and secure it in place with the clips.

16. Check the dwell angle and ignition timing. Adjust if necessary.

ADJUSTMENT

Feeler Gauge Method

♦ **See Figures 5 and 6**

Perform the gap adjustment procedure whenever new points are installed, or as part of routine maintenance. If you are adjusting an old set of points, you *must* check the dwell as well, since the feeler gauge is really only accurate with a new point set.

1. Rotate the engine by hand or by using a remote starter switch, so that the rubbing block is on the high point of the cam lobe.

2. Insert a feeler gauge between the points; a slight drag should be felt.

3. If no drag is felt or if the feeler gauge cannot be inserted at all, loosen, but do not remove, the point hold-down screw.

4. Insert a screwdriver into the adjustment slot. Rotate the screwdriver until the proper point gap is attained. The point gap is increased by rotating the screwdriver counterclockwise and decreased by rotating it clockwise. On some models it is possible to adjust the point gap by means of an eccentric adjustment screw provided for this purpose in the breaker plate.

5. Tighten the point hold-down screw.

Lubricate the cam lobes, breaker arm, rubbing block, arm

pivot, and distributor shaft with special high-temperature distributor grease. Check the dwell.

Dwell Meter Method
♦ See Figure 7

A dwell meter virtually eliminates errors in point gap caused by the distributor cam lobes being unequally worn, or human error. In any case, point dwell should be checked as soon as possible after setting with a feeler gauge because it is a far more accurate check of point operation under normal operating conditions.

The dwell meter, actually a modified voltmeter, depends on the nature of contact point operation for its usefulness. In this electro-mechanical system, a fiber block slides under tension, over a cam (see illustrations). The angle (in black) that the block traverses on the cam, during which time current is made available to the coil primary winding, is an inverse function of point gap. In other words, the wider the gap, the smaller the "dwell" (expressed in degrees); the closer the gap, the greater the "dwell."

Because the fiber block wears down gradually in service, it is a good practice to set the dwell on the low side of any dwell range (smaller number of degrees) given in specifications. As the block wears, the dwell becomes greater (toward the center of the range) and point life is increased between adjustments.

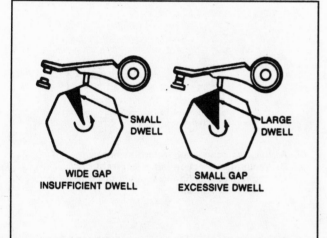

Fig. 7 Dwell is the amount of time the points are open (shaded areas)

To connect the dwell meter, switch the meter to the six-, four- or eight-cylinder range, as the case may be, and connect one lead to ground. The other lead should be connected to the coil distributor terminal (the one having the wire going to contact points). Follow the manufacturer's instructions if they differ from those listed. Zero the meter, start the engine and gradually allow it to assume normal idle speed. (See "Tune-Up Specifications.") The meter should agree with the specifications. Any excessive variation in dwell indicates a worn distributor shaft or bushings, or perhaps a worn distributor cam or breaker plate.

➡**Up until 1976 (V8), 1977 (6-cylinder) or 1977 (4-cylinder), Mercedes-Benz engines use transistorized ignitions. These can be identified by a "blue" ignition coil. Occasionally, a dwell meter or tachometer will not work on these ignitions because of internal design.**

It is obvious from the above procedure that some means of measuring engine rpm must also be employed when checking dwell. An external tachometer should be employed. Hook-up is the same as for the dwell meter and both can be used in conjunction. Most commercial dwell meters have a tachometer scale built in and switching between them is possible.

➡**Diesel engines, 1976 and later V8's, 1977 and later 6-cylinder engines and 1977 and later 4-cylinder engines have no provision for adjusting dwell.**

1. The dwell angle should be measured at idle speed.
2. Raise the hood and connect a dwell meter/tachometer.
3. Start the engine and allow it to reach normal idle speed. Read the dwell angle from the meter on the appropriate scale.
4. If the dwell angle is not according to specifications, remove the distributor cap and adjust the dwell angle. Reduce the point gap if the dwell angle is too small, or increase the contact point gap if the dwell angle is too large.
5. To actually adjust the point gap, stop the engine and loosen the hold-down screw and insert a screwdriver between the lugs on the breaker plate. Move the plate to the desired location. Tighten the hold-down screw. On some models it is possible to adjust the point gap by means of the eccentric screw provided for this purpose in the breaker plate.
6. Recheck the dwell angle and adjust the gap again if it is still not satisfactory. Repeat the process until the dwell angle is as specified.

IGNITION TIMING

Timing

Ignition timing is the measurement in degrees of crankshaft rotation of the instant the spark plugs in the cylinders fire, in relation to the location of the piston, while the piston is on its compression stroke.

➡**Diesel engines use no distributor, so they require no ignition timing adjustment.**

Ignition timing is adjusted by loosening the distributor locking device and turning the distributor in the engine.

Ideally, the air/fuel mixture in the cylinder will be ignited (by the spark plug) and just beginning its rapid expansion as the pis-

ton passes top dead center (TDC) of the compression stroke. If this happens, the piston will be beginning the power stroke just as the compressed (by the movement of the piston) and ignited (by the spark plug) air/fuel mixture starts to expand. The expansion of the air/fuel mixture will then force the piston down on the power stroke and turn the crankshaft.

It takes a fraction of a second for the spark from the plug to completely ignite the mixture in the cylinder. Because of this, the spark plug must fire before the piston reaches TDC, if the mixture is to be completely ignited as the piston passes TDC. This measurement is given in degrees (of crankshaft rotation) *before* the piston reaches *top dead center* (BTDC). If the ignition timing setting for your engine is seven degrees (7°) BTDC, this means that the spark plug must fire at a time when the piston for that cylinder is 7° before top dead center of its compression stroke. However, this only holds true while your engine is at idle speed.

As you accelerate from idle, the speed of your engine (rpm) increases. The increase in rpm means that the pistons are now traveling up and down much faster. Because of this, the spark plugs will have to fire even sooner if the mixture is to be completely ignited as the piston passes TDC. To accomplish this, the distributor incorporates means to advance the timing of the spark as engine speed increases.

The distributor in your Mercedes-Benz has two means of advancing the ignition timing. One is called centrifugal advance and is actuated by weights in the distributor. The other is called vacuum advance and is controlled by that larger circular housing on the side of the distributor.

In addition, some distributors have a vacuum-retard mechanism which is contained in the same housing on the side of the distributor as the vacuum advance. The function of this mechanism is to retard the timing of the ignition spark under certain engine conditions. This causes more complete burning of the air/fuel mixture in the cylinder and consequently lowers exhaust emissions.

Because these mechanisms change ignition timing, it is necessary to disconnect and plug the one or two vacuum lines from the distributor when setting the basic ignition timing.

If ignition timing is set too far advanced (BTDC), the ignition and expansion of the air/fuel mixture in the cylinder will try to force the piston down the cylinder while it is still traveling upward. This causes engine "ping," a sound which resembles marbles being dropped into an empty tin can. If the ignition timing is too far retarded (after, or ATDC), the piston will have already started down on the power stroke when the air/fuel mixture ignites and expands. This will cause the piston to be forced down only a portion of its travel. This will result in poor engine performance and lack of power.

Ignition timing adjustment is checked with a timing light. This instrument is connected to the number one (No. 1) spark plug of the engine. The timing light flashes every time an electrical current is sent from the distributor, through the No. 1 spark plug wire, to the spark plug. The vibration damper or balancing plate are marked with a timing pointer and a timing scale. When the timing pointer is aligned with the mark (pin) on the timing scale, the piston in No. 1 cylinder is at TDC of its compression stroke. With the engine running, and the timing light aimed at the timing pointer and timing scale, the stroboscopic flashes from the timing light will allow you to check the ignition timing setting of the engine. The timing light flashes every time the spark plug in the No. 1 cylinder of the engine fires. Since the flash from the timing light makes the crankshaft pulley seem stationary for a moment, you will be able to read the exact position of the piston in the No. 1 cylinder on the timing scale on the front of the engine.

There are three basic types of timing light available. The first is a simple neon bulb with two wire connections (one for the spark plug and one for the plug wire, connecting the light in series). This type of light is quite dim, and must be held closely to the marks to be seen, but it is inexpensive. The second type of light operates from the car battery. Two alligator clips connect to the battery terminals, while a third wire connects to the spark plug with an adapter. This type of light is more expensive, but the zenon bulb provides a nice bright flash which can even be seen in sunlight. The third type replaces the battery source with 110 volt house current. Some timing lights have other functions built into them, such as dwell meters, tachometers, or remote starting

switches. These are convenient, in that they reduce the tangle of wires under the hood, but may duplicate the functions of tools you already have.

If your Mercedes has electronic ignition, you should use a timing light with an inductive pickup. This pickup simply clamps onto the No. 1 plug wire, eliminating the adapter. It is not susceptible to crossfiring or false triggering, which may occur with a conventional light, due to the greater voltages produced by electronic ignition.

INSPECTION & ADJUSTMENT

All Engines (Except Diesels)
▶ **See Figure 8**

1. Warm-up the engine. Connect a tachometer and check the engine idle speed to be sure that it is within the specification given in the "Tune-Up Specifications" chart at the beginning of the section.

2. If the timing marks are difficult to see use a dab of paint or chalk to make them more visible.

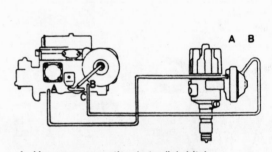

A. Vacuum connection (retard) (white)
B. Vacuum connection (advance) (red)
C. Vacuum connection to vacuum governor and fuel return valve

Fig. 8 Disconnect and plug both vacuum lines when adjusting the timing—280, 280C and 280S engines

3. Connect a timing light according to the manufacturer's instructions.

4. Disconnect the vacuum line(s) from the distributor vacuum unit. Plug it (them) with a pencil or golf tee(s).

5. Be sure that the timing light wires are clear of the fan and start the engine.

❋❋❋ CAUTION

Keep fingers, clothes, tools, hair, and leads clear of the spinning engine fan. Be sure that you are running the engine in a well-ventilated area.

6. Allow the engine to run at the specified idle speed with the gearshift in Neutral with manual transmission and Drive (D) with automatic transmission.

❊❊ CAUTION

Be sure that the parking brake is set and that the front wheels are blocked to prevent the car from rolling forward, especially when Drive is selected with an automatic.

7. Point the timing light at the mark indicated previously. With the engine at idle, timing should be at the specification given on the "Tune-Up Specifications" chart at the beginning of the section.

➡ **The balancer on some engines has two timing scales. If in doubt as to which scale to use, rotate the crankshaft (in the direction of rotation only) until the distributor rotor is** aligned with the notch on the distributor housing (No. 1 cylinder). In this position, the timing pointer should be at TDC on the proper timing scale.

8. If the timing is not at the specification, loosen the pinchbolt at the base of the distributor just enough so that the distributor can be turned. Turn the distributor to advance or retard the timing as required. Once the proper marks are seen to align with the timing light, timing is correct.

9. Stop the engine and tighten the pinchbolt. Start the engine and recheck timing. Stop the engine; disconnect the tachometer and timing light. Connect the vacuum line(s) to the distributor vacuum unit.

VALVE LASH

Description

The valve lash (clearance) can be checked with a feeler gauge on a hot or cold engine. Be sure to consult the illustrations of valve placement; the clearance on intake and exhaust valves is different.

Valve lash is one factor which determines how far the intake and exhaust valves will open into the cylinder.

If the valve clearance is too large, part of the lift of the camshaft will be used up in removing the excessive clearance, thus the valves will not be opened far enough. This condition has two effects, the valve train components will emit a tapping noise as they take up the excessive clearance, and the engine will perform poorly, since the less the intake valves open, the smaller the amount of air/fuel mixture admitted to the cylinders will be. The less the exhaust valves open, the greater the back-pressure in the cylinder which prevents the proper air/fuel mixture from entering the cylinder.

If the valve clearance is too small, the intake and exhaust valves will not fully seat on the cylinder head when they close. When a valve seats on the cylinder head it does two things; it seals the combustion chamber so none of the gases in the cylinder can escape and it cools itself by transferring some of the heat it absorbed from the combustion process through the cylinder head and into the engine cooling system. Therefore, if the valve clearance is too small, the engine will run poorly (due to gases escaping from the combustion chamber), and the valves will overheat and warp (since they cannot transfer heat unless they are touching the seat in the cylinder head).

➡ **While all valve adjustments must be as accurate as possible, it is better to have the valve adjustment slightly loose than slightly tight, as burnt valves may result from overly tight adjustments.**

ADJUSTMENT

4 and 6-Cylinder Gasoline Engines
♦ **See Figures 9, 10, 11 and 12**

➡ **The 190E has hydraulic valve clearance compensation. No adjustment is either possible or necessary.**

The valve clearance is measured between the sliding surface of the rocker arm and the heel of the camshaft lobe. The highest point of the camshaft lobe should be at a 90° angle to the sliding surface of the rocker arm.

➡ **Prior to rotating the 6 cyl. engine manually, disconnect the transmitter ignition distributor (green) plug from the switching unit.**

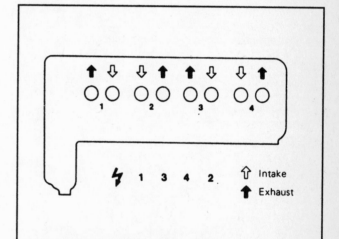

Fig. 9 Location of the intake and exhaust valves—4-cyl. gasoline engines

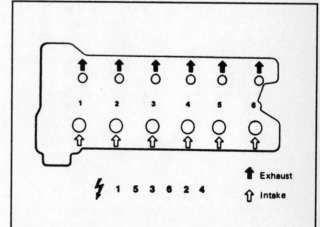

Fig. 10 Location of the intake and exhaust valves—6-cyl. gasoline engines

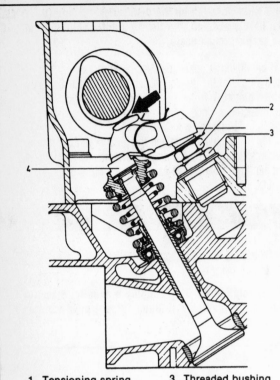

1. Tensioning spring   3. Threaded bushing
2. Adjusting nut   4. Thrust piece

Fig. 11 Insert a feeler gauge between the heel of the camshaft lobe and the sliding surface of the rocker arm (at the arrow)

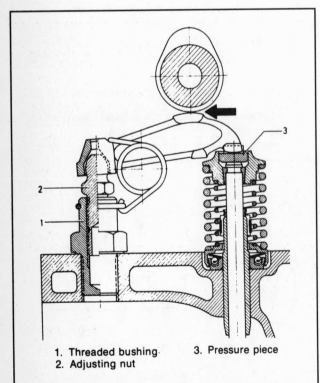

1. Threaded bushing   3. Pressure piece
2. Adjusting nut

Fig. 12 Measure the valve clearance with a feeler gauge at the arrow—4-cyl. engines (except 190)

1. Remove the air vent hose and air cleaner from the valve cover. Remove the spark plugs. This makes it easier to crank the engine by hand.

2. Remove the valve cover and gasket.

3. Note the position of the intake and exhaust valves.

4. Rotate the crankshaft with a socket wrench on the crankshaft pulley bolt until the heel of the camshaft lobe is perpendicular to the sliding surface of the rocker arm.

➡**Do not rotate the engine using the camshaft sprocket bolt. The strain will distort the timing chain tensioner rail. Always rotate the engine in the direction of normal rotation only.**

5. Some models have holes in the vibration damper plate to assist in crankshaft rotation. In this case, a screwdriver can be used to carefully rotate the crankshaft.

6. To measure the valve clearance, insert a feeler blade of the specified thickness between the heel of the camshaft lobe and the sliding surface of the rocker arm. The clearance is correct if the blade can be inserted and withdrawn with a very slight drag.

7. If adjustment is necessary, it can be done by turning the ball pin head at the hex collar. If the clearance is too small, increase it by turning the ball pin head in. If the clearance is too large, decrease it by turning the ball pin head out.

8. If the adjuster turns too easily or the proper clearance cannot be obtained, check the torque of the adjuster.

➡**This adjustment is ideally made with a special adaptor ("crow's foot") and a torque wrench. The shape of the adaptor is dictated by the need for accurate torque readings and, by using it, the torque wrench can be directly aligned with the ball pin head.**

If the torque is less than 14.8 ft. lbs., the adjuster will vibrate and the clearance will not remain as set. If the valve clearance is too small, and the ball pin head cannot be screwed in far enough to correct it, a thinner pressure piece should be installed in the spring retainer. To replace the pressure piece, the rocker arm must be removed. Refer to Section 3 for this operation.

9. After all the valves have been checked and adjusted, install the valve cover. Be sure that the gaskets are seated properly. It is best to use a new gasket whenever the valve cover is removed.

➡**Two types of triangular rubber gaskets are used on 6-cylinder DOHC engines, but only the later type with 3 notches are supplied for service.**

10. Install the spark plugs.

11. Reconnect the air vent line to the valve cover and install the air cleaner, if removed.

12. Run the engine and check for leaks at the rocker arm cover.

V-8 Engines

♦ **See Figures 13, 14 and 15**

➡**1976 and later V-8 engines use hydraulic valve lifters that require no periodic adjustment.**

Valve clearance is measured between the sliding surface of the rocker arm and the heel of the camshaft lobe. The highest point of the camshaft lobe should be at a 90° angle to the sliding surface of the rocker arm.

1. Loosen the venting line and disconnect the regulating linkage. Remove the valve cover.

2. Disconnect the cable from the ignition coil.

3. Identify all of the valves as intake or exhaust.

4. Beginning with No. 1 cylinder, crank the engine with the starter to position the heel of the camshaft approximately over the sliding surface of the rocker arm.

5. Rotate the crankshaft by using a socket wrench on the crankshaft pulley bolt until the heel of the camshaft lobe is perpendicular to the sliding surface of the rocker arm.

➡**Do not rotate the engine using the camshaft sprocket bolt. The strain will distort the timing chain tensioner rail. Always rotate the engine in the direction of normal rotation only.**

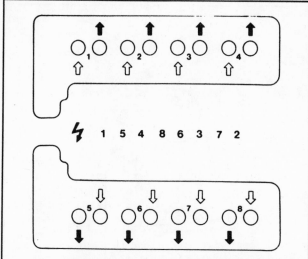

Fig. 13 Location of the intake and exhaust valves—6.9 V8 engines. Black arrows indicate exhaust valves

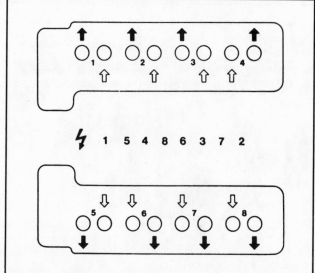

Fig. 14 Location of the intake and exhaust valves—V8 engines (except 6.9). Black arrows indicate exhaust valves

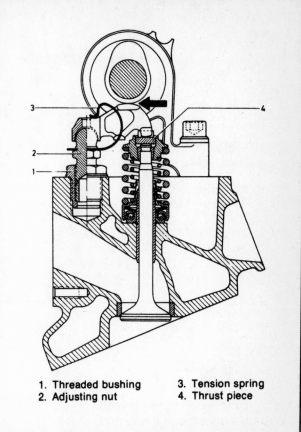

1. Threaded bushing
2. Adjusting nut
3. Tension spring
4. Thrust piece

Fig. 15 On 1974–75 V8 models, measure the valve clearance at the arrow. 1976–84 models use hydraulic lifters which require no adjustment

6. Some models have holes in the vibration damper plate to assist in crankshaft rotation. In this case, a screwdriver can be used to carefully rotate the crankshaft.

7. To measure the valve clearance, insert a feeler blade of the specified thickness between the heel of the camshaft lobe and the sliding surface of the rocker arm. The clearance is correct if the blade can be inserted and withdrawn with a very slight drag.

8. If adjustment is necessary, it can be done by turning the ball pin head at the hex collar. If the clearance is too small, increase it by turning the ball pin head in. If the clearance is too large, decrease it by turning the ball pin head out.

➡**If the adjuster turns very easily or if the proper clearance cannot be obtained check the torque on the adjuster with a special adaptor ("crow's foot").**

The shape of the adapter is dictated by the need for accurate torque readings and, by using it, the torque wrench can be directly aligned with the ball pin head.

9. When the ball pin head is turned, if the torque is less than 14.4 ft. lbs., either the adjusting screw, the threaded bolt, or both will have to be replaced. If the valve clearance is too small, and the ball pin head cannot be screwed in far enough to correct it, a thinner pressure piece should be installed in the spring retainer. To replace the pressure piece, the rocker arm must be removed.

See Section 3 for this operation.

10. Install the regulating linkage, valve cover gasket, and valve cover. Be sure the gasket is seated properly.

11. Connect the cable to the coil, the venting line and the regulating linkage. Run the engine and check for leaks at the valve cover.

Diesel Engines

▶ **See Figures 16, 17 and 18**

➡**The 190D utilizes hydraulic valve clearance compensators. No adjustment is either necessary or possible.**

1. Remove the valve cover and note the position of the intake and exhaust valves.

2. Turn the engine with a socket and breaker bar on the crankshaft pulley or by using a remote starter, hooked to the battery (+) terminal and the large, uppermost starter solenoid terminal. Due to the extremely high compression pressures in the diesel engine, it will be considerably easier to use a remote starter. If a remote starter is not available, the engine can be bumped into position with the normal starter.

➡**Do not turn the engine backwards or use the camshaft sprocket bolt to rotate the engine.**

3. Measure the valve clearance when the heel of the camshaft lobe is directly over the sliding surface of the rocker arm. The lobe of the camshaft should be vertical to the surface of the rocker arm. The clearance is correct when the specified feeler gauge can be pulled out with a very slight drag.

4. To adjust the clearance, loosen the cap nut while holding the hex nut. Adjust the valve clearance by turning the hex nut.

5. After adjustment hold the cap nut and lock it in place with the nex nut. Recheck the clearance.

6. Check the gasket and install the rocker arm cover.

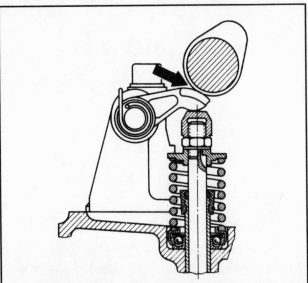

Fig. 18 Measure the valve clearance with a feeler gauge at the arrow—diesel engines

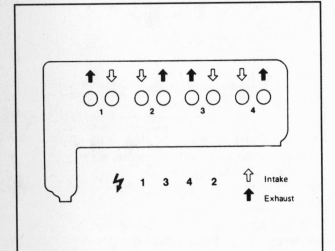

Fig. 16 Location of the intake and exhaust valves—4-cyl. diesel engines

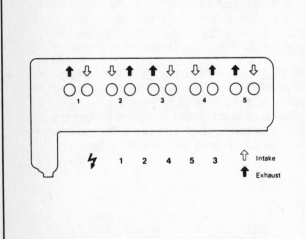

Fig. 17 Location of the intake and exhaust valves—5-cyl. diesel engines

1. Camshaft
2. Cam follower
3. Feeler gauge
4. Adjusting nut

To check the valve clearance, use a feeler gauge and adjust the hex nut until a slight drag is felt on the gauge

IDLE SPEED AND MIXTURE ADJUSTMENTS

The adjustments given here are intended to include only those which would be performed in the course of a normal tune-up, after the spark plugs, dwell angle, and ignition timing have been adjusted. Obviously, there are other adjustments which can and should be made for various reasons. These can be found in Section 5. The following chart gives the applications of various carburetors.

➡**Idle speed and fuel mixture are best set with a CO meter to comply with federal emission regulations. Follow the instructions that are packaged with the meter.**

Catalytic Converter

PRECAUTIONS

With the exception of diesels, most Mercedes-Benz cars are equipped with catalysts. The following points should be adhered to:

1. Use only unleaded gas.
2. Maintain the engine at the specified intervals.
3. Avoid running the engine with an excessively rich mixture. Do not run the engine excessively on fast idle.
4. Prolonged warm-up after a cold start should be avoided.
5. Do not check exhaust emissions over a long period of time without air injection.
6. Do not alter the emission control system in any way.

Carburetors

ADJUSTMENTS

◆ **See Figure 19**

Stromberg 175 CDT

1. Turn off the heater and A/C and run the vehicle to normal operating temperature.
2. Check the throttle valve for ease of operation.
3. Connect a tachometer. Adjust the idle speed to specifications with the idle speed adjusting screw.
4. See whether the idle speed stop is resting against the throttle valve lever and not against the vacuum governor. Set the vacuum governor back if required.
5. If an exhaust gas analyzer (CO meter) is available, check the exhaust gas for percentage of Carbon monoxide (CO). On 1975–76 models, check CO without air injection. Disconnect and plug the centerline from the blue switch-over valve. On 1977 models, be sure the wheel for altitude compensation is set properly.
6. Remove the plug in the exhaust gas tapping pipe and connect a tester to the hose.
7. If required, adjust the CO by means of the adjusting screw. Loosen the locknut while simultaneously holding the nozzle screw and turning the fuel shutoff valve. Accelerate a brief instant after each adjustment of the idle speed and fuel control screw to stabilize the mixture.

Carburetor Applications

Model	Year	Carburetor
230	1973–78	1 Stromberg 175 CDT
280	1973–76	1 Solex 4A1
280C	1973–76	

Fig. 19 Carburetor applications chart

8. Check the idle speed again and adjust with the idle speed adjusting screw, if required.
9. Adjust the control linkage as follows:
   a. On vehicles with a manual transmission, attach the control rod and adjust it so that the roller rests in the gate lever without binding. The control lever is equipped with right and left-hand threads.
   b. On vehicles with an automatic transmission, run the engine at idle speed. Set the control rod so that it can be attached with no binding.

Solex 4A 1

1. The idle speed adjustment on this carburetor is made with the air cleaner installed and the crankcase breather connected.
2. Warm the engine to normal operating temperature. Do not adjust the idle after the engine has been driven very far or the engine will be too hot.
3. Check the throttle valve shaft for binding.
4. Adjust the idle speed to specifications with the idle speed adjusting screw. This should be done with a tachometer installed. Be sure that the idle speed stop is on the throttle valve lever and not on the vacuum governor. Loosen the spring of the vacuum governor, if necessary, by altering the setting of the adjusting nut.
5. If a CO meter is available, check the Carbon monoxide (CO) content of the exhaust gas without air injection. To cancel air injection, disconnect the red vacuum line (1974) or blue-violet line (1975–76). Follow the manufacturer's directions for use. If necessary, turn both mixture control screws to the right against the stop. Turn both screws simultaneously to the left until the CO percentage is within specifications. Turning the screws out will give a richer mixture and turning the screws in will give a leaner mixture.
6. Check the idle speed again until both the idle speed and CO percentage of the exhaust gas are as specified.

Fuel Injection

ADJUSTMENTS

Gasoline Engines

1974–75 MODELS

Adjustment should be made with the air conditioner off and transmission in park.

1. Run the engine to normal operating temperature. The idle speed should not be adjusted immediately after hard driving for extended periods of time or when extremely hot. Be sure the cruise control cable is attached free of tension.
2. Remove the air cleaner.
3. Disconnect the connecting rod from the valve connection and check to be sure that the throttle valve closes completely without binding.
4. Reattach the connecting rod so that it does not bind.
5. Connect a tachometer and adjust the idle speed to specifications with the idle speed air screw.
6. Check the exhaust gas content with a Carbon monoxide (CO) meter. On 1975 cars, check the CO without air injection. Pull the plug from the oil temperature switch on the right-hand wheel well and ground it to cancel air injection. If necessary, adjust the CO content with the adjusting screw on the control unit. Turning the screw clockwise will give a richer mixture, while turning the screw counterclockwise will give a leaner mixture.
7. On 450SL and 450SLC, the control unit can be reached after removing the inner lining below the glove-box. On others, the control unit adjusting screw is behind a piece of trim on the right front kick panel.
8. Check and, if necessary, readjust the idle speed.
9. Install the air cleaner. Check the idle speed and exhaust emissions values and readjust if necessary.
10. Remove the tachometer.
11. Adjust the regulating linkage (on cars with a gate lever) so that the roller in the gate lever rests free in the gate. Move the transmission lever to Drive and switch on the A/C. Move the power steering to full lock. Adjust the speed so the engine runs smoothly.

1976–79 MODELS

The mechanical fuel injection is the airflow controlled type known as Bosch K-Jetronic®. The idle speed should be adjusted with the air conditioner off and the transmission in Park.

1. Connect a tachometer.
2. Be sure the cruise control cable is connected to the regulating lever with no binding or kinking.
3. Run the engine to normal operating temperature.
4. Be sure the throttle valve rests against the idle speed stop.
5. Set the idle speed to specifications with the idle air screw.
6. If possible, check the Carbon monoxide (CO) level.

All 1976 engines—Check CO without air injection. Disconnect the blue/purple vacuum line at the blue thermal valve and plug the opening at the thermal valve to stop air injection.

1977–79 models—Disconnect the hose at the exhaust back pressure line and connect the CO tester to the line. On Federal V-8 engines, check CO with air injection connected. On all others, disconnect the blue/purple vacuum line from the blue thermal valve and plug the thermo valve to cancel air injection.

7. Adjust the CO valve by unscrewing the plug and inserting the special adjusting tool (allen wrench). Turn the screw in to richen the mixture and out to lean the mixture.
8. Accelerate briefly and check the speed and CO again.
9. Reconnect the vacuum lines and check the CO value again. It should be below the specified value.
10. Adjust the regulating lever so that the roller rests in the gate lever without binding. Put the transmission in Drive and turn on the A/C. Turn the wheels to full lock and adjust the idle speed so the engine runs smoothly.

1980 6-CYLINDER AND V8 MODELS

1. Connect a tachometer and remote oil temperature gauge.
2. Run the engine to approximately 176°F oil temperature.
3. The automatic transmission should be in Park and the A/C off.
4. Be sure the throttle valve lever rests against the idle stop.
5. Adjust the Bowden cable with the adjusting screw so there is no tension against the throttle valve lever.
6. Check the idle speed. If necessary, adjust with the idle air adjustment screw.

1981 6-CYLINDER MODELS

1. Run the engine to normal operating temperature (167°–185° oil temperature) and connect a tachometer.
2. The automatic transmission should be in Park and A/C off.
3. Be sure the throttle valve lever rests against the idle speed stop.
4. Be sure the cruise control actuating rod rests against the idle speed stop. Disconnect the connecting rod and push the lever of the actuating lever clockwise to the idle speed position.
5. Reconnect the connecting rod; make sure that the actuating element is approximately 0.04 inch from the idle speed stop. Adjust this clearance with the pull rod.
6. Check and adjust the idle speed. Idle speed is adjusted at the idle speed air screw.

1981–84 MODELS

These engines have electronically controlled idle speed, using a solenoid connected to terminals 1 and 5 of the control unit.

Diesel Engines

1973–80 MODELS (EXCEPT 1980 300 SD)
▶ See Figure 20

Since the diesel engine has no ignition distributor or ignition coil there is no way to connect an external tachometer to measure idle speed. While using the built-in tachometer on the dash is not the most accurate way, the only other possibility is to set the idle speed by ear.

1. On models before 1977, turn the knob on the instrument panel completely clockwise. Turn it again counterclockwise. The travel before the idle speed is raised should not exceed about ½ turn. If required, adjust the travel with the nut.
2. On 1977–80 models, turn the knob on the instrument panel completely clockwise and check the distance between the adjusting ring and the specially shaped spring. It should be approximately 0.04 inch.
3. With the engine stopped, depress the accelerator pedal while turning the idle knob counterclockwise.
4. Start the engine. The idle should be 1,000–1,100 rpm. Adjust this with the adjusting screw, but do not exceed 1,100 rpm.
5. On 1977–80 models, be sure the special spring is installed correctly.
6. Run the engine to operating temperature.

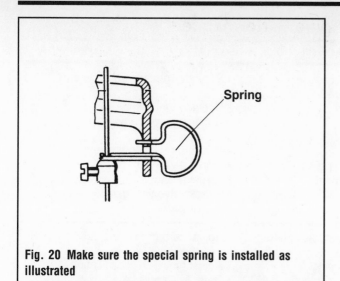

Fig. 20 Make sure the special spring is installed as illustrated

7. Turn the idle adjusting knob on the dash fully to the right.

8. Disconnect the regulating rod and adjust the idle speed with the idle speed adjusting screw. 1977–80 models have a locknut on the idle speed adjusting screw.

9. Reconnect the regulating rod.

1980 300SD AND 1981–84 DIESELS EXCEPT 1982–83 240D AND 1984 190D MODELS

1. Run the engine to normal operating temperature.

2. On normally aspirated engines, turn the idle speed adjuster on the dash completely to the right.

3. Disconnect the pushrod at the angle lever.

4. Check the idle speed. Adjust by loosening the locknut and adjusting the idle speed screw. Tighten the locknut.

5. On all except Turbodiesels, adjust the pushrod so that a clearance of approximately 0.2 inch exists between the cam on the lever and the actuator on the switchover valve. The lever on the fuel injection pump must rest against the idle stop.

6. On all models except the 1981 turbodiesel, depress the stop lever as far as possible. The cruise control Bowden cable should be free of tension against the angle lever. Use the adjusting screw to alter the tension. Let go of the stop lever. The Bowden cable should have a slight amount of play.

7. On turbodiesels, adjust the pushrod so that the roller in the guide lever rests free of tension against the stop.

8. Put the automatic transmission in Drive and turn the steering wheel to full lock. The engine should run smoothly. If not, adjust the idle speed. Disconnect the cruise control connecting rod, and push the lever clockwise to the idle stop. Attach the connecting rod, making sure the lever is about 0.04 inch from the idle speed stop.

✳✳ WARNING

If the engine speed is adjusted higher, it will be above the controlled idle speed range of the governor and the engine can increase in speed to maximum rpm.

1982–83 240D MODELS

1. Run the engine to normal operating temperature.

2. Turn the idle speed adjuster knob on the dashboard completely to the right.

3. Disconnect the pushrod at the operating lever.

4. Move the guide lever to the idle speed position. Set the edge of the guide lever at the mark (arrow) on the cap.

5. Check, and if necessary, adjust the idle speed. Use the idle speed adjusting screw.

6. Attach the pushrod to the injection pump lever so that the rod is free of tension when the lever is against the idle speed stop.

7. Check to be sure the cruise control rods are free of tension.

8. Move the automatic transmission into Drive. Turn on the A/C and turn the wheels to full lock. The engine should run smoothly. Adjust the idle speed if necessary.

1984 190D MODELS

♦ See Figure 21

➡Testing the idle speed on the 190D will require two special tools. A digital tester (Sun-1019, 2110 or All-Test 3610-MB) and a TDC impulse transmitter; not commonly available tools. Without these two special tools, idle speed adjustment is impossible and should not be attempted.

1. Run the engine until it reaches normal operating temperature.

2. Connect the digital tester and the TDC impulse transmitter as indicated in the illustration.

3. Check all linkages for ease of operation.

4. Disconnect the pushrod from the adjusting lever.

5. Start the engine and check the idle speed. If required, adjust by loosening the locknut on the vacuum control unit and turning the unit itself in or out.

6. After the idle speed is correct, tighten the vacuum control unit locknut and reconnect the pushrod so that it is tension free when the lever is against the idle speed stop.

7. Switch on all auxiliary power accessories and check that the engine continues to run smoothly. Readjust the idle speed if necessary.

8. Disconnect the two special tools and turn off the engine.

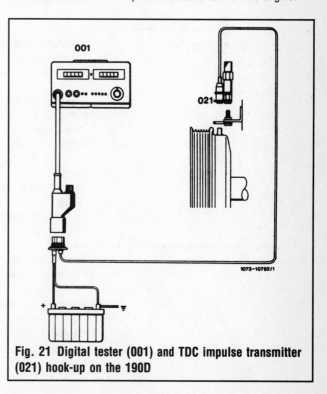

Fig. 21 Digital tester (001) and TDC impulse transmitter (021) hook-up on the 190D

Troubleshooting Engine Performance

Problem	Cause	Solution
Hard starting (engine cranks normally)	• Faulty engine control system component	• Repair or replace as necessary
	• Faulty fuel pump	• Replace fuel pump
	• Faulty fuel system component	• Repair or replace as necessary
	• Faulty ignition coil	• Test and replace as necessary
	• Improper spark plug gap	• Adjust gap
	• Incorrect ignition timing	• Adjust timing
	• Incorrect valve timing	• Check valve timing; repair as necessary
Rough idle or stalling	• Incorrect curb or fast idle speed	• Adjust curb or fast idle speed (If possible)
	• Incorrect ignition timing	• Adjust timing to specification
	• Improper feedback system operation	• Refer to Chapter 4
	• Faulty EGR valve operation	• Test EGR system and replace as necessary
	• Faulty PCV valve air flow	• Test PCV valve and replace as necessary
	• Faulty TAC vacuum motor or valve	• Repair as necessary
	• Air leak into manifold vacuum	• Inspect manifold vacuum connections and repair as necessary
	• Faulty distributor rotor or cap	• Replace rotor or cap (Distributor systems only)
	• Improperly seated valves	• Test cylinder compression, repair as necessary
	• Incorrect ignition wiring	• Inspect wiring and correct as necessary
	• Faulty ignition coil	• Test coil and replace as necessary
	• Restricted air vent or idle passages	• Clean passages
	• Restricted air cleaner	• Clean or replace air cleaner filter element
Faulty low-speed operation	• Restricted idle air vents and passages	• Clean air vents and passages
	• Restricted air cleaner	• Clean or replace air cleaner filter element
	• Faulty spark plugs	• Clean or replace spark plugs
	• Dirty, corroded, or loose ignition secondary circuit wire connections	• Clean or tighten secondary circuit wire connections
	• Improper feedback system operation	• Refer to Chapter 4
	• Faulty ignition coil high voltage wire	• Replace ignition coil high voltage wire (Distributor systems only)
	• Faulty distributor cap	• Replace cap (Distributor systems only)
Faulty acceleration	• Incorrect ignition timing	• Adjust timing
	• Faulty fuel system component	• Repair or replace as necessary
	• Faulty spark plug(s)	• Clean or replace spark plug(s)
	• Improperly seated valves	• Test cylinder compression, repair as necessary
	• Faulty ignition coil	• Test coil and replace as necessary

Troubleshooting Engine Performance

Problem	Cause	Solution
Faulty acceleration (cont.)	• Improper feedback system operation	• Refer to Chapter 4
Faulty high speed operation	• Incorrect ignition timing • Faulty advance mechanism	• Adjust timing (if possible) • Check advance mechanism and repair as necessary (Distributor systems only)
	• Low fuel pump volume • Wrong spark plug air gap or wrong plug	• Replace fuel pump • Adjust air gap or install correct plug
	• Partially restricted exhaust manifold, exhaust pipe, catalytic converter, muffler, or tailpipe	• Eliminate restriction
	• Restricted vacuum passages • Restricted air cleaner	• Clean passages • Cleaner or replace filter element as necessary
	• Faulty distributor rotor or cap	• Replace rotor or cap (Distributor systems only)
	• Faulty ignition coil • Improperly seated valve(s)	• Test coil and replace as necessary • Test cylinder compression, repair as necessary
	• Faulty valve spring(s)	• Inspect and test valve spring tension, replace as necessary
	• Incorrect valve timing	• Check valve timing and repair as necessary
	• Intake manifold restricted	• Remove restriction or replace manifold
	• Worn distributor shaft	• Replace shaft (Distributor systems only)
	• Improper feedback system operation	• Refer to Chapter 4
Misfire at all speeds	• Faulty spark plug(s) • Faulty spark plug wire(s) • Faulty distributor cap or rotor	• Clean or relace spark plug(s) • Replace as necessary • Replace cap or rotor (Distributor systems only)
	• Faulty ignition coil • Primary ignition circuit shorted or open intermittently • Improperly seated valve(s)	• Test coil and replace as necessary • Troubleshoot primary circuit and repair as necessary • Test cylinder compression, repair as necessary
	• Faulty hydraulic tappet(s) • Improper feedback system operation • Faulty valve spring(s)	• Clean or replace tappet(s) • Refer to Chapter 4 • Inspect and test valve spring tension, repair as necessary
	• Worn camshaft lobes • Air leak into manifold	• Replace camshaft • Check manifold vacuum and repair as necessary
	• Fuel pump volume or pressure low • Blown cylinder head gasket • Intake or exhaust manifold passage(s) restricted	• Replace fuel pump • Replace gasket • Pass chain through passage(s) and repair as necessary
Power not up to normal	• Incorrect ignition timing • Faulty distributor rotor	• Adjust timing • Replace rotor (Distributor systems only)

Troubleshooting Engine Performance

Problem	Cause	Solution
Power not up to normal (cont.)	• Incorrect spark plug gap	• Adjust gap
	• Faulty fuel pump	• Replace fuel pump
	• Faulty fuel pump	• Replace fuel pump
	• Incorrect valve timing	• Check valve timing and repair as necessary
	• Faulty ignition coil	• Test coil and replace as necessary
	• Faulty ignition wires	• Test wires and replace as necessary
	• Improperly seated valves	• Test cylinder compression and repair as necessary
	• Blown cylinder head gasket	• Replace gasket
	• Leaking piston rings	• Test compression and repair as necessary
	• Improper feedback system operation	• Refer to Chapter 4
Intake backfire	• Improper ignition timing	• Adjust timing
	• Defective EGR component	• Repair as necessary
	• Defective TAC vacuum motor or valve	• Repair as necessary
Exhaust backfire	• Air leak into manifold vacuum	• Check manifold vacuum and repair as necessary
	• Faulty air injection diverter valve	• Test diverter valve and replace as necessary
	• Exhaust leak	• Locate and eliminate leak
Ping or spark knock	• Incorrect ignition timing	• Adjust timing
	• Distributor advance malfunction	• Inspect advance mechanism and repair as necessary (Distributor systems only)
	• Excessive combustion chamber deposits	• Remove with combustion chamber cleaner
	• Air leak into manifold vacuum	• Check manifold vacuum and repair as necessary
	• Excessively high compression	• Test compression and repair as necessary
	• Fuel octane rating excessively low	• Try alternate fuel source
	• Sharp edges in combustion chamber	• Grind smooth
	• EGR valve not functioning properly	• Test EGR system and replace as necessary
Surging (at cruising to top speeds)	• Low fuel pump pressure or volume	• Replace fuel pump
	• Improper PCV valve air flow	• Test PCV valve and replace as necessary
	• Air leak into manifold vacuum	• Check manifold vacuum and repair as necessary
	• Incorrect spark advance	• Test and replace as necessary
	• Restricted fuel filter	• Replace fuel filter
	• Restricted air cleaner	• Clean or replace air cleaner filter element
	• EGR valve not functioning properly	• Test EGR system and replace as necessary
	• Improper feedback system operation	• Refer to Chapter 4

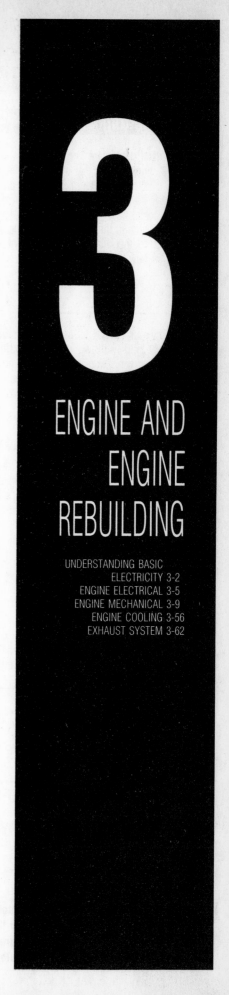

3

ENGINE AND ENGINE REBUILDING

UNDERSTANDING BASIC ELECTRICITY

Understanding Electricity

For any electrical system to operate, there must be a complete circuit. This simply means that the power flow from the battery must make a full circle. When an electrical component is operating, power flows from the battery to the components, passes through the component (load) causing it to function, and returns to the battery through the ground path of the circuit. This ground may be either another wire or a metal part of the vehicle (depending upon how the component is designed).

BASIC CIRCUITS

Perhaps the easiest way to visualize a circuit is to think of connecting a light bulb (with two wires attached to it) to the battery. If one of the two wires was attached to the negative post (−) of the battery and the other wire to the positive post (+), the circuit would be complete and the light bulb would illuminate. Electricity could follow a path from the battery to the bulb and back to the battery. It's not hard to see that with longer wires on our light bulb, it could be mounted anywhere on the vehicle. Further, one wire could be fitted with a switch so that the light could be turned on and off. Various other items could be added to our primitive circuit to make the light flash, become brighter or dimmer under certain conditions, or advise the user that it's burned out.

Ground

Some automotive components are grounded through their mounting points. The electrical current runs through the chassis of the vehicle and returns to the battery through the ground (−) cable; if you look, you'll see that the battery ground cable connects between the battery and the body of the vehicle.

Load

Every complete circuit must include a "load" (something to use the electricity coming from the source). If you were to connect a

Damaged insulation can allow wires to break (causing an open circuit) or touch (causing a short circuit)

wire between the two terminals of the battery (DON'T do this, but take our word for it) without the light bulb, the battery would attempt to deliver its entire power supply from one pole to another almost instantly. This is a short circuit. The electricity is taking a short cut to get to ground and is not being used by any load in the circuit. This sudden and uncontrolled electrical flow can cause great damage to other components in the circuit and can develop a tremendous amount of heat. A short in an automotive wiring harness can develop sufficient heat to melt the insulation on all the surrounding wires and reduce a multiple wire cable to one sad lump of plastic and copper. Two common causes of shorts are broken insulation (thereby exposing the wire to contact with surrounding metal surfaces or other wires) or a failed switch (the pins inside the switch come out of place and touch each other).

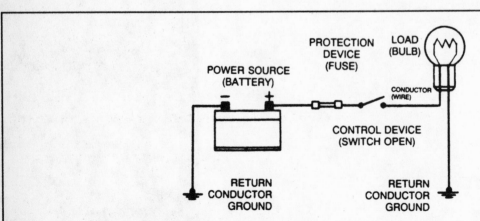

Here is an example of a simple automotive circuit. When the switch is closed, power from the positive battery terminal flows through the fuse, the switch and then the load (light bulb). The light illuminates and the circuit is completed through the return conductor and the vehicle ground. If the light did not work, the tests could be made with a voltmeter or test light at the battery, fuse, switch or bulb socket

Switches and Relays

Some electrical components which require a large amount of current to operate also have a relay in their circuit. Since these circuits carry a large amount of current (amperage or amps), the thickness of the wire in the circuit (wire gauge) is also greater. If this large wire were connected from the load to the control switch on the dash, the switch would have to carry the high amperage load and the dash would be twice as large to accommodate wiring harnesses as thick as your wrist. To prevent these problems, a relay is used. The large wires in the circuit are connected from the battery to one side of the relay and from the opposite side of the relay to the load. The relay is normally open, preventing current from passing through the circuit. An additional, smaller wire is connected from the relay to the control switch for the circuit. When the control switch is turned on, it grounds the smaller wire to the relay and completes its circuit. The main switch inside the relay closes, sending power to the component without routing the main power through the inside of the vehicle. Some common circuits which may use relays are the horn, headlights, starter and rear window defogger systems.

Protective Devices

It is possible for larger surges of current to pass through the electrical system of your vehicle. If this surge of current were to reach the load in the circuit, it could burn it out or severely damage it. To prevent this, fuses, circuit breakers and/or fusible links are connected into the supply wires of the electrical system. These items are nothing more than a built-in weak spot in the system. It's much easier to go to a known location (the fusebox) to see why a circuit is inoperative than to dissect 15 feet of wiring under the dashboard, looking for what happened.

When an electrical current of excessive power passes through the fuse, the fuse blows (the conductor melts) and breaks the circuit, preventing the passage of current and protecting the components.

A circuit breaker is basically a self repairing fuse. It will open the circuit in the same fashion as a fuse, but when either the short is removed or the surge subsides, the circuit breaker resets itself and does not need replacement.

A fuse link (fusible link or main link) is a wire that acts as a fuse. One of these is normally connected between the starter relay and the main wiring harness under the hood. Since the starter is usually the highest electrical draw on the vehicle, an internal short during starting could direct about 130 amps into the wrong places. Consider the damage potential of introducing this current into a system whose wiring is rated at 15 amps and you'll understand the need for protection. Since this link is very early in the electrical path, it's the first place to look if nothing on the vehicle works, but the battery seems to be charged and is properly connected.

TROUBLESHOOTING

Electrical problems generally fall into one of three areas:
• The component that is not functioning is not receiving current.
• The component is receiving power but is not using it or is using it incorrectly (component failure).
• The component is improperly grounded.
The circuit can be can be checked with a test light and a

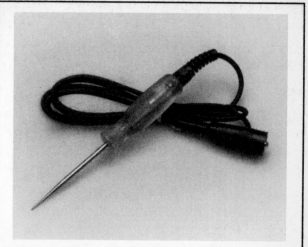

A 12 volt test light is useful when checking parts of a circuit for power

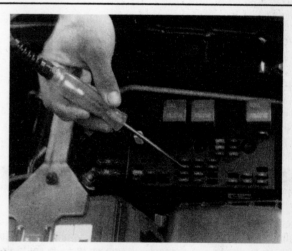

Here, someone is checking a circuit by making sure there is power to the component's fuse

jumper wire. The test light is a device that looks like a pointed screwdriver with a wire on one end and a bulb in its handle. A jumper wire is simply a piece of wire with alligator clips or special terminals on each end. If a component is not working, you must follow a systematic plan to determine which of the three causes is the villain.

1. Turn ON the switch that controls the item not working.

➡**Some items only work when the ignition switch is turned ON.**

2. Disconnect the power supply wire from the component.
3. Attach the ground wire of a test light or a voltmeter to a good metal ground.
4. Touch the end probe of the test light (or the positive lead of the voltmeter) to the power wire; if there is current in the wire, the light in the test light will come on (or the voltmeter will indicate the amount of voltage). You have now established that current is getting to the component.
5. Turn the ignition or dash switch **OFF** and reconnect the wire to the component.

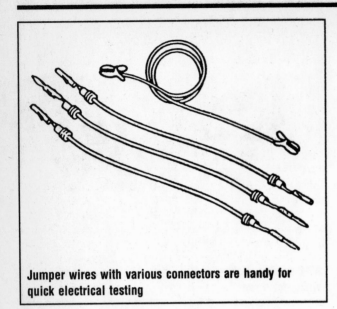

Jumper wires with various connectors are handy for quick electrical testing

If there was no power, then the problem is between the battery and the component. This includes all the switches, fuses, relays and the battery itself. The next place to look is the fusebox; check carefully either by eye or by using the test light across the fuse clips. The easiest way to check is to simply replace the fuse. If the fuse is blown, and upon replacement, immediately blows again, there is a short between the fuse and the component. This is generally (not always) a sign of an internal short in the component. Disconnect the power wire at the component again and replace the fuse; if the fuse holds, the component is the problem.

✳✳ WARNING

DO NOT test a component by running a jumper wire from the battery UNLESS you are certain that it operates on 12 volts. Many electronic components are designed to operate with less voltage and connecting them to 12 volts could destroy them. Jumper wires are best used to bypass a portion of the circuit (such as a stretch of wire or a switch) that DOES NOT contain a resistor and is suspected to be bad.

If all the fuses are good and the component is not receiving power, find the switch for the circuit. Bypass the switch with the jumper wire. This is done by connecting one end of the jumper to the power wire coming into the switch and the other end to the wire leaving the switch. If the component comes to life, the switch has failed.

✳✳ WARNING

Never substitute the jumper for the component. The circuit needs the electrical load of the component. If you bypass it, you will cause a short circuit.

Checking the ground for any circuit can mean tracing wires to the body, cleaning connections or tightening mounting bolts for the component itself. If the jumper wire can be connected to the case of the component or the ground connector, you can ground the other end to a piece of clean, solid metal on the vehicle. Again, if the component starts working, you've found the problem. A systematic search through the fuse, connectors, switches and

the component itself will almost always yield an answer. Loose and/or corroded connectors, particularly in ground circuits, are becoming a larger problem in modern vehicles. The computers and on-board electronic (solid state) systems are highly sensitive to improper grounds and will change their function drastically if one occurs.

Remember that for any electrical circuit to work, ALL the connections must be clean and tight.

➡**For more information on Understanding and Troubleshooting Electrical Systems, please refer to Section 6 of this manual.**

Battery, Starting and Charging Systems

BASIC OPERATING PRINCIPLES

Battery

The battery is the first link in the chain of mechanisms which work together to provide cranking of the automobile engine. In most modern vehicles, the battery is a lead/acid electrochemical device consisting of six 2v subsections (cells) connected in series so the unit is capable of producing approximately 12v of electrical pressure. Each subsection consists of a series of positive and negative plates held a short distance apart in a solution of sulfuric acid and water.

The two types of plates are of dissimilar metals. This sets-up a chemical reaction, and it is this reaction which produces current flow from the battery when its positive and negative terminals are connected to an electrical accessory such as a lamp or motor. The continued transfer of electrons would eventually convert the sulfuric acid to water, and make the two plates identical in chemical composition. As electrical energy is removed from the battery, its voltage output tends to drop. Thus, measuring battery voltage and battery electrolyte composition are two ways of checking the ability of the unit to supply power. During engine cranking, electrical energy is removed from the battery. However, if the charging circuit is in good condition and the operating conditions are normal, the power removed from the battery will be replaced by the alternator which will force electrons back through the battery, reversing the normal flow, and restoring the battery to its original chemical state.

Starting System

The battery and starting motor are linked by very heavy electrical cables designed to minimize resistance to the flow of current. Generally, the major power supply cable that leaves the battery goes directly to the starter, while other electrical system needs are supplied by a smaller cable. During starter operation, power flows from the battery to the starter and is grounded through the vehicle's frame/body or engine and the battery's negative ground strap.

The starter is a specially designed, direct current electric motor capable of producing a great amount of power for its size. One thing that allows the motor to produce a great deal of power is its tremendous rotating speed. It drives the engine through a tiny pinion gear (attached to the starter's armature), which drives the very large flywheel ring gear at a greatly reduced speed. Another factor allowing it to produce so much power is that only intermittent operation is required of it. Thus, little allowance for air circulation is necessary, and the windings can be built into a very small space.

The starter solenoid is a magnetic device which employs the small current supplied by the start circuit of the ignition switch. This magnetic action moves a plunger which mechanically engages the starter and closes the heavy switch connecting it to the battery. The starting switch circuit usually consists of the starting switch contained within the ignition switch, a neutral safety switch or clutch pedal switch, and the wiring necessary to connect these in series with the starter solenoid or relay.

The pinion, a small gear, is mounted to a one way drive clutch. This clutch is splined to the starter armature shaft. When the ignition switch is moved to the **START** position, the solenoid plunger slides the pinion toward the flywheel ring gear via a collar and spring. If the teeth on the pinion and flywheel match properly, the pinion will engage the flywheel immediately. If the gear teeth butt one another, the spring will be compressed and will force the gears to mesh as soon as the starter turns far enough to allow them to do so. As the solenoid plunger reaches the end of its travel, it closes the contacts that connect the battery and starter, then the engine is cranked.

As soon as the engine starts, the flywheel ring gear begins turning fast enough to drive the pinion at an extremely high rate of speed. At this point, the one-way clutch begins allowing the pinion to spin faster than the starter shaft so that the starter will not operate at excessive speed. When the ignition switch is released from the starter position, the solenoid is de-energized, and a spring pulls the gear out of mesh interrupting the current flow to the starter.

Some starters employ a separate relay, mounted away from the starter, to switch the motor and solenoid current on and off. The relay replaces the solenoid electrical switch, but does not eliminate the need for a solenoid mounted on the starter used to mechanically engage the starter drive gears. The relay is used to reduce the amount of current the starting switch must carry.

Charging System

The automobile charging system provides electrical power for operation of the vehicle's ignition system, starting system and all electrical accessories. The battery serves as an electrical surge or storage tank, storing (in chemical form) the energy originally produced by the engine driven generator. The system also provides a means of regulating output to protect the battery from being overcharged and to avoid excessive voltage to the accessories.

The storage battery is a chemical device incorporating parallel lead plates in a tank containing a sulfuric acid/water solution. Adjacent plates are slightly dissimilar, and the chemical reaction of the two dissimilar plates produces electrical energy when the battery is connected to a load such as the starter motor. The chemical reaction is reversible, so that when the generator is producing a voltage (electrical pressure) greater than that produced by the battery, electricity is forced into the battery, and the battery is returned to its fully charged state.

Newer automobiles use alternating current generators or alternators, because they are more efficient, can be rotated at higher speeds, and have fewer brush problems. In an alternator, the field usually rotates while all the current produced passes only through the stator winding. The brushes bear against continuous slip rings. This causes the current produced to periodically reverse the direction of its flow. Diodes (electrical one way valves) block the flow of current from traveling in the wrong direction. A series of diodes is wired together to permit the alternating flow of the stator to be rectified back to 12 volts DC for use by the vehicle's electrical system.

The voltage regulating function is performed by a regulator. The regulator is often built in to the alternator; this system is termed an integrated or internal regulator.

ENGINE ELECTRICAL

Distributor

REMOVAL & INSTALLATION

The removal and installation procedures for all distributors on Mercedes-Benz vehicles are basically similar. However, certain minor differences may exist from model to model.

1. The distributor (on most models) is located on the front of the engine.
2. Remove the dust cover, distributor cap, cable plug connections and vacuum line.
3. Rotating the engine in the direction of normal rotation, crank it around until the markings on the distributor rotor and distributor housing are aligned.
4. The engine can be cranked with a socket wrench on the balancer bolt or with a small prybar inserted in the balancer.
5. Matchmark the distributor body and the engine so that the distributor can be returned to its original position. White paint can be used for this purpose. The notch on the rim of the distributor housing indicates No. 1 cylinder.

6. Remove the distributor hold-down bolt and withdraw the distributor from the engine.

➡**Do not crank the engine while the distributor is removed.**

7. To install the distributor, reverse the removal instructions. Insert the distributor so that the matchmarks on the distributor and engine are aligned.
8. Tighten the clamp bolt and check the dwell angle and ignition timing.

TESTING

➡**The following testing procedures apply only to electronic ignition distributors.**

Except 1981 6-Cyl. and 1984 4-Cyl. Engines
◆ **See Figures 1 and 2**

1. Check the screw type plug terminals and the plug wires.
2. With the ignition **ON,** a primary current of about 8 amps will flow continuously through the system.

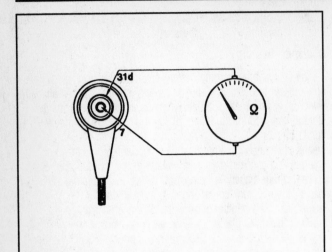

Fig. 1 Use an ohmmeter to check armature resistance—pre-1980 electronic ignition

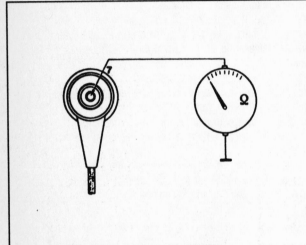

Fig. 2 Use an ohmmeter to check pick-up coil resistance—pre-1980 electronic ignition

3. Check the input voltage at the terminal block. Terminal 15 should show 4.5 volts and terminal 1 should show 0.5–2.0 volts. If the voltage at terminal 1 is excessive, replace the switching unit.

4. If there is no spark but terminal 1 voltage is OK, check the armature resistance (terminal 7 and 31d). Resistance should be 450–750 ohms.

5. Test the pick-up coil resistance. There should be infinite resistance between terminal 7 and ground.

6. Check the armature and pick-up coil for mechanical damage. An air gap should exist between them.

7. Check the dwell angle. Even though it cannot be adjusted, it should be 25–39° at 1,400–1,500 rpm.

8. If the armature and pick up coil are functioning, replace the switching unit. If the armature and pick-up coil indicate no damage, replace the switching unit. If the armature or pick-up coil are defective, replace the distributor.

1981 6-Cylinder Engines

This engine uses a new breakerless transistorized ignition system with no preresistance and no current flow unless the engine

is running. The new system consists of ignition coil, distributor, harness and switching unit. Do not replace the coil with a previously used coil. Also, see the ignition system precautions given previously.

1. Test the voltage between bushing 5 of the diagnosis plug and ground with the ignition **ON.** Nominal battery voltage should be indicated. If not, test the voltage via the ignition switch. If voltage is correct, go to Step 2.

2. Test the voltage between bushing 4 and 5 of the diagnosis plug socket. Zero voltage should be indicated. If voltage is more than 0.1 volt, switch off the ignition immediately. Renew the switching unit. Check the pressure relief plug in the ignition coil and the ohmic value of the ignition coil between terminals 1 and 15. If the pressure relief plug has popped out or the resistance is not .7Ω, replace the ignition coil.

3. Test the dwell angle. It should be 7–25°. If more than 25°, replace the switching unit. If no reading or the reading is correct, go to Step 4.

4. Disconnect the green control line from the switching unit and test the resistance between terminals 3 and 7. Resistance should be 500–700ohms. If the resistance is wrong, pull the green cable from the distributor and see if there are 500–700 ohms present at the connector plugs. If so, replace the green cable. If not, replace the distributor.

5. Remove the green cable from the control unit. There should be 200 kΩ between terminals 3 or 7 and ground. If not, disconnect the green cable from the distributor and test the resistance between any of the plugs and ground. If 200 kΩ are not present, replace the distributor.

1984 4-Cylinder Engines

The electronic ignition system on the 190E differs from the previous systems with the addition of a small switching unit.

➡**The base plate on this switching unit serves as a heat sink; periodic cleaning will ensure proper heat flow between it and the wheel arch.**

The ignition coil and all testing procedures are similar to those given for the 1981 6-cylinder engine.

Alternator

Since 1968, all Mercedes-Benz cars imported into the United States use 12 volt alternators, sometimes in conjunction with the transistorized (electronic) ignition system.

PRECAUTIONS

Some precautions that should be taken into consideration when working on this, or any other, AC charging system are as follows:

1. Never switch battery polarity.

2. When installing a battery, always connect the grounded terminal first.

3. Never disconnect the battery while the engine is running.

4. If the molded connector is disconnected from the alternator, do not ground the hot wire.

5. Never run the alternator with the main output cable disconnected.

6. Never electric weld around the car without disconnecting the alternator.

7. Never apply any voltage in excess of battery voltage during testing.

8. Never "jump" a battery for starting purposes with more than 12 volts.

REMOVAL & INSTALLATION

The alternator is located on the left or right-hand side, usually down low. Because of the location, it is sometimes easier to remove the alternator from below the vehicle. The following is a general procedure for all models.

1. Locate the alternator and disconnect and tag all wires.

2. Loosen the adjusting (pivot) bolt or the adjusting mechanism and swing the alternator in toward the engine.

3. Remove the drive belt from the alternator pulley.

4. The alternator can now be removed from its mounting bracket or the bracket and alternator can be removed from the engine.

Using a ratchet, socket and a back-up wrench, loosen . . .

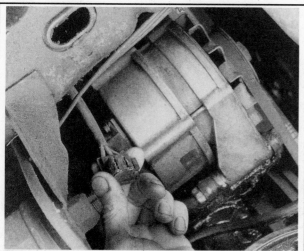

To remove the alternator, disengage the electrical connections . . .

. . . then remove the mounting bolt

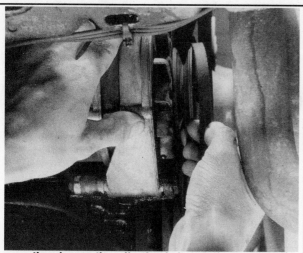

. . . then loosen the adjusting bolt and disconnect the drive belt

Remove the alternator from the engine

5. Installation is the reverse of removal.

6. Re-tension all of the drive belts that were loosened. See Section 1.

BELT TENSION ADJUSTMENT

All alternator drive belts should be tensioned to the specified deflection under thumb pressure at the middle of its longest span. See Section 1 for exact drive belt adjustment procedures.

➡ **The 190D utilizes a single V-belt with automatic tensioning. No adjustment is necessary.**

Starter

All Mercedes-Benz passenger cars are equipped with 12-volt Bosch electric starters of various rated outputs. The starter motor is actually nothing but a simple series-wound electric motor of high torque output, fitted with a drive pinion and a device to mesh the pinion with the flywheel ring gear. The carrier, which is connected to the pinion through the overrunning clutch, runs in splines machined in the armature shaft. When the armature rotates, these splines force the pinion into mesh. When the engine starts, the overrunning (one-way) clutch releases the pinion and the unit disengages. The starter is actuated and the pinion engaged by an electric solenoid mounted on top of the starter motor.

When removing the starter, note the exact position of all wires and washers, since they should be installed in their original locations. On some models it may be necessary to also position the front wheels to the left or right to provide working clearance.

REMOVAL & INSTALLATION

1. Remove all wires from the starter and tag them as to location.

2. Disconnect the battery cable.

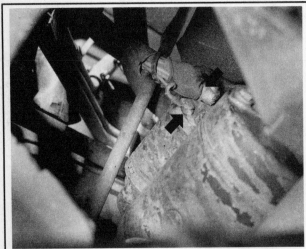

To remove the starter, disengage its electrical connections . . .

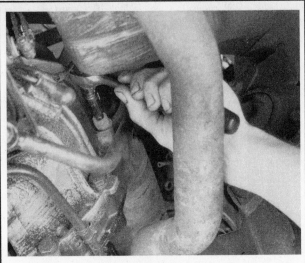

. . . then unfasten the retaining bolts

Remove the starter motor from the engine

3. Unbolt the starter from the bell housing and remove the starter from underneath the car.

4. Installation is the reverse of removal. Be sure to replace all wires and washers in their original locations.

Battery

REMOVAL & INSTALLATION

The battery is located in the engine compartment and can be easily removed by disconnecting the battery cables (negative cable first) and removing the hold-down clamp. To install the battery, position it in its tray and fasten the hold-down clamp, then connect the positive cable, followed by the negative cable.

Battery and Starter Specifications
All cars use 12 volt, negative ground electrical systems

Engine Model	Battery AMP Hour Capacity	Starter							Brush Spring Tension (oz)	Min Brush Length (in.)
		Lock Test			No Load Test					
		Amps	Volts	Torque (ft/lbs)	Amps	Volts	RPM			
All w/Diesel Engine	88	650–750	9.0	1000–1200	80–95	12	7500–8500		NA	NA
All w/Gas Engine	66	290–300	9.0	1600–1800	50–70	12	9000–11000		NA	.05

NA—Not specified by manufacturer

ENGINE MECHANICAL

Engine Overhaul Tips

Most engine overhaul procedures are fairly standard. In addition to specific parts replacement procedures and specifications for your individual engine, this section is also a guide to acceptable rebuilding procedures. Examples of standard rebuilding practice are given and should be used along with specific details concerning your particular engine.

Competent and accurate machine shop services will ensure maximum performance, reliability and engine life. In most instances it is more profitable for the do-it-yourself mechanic to remove, clean and inspect the component, buy the necessary parts and deliver these to a shop for actual machine work.

On the other hand, much of the rebuilding work (crankshaft, block, bearings, piston rods, and other components) is well within the scope of the do-it-yourself mechanic's tools and abilities. You will have to decide for yourself the depth of involvement you desire in an engine repair or rebuild.

TOOLS

The tools required for an engine overhaul or parts replacement will depend on the depth of your involvement. With a few exceptions, they will be the tools found in a mechanic's tool kit (see Section 1 of this manual). More in-depth work will require some or all of the following:
- A dial indicator (reading in thousandths) mounted on a universal base
- Micrometers and telescope gauges
- Jaw and screw-type pullers
- Scraper
- Valve spring compressor
- Ring groove cleaner
- Piston ring expander and compressor
- Ridge reamer
- Cylinder hone or glaze breaker
- Plastigage®
- Engine stand

The use of most of these tools is illustrated in this chapter. Many can be rented for a one-time use from a local parts jobber or tool supply house specializing in automotive work.

Occasionally, the use of special tools is called for. See the information on Special Tools and the Safety Notice in the front of this book before substituting another tool.

INSPECTION TECHNIQUES

Procedures and specifications are given in this chapter for inspecting, cleaning and assessing the wear limits of most major components. Other procedures such as Magnaflux® and Zyglo® can be used to locate material flaws and stress cracks. Magnaflux® is a magnetic process applicable only to ferrous materials. The Zyglo® process coats the material with a fluorescent dye penetrant and can be used on any material.

Checking for suspected surface cracks can be more readily made using spot check dye. The dye is sprayed onto the suspected area, wiped off and the area sprayed with a developer. Cracks will show up brightly.

OVERHAUL TIPS

Aluminum has become extremely popular for use in engines, due to its low weight. Observe the following precautions when handling aluminum parts:
- Never hot tank aluminum parts (the caustic hot tank solution will eat the aluminum.
- Remove all aluminum parts (identification tag, etc.) from engine parts prior to the tanking.
- Always coat threads lightly with engine oil or anti-seize compounds before installation, to prevent seizure.
- Never overtorque bolts or spark plugs especially in aluminum threads.

Stripped threads in any component can be repaired using any of several commercial repair kits (Heli-Coil®, Microdot®, Keenserts®, etc.).

When assembling the engine, any parts that will be exposed to frictional contact must be prelubed to provide lubrication at initial start-up. Any product specifically formulated for this purpose can be used, but engine oil is not recommended as a prelube in most cases.

When semi-permanent (locked, but removable) installation of

bolts or nuts is desired, threads should be cleaned and coated with Loctite® or another similar, commercial non-hardening sealant.

REPAIRING DAMAGED THREADS

Several methods of repairing damaged threads are available. Heli-Coil® (shown here), Keenserts® and Microdot® are among the most widely used. All involve basically the same principle—drilling out stripped threads, tapping the hole and installing a prewound insert—making welding, plugging and oversize fasteners unnecessary.

Two types of thread repair inserts are usually supplied: a standard type for most inch coarse, inch fine, metric course and metric fine thread sizes and a spark lug type to fit most spark plug port sizes. Consult the individual tool manufacturer's catalog to determine exact applications. Typical thread repair kits will contain a selection of prewound threaded inserts, a tap (corresponding to

Drill out the damaged threads with the specified size bit. Be sure to drill completely through the hole or to the bottom of a blind hole

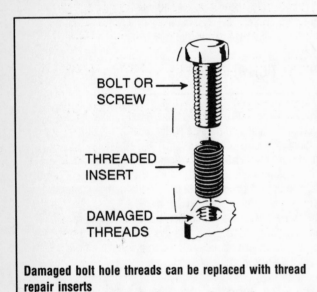

Damaged bolt hole threads can be replaced with thread repair inserts

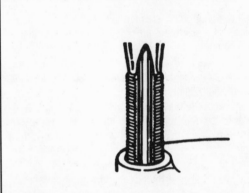

Using the kit, tap the hole in order to receive the thread insert. Keep the tap well oiled and back it out frequently to avoid clogging the threads

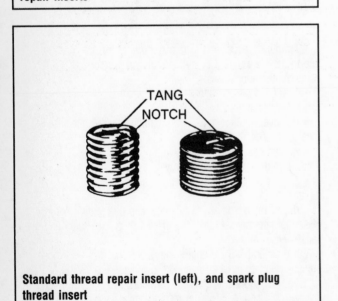

Standard thread repair insert (left), and spark plug thread insert

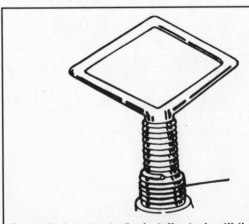

Screw the insert onto the installer tool until the tang engages the slot. Thread the insert into the hole until it is 1/4–1/2 turn below the top surface, then remove the tool and break off the tang using a punch

the outside diameter threads of the insert) and an installation tool. Spark plug inserts usually differ because they require a tap equipped with pilot threads and a combined reamer/tap section. Most manufacturers also supply blister-packed thread repair inserts separately in addition to a master kit containing a variety of taps and inserts plus installation tools.

Before attempting to repair a threaded hole, remove any

snapped, broken or damaged bolts or studs. Penetrating oil can be used to free frozen threads. The offending item can usually be removed with locking pliers or using a screw/stud extractor. After the hole is clear, the thread can be repaired, as shown in the series of accompanying illustrations and in the kit manufacturer's instructions.

General Gasoline Engine Specifications

Year Model	Engine Model	Engine Displacement (cc)	Carburetor Type	Horsepower @ rpm	Torque @ rpm (ft lbs)	Bore x Stroke (mm)	Compression Ratio	Firing Order
190E	M102	2299	Fuel Injection	113 @ 5000	133 @ 3500	95.50 x 80.25	8.0:1	1342
230	M115	2307	Stromberg 175 CDT	95 @ 4800 ③	128 @ 2500 ④	93.75 x 83.6	8.0:1	1342
280S (1975–76)	M110	2746	Solex 4-bbl	120 @ 4800	143 @ 2800	86.00 x 78.80	8.0:1	153624
280, 280C (1974–76)	M110	2746	Solex 4-bbl	120 @ 4800	143 @ 2800	86.00 x 78.80	8.0:1	153624
280E, 280CE (1977–79) 280SE (1977–79)	M110	2746	Fuel Injection	142 @ 5750 ⑤	149 @ 4600 ⑥	86.00 x 78.80	8.0:1	153624
380SE, 380SEC, 380SEL, 380SL, 380SLC	M116	3839	Fuel Injection	155 @ 4750	196 @ 2750	88.0 x 78.9	8.3:1	15486372
1974 450SE 450SEL 450SL 450SLC	M117	4520	Fuel Injection	190 @ 4750 ①	240 @ 3000 ②	92.00 x 85.00	8.0:	15486372
1975–79 450SE 450SEL 450SL 450SLC	M117	4520	Fuel Injection	180 @ 4750	220 @ 3000	92.00 x 85.00	8.0:1	15486372
450SEL 6.9	M100	6834	Fuel Injection	250 @ 4000	360 @ 2500	107.00 x 95.00	8.0:1	15486372
500SEC, 500SEL	M117	4973	Fuel Injection	184 @ 4500	247 @ 2000	96.5 x 85.0	8.0:1	1548672

① California—180 @ 4750
② California—232 @ 3000
③ 1975 California—85 @ 4800
④ 1975–77 California—122 @ 2500
⑤ 1977 and later California—137 @ 5750
⑥ 1977 and later California—142 @ 4600

General Diesel Engine Specifications

Car Model	Engine Model	Engine Displacement (cc)	Fuel Delivery	Horsepower @ rpm	Torque @ rpm (ft. lbs.)	Bore x Stroke (mm)	Compression Ratio	Firing Order
190D	OM601	2197	Fuel Injection	72 @ 4200	96 @ 2800	87.0 x 92.4	22.0:1	1342
240D	OM616	2404	Fuel Injection	62–67 @ 4000	97 @ 2400	91.0 x 92.4	21:1	1342
300D ('77–'81) 300CD ('78–'81) 300TD ('79–'80)	OM617	3005 ①	Fuel Injection	77–83 @ 4000	115–120 @ 2400	91.0 x 92.4 ②	21:1	12453
300 TD Turbo ('81–'84) 300D ('82–'84) 300CD ('82–'84)	OM617	2998	Fuel Inj. Turbocharged	120 @ 4350 ③	170 @ 2400 ④	90.0 x 92.4	21:1 ⑤	12453
300SD	OM617	2998	Fuel Inj. Turbocharged	110–120 @ 4200 ③	168–170 @ 2400 ④	90.9 x 92.4	21:1 ⑤	12453

NOTE: *Horsepower may vary depending on year and application.*
① 1979 and later: 2998
② 1979 and later: 90.0 x 92.4
③ 1984: 123 @ 4350
④ 1984: 184 @ 2400
⑤ 1984: 21.5:1

Valve Specifications

Car Model	Engine Displacement (cc)	Seat Angle (deg)	Spring Test Pressure (mm @ KP)	Stem Diameter (mm) Intake	Stem Diameter (mm) Exhaust
190E	2299	45	30.5 @ 85.96–91.98	7.97	8.96
190D	2197	45	27 @ 73.42–78.52	7.97	8.96
230	2307	45 + 15'	39 @ 36 ①	8.948–8.970	10.918–10.940
240D	2404	30 + 15'	38.4 @ 23–26.4	9.920–9.905	9.918–9.940
280, 280C, 280CE, 280E, 280S, 290SE	2746	45 + 15'	84–92 @ 30.5	8.950–8.970	③
300D, 300CD, 300TD, 300SD	3005 ②	30 + 15'	38.4 @ 23–26.4	9.920–9.940	9.918–9.940
380SE 380SL 380SLC 380SEL 380SEC	3839	45	30.5 @ 88 ①	8.955–8.970	8.935–8.960
450SL 450SLC 450SEL	4520	45 + 15'	42 @ 29.5–32.5 ①	8.955–8.970	10.940–10.960
500SEC 500SEL	4973	45 + 15'	30.5 @ 88 ①	8.955–8.970	8.935–8.960
6.9	6834	45 + 15'	44.5 2.3	8.948–8.970	11.932–11.950

① Outer spring—the spring should be installed so that the close coils are in contact with the cylinder head
② 1979 and later: 2998
③ Thru 1979: 10.940–10.960
   1980 and later: 8.940–8.960
④ 1980 and later: 28.0

Valve Timing Specifications▲

Model	Camshaft Code Number●	Intake Valve		Exhaust Valve	
		Opens ATDC*	Closes ABDC*	Opens BBDC*	Closes BTDC*
190D	05	11/12	17/18	28/27	15/14
190E	20①, 21②	17/18	11/12	17.5/16.5	12/11
230	05	14	20	22	12
240D	02, 06③	11.5/13.5	13.5/15.5	21/19	19/17
280, 280C ('74 Fed.)	30④, 33④	11	15	22	24
280, 280C ('74 Calif.)	25④, 24④	6	21	30	13
280, 280C, 280E, 280CE, 280S, 280SE ('75 and later)	64④, 71④	7	21	30	12
300D ('75–'81), 300CD ('78–'81), 300SD ('78–'79), 300TD ('79–'80)	00, 08③	11.5/13.5	13.5/15.5	21/19	19/17
300D ('82–'84), 300CD ('82–'84), 300SD ('80–'84), 300TD ('81–'84)	05③	9/11	15/17	27/25	16/14
380SEL, 380SL, 38SLC	62/63, 68/69 L R L R	L-24 R-22	L-7.5 R-5.5	L-4 R-6	L-12.5 R-14.5
380SE, 380SEC	70/71 L R	L-16 R-14	L-15 R-13	L-16 R-18	L-17 R-19
450SE, 450SEL, 450SL, 450SLC ('74)	52/53 L R	4	14	30	16
450SE ('75–'76) 450SEL, 450SL, 450SLC ('75–'77)	54/55, 56/57 L R L R	5	21	25	5
450SEL, 450SL, 450SLC ('78–'80)	00/01 L R	L-6.5 R-4.5	L-18.5 R-16.5	L-23 R-25	L-8 R-10
500SEC, 500SEL	08/09 L R	L-22 R-20	L-21 R-19	L-10 R-12	L-15 R-17
6.9	36/37 L R	L-12 R-10	L-25 R-23	L-32 R-34	L-19 R-21

▲ Taken at 2mm valve lift

● Camshaft code number is stamped into rear face of camshaft

* When numbers are separated by a slash, first figure is for new timing chain and second figure is for a used timing chain (approx. 20,000 km). When no slash is used, the figure is for a new timing chain.

L—Left

R—Right

ATDC—After Top Dead Center

ABDC—After Bottom Dead Center

BBDC—Before Bottom Dead Center

BTDC—Before Top Dead Center

① Camshaft with 32mm bearing diameter (standard)

② Camshaft with 32.5mm bearing diameter (repair version)

③ Camshaft made of chilled cast iron

④ 1st figure: exhaust camshaft
   2nd figure: intake camshaft

Crankshaft and Connecting Rod Specifications

(All measurements are given in millimeters)

Car Model	Engine Displace (cc)	Engine Model	Crankshaft				Connecting Rod		
			Main Brg. Journal Dia.	Main Brg. Oil Clearance	Shaft End-Play	Thrust on No.	Journal Diameter	Oil Clearance	Side Clearance
190D	2197	OM601	57.960– 57.965	0.031– 0.073	0.100– 0.250	①	47.950– 47.965	0.031– 0.073	N.A.
190E	2299	M102							
230	2307	M115	69.955– 69.965	0.045– 0.065	0.100– 0.240	①	51.955– 51.965	0.035– 0.055	0.110– 0.260
240D	2404	OM616	69.955– 69.965	0.045– 0.065	0.100– 0.240	①	51.955– 51.965	0.035– 0.055	0.110– 0.260
280E, 280 280CE, 280C 280SE, 280S	2746	M110	59.96– 59.95	0.03– 0.07	0.10– 0.24	①	47.95– 47.96	0.15– 0.50	0.11– 0.23
300D, 300CD, 300TD, 300SD	3005 ②	OM617	69.955– 69.965	0.045– 0.065	0.100– 0.240	①	51.955– 51.965	0.035– 0.055	0.110– 0.260
380SE 380SEL 380SL 380SLC 380SEC	3839	M116	63.950– 63.965	0.045– 0.065	0.100– 0.240	①	47.945– 47.965	0.045– 0.065	0.220– 0.359
450SL 450SLC 450SEL	4520	M117	63.955– 63.965	0.035– 0.075	0.100– 0.240	①	51.955– 51.965	0.035– 0.065	0.220– 0.380
500SEC 500SEL	4973	M117	63.950– 63.965	0.045– 0.065	0.100– 0.240	①	47.945– 47.965	0.045– 0.065	0.220– 0.359
6.9	6836	M100	69.945– 69.965	0.045– 0.065	0.100– 0.240	①	54.940– 54.600	0.045– 0.065	0.220– 0.359

N.A. Not Available

① Center main on 5 main bearing engines;
   rear main on 7 main bearing engines; 3rd
   from front on 300D (5-cylinder)

② 1979 and later: 2998

Torque Specifications
(All reading in ft. lbs.)

Car Model	Engine Model	Cylinder Head Bolts	Rod Bearing Bolts	Main Bearing Bolts	Crankshaft Pulley Bolt	Flywheel to Crankshaft Bolts	Cam Sprocket Bolt(s)	Exhaust Manifold Bolts
190D	OM601	⑦ ①	⑧	65	195–239	⑨	33	N.A.
190E	M102	⑩ ①	⑨	65	195–239	⑨	58	N.A.
230	M115	58	①	58 ③	151–158	①	18	18–21
240D	OM616	65 ⑬	①	65	151–158	①	18	18–21
280E, 280 280CE, 280C 280SE, 280S	M110	58	①	58	206–226	①	58	N.A.
300D, 300CD 300TD, 300SD	OM617	65 ⑬	①	65	195–240	①	18	18–21
380SE 380SL 380SEL 380SLC 380SEC	M116	⑫	30–37 ①	⑤	289	①	74	N.A.
450SL 450SLC 450SEL	M117	⑪	①	④	180–194	①	36	18–21
500SEC 500SEL	M117	⑫	①	④	180–194	①	36	18–21
6.9	M100	65	①	⑤	289	①	72	N.A.

N.A. Not Available at time of publication
① See text
② With cold engine; cylinder head bolts should be tightened in at least 3 stages
③ 65 on M115 engines
④ M 10 bolts—37 ft. lbs.
M 12 bolts—72 ft. lbs.
⑤ M 10 bolts—43 ft. lbs
M 12 bolts—58 ft. lbs.
⑥ Tighten to 22 ft. lbs. then to 45 ft. lbs. in proper sequence. After 10 mins. loosen and tighten again to 45 ft. lbs.
⑦ M 10 bolts: 1st step—18 ft. lbs.
2nd step—29 ft. lbs.
Setting time—10 min.
3rd step—90° torquing angle
4th step—90° torquing angle
M 8 bolts: 18 ft. lbs.
⑧ 1st step: 22–25 ft. lbs.
2nd step: 90–100° torquing angle
⑨ 1st step: 22–29 ft. lbs.
2nd step: 90–100° torquing angle

⑩ M 12 bolts: 1st step—29 ft. lbs.
2nd step—51 ft. lbs.
Setting time—10 min.
3rd step—90° torquing angle
4th step—90° torquing angle
M 8 bolts: 18 ft. lbs.
⑪ 1st step: 22 ft. lbs.
2nd step: 44 ft. lbs.
setting time: 10 min.
3rd step: warm engine, loosen bolts and retighten to 44 ft. lbs.
⑫ 1st step: 22 ft. lbs.
2nd step: 44 ft. lbs.
setting time: 10 min.
3rd step: loosen bolts and retighten to 44 ft. lbs.
⑬ All vehicles manufactured after Feb. 1979:
1st step:—29 ft. lbs.
2nd step—51 ft. lbs.
setting time—10 min.
3rd step—90° torquing angle
4th step—90° torquing angle

Engine

REMOVAL & INSTALLATION

➡In all cases, Mercedes-Benz engines and transmissions are removed as a unit.

190D, 190E, 230, 240D, 300D, 300CD, 300TD and 300SD Models

◗ **See Figure 3**

Remove the engine/transmission as a unit.

1. Remove the hood, then drain the cooling system and disconnect the battery.

To remove the engine, the battery cables must be disconnected

✳✳ CAUTION

When draining engine coolant, keep in mind that cats and dogs are attracted to ethylene glycol antifreeze and could drink any that is left in an uncovered container or in puddles on the ground. This will prove fatal in sufficient quantity. Always drain coolant into a sealable container. Coolant should be reused unless it is contaminated or is several years old.

2. Remove the fan shroud, radiator, and disconnect all heater hoses and oil cooler lines. Plug all openings to keep out dirt.

3. Remove the air cleaner and all fuel, vacuum and oil hoses. Swing the A/C compressor aside. Leave lines connected. Disconnect all other fluid lines and hoses. Plug all openings to keep out dirt.

4. Remove the viscous coupling and fan and disconnect the carburetor choke cable (if so equipped).

5. On diesel engines, disconnect the idle control and starting cables. On the 300SD, loosen the oil filter cover slightly. Siphon off the power steering fluid and disconnect the hoses.

6. On all engines, disconnect the accelerator linkage.

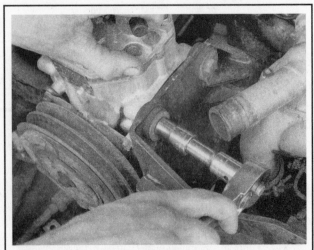

Loosen the air conditioning compressor retaining bolts . . .

1. U-joint flange   3. Wooden block
2. U-joint plate

Fig. 3 When removing the engine, use a wood-padded jack under the transmission to support the weight

. . . and move the compressor to one side without disconnecting the refrigerant lines

7. Disconnect all ground straps and electrical connections. Tag each wire for easy reassembly.

8. Detach the gearshift linkage and the exhaust pipes.

9. Loosen the steering relay arm and pull it down out of the way, along with the center steering rod and hydraulic steering damper.

10. The hydraulic engine shock absorber should be removed.

11. Remove the hydraulic line from the clutch housing and the oil line connectors from the automatic transmission.

12. Unbolt the clutch slave cylinder from the bellhousing after removing the return spring.

13. Remove the exhaust pipe bracket attached to the transmission and place a wood-padded jack under the bellhousing, or place a cable sling under the oil pan, to support the engine. On turbocharged models, disconnect the exhaust pipes at the turbo charger.

14. Mark the position of the rear engine support and unbolt the two outer bolts, then remove the top bolt at the transmission and pull the support out.

15. Disconnect the speedometer cable and the front driveshaft U-joint. Push the driveshaft back and wire it out of the way.

16. Unbolt the engine mounts on both sides and, on four-cylinder engines, the front limit stop.

17. Unbolt the power steering fluid reservoir and swing it out of the way; then, using a chain hoist and cable, lift the engine and transmission upward and outward. An angle of about 45° will allow the car to be pushed backward while the engine is coming up.

18. Reverse the procedure to install, making sure to bleed the hydraulic clutch, power steering, power brakes and fuel system.

280, 280C, 280E, 280CE, 280SE & 280S MODELS

1. Scribe alignment marks on the hood hinges and remove the hood. Drain the coolant from the radiator and block.

✳✳ CAUTION

When draining engine coolant, keep in mind that cats and dogs are attracted to ethylene glycol antifreeze and could drink any that is left in an uncovered container or in puddles on the ground. This will prove fatal in sufficient quantity. Always drain coolant into a sealable container. Coolant should be reused unless it is contaminated or is several years old.

2. Remove the radiator.

3. Disconnect the lines from the vacuum pump.

4. On vehicles with air conditioning, remove the compressor and place it aside.

✳✳ CAUTION

Please refer to Section 1 before discharging the compressor or disconnecting air conditioning lines. Damage to the air conditioning system or personal injury could result. Consult your local laws concerning refrigerant discharge and recycling. In many areas it may be illegal for anyone but a certified technician to service the A/C system. Always use an approved recovery station when discharging the air conditioning.

5. Disconnect and tag all electrical connections from the engine.

6. Disconnect all coolant and vacuum lines from the engine.

7. Disconnect and plug the pressure oil lines from the power steering pump, after draining the pump reservoir.

8. Remove the accelerator linkage control rod by pulling off the lock-ring and pushing the shaft in the direction of the firewall.

9. Loosen and remove the exhaust pipes from the manifold and transmission supports.

10. Disconnect the transmission linkage and all other connections.

11. Loosen the front right (driving direction) shock absorber from the front axle carrier.

12. Remove the left-hand engine shock absorber from the engine mount.

13. Attach a lifting device to the engine and tension the cables.

14. Unbolt the engine and transmission mounts and remove the engine at a 45° angle.

15. Installation is the reverse of removal. Be sure to check all fluids and fill or top up as necessary. Check all adjustments on the engine.

V8 Engines

➡**Removal of a V-8 engine equipped with air conditioning, requires disconnecting the air conditioning system.**

✳✳ CAUTION

Please refer to Section 1 before discharging the compressor or disconnecting air conditioning lines. Damage to the air conditioning system or personal injury could result. Consult your local laws concerning refrigerant discharge and recycling. In many areas it may be illegal for anyone but a certified technician to service the A/C system. Always use an approved recovery station when discharging the air conditioning.

1. Remove the hood. On the 380 SEC, the hood can be tilted back 90° and does not need to be removed.

2. Drain the cooling system.

✳✳ CAUTION

When draining engine coolant, keep in mind that cats and dogs are attracted to ethylene glycol antifreeze and could drink any that is left in an uncovered container or in puddles on the ground. This will prove fatal in sufficient quantity. Always drain coolant into a sealable container. Coolant should be reused unless it is contaminated or is several years old.

3. Remove the radiator and fan shroud.

4. Remove the cable plug from the temperature switch.

5. Remove the battery, battery frame and air filter.

6. Drain the power steering reservoir and windshield washer reservoir.

7. Disconnect and plug the high pressure and return lines on the power steering pump.

8. Detach the fuel lines from the fuel filter, pressure regulator, and pressure sensor.

9. If equipped, loosen the line to the supply and anti-freeze tanks. On models so equipped, disconnect the lines to the hydro-pneumatic suspension.

10. Disconnect the cables from the ignition coil and transistor ignition switchbox.

11. Disconnect the brake vacuum lines.

12. Detach the cable connections for the following:
   a. venturi control unit
   b. temperature sensor
   c. distributor
   d. temperature switch
   e. cold starting valve
   f. speedometer inductance transmitter (380 series only)

13. Remove the regulating shaft by pushing it in the direction of the firewall.

14. Disconnect the thrust and pullrods.

15. Disconnect the heater lines.

16. Detach the lines to the oil pressure and temperature gauges.

17. Remove the ground strap from the vehicle.

18. Detach the cables from the alternator, terminal bridge, and battery. Remove the battery.

19. On the 6.9, remove the oil line shield and disconnect the oil lines between the oil pan and oil reservoir.

20. Position a lifting sling on the engine and take up the slack in the chain.

21. Remove the left-hand engine mount and loosen the hex nut on the right-hand mount.

22. Remove the exhaust system. Remove the connecting rod chain on the rear level control valve and loosen the torsion bar slightly. Raise the vehicle slightly at the rear and remove the exhaust system in a rearward direction.

23. Disconnect the handbrake cable.

24. Remove the shield plate from the transmission tunnel.

25. Place a block of wood between the transmission and cross yoke so the engine will not sag, when the rear mount is removed.

26. Loosen the driveshaft intermediate bearing and the driveshaft slide.

27. Support the transmission with a jack.

28. Mark the installation of the crossmember and remove the crossmember. Remove the rear engine carrier with the engine mount.

29. Unbolt the front U-joint flange on the transmission and push it back. Do not loosen the clamp nut on the intermediate bearing. Support the driveshaft.

30. Disconnect the speedometer shaft, shift rod, control pressure rod, regulating linkage (on automatic transmissions), kickdown switch cable, starter lockout switch cable, and the cable for the back-up light switch.

31. Remove the front engine mounting bolt and remove the engine at approximately a 45° angle.

32. Installation is the reverse of removal. Lower the engine until it is behind the front axle carrier. Place a jack under the transmission and lower the engine into its compartment. While lowering the engine, install the right-hand shock mount.

Fill the engine with all required fluids and start the engine. Check for leaks.

Rocker Arms and Shafts

REMOVAL & INSTALLATION

Diesel Engines

Rocker arms on diesel engines can only be removed as a unit with the respective rocker arm blocks.

➡**The 1984 190D does not use rocker arms. The camshaft acts directly on the hydraulic valve tappet.**

1. Detach the connecting rod for the venturi control unit from the bearing bracket lever and remove the bearing bracket from the rocker arm cover.

2. Remove the air vent line from the rocker arm cover and remove the rocker arm cover.

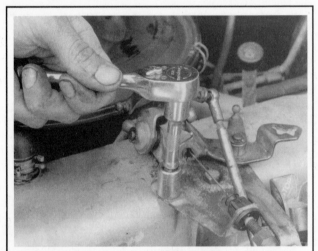

To remove the rocker cover arms and shafts, unbolt the venturi linkage and set it to one side

Unfasten the rocker cover retaining bolts . . .

. . . then remove the rocker arm cover

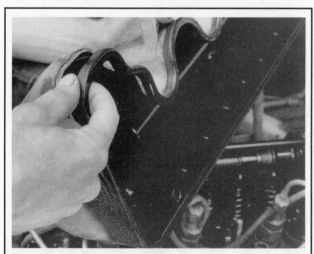

Remove the old gasket material from the rocker arm cover and cylinder head

Remove the bolts from the rocker arm blocks . . .

. . . then remove the rocker arm shafts and bolts

3. Remove the stretchbolts from the rocker arm blocks and remove the blocks with the rocker arms. Turn the crankshaft in each case so that the camshaft does not put any load on the rocker arms.

➡**Turn the crankshaft with a socket wrench on the crankshaft pulley bolt. Do not rotate the engine by turning the camshaft sprocket.**

4. Before installing the rocker arms, check the sliding surfaces of the ball cup and rocker arms. Replace any defective parts.
To install:
5. Assemble the rocker arm blocks and insert new stretchbolts.
6. Tighten the stretchbolts. In each case, position the camshaft so that there is no load on the rocker arms. Refer to the previous NOTE.
7. Check to be sure that the tension clamps have engaged with the notches of the rocker arm blocks.
8. Adjust the valve clearance.
9. Reinstall the rocker arm cover, air vent line, and bearing bracket for the reverse lever. Attach the connecting rod for the venturi control unit to the reversing lever.
10. Make sure that during acceleration, the control cable can move freely without binding.
11. Start the engine and check the rocker arm cover for leaks.

Gasoline Engines—Except 190E Models

➡**1976 and later V8's use hydraulic valve lifters.**

Before removing the rocker arm(s), be sure that they are identified as to their position relative to the camshaft lobe. They should be installed in the same place as they were before disassembly.
Be very careful removing the thrust pieces. They can easily fall into the engine.
1. Remove the rocker arm cover or covers.
2. Force the clamping spring out of the notch in the top of the rocker arm. Slide it in an outward direction across the ball socket or the rocker arm.

➡ **Turn the engine over each time to relieve any load from the rocker arm.**

3. On V8 models, the clamping spring must be forced from the adjusting screw with a small prybar.

4. Force the valve down to remove load from the rocker arm.

➡ **Don't depress the spring too far. When the piston is up as it should be, the valve will hit the piston. As the spring goes down the thrust piece will fall off into the engine.**

5. Lift the rocker arm from the ball pin and remove the rocker arm.

To install:

6. When installing the rocker arm(s), force the rocker arm down until the rocker arm and its ball socket can be installed in the top of the ball pin.

7. Install the rocker arms.

8. Slide the clamping spring across the ball socket of the rocker arm until it rests in the notch of the rocker arm.

9. On V8 models, engage the clamping spring into the recess of the adjusting screw.

10. Check and, if necessary, adjust the valve clearance.

11. After completion of the adjustment, check to be sure that the clamping springs are correctly seated.

12. Install the rocker arm cover and connect any hoses or lines that were disconnected.

13. Run the engine and check for leaks at the rocker arm cover.

190E Models

Rocker arms on this engine are individually mounted on rocker arm shafts that fit into either side of the camshaft bearing brackets.

1. Remove the cylinder head cover. The cover on the 190E is removed with the spark plug wires and distributor cap still connected.

2. Tag each rocker arm and shaft so that they are identified as to their position relative to the camshaft. They should always be installed in the same place as they were before disassembly.

3. The rocker arm shaft is held axially and rotationally by a bearing bracket fastening bolt. Remove the bolt on the side of the bearing bracket that allows access to the exposed end of the rocker shaft.

4. Thread a bolt (M8) into the end of the rocker arm shaft and slowly ease the shaft out of the bearing bracket.

✳✳ CAUTION

Support the rocker arm/lifter assembly while removing the shaft so it will not drop onto the cylinder head.

➡ **Carefully forcing the valve down with a small prybar will remove the load on the hydraulic valve tappet and ease the removal of the shaft. Don't depress the spring too far. When the piston is up as it should be, the valve will hit the piston. As the spring goes down the thrust piece will fall off into the engine.**

5. Replace the bearing bracket bolt and tighten it to 11 ft. lbs. (15 Nm) until ready to replace the rocker shaft.

6. To install, position the rocker arm between the two bearing brackets and slide the shaft into place.

➡ **The circular groove on the end of the rocker shaft must line up with the mounting bolt shank to ensure proper positioning.**

7. Replace the bearing bracket mounting bolt.

8. Repeat Steps 3–7 for all remaining rocker arm/shaft assemblies. Turn the engine over each time to relieve any load from the rocker arm.

9. Replace the cylinder head cover.

Intake Manifold

REMOVAL & INSTALLATION

V8 Engine

◆ **See Figure 4**

1. Partially drain the coolant.

2. Remove the air cleaner.

3. Disconnect the regulating linkage and remove the longitudinal regulating shaft.

4. Pull off all cable plug connections.

5. Disconnect and plug the fuel lines on the pressure regulator and starting valve.

6. Unscrew the nuts on the injection valves and set the injection valves aside.

7. Remove the 16 attaching bolts from the intake manifold.

8. Loosen the hose clip on the thermostat housing hose and disconnect the hose.

9. Remove the intake manifold. If a portion of the manifold must be replaced, disassemble the intake manifold. Replace the rubber connections during reassembly.

10. Intake manifold installation is the reverse of removal. Replace all seals and gaskets. Adjust the linkage and idle speed.

Exhaust Manifold

REMOVAL & INSTALLATION

V8 Engine

1. Unbolt the exhaust pipes from the manifolds.

2. Disconnect the rubber mounting ring from the exhaust system.

3. Loosen the shield plate on the exhaust manifold.

4. When removing the left-hand exhaust manifold, remove the shield plate for the engine mount together with the engine damper.

5. Unbolt the manifold from the engine.

6. Pull the manifolds off of the mounting studs by turning the left-hand exhaust manifold forward and down and removing it upward. Remove the right-hand manifold down and toward the rear.

7. Installation is the reverse of removal. Replace all gaskets and nuts. Mount the flanged gaskets between the exhaust manifold and the cylinder head with their flat sides toward the exhaust manifold.

8. Tighten all nuts evenly and to the specified torque. Run the engine and check for a tight fit.

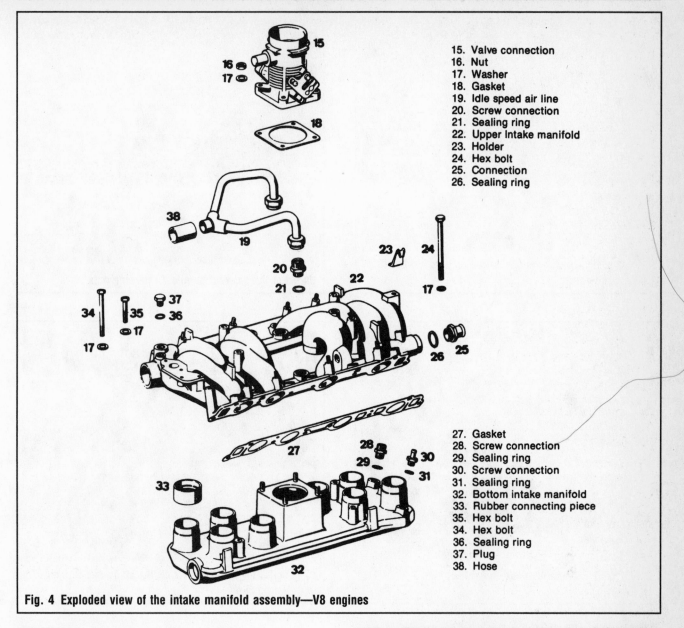

15.	Valve connection
16.	Nut
17.	Washer
18.	Gasket
19.	Idle speed air line
20.	Screw connection
21.	Sealing ring
22.	Upper Intake manifold
23.	Holder
24.	Hex bolt
25.	Connection
26.	Sealing ring

27.	Gasket
28.	Screw connection
29.	Sealing ring
30.	Screw connection
31.	Sealing ring
32.	Bottom intake manifold
33.	Rubber connecting piece
35.	Hex bolt
34.	Hex bolt
36.	Sealing ring
37.	Plug
38.	Hose

Fig. 4 Exploded view of the intake manifold assembly—V8 engines

Diesel Engine

1. Remove the air filter housing.
2. Disconnect the exhaust pipe from the manifolds.
3. Unfasten the oil dipstick tube bracket bolt and separate the tube from the exhaust manifold.
4. Remove the exhaust manifold retaining nuts.
5. Pull the manifold off the mounting studs and remove it from the engine.

To install:

6. Clean the old gasket material from both mounting surfaces.
7. Position a new gasket on the manifold and install the manifold on the mounting studs.
8. Use new retaining nuts and tighten them to the proper specification.
9. Connect the exhaust pipe to the manifold and tighten the fasteners.
10. Engage the oil dipstick bracket to the manifold and tighten the bolt.

To remove the exhaust manifold, unbolt the air cleaner housing . . .

. . . then disconnect the hoses and remove the housing from the engine

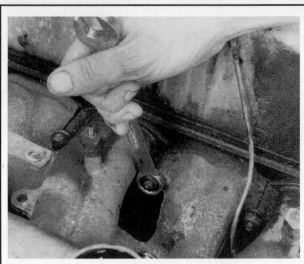

Unfasten the exhaust manifold retaining nuts . . .

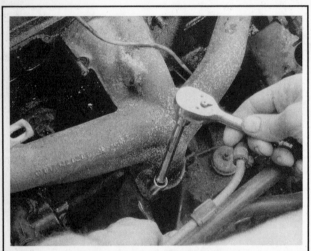

Remove the exhaust manifold-to-exhaust pipe retainers . . .

. . . then pull the manifold off the studs and remove it from the engine

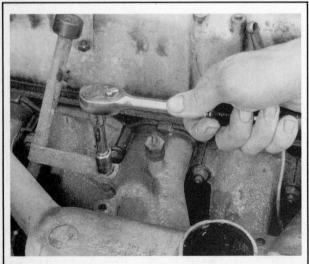

. . . then detach the oil dipstick tube from the manifold

11. Install the air filter housing and start the vehicle to check for proper operation.

Turbocharger

TURBO-DIESEL MODELS

♦ See Figure 5

➡There is no particular maintenance associated with the turbocharger. It should also be noted that a turbocharger cannot be installed on an engine that was not meant for one, without incurring serious engine damage.

The exhaust gas turbocharger is a Garret Model TA 0301. It uses the aerodynamic energy of the exhaust gases to drive a centrifugal compressor which in turn delivers high pressure air to the cylinders of the diesel engine. The turbine wheel and the compressor wheel are mounted on a common shaft. The turbocharger is

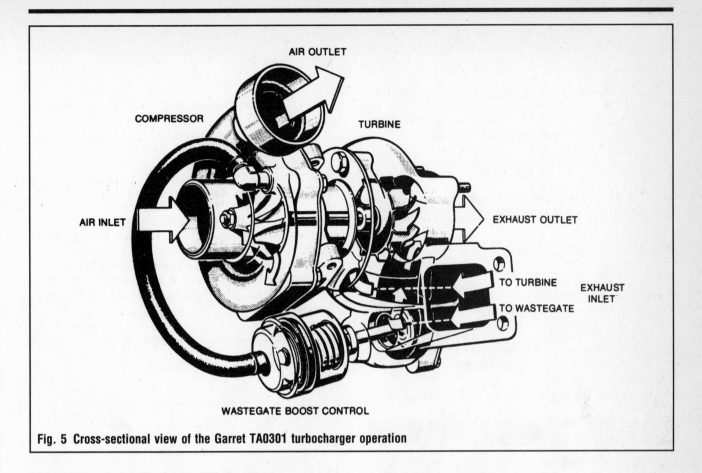

Fig. 5 Cross-sectional view of the Garret TA0301 turbocharger operation

mounted between the exhaust manifold and the exhaust pipe. For lubrication and cooling, the turbocharger is connected directly to the engine lubrication system.

A boost pressure control valve (wastegate valve) is attached to the turbine housing to insure that a certain boost pressure is not exceeded. Should the boost pressure control valve malfunction, an engine overload protection system will prevent a failure of the engine.

OPERATION

Turbocharger

The exhaust gases of the engine are routed via the exhaust manifold directly into the turbine housing and to the turbine wheel. The velocity of the exhaust gases causes the turbine wheel to turn. This turns the compressor wheel which is directly connected to the turbine wheel via the shaft. The turbocharger can obtain a maximum of approximately 100,000 rpm; the fresh air drawn in by the compressor wheel is compressed and delivered to the pistons of the engine.

At idle speed, the engine operates as a naturally aspirated engine. With increasing load and engine rpm, (increasing velocity of the exhaust gases), the turbine wheel accelerates and boost pressure is produced by the compressor wheel. The boost pressure is routed via the intake manifold to the individual cylinders.

The exhaust gases produced by the combustion are routed into the turbine housing and from there into the exhaust pipe.

Boost Pressure Control Valve

In order not to exceed the designed boost pressure, a boost pressure control valve is installed on the turbine housing. The boost pressure is picked up at the compressor housing and connected to the boost pressure control valve via a connecting hose. If the maximum permissible boost pressure is obtained, the boost pressure control valve starts to open the bypass canal for the exhaust gas around the turbine wheel. A part of the exhaust gas flows now directly into the exhaust pipe. This keeps the boost pressure constant and prevents it from increasing beyond its designed limits.

REMOVAL & INSTALLATION

1. Remove the air filter.
2. Disconnect the electrical cable from the temperature switch.
3. Loosen the lower hose clamp on the air duct that connects the air filter with the compressor housing.
4. Remove the vacuum line and crankcase breather pipe.
5. Remove the air filter and air intake duct.
6. Disconnect the oil line at the turbocharger.
7. Remove the air filter mounting bracket.
8. Disconnect the turbocharger at the exhaust flange.
9. Disconnect and remove the pipe bracket on the automatic transmission.
10. Push the exhaust pipe rearward.
11. Remove the mounting bracket at the intermediate flange.

12. Unbolt and remove the turbocharger.

13. Remove the intermediate flange and oil return line at the turbocharger.

To install:

14. Installation is the reverse of removal. Before installing the turbocharger, install the oil return line and intermediate flange. Install the flange gasket between the turbocharger and exhaust manifold with the reinforcing bead toward the exhaust manifold.

Use only heatproof nuts and bolts and fill a new turbocharger with ¼ pint of engine oil through the engine oil supply bore before operating.

Cylinder Head

REMOVAL & INSTALLATION

4 and 5-Cylinder Engines

♦ **See Figures 6 thru 14 (p. 24–26)**

In order to perform a valve job or to inspect cylinder bores for wear, the head must be removed. While this may seem fairly straightforward, some caution must be observed to ensure that valve timing is not disturbed.

1. Drain the radiator and remove all hoses and wires (tag all wires).

✳✳ CAUTION

When draining engine coolant, keep in mind that cats and dogs are attracted to ethylene glycol antifreeze and could drink any that is left in an uncovered container or in puddles on the ground. This will prove fatal in sufficient quantity. Always drain coolant into a sealable container. Coolant should be reused unless it is contaminated or is several years old.

2. Remove the camshaft cover and associated throttle linkage, then press out the spring clamp from the notch in the rocker arm (all except 190 series).

➡**The cylinder head cover on the 190E is removed with the spark plug cables and distributor cap still attached to it.**

3. Push the clamp outward over the ball cap of the rocker, then depress the valve with a large screwdriver and lift the rocker arm out of the ball pin head (all except 190 series).

4. Remove the rocker arm supports (all except 190 series) and the camshaft sprocket nut.

5. On all 5 cyl. engines and the 190E, the rockers and their supports must be removed together.

6. Using a suitable puller, remove the camshaft sprocket, after having first marked the chain, sprocket and cam for ease in assembly.

7. Remove the sprocket and chain and wire it out of the way.

✳✳ WARNING

Make sure the chain is securely wired so that it will not slide down into the engine.

8. Unbolt the manifolds and exhaust header pipe and push them out of the way.

9. Then loosen the cylinder head hold-down bolts in the reverse order of that shown in torque diagrams for each model. It is good practice to loosen each bolt a little at a time, working round the head, until all are free. This prevents unequal stresses in the metal.

10. Reach into the engine compartment and gradually work the head loose from each end by rocking it. Never, under any circumstances, use a screwdriver between the head and block to pry, as the head will be scarred badly and may be ruined.

11. Installation is the reverse of removal.

➡**All diesel engines manufactured after 2/79 utilize cylinder head "stretch" bolts. These bolts undergo a permanent stretch each time they are tightened. When a maximum length is reached, they must be scrapped and replaced with new bolts. When tightening the head bolts on these engines, be sure to follow the steps listed under "Torque Specifications" exactly. Under no circumstances may the older type cylinder head bolts be exchanged with the newer "stretch" bolts.**

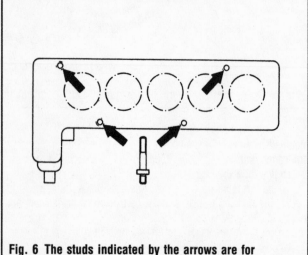

Fig. 6 The studs indicated by the arrows are for attaching the rocker cover on 5-cylinder engines

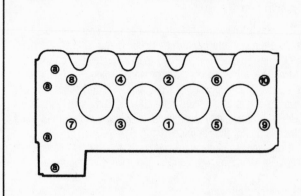

Fig. 7 Cylinder head bolt tightening sequence—190E models (bolts "a" are tightened to 25 Nm)

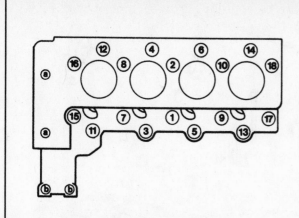

Fig. 8 Cylinder head bolt tightening sequence—190D models (bolts "a" and "b" are tightened to 25 Nm)

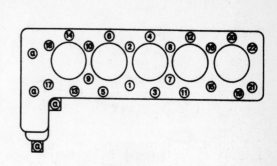

Fig. 11 Cylinder head bolt tightening sequence—5-cylinder engines (bolts marked "a" are tightened with a Hex bit)

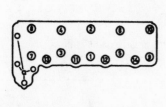

Fig. 9 Cylinder head bolt tightening sequence—4-cylinder gasoline engines (except 190E)

Model	Length when new (mm)	Maximum (mm)
190E	119	122
190D	80	83.6
	102	105.6
	115	118.6
240D, 300D, 300CD, 300SD, 300TD	104	105.5
	119	120.5
	144	145.5

Fig. 12 Cylinder head stretch bolt specifications

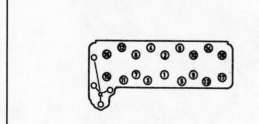

Fig. 10 Cylinder head bolt tightening sequence—4-cylinder diesel engines (except 190D)

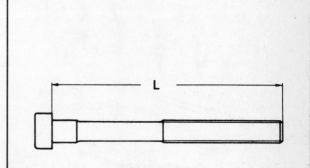

Fig. 12a The cylinder head bolt stretch is measured at dimension "L"

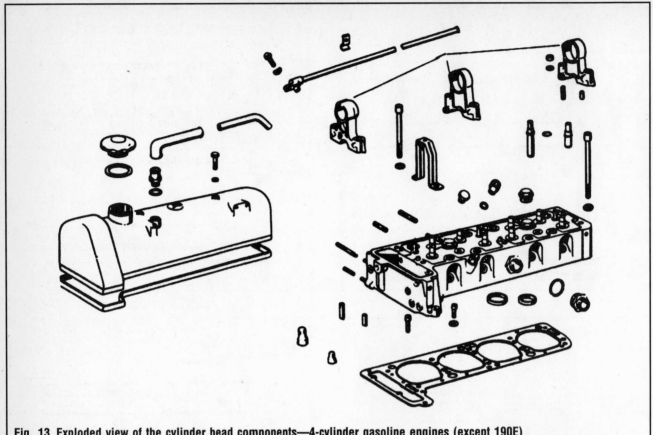

Fig. 13 Exploded view of the cylinder head components—4-cylinder gasoline engines (except 190E)

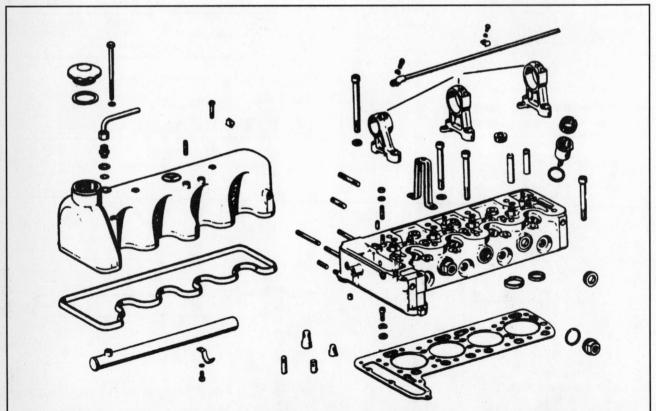

Fig. 14 Exploded view of the cylinder head components—4-cylinder diesel engines (except 190D); 5-cylinder engines are similar

Remove the cylinder head after unfastening the bolts in the proper sequence

Remove the old gasket from the engine block . . .

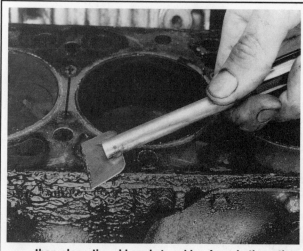

. . . then clean the old gasket residue from both mating surfaces

V8 Engines

◆ See Figures 15, 16, 17 and 18 (p. 27–29)

➡Before removing the cylinder head from a V8, be sure you have the 4 special tools necessary to torque the head bolts; without them it will be impossible. Do not confuse the left and right-hand head gaskets—the left side has 2 attaching holes in the timing chain cover, the right side has only 1 hole. Cylinder heads on the 3.8, 4.5 and 5.0 liter V8's are not interchangeable.

➡Cylinder heads can only be removed with the engine cold.

1. Drain the cooling system.

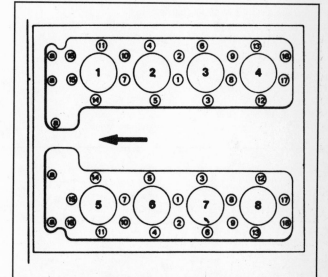

Fig. 15 Cylinder head bolt tightening sequence—V8 engines (except 6.9)

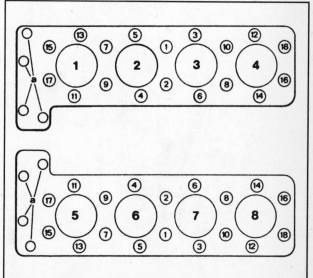

Fig. 16 Cylinder head bolt tightening sequence—model 6.9 V8 engines

❈❈ CAUTION

When draining engine coolant, keep in mind that cats and dogs are attracted to ethylene glycol antifreeze and could drink any that is left in an uncovered container or in puddles on the ground. This will prove fatal in sufficient quantity. Always drain coolant into a sealable container. Coolant should be reused unless it is contaminated or is several years old.

2. Remove the battery.

3. Remove the air cleaner. Remove the fan and fan shroud.

4. Pull the cable plug from the temperature sensor.

5. On the 6.9, to remove the right-hand head, remove the alternator (with bracket), windshield washer reservoir and bracket and automatic transmission dipstick tube.

6. Detach the vacuum hose from the venturi control unit.

7. Remove the following electrical connections:
   a. injection valves
   b. distributor
   c. venturi control unit
   d. temperature sensor and temperature switch
   e. starting valve
   f. temperature switch for the auxiliary fan.

8. Loosen the ring line on the fuel distributor.

9. Loosen the screws on the injection valves and pressure regulator or mixture regulator. Remove the ring line with the injection valves and pressure regulator.

10. Plug the holes for the injection valves in the cylinder head.

11. Remove the regulating shaft by disconnecting the pull rod and the thrust rod.

12. Remove the ignition cable plug.

13. Loosen the heating connection on the intake manifold.

14. Loosen the vacuum connection for the central lock at the transmission.

15. Remove the oil filler tube from the right-hand cylinder head and remove the temperature connector.

16. Remove the oil pressure gauge line from the left-hand cylinder head.

17. Loosen the coolant connection on the intake manifold.

18. Remove the intake manifold. This is not necessary on 3.8L and 5.0L V8's although the bolts must still be removed.

19. Loosen the alternator belt and remove the alternator and mounting bracket.

20. Remove the electrical connections from the distributor and electronic ignition switchgear.

21. Drain some fluid from the power steering reservoir and disconnect and plug the return hose and high pressure supply line.

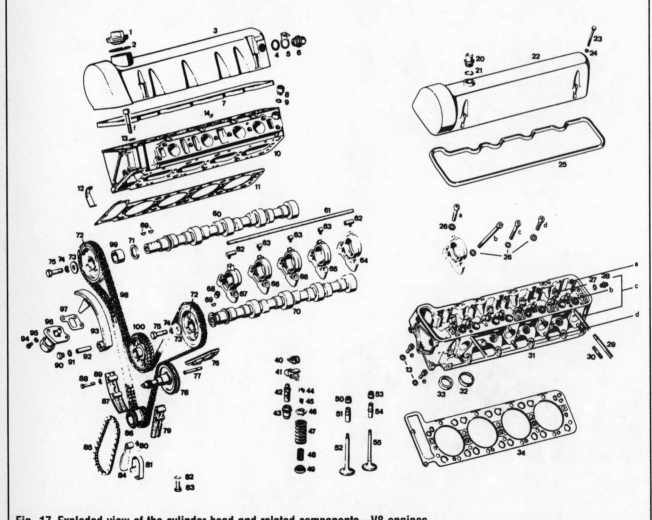

Fig. 17 Exploded view of the cylinder head and related components—V8 engines

Right cylinder head 1–14

1. Filler plug
2. Sealing ring
3. Cylinder head cover
4. Sealing ring
5. Holder for cable to injection valves
6. Connection
7. Valve cover gasket
8. Connection to temperature sensor
9. Sealing ring
10. Cylinder head
11. Cylinder head gasket
12. Cable holder
13. 5 Washers
14. 4 Hollow dowel pins

Left cylinder head 20–34

20. Connection
21. Sealing ring
22. Cylinder head cover
23. 8 Screws
24. 8 Sealing rings
25. Cylinder head cover gasket
26. 36 Washers
27. Sealing ring
28. Screw connection oil pressure gauge
29. 3 Studs
30. 13 Studs
31. Cylinder head
32. Valve seat ring—intake
33. Valve seat ring—exhaust
34. Cylinder head gasket

Cylinder head bolts (mm)

a. 10 M 10 × 50 (camshaft bearing fastening bolts)
b. 10 M 10 × 155
c. 18 M 10 × 80
d. 8 M 10 × 55
e. 4 M 8 × 30
f. 1 M 8 × 70

Valve arrangement 40–55

40. Tensioning spring
41. Rocker arm
42. Adjusting screw
43. Threaded bushing
44. Thrust piece
45. Valve cone piece
46. Valve spring retainer
47. Outer valve spring
48. Inner valve spring
49. Rotator
50. Intake valve seal
51. Exhaust valve guide
52. Intake valve
53. Exhaust valve seal
54. Exhaust valve guide
55. Exhaust valve

Engine timing 60–100

60. Right camshaft
61. Oil pipe (external lubrication) Oil pipe to camshaft bearing
62. Connecting piece
63. Connecting piece
64. Camshaft bearing-flywheel end
65. Camshaft bearing 4
66. Camshaft bearing 2 and 3
67. Camshaft bearing-cranking end
68. 5 hollow dowel pins
69. Spring washer
70. Left camshaft
71. Compensating washer
72. Camshaft gear
73. Camshaft gear washer
74. Spring washer
75. Bolt
76. 3 Slide rails
77. 6 Bearing bolts
78. Distributor drive gear
79. Guide rail
80. Lockwasher
81. Spring—chain tensioner, oil pump
82. Washer
83. Screw
84. Clamp
85. Single roller chain (oil pump drive)
86. Crankshaft gear
87. Slide rail
88. 4 screws
89. 4 spring washers
90. Plug
91. Sealing ring
92. Bearing bolt
93. Tensioning lever
94. 2 Bolts
95. 2 Spring washers
96. Chain tensioner
97. Gasket
98. Double roller chain
99. Spacer ring
100. Idler gear

Fig. 18 V8 engine cylinder head component keylist

22. Disconnect the exhaust system. On 3.8 and 5.0L V8's, you need only remove the manifolds.

23. Loosen the right-hand holder for the engine damper.

24. Remove the right-hand chain tensioner.

25. Matchmark the camshaft, camshaft sprocket, and chain. Remove the camshaft sprocket and chain after removing the cylinder head cover. Be sure to hang the chain and sprocket to prevent it from falling into the timing chain case.

26. Remove the upper slide rail. On 3.8 and 5.0L V8's, remove the distributor and remove the inner slide rail on the left cylinder head. Remove the rail after the camshaft sprocket.

27. Unscrew the cylinder head bolts. This should be done with a cold engine. Unscrew the bolts in the reverse order of the illustrated torque sequences. Unscrew all the bolts a little at a time

and proceed in this manner until all the bolts have been removed. On the 6.9, you'll need to raise the engine to remove No. 12 and 18 bolts on the left-side head. To do this, place the level adjusting switch at "S" (first notch).

➡**Cylinder head bolts on 3.8 and 5.0L V8's are nickel plated and 10 mm longer than those for previous engines.**

28. Remove the cylinder head. Do not pry on the cylinder head.

29. Remove the cylinder head gasket.

30. Clean the cylinder head and cylinder block joint faces.

To install:

31. Position the cylinder head gasket.

32. Do not confuse the cylinder head gaskets. The left-hand

head has two attaching holes in the timing chain cover while the right-hand head has three.

33. Install the cylinder head and torque the bolts according to the illustrated torque sequence.

34. Further installation is the reverse of removal. On 3.8 and 5.0L V8's, insert the rear cam bearing cylinder head bolt before positioning the cylinder head. Also, install the exhaust manifolds only after the cylinder head bolts have been tightened. The camshaft sprocket should be installed so that the flange faces the camshaft. Check the valve clearance and fill the engine with oil. Top up the power steering tank and bleed the power steering system.

35. Run the engine and check for leaks.

6-Cylinder Engines

▶ See Figures 19, 20, 21 and 22

➡Two people are best for this job. The head must be removed STRAIGHT up. The 2 bolts in the chain case are removed with a magnet.

To install, use 2 pieces of wood ½ inch × 1½ inch × 9 inch to lay the head on while aligning the bolt holes. The exhaust camshaft gear bolt is 0.2 inch shorter.

1. Completely drain the cooling system.

✳✳ CAUTION

When draining engine coolant, keep in mind that cats and dogs are attracted to ethylene glycol antifreeze and could drink any that is left in an uncovered container or in puddles on the ground. This will prove fatal in sufficient quantity. Always drain coolant into a sealable container. Coolant should be reused unless it is contaminated or is several years old.

2. Remove the air filter.
3. Remove the radiator.
4. Remove the rocker arm cover.
5. Remove the battery. Remove the idler pulley and the holding bracket for the compresser.
6. Remove the compressor and bracket and lay it aside without disconnecting any of the lines.

✳✳ CAUTION

Disconnecting any of the refrigerant lines could result in physical harm.

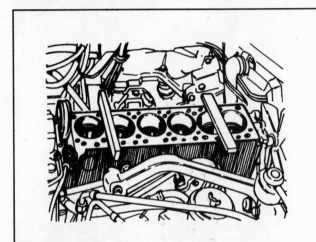

Fig. 20 Fabricated tools for installing the cylinder head—6-cylinder engines

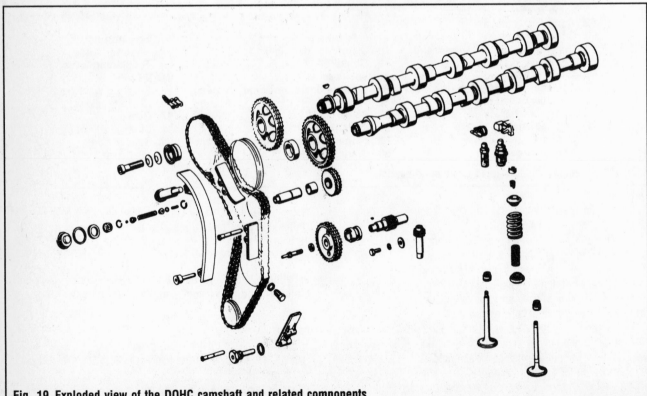

Fig. 19 Exploded view of the DOHC camshaft and related components

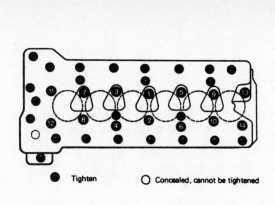

Fig. 21 Cylinder head and camshaft housing tightening sequence—6-cylinder engines

Fig. 22 Make sure the marks on the camshaft and bearing housing are aligned when the engine is at TDC—6-cylinder engines

7. Unbolt the cover from the camshaft housing.

8. Disconnect the heated water line from the carburetor, the vacuum line on the starter housing, and the distributor vacuum line.

9. Disconnect all electrical connections, water lines, fuel lines, and vacuum lines which are connected to the cylinder head. Tag these for reassembly.

10. Remove the regulating linkage shaft.

11. Remove the EGR line between the exhaust return valve and the exhaust pipe.

12. Disconnect and plug the oil return line at the cylinder head.

13. At the thermostat housing, loosen the hose which passes between the thermostat housing and the water pump. Unscrew the bypass line on the water pump.

14. Loosen the oil dipstick tube from the clamp and bend it slightly sidewards.

15. Unbolt the exhaust pipes from the exhaust manifolds and bracket on the transmission.

16. Force the tension springs out of the rocker arm with a small prybar.

17. Remove all of the rocker arms.

18. Crank the engine to TDC. This can be done with a socket wrench on the crankshaft pulley bolt. The marks on the camshaft sprockets and bearing housings must be aligned.

19. Hold the camshafts and remove the bolt which holds each camshaft gear to the camshaft.

20. Remove the upper slide rail. Knock out the bearing bolts with a puller.

21. Remove the chain tensioner.

22. Push both camshafts toward the rear and remove the camshafts' sprockets.

23. Remove the spacer sleeves on both camshafts. The sleeves are located in front of the camshaft bearings.

24. Remove the guide wheel by unscrewing the plug and removing the bearing bolt.

25. Lift off the timing chain and suspend the chain from the hood with a piece of wire. Pull out the guide gear.

26. Remove the slide rail in the cylinder head by removing the bearing pin with a puller.

27. Loosen the cylinder head bolts in small increments, using the reverse order of the tightening sequence. This should be done on a cold engine to prevent the possibility of head warpage.

28. Pull out the two bolts in the chain case with a magnet. Be careful not to drop the washers.

29. Pull up on the timing chain and force the tensioning rail toward the center of the engine.

30. Lift the cylinder head up in a vertical direction.

➡**Mercedes-Benz recommends two people for this job.**

31. Remove the cylinder head gasket and clean the joint faces of the block and head.

To install:

32. Cut two pieces of wood ½ inch × 1-½ inch × 9-½ inch Lay one piece upright between cylinders 1 and 2; lay the other flat between cylinders 5 and 6.

33. Install the cylinder head in an inclined position so that the timing chain and tensioning rail can be inserted.

34. Lift the cylinder head at the front and remove the front piece of wood toward the exhaust side. Carefully lower the cylinder head until the bolt holes align.

35. Lift the head at the rear so that the board can be moved toward the exhaust side. Carefully lower the cylinder head until all the bolt holes align.

36. Tighten the cylinder head bolts in gradual steps until they are fully tightened. Follow the torque sequence illustrated.

37. Check to be sure that both camshafts rotate freely after the bolts are tight.

38. The remainder of installation is the reverse of removal. Be sure that the spacer for the camshaft gear with the engaging lugs for the vacuum pump drive gear is installed on the exhaust side. Also, the washers for the bolts attaching the camshaft gears to the camshafts must be installed with the domed side against the head of the bolt.

39. Note that the attaching bolt for the exhaust camshaft gear is 0.2 in. shorter.

40. Be sure to adjust the valve clearance and fill the cooling system. Run the engine and check for leaks.

CHECKING ENGINE COMPRESSION

Gasoline Engines Only

A noticeable lack of engine power, excessive oil consumption and/or poor fuel mileage measured over an extended period are all indicators of internal engine wear. Worn piston rings, scored and worn cylinder bores, blown head gaskets, sticking or burnt valves and worn valve seats are all possible culprits here. A check of each cylinder's compression will help you locate the problems.

As mentioned in the "Tools and Equipment" portion of Section 1, a screw-in compression gauge is more accurate than the type you simply hold against the spark plug hole, although it takes slightly longer to use (it's worth it). To check compression:

1. Warm the engine up to operating temperature.
2. Remove spark plugs.

A screw-in type compression gauge is more accurate and easier to use without an assistant

3. Disconnect the high tension wire from the ignition coil.
4. Screw the compression gauge into the No. 1 spark plug hole until the fitting is snug. Be very careful not to crossthread the hole, as most heads are aluminum.
5. Fully open the throttle either by operating the carburetor throttle linkage by hand, or on fuel injected cars having an assistant "floor" the accelerator pedal.
6. Ask your assistant to crank the engine a few times using the ignition switch.
7. Record the highest reading on the gauge, and compare it to the compression specifications. The specs listed are maximum, and a cylinder is usually acceptable if its compression is within about 20 pounds of maximum.
8. Repeat the procedure for the remaining cylinders, recording each cylinder's compression. The difference between each cylinder should be no more than 14 pounds. If a cylinder is unusually low, pour a tablespoon of clean engine oil into the cylinder through the spark plug hole and repeat the compression test. If the compression comes up after adding the oil, it appears that that cylinder's piston rings or bore are damaged or worn. If the pressure remains low, the valves may not be seating properly (a valve job is needed) or the head gasket may be blown near that cylinder.

CLEANING & INSPECTION

◆ See Figures 23 and 24

Carefully chip carbon away from the valve heads, combustion chambers and ports by using a chisel made of hardwood. Remove the remaining deposits with a stiff wire brush or a wire brush attachment for a hand drill.

➡**Always make sure that the deposits are actually removed, rather than just burnished.**

Clean the remaining cylinder head components in an engine cleaning solvent. Do not remove the protective coating from the valve springs.

❊❊ WARNING

As most Mercedes-Benz cylinder heads are made out of aluminum, NEVER "hot tank" the cylinder head as is a common process with cast iron heads.

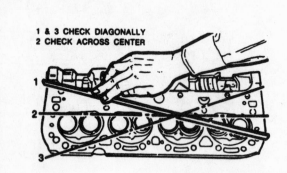

Fig. 23 Use a straightedge to check the cylinder head for warpage

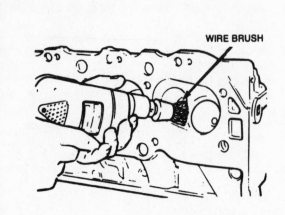

Fig. 24 A wire brush mounted in a drill can be used to remove carbon from the cylinder head

A wire wheel may be used to clean the combustion chambers of carbon deposits

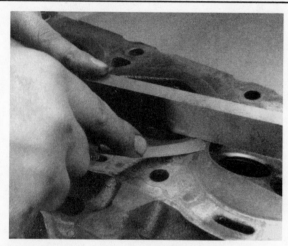

Check the cylinder head for flatness across the head surface

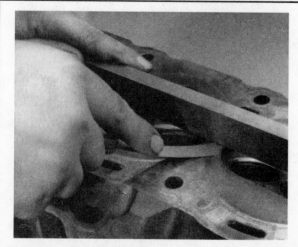

Checks should be made both straight across the cylinder head and at both diagonals

Place a straight-edge across the gasket surface of the cylinder head. Using feeler gauges, determine the clearance at the center of the straight-edge. If warpage exceeds .003 inch in a 6 inch span, or .006 inch over the total length the cylinder head will require resurfacing.

➡**If warpage exceeds the manufacturer's tolerance for material removal, the cylinder head must be replaced.**

Cylinder head resurfacing should be performed by a reputable machine shop in your area.

Valves and Springs

REMOVAL & INSTALLATION

1. Remove the cylinder head. Remove the rocker arms and shafts (all except 190D). Remove the camshaft (190D only).

On gasoline engines only:
2. Using a valve spring compressor, compress the spring and remove the valve cone halves (be careful not to lose the two valve cone halves).
3. Remove the spring retainer and then lift out the spring.
4. Pry off the valve stem oil seal and lift out the lower spring seat (thrust ring). Remove the valve through the bottom of the cylinder head.

➡**Then removing the valve stem seal and the thrust ring, a small screwdriver and a magnet may come in handy.**

On the 190D:
5. Remove the hydraulic valve tappet with Special Tool #601 589 05 33 00. After the tappet has been removed, follow the procedures detailed for gasoline engines.

On all other diesel engines:
6. Position an open-end wrench on the valve spring retainer; while holding the retainer, unscrew the capnut with a valve adjusting wrench.

➡**A second valve adjusting wrench will be required to hold the counternut while loosening the capnut.**

7. Loosen and remove the counternut.
8. Lift out the valve spring and lower spring seat. Remove the valve through the bottom of the cylinder head.

On all engines:
9. Inspect the valve and spring. Clean the valve guide with a cotton swab and solvent. Inspect the valve guide and seat and check the valve guide-to-stem clearance.
10. Lubricate the valve stem and guide with engine oil. Install the valve into the cylinder head through the bottom and position the lower spring seat (thrust ring).
11. Lubricate the valve stem oil seal with engine oil, slide it down over the stem and then install it into position over the spring seat.

➡**When installing seals, always ensure that a small amount of oil is able to pass the seal so as to lubricate the valve guides; otherwise, excessive wear may result.**

➡**Intake and exhaust valve stem seals on the 190 series engines are not interchangeable.**

12. Position the valve spring onto the spring seat with the tight coils facing the cylinder head.

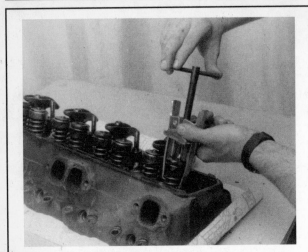

Use a valve spring compressor tool to relieve spring tension from the valve caps

Once the spring has been removed, the O-ring may be removed from the valve stem

A small magnet will help in removal of the valve keepers

A magnet may be helpful in removing the valve keepers

Be careful not to lose the valve keepers

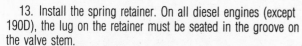
Remove the spring from the valve stem in order to access the seal

Remove the valve stem seal from the cylinder head

13. Install the spring retainer. On all diesel engines (except 190D), the lug on the retainer must be seated in the groove on the valve stem.

14. Further installation is the reverse of the removal procedures detailed previously for the individual engine groups.

➡️**Tap the installed valve stem lightly with a rubber mallet to ensure a proper fit.**

INSPECTION

◆ **See Figures 25 thru 30 (p. 36–37)**

Inspect the valve faces and seats (in the cylinder head) for pits, burned spots and other evidence of poor seating. If the valve face is in such bad shape that the head of the valve must be ground in order to true up the face, discard the valve because the sharp edge will run too hot. The correct angle for valve faces is given in the specification section at the front of this chapter. It is recommended that any reaming or resurfacing (grinding) be performed by a reputable machine shop.

Check the valve stem for scoring and/or burned spots. If not noticeably scored or damaged, clean the valve stem with a suitable solvent to remove all gum and varnish. Clean the valve guides using a suitable solvent and an expanding wire-type valve guide cleaner (generally available at a local automotive supply store). If you have access to a dial indicator for measuring valve stem-to-guide clearance, mount it so that the stem of the indicator is at a 90° angle to the valve stem and as close to the valve guide as possible. Move the valve off its seat slightly and measure the valve guide-to-stem clearance by rocking the valve back and forth so that the stem actuates the dial indicator. Measure the valve stem using a micrometer, and compare to specifications in order to determine whether the stem or the guide is responsible for the excess clearance. If a dial indicator and a micrometer are not available, take the cylinder head and valves to a reputable machine shop.

Using a steel square, check the squareness of the valve spring. If the spring is out of square more than the maximum allowable, it will require replacement. Check that the spring free height is up to specifications. Measure the distance between the thrust ring and the lower edge of the spring retainer, and compare to specifications.

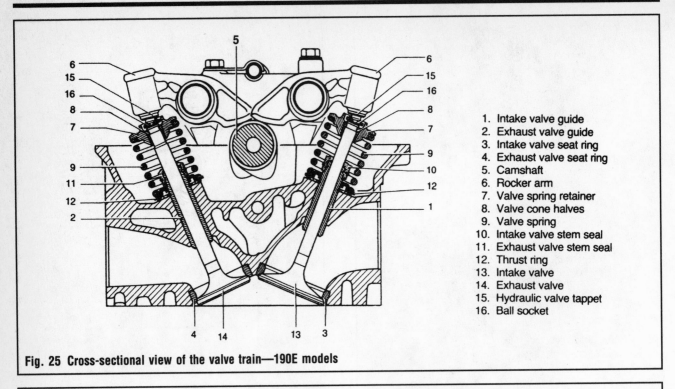

1. Intake valve guide
2. Exhaust valve guide
3. Intake valve seat ring
4. Exhaust valve seat ring
5. Camshaft
6. Rocker arm
7. Valve spring retainer
8. Valve cone halves
9. Valve spring
10. Intake valve stem seal
11. Exhaust valve stem seal
12. Thrust ring
13. Intake valve
14. Exhaust valve
15. Hydraulic valve tappet
16. Ball socket

Fig. 25 Cross-sectional view of the valve train—190E models

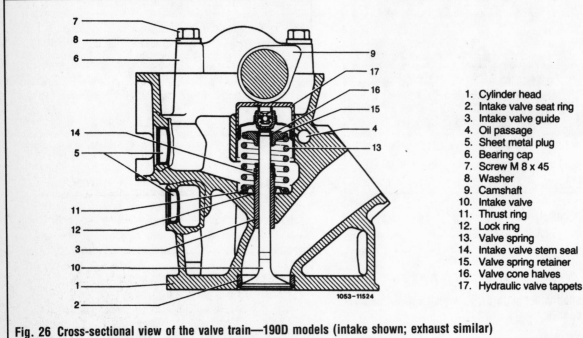

1. Cylinder head
2. Intake valve seat ring
3. Intake valve guide
4. Oil passage
5. Sheet metal plug
6. Bearing cap
7. Screw M 8 x 45
8. Washer
9. Camshaft
10. Intake valve
11. Thrust ring
12. Lock ring
13. Valve spring
14. Intake valve stem seal
15. Valve spring retainer
16. Valve cone halves
17. Hydraulic valve tappets

1053-11524

Fig. 26 Cross-sectional view of the valve train—190D models (intake shown; exhaust similar)

Valve Guides

REMOVAL & INSTALLATION

All Models

1. Remove the cylinder head.
2. Clean the valve guide with a brush, knocking away all loose carbon and oil deposits.
3. Knock out the old valve guide with a drift.

To install:

4. Check the bore in the cylinder head and clean up any rough spots. Use a reamer for this purpose. If necessary, the valve guide bore can be reamed for oversize valve guides.
5. Clean the basic bores for the valve guides.
6. Heat the cylinder head in water to approximately 176–194°F.
7. If possible, cool the valve guides slightly.
8. Drive the valve guides into the bores with a drift. Coat the bores in the cylinder head with wax prior to installation and be sure that the circlip rests against the cylinder head.

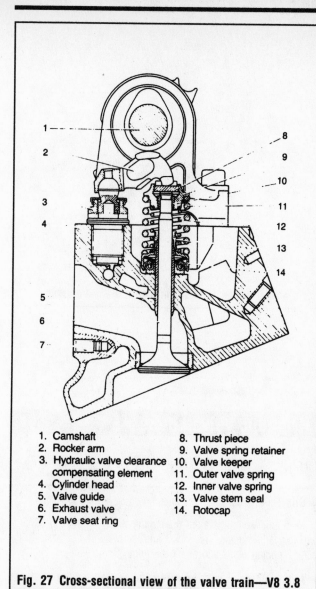

1. Camshaft
2. Rocker arm
3. Hydraulic valve clearance compensating element
4. Cylinder head
5. Valve guide
6. Exhaust valve
7. Valve seat ring
8. Thrust piece
9. Valve spring retainer
10. Valve keeper
11. Outer valve spring
12. Inner valve spring
13. Valve stem seal
14. Rotocap

Fig. 27 Cross-sectional view of the valve train—V8 3.8 engine (all V8 engines are similar)

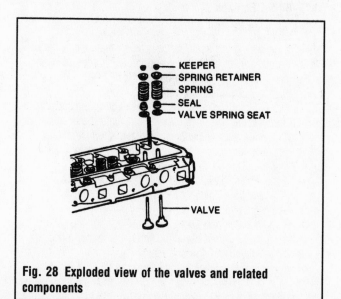

Fig. 28 Exploded view of the valves and related components

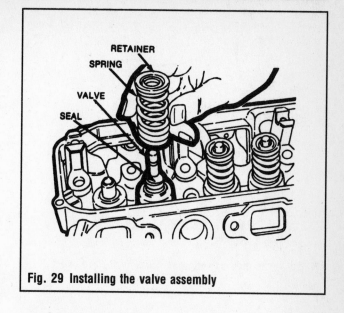

Fig. 29 Installing the valve assembly

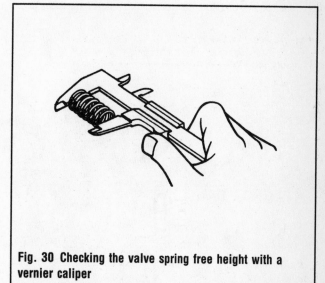

Fig. 30 Checking the valve spring free height with a vernier caliper

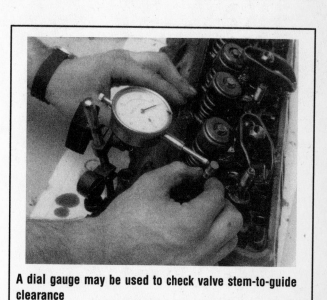

A dial gauge may be used to check valve stem-to-guide clearance

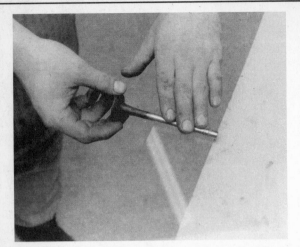

Valve stems may be rolled on a flat surface to check for bends

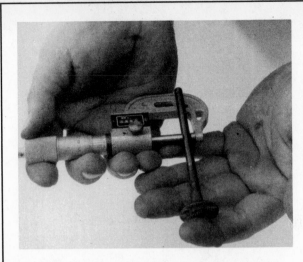

Use a micrometer to check the valve stem diameter

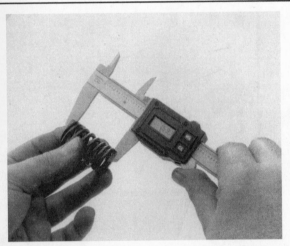

Use a caliper gauge to check the valve spring free-length

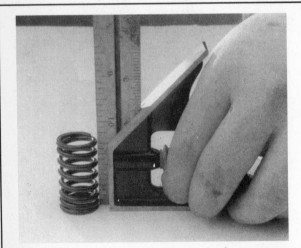

Check the valve spring for squareness on a flat surface; a carpenter's square can be used

9. Let the head cool and try to knock the valve guide out with light hammer blows and a plastic drift. If the guide can be knocked out, try another guide with a tighter fit.

10. Install the cylinder head.

Hydraulic Valve Lifters

CHECKING BASE SETTING

▶ **See Figure 31**

Hydraulic valve lifters are used with overhead cams on 1976 and later V8 engines. The rocker arm is always in contact with the cam, reducing noise and eliminating operating clearance.

➡**A dial indicator with an extension and a measuring thrust piece (MBNA #100 589 16 63 00, 0.187 in. thick are necessary to perform this adjustment.**

1976–84 V8 Engines
▶ **See Figures 32 and 33**

The base setting is the clearance between the upper edge of the cylindrical part of the plunger and the lower edge of the retaining cap (dimension A) when the cam lobe is vertical.

1. Turn the cam lobe to a vertical position.

2. Attach a dial indicator and tip extension and insert the extension through the bore in the rocker arm onto the head plunger. Preload the dial indicator by 2 mm and zero the instrument.

3. Depress the valve with a valve spring compressor. The lift on the dial indicator should be 0.028–0.075 inch.

4. If the lift is excessive, the base setting can be changed by installing a new thrust piece.

5. Remove the dial indicator.

6. Remove the rocker arm.

7. Remove the thrust piece and insert the measuring disc.

8. Install the rocker arm and repeat Steps 1–3.

9. Select a thrust piece according to the table. If the measured value is 0–0.002 inch and the 0.2146 inch thrust piece will not give the proper base setting, use the 0.2883 inch thrust piece.

10. Remove the dial indicator and the rocker arm. Install the selected thrust piece.

11. Reinstall the rocker arm and dial indicator and repeat Steps 1–3.

REMOVAL & INSTALLATION

Temporarily removed valve lifters must be reinstalled in their original locations. When replacing worn rocker arms, the camshaft must also be replaced. If the rocker arm, or hydraulic lifter is replaced, check the base setting.

Remove the rocker arm and unscrew the valve lifter with a 24 mm socket.

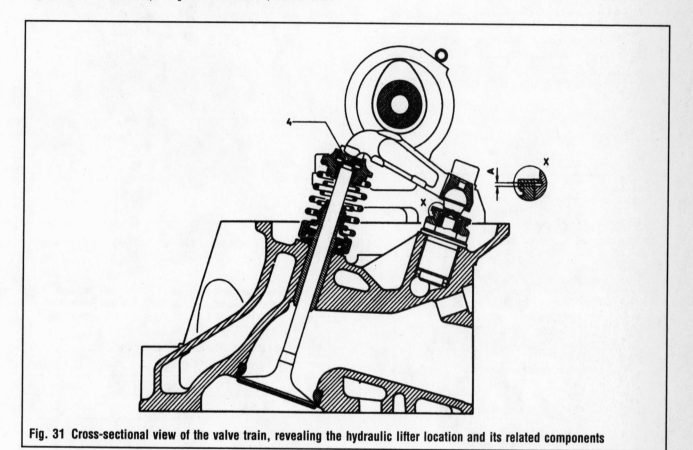

Fig. 31 Cross-sectional view of the valve train, revealing the hydraulic lifter location and its related components

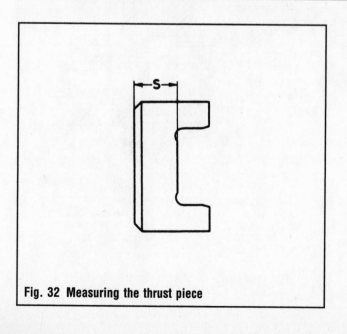

Fig. 32 Measuring the thrust piece

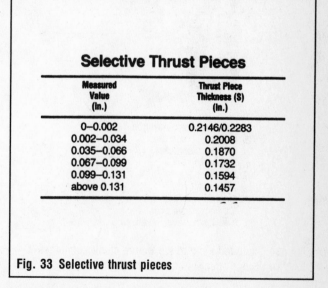

Selective Thrust Pieces

Measured Value (In.)	Thrust Piece Thickness (S) (in.)
0–0.002	0.2146/0.2283
0.002–0.034	0.2008
0.035–0.066	0.1870
0.067–0.099	0.1732
0.099–0.131	0.1594
above 0.131	0.1457

Fig. 33 Selective thrust pieces

Timing Chain Tensioner

REMOVAL & INSTALLATION

4 and 5-Cylinder Engines

▶ **See Figures 34, 35 and 36**

There are 2 kinds of timing chain tensioners. One uses an O-ring seal and the other a flat gasket. Do not install a flat gasket on a tensioner meant to be used with an O-ring.

Chain tensioners should be replaced as a unit if defective.

1. Drain the coolant. If the car has air conditioning, disconnect the compressor and mounting bracket and lay it aside. Do not disconnect the refrigerant lines. On diesel engines, drain the coolant from the block.

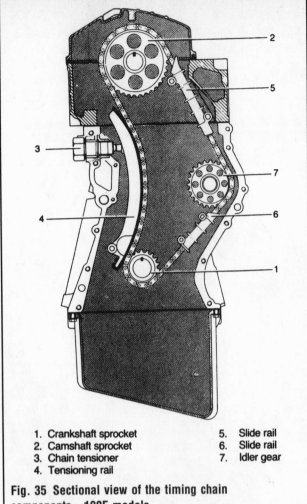

1. Crankshaft sprocket
2. Camshaft sprocket
3. Chain tensioner
4. Tensioning rail
5. Slide rail
6. Slide rail
7. Idler gear

Fig. 35 Sectional view of the timing chain components—190E models

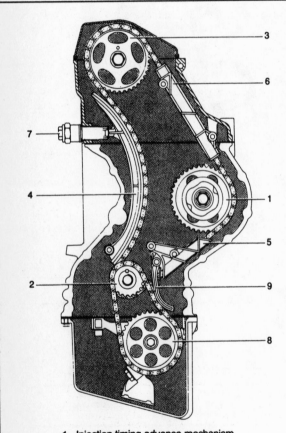

1. Injection timing advance mechanism
2. Crankshaft sprocket
3. Camshaft sprocket
4. Tensioning rail
5. Slide rail
6. Slide rail
7. Chain tensioner
8. Oil pump drive gear
9. Tensioning lever, chain, oil pump drive

Fig. 34 Exploded view of the timing chain components—190D models

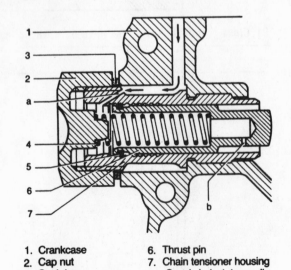

1. Crankcase
2. Cap nut
3. Seal ring
4. Compression spring
5. Detent spring
6. Thrust pin
7. Chain tensioner housing
a. Supply hole 1.1 mm dia.
b. Orifice 1.2 mm dia.

Fig. 36 Cross-sectional view of the timing chain tensioner—190E models (190D similar)

When draining engine coolant, keep in mind that cats and dogs are attracted to ethylene glycol antifreeze and could drink any that is left in an uncovered container or in puddles on the ground. This will prove fatal in sufficient quantity. Always drain coolant into a sealable container. Coolant should be reused unless it is contaminated or is several years old.

2. Remove the thermostat housing.

3. Loosen and remove the chain tensioner. Be careful of loose O-rings. On the 190 series you must first remove the tensioner capnut and then the tension spring. The tensioner body can now be unscrewed with an Allen wrench.

4. Check the O-rings or gasket and replace if necessary.

5. To fill the chain tensioner, place the tensioner (pressure bolt down) in a container of SAE 10 engine oil, at least up to the flat flange. Using a drill press, depress the pressure bolt slowly, about 7–10 times. Be sure this is done slowly and uniformly.

When removing the timing belt tensioner, unbolt the air conditioning mounting bracket . . .

. . . then move the air conditioning unit to one side without disconnecting any lines

6. Install the chain tensioner. Tighten the bolts evenly. Tighten the capnut on the 190 to 51 ft. lbs. (70 Nm).

V8 Engines

The chain tensioner is connected to the engine oil circuit. Bleeding occurs once oil pressure has been established and the tensioner is filling with oil.

Since December of 1974, a venting hole has been installed in the tensioner to prevent oil foaming. If you have a lot of timing chain noise, use this type of tensioner, which is identified by a white paint dot on the cap.

Service procedures for tensioners and rails on the different V8's are all similar. Arrangement and shape and size of parts however, is slightly different.

1. On California models, disconnect the line from the tensioner.

2. Remove the attaching bolts and remove the tensioner. The inside bolts will probably require a long, straight 6 mm allen key to bypass the exhaust manifold. It is a tight fit.

3. Place the tensioner vertically in a container of engine oil. Operate the pressure bolt to fill the tensioner. After filling, it should permit compression very slowly under considerable force. If not, replace the tensioner with a new unit.

4. Install the tensioner and tighten the bolts evenly.

6-Cylinder Engines
▶ See Figure 37

1. On A/C vehicles, remove the battery. Unbolt the refrigerant compressor and lay it aside. Do not disconnect the refrigerant lines.

2. Remove the plug with a 17 mm allen key.

3. Tighten the threaded ring and loosen the ball seat ring.

4. Remove the threaded ring.

5. Remove the chain tensioner with a 10 mm allen key.

6. Be sure the tight side of the chain is tight.

7. Compress the tensioner and install the chain tensioner with a 10 mm allen key. Do not bump the allen key or the tensioner will release.

8. Screw in the threaded ring and tighten it to 44 ft. lbs.

9. Tighten the ball seat ring to 18 ft. lbs. The pressure bolt

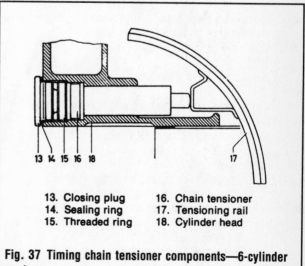

13. Closing plug
14. Sealing ring
15. Threaded ring
16. Chain tensioner
17. Tensioning rail
18. Cylinder head

Fig. 37 Timing chain tensioner components—6-cylinder engines

should jump forward with an audible clock. If it does not, the assembly must be removed and the installation repeated until it does click.

10. Install the plug.
11. Reinstall the A/C compressor, battery and air cleaner.

Timing Chain

REMOVAL & INSTALLATION

All Models
♦ See Figure 38

An endless timing chain is used on production engines, but a split chain with a connecting link is used for service. The endless chain can be separated with a "chain-breaker". Only one mast link (connecting link) should be used on a chain.

1. Remove the spark plugs.
2. Remove the valve cover(s).

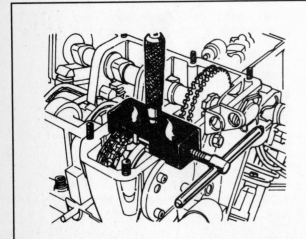

Fig. 38 Use a chain breaker to disengage a link and remove the timing chain

3. Clamp the chain to the cam gear and cover the opening of the timing chain case with rags. On 6-cylinder and V8 engines, remove the rocker arms from the right-hand camshaft.
4. Separate the chain with a chain breaker.
To install:
5. Attach a new timing chain to the old chain with a master link.
6. Using a socket wrench on the crankshaft, slowly rotate the engine in the direction of normal rotation. Simultaneously, pull the old chain through until the master link is uppermost on the camshaft sprocket. Be sure to keep tension on the chain throughout this procedure.
7. Disconnect the old timing chain and connect the ends of the new chain with the master link. Insert the new connecting link from the rear, so that the lockwashers can be seen from the front.
8. Rotate the engine until the timing marks align. Check the valve timing. Once the new chain is assembled, rotate the engine (by hand) through at least one complete revolution to be sure everything is OK. Refer to the valve timing procedure for illustrations.

Camshaft

REMOVAL & INSTALLATION

4 and 5-Cylinder Engines

EXCEPT 190D AND 190E MODELS

When the camshaft is replaced, be sure the rocker arms are also replaced.

1. Remove the valve cover.
2. Remove the chain tensioner.
3. Remove the rocker arms.
4. Set the crankshaft at TDC for No. 1 cylinder and be sure that the camshaft timing marks are aligned.
5. Hold the camshaft and loosen the cam gear bolt. Remove the cam gear and wire it securely so that the chain does not loose tension nor slip down into the chain case.
6. Remove the camshaft.
7. Installation is the reverse of removal. Be sure to check that

When removing the camshaft, first drain the coolant

Loosen the thermostat housing hose clamp . . .

1. Timing chain guide

Remove the timing chain guide retaining bolt . . .

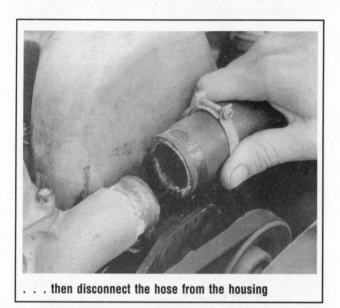

. . . then disconnect the hose from the housing

. . . then remove the timing chain guide

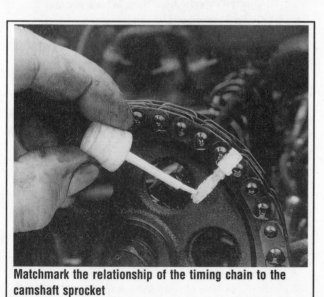

Matchmark the relationship of the timing chain to the camshaft sprocket

Remove the camshaft gear retaining bolt . . .

. . . then remove the gear from the camshaft while still keeping tension on the timing chain

Keep tension on the timing chain and secure it with a wire, so it does not slip down into the chain case

the valve timing marks align when No. 1 cylinder is at TDC. Check the valve clearance.

190D AND 190E MODELS

➡On the 190E it is always a good idea to replace the rocker arms and shafts whenever the camshaft is replaced.

1. Remove the valve cover.
2. Remove the chain tensioner.
3. On the 190E, remove the rocker arms and shafts.
4. Set the crankshaft at TDC for the No. 1 piston and make sure that the timing marks on the camshaft are in alignment.
5. Using a 24mm open-end wrench, hold the rear of the camshaft (flats are provided) and then loosen and remove the camshaft retaining bolt. Carefully slide the gear and chain off the shaft and wire them securely so they won't slip down into the case.

➡Be careful not to lose the Woodruff key while removing the gear on the 190E.

6. The camshaft is secured on the cylinder head by means of the bearing caps. Remove them and keep them in their proper or-

der. Each cap is marked by a number punched into its side; this number must match the number cast into the cylinder head.

➡When removing the bearing caps on the 190D, always loosen the center two first and then move on to the outer ones.

7. Remove the camshaft.
8. Installation is in the reverse order of removal. Always make sure that the No. 1 cylinder is at TDC and all timing marks are aligned. Tighten the bearing caps to 15 ft. lbs. (21 Nm) on the 190E and 18 ft. lbs. (25 Nm) on the 190D. The camshaft gear retaining bolt should be tightened to 58 ft. lbs. (80 Nm) on the 190E and 33 ft. lbs. (45 Nm) on the 190D.

➡Be certain not to forget the Woodruff key on the 190E.

6-Cylinder Engines
◆ See Figure 39

With the engine installed in the car, the camshafts can only be removed together with the camshaft housing. If a new camshaft is installed, be sure to use new rocker arms.

1. Remove the refrigerant compressor but do not disconnect the refrigerant lines.
2. Remove the battery.
3. Remove the vacuum pump from the right-hand cylinder head.
4. Drain the coolant and remove the water hoses.

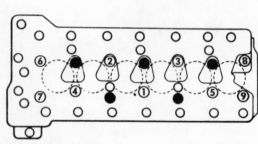

○ Unscrew M 8 bolts
① Unscrew cylinder head bolts in reverse order
● Do not loosen bolts

Fig. 39 When removing the camshaft, unfasten the bolts in the sequence illustrated—6-cylinder engines

✳✳ CAUTION

When draining engine coolant, keep in mind that cats and dogs are attracted to ethylene glycol antifreeze and could drink any that is left in an uncovered container or in puddles on the ground. This will prove fatal in sufficient quantity. Always drain coolant into a sealable container. Coolant should be reused unless it is contaminated or is several years old.

5. Remove the rocker arm cover.
6. Remove the cover from the front of the camshaft housing.
7. Remove the rocker arm springs.

8. Remove the rocker arms.

9. Crank the engine around in the normal direction of rotation (using the crankshaft bolt) until No. 1 piston is at TDC, the pointer aligns with the TDC mark on the crankshaft pulley and the camshaft timing marks are aligned.

10. Hold the camshaft(s) and loosen the camshaft bolts.

➡**Wire the camshaft gears up so that tension applied to the chain. The chain must not be allowed to slip off the camshaft or crankshaft gears.**

11. Remove the chain tensioner.

12. Remove the slide rail from the camshaft housing. You'll need a small puller for this.

13. Loosen the cover at the right-hand rear side of the camshaft housing and push the right-hand camshaft toward the rear. Remove the camshaft gear.

14. Loosen the camshaft housing retaining bolts. Do not loosen the 5 lower cylinder head bolts or the 2 M8 bolts.

15. Remove the camshaft housing with the camshafts.

16. Remove the rear covers from the camshaft housing.

17. Hold the left-hand camshaft and loosen the attaching bolt.

18. Push the camshaft rearward and remove the camshaft gear. Remove the spacer from the intake camshaft.

19. Remove both camshafts from the housing.

To install:

20. Oil the bearings and install the intake camshaft (left-hand) with cam gear and spacer. Use retaining bolt and washer (not springs).

21. Install the exhaust (right-hand) camshaft. Do not install the gear until the housing is installed.

22. Install the rear camshaft covers. Do not tighten the one on the right-hand side.

23. Install the camshaft housing.

24. Lubricate the bolts and tighten them in 3 stages:
• Starting with Bolt #2, tighten to 30 ft. lbs.
• Starting with Bolt #2, tighten to 44 ft. lbs.
• Starting with Bolt #1, tighten to 67 ft. lbs. First, slightly loosen the 5 lower cylinder head bolts.

25. When you are finished torquing the camshaft housing bolts, torque the cylinder head bolts. When all bolts have finally been tightened, the camshafts should rotate easily and freely.

26. Install the righthand camshaft gear. Be sure the cam timing is accurate and the engine is set at TDC on No. 1 cylinder.

➡**Some engines have a scale for BDC as well as one for TDC. The TDC mark is next to the pin in the balancer.**

27. Install the timing chain rail.

28. Install the rockers and tension springs. Adjust the valves.

29. Crank the engine by hand and check the valve timing.

30. Tighten the camshaft gear bolts to 59 ft. lbs.

31. Install the chain tensioner.

32. Install the camshaft rear housing covers (if not already done) and the vacuum pump.

33. Install the rocker covers.

V8 Engines

♦ **See Figure 40**

Experience shows that the right-hand camshaft is always the first one to require replacement. When the V8 camshaft is re-

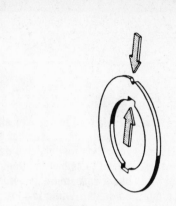

Fig. 40 Install the compensating washer so that the keyway below the notch slides over the Woodruff key

moved, keep the pedestals with the camshaft. In particular, make sure that the 2 left-hand rear cam pedestals are not swapped. The result will be no oil pressure. Always replace the oil gallery pipe with the camshaft.

1. Remove the valve cover.

2. Remove the tensioning springs and rocker arms.

3. Using a wrench on the crankshaft pulley, crank the engine around until No. 1 piston is at TDC on compression. Using some stiff wire, hang the camshaft gear so that the chain will not slip off the gears.

4. Remove the camshaft gear.

5. Unbolt the camshaft, camshaft bearing pedestals and the oil pipe. Note the angle of the bolts holding the cam bearing pedestals to the engine. The inner row of bolts are the only bolts that do not hold the head to the block.

To install:

6. Install the bearing pedestals and camshaft. On the left-hand camshaft, the outer bolt on the rear bearing must be inserted prior to installing the bearings or it will not clear the power brake unit. Tighten the bolts from the inside out. When finished tightening, the camshaft should rotate freely.

7. Check the oil pipes for obstructions and replace if necessary.

8. When installing the oil pipes, also check the 3 inner connecting pipes.

9. Install the compensating washer so that the keyway below the notch slides over the Woodruff key of the camshaft.

10. Install the rocker arms and tensioning springs.

11. Adjust the valve clearance and check the valve timing. See Valve Timing for illustrations.

Engine

DISASSEMBLY

All Models

▸ **See Figures 41 thru 47 (p. 46–50**

➡**This procedure is general and intended to apply to all Mercedes-Benz engines. It is suggested however, that you be entirely familiar with Mercedes-Benz engines and be equipped with the numerous special tools before attempting an engine rebuild. If at all in doubt concerning any procedure, refer the job to a qualified dealer. While this may be more expensive, it will probably produce better results in the end.**

1. Remove the engine and support it on an engine stand or other suitable support.

2. Set the engine at TDC and matchmark the timing chain and timing gear(s). Be sure the timing marks align. Remove the cylinder head(s) and gasket(s).

3. Remove the oil pan bolts, the pan, and, on most models, the lower crankcase section.

4. Remove the oil pump.

5. Matchmark the connecting rod bearing caps to identify the proper cylinder for reassembly. Matchmark the sides of the connecting rod and the side of the bearing cap for proper alignment. Pistons should bear an arrow indicating the front. If not, mark the front of the piston with an arrow with magic marker. Also identify pistons as to cylinder, so they may be replaced in their original location.

6. Remove the connecting rod nuts, bearing caps, and lower bearing shells.

7. Place small pieces of plastic tubing on rod bolts to prevent crankshaft damage.

8. Inspect the crankshaft journals for nicks and roughness and measure diameters.

9. Turn the engine over and ream the ridge from the top of the cylinders to remove all carbon deposits.

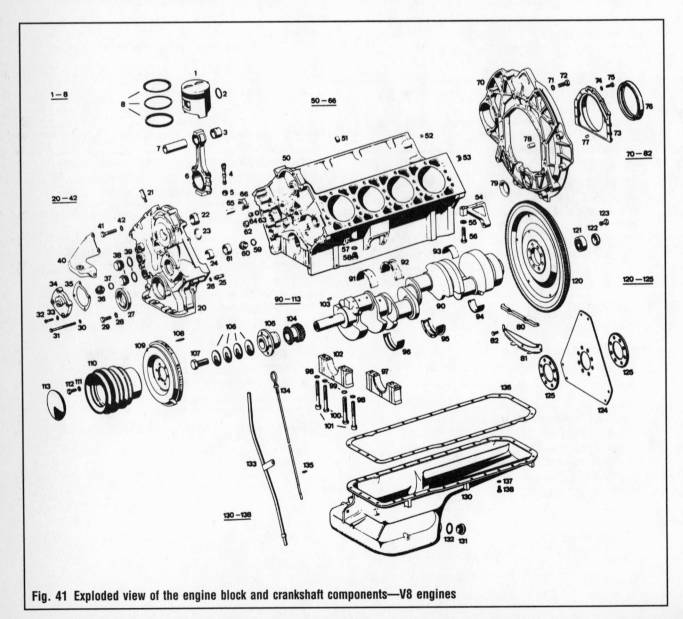

Fig. 41 Exploded view of the engine block and crankshaft components—V8 engines

Piston and connecting rod 1–8

1. Piston
2. Circlip
3. Connecting rod bearing
4. Connecting rod bolt
5. Nut
6. Connecting rod
7. Wrist pin
8. Piston rings

Timing housing cover 20–42

20. Timing housing cover
21. Threaded bolts for adjusting lever of ignition distributor
22. Bearing bushing (guidewheel bearing)
23. 2 O-rings
24. Bearing bushing (intermediate gear shaft)
25. Bolt
26. Spring plate
27. Crankshaft sealing ring (front)
28. Washer
29. Screw
30. Washer
31. Screw
32. 4 screws
33. 4 washers
34. End cover
35. Gasket
36. Screw connection
37. Sealing ring
38. Plug
39. Sealing ring
40. Holder-engine damper
41. 6 screws
42. 6 washers

Cylinder crankcase 50–66

50. Cylinder block
51. 4 Hollow dowel pins
52. 3 plugs (oil duct)
53. Plug (rear main oil duct)
54. 2 Supporting angle pieces
55. 2 washers
56. 2 screws
57. 2 sealing rings
58. 2 plugs
59. Sealing ring
60. Screw connection
61. Bearing bushing intermediate gear shaft rear
62. Plug (front main oil duct)
63. Sealing ring
64. Plug
65. 2 cylinder pins
66. Idler gear bearing

Intermediate flange 70–82

70. Intermediate flange
71. 4 spring washers
72. 4 screws
73. Cover (crankcase sealing ring, rear)
74. 8 washers
75. 3 screws
76. Crankshaft sealing ring (rear)
77. 2 cylinder pins
78. 2 set pins
79. Cover
80. Sealing strip
81. Cover plate
82. 3 screws

Crankshaft 90–113

90. Crankshaft
91. Main bearing shell (top)
92. Fitted bearing shell (top)
93. Connecting rod bearing shell (top)
94. Connecting rod bearing shell (bottom)
95. Fitted bearing shell (bottom)
96. Main bearing shell (bottom)
97. Crankshaft bearing cap (fitted bearing)
98. 10 washers
99. 10 washers
100. 10 Hex bolts
101. 10 Hex socket bolts
102. Crankshaft bearing cap (main bearing)
103. Key
104. Crankshaft gear
105. Vibration damper pulley
106. Plate springs
107. Bolt
108. Indicating needle
109. Vibration damper
110. Pulley
111. 6 circlips
112. 6 screws
113. Pulley cover

Flywheel and driven plate 120–125

120. Flywheel
121. Ball bearing
122. Closing ring
123. 8 bolts
124. Driven plate
125. Spacers

Oil pan 130–138

130. Oil pan
131. Oil drain plug
132. Sealing ring
133. Guide tube (oil dipstick)
134. Oil dipstick
135. Stop-ring (oil dipstick)
136. Oil pan gasket
137. 30 washers
138. 30 screws

Fig. 42 V8 engine block and crankshaft component keylist

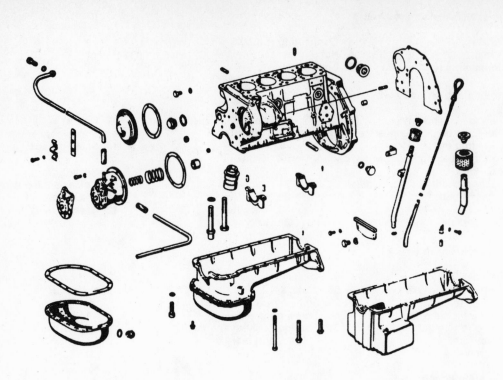

Fig. 43 Exploded view of engine block components—4-cylinder diesel engines (5-cylinder models are similar)

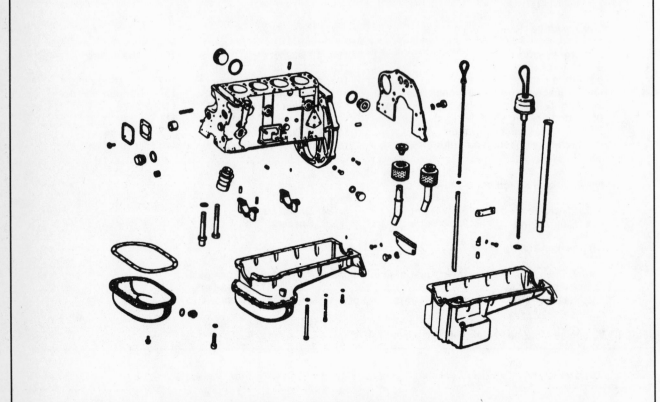

Fig. 44 Exploded view of engine block components—4-cylinder gasoline engines

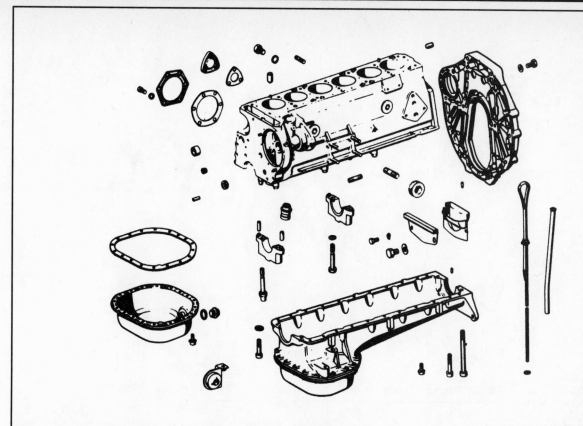

Fig. 45 Exploded view of engine block components—6-cylinder engines

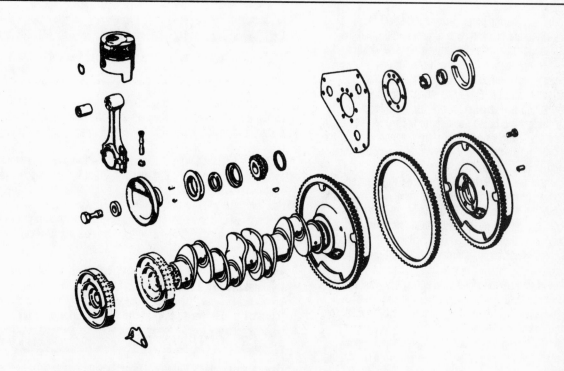

Fig. 46 Crankshaft and related components—4-cylinder diesel engines (5-cylinder models are similar)

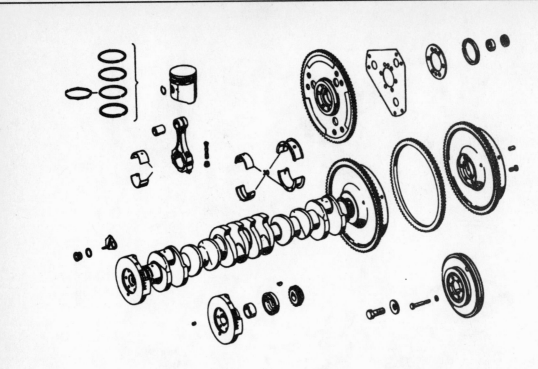

Fig. 47 Crankshaft and related components—6-cylinder engines (4-cylinder gasoline models are similar)

10. Using a hammer handle or other piece of hardwood, gently tap the pistons and rods out from the bottom.

11. The cylinder bores can be inspected at this time for taper and general wear.

12. Check the pistons for proper size and inspect the ring grooves. If any rings are cracked, it is almost certain that the grooves are no longer true, because broken rings work up and down. It is best to replace any such worn pistons.

13. The pistons, wrist pins, and connecting rods may be marked with a color dot assembly code. If a color code is present, only parts having the same color may be used together.

14. If the cylinders are bored, make sure the machinist has the pistons beforehand—cylinder bore sizes are nominal and the pistons must be individually fitted to the block. Maximum piston weight deviation in any one engine is 4 grams.

15. The flywheel and crankshaft are balanced together as a unit. Matchmark the location of the flywheel relative to the crankshaft and remove the flywheel. Stretch bolts are used on some newer flywheels and can be identified by their "hourglass" shape. Once used, they should be discarded and replaced at assembly.

16. Remove the water pump, alternator, and fuel pump, if not done previously.

17. Unbolt and remove the vibration damper and crankshaft pulley. On certain models, it is necessary to clamp the vibration damper with C-clamps before removing the bolts. Otherwise, the vibration damper may come apart.

18. Remove the timing chain tensioner and chain cover.

19. Matchmark the position of the timing chain on the timing gear of the crankshaft.

20. Matchmark the main bearing caps for number and position in the block. It is important that they are installed in their original positions. Most bearing caps are numbered for position. Remove the bearing caps.

21. Lift the crankshaft out of the block in a forward direction.

22. With the block completely disassembled, inspect the water passages and bearing webs for cracks. If the water passages are plugged with rust, they can be cleaned out by boiling the block at a radiator shop.

✳✳ WARNING

Aluminum parts must not be boiled out because they will be eroded by chemicals.

23. Measure piston ring end-gap by sliding a new ring into the bore and measuring. Measure the gap at the top, bottom, and midpoint of piston travel and correct by filing or grinding the ring ends.

24. To check bearing clearances, use Plastigage® inserted between the bearing and the crankshaft journal. Blow out all crankshaft oil passages before measuring; torque the bolts to specification. Plastigage® is a thin plastic strip that is crushed by the bearing cap and spreads out an amount in proportion to clearance. After torquing the bearing cap, remove the cap and compare the width of the Plastigage® with the scale.

➡Do not rotate the crankshaft. Bearing shells of various thicknesses are available and should be used to correct clearance; it may be necessary to machine the crankshaft journals undersize to obtain the proper oil clearance.

✳✳ WARNING

Use of shim stock between bearings and caps to decrease clearance is not a good practice.

25. Check crankshaft end-play using a feeler gauge.

26. When installing new piston rings, ring grooves must be cleaned out, preferably using a special groove cleaner, although a

Place rubber hose over the connecting rod studs to protect the crank and bores from damage

Use a ring expander tool to remove the piston rings

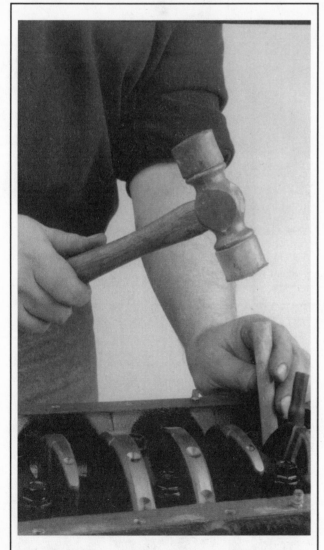

Carefully tap the piston out of the bore using a wooden dowel

Clean the piston grooves using a ring groove cleaner

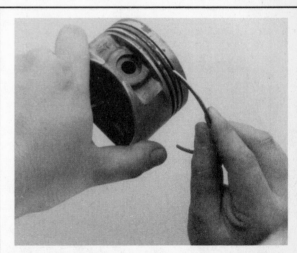

You can use a piece of an old ring to clean the piston grooves, BUT be careful, the ring is sharp

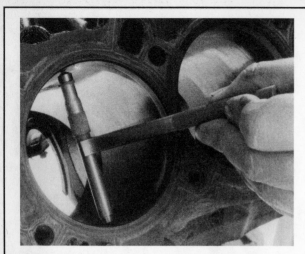

A telescoping gauge may be used to measure the cylinder bore diameter

Measure the piston's outer diameter using a micrometer

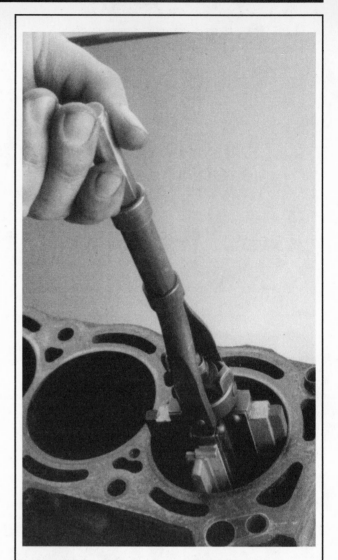

A solid hone can also be used to cross-hatch the cylinder bore

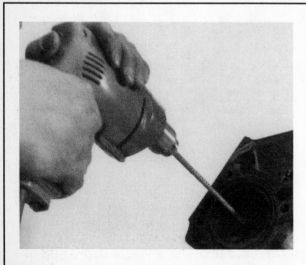

Removing cylinder glazing using a flexible hone

Use a reamer to remove the ridge in the cylinder bore

A properly cross-hatched cylinder bore

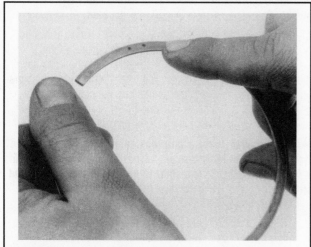

Most rings are marked to show which side should face upward

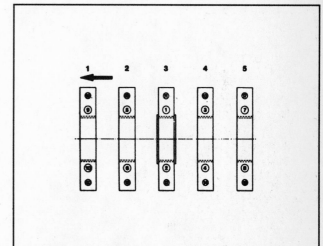

Fig. 48 An angle rotation tool, rather than a torque wrench, is used to tighten the connecting rods stretch bolts

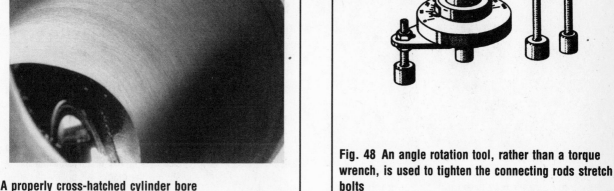

Fig. 49 Main bearing bolt tightening sequence—V8 engines

broken ring will work as well. After installing the rings, check ring side clearance.

ASSEMBLY

▶ **See Figures 48 and 49**

1. Assemble the engine using all new gaskets and seals, and make sure all parts are properly lubricated. Bearing shells and cylinder walls must be lubricated with engine oil before assembly. Make sure no metal chips remain in the cylinder bores or the crankcase.

2. To install the piston and rod, turn the engine right side up and insert the rod into the cylinder. Clamp the rings to the piston, with their gaps equally spaced around the circumference, using a piston ring compressor. Gently tap the piston into the bore, using a hammer handle or similar hard wood, making sure the rings clear the edge.

➡**Pistons on the 3.8 and 5.0L V-8's are installed with the arrow facing in the driving direction.**

3. Torque the rod and main caps to specification and try to turn the crankshaft by hand. It should turn with moderate resistance, not spin freely or be locked up. Stretch bolts are used for the connecting rods. These bolts are tightened by angle of rotation rather than by use of a torque wrench. Make sure the stretch section diameter is greater than 0.35 inch (−0.003 inch). Remove the bolt from the rod and measure the diameter at the point normally covered by the rod; it should be at least 0.31 in. For reasons of standardization, the angle of rotation for all the screw connections tightened according to angle of rotation has been set to 90° + 10°. Initially, the bolts should be torqued to 22–25 ft. lbs., then 90° past that point.

➡**The bearing shells on the 3rd main bearing of the 190E series engines are fitted with thrust washers. The thrust washers in the bearing cap have two locating tabs to keep them from rotating. During assembly the grooves in the washers should face the crankcase thrust surfaces.**

4. Disassemble the oil pump and check the gear backlash. Place a straightedge on the cover and check for warpage. Deep

Most pistons are marked to indicate positioning in the engine (usually a mark means the side facing front)

Installing the piston into the block using a ring compressor and the handle of a hammer

scoring on the cover usually indicates that metal or dirt particles have been circulating through the oil system. Covers can be machined, but it is best to replace them if damaged.

5. Install the oil pump.

6. Install the oil pan and lower crankcase and tighten the bolts evenly all around, then turn the engine right side up and install the cylinder head gasket and head. Make sure the gasket surfaces are clean before installation—a small dirt particle could cause gasket failure. Tighten the cylinder heat bolts in sequence to insure against distortion. Don't forget the small bolts at the front of the head.

7. Install the engine into the vehicle.

➡It is a good practice to use a good break-in oil after an engine overhaul. Be sure that all fluids have been replaced and perform a general tune-up. Check the valve timing.

Valve Timing

GASOLINE ENGINES

♦ **See Figures 50, 51 and 52**

Ideally, this operation should be performed by a dealer, who is equipped with the necessary tools and knowledge to do the job properly.

Checking valve timing is too inaccurate at the standard tappet clearance, therefore timing values are given for an assumed tappet clearance of 0.4mm. The engines are not measured at 0.4mm but rather at 2mm.

1. To check timing, remove the rocker arm cover and spark plugs. Remove the tensioning springs. On the 6-cylinder engine install the testing thrust pieces. Eliminate all valve clearance.

2. Set up a degree wheel on the crankshaft pulley or cam shaft pulley.

➡If the degree wheel is attached to the camshaft as shown, valves read from it must be doubled.

3. A pointer must be made out of a bent section of 3/16 in. brazing rod or coathanger wire, and attached to the engine.

4. With a 22mm wrench on the crankshaft pulley, turn the engine, in the direction of rotation, until the TDC mark on the vibration damper registers with the pointer and the distributor rotor points to the No. 1 cylinder mark on the housing. The camshaft timing marks should also align at this point.

➡Due to design of the chain tensioner on V-8 engines, the right side of the chain travels farther than the left side. This means the right-side camshaft is approximately 7° retarded compared to the left-side, and both marks on each side will not simultaneously align.

5. Turn the loosened degree wheel until the pointer lines up with the 0° (OT) mark, then tighten it in this position.

6. Continue turning the crankshaft in the direction of rotation until the camshaft lobe of the associated valve is vertical (i.e., points away from the rocker arm surface). To take up tappet clearance, insert a feeler gauge thick enough to raise the valve slightly from its seat between the rocker arm cone and the pressure piece.

7. Attach the indicator to the cylinder head so that the feeler rests against the valve spring retainer of No. 1 cylinder intake valve. Preload the indicator at least 0.008 inch then set to zero, making sure the feeler is exactly perpendicular on the valve spring retainer. It may be necessary to bleed down the chain tensioner at this time to facilitate readings.

8. Turn the crankshaft in the normal direction of rotation, again using a wrench on the crankshaft pulley, until the indicator reads 0.016 inch less than zero reading.

9. Note the reading of the degree wheel at this time, remembering to double the reading if the wheel is mounted to the camshaft sprocket.

10. Again turn the crankshaft until the valve is closing and the indicator again reads 0.016 inch less than zero reading. Make sure, at this time, that preload has remained constant, then note the reading of the degree wheel. The difference between the two degree wheel readings is the timing angle (number of degrees the valve is open) for that valve.

11. The other valves may be checked in the same manner, comparing them against each other and the opening values given

in the "Specifications." It must be remembered that turning the crankshaft contrary to the normal direction of rotation results in inaccurate readings and damage to the engine.

12. If valve timing is not to specification, the easiest way of bringing it in line is to install an offset Woodruff key in the camshaft sprocket. This is far simpler than replacing the entire timing chain, and it is the factory-recommended way of changing valve timing provided the timing chain is not stretched too far or worn out. Offset keys are available in the following sizes:

Offset	Part No.	For a Correction at Crankshaft of
2° (0.7 mm)	621 991 04 67	4°
3° 20' (0.9 mm)	621 991 02 67	6½°
4° (1.1 mm)	621 991 01 67	8°
5° (1.3mm)	621 991 00 67	10°

Fig. 50 Offset Woodruff key specifications

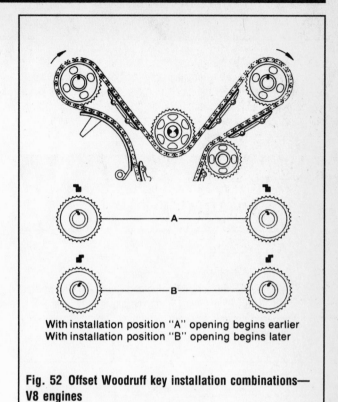

With installation position ''A'' opening begins earlier
With installation position ''B'' opening begins later

Fig. 52 Offset Woodruff key installation combinations—V8 engines

13. The Woodruff key must be installed with the offset toward the "right", in the normal direction of rotation, to effect advanced valve opening; toward the "left" to retard.

14. Advancing the intake valve opening too much can result in piston and/or valve damage (the valve will hit the piston). To check the clearance between the valve head and the piston, the crankshaft must be positioned at 5° ATDC (on intake stroke). The procedure is essentially the same as for measuring valve timing.

15. As before, the dial indicator is set to zero after being preloaded, then the valve is depressed until it touches the top of the piston. As the normal valve head-to-piston clearance is approximately 0.035 inch, you can see that the dial indicator must be preloaded at least 0.042 inch so there will be enough movement for the feeler.

If the clearance is much less than 0.035 in., the cylinder head must be removed and checked for carbon deposits. If none exist, the valve seat must be cut deeper into the head. Always set the ignition timing after installing an offset key.

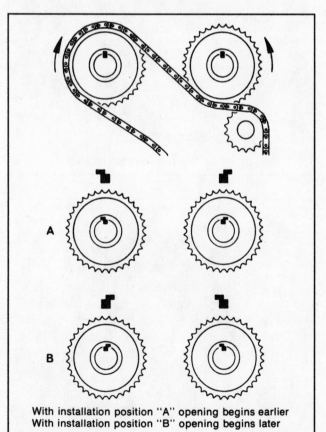

With installation position ''A'' opening begins earlier
With installation position ''B'' opening begins later

Fig. 51 Offset Woodruff key installation combinations—6-cylinder engines

ENGINE COOLING

Mercedes-Benz passenger car engines are all equipped with closed, pressurized, water cooling systems. Care should be exercised when dealing with the cooling system. Always turn the radiator cap to the first notch and allow the pressure to decrease before completely removing the cap. An audible hiss indicates that pressure is being released from the system.

Radiator

REMOVAL & INSTALLATION

All Models

1. Remove the radiator cap.
2. Unscrew the radiator drain plug and drain the coolant from the radiator. If all of the coolant in the system is to be drained, move the heater controls to "warm" and open the draincocks on the engine block.

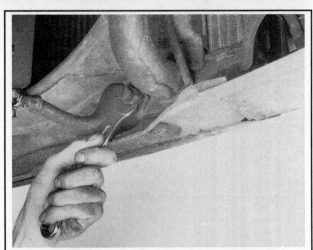

Use a wrench to loosen the transmission coolant line nut . . .

1. Drain plug

To remove the radiator, position a drain pan, then open the drain plug on the bottom of the radiator

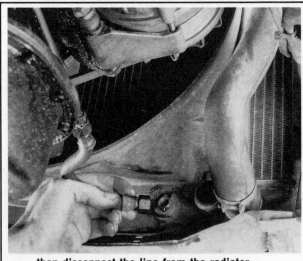

. . . then disconnect the line from the radiator

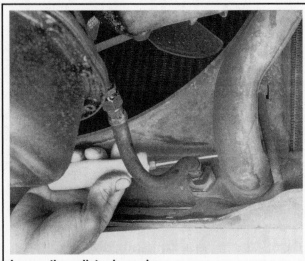

Loosen the radiator hose clamp screws . . .

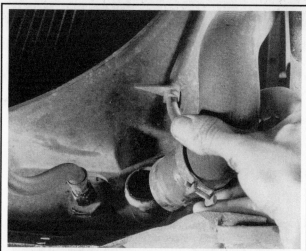

. . . then slide back the clamps and detach the hoses from the radiator

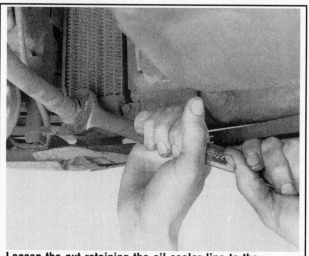

Loosen the nut retaining the oil cooler line to the radiator . . .

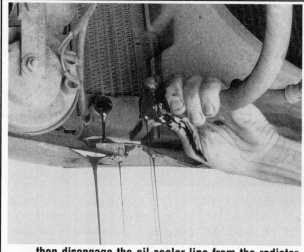

. . . then disengage the oil cooler line from the radiator and drain the oil into an approved container

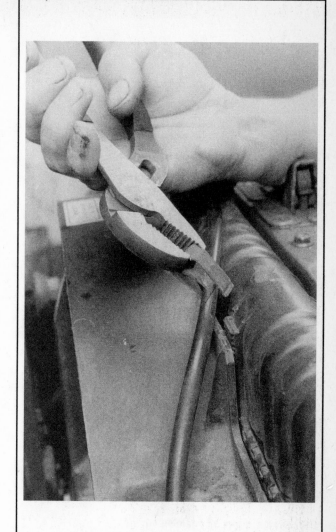

Use a pair of pliers to remove the fan shroud retaining clips . . .

. . . then remove the fan shroud from the engine compartment

Remove the radiator retaining clips . . .

. . . then remove the radiator from the vehicle

3. If the car is equipped with an oil cooler, drain the oil from the cooler.

4. If equipped, loosen the radiator shell.

5. Loosen the hose clips on the top and bottom radiator hoses and remove the hoses from the connections on the radiator.

6. Unscrew and plug the bottom line on the oil cooler.

7. If the car is equipped with an automatic transmission, unscrew and plug the lines on the transmission oil cooler.

8. Disconnect the right-hand and left-hand rubber loops and pull the radiator up and out of the body. On 450 SL and SLC models, push the retaining springs toward the fenders to remove the radiator from the shell.

To install:

9. Inspect and replace any hoses which have become hardened or spongy.

10. Install the radiator shell and radiator (if the shell was removed) from the top and connect the top and bottom hoses to the radiator.

11. Bolt the shell to the radiator.

12. Attach the rubber loops or position the retaining springs as applicable.

13. Position the hose clips on the top and bottom hoses.

14. Attach the lines to the oil cooler.

15. On cars with automatic transmissions, connect the lines to the transmission oil cooler.

16. Move the heater levers to the "warm" position and slowly add coolant, allowing air to escape.

17. Check the oil level and fill if necessary. Run the engine for about one minute at idle with the filler neck open.

18. Add coolant to the level specified in Chapter One. Install the radiator cap and turn it until it seats in the second notch. Run the engine and check for leaks.

Water Pump

REMOVAL & INSTALLATION

Except V8 Engines

1. Drain the coolant from the radiator.

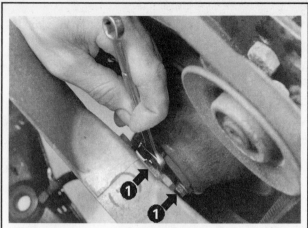

1. Retaining bolts

To remove the radiator, unfasten the cooling fan retaining bolts . . .

Unfasten the water pump retaining bolts . . .

. . . then remove the cooling fan from the vehicle

. . . then remove the water pump from the engine

Disconnect the water pump drive belt and remove the pulley

Use a scraper to clean the old gasket residue from both the water pump and its mating surface

2. Loosen the radiator shell and remove the radiator.

3. Remove the fan with the coupling and set it aside in an upright position.

4. Loosen the belt around the water pump pulley and remove the belt.

5. Remove the bolts from the harmonic balancer and remove the balancer and pulley.

6. Unbolt and remove the water pump.

7. Installation is the reverse of removal. Tighten the belt and fill the cooling system.

V8 Models

1. Drain the coolant from the radiator and block.

✳✳ CAUTION

When draining engine coolant, keep in mind that cats and dogs are attracted to ethylene glycol antifreeze and could drink any that is left in an uncovered container or in puddles on the ground. This will prove fatal in sufficient quantity. Always drain coolant into a sealable container. Coolant should be reused unless it is contaminated or is several years old.

2. Remove the air cleaner.

3. Loosen and remove the power steering pump drive belt.

4. Disconnect the upper water hose from the radiator and thermostat housing.

5. Remove the fan and coupling.

6. Remove the bottom water hose from the water pump housing.

7. Remove the hose from the intake (top) connection from the water pump.

8. Set the engine at TDC. Matchmark the distributor and engine and remove the distributor. Crank the engine with a socket wrench on the crankshaft pulley bolt or with a screwdriver inserted in the balancer. Crank in the normal direction of rotation only.

9. Turn the balancer so that the recesses provide access to the mounting bolts. Remove the mounting bolts. Rotate the engine in the normal direction of rotation only.

10. Remove the water pump.

11. Clean the mounting surfaces of the water pump and block.

12. Installation is the reverse of removal. Always use a new gasket. Set the engine at TDC and install the distributor so that the distributor rotor points to the notch on the distributor housing. Fill the cooling system and check and adjust the ignition timing.

Thermostat

REMOVAL & INSTALLATION

4 and 5-Cylinder Engines

▶ See Figure 53

The thermostat housing is a light metal casting attached directly to the cylinder head, except on the 190D where it is attached to the side of the water pump housing.

1. Open the radiator cap and depressurize the system.

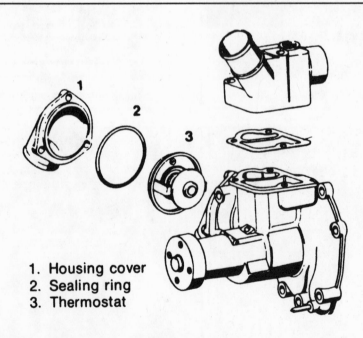

1. Housing cover
2. Sealing ring
3. Thermostat

Fig. 53 Exploded view of the thermostat housing and related components—V8 engines

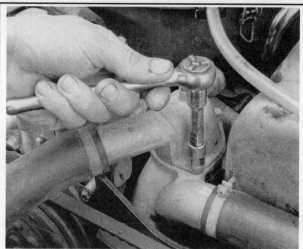

To remove the thermostat, loosen the housing retaining bolts . . .

. . . then remove the thermostat housing

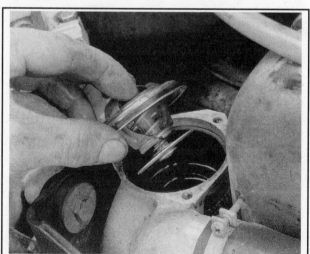

Remove the thermostat from the engine block and clean the old gasket from the mating surfaces

2. Open the radiator draincock and partially drain the coolant. Drain enough coolant to bring the coolant level below the level of the thermostat housing.

✳✳ CAUTION

When draining engine coolant, keep in mind that cats and dogs are attracted to ethylene glycol antifreeze and could drink any that is left in an uncovered container or in puddles on the ground. This will prove fatal in sufficient quantity. Always drain coolant into a sealable container. Coolant should be reused unless it is contaminated or is several years old.

3. Remove the bolts on the thermostat housing cover and remove the cover.

4. Note the installation position of the thermostat and remove the thermostat.

5. Installation is the reverse of removal. Be sure that the thermostat is positioned with the ball valve at the highest point and that the bolts are tightened evenly against the seal. On the 190D, the recess in the thermostat casing should be located above the lug in the thermostat housing.

6. Refill the cooling system and check for leaks.

V8 Engines

1. Drain the coolant from the radiator and block.

✳✳ CAUTION

When draining engine coolant, keep in mind that cats and dogs are attracted to ethylene glycol antifreeze and could drink any that is left in an uncovered container or in puddles on the ground. This will prove fatal in sufficient quantity. Always drain coolant into a sealable container. Coolant should be reused unless it is contaminated or is several years old.

2. Remove the air cleaner.

3. Disconnect the battery and remove the alternator. Usually this need not be done on V8 Engines.

4. Unscrew the housing cover on the side of the water pump and remove the thermostat. Note that the thermostat used on 4.5 liter V8 models differs from the one used on other models by a different positioning of the ball valve.

5. If a new thermostat is to be installed, always install a new sealing ring.

6. Installation is the reverse of removal. Be sure to tighten the screws on the housing cover evenly to prevent leaks. Refill the cooling system and check for leaks.

6-Cylinder Engines

1. Drain the coolant from the radiator.

✳✳ CAUTION

When draining engine coolant, keep in mind that cats and dogs are attracted to ethylene glycol antifreeze and could drink any that is left in an uncovered container or in puddles on the ground. This will prove fatal in sufficient quantity. Always drain coolant into a sealable container. Coolant should be reused unless it is contaminated or is several years old.

2. Remove the vacuum pump and put the pump aside.
3. Remove the three bolts on the thermostat housing.
4. Remove the cover and the thermostat.
5. Installation is the reverse of removal. Install the thermostat so that the ball valve is at the highest point. Refill the cooling system.

EXHAUST SYSTEM

General Information

➡Safety glasses should be worn at all times when working on or near the exhaust system. Older exhaust systems will almost always be covered with loose rust particles which will shower you when disturbed. These particles are more than a nuisance and could injure your eye.

Whenever working on the exhaust system always keep the following in mind:

• Check the complete exhaust system for open seams, holes loose connections, or other deterioration which could permit exhaust fumes to seep into the passenger compartment.

• The exhaust system is usually supported by free-hanging rubber mountings which permit some movement of the exhaust system, but does not permit transfer of noise and vibration into the passenger compartment. Do not replace the rubber mounts with solid ones.

• Before removing any component of the exhaust system, ALWAYS squirt a liquid rust dissolving agent onto the fasteners for ease of removal. A lot of knuckle skin will be saved by following this rule. It may even be wise to spray the fasteners and allow them to sit overnight.

✳✳ CAUTION

Allow the exhaust system to cool sufficiently before spraying a solvent exhaust fasteners. Some solvents are highly flammable and could ignite when sprayed on hot exhaust components.

• Annoying rattles and noise vibrations in the exhaust system are usually caused by misalignment of the parts. When aligning the system, leave all bolts and nuts loose until all parts are properly aligned, then tighten, working from front to rear.

• When installing exhaust system parts, make sure there is enough clearance between the hot exhaust parts and pipes and hoses that would be adversely affected by excessive heat. Also make sure there is adequate clearance from the floor pan to avoid possible overheating of the floor.

USING A VACUUM GAUGE

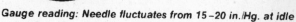

White needle = steady needle   *Dark needle = drifting needle*

The vacuum gauge is one of the most useful and easy-to-use diagnostic tools. It is inexpensive, easy to hook up, and provides valuable information about the condition of your engine.

Indication: Normal engine in good condition

Gauge reading: Steady, from 17–22 in./Hg.

Indication: Sticking valve or ignition miss

Gauge reading: Needle fluctuates from 15–20 in./Hg. at idle

Indication: Late ignition or valve timing, low compression, stuck throttle valve, leaking carburetor or manifold gasket.

Gauge reading: Low (15–20 in./Hg.) but steady

Indication: Improper carburetor adjustment, or minor intake leak at carburetor or manifold

NOTE: Bad fuel injector O-rings may also cause this reading.

Gauge reading: Drifting needle

Indication: Weak valve springs, worn valve stem guides, or leaky cylinder head gasket (vibrating excessively at all speeds).

NOTE: A plugged catalytic converter may also cause this reading.

Gauge reading: Needle fluctuates as engine speed increases

Indication: Burnt valve or improper valve clearance. The needle will drop when the defective valve operates.

Gauge reading: Steady needle, but drops regularly

Indication: Choked muffler or obstruction in system. Speed up the engine. Choked muffler will exhibit a slow drop of vacuum to zero.

Gauge reading: Gradual drop in reading at idle

Indication: Worn valve guides

Gauge reading: Needle vibrates excessively at idle, but steadies as engine speed increases

Troubleshooting Engine Mechanical Problems

Problem	Cause	Solution
External oil leaks	• Cylinder head cover RTV sealant broken or improperly seated	• Replace sealant; inspect cylinder head cover sealant flange and cylinder head sealant surface for distortion and cracks
	• Oil filler cap leaking or missing	• Replace cap
	• Oil filter gasket broken or improperly seated	• Replace oil filter
	• Oil pan side gasket broken, improperly seated or opening in RTV sealant	• Replace gasket or repair opening in sealant; inspect oil pan gasket flange for distortion
	• Oil pan front oil seal broken or improperly seated	• Replace seal; inspect timing case cover and oil pan seal flange for distortion
	• Oil pan rear oil seal broken or improperly seated	• Replace seal; inspect oil pan rear oil seal flange; inspect rear main bearing cap for cracks, plugged oil return channels, or distortion in seal groove
	• Timing case cover oil seal broken or improperly seated	• Replace seal
	• Excess oil pressure because of restricted PCV valve	• Replace PCV valve
	• Oil pan drain plug loose or has stripped threads	• Repair as necessary and tighten
	• Rear oil gallery plug loose	• Use appropriate sealant on gallery plug and tighten
	• Rear camshaft plug loose or improperly seated	• Seat camshaft plug or replace and seal, as necessary
Excessive oil consumption	• Oil level too high	• Drain oil to specified level
	• Oil with wrong viscosity being used	• Replace with specified oil
	• PCV valve stuck closed	• Replace PCV valve
	• Valve stem oil deflectors (or seals) are damaged, missing, or incorrect type	• Replace valve stem oil deflectors
	• Valve stems or valve guides worn	• Measure stem-to-guide clearance and repair as necessary
	• Poorly fitted or missing valve cover baffles	• Replace valve cover
	• Piston rings broken or missing	• Replace broken or missing rings
	• Scuffed piston	• Replace piston
	• Incorrect piston ring gap	• Measure ring gap, repair as necessary
	• Piston rings sticking or excessively loose in grooves	• Measure ring side clearance, repair as necessary
	• Compression rings installed upside down	• Repair as necessary
	• Cylinder walls worn, scored, or glazed	• Repair as necessary

Troubleshooting Engine Mechanical Problems

Problem	Cause	Solution
Excessive oil consumption (cont.)	• Piston ring gaps not properly staggered	• Repair as necessary
	• Excessive main or connecting rod bearing clearance	• Measure bearing clearance, repair as necessary
No oil pressure	• Low oil level	• Add oil to correct level
	• Oil pressure gauge, warning lamp or sending unit inaccurate	• Replace oil pressure gauge or warning lamp
	• Oil pump malfunction	• Replace oil pump
	• Oil pressure relief valve sticking	• Remove and inspect oil pressure relief valve assembly
	• Oil passages on pressure side of pump obstructed	• Inspect oil passages for obstruction
	• Oil pickup screen or tube obstructed	• Inspect oil pickup for obstruction
	• Loose oil inlet tube	• Tighten or seal inlet tube
Low oil pressure	• Low oil level	• Add oil to correct level
	• Inaccurate gauge, warning lamp or sending unit	• Replace oil pressure gauge or warning lamp
	• Oil excessively thin because of dilution, poor quality, or improper grade	• Drain and refill crankcase with recommended oil
	• Excessive oil temperature	• Correct cause of overheating engine
	• Oil pressure relief spring weak or sticking	• Remove and inspect oil pressure relief valve assembly
	• Oil inlet tube and screen assembly has restriction or air leak	• Remove and inspect oil inlet tube and screen assembly. (Fill inlet tube with lacquer thinner to locate leaks.)
	• Excessive oil pump clearance	• Measure clearances
	• Excessive main, rod, or camshaft bearing clearance	• Measure bearing clearances, repair as necessary
High oil pressure	• Improper oil viscosity	• Drain and refill crankcase with correct viscosity oil
	• Oil pressure gauge or sending unit inaccurate	• Replace oil pressure gauge
	• Oil pressure relief valve sticking closed	• Remove and inspect oil pressure relief valve assembly
Main bearing noise	• Insufficient oil supply	• Inspect for low oil level and low oil pressure
	• Main bearing clearance excessive	• Measure main bearing clearance, repair as necessary
	• Bearing insert missing	• Replace missing insert
	• Crankshaft end-play excessive	• Measure end-play, repair as necessary
	• Improperly tightened main bearing cap bolts	• Tighten bolts with specified torque
	• Loose flywheel or drive plate	• Tighten flywheel or drive plate attaching bolts
	• Loose or damaged vibration damper	• Repair as necessary

Troubleshooting Engine Mechanical Problems

Problem	Cause	Solution
Connecting rod bearing noise	• Insufficient oil supply	• Inspect for low oil level and low oil pressure
	• Carbon build-up on piston	• Remove carbon from piston crown
	• Bearing clearance excessive or bearing missing	• Measure clearance, repair as necessary
	• Crankshaft connecting rod journal out-of-round	• Measure journal dimensions, repair or replace as necessary
	• Misaligned connecting rod or cap	• Repair as necessary
	• Connecting rod bolts tightened improperly	• Tighten bolts with specified torque
Piston noise	• Piston-to-cylinder wall clearance excessive (scuffed piston)	• Measure clearance and examine piston
	• Cylinder walls excessively tapered or out-of-round	• Measure cylinder wall dimensions, rebore cylinder
	• Piston ring broken	• Replace all rings on piston
	• Loose or seized piston pin	• Measure piston-to-pin clearance, repair as necessary
	• Connecting rods misaligned	• Measure rod alignment, straighten or replace
	• Piston ring side clearance excessively loose or tight	• Measure ring side clearance, repair as necessary
	• Carbon build-up on piston is excessive	• Remove carbon from piston
Valve actuating component noise	• Insufficient oil supply	• Check for: (a) Low oil level (b) Low oil pressure (c) Wrong hydraulic tappets (d) Restricted oil gallery (e) Excessive tappet to bore clearance
	• Rocker arms or pivots worn	• Replace worn rocker arms or pivots
	• Foreign objects or chips in hydraulic tappets	• Clean tappets
	• Excessive tappet leak-down	• Replace valve tappet
	• Tappet face worn	• Replace tappet; inspect corresponding cam lobe for wear
	• Broken or cocked valve springs	• Properly seat cocked springs; replace broken springs
	• Stem-to-guide clearance excessive	• Measure stem-to-guide clearance, repair as required
	• Valve bent	• Replace valve
	• Loose rocker arms	• Check and repair as necessary
	• Valve seat runout excessive	• Regrind valve seat/valves
	• Missing valve lock	• Install valve lock
	• Excessive engine oil	• Correct oil level

Troubleshooting the Serpentine Drive Belt

Problem	Cause	Solution
Tension sheeting fabric failure (woven fabric on outside circumference of belt has cracked or separated from body of belt)	• Grooved or backside idler pulley diameters are less than minimum recommended • Tension sheeting contacting (rubbing) stationary object • Excessive heat causing woven fabric to age • Tension sheeting splice has fractured	• Replace pulley(s) not conforming to specification • Correct rubbing condition • Replace belt • Replace belt
Noise (objectional squeal, squeak, or rumble is heard or felt while drive belt is in operation)	• Belt slippage • Bearing noise • Belt misalignment • Belt-to-pulley mismatch • Driven component inducing vibration • System resonant frequency inducing vibration	• Adjust belt • Locate and repair • Align belt/pulley(s) • Install correct belt • Locate defective driven component and repair • Vary belt tension within specifications. Replace belt.
Rib chunking (one or more ribs has separated from belt body)	• Foreign objects imbedded in pulley grooves • Installation damage • Drive loads in excess of design specifications • Insufficient internal belt adhesion	• Remove foreign objects from pulley grooves • Replace belt • Adjust belt tension • Replace belt
Rib or belt wear (belt ribs contact bottom of pulley grooves)	• Pulley(s) misaligned • Mismatch of belt and pulley groove widths • Abrasive environment • Rusted pulley(s) • Sharp or jagged pulley groove tips • Rubber deteriorated	• Align pulley(s) • Replace belt • Replace belt • Clean rust from pulley(s) • Replace pulley • Replace belt
Longitudinal belt cracking (cracks between two ribs)	• Belt has mistracked from pulley groove • Pulley groove tip has worn away rubber-to-tensile member	• Replace belt • Replace belt
Belt slips	• Belt slipping because of insufficient tension • Belt or pulley subjected to substance (belt dressing, oil, ethylene glycol) that has reduced friction • Driven component bearing failure • Belt glazed and hardened from heat and excessive slippage	• Adjust tension • Replace belt and clean pulleys • Replace faulty component bearing • Replace belt
"Groove jumping" (belt does not maintain correct position on pulley, or turns over and/or runs off pulleys)	• Insufficient belt tension • Pulley(s) not within design tolerance • Foreign object(s) in grooves	• Adjust belt tension • Replace pulley(s) • Remove foreign objects from grooves

Troubleshooting the Serpentine Drive Belt

Problem	Cause	Solution
"Groove jumping" (belt does not maintain correct position on pulley, or turns over and/or runs off pulleys)	• Excessive belt speed • Pulley misalignment • Belt-to-pulley profile mismatched • Belt cordline is distorted	• Avoid excessive engine acceleration • Align pulley(s) • Install correct belt • Replace belt
Belt broken (Note: identify and correct problem before replacement belt is installed)	• Excessive tension • Tensile members damaged during belt installation • Belt turnover • Severe pulley misalignment • Bracket, pulley, or bearing failure	• Replace belt and adjust tension to specification • Replace belt • Replace belt • Align pulley(s) • Replace defective component and belt
Cord edge failure (tensile member exposed at edges of belt or separated from belt body)	• Excessive tension • Drive pulley misalignment • Belt contacting stationary object • Pulley irregularities • Improper pulley construction • Insufficient adhesion between tensile member and rubber matrix	• Adjust belt tension • Align pulley • Correct as necessary • Replace pulley • Replace pulley • Replace belt and adjust tension to specifications
Sporadic rib cracking (multiple cracks in belt ribs at random intervals)	• Ribbed pulley(s) diameter less than minimum specification • Backside bend flat pulley(s) diameter less than minimum • Excessive heat condition causing rubber to harden • Excessive belt thickness • Belt overcured • Excessive tension	• Replace pulley(s) • Replace pulley(s) • Correct heat condition as necessary • Replace belt • Replace belt • Adjust belt tension

Troubleshooting the Cooling System

Problem	Cause	Solution
High temperature gauge indication— overheating	• Coolant level low • Improper fan operation • Radiator hose(s) collapsed • Radiator airflow blocked	• Replenish coolant • Repair or replace as necessary • Replace hose(s) • Remove restriction (bug screen, fog lamps, etc.)
	• Faulty pressure cap • Ignition timing incorrect • Air trapped in cooling system • Heavy traffic driving	• Replace pressure cap • Adjust ignition timing • Purge air • Operate at fast idle in neutral intermittently to cool engine • Install proper component(s)
	• Incorrect cooling system component(s) installed • Faulty thermostat • Water pump shaft broken or impeller loose • Radiator tubes clogged • Cooling system clogged • Casting flash in cooling passages	• Replace thermostat • Replace water pump • Flush radiator • Flush system • Repair or replace as necessary. Flash may be visible by removing cooling system components or removing core plugs.
	• Brakes dragging • Excessive engine friction • Antifreeze concentration over 68% • Missing air seals • Faulty gauge or sending unit • Loss of coolant flow caused by leakage or foaming • Viscous fan drive failed	• Repair brakes • Repair engine • Lower antifreeze concentration percentage • Replace air seals • Repair or replace faulty component • Repair or replace leaking component, replace coolant • Replace unit
Low temperature indication— undercooling	• Thermostat stuck open • Faulty gauge or sending unit	• Replace thermostat • Repair or replace faulty component
Coolant loss—boilover	• Overfilled cooling system • Quick shutdown after hard (hot) run • Air in system resulting in occasional "burping" of coolant • Insufficient antifreeze allowing coolant boiling point to be too low • Antifreeze deteriorated because of age or contamination • Leaks due to loose hose clamps, loose nuts, bolts, drain plugs, faulty hoses, or defective radiator	• Reduce coolant level to proper specification • Allow engine to run at fast idle prior to shutdown • Purge system • Add antifreeze to raise boiling point • Replace coolant • Pressure test system to locate source of leak(s) then repair as necessary

Troubleshooting the Cooling System (cont.)

Problem	Cause	Solution
Coolant loss—boilover	• Faulty head gasket • Cracked head, manifold, or block • Faulty radiator cap	• Replace head gasket • Replace as necessary • Replace cap
Coolant entry into crankcase or cylinder(s)	• Faulty head gasket • Crack in head, manifold or block	• Replace head gasket • Replace as necessary
Coolant recovery system inoperative	• Coolant level low • Leak in system • Pressure cap not tight or seal missing, or leaking • Pressure cap defective • Overflow tube clogged or leaking • Recovery bottle vent restricted	• Replenish coolant to FULL mark • Pressure test to isolate leak and repair as necessary • Repair as necessary • Replace cap • Repair as necessary • Remove restriction
Noise	• Fan contacting shroud • Loose water pump impeller • Glazed fan belt • Loose fan belt • Rough surface on drive pulley • Water pump bearing worn • Belt alignment	• Reposition shroud and inspect engine mounts (on electric fans inspect assembly) • Replace pump • Apply silicone or replace belt • Adjust fan belt tension • Replace pulley • Remove belt to isolate. Replace pump. • Check pulley alignment. Repair as necessary.
No coolant flow through heater core	• Restricted return inlet in water pump • Heater hose collapsed or restricted • Restricted heater core • Restricted outlet in thermostat housing • Intake manifold bypass hole in cylinder head restricted • Faulty heater control valve • Intake manifold coolant passage restricted	• Remove restriction • Remove restriction or replace hose • Remove restriction or replace core • Remove flash or restriction • Remove restriction • Replace valve • Remove restriction or replace intake manifold

NOTE: *Immediately after shutdown, the engine enters a condition known as heat soak. This is caused by the cooling system being inoperative while engine temperature is still high. If coolant temperature rises above boiling point, expansion and pressure may push some coolant out of the radiator overflow tube. If this does not occur frequently it is considered normal.*

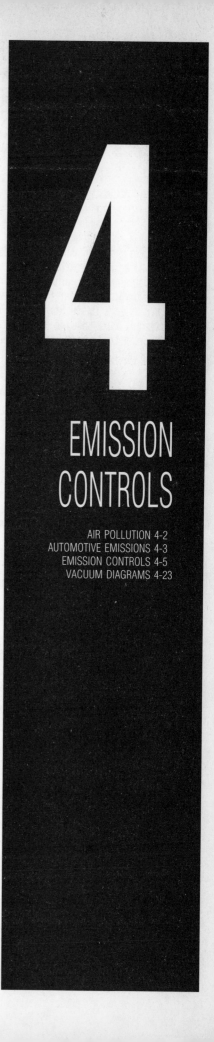

4

EMISSION CONTROLS

AIR POLLUTION 4-2
AUTOMOTIVE EMISSIONS 4-3
EMISSION CONTROLS 4-5
VACUUM DIAGRAMS 4-23

AIR POLLUTION

The earth's atmosphere, at or near sea level, consists approximately of 78 percent nitrogen, 21 percent oxygen and 1 percent other gases. If it were possible to remain in this state, 100 percent clean air would result. However, many varied sources allow other gases and particulates to mix with the clean air, causing our atmosphere to become unclean or polluted.

Some of these pollutants are visible while others are invisible, with each having the capability of causing distress to the eyes, ears, throat, skin and respiratory system. Should these pollutants become concentrated in a specific area and under certain conditions, death could result due to the displacement or chemical change of the oxygen content in the air. These pollutants can also cause great damage to the environment and to the many man made objects that are exposed to the elements.

To better understand the causes of air pollution, the pollutants can be categorized into 3 separate types, natural, industrial and automotive.

Natural Pollutants

Natural pollution has been present on earth since before man appeared and continues to be a factor when discussing air pollution, although it causes only a small percentage of the overall pollution problem. It is the direct result of decaying organic matter, wind born smoke and particulates from such natural events as plain and forest fires (ignited by heat or lightning), volcanic ash, sand and dust which can spread over a large area of the countryside.

Such a phenomenon of natural pollution has been seen in the form of volcanic eruptions, with the resulting plume of smoke, steam and volcanic ash blotting out the sun's rays as it spreads and rises higher into the atmosphere. As it travels into the atmosphere the upper air currents catch and carry the smoke and ash, while condensing the steam back into water vapor. As the water vapor, smoke and ash travel on their journey, the smoke dissipates into the atmosphere while the ash and moisture settle back to earth in a trail hundreds of miles long. In some cases, lives are lost and millions of dollars of property damage result.

Industrial Pollutants

Industrial pollution is caused primarily by industrial processes, the burning of coal, oil and natural gas, which in turn produce smoke and fumes. Because the burning fuels contain large amounts of sulfur, the principal ingredients of smoke and fumes are sulfur dioxide and particulate matter. This type of pollutant occurs most severely during still, damp and cool weather, such as at night. Even in its less severe form, this pollutant is not confined to just cities. Because of air movements, the pollutants move for miles over the surrounding countryside, leaving in its path a barren and unhealthy environment for all living things.

Working with Federal, State and Local mandated regulations and by carefully monitoring emissions, big business has greatly reduced the amount of pollutant introduced from its industrial sources, striving to obtain an acceptable level. Because of the mandated industrial emission clean up, many land areas and streams in and around the cities that were formerly barren of vegetation and life, have now begun to move back in the direction of nature's intended balance.

Automotive Pollutants

The third major source of air pollution is automotive emissions. The emissions from the internal combustion engines were not an appreciable problem years ago because of the small number of registered vehicles and the nation's small highway system. However, during the early 1950's, the trend of the American people was to move from the cities to the surrounding suburbs. This caused an immediate problem in transportation because the majority of suburbs were not afforded mass transit conveniences. This lack of transportation created an attractive market for the automobile manufacturers, which resulted in a dramatic increase in the number of vehicles produced and sold, along with a marked increase in highway construction between cities and the suburbs. Multi-vehicle families emerged with a growing emphasis placed on an individual vehicle per family member. As the increase in vehicle ownership and usage occurred, so did pollutant levels in and around the cities, as suburbanites drove daily to their businesses and employment, returning at the end of the day to their homes in the suburbs.

It was noted that a smoke and fog type haze was being formed and at times, remained in suspension over the cities, taking time to dissipate. At first this "smog," derived from the words "smoke" and "fog," was thought to result from industrial pollution but it was determined that automobile emissions shared the blame. It was discovered that when normal automobile emissions were exposed to sunlight for a period of time, complex chemical reactions would take place.

It is now known that smog is a photo chemical layer which develops when certain oxides of nitrogen (NOx) and unburned hydrocarbons (HC) from automobile emissions are exposed to sunlight. Pollution was more severe when smog would become stagnant over an area in which a warm layer of air settled over the top of the cooler air mass, trapping and holding the cooler mass at ground level. The trapped cooler air would keep the emissions from being dispersed and diluted through normal air flows. This type of air stagnation was given the name "Temperature Inversion."

TEMPERATURE INVERSION

In normal weather situations, surface air is warmed by heat radiating from the earth's surface and the sun's rays. This causes it to rise upward, into the atmosphere. Upon rising it will cool through a convection type heat exchange with the cooler upper air. As warm air rises, the surface pollutants are carried upward and dissipated into the atmosphere.

When a temperature inversion occurs, we find the higher air is no longer cooler, but is warmer than the surface air, causing the cooler surface air to become trapped. This warm air blanket can extend from above ground level to a few hundred or even a few thousand feet into the air. As the surface air is trapped, so are the pollutants, causing a severe smog condition. Should this stagnant air mass extend to a few thousand feet high, enough air movement with the inversion takes place to allow the smog layer to rise above ground level but the pollutants still cannot dissipate. This inversion can remain for days over an area, with the smog level only rising or lowering from ground level to a few hundred feet high. Meanwhile, the pollutant levels increase, causing eye irritation, respiratory problems, reduced visibility, plant damage and in some cases, even disease.

This inversion phenomenon was first noted in the Los Angeles, California area. The city lies in terrain resembling a basin and with certain weather conditions, a cold air mass is held in the basin while a warmer air mass covers it like a lid.

Because this type of condition was first documented as prevalent in the Los Angeles area, this type of trapped pollution was named Los Angeles Smog, although it occurs in other areas where a large concentration of automobiles are used and the air remains stagnant for any length of time.

HEAT TRANSFER

Consider the internal combustion engine as a machine in which raw materials must be placed so a finished product comes out. As in any machine operation, a certain amount of wasted material is formed. When we relate this to the internal combustion engine, we find that through the input of air and fuel, we obtain power during the combustion process to drive the vehicle. The by-product or waste of this power is, in part, heat and exhaust gases with which we must dispose.

The heat from the combustion process can rise to over 4000°F (2204°C). The dissipation of this heat is controlled by a ram air effect, the use of cooling fans to cause air flow and a liquid coolant solution surrounding the combustion area to transfer the heat of combustion through the cylinder walls and into the coolant. The coolant is then directed to a thin-finned, multi-tubed radiator, from which the excess heat is transferred to the atmosphere by 1 of the 3 heat transfer methods, conduction, convection or radiation.

The cooling of the combustion area is an important part in the control of exhaust emissions. To understand the behavior of the combustion and transfer of its heat, consider the air/fuel charge. It is ignited and the flame front burns progressively across the combustion chamber until the burning charge reaches the cylinder walls. Some of the fuel in contact with the walls is not hot enough to burn, thereby snuffing out or quenching the combustion process. This leaves unburned fuel in the combustion chamber. This unburned fuel is then forced out of the cylinder and into the exhaust system, along with the exhaust gases.

Many attempts have been made to minimize the amount of unburned fuel in the combustion chambers due to quenching, by increasing the coolant temperature and lessening the contact area of the coolant around the combustion area. However, design limitations within the combustion chambers prevent the complete burning of the air/fuel charge, so a certain amount of the unburned fuel is still expelled into the exhaust system, regardless of modifications to the engine.

AUTOMOTIVE EMISSIONS

Before emission controls were mandated on internal combustion engines, other sources of engine pollutants were discovered along with the exhaust emissions. It was determined that engine combustion exhaust produced approximately 60 percent of the total emission pollutants, fuel evaporation from the fuel tank and carburetor vents produced 20 percent, with the final 20 percent being produced through the crankcase as a by-product of the combustion process.

Exhaust Gases

The exhaust gases emitted into the atmosphere are a combination of burned and unburned fuel. To understand the exhaust emission and its composition, we must review some basic chemistry.

When the air/fuel mixture is introduced into the engine, we are mixing air, composed of nitrogen (78 percent), oxygen (21 percent) and other gases (1 percent) with the fuel, which is 100 percent hydrocarbons (HC), in a semi-controlled ratio. As the combustion process is accomplished, power is produced to move the vehicle while the heat of combustion is transferred to the cooling system. The exhaust gases are then composed of nitrogen, a diatomic gas (N_2), the same as was introduced in the engine, carbon dioxide (CO_2), the same gas that is used in beverage carbonation, and water vapor (H_2O). The nitrogen (N_2), for the most part, passes through the engine unchanged, while the oxygen (O_2) reacts (burns) with the hydrocarbons (HC) and produces the carbon dioxide (CO_2) and the water vapors (H_2O). If this chemical process would be the only process to take place, the exhaust emissions would be harmless. However, during the combustion process, other compounds are formed which are considered dangerous. These pollutants are hydrocarbons (HC), carbon monoxide (CO), oxides of nitrogen (NOx) oxides of sulfur (SOx) and engine particulates.

HYDROCARBONS

Hydrocarbons (HC) are essentially fuel which was not burned during the combustion process or which has escaped into the atmosphere through fuel evaporation. The main sources of incomplete combustion are rich air/fuel mixtures, low engine temperatures and improper spark timing. The main sources of hydrocarbon emission through fuel evaporation on most vehicles used to be the vehicle's fuel tank and carburetor float bowl.

To reduce combustion hydrocarbon emission, engine modifications were made to minimize dead space and surface area in the combustion chamber. In addition, the air/fuel mixture was made more lean through the improved control which feedback carburetion and fuel injection offers and by the addition of external controls to aid in further combustion of the hydrocarbons outside the engine. Two such methods were the addition of air injection systems, to inject fresh air into the exhaust manifolds and the installation of catalytic converters, units that are able to burn traces of hydrocarbons without affecting the internal combustion process or fuel economy.

To control hydrocarbon emissions through fuel evaporation,

modifications were made to the fuel tank to allow storage of the fuel vapors during periods of engine shut-down. Modifications were also made to the air intake system so that at specific times during engine operation, these vapors may be purged and burned by blending them with the air/fuel mixture.

CARBON MONOXIDE

Carbon monoxide is formed when not enough oxygen is present during the combustion process to convert carbon (C) to carbon dioxide (CO_2). An increase in the carbon monoxide (CO) emission is normally accompanied by an increase in the hydrocarbon (HC) emission because of the lack of oxygen to completely burn all of the fuel mixture.

Carbon monoxide (CO) also increases the rate at which the photo chemical smog is formed by speeding up the conversion of nitric oxide (NO) to nitrogen dioxide (NO_2). To accomplish this, carbon monoxide (CO) combines with oxygen (O_2) and nitric oxide (NO) to produce carbon dioxide (CO_2) and nitrogen dioxide (NO_2). ($CO + O_2 + NO \rightarrow CO_2 + NO_2$).

The dangers of carbon monoxide, which is an odorless and colorless toxic gas are many. When carbon monoxide is inhaled into the lungs and passed into the blood stream, oxygen is replaced by the carbon monoxide in the red blood cells, causing a reduction in the amount of oxygen supplied to the many parts of the body. This lack of oxygen causes headaches, lack of coordination, reduced mental alertness and, should the carbon monoxide concentration be high enough, death could result.

NITROGEN

Normally, nitrogen is an inert gas. When heated to approximately 2500°F (1371°C) through the combustion process, this gas becomes active and causes an increase in the nitric oxide (NO) emission.

Oxides of nitrogen (NOx) are composed of approximately 97–98 percent nitric oxide (NO). Nitric oxide is a colorless gas but when it is passed into the atmosphere, it combines with oxygen and forms nitrogen dioxide (NO_2). The nitrogen dioxide then combines with chemically active hydrocarbons (HC) and when in the presence of sunlight, causes the formation of photo-chemical smog.

Ozone

To further complicate matters, some of the nitrogen dioxide (NO_2) is broken apart by the sunlight to form nitric oxide and oxygen. (NO_2 + sunlight $\rightarrow$ NO + O). This single atom of oxygen then combines with diatomic (meaning 2 atoms) oxygen (O_2) to form ozone (O_3). Ozone is one of the smells associated with smog. It has a pungent and offensive odor, irritates the eyes and lung tissues, affects the growth of plant life and causes rapid deterioration of rubber products. Ozone can be formed by sunlight as well as electrical discharge into the air.

The most common discharge area on the automobile engine is the secondary ignition electrical system, especially when inferior quality spark plug cables are used. As the surge of high voltage is routed through the secondary cable, the circuit builds up an electrical field around the wire, which acts upon the oxygen in the surrounding air to form the ozone. The faint glow along the cable

with the engine running that may be visible on a dark night, is called the "corona discharge." It is the result of the electrical field passing from a high along the cable, to a low in the surrounding air, which forms the ozone gas. The combination of corona and ozone has been a major cause of cable deterioration. Recently, different and better quality insulating materials have lengthened the life of the electrical cables.

Although ozone at ground level can be harmful, ozone is beneficial to the earth's inhabitants. By having a concentrated ozone layer called the "ozonosphere," between 10 and 20 miles (16–32 km) up in the atmosphere, much of the ultra violet radiation from the sun's rays are absorbed and screened. If this ozone layer were not present, much of the earth's surface would be burned, dried and unfit for human life.

OXIDES OF SULFUR

Oxides of sulfur (SOx) were initially ignored in the exhaust system emissions, since the sulfur content of gasoline as a fuel is less than 1/10 of 1 percent. Because of this small amount, it was felt that it contributed very little to the overall pollution problem. However, because of the difficulty in solving the sulfur emissions in industrial pollutions and the introduction of catalytic converter to the automobile exhaust systems, a change was mandated. The automobile exhaust system, when equipped with a catalytic converter, changes the sulfur dioxide (SO_2) into sulfur trioxide (SO_3).

When this combines with water vapors (H_2O), a sulfuric acid mist (H_2SO_4) is formed and is a very difficult pollutant to handle since it is extremely corrosive. This sulfuric acid mist that is formed, is the same mist that rises from the vents of an automobile battery when an active chemical reaction takes place within the battery cells.

When a large concentration of vehicles equipped with catalytic converters are operating in an area, this acid mist may rise and be distributed over a large ground area causing land, plant, crop, paint and building damage.

PARTICULATE MATTER

A certain amount of particulate matter is present in the burning of any fuel, with carbon constituting the largest percentage of the particulates. In gasoline, the remaining particulates are the burned remains of the various other compounds used in its manufacture. When a gasoline engine is in good internal condition, the particulate emissions are low but as the engine wears internally, the particulate emissions increase. By visually inspecting the tail pipe emissions, a determination can be made as to where an engine defect may exist. An engine with light gray or blue smoke emitting from the tail pipe normally indicates an increase in the oil consumption through burning due to internal engine wear. Black smoke would indicate a defective fuel delivery system, causing the engine to operate in a rich mode. Regardless of the color of the smoke, the internal part of the engine or the fuel delivery system should be repaired to prevent excess particulate emissions.

Diesel and turbine engines emit a darkened plume of smoke from the exhaust system because of the type of fuel used. Emission control regulations are mandated for this type of emission and more stringent measures are being used to prevent excess emission of the particulate matter. Electronic components are being introduced to control the injection of the fuel at precisely the proper time of piston travel, to achieve the optimum in fuel ignition and fuel usage. Other particulate after-burning components are being tested to achieve a cleaner emission.

Good grades of engine lubricating oils should be used, which meet the manufacturers specification. Cut-rate oils can contribute to the particulate emission problem because of their low flash or ignition temperature point. Such oils burn prematurely during the combustion process causing emission of particulate matter.

The cooling system is an important factor in the reduction of particulate matter. The optimum combustion will occur, with the cooling system operating at a temperature specified by the manufacturer. The cooling system must be maintained in the same manner as the engine oiling system, as each system is required to perform properly in order for the engine to operate efficiently for a long time.

Crankcase Emissions

Crankcase emissions are made up of water, acids, unburned fuel, oil fumes and particulates. These emissions are classified as hydrocarbons (HC) and are formed by the small amount of unburned, compressed air/fuel mixture entering the crankcase from the combustion area (between the cylinder walls and piston rings) during the compression and power strokes. The head of the compression and combustion help to form the remaining crankcase emissions.

Since the first engines, crankcase emissions were allowed into the atmosphere through a road draft tube, mounted on the lower side of the engine block. Fresh air came in through an open oil filler cap or breather. The air passed through the crankcase mixing with blow-by gases. The motion of the vehicle and the air blowing past the open end of the road draft tube caused a low pressure area (vacuum) at the end of the tube. Crankcase emissions were simply drawn out of the road draft tube into the air.

To control the crankcase emission, the road draft tube was deleted. A hose and/or tubing was routed from the crankcase to the intake manifold so the blow-by emission could be burned with the air/fuel mixture. However, it was found that intake manifold vacuum, used to draw the crankcase emissions into the manifold, would vary in strength at the wrong time and not allow the proper emission flow. A regulating valve was needed to control the flow of air through the crankcase.

Testing, showed the removal of the blow-by gases from the crankcase as quickly as possible, was most important to the longevity of the engine. Should large accumulations of blow-by

gases remain and condense, dilution of the engine oil would occur to form water, soots, resins, acids and lead salts, resulting in the formation of sludge and varnishes. This condensation of the blow-by gases occurs more frequently on vehicles used in numerous starting and stopping conditions, excessive idling and when the engine is not allowed to attain normal operating temperature through short runs.

Evaporative Emissions

Gasoline fuel is a major source of pollution, before and after it is burned in the automobile engine. From the time the fuel is refined, stored, pumped and transported, again stored until it is pumped into the fuel tank of the vehicle, the gasoline gives off unburned hydrocarbons (HC) into the atmosphere. Through the redesign of storage areas and venting systems, the pollution factor was diminished, but not eliminated, from the refinery standpoint. However, the automobile still remained the primary source of vaporized, unburned hydrocarbon (HC) emissions.

Fuel pumped from an underground storage tank is cool but when exposed to a warmer ambient temperature, will expand. Before controls were mandated, an owner might fill the fuel tank with fuel from an underground storage tank and park the vehicle for some time in warm area, such as a parking lot. As the fuel would warm, it would expand and should no provisions or area be provided for the expansion, the fuel would spill out of the filler neck and onto the ground, causing hydrocarbon (HC) pollution and creating a severe fire hazard. To correct this condition, the vehicle manufacturers added overflow plumbing and/or gasoline tanks with built in expansion areas or domes.

However, this did not control the fuel vapor emission from the fuel tank. It was determined that most of the fuel evaporation occurred when the vehicle was stationary and the engine not operating. Most vehicles carry 5–25 gallons (19–95 liters) of gasoline. Should a large concentration of vehicles be parked in one area, such as a large parking lot, excessive fuel vapor emissions would take place, increasing as the temperature increases.

To prevent the vapor emission from escaping into the atmosphere, the fuel systems were designed to trap the vapors while the vehicle is stationary, by sealing the system from the atmosphere. A storage system is used to collect and hold the fuel vapors from the carburetor (if equipped) and the fuel tank when the engine is not operating. When the engine is started, the storage system is then purged of the fuel vapors, which are drawn into the engine and burned with the air/fuel mixture.

EMISSION CONTROLS

Description

Beginning in 1968, various modifications were incorporated on Mercedes-Benz engines to meet Federal emissions control regulations. Since 1968, these modifications have been continually updated and improved.

The following emission controls and modifications were used on 1968 carbureted engines:
• Modifications to the Manifold Air-Oxidation System.

• Changes to the ignition timing and distributor advance curves to provide better combustion in the middle rpm ranges.
• A Port Burning System, which uses a belt driven pump to force in air directly behind the exhaust valves, creating an afterburning effect.
• Modified carburetor jets to provide a leaner carburetor mixture.

Fuel injected engines required no modifications in 1968.

In 1971, the design of the combustion chambers was changed

and the spark plugs were set deeper on 6-cylinder engines. Better cooling is accomplished by adding more cooling jackets. All 4 and 6-cylinder engines are equipped with a Fuel Evaporation Control System.

In 1972, the engine compression ratio was reduced to 8.0:1 on all engines except the diesel. Automatic transmission shift points were modified. The fuel evaporation control system remained unchanged, although the evaporation control valve was redesigned and relocated under the rear seat.

The fuel evaporation system remained unchanged in 1973, but the 2-way valves previously used were replaced by switchover valves that are identical in appearance. To be able to distinguish the function of the individual valves, the covers are color coded according to valve function, as follows:

- WHITE—advanced ignition valve
- RED—retarded ignition valve
- GRAY—throttle opening valve
- BROWN—exhaust gas recycling (EGR) valve

➡**It is important that the vacuum line always be connected to the center connection, whether it is on the top or the bottom.**

1974 Vehicles

Design and function of the system remains basically unchanged from 1973, except for the addition of an air pump on 280, 280C and 450 California models.

It is impossible to list test procedures for all the various switches and valves in this book, so only basic tests and results appear here.

The following tests should be performed on a warm engine at normal operating temperature, and should be performed in the sequence listed. Be sure to check the fuses if a malfunction is suspected.

230 MODELS

◆ **See Figure 1**

Ignition changeover is accomplished through vacuum and oil temperature. Vacuum retard is only activated during acceleration, while vacuum advance is activated under the following conditions:

- Oil temperature below 77°F.
- Oil temperature above 77°F and engine speed above 2000 rpm.

The throttle valve is also opened slightly during coasting, through a vacuum governor on the carburetor.

Exhaust gas is being recycled by the EGR valve under the following condition:

- Oil temperature above 77°F up to 3600 rpm.

Exhaust gas recirculation is not effective under the following conditions:

- Oil temperature above 77°F up to 3600.
- Speed above 3600 rpm.

Testing the System

77°F TEMPERATURE SWITCH

1. Disconnect the plug to the temperature switch in the oil filter housing and ground it. The engine rpm should increase, indicating that vacuum advance is present.

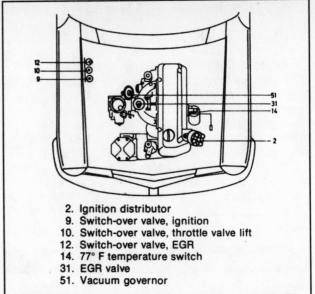

2. Ignition distributor
9. Switch-over valve, ignition
10. Switch-over valve, throttle valve lift
12. Switch-over valve, EGR
14. 77° F temperature switch
31. EGR valve
51. Vacuum governor

Fig. 1 Emission control component locations—1974 230 models

2. Increase the engine speed to about 2500 rpm and remove the red vacuum line at the distributor. The engine rpm should drop slightly, indicating that vacuum advance is no longer present.

If the results are not as specified, check the connections of the vacuum lines. The blue line from the carburetor should go to the center port of the red switchover valve and the red line should go from the outer port of the switchover valve to the distributor.

EGR SWITCHOVER VALVE

1. Place your hand over the brown EGR switchover valve. It may be necessary to remove the valve to isolate its operation. Increase the engine speed. The valve should be felt to switch.

2. If it does not function, check the voltage at the plug. If no voltage is measured at the plug, below 3600 rpm, replace the rpm relay.

EGR VALVE

1. Connect the EGR valve directly to intake manifold vacuum with the blue vacuum line. The engine should run poorly or stall, indicating that the valve is open.

2. If the speed does not change, remove the valve and connect it to vacuum. The valve stem should lift from its seat. Remove exhaust deposits from the valve with a 10mm drill and blow it clean with compressed air.

VACUUM GOVERNOR

1. Connect a tachometer and increase engine speed to about 2500 rpm and release the throttle slowly. The vacuum governor should pop out above 2000 rpm and retract below 1800 rpm.

If not, check the vacuum lines. The blue line should connect the center port of the gray switchover valve. The gray line should connect the vacuum governor and the outer port of the switchover valve.

2. If the vacuum lines are connected properly, remove the relay box plug and connect terminals 2 and 8. With the ignition **ON**, the switchover valve should click. If the switchover valve functions properly, the relay box is defective.

280 & 280C MODELS (FEDERAL)

♦ **See Figure 2**

An ignition changeover is installed to retard or advance the ignition. Ignition is retarded under the following conditions:

1. When the oil temperature is above 62°F and coolant temperature is below 212°F.
2. Engine speed is below 3200 rpm.

Ignition retard is negated under the following conditions:
- Oil temperature below 62°F.
- Coolant temperature above 212°F.
- Engine speed above 3200 rpm and oil temperature above 62°F, and coolant temperature below 212°F.
- When shifting into fourth gear.
- When switching on the air conditioner.
- With vacuum between 0 and 2.8 psi.

A throttle positioner is installed which will open the throttle slightly when the oil temperature is above 62°F, when the coolant temperature is below 212°F and when engine speed exceeds 200 rpm.

Exhaust gases are recycled when engine oil temperature is above 62°F, when coolant temperature is below 212°F and when manifold vacuum is between 0 and 2.8 psi, up to 3200 rpm.

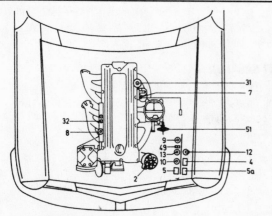

2. Distributor
4. RPM relay
5. Relay box (8 prong)
5a. Relay box (12 prong)
7. 62° F temperature switch
8. 212° F temperature switch
9. Ignition switch-over valve
10. Throttle valve lift switch-over valve
12. EGR switch-over valve
13. Vacuum switch
31. EGR valve
32. 149° F temperature switch
49. Connection at relay support
51. Vacuum governor

Fig. 2 Emission control component locations—1974 280 and 280C models (Federal)

Testing the System

IGNITION TIMING

1. Check the ignition timing. It should be as specified.
2. If not, check all vacuum connections and the temperature switches before adjusting the timing.

62°F TEMPERATURE SWITCH

1. Disconnect the plug of the relay box.
2. Connect a voltmeter to terminals 5 and 8.
3. The voltmeter should indicate 0 volts when the oil temperature is above 62°F.

212°F TEMPERATURE SWITCH

1. Disconnect the plug from the relay box.
2. Connect a test lamp to terminals 4 and 8.
3. Switch on the ignition.
4. The test lamp should light when coolant temperature is above 212°F.

THROTTLE POSITIONER

1. Connect a tachometer to the engine.
2. Start the engine and increase the speed to approximately 2500 rpm.
3. Release the accelerator linkage and observe the tachometer. At speeds above 1800 rpm, the adjusting screw should rest against the actuating lever. At speeds below 1800 rpm, the adjusting screw should be off the actuating lever.

RPM SWITCH

Use only a voltmeter to test the rpm switch.

1. Disconnect the plug of the switch valve and connect a voltmeter.
2. Start the engine and increase speed.
3. The voltmeter should indicate about 13 volts, above 2000 rpm.
4. Decrease speed below about 1800 rpm and the voltmeter should read approximately 0 volts.

EGR SWITCH VALVE

1. Disconnect the plug from the switch valve and connect a tachometer.
2. Connect a voltmeter and increase rpm.
3. The voltmeter should read about 13 volts up to 3200 rpm.

149°F TEMPERATURE SWITCH

1. Disconnect the plug from the relay box and connect a voltmeter to terminals 6 and 8.
2. The voltmeter should indicate approximately 13 volts above 149°F.

VACUUM SWITCH

1. Disconnect the plug from the relay box and connect a voltmeter to terminals 7 and 8.
2. Idle the engine.
3. The voltmeter should indicate 0 volts.
4. Disconnect the vacuum line from the switch. The voltmeter should now indicate about 13 volts.

EGR RPM SWITCH

1. Disconnect the plug from the relay box.
2. Connect a voltmeter to terminals 1 and 3.
3. Start the engine and increase speed.
4. The voltmeter should indicate 0 volts up to approximately 3200 rpm. Beyond that, voltage should be about 13 volts.
5. When rpm decreases, the voltmeter should return to 0 volts at about 2800 rpm.

EGR VALVE

1. Start the engine and run it at idle.
2. Remove the lower, brown vacuum line from the EGR switchover valve and connect it to the carburetor in place of the blue vacuum line.
3. If the EGR valve is working, the engine will idle roughly or stop running. If the engine does not do one or the other, replace the EGR valve.
4. Do not forget to replace the vacuum lines.

280 & 280C MODELS (CALIFORNIA)

‣ **See Figure 2a**

The California system for these cars is a modification of the Federal system. A Saginaw air pump is used and a reactor with injection tubes is used in place of an exhaust manifold.

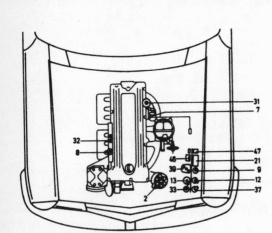

2. Distributor
7. 62° F temperature switch
8. 212° F temperature switch
9. Switchover valve, ignition
12. Switchover valve, EGR
13. Vacuum switch
21. Relay box
31. EGR valve
32. 149° F temperature switch
33. Switchover valve, air injection
37. Switchover valve, fuel evaporation system
39. Charcoal canister
46. Resistor for automatic choke
47. Relay for resistor, automatic choke

Fig. 2a Emission control component locations—1974 280 and 280C models (California)

Testing the System

62°F TEMPERATURE SWITCH

1. Disconnect and ground the plug to the switch in the oil filter housing. The engine rpm should increase. If not disconnect the relay box plug and connect terminals 2 and 10. With the ignition **ON** the valve should click. If the valve clicks, replace the relay box.

212°F TEMPERATURE SWITCH

1. Unplug and ground the temperature switch. The engine should increase and the auxiliary should run. If not, replace the relay box.

RELAY BOX VOLTAGE

1. Turn the air conditioner ON. The engine speed should not drop. If the engine speed decreases, remove the relay box plug and connect a voltmeter to terminals 3 and 8 of the plug. If less than 13 volts is present, replace the relay box, or, if no voltage is present, check the air conditioner circuit.

VACUUM SWITCHOVER VALVE

1. Remove the vacuum line from the top of the switchover valve and remove the blue line from the vacuum switch. The engine speed should increase. A voltmeter should read 13 volts between terminals 11 and 2 of the relay box plug with the engine running. Remove the vacuum line from the vacuum switch. No voltage should be present. If both readings are correct, replace the relay box.

EGR VALVE AND VACUUM SWITCHOVER VALVE

1. Remove the blue vacuum line from the vacuum switch. The engine should run poorly or stall.
2. Unplug the brown vacuum line at the connection on the firewall and connect it to the vacuum line for air conditioning. The engine should run poorly or stall. If the switchover valve and EGR valve are functioning, replace the relay box.

ANTI-BACKFIRE VALVE

1. Disconnect the center hose on the air filter. There should be no air flow. If the switchover valve clicks by bridging terminals 1 and 2 of the relay box plug, the anti-backfire valve must be replaced.

AIR INJECTION SWITCHOVER VALVE

1. Increase engine speed slowly to above 3450 rpm. The air flow should stop in the injection line at about 3450 rpm.

AUTOMATIC CHOKE RELAY

1. Disconnect the plug to the 62°F temperature switch in the oil filter housing and ground the switch. The automatic choke resistor relay should click. Voltage at the switch should be about 13 volts. If none is present, replace the relay box.

FLOAT CHAMBER VENT VALVE

1. Shut the engine OFF. Disconnect the gray vacuum line at the float chamber vent valve on the carburetor. No vacuum should be present. Reconnect the line.
2. Start the engine and remove the line again. A hissing sound should indicate the presence of vacuum. If no vacuum is present, remove the float chamber vent valve. With the vacuum lines connected, turn the ignition **ON** and **OFF**. The valve stem should move in and out. If not, replace the vent valve diaphragm.

CHARCOAL CANISTER PURGE VALVE

1. Remove the thin center hose from the charcoal canister and close the end of the hose with your finger. Increase engine speed to more than 2000 rpm. At idle, slight vacuum should be felt, increasing with engine speed. If not, the purge valve should be replaced, or there is a restriction in the line.

450SL, 450SLC, 450SE & 450SEL MODELS (FEDERAL)

♦ **See Figure 3**

A two-way valve is installed in the vacuum line between the venturi control unit and the distributor. Ignition timing is retarded when the two-way valve is not energized, and advanced when the valve is energized (circuit completed to ground). The valve is controlled by a 212°F temperature switch in the thermostat housing, which activates the valve above coolant temperatures of 212°F.

A fuel shut-off solenoid cuts off the delivery of fuel under the following conditions:

1. Accelerator pedal is in the idling position.
2. Engine speed is above 1500 rpm, determined by an electronic control unit. There is no fuel shut-off when coolant temperature is below −4°F.

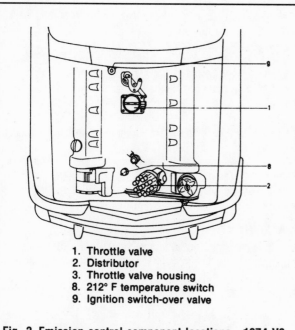

1. Throttle valve
2. Distributor
3. Throttle valve housing
8. 212° F temperature switch
9. Ignition switch-over valve

Fig. 3 Emission control component locations—1974 V8 engines (Federal)

Testing the System

IGNITION CHANGEOVER DEVICE

1. Connect a timing light and check the timing at idle. It should be as specified.
2. Ground the connection of the 212°F temperature switch. The ignition timing should advance by 15° and engine speed should increase by about 300 rpm.
3. Check the oil pressure switch. This can only be done on the road or on a dynamometer. Connect a test lamp to the B+ terminal and terminal 87 of the relay. Disconnect the relay. Above a speed of 40 mph, the test lamp should light. Below approximately 30 mph, the light should go out.
4. Check the 212°F switch by connecting a test lamp to the B+ terminal and to the switch. At a coolant temperature above 212°F, the light should come on.

5. If there is no ignition changeover and the oil pressure switch is working, check the following:
   a. Fuse No. 6 in the main fuse box.
   b. All vacuum and electrical connections on the two-way valve.
   c. The two-way valve. Switch on the ignition and ground the oil pressure switch. This should energize the two-way valve.
   d. The relay. Connect a test lamp to the plug of the two-way valve. Switch on the ignition and ground the 212°F temperature switch. The relay is working if the lamp lights.

450SE, SEL, SL & SLC MODELS (CALIFORNIA)

♦ **See Figures 4 and 5**

The California system is a refinement of the Federal system and closely resembles it, with an added air pump.

Testing the System

212°F TEMPERATURE SWITCH

1. Unplug the temperature switch and ground it. The engine rpm should increase and the auxiliary fan should run on the 450SE and 450SEL. If not, connect terminals 3 and 4 of the relay box plug. With the ignition **ON**, the switchover valve should click. If not, replace the relay.
2. Switch ON the air conditioning. The engine rpm should rise slightly. If the engine rpm does not increase, check the air conditioning. If the air conditioning works, replace the relay.

EGR

1. Remove the air filter top cover and check that exhaust gas is emitted from the recirculation line in the throttle valve housing.

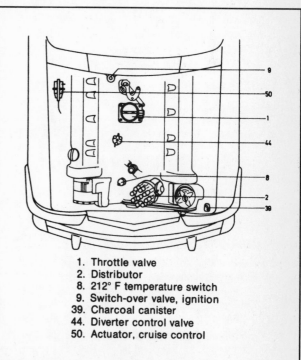

1. Throttle valve
2. Distributor
8. 212° F temperature switch
9. Switch-over valve, ignition
39. Charcoal canister
44. Diverter control valve
50. Actuator, cruise control

Fig. 4 Emission control component locations—1974 450SE and SEL models (California)

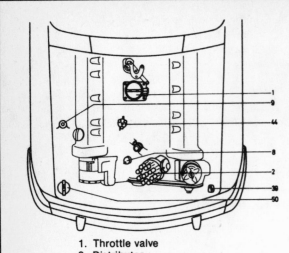

1. Throttle valve
2. Distributor
8. 212° F temperature switch
9. Switch-over valve, ignition
39. Charcoal canister
44. Diverter control valve
50. Actuator, cruise control

Fig. 5 Emission control component locations—1974 450SL and SLC models (California)

If no exhaust is emitted into the throttle valve housing, clean the throttle housing and EGR line.

DIVERTER CONTROL VALVE

1. Remove the air filter housing and lay it aside without unplugging the warm air sensor. Disconnect the brown vacuum line at the diverter control valve. Increase the rpm to over 2000 and release the throttle linkage. Vacuum should be present at the port of the diverter valve only when the throttle linkage is released. A hissing sound should be heard.

2. If no vacuum is present, replace the diverter valve.

CO CONTENT

1. Check the CO content of the exhaust gas. It should be a maximum of 1.0% WITH OR WITHOUT air injection. To check the CO, remove the air filter housing and lay it aside without unplugging the warm air sensor. Disconnect the brown vacuum line at the diverter valve and connect this to the vacuum supply line for the cruise control actuator.

2. If the CO content varies with or without air injection, check the brown vacuum line to the diverter valve for tightness. Also check the diverter valve.

CHARCOAL CANISTER PURGE VALVE

See this test under "280 and 280C (California Only)." The 1975 emission control equipment closely resembles that for 1974. The 230 (California only) and all other gasoline engines are equipped with catalysts. These models must be operated only with unleaded gasoline.

All of the following tests should be made in the specified sequence with the engine at operating temperature.

As of 1975, the base color of vacuum lines for emission control is white. Lines originating at a vacuum source have only one color stripe. These lines are connected to the center connection of the switchover valve of the same color. Lines terminating at a vac-

uum operated device have 2 color stripes. Purple is always the second color. The lines are connected to the outer connection of the switchover valve of the same color.

Switchover valve filter caps are color coded as follows:
- RED—Valve for ignition advance
- GRAY—Valve for throttle lift
- BROWN—Valve for EGR
- BLUE—Valve for air injection

1975 Vehicles

230 MODELS

◆ **See Figure 6**

Testing the System

77°F TEMPERATURE SWITCH

1. Disconnect the temperature switch plug and ground the switch. The engine rpm should increase.

2. If not, check the vacuum line connections.

3. Unplug the relay box and connect terminals 7 and 1; an audible click should be heard. If not, replace the relay box.

4. Disconnect and ground the temperature switch. Place your hand over the air pump muffler. A light air flow should be present.

5. If no air flow is present, check the vacuum line connections (see Step 2).

6. Disconnect the plug from the relay box and connect terminals 6 and 7. The blue switchover valve should click. If not, replace the switchover valve. If the valve does click, the relay is defective.

RPM SWITCH

1. Increase engine speed to about 2500 rpm and remove the red/purple vacuum line from the distributor. The engine speed

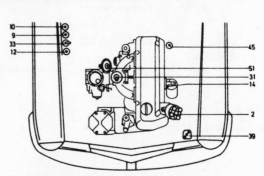

2. Distributor
9. Switch-over valve, ignition (red)
10. Switch-over valve, throttle lift (gray)
12. Switch-over valve, EGR (brown)
14. 77° F temperature switch
31. EGR valve
33. Switch-over valve, air injection (blue)
45. Muffler (air filter for noise suppression)
51. Vacuum control, throttle lift

Fig. 6 Emission control component locations—1975–76 230 models

should drop slightly. Below about 2000 rpm, there should be 13 volts at the switch. If there is less than 11 volts, temporarily replace the rpm relay or relay box and repeat the test.

EGR SWITCHOVER VALVE

1. Disconnect the brown vacuum line at the carburetor and brown/purple vacuum line at the carburetor. Blow into the brown vacuum line and simultaneously increase the rpm to about 3600. At idle, air can be blown through the line, while above 3600, no air should pass.

EGR VALVE

1. Connect the EGR valve to intake manifold vacuum. Disconnect the red line at the carburetor and the brown/purple line at the carburetor. Connect both lines together. The engine should run poorly or stall. If not be sure that the valve stem is moving and if not, replace the valve. If the valve works, clean the EGR valve with a 10 mm drill.

VACUUM GOVERNOR

1. Increase the engine speed to about 2500 rpm and release the throttle slowly. At the same time watch the vacuum control on the carburetor. It should pop out above 2000 rpm and retract below 1800 rpm. If not, remove the plug from the relay box and connect terminals 2 and 7. With the ignition **ON,** the valve should click audibly. If it does, replace the relay box.

280, 280C & 280S MODELS

♦ **See Figures 7 and 8**

The system remains basically unchanged except for different color coding of vacuum lines and addition of a catalytic converter in all states.

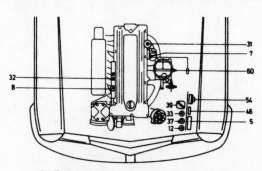

5. Relay box
7. 62° F temperature switch
8. 212° F temperature switch
12. Switch-over valve, EGR (brown)
31. EGR valve
32. 149° F temperature switch
33. Switch-over valve, air injection (blue)
37. Switch-over valve, fuel evaporation control system (green)
39. Charcoal canister
46. Resistor, automatic choke cover
54. Vacuum booster
60. Venturi connection

Fig. 7 Emission control component locations—1975–76 280 and 280C models

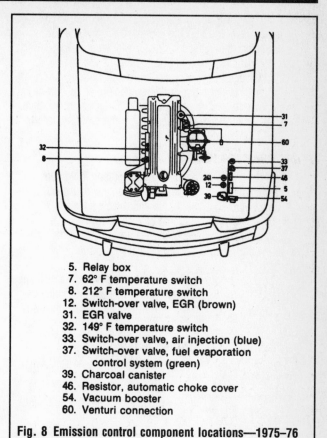

5. Relay box
7. 62° F temperature switch
8. 212° F temperature switch
12. Switch-over valve, EGR (brown)
31. EGR valve
32. 149° F temperature switch
33. Switch-over valve, air injection (blue)
37. Switch-over valve, fuel evaporation control system (green)
39. Charcoal canister
46. Resistor, automatic choke cover
54. Vacuum booster
60. Venturi connection

Fig. 8 Emission control component locations—1975–76 280S models

Testing the System

EGR VALVE

1. Remove the brown/purple vacuum line from the EGR valve and turn the ignition **ON.** Blow air into the line. Place the gear selector in a driving position (not N or P). The line should be closed.

2. Remove the brown vacuum line on the carburetor and the green line on the carburetor. Connect the brown line in place of the green line. Start the engine and place the gear selector in a driving position (not N or P).

3. The engine should run roughly or stall. If not, either the vacuum booster or the EGR valve is at fault.

AIR INJECTION

1. Remove the air injection hose at the air filter (center hose) and run the engine at idle. There should be no air flow present. If air is discharged at idle, replace the diverter valve.

62°F. TEMPERATURE SWITCH

1. Disconnect the plug from the switch in the oil filter housing and ground the switch. Air flow in the injection line should cease. If it does not, disconnect the plug from the blue switchover valve and connect a voltmeter. Disconnect and ground the temperature switch. Turn the ignition **ON;** the voltmeter should read about 12 volts. If no voltage is present, replace the relay box.

AUTOMATIC CHOKE RESISTOR

1. Connect a voltmeter to the resistor outlet (top connection) and to ground. Disconnect the plug of the 62°F temperature

switch and connect it to ground. Disconnect the plug of the 149°F temperature switch and turn the ignition **ON.** With the 62°F switch grounded, the voltmeter should read about 7–8 volts. If the ground is interrupted, it should read about 12 volts.

2. If the voltage is not as specified, check the relay box. Connect a voltmeter to the input of the resistor (lower connection) and to ground. Ground the plug of the 62°F temperature switch and the voltmeter should read about 12 volts. If not, replace the relay box.

FLOAT CHAMBER VENT VALVE

1. Connect a vacuum gauge to the green/purple vacuum line to the float chamber vent valve. Start the engine and briefly accelerate. The vacuum should build up and remain constant. With the ignition **OFF,** the vacuum should drop to zero.

2. If no vacuum is present, connect a voltmeter to the switchover valve. About 13 volts should be present, and the valve should click audibly.

If vacuum does not remain constant, unscrew the float chamber vent valve. With the vacuum line connected, run the engine at idle. The valve rod should move. If necessary, replace the valve vacuum diaphragm.

CHARCOAL CANISTER PURGE VALVE

See this test under "1974 280 and 280C Models (California)." The test is the same.

450SE, SEL, SL & SLC MODELS

◗ **See Figures 9 and 10**

This system is basically the same as the 1974 system with the addition of a dual diaphragm distributor and catalytic converter.

Testing the System

212°F TEMPERATURE SWITCH

See this test under "1974 450SL, SLC and 450SE, SEL." It is identical, except for color coding.

VACUUM CONTROL UNIT

1. Remove the yellow/purple and red/purple vacuum lines from the vacuum control on the distributor. The engine rpm should increase slightly. Connect the yellow/purple vacuum line to the upper connection of the vacuum control unit. The engine speed should increase slightly. If not, replace the vacuum control unit.

EGR SWITCHOVER VALVE

1. Remove the red/purple vacuum line at the EGR valve. Connect a vacuum gauge to the red/purple line and to the red connection of the EGR valve. Run the engine at idle and increase the rpm to 2500. At idle, the gauge should show no vacuum. At higher rpm, there should be some vacuum.

2. If not, shut the engine **OFF** and turn the ignition to **ON.** Remove the plug from the 104°F. temperature switch. The switchover valve should click. If it does not click, replace the switchover valve with a new one and repeat the test. If it still does not click, replace the relay.

EGR VACUUM CONTROL SWITCH

1. Remove the brown/purple vacuum line from the EGR valve. Connect a vacuum gauge to the brown/purple line and to the bottom of the EGR valve. Start the engine and increase speed to

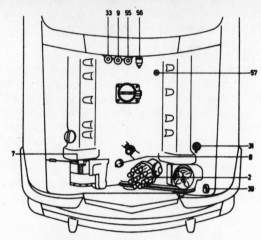

2. Distributor
7. 62° F (17° C) temperature switch
8. 202° F (100° C) temperature switch
9. Switch-over valve, ignition retard (yellow)
31. EGR valve
33. Switch-over valve, air injection (blue)
39. Charcoal canister
55. Switch-over valve, EGR/ ignition advance (red)
56. Vacuum control switch
57. 104° F (40° C) temperature switch

Fig. 9 Emission control component locations—1975 450SE and SEL models

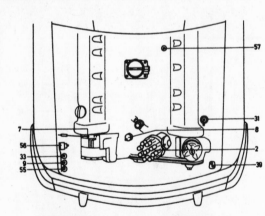

2. Distributor
7. 62° F (17° C) temperature switch
8. 202° F (100° C) temperature switch
9. Switch-over valve, ignition retard (yellow)
31. EGR valve
33. Switch-over valve, air injection (blue)
39. Charcoal canister
55. Switch-over valve, EGR/ ignition advance (red)
56. Vacuum control switch
57. 104° F (40° C) temperature switch

Fig. 10 Emission control component locations—1975 450SL and SLC models

2500 rpm. At idle, the gauge should show no vacuum. During acceleration, vacuum should be present for a brief period until engine rpm stabilizes at a higher speed.

2. If no vacuum can be measured and the vacuum lines are correctly attached, the vacuum control switch is defective.

EGR VALVE

1. Remove the yellow/purple vacuum line from the vacuum control unit on the distributor. Disconnect the vacuum lines from the EGR valve. With a vacuum test line, connect the yellow/purple line with the upper, and then the lower connection of the EGR valve. The engine should run roughly or stall in both operating phases of the EGR valve.

3. If the engine does not run roughly or stall, the EGR valve should be replaced.

CO EXHAUST GAS CONTENT

1. Run the engine at idle. Test the CO content of the exhaust gas. Disconnect the plug for the 62°F temperature switch and ground it with a test cable. Measure the CO again without air injection. The CO content should change noticeably.

2. If it does not change noticeably, disconnect and ground the 62° temperature switch. The blue switchover valve should click. If it doesn't, replace the switchover valve.

3. If the switchover valve functions, remove the air filter on the diverter valve. Disconnect and ground the 62°F temperature switch. Air should exit from the diverter valve. If there is no air flow, replace the diverter valve and repeat the test. Also, check the air pump and air pump drive belt tension.

CHARCOAL CANISTER PURGE VALVE

Refer to this test under "1974 280 and 280C Models (California)."

1976 Vehicles

The 1976 emission control system is close to the system used in 1975. Catalytic converters are used on all engines, but the 450 series cars have the catalysts installed on the exhaust manifold. Due to Federal regulations, the routing of the fuel evaporation lines has been changed.

230 MODELS

▶ **See Figure 6**

Refer to the 1975 230 model Emission Control System testing procedures.

280, 280C & 280S MODELS

▶ **See Figures 7 and 8**

Refer to the 1975 280, 280C and 280S model Emission Control System testing procedures.

450SE, SEL, SL & SLC MODELS

▶ **See Figure 11**

These cars with the M117 engine use one emission system for the entire U.S. market, including California.

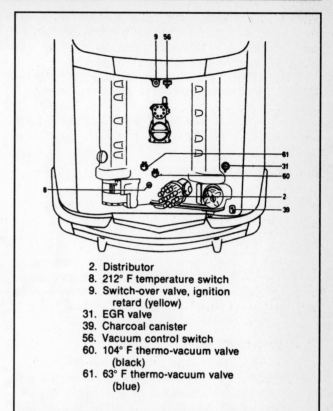

2. Distributor
8. 212° F temperature switch
9. Switch-over valve, ignition retard (yellow)
31. EGR valve
39. Charcoal canister
56. Vacuum control switch
60. 104° F thermo-vacuum valve (black)
61. 63° F thermo-vacuum valve (blue)

Fig. 11 Emission control component locations—1976 450SE, SEL, SL and SLC models

The base color of the vacuum lines is opaque (white). Lines originating at a vacuum source have only one color stripe; lines terminating at a vacuum source have 2-color stripes. Purple is always the second color.

Thermo vacuum valves are used to control the ignition changeover, EGR and air injection. They are color coded:

Black—104°F valve
Blue—63°F valve

The retard side of the vacuum control unit is only activated when the coolant is below 212°F during deceleration with the A/C off. The advance side of the vacuum control unit is activated when temperatures at the thermo-valve are 104°F or above and the advance is determined by the position of the throttle plate.

The EGR valve works in 2 stages. The first stage (small amount) takes place with coolant temperature above 104°F. There is no EGR with coolant temperature below 86°F.

The second (larger) stage of EGR occurs during acceleration with coolant temperature above 140°F and vacuum less than 7.9 in. Hg.

Air injection takes place above 62°F and is cancelled below 50°F (coolant temperatures).

Testing the System

IGNITION CHANGEOVER SWITCH

Unplug and ground the temperature switch. The engine rpm should increase and the auxiliary fan should operate.

If the engine speed does not increase, check the vacuum lines. The yellow line from the throttle valve housing should go to the center of the yellow switchover valve. The yellow/purple line goes to the outer connection of the switchover valve to the inner chamber of the vacuum unit (retard). Disconnect the plug from the relay and bridge terminals 3 and 4. With the ignition **ON,** the switchover valve should click. If not, replace the relay. If the switchover valve does not function, replace the valve.

Check the auxiliary fan. Disconnect the relay and bridge terminals 1 and 3. With ignition **ON;** the fan should run. If not, replace the fan.

Check othe relay. Remove the plug and bridge terminals 1 and 3. With the ignition **ON,** the fans hould run. If so, replace the relay.

IGNITION RETARD RELAY

Switch on the A/C. The engine rpm should increase slightly. If not, check that the A/C is operating. If the A/C is operating, replace the relay.

IGNITION ADVANCE

Remove the yellow/purple and red/purple vacuum lines from the distributor. The engine speed should increase slightly. Connect the yellow/purple vacuum line to the upper connection at the vacuum diaphragm. The engine speed should increase.

If not, replace the 2-way vacuum diaphragm.

EGR SWITCHOVER VALVE

Remove the red/purple vacuum line at the EGR valve. Connect a vacuum gauge to the red/purple line and run the engine at idle. Increase speed to 2500 rpm. At idle, the gauge should show no vacuum; at 2500 rpm, vacuum should be present.

If no vacuum is indicated, check the line connections. The red line from the red connection at the throttle valve housing should go to the angular connection of the thermovacuum valve. The red/purple line should be attached to the vertical connection at the thermo-vacuum valve, to the red connection of the vacuum control switch and red connection of the EGR valve.

Check the 104°F thermo-vacuum valve. It should open if the surrounding temperature is above 104°F. It should close below 86°F. If the valve is not functioning properly, check the bore of the throttle housing vacuum connection.

VACUUM CONTROL SWITCH

Remove the brown/purple vacuum line from the EGR valve. Connect a vacuum gauge between the line and the bottom of the EGR valve. Increase engine speed to 2500 rpm. At idle, vacuum should not be present. During acceleration, vacuum should be present briefly until the rpm stabilizes. If no vacuum is present, check the vacuum lines. The red/purple line should be connected to the red connection at the vacuum control switch, the white line to the center of the vacuum control switch and the red/purple line to the brown control switch connection. If vacuum still is not present, replace the control switch.

EGR VALVE

Disconnect the yellow/purple line from the distributor diaphragm. Disconnect both vacuum lines at the EGR valve. Connect the yellow/purple line with the upper, then the lower connection of the EGR valve. The engine should run rough or stall in both cases. If not, replace the EGR valve.

DIVERTER VALVE

Run the engine at idle. Connect a CO tester. Note the reading. Remove the blue/purple vacuum line from the blue thermo-valve and note the reading again. It should change noticeably.

If not, check the vacuum lines. The blue line runs to the angu-

lar connection on the blue thermo-vacuum valve. The blue/purple line goes to the vertical connection of the same valve.

Check the diverter valve. Remove the muffler on the valve. Disconnect the blue/purple vacuum line at the blue thermo-vacuum valve. Air should flow from the diverter valve. If there is no air flow, replace the diverter valve. If necessary, check the drive belt tension.

CHARCOAL CANISTER

Remove the thin hose from the charcoal canister. Cover the hose opening with your finger or connect a vacuum gauge. Slowly increase rpm to 2,500. At idle, a small amount of vacuum should be present, and vacuum should increase with engine speed.

If no vacuum is present at idle, check the purge line to the intake manifold. Disconnect the charcoal canister hose at the purge valve and clean it by blowing through with compressed air in the direction of the intake manifold. Replace the purge valve if necessary.

If vacuum does not increase at idle, check the vacuum at the purge valve. Disconnect the white vacuum line at the purge valve. Connect a vacuum gauge or close the line with a finger. Increase engine speed. At idle, there should be no vacuum. With increasing engine speed, vacuum should increase. If vacuum is present, replace the purge valve. If no vacuum is present, blow through the line towards the throttle valve housing.

1977 Vehicles

The following tests should be performed in the order given with the engine at normal operating temperature.

230 MODELS

▶ **See Figure 12**

Testing the System

EGR VALVE

1. Run the engine at idle speed.
2. Remove the brown vacuum line at the carburetor and the gray vacuum line at the intake manifold. Connect the brown line at the intake manifold.
3. The engine should run roughly or stall. If the rpm does not change, check the vacuum line connections. Check for leaks and blow through the vacuum connection on the carburetor.
4. Check the thermo-vacuum valve (blue plastic portion and "50AB5" stamped in metal housing). Remove the brown/purple vacuum line and race the engine. Vacuum must be present at the open connection when accelerating.
5. Check the EGR valve. Remove the EGR valve. Connect the brown/purple vacuum line to the EGR valve and slowly increase engine rpm. Cover the bores in the intake manifold. The valve stem should lift from its seat; if not replace the EGR valve with a new one.

AIR INJECTION

1. Connect a CO tester to the test connection and remove the vacuum hose from the vertical connection of the thermo-vacuum valve. The air injection thermo-vacuum valve has "50AA13" stamped in the metal housing. Plug the connection on the valve. The CO reading should drop noticeably.

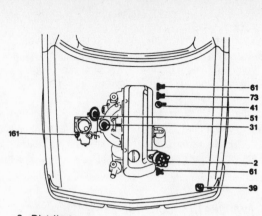

2. Distributor
31. EGR valve
39. Charcoal canister
41. Diverter valve
51. Vacuum governor
61. 62° F thermo-vacuum valve (blue); for EGR, located at front of engine next to distributor
61. 62° F thermo-vacuum valve (blue), for air
73. 122° F thermo-vacuum valve (black with green dot)
161. Float chamber vent valve

Fig. 12 Emission control component locations—1977–79 230 models

2. If the CO does not drop, and vacuum IS indicated, replace the thermo-vacuum valve. If the CO does not drop and vacuum is NOT indicated, clean the vacuum line to the intake manifold with compressed air.

3. Check the connection of the vacuum lines.

4. Check the vertical connection of the thermal vacuum valve for vacuum. If vacuum is present, replace the diverter valve. If no vacuum is present, remove the blue vacuum line from the thermo-vacuum valve and check for vacuum at the line.

5. If the CO still does not decrease, check that the thermo-vacuum valve is open; if not, replace the valve.

➡ **Below approximately 120°F, the valve should be open; above that, it should be closed.**

THROTTLE VALVE LIFT

1. Remove the vacuum hose from the vacuum governor on the carburetor. The idle speed should increase. Reconnect the hose. The idle speed should decrease.

2. If the rpm does not increase, check the connection of the hose. Check the hose for leaks.

3. Run the engine at idle. Remove the vacuum line on the carburetor; the idle speed should increase. If not, replace the vacuum governor.

FUEL EVAPORATION CONTROL SYSTEM

1. Remove the solenoid plug from the float chamber vent valve. Reconnect the solenoid; it should click audibly.

2. If the solenoid does not click, turn on the ignition and connect a test lamp to the plug. The test lamp should light with the ignition **ON.** If not, check the proper fuse. If the lamp still does not light, replace the solenoid.

3. Remove the middle purge hose to the carburetor from the charcoal canister and cover the hose opening with your finger. Slowly increase engine speed to over 2000 rpm. At idle no vacuum should be present. As engine speed increases, vacuum should increase. If no vacuum is present as the engine speed increases, check the connection of the purge hose. Check the hose for leaks and clean it out with compressed air.

4. On 1978–79 models remove the hose from the purge valve and repeat the test. If vacuum is present, replace the purge valve.

280E & 280SE MODELS (FEDERAL)

➧ **See Figure 13**

Testing the System

The following tests should be performed with the engine at idle speed, at operating temperature and in the order listed.

EGR VALVE

1. Remove the brown vacuum line from the EGR valve and slowly increase engine rpm. At about 1200 rpm, the engine should run roughly or stall.

2. If it does not run roughly or stall, check the vacuum line connections. The connections at the exhaust pressure transducer are marked with colored rings and must be connected to the same color code.

3. Disconnect the vacuum line from the vertical connection of the thermo-vacuum valve marked "50AA4" in the metal housing. Run the engine and increase rpm. Vacuum should be present at the connection.

4. Run the engine at idle and disconnect the brown line between the EGR valve and exhaust pressure transducer. Cover the line with your finger; vacuum must be present at idle. If not, replace the exhaust pressure transducer.

5. Run the engine at idle and remove both vacuum lines from the EGR valve. Connect the brown line to the connection on the red/purple line on the EGR valve. The engine should run roughly or stall. If not, replace the EGR valve.

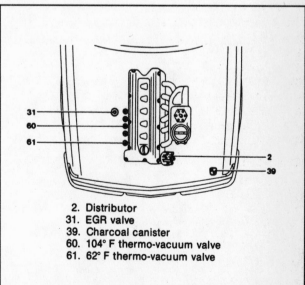

2. Distributor
31. EGR valve
39. Charcoal canister
60. 104° F thermo-vacuum valve
61. 62° F thermo-vacuum valve

Fig. 13 Emission control component locations—1977–79 280E, CE and SE models (Federal)

AIR INJECTION

1. Connect a CO tester to the exhaust back pressure line. Remove and plug the vacuum hose from the vertical connection at the thermo-vacuum valve. The CO should increase.

2. If not, check the vacuum line connections. The (large) cap end connection of the check valve must face the intake manifold (Federal only).

3. Remove the blue vacuum line from the thermo-vacuum valve and cover it with your finger. Vacuum must be present at idle; if not, check for leaks and clean the line with compressed air.

4. If vacuum is present, check the thermo-vacuum valve and replace if necessary.

5. Disconnect the blue/purple line from the thermo-vacuum valve marked "50AB5" on the metal housing. Run the engine. Vacuum should be present at the vertical connection. If not, replace the diverter valve.

FUEL EVAPORATION CONTROL SYSTEM

1. Remove the black purge line from the charcoal canister. Cover the opening with your finger and increase rpm to over 2000 rpm. No vacuum should be present at idle and vacuum should increase with engine speed. If not, check the vacuum line connections, check for leaks and clean the line with compressed air.

280E & 280SE MODELS (CALIFORNIA)

▶ **See Figure 14**

Testing the System

EGR VALVE

Refer to the 280E and 280SE Federal models procedure.

AIR INJECTION

1. Connect a CO tester to the exhaust pressure transducer. Remove the vacuum line from the vertical connection of the 122°F thermo-vacuum valve and connect it to the vertical connection of the 62°F thermo-vacuum valve. The CO should drop.

2. If not, check the vacuum line connections.

3. Run the engine at idle and check for vacuum at the vertical connection of the 62°F thermo-vacuum valve. If vacuum is present, replace the diverter valve.

If no vacuum is present, remove the blue line from the 62°F thermo-vacuum valve and check for vacuum at the valve. If vacuum is present, replace the thermo-vacuum valve. If no vacuum is present, remove the line from the intake manifold and clean it with compressed air.

4. If the CO still does not drop, check the 122°F thermo-vacuum valve. It will have "50AA13" stamped in the metal housing. Above 122°F, the valve is closed and no vacuum should be present at the vertical connection. Below 122°F, vacuum should be present at the vertical connection. If these conditions are not met, replace the valve.

FUEL EVAPORATION CONTROL SYSTEM

Refer to the 280E and 280SE Federal models procedure.

450SEL, 450SL & 450SLC MODELS (FEDERAL)

▶ **See Figure 15**

Testing the System

The following tests should be performed with the engine running at normal operating temperature in the order given.

EGR VALVE

1. Remove the brown line at the EGR valve and slowly increase engine speed. Above 1200 rpm, the engine should run roughly or stall. If not check the vacuum line connections.

2. Check the thermo vacuum valve with "50AA4" stamped in the metal housing (104°F valve). Remove the red/purple line from the vertical connection, run the engine and accelerate briefly. Vacuum should be present at the vertical connection.

3. Run the engine at idle and remove the brown vacuum line at the EGR valve. If no vacuum is present at idle, replace the exhaust pressure transducer.

4. Run the engine at idle and remove both lines from the EGR valve. Connect the brown line to the connection for the red/purple line. The engine should run roughly or stall. If not, replace the EGR valve.

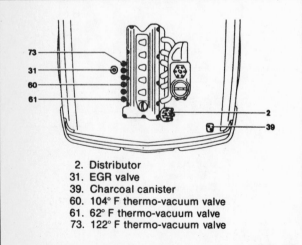

2. Distributor
31. EGR valve
39. Charcoal canister
60. 104° F thermo-vacuum valve
61. 62° F thermo-vacuum valve
73. 122° F thermo-vacuum valve

Fig. 14 Emission control component locations—1977–79 280E, CE and SE models (California)

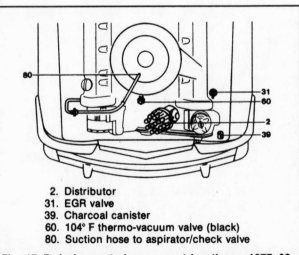

2. Distributor
31. EGR valve
39. Charcoal canister
60. 104° F thermo-vacuum valve (black)
80. Suction hose to aspirator/check valve

Fig. 15 Emission control component locations—1977–80 4.5L V8 models (Federal)

AIR INJECTION

1. Remove the suction hose from the aspirator/check valve in the air cleaner and cover with your finger. Vacuum should be present and a suction noise should be audible. If no vacuum is present, replace the aspirator/check valve.

FUEL EVAPORATION CONTROL SYSTEM

Refer to the 280E and 280SE Federal models procedure.

450SEL, 450SL, 450SLC (CALIFORNIA) & 6.9 MODELS

♦ See Figures 16 and 17

Testing the System

EGR VALVE

Refer to the 450SEL, 450SL and 450 SLC Federal models procedure.

AIR INJECTION

1. Connect a CO tester to the exhaust gas back pressure line and remove the blue/purple vacuum line from the vertical connection of the 62°F thermo-vacuum valve. Plug the connection. The CO should increase.

2. If not, check the vacuum line connections. The check valve must be installed with the larger (cap) end toward the intake manifold.

3. Remove the vacuum line from the angular connection of the 62°F thermo-vacuum valve and cover the valve with your finger. If no vacuum is present at idle, check the lines for leaks and clean the vacuum pick-up bore with compressed air.

4. If vacuum is present, check the thermo-vacuum valve and replace if necessary.

5. The thermo-vacuum valve can be identified by the "50AB5" stamped in the metal body. Remove the blue/purple vacuum line, run the engine at idle and accelerate briefly. Vacuum should be present at the vertical connection; if not, replace the diverter valve.

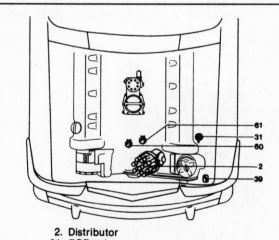

2. Distributor
31. EGR valve
39. Charcoal canister
60. 104° F thermo-vacuum valve (black)
61. 62° F thermo-vacuum valve (blue)

Fig. 16 Emission control component locations—1977–80 4.5L V8 models (California)

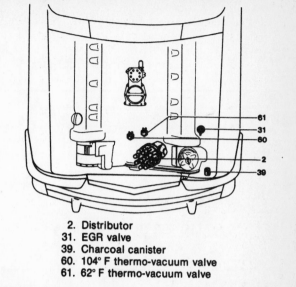

2. Distributor
31. EGR valve
39. Charcoal canister
60. 104° F thermo-vacuum valve
61. 62° F thermo-vacuum valve

Fig. 17 Emission control component locations—1978 6.9 models

FUEL EVAPORATION CONTROL SYSTEM

Refer to this test under 280E and 280SE (Federal).

1978–79 Vehicles

The emission control system for 1978–79 models is very similar in components and operation to the 1977 version.

230 MODELS

♦ See Figure 12

Perform the following tests in the order given with the engine at idle at normal operating temperature.

Testing the System

Refer to the 1977 230 model procedures for "Testing the System."

280E, 280CE & 280SE (FEDERAL) MODELS

♦ See Figure 13

Perform the following tests in the order given with the engine at normal operating temperature and idling.

Testing the System

Refer to the 1977 280E and 280SE (Federal) model procedures for "Testing the System."

280E, 280CE & 280SE MODELS (CALIFORNIA)

♦ See Figure 14

Perform the following tests in the order given with the engine at idle and at normal operating temperature.

Testing the System

Refer to the procedures under "Testing the System" for 1977 280E and 280SE California models.

450SEL, 450SL & 450SLC MODELS (FEDERAL)

◆ **See Figure 15**

Perform the following tests in the order given with the engine idling at normal operating temperature.

Testing the System

Refer to the procedures for "Testing the System" under 1977 450SL, 450SLC, 450SEL (Federal) models.

450SEL, 450SL, 450SLC (CALIFORNIA) & 6.9 MODELS

◆ **See Figures 16 and 17**

Perform the following tests in the order given with the engine idling at normal operating temperature.

Testing the System

Refer to the procedures for "Testing the System" under 1977 450SL, 450SLC, 450SEL (California) and 6.9 models.

CATALYST REPLACEMENT WARNING INDICATOR

A warning light in the instrument cluster comes on at 37,500 mile intervals, indicating that the catalyst should be replaced. The catalyst mileage counter is located under the dash and is driven by the speedometer cable. To reset the mileage counter, push the reset pin on the counter.

1980 Vehicles

6-CYLINDER ENGINES

The base color of the emission control vacuum lines is white. Colored stripes identify various functions:
- Advanced timing = red
- Retarded timing = yellow/purple
- Air injection = blue

A Lambda oxygen sensor control system ensures a constant air fuel ratio of approximately 14.5:1. The oxygen sensor is screwed into the front part of the exhaust pipe to constantly monitor the oxygen content of the exhaust gases. An electronic control unit, located behind the kick panel, receives input from a throttle valve switch and oil temperature switch to maintain an ideal fuel mixture in conjunction with the 3-way catalyst. The oxygen sensor must be replaced every 30,000 miles (light on the dash warns driver).

An air injection system is used, the components of which are very similar to those used in 1979.

Testing the System

A special test adaptor that connects to the electronic control unit plug and a special test meter that connects to the adaptor are necessary to properly test the emission system. Do not attempt to try and test electrical components of the system with an ordinary volt-ohmmeter.

The only tests that can be performed without special equipment are as follows:

AIR INJECTION

1. Pull the Y-fitting from the angled connections at the thermo-vacuum valves and check for vacuum at the Y-fitting. If no vacuum is present, clean the connection at the intake manifold with compressed air.
2. Be sure the fitting and connecting lines are not plugged. If vacuum is present, the thermo-vacuum valves should be open. If the valves are open, replace the diverter valve.

FUEL EVAPORATION CONTROL SYSTEM

1. Remove the purge line from the charcoal canister (connected to the throttle valve housing) and block it with your finger. Slowly increase the engine speed to more than 2000 rpm.
2. There should be no vacuum at idle, but vacuum should increase with rpm.
3. If vacuum does not increase with rpm, test the purge line connection and purge valve. The purge line must be connected to the throttle valve housing, and must not leak. Clean out the throttle valve housing with compressed air. If vacuum is still not present, remove the purge line from the front of the purge valve. If vacuum is present, replace the purge valve.

V8 ENGINES

◆ **See Figures 15 and 16**

Color coding of the vacuum lines is identical to the 6-cylinder engines and operation of the Lambda oxygen sensor control system is the same as 6-cylinder engines.

Air injection uses a shut-off valve in a special shaped hose between the air filter and the aspirator valve, which is in the air injection line leading to the cylinder head.

Primary, underfloor and catalyst/muffler combination catalytic converters are used, depending on application.

The fuel evaporation control system is identical to the 1979 system.

Testing the System

A special test adapter that connects to the electronic control unit plug and a special test meter that connects to the adapter are necessary to properly test the emission control system. Do not attempt to try and test electrical components of the system with an ordinary volt-ohmmeter.

The only tests that can be performed without special equipment are as follows:

FREQUENCY VALVE

1. With the engine idling at normal operating temperature, place your hand on the frequency valve.
2. Operation of the frequency valve can be felt. If not replace the valve.

AIR INJECTION

1. Idle the engine and remove the specially shaped hose from the air shut-off valve. A suction sound should be audible.
2. If there is no suction sound, check the vacuum lines and

vacuum supply. Check the blue line connected to the air shut-off valve. Disconnect the line at the air shut-off valve. If vacuum is not present, clean out the vacuum connection at the throttle valve housing.

3. If vacuum is present at the air shut-off valve, remove the valve. If the suction sound is still audible, replace the air shutoff valve. If no suction sound could be heard at the air shut-off valve, replace the aspirator valve.

1981–84 Vehicles

6-CYLINDER ENGINES

♦ See Figure 18

The emission control system is the same as 1980, with two exceptions. The air pump intake is connected to the clean side of the air cleaner. A rubber scoop inside the air cleaner facilitates air intake. The second change is that the fuel evaporation control purge system is controlled by a thermo valve and is effective only at temperatures above 122°F.

➡Color coding of the vacuum lines is as indicated in the accompanying chart.

Lines originating at a vacuum source have only one color stripe; lines terminating at a vacuum operated device have 2 color stripes and purple is always the second color.

Testing the System

Refer to the testing procedures for 1980 models.

V8 ENGINES

Color coding of the vacuum lines is identical to the 6-cylinder engines. Operation of the Lambda oxygen sensor control system is the same as 1980. Only the oxygen sensor itself has been modified for production reasons. All models in 1983 are equipped with a standardized O_2 sensor, with a new plug connection. The plug is no longer below the vehicle, but inside the passenger com-

Device	Color of Line Originating at a Vacuum Source	Color of Line Terminating at a Vacuum Operated Device
Ignition advance	Red	
Ignition retard	Yellow	
Air injection	Blue	Blue/purple
Fuel evaporation thermo valve	Black	Black/purple

Fig. 18 Vacuum line color coding chart

partment, accessible after removing the control unit cover plate. The air pump is a maintenance-free vane type pump, similar in operation to the 1980 system. Three-way-catalysts have been slightly modified dimensionally, but operate the same as those in 1980. The fuel evaporation control system is the same as 1980, except that the purge system is controlled by a thermo valve that allows purge only at coolant temperatures below approximately 122°F.

Testing the System

Refer to the testing procedures for 1980 models.

ELECTRONIC IDLE SPEED CONTROL

♦ See Figures 19, 20, 21 and 22 (p. 19–21)

1981–82 Models

1. The engine should be at operating temperature with the ignition **ON**.
2. Pull the plug from the idle speed adjuster and check the voltage. If 12 volts are present, go to Step 4.

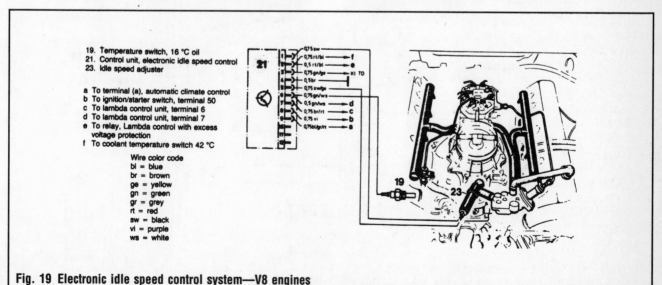

19. Temperature switch, 16 °C oil
21. Control unit, electronic idle speed control
23. Idle speed adjuster

a To terminal (a), automatic climate control
b To ignition/starter switch, terminal 50
c To lambda control unit, terminal 6
d To lambda control unit, terminal 7
e To relay, Lambda control with excess voltage protection
f To coolant temperature switch 42 °C

Wire color code
bl = blue
br = brown
ge = yellow
gn = green
gr = grey
rt = red
sw = black
vi = purple
ws = white

Fig. 19 Electronic idle speed control system—V8 engines

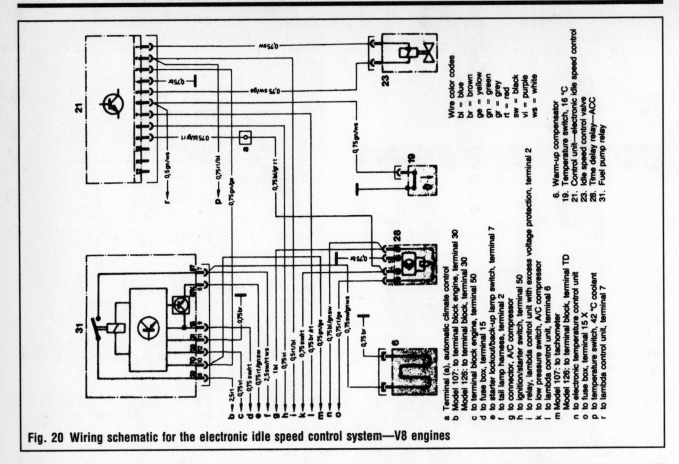

Fig. 20 Wiring schematic for the electronic idle speed control system—V8 engines

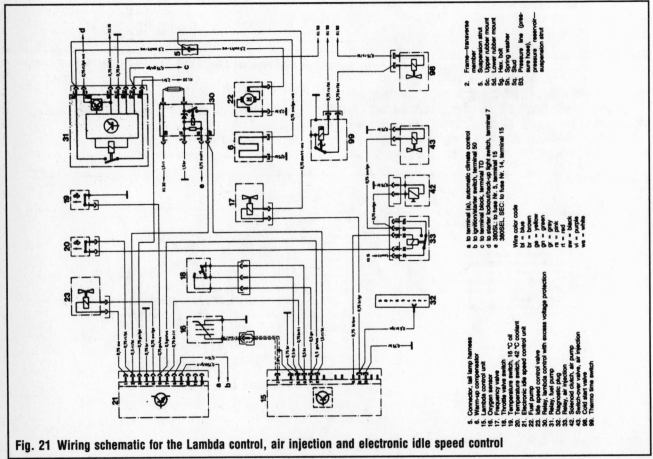

Fig. 21 Wiring schematic for the Lambda control, air injection and electronic idle speed control

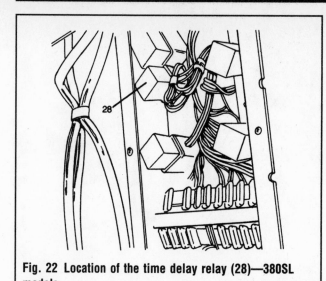

Fig. 22 Location of the time delay relay (28)—380SL models

3. If there is no voltage, pull the plug from the control unit and check the voltage between terminals 2 and 4 (arrows). There should be approximately 12 volts. If there is no voltage, check the voltage supply and replace any defective parts. If 12 volts are present, check the wires from the plug of the idle speed adjuster and the control unit plug (black/yellow wire to terminal 5 of the control unit and the black wire to terminal 1 of the control unit). If there are infinite ohms, replace the wire. If there are 0 ohms, connect the coupling to the control unit and measure the voltage at the idle speed adjuster. If there are 0 volts, replace the control unit.

4. Check the control unit. With the engine idling at operating temperature, connect the plug to the idle speed adjuster so that you can check voltage at the plug. If there are 4–6 volts, go to Step 5. If there are no volts, replace the control unit.

5. Check the idle speed adjuster. Idle the engine and pull the plug from the coolant temperature switch. Bridge the terminals. The idle speed should increase. If not, apply battery voltage to the idle speed adjuster (for no more than 5 seconds). If the speed drops or the engine stops, replace the control unit. If the idle speed does not drop, replace the idle speed adjuster.

1983–84 Models

The electronic idle speed control system has been slightly modified. A new control unit on V8's, processes the following inputs:
- Engine speed (rpm)
- Idle and partial load
- Engine oil temperature
- Transmission shift lever position
- Engagement of A/C compressor

The signal for engine rpm is controlled by the oil temperature switch, which also sends a signal to the Lambda system control unit at the same time.

The A/C compressor has a time delay relay in place of the relay used in '82. Through the relay, voltage is supplied to the idle speed control unit prior to engagement of the compressor clutch. The idle speed solenoid will already be maintaining sufficient rpm when the clutch is engaged.

When the automatic transmission shift lever is in P or N, the starter lockout is closed and the solenoid is ground. When the shift lever is in a driving position, the starter lockout switch is open and the idle speed is lowered.

This new version of the electronic control unit cannot be used on older model vehicles.

Troubleshooting

ENGINE STALLS OR WILL NOT START

1. Turn the ignition on and off. The idle speed control valve switch on and off noticeably (audibly).

2. If not, remove the valve and see if the aperture is open. If not, follow the Idle Speed Control Test.

ENGINE SURGES OR SHAKES AT IDLE

Perform the Idle Speed Control Test.

IDLE SPEED TOO HIGH OR LOW, ENGINE STALLS

◆ See Figure 23

1. Disconnect the plug from the idle speed control valve and reconnect it.

2. The idle speed should increase to about 1500 rpm.

3. If no change in idle speed occurs, replace the control valve.

4. Put the transmission in a driving gear. The idle speed should drop to about 500 rpm. If not, perform the Idle Speed Control Test.

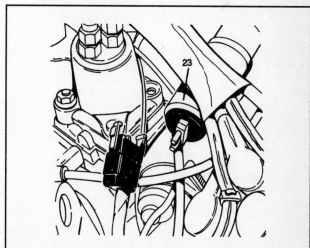

Fig. 23 Disengage the wiring harness from the idle control solenoid (23)

IDLE SPEED TO HIGH, ENGINE AT NORMAL TEMPERATURE

1. Disconnect the plug from the temperature switch.

2. If the engine rpm drops with the automatic transmission in P or N, replace the temperature switch. If the engine rpm does not drop, perform the Idle Speed Control Test.

Idle Speed Control Test

CHECK VOLTAGE TO CONTROL VALVE

◆ See Figure 24

1. Turn the ignition on and off.

2. The idle speed control valve should switch on and off audibly.

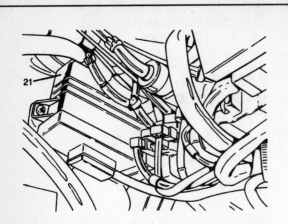

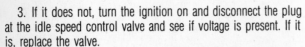

Fig. 24 The control unit on the 380SL models is located under a cover (21) on the right side of the passenger compartment

Fig. 25 The control unit is located under the cowl panel on 380SEC and SEL models

3. If it does not, turn the ignition on and disconnect the plug at the idle speed control valve and see if voltage is present. If it is, replace the valve.

4. If no voltage is present, disconnect the plug on the control unit and check battery voltage between pins 2 (positive) and 4 (negative). If no voltage is present, check the power supply according to the wiring diagram.

5. If there is voltage at pins 2 and 4, bridge pins 1 and 2 and 4 and 5 simultaneously for a maximum of 5 seconds. The idle speed valve should switch audibly.

6. If the valve switches, replace the control unit.

7. If the valve does not switch, check the black and the black/yellow wires to the idle speed valve for continuity and repair if necessary.

CHECK IDLE AND PART LOAD

♦ **See Figures 25, 26 and 27**

A special M-B test cable is necessary for this test. The engine should be running at idle (with accessories turned off) at normal operating temperature. The transmission should be in P or N. Con-

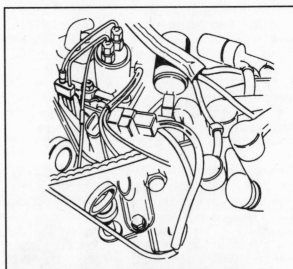

Fig. 26 Turn the engine off before disengaging the control unit's electrical connection

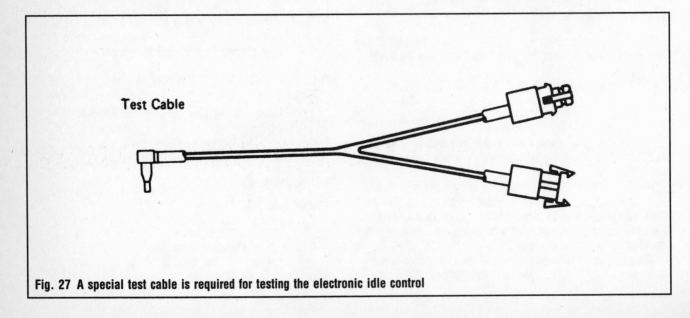

Test Cable

Fig. 27 A special test cable is required for testing the electronic idle control

nect a multimeter to a test cable and connect the test cable between the idle speed valve and the wiring harness.

1. The reading on the meter should be above 400 mA at about 650 rpm.

2. If the reading fluctuates and the engine surges, replace the idle speed valve or the control unit.

3. If the reading is 0 mA, perform the Idle Speed Control Test.

4. Disconnect the throttle valve switch connector and check the idle speed. The idle speed should increase to about 850 rpm.

5. If the idle speed does not increase, turn off the engine and disconnect the plug from the control unit. Set the multimeter on the 0 to infinite ohms scale and connect it to bushings 4 and 7. With the throttle valve against the stop, the meter should read 0 ohms. With the throttle valve slightly opened the meter should read infinite ohms. If the readings are not present, adjust the throttle valve switch, or if necessary replace it. Check the wires to the throttle valve switch.

6. Reconnect the plug to the control unit. Start the engine.

7. The idle speed should increase to approximately 850 rpm.

8. If not, replace the control unit.

CHECK FAST IDLE

▶ See Figure 28

The engine should be idling at normal operating temperature with the shift lever in P or N. Connect the plug of the temperature switch to ground to simulate an oil temperature of less than 16°C.

1. If the idle speed increases to about 800–900 rpm, check the temperature switch and replace if necessary. Below an actual oil

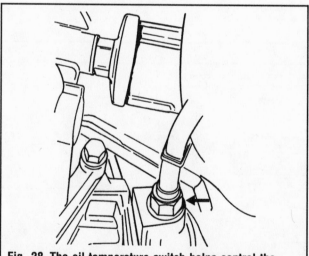

Fig. 28 The oil temperature switch helps control the engine RPM

temperature of 16°C, the switch contacts should be closed. Above an actual oil temperature of 16°C, the switch contacts should be open.

2. If the idle speed does not increase, disconnect the plug from the control unit and check the wire from pin #6 to the temperature switch for continuity. If 0 ohms are present, replace the control unit. If infinite ohms are present, check the wire to the temperature switch.

CHECK IDLE SPEED WITH AND WITHOUT THE TRANSMISSION ENGAGED

The engine should be running at idle, at normal operating temperature, and the wheels blocked.

1. Put the car in gear. The idle speed should drop to about 500 rpm.

2. If the idle speed does not drop, disconnect the plug from the control unit. Turn the engine off, then on.

3. Connect a voltmeter between pins 8 (negative) and 2 (positive). Battery voltage should be present with the transmission in P or N.

4. If battery voltage is present, replace the control unit. If battery voltage is not present, and no voltage is present at pin #2, check the wiring according to the wiring diagram.

5. If no ground is made at pin #8, check the writing to the starter lockout/back-up light switch.

CHECK IDLE SPEED WHEN A/C COMPRESSOR IS ENGAGED

1. Turn the ignition on and engage the A/C compressor. Disconnect the plug from the control unit. Battery voltage should be present at pin #9.

2. If battery voltage is not present, check the voltage supply on the wiring diagram.

3. If battery voltage is present, but the idle speed drop is too much when the compressor is engaged, replace the ACC time delay relay or the control unit.

IDLE SPEED TOO HIGH ON WARM ENGINE

The engine should be running at idle, at normal operating temperature. The transmission should be in P or N.

1. Disconnect the plug on the temperature switch.

2. If the idle speed drops to about 500 rpm, replace the temperature switch.

3. If the idle speed does not drop, disconnect the plug from the control unit. Check the wire from pin #6 to the temperature switch for continuity.

4. If 0 ohms are present, replace the control unit.

5. If infinite ohms are present, check the wire to the temperature switch.

VACUUM DIAGRAMS

Following are vacuum diagrams for most of the engine and emissions package combinations covered by this manual. Because vacuum circuits will vary based on various engine and vehicle options, always refer first to the vehicle emission control information label, if present. Should the label be missing, or should vehicle be equipped with a different engine from the vehicle's original

equipment, refer to the diagrams below for the same or similar configuration.

If you wish to obtain a replacement emissions label, most manufacturers make the labels available for purchase. The labels can usually be ordered from a local dealer.

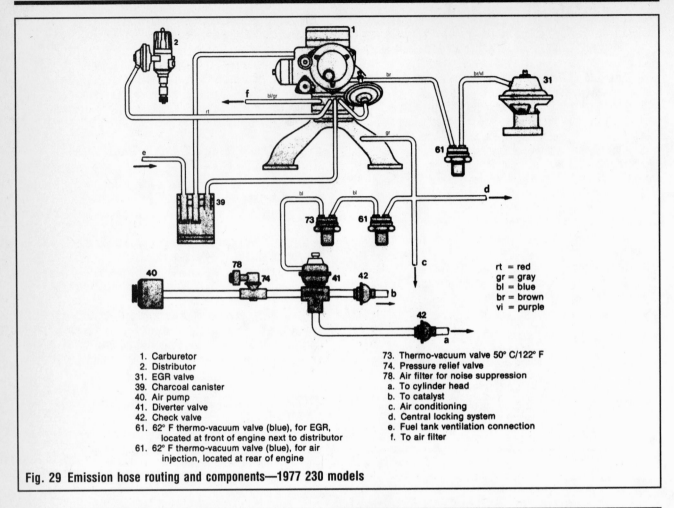

1. Carburetor
2. Distributor
31. EGR valve
39. Charcoal canister
40. Air pump
41. Diverter valve
42. Check valve
61. 62° F thermo-vacuum valve (blue), for EGR, located at front of engine next to distributor
61. 62° F thermo-vacuum valve (blue), for air injection, located at rear of engine

73. Thermo-vacuum valve 50° C/122° F
74. Pressure relief valve
78. Air filter for noise suppression
a. To cylinder head
b. To catalyst
c. Air conditioning
d. Central locking system
e. Fuel tank ventilation connection
f. To air filter

rt = red
gr = gray
bl = blue
br = brown
vi = purple

Fig. 29 Emission hose routing and components—1977 230 models

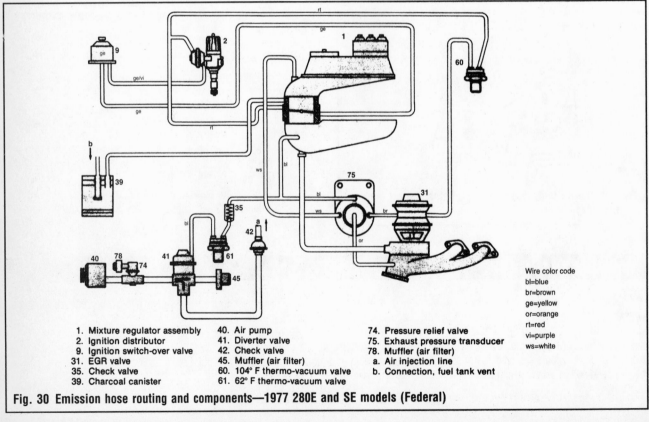

1. Mixture regulator assembly
2. Ignition distributor
9. Ignition switch-over valve
31. EGR valve
35. Check valve
39. Charcoal canister

40. Air pump
41. Diverter valve
42. Check valve
45. Muffler (air filter)
60. 104° F thermo-vacuum valve
61. 62° F thermo-vacuum valve

74. Pressure relief valve
75. Exhaust pressure transducer
78. Muffler (air filter)
a. Air injection line
b. Connection, fuel tank vent

Wire color code
bl=blue
br=brown
ge=yellow
or=orange
rt=red
vi=purple
ws=white

Fig. 30 Emission hose routing and components—1977 280E and SE models (Federal)

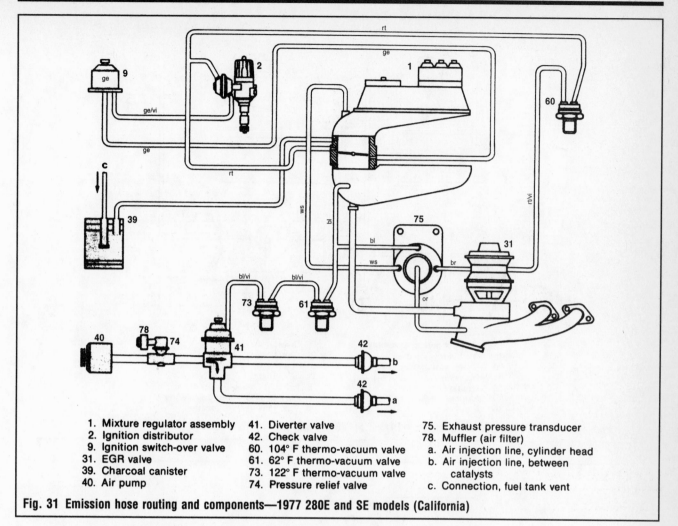

Fig. 31 Emission hose routing and components—1977 280E and SE models (California)

1. Mixture regulator assembly	41. Diverter valve	75. Exhaust pressure transducer
2. Ignition distributor	42. Check valve	78. Muffler (air filter)
9. Ignition switch-over valve	60. 104° F thermo-vacuum valve	a. Air injection line, cylinder head
31. EGR valve	61. 62° F thermo-vacuum valve	b. Air injection line, between
39. Charcoal canister	73. 122° F thermo-vacuum valve	catalysts
40. Air pump	74. Pressure relief valve	c. Connection, fuel tank vent

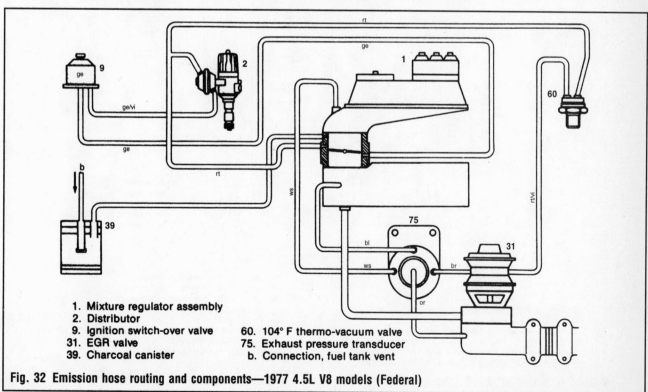

1. Mixture regulator assembly	
2. Distributor	
9. Ignition switch-over valve	60. 104° F thermo-vacuum valve
31. EGR valve	75. Exhaust pressure transducer
39. Charcoal canister	b. Connection, fuel tank vent

Fig. 32 Emission hose routing and components—1977 4.5L V8 models (Federal)

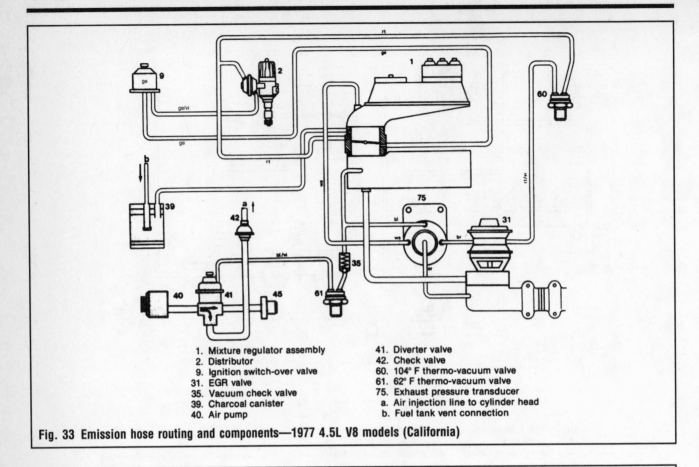

1. Mixture regulator assembly
2. Distributor
9. Ignition switch-over valve
31. EGR valve
35. Vacuum check valve
39. Charcoal canister
40. Air pump
41. Diverter valve
42. Check valve
60. 104° F thermo-vacuum valve
61. 62° F thermo-vacuum valve
75. Exhaust pressure transducer
a. Air injection line to cylinder head
b. Fuel tank vent connection

Fig. 33 Emission hose routing and components—1977 4.5L V8 models (California)

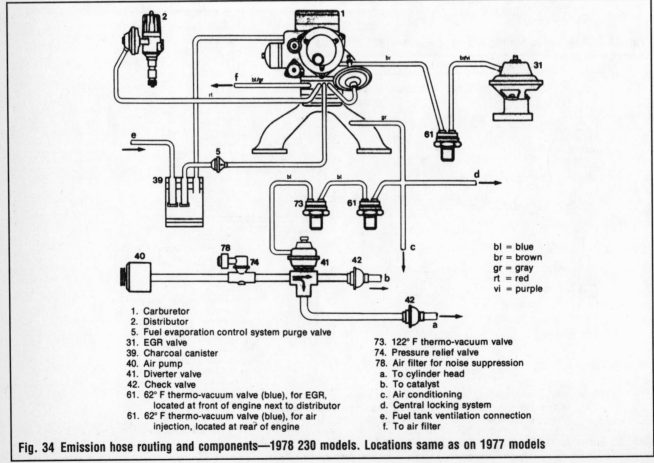

bl = blue
br = brown
gr = gray
rt = red
vi = purple

1. Carburetor
2. Distributor
5. Fuel evaporation control system purge valve
31. EGR valve
39. Charcoal canister
40. Air pump
41. Diverter valve
42. Check valve
61. 62° F thermo-vacuum valve (blue), for EGR, located at front of engine next to distributor
61. 62° F thermo-vacuum valve (blue), for air injection, located at rear of engine
73. 122° F thermo-vacuum valve
74. Pressure relief valve
78. Air filter for noise suppression
a. To cylinder head
b. To catalyst
c. Air conditioning
d. Central locking system
e. Fuel tank ventilation connection
f. To air filter

Fig. 34 Emission hose routing and components—1978 230 models. Locations same as on 1977 models

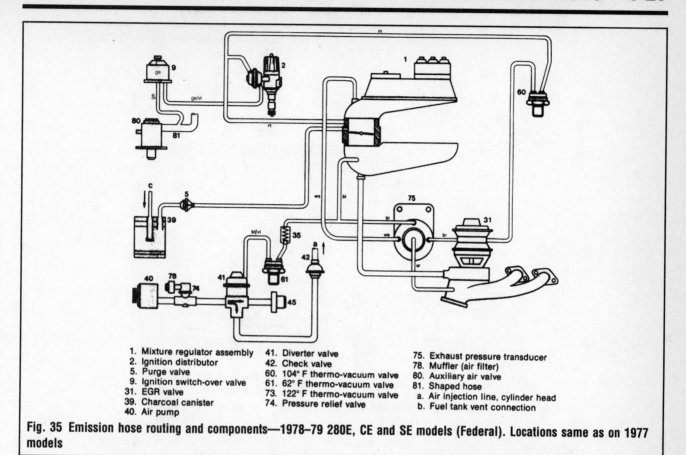

Fig. 35 Emission hose routing and components—1978–79 280E, CE and SE models (Federal). Locations same as on 1977 models

1. Mixture regulator assembly
2. Ignition distributor
5. Purge valve
9. Ignition switch-over valve
31. EGR valve
39. Charcoal canister
40. Air pump
41. Diverter valve
42. Check valve
60. 104° F thermo-vacuum valve
61. 62° F thermo-vacuum valve
73. 122° F thermo-vacuum valve
74. Pressure relief valve
75. Exhaust pressure transducer
78. Muffler (air filter)
80. Auxiliary air valve
81. Shaped hose
a. Air injection line, cylinder head
b. Fuel tank vent connection

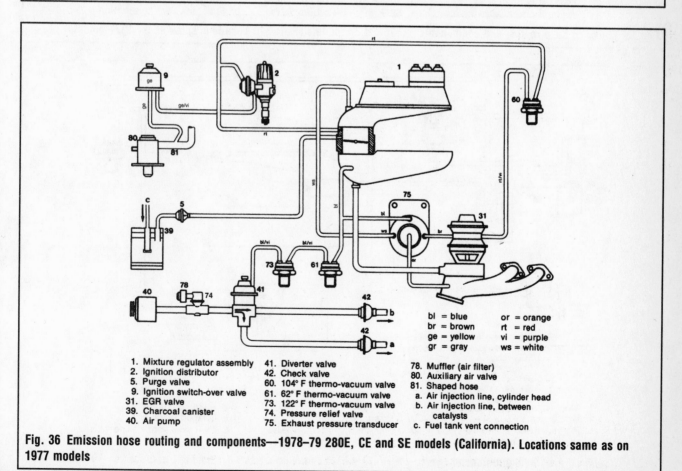

Fig. 36 Emission hose routing and components—1978–79 280E, CE and SE models (California). Locations same as on 1977 models

1. Mixture regulator assembly
2. Ignition distributor
5. Purge valve
9. Ignition switch-over valve
31. EGR valve
39. Charcoal canister
40. Air pump
41. Diverter valve
42. Check valve
60. 104° F thermo-vacuum valve
61. 62° F thermo-vacuum valve
73. 122° F thermo-vacuum valve
74. Pressure relief valve
75. Exhaust pressure transducer
78. Muffler (air filter)
80. Auxiliary air valve
81. Shaped hose
a. Air injection line, cylinder head
b. Air injection line, between catalysts
c. Fuel tank vent connection

bl = blue
br = brown
ge = yellow
gr = gray
or = orange
rt = red
vi = purple
ws = white

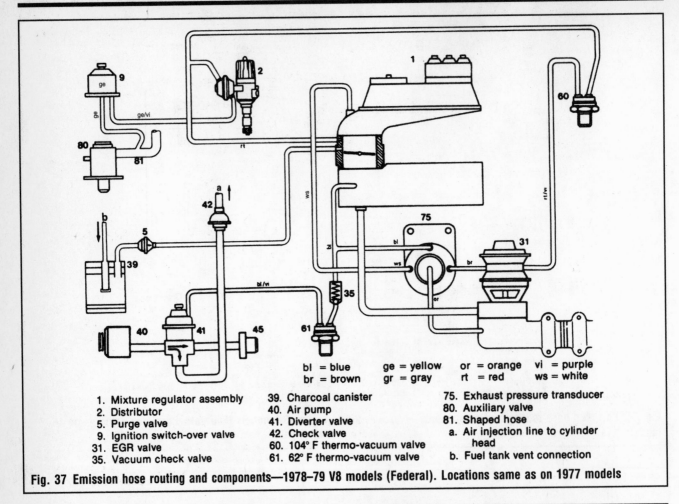

bl = blue   ge = yellow   or = orange   vi = purple
br = brown   gr = gray   rt = red   ws = white

1. Mixture regulator assembly
2. Distributor
5. Purge valve
9. Ignition switch-over valve
31. EGR valve
35. Vacuum check valve

39. Charcoal canister
40. Air pump
41. Diverter valve
42. Check valve
60. 104° F thermo-vacuum valve
61. 62° F thermo-vacuum valve

75. Exhaust pressure transducer
80. Auxiliary valve
81. Shaped hose
a. Air injection line to cylinder head
b. Fuel tank vent connection

Fig. 37 Emission hose routing and components—1978–79 V8 models (Federal). Locations same as on 1977 models

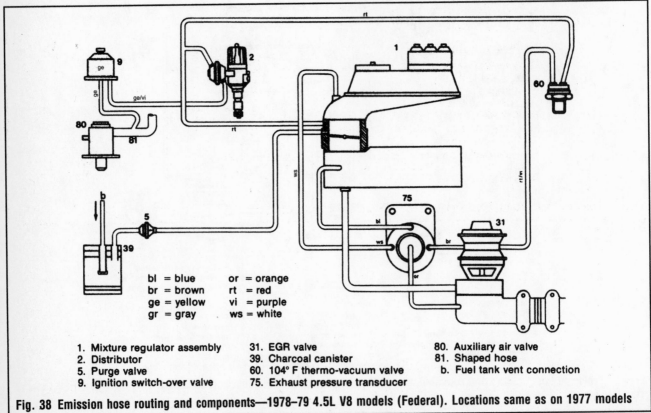

bl = blue   or = orange
br = brown   rt = red
ge = yellow   vi = purple
gr = gray   ws = white

1. Mixture regulator assembly
2. Distributor
5. Purge valve
9. Ignition switch-over valve

31. EGR valve
39. Charcoal canister
60. 104° F thermo-vacuum valve
75. Exhaust pressure transducer

80. Auxiliary air valve
81. Shaped hose
b. Fuel tank vent connection

Fig. 38 Emission hose routing and components—1978–79 4.5L V8 models (Federal). Locations same as on 1977 models

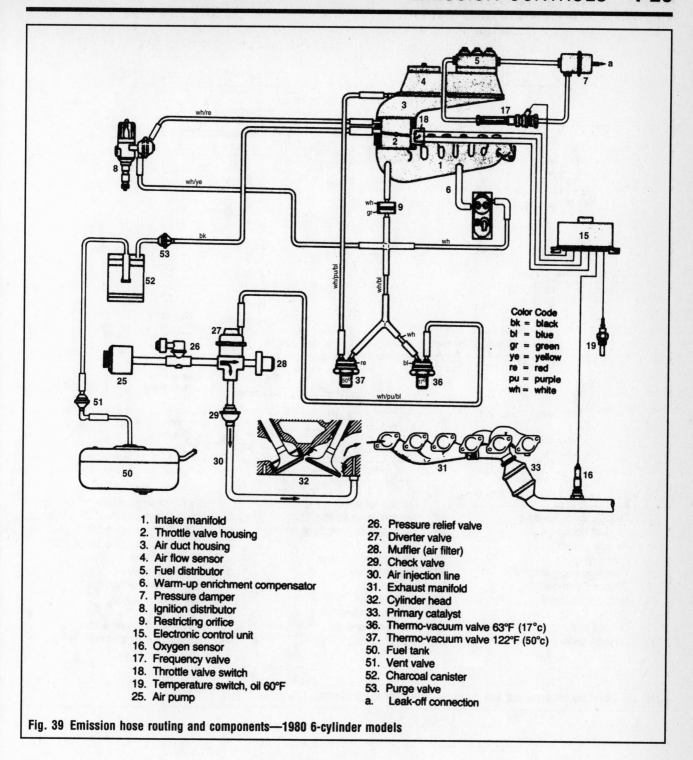

1. Intake manifold
2. Throttle valve housing
3. Air duct housing
4. Air flow sensor
5. Fuel distributor
6. Warm-up enrichment compensator
7. Pressure damper
8. Ignition distributor
9. Restricting orifice
15. Electronic control unit
16. Oxygen sensor
17. Frequency valve
18. Throttle valve switch
19. Temperature switch, oil 60°F
25. Air pump

26. Pressure relief valve
27. Diverter valve
28. Muffler (air filter)
29. Check valve
30. Air injection line
31. Exhaust manifold
32. Cylinder head
33. Primary catalyst
36. Thermo-vacuum valve 63°F (17°c)
37. Thermo-vacuum valve 122°F (50°c)
50. Fuel tank
51. Vent valve
52. Charcoal canister
53. Purge valve
a. Leak-off connection

Fig. 39 Emission hose routing and components—1980 6-cylinder models

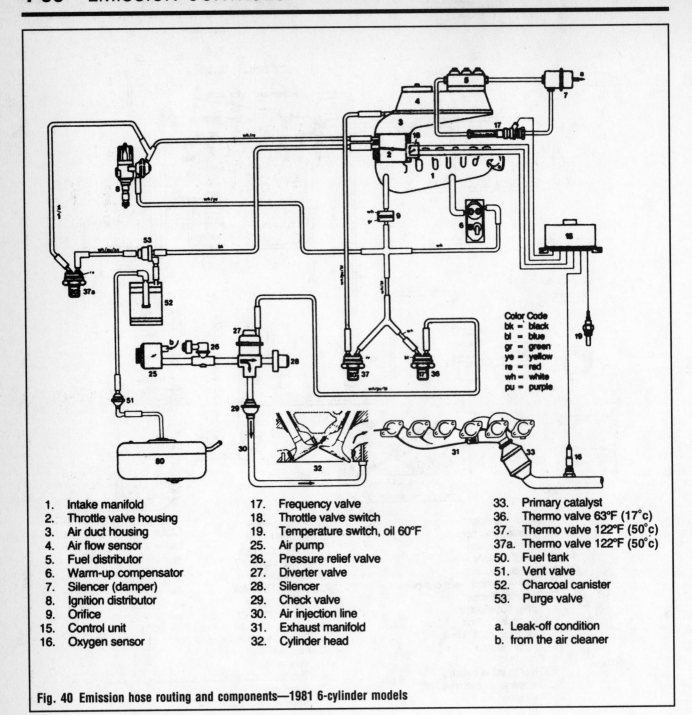

1.	Intake manifold	17.	Frequency valve	33.	Primary catalyst
2.	Throttle valve housing	18.	Throttle valve switch	36.	Thermo valve 63°F (17°c)
3.	Air duct housing	19.	Temperature switch, oil 60°F	37.	Thermo valve 122°F (50°c)
4.	Air flow sensor	25.	Air pump	37a.	Thermo valve 122°F (50°c)
5.	Fuel distributor	26.	Pressure relief valve	50.	Fuel tank
6.	Warm-up compensator	27.	Diverter valve	51.	Vent valve
7.	Silencer (damper)	28.	Silencer	52.	Charcoal canister
8.	Ignition distributor	29.	Check valve	53.	Purge valve
9.	Orifice	30.	Air injection line		
15.	Control unit	31.	Exhaust manifold	a.	Leak-off condition
16.	Oxygen sensor	32.	Cylinder head	b.	from the air cleaner

Fig. 40 Emission hose routing and components—1981 6-cylinder models

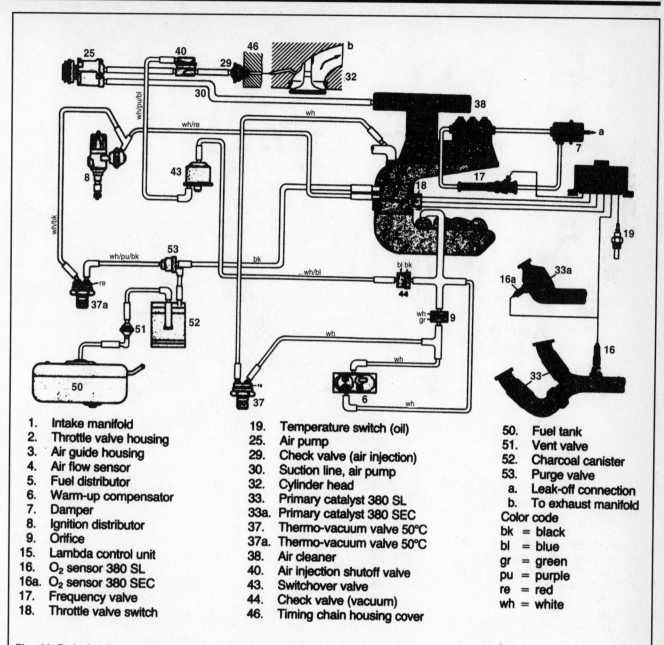

1. Intake manifold
2. Throttle valve housing
3. Air guide housing
4. Air flow sensor
5. Fuel distributor
6. Warm-up compensator
7. Damper
8. Ignition distributor
9. Orifice
15. Lambda control unit
16. O₂ sensor 380 SL
16a. O₂ sensor 380 SEC
17. Frequency valve
18. Throttle valve switch

19. Temperature switch (oil)
25. Air pump
29. Check valve (air injection)
30. Suction line, air pump
32. Cylinder head
33. Primary catalyst 380 SL
33a. Primary catalyst 380 SEC
37. Thermo-vacuum valve 50°C
37a. Thermo-vacuum valve 50°C
38. Air cleaner
40. Air injection shutoff valve
43. Switchover valve
44. Check valve (vacuum)
46. Timing chain housing cover

50. Fuel tank
51. Vent valve
52. Charcoal canister
53. Purge valve
a. Leak-off connection
b. To exhaust manifold
Color code
bk = black
bl = blue
gr = green
pu = purple
re = red
wh = white

Fig. 41 Emission hose routing and components—1982–83 3.8L V8 models

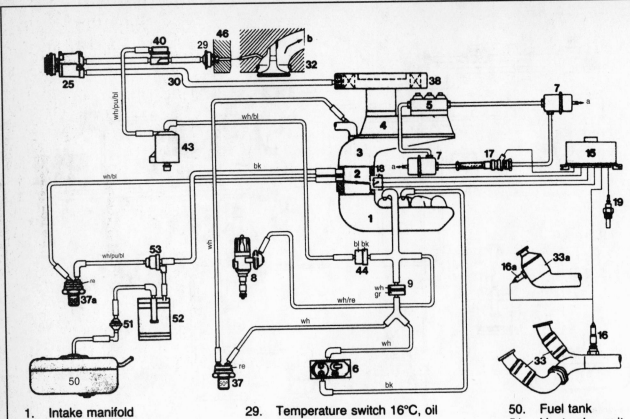

1.	Intake manifold	29.
2.	Throttle valve housing	25.
3.	Air guide housing	29.
4.	Air flow sensor	30.
5.	Fuel distributor	32.
6.	Warm-up compensator	33.
7.	Damper	33a.
8.	Ignition distributor	37.
9.	Throttle (orifice)	37a.
15.	Control unit	38.
16.	O₂-sensor (model 107)	40.
16a.	O₂-sensor (model 126)	43.
17.	Frequency valve	44.
18.	Throttle valve switch	46.

1. Intake manifold
2. Throttle valve housing
3. Air guide housing
4. Air flow sensor
5. Fuel distributor
6. Warm-up compensator
7. Damper
8. Ignition distributor
9. Throttle (orifice)
15. Control unit
16. O$_2$-sensor (model 107)
16a. O$_2$-sensor (model 126)
17. Frequency valve
18. Throttle valve switch

29. Temperature switch 16°C, oil
25. Air pump
29. Check valve (Air injection)
30. Intake line
32. Cylinder head
33. Primary catalyst (model 107)
33a. Primary catalyst (model 126)
37. Thermovalve 50°C
37a. Thermovalve 50°C
38. Air cleaner
40. Air shutoff valve
43. Switchover valve
44. Check valve (vacuum)
46. Timing housing cover

50. Fuel tank
51. Vent valve unit
53. Purge valve

a. Leak connection
b. To exhaust manifold

bk = black
bl = blue
gr = green
pu = purple
re = red
wh = white

Fig. 42 Emission hose routing and components—1984 V8 models

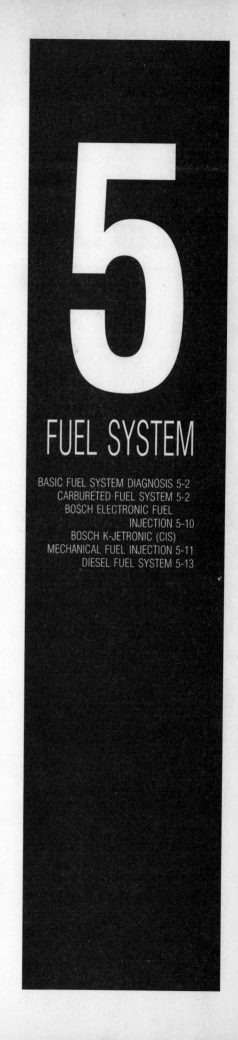

5
FUEL SYSTEM

BASIC FUEL SYSTEM DIAGNOSIS

When there is a problem starting or driving a vehicle, two of the most important checks involve the ignition and the fuel systems. The questions most mechanics attempt to answer first, "is there spark?" and "is there fuel?" will often lead to solving most basic problems. For ignition system diagnosis and testing, please refer to the information on engine electrical components and ignition systems found earlier in this manual. If the ignition system checks out (there is spark), then you must determine if the fuel system is operating properly (is there fuel?).

CARBURETED FUEL SYSTEM

Mechanical Fuel Pump

All Mercedes-Benz carbureted engines use a diaphragm type fuel pump, which is mounted on the side of the block. It is operated by a gear driven eccentric shaft through a rocker arm on the fuel pump.

REMOVAL & INSTALLATION

1. Clean the joint around the fuel pump base and cylinder block.
2. One at a time, remove and plug the intake and outlet lines from the fuel pump.
3. Unbolt the retaining bolts and remove the fuel pump and gasket from the cylinder block.
   To install:
4. Clean the mating surfaces of the engine and cylinder block.
5. Install a new gasket.
6. Insert the fuel pump into the block and install the retaining bolts. Be sure that the bolts are tightened evenly.
7. Reconnect the intake and outlet lines to the fuel pump.
8. Run the engine and check for leaks.

TESTING DELIVERY PRESSURE

1. Remove the wire from the coil to prevent starting.
2. Connect a pressure gauge into the output line of the fuel pump.
3. Crank the engine and read the delivery pressure on the pressure gauge. The pressure should be a constant 1.5–2.5 psi.
4. If the pressure is not within specifications or is erratic, remove the pump for service or for replacement with a new or rebuilt unit. No adjustment is provided.

Carburetors

♦ **See Figure 1**

REMOVAL & INSTALLATION

1974–78 Stromberg 175CDT

♦ **See Figure 2**

1. Remove the air cleaner.
2. Remove and plug the fuel lines.

✸✸ WARNING

Do not pull off the fuel lines. They should be pried off along with the securing discs.

3. Disconnect the control linkage.
4. Remove the vacuum lines.
5. Disconnect the water hoses for the automatic choke.
6. Disconnect the leads for the automatic choke and fuel shut-off valve.
7. Remove the carburetor retaining nuts and remove the carburetor.
8. Installation is the reverse of removal. Adjust the carburetor. Refer to the "Tune-Up Specifications" in Section 2.

SOLEX 4 A 1 (280, 280C AND 280S)

♦ **See Figure 3 (p. 4)**

1. Remove the air filter.
2. Remove the electric cable from the starter cover and cut-off valves.
3. Remove the vacuum lines.
4. To prevent corrosion from leaked coolant, cover the starter housing with a rag. Release the pressure in the cooling system by cracking the radiator cap until pressure has escaped. Install and tighten the radiator cap. Remove and plug the coolant water hoses from the carburetor.
5. Remove and plug the fuel lines.

Carburetor Applications

Model	Year	Carburetor
230	1974–78	1 Stromberg 175 CDT
280	1974–76	1 Solex 4A1
280C	1974–76	
280S	1975–76	

Fig. 1 Carburetor applications chart

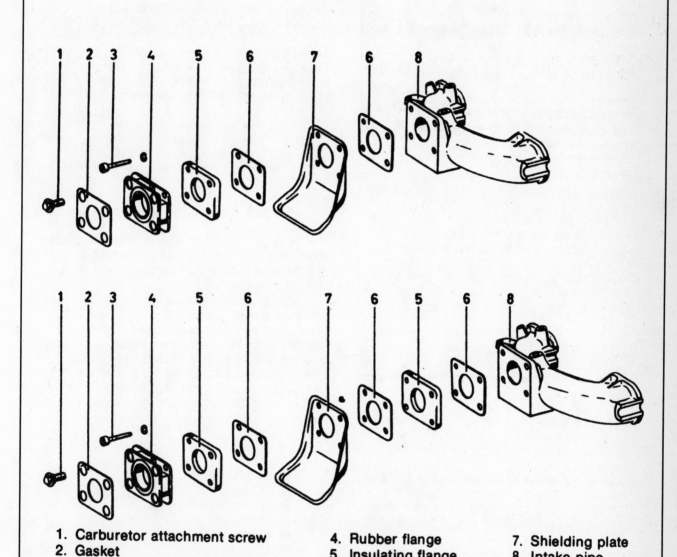

Fig. 2 Exploded view of the Stromberg 175 CDT gasket and flange mounting on 1974 (top) and 1975–78 (bottom) models

1. Carburetor attachment screw
2. Gasket
3. Rubber flange fastening screw
4. Rubber flange
5. Insulating flange
6. Gasket
7. Shielding plate
8. Intake pipe

Fig. 3 A new gasket was introduced in 1974 for the Solex 4A1. The top side is shown on the left and the bottom side on the right

6. Remove the retaining nuts and remove the carburetor from the manifold.

7. Installation is the reverse of removal. Install the insulating flange on the intake manifold as shown. The paper side of the insulating flange must face UP. In 1974, a new style insulating flange was used, which can be installed on previous engines.

8. Install the retaining nuts and tighten evenly, torquing the nuts in a crossing pattern. Torque the nuts to 7–11 ft. lbs.

9. Be sure to adjust the idle speed. Refer to Section 2 for these procedures.

OVERHAUL

All Models

Efficient carburetion depends greatly on careful cleaning and inspection during overhaul. Since dirt, gum, water, or varnish in or on the carburetor parts are often responsible for poor performance.

Overhaul your carburetor in a clean, dust-free area. Carefully disassemble the carburetor, referring often to the exploded views. Keep all similar and lookalike parts segregated during disassembly and cleaning to avoid accidental interchange during assembly. Make a note of all jet sizes.

When the carburetor is assembled, wash all parts (except diaphragms, electric choke units, pump plunger, and any other plastic, leather, fiber, or rubber parts) in clean carburetor solvent. Do not leave parts in the solvent any longer than is necessary to sufficiently loosen the deposits. Excessive cleaning may remove the special finish from the float bowl and choke valve bodies, leaving these parts unfit for service. Rinse all parts in clean solvent and blow them dry with compressed air or allow them to air dry. Wipe clean all cork, plastic, leather, and fiber parts with a clean, lint-free cloth.

Blow out all passages and jets with compressed air and be sure that there are no restrictions or blockages. Never use wire or similar tools to clean jets, fuel passages, or air bleeds. Clean all jets and valves separately to avoid accidental interchange.

Check all parts for wear or damage. If wear or damage is found, replace the defective parts. Especially check the following:

1. Check the float needle and seat for wear. If wear is found, replace the complete assembly.

2. Check the float hinge pin for wear and the float(s) for dents or distortion. Replace the float if fuel has leaked into it.

3. Check the throttle and choke shaft bores for wear or an out-of-round condition. Damage or wear to the throttle arm, shaft, or shaft bore will often require replacement of the throttle body. These parts require a close tolerance of fit; wear may allow air leakage, which could affect starting and idling.

➡**Throttle shafts and bushings are not included in overhaul kits. They can be purchased separately.**

4. Inspect the idle mixture adjusting needles for burrs or grooves. Any such condition requires replacement of the needle, since you will not be able to obtain a satisfactory idle.

5. Test the accelerator pump check valves. They should pass air one way but not the other. Test for proper seating by blowing and sucking on the valve. Replace the valve if necessary. If the valve is satisfactory, wash the valve again to remove breath moisture.

6. Check the bowl cover for warped surfaces with a straightedge.

7. Closely inspect the valves and seats for wear and damage, replacing as necessary.

8. After the carburetor is assembled, check the choke valve for freedom of operation.

Carburetor overhaul kits are recommended for each overhaul. These kits contain all gaskets and new parts to replace those that deteriorate most rapidly. Failure to replace all parts supplied with the kit (especially gaskets) can result in poor performance later.

Some carburetor manufacturers supply overhaul kits of three basic types: minor repair; major repair; and gasket kits. Basically, they contain the following:

Minor Repair Kits:
- All gaskets
- Float needle valve
- Volume control screw
- All diaphragms
- Spring for the pump diaphragm

Major Repair Kits:
- All jets and gaskets
- All diaphragms
- Float needle valve
- Volume control screw
- Pump ball valve
- Main jet carrier
- Float
- Complete intermediate rod
- Intermediate pump lever
- Complete injector tube
- Some cover hold-down screws and washers

Gasket Kits:
- All gaskets

After cleaning and checking all components, reassemble the carburetor, using new parts and referring to the exploded view. When reassembling, make sure that all screws and jets are tight in their seats, but do not overtighten, as the tips will be distorted. Tighten all screws gradually, in rotation. Do not tighten needle valves into their seats; uneven jetting will result. Always use new gaskets. Be sure to adjust the float level when reassembling.

STROMBERG 175CDT CARBURETOR ONLY

▶ See Figures 4 and 5 (p. 6–7))

The preceding information applies to Stomberg carburetors also, but the following, additional suggestions should be followed.

1. Soak the small cork gaskets (jet gland washers) in penetrating oil or hot water for at least a half-hour prior to assembly, or they will invariably split.

2. When the jet is fully assembled, the jet tube should be a close fit without any lateral play, but it should be free to move smoothly. A few drops of oil or polishing of the tube may be necessary to achieve this.

3. If the jet sealing ring washer is made of cork, soak it in hot water for a minute or two prior to installation.

4. Adjust the float height.

5. Center the jet so that the piston will fall freely (when raised) and seat with a distinct click. If the jet is not centered properly, it will hang up in the tube.

ADJUSTMENTS

Stromberg 175CDT Carburetor

DAMPER FLUID LEVEL

1. Unscrew the top of the damper and check the fluid level. See Chapter 1.

2. If necessary, top up the reservoir with Automatic Transmission Fluid (ATF).

3. The fluid level should be to the top edge of the piston ring or on 1977–78 models, to the lower edge of the filler plug threads.

4. Replace the top on the reservoir.

FLOAT LEVEL

▶ See Figure 6 (p. 7)

1. Remove the carburetor.

2. Remove the float chamber cover and idling speed cut-off valve.

3. Do not loosen the lock screw from the needle, or the needle will have to be recentered.

4. Remove the fuel nozzle and compensating element.

5. Push the float down until the float needle valve ball is fully pushed in.

6. Check the float level with a home-made gauge.

7. To correct the float level, bend the float arm at the tang over the needle valve. The float arm must always remain perpendicular to the needle valve. Also check the sealing ring under the needle valve for specified thickness (1.5 mm) and replace if necessary.

8. Replace the float chamber cover and install the carburetor.

9. Adjust the idle.

AUTOMATIC CHOKE

1. The idle should be set and the engine should be at normal operating temperature.

2. On vehicles with air conditioning, remove the air cleaner and air intake.

3. Check the adjustment of the choke cover. The index marks should be aligned.

4. Raise the throttle linkage slightly and insert a screwdriver through the slot of the starter housing on the carburetor. Push the screwdriver against the engaging lever in the direction of the engine. Release the throttle linkage and engaging lever. This will set the engine at fast idle.

5. The fast idle speed should be 3300–3600 rpm. If the speed requires adjustment, loosen both locknuts on the connecting rod and turn the threaded bolt. ½ turn of the bolt will change the engine rpm by about 200–300 rpm. Decreasing the length of the bolt will decrease rpm and increasing the length will increase rpm.

FAST IDLE (1975–78 MODELS ONLY)

The fast idle adjustment is done with the cam on the second step.

1. Run the engine to normal operating temperature.

2. With the engine idling, raise the throttle linkage slightly.

3. At the same time, push the engaging lever with a small screwdriver, through the slot of the choke housing in the direction of the engine, against the stop on the full down diaphragm rod. Do not force it past the stop.

4. Raise the throttle linkage, while holding the engaging lever against the stop.

5. Check the CO and fast idle.

6. Adjust the fast idle speed with the upper adjusting screw to 1600–1800 rpm.

7. Adjust the CO with the mixture adjusting screw to 5–8%. To check the CO, the center vacuum line for the air injection switchover valve must be disconnected and plugged.

FULL THROTTLE STOP (1975–78 CALIFORNIA ONLY)

1. With the accelerator pedal fully depressed, adjust the full throttle stop screw so that a clearance of .02 in. exists between the throttle valve lever and carburetor housing.

THERMO AIR VALVE

1. Disconnect the hoses from the thermo air valve and blow into one hose. If the valve is cold, no air can pass through the valve. If the valve is warm (slightly above room temperature) air should pass through the valve.

Solex 4A1 Carburetor
▶ See Figures 7 and 8 (p. 8–9)

FUEL LEVEL
▶ See Figure 9 (p. 9)

1. There is no provision for measuring the fuel level, other than with the special Mercedes-Benz tool. It is a measuring rod which is inserted through the bore of the carburetor cover, and can be purchased from a dealer or fabricated.

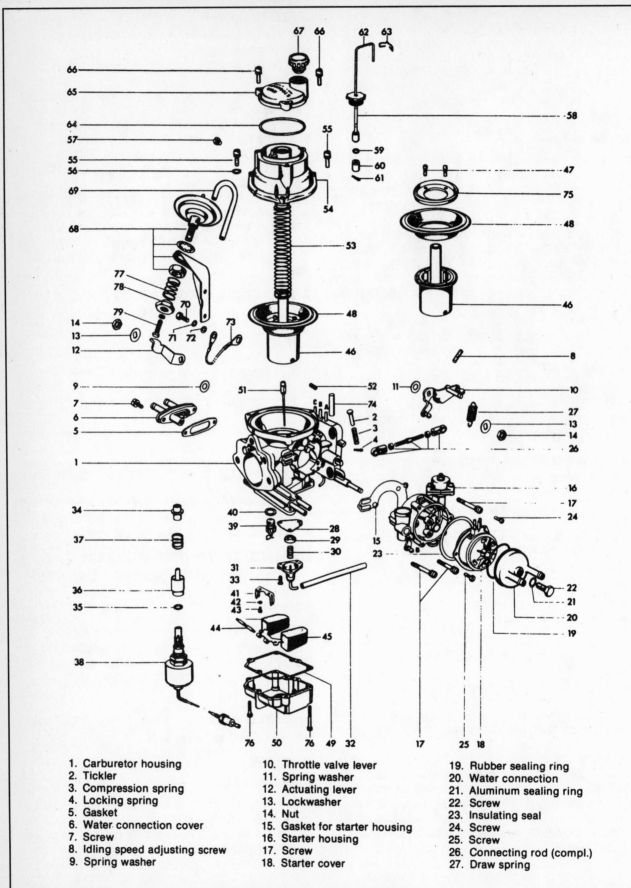

Fig. 4 Exploded view of the Stromberg 175 CDT carburetor and component list

1. Carburetor housing
2. Tickler
3. Compression spring
4. Locking spring
5. Gasket
6. Water connection cover
7. Screw
8. Idling speed adjusting screw
9. Spring washer
10. Throttle valve lever
11. Spring washer
12. Actuating lever
13. Lockwasher
14. Nut
15. Gasket for starter housing
16. Starter housing
17. Screw
18. Starter cover
19. Rubber sealing ring
20. Water connection
21. Aluminum sealing ring
22. Screw
23. Insulating seal
24. Screw
25. Screw
26. Connecting rod (compl.)
27. Draw spring

28. Diaphragm for fuel return valve	44. Float shaft	62. Capillary pipe
29. Spring plate	45. Float	63. Spring clip
30. Compression spring	46. Air piston	64. Rubber sealing ring
31. Valve cover	47. Screw	65. Closing cover
32. Vacuum hose	48. Vacuum diaphragm	66. Screw
33. Countersunk head screw	49. Gasket for float chamber	67. Damper oil filler plug
34. Guide bushing for fuel nozzle (pressed-in)	50. Float chamber	68. Vacuum box with fastening elements
35. Rubber sealing ring	51. Nozzle needle	69. Vacuum hose
36. Temperature-controlled compensating element with fuel nozzle	52. Stud for attaching nozzle needle	70. Screw
	53. Compression spring	71. Snap-ring
37. Compression spring	54. Carburetor cover	72. Washer
38. Idling speed shutoff valve	55. Screw	73. Grounding cable
39. Float needle valve	56. Washer	74. Rubber closing cap
40. Sealing ring	57. Cheese head screw	75. Holding disc
41. Bracket for float shaft	58. Damper for air piston	76. Cheese head screw
42. Snap ring	59. Washer	77. Compression spring
43. Screw	60. Damper piston	78. Adjusting nut
	61. Locking spring	79. Thrust bolt

Fig. 5 Stromberg 175 CDT carburetor component list (continued)

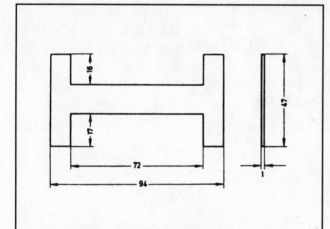

Fig. 6 Fabricate a gauge to these specifications to measure the Stromberg 175 CDT float level (dimensions in mm)

2. Run the engine briefly at fast idle and shut off the ignition.

3. Insert the measuring gauge through the bore of the carburetor cover as far as it will go.

4. Remove the gauge and read the fuel level. The reading should be within the tolerance range marked on the stick.

5. To adjust the level, remove the carburetor cover and adjust the float by bending it on the hinge.

6. Reinstall the cover and test the level again.

FLOAT LEVEL

▶ **See Figures 10 and 11 (p. 9)**

1. Remove the carburetor cover. The carburetor does not have to be removed.

2. With the float needle valve installed, push the connecting web of the float arms down until a noticeable stop. Be sure to push at the web. If not, the float shaft will lift from the bottom and result in an incorrect measurement.

3. Using a T-gauge or a homemade gauge, measure the level of the float below the carburetor housing without the gasket installed.

4. If the float level is not correct, remove the float in the desired direction.

5. Reinstall the carburetor cover.

VACUUM GOVERNOR

1. Set the idle speed and make sure that the engine is at normal operating temperature.

2. Run the engine at idle and pull the vacuum hose from the governor.

3. Set the engine speed to approximately 1200–1400 rpm. Loosen the locknut and adjust the rpm with the adjusting screw. Hold the diaphragm rod and turn the adjusting nut.

4. Adjust the compression spring with the transmission in gear.

5. The speed should be 600–700 rpm. If necessary, adjust the compression spring with the adjusting nut.

6. Turn on the air conditioning, and turn the wheels to full lock. The engine should keep running. If it does not, adjust the speed with the adjusting nut again. Refer to Step 3.

AUTOMATIC CHOKE

1. Check the choke for ease of operation.

2. Switch on the ignition and check to be sure that the choke opens after a minute or so.

3. Check the adjustment on the choke cover. The markings on the housing and cover should be aligned.

CHOKE GAP

1. Run the engine at idle until the diaphragm in the vacuum unit has been pulled completely against the stop.

2. Then clamp the hose to block all vacuum.

3. Be sure that the diaphragm is still against the stop and

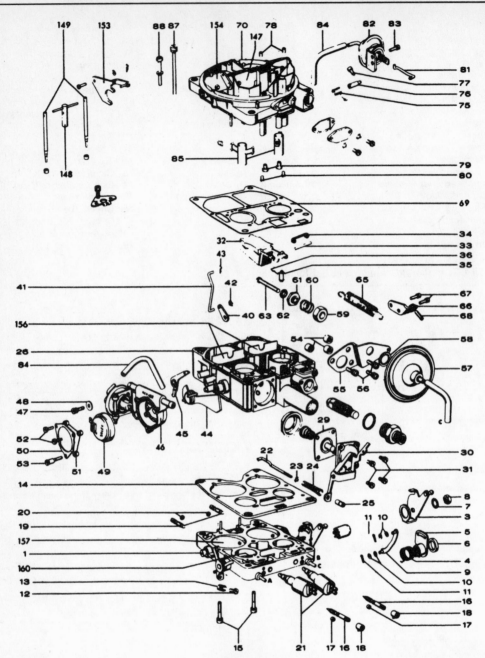

Fig. 7 Exploded view of the Solex 4A1 carburetor and component list

1. Throttle valve housing
3. Bracket
4. Spring
5. Cam lever
6. Bushing
7. Washer
8. Nut
9. Secondary connecting rod
10. Washer
11. Cotter pin
12. Screw
13. Spring
14. Plate
15. Screw
16. Idle mixture adjusting screws
17. Idle mixture adjusting screws
18. Idle mixture adjusting screws

19. Secondary jets
20. Secondary jets
21. Idle speed solenoid
22. Actuating levers for accelerator pump
23. Actuating levers for accelerator pump
24. Actuating levers for accelerator pump
25. Actuating levers for accelerator pump
26. Float housing
29. Diaphragm
30. Accelerator pump cover
31. Screws
32. Float
33. Float shaft

34. Hold-down clamp
35. Float needle
36. Float needle
40. Choke connecting rod
41. Choke connecting rod
42. Circlip
43. Cotter pin
44. Cam lever
45. Step lever
46. Thermostat housing
47. Screw
48. Washer
49. Thermostat cover
50. Attaching plate
51. Bushing
52. Screws (short)
53. Screw (long)

54. Vacuum regulator with bracket	69. Gasket	85. Emulsion Tube
55. Vacuum regulator with bracket	70. Carburetor cover	87. Screw
56. Vacuum regulator with bracket	75. Spring	88. Screw
57. Vacuum regulator with bracket	76. Eccentric pin	147. Choke plate
58. Vacuum regulator with bracket	77. Clamp screw	148. Guide pin
59. Nut	78. Primary idle air jets	149. Secondary needle valve
60. Spring	79. Main jets	153. Lever
61, 62. Nut	80. Screws	154. Secondary choke plate
63. Screw	81. Vacuum diaphragm connecting	156. Secondary baffle plates
65. Throttle return spring	rod	157. Throttle valve (primary)
66. Idle stop screw with bracket	82. Vacuum diaphragm	160. Throttle valve (secondary)
67. Idle stop screw with bracket	83. Screw	
68. Idle stop screw with bracket	84. Vacuum line	

Fig. 8 Solex 4A1 carburetor component list (continued)

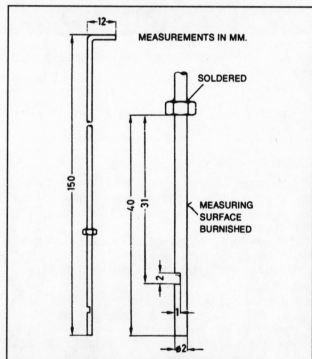

Fig. 9 Fabricate a tool to measure the fuel level on Solex 4A1 carburetors using the specifications illustrated

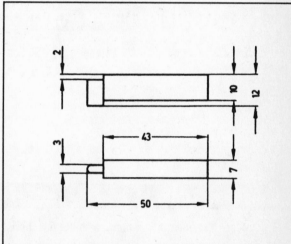

Fig. 10 Fabricate a tool to measure the float level on Solex 4A1 carburetors using these specifications

slightly raise the throttle valve lever. Position the stepped disc upward against the top stop. Release the throttle valve lever.

4. Push the lever of the bi-metallic spring until the stop is felt. The connecting rod will now be against the stop in the slot of the lever.

5. Measure the choke gap with a drill (0.060 in.—1974 Federal; 0.10 in.—1974 California; 0.108–0.120 in.—1975–76) between the choke plate and the wall of the air horn.

6. To adjust the gap, remove the coolant hose from the choke housing. Cover the choke housing with a rag and release the pressure in the radiator. Tighten the radiator cap again. Remove the coolant hose and clamp it shut.

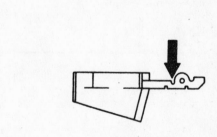

Fig. 11 To adjust the float level on a Solex 4A1 carburetor, bend the float at the point illustrated (arrow)

7. Bend the connecting rod with a pair of pliers. On later models, the adjustment is made by turning the adjusting screw in the choke housing cover in (decrease gap) or out (increase gap).

8. While making the adjustment, be sure that the diaphragm in the vacuum unit is still against its stop.

FAST IDLE

1. Adjust the idle speed and be sure that the engine is at normal operating temperature.

2. Run the engine at idle speed.

3. Raise the throttle valve lever slightly and position the stepped disc completely upward against the top stop.

4. Release the throttle valve lever.

5. Connect a tachometer and measure the engine speed. It should be 2400–2600 rpm. If required, adjust the fast idle with the fast idle speed adjusting screw.

ACCELERATOR PUMP

1. Move the throttle valve lever several times. A strong jet of fuel should be forced out of the fuel outlets.

2. If not, remove the accelerator pump cover and check the diaphragm. Blow out the ducts with compressed air.

3. Install the accelerator pump cover.

4. If there still is no fuel from the injection tube, remove the carburetor cover.

5. Actuate the accelerator pump. If fuel emerges from the ball valves, blow out the injection holes in the carburetor cover with compressed air.

6. Install the carburetor cover. Tighten the screws evenly to 11 ft. lbs.

FUEL RETURN VALVE

1. Pull the fuel return hose from the connection to the return line below the fuel pump.

2. Hold the return hose in a container and check whether a strong fuel jet comes from the line with the automatic transmission in Drive and the air conditioning on.

BOSCH ELECTRONIC FUEL INJECTION

➡**This system was used on 1974–75 V8 engines.**

This system is a constant pressure, electronically controlled unit. The "brain" of the system, actually a small computer that senses the determining factors for fuel delivery, is located behind the passenger kick panel on the right-hand side.

A Bosch tester is necessary to accurately test the solid state circuitry and components, but there are a few checks that can be carried out independently of the tester.

Electric Fuel Pump

➡**Do not confuse the electric fuel pump with the injection pump.**

All Mercedes-Benz fuel injected engines are equipped with electric fuel pumps. The electric fuel pump is located underneath the rear floor panel. The fuel return line was also eliminated and a check ball installed in its place.

Two types of fuel pumps have been used. One, the large pump, has been replaced with a new small design which has a bypass system to prevent vapor lock.

REMOVAL & INSTALLATION

1. Jack the left rear of the car and support it on jackstands. This will provide sufficient working clearance.

2. Remove and plug the intake, outlet, and bypass lines from the pump.

3. Disconnect the electrical leads.

4. Unbolt and remove the fuel pump and vibration pads.

5. Install the fuel pump in the reverse order of removal. Be sure that the electrical leads are connected to the proper terminals. The negative wire (brown) is connected to the negative terminal (brown plastic plate) and the positive wire (black/red) is connected to the positive terminal (red plastic plate). If the terminals

are reversed, the pump will operate in the reverse direction of normal rotation and will deliver no fuel.

TESTING

Fuel Pump Pressure

Temporarily reduce the pressure in the ring line by unplugging the connection at the starting valve. Connect the terminals of the starting valve to the battery for approximately 20 seconds. Reconnect the starting valve.

1. Remove the air filter and connect a pressure gauge at the branch connection at the ring line.

2. Run the engine and measure the pressure. It should be 26.5–29.5 psi.

3. Stop the engine. The fuel pressure may drop to 21 psi, after approximately 5 minutes. If the fuel pressure drops uniformly to 0, check the following points for leaks.

Starting valve—Switch on ignition and disconnect hose at starting valve. If there is no drop in pressure, the valve leaks.

Pressure regulator—Switch on the ignition and disconnect the fuel return hose, as soon as the fuel pump stops. If there is no drop in pressure, the regulator leaks.

Ball valve in delivery connection of fuel pump—Switch on the ignition and disconnect the fuel hose in front of the ring line the moment the fuel pump stops. If there is no drop in pressure, replace the fuel pump.

Injection Valves—remove the kick panel and bridge terminals 1 and 3 on the relay shown. This will energize the fuel pump with the engine stopped, and ignition **ON**. Check the valves for leaks.

4. Before removing the gauge, reduce the pressure in the ring line.

The fuel pressure can be adjusted on the regulator with the adjusting screw. Adjust to 28 psi. If a slight turn of the screw shows no change of pressure replace the regulator.

ADJUSTMENTS

Fuel Pressure
⊳ See Figure 12

The fuel pressure can be adjusted on the regulator with the adjusting screw. Adjust to 28 psi. If a slight turn of the screw shows no change of pressure replace the regulator.

Before replacing the regulator or removing the pressure gauge, reduce the pressure in the ring line by unplugging the starting valve and connecting it to battery voltage for 20 seconds.

Fig. 12 To check the fuel pump pressure, disconnect the fuel return hose from the fuel distributor (arrow)

Regulating Shaft

Step on the accelerator pedal up to the kickdown. The regulating lever should rest against the fuel throttle stop of the valve.

Loosen the hex bolt and push the linkage up to the full throttle stop if adjustment is required.

Regulating Linkage
⊳ See Figure 13

1. Check the linkage for ease of operation.
2. Check that the throttle valve closes completely. Disconnect the regulating rods.

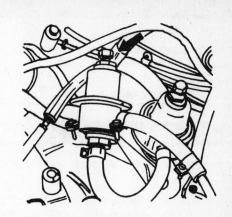

Fig. 13 Location of the adjusting screw on the fuel pressure regulator—Bosch electronic fuel injected models

3. Adjust the pushrod to a length of 4 in. from the center of the rubber mount to the center of the ball socket and attach.

On vehicles with manual transmission:

4. Adjust the connecting rod to a length of 3.5 in. (4.1 in. for cars with gate shift lever with bore next to ball head) and attach it.
5. Push the throttle lever against the idle speed stop. Adjust the connecting rod so that the regulating lever rests with the roller against the end stop of the gate shift lever.

On cars with automatic transmission and no gate shift lever:

6. Adjust the connecting rod (31) to 4.2 in. and the connecting rod (11) to 2.7 in. and attach.
7. Push the control rod to the rear against the stop and attach it tension free. During adjustment of the control pushrod, the ball socket must be held next to the ball head.

On cars with automatic transmission and gate shift lever:

8. Adjust the connecting rod to 4.2 in. and attach.
9. Push the throttle valve lever against the idle speed stop. Adjust the connecting rod so that the regulating lever rests with the roller against the end stop of the gate lever. Push the regulating lever to the rear against the stop pin.
10. Push the control pushrod against the stop and connect it tension free. The ball socket must be held next to the ball head.

BOSCH K-JETRONIC (CIS) MECHANICAL FUEL INJECTION

➡ This system was used on 1976–84 vehicles.

This system replaces the electronic system of earlier years. In contrast to the intermittent type fuel injection, this system measures air volume through and air flow sensor and injects fuel continuously in front of the intake valves, regardless of firing position.

Minor running changes and improvements are made during production, but essential operation and service of the system remains alike on all vehicles equipped with the CIS injection.

The 190E utilizes an electronically controlled version of the K-Jetronic injection system called KE-Jetronic (CIS-E). This system is a further development of the mechanically controlled CIS system. The essential difference between the two is mixture correction by means of electronically controlled correction functions (CIS-E). An electronic control unit sends out impulses which effect the amount of fuel being injected. Since only the mixture corrections are controlled by this new system, the vehicle will continue to operate if there is an electronic malfunction.

✳✳ CAUTION

Even a seemingly minor adjustment, such as idle speed, can necessitate adjustments to other portions of the fuel injection system. Be extremely careful when adjusting the idle. If any difficulty at all is experienced, it will only upset the balance of an already delicate system.

Electric Fuel Pump

➡Do not confuse the electric fuel pump with the injection pump.

All Mercedes-Benz fuel injected engines are equipped with electric fuel pumps. The electric fuel pump is located underneath the rear floor panel. The fuel return line was also eliminated and a check ball installed in its place.

Two types of fuel pumps have been used. One, the large pump, has been replaced with a new small design which has a bypass system to prevent vapor lock.

REMOVAL & INSTALLATION

1. Jack the left rear of the car and support it on jackstands. This will provide sufficient working clearance.
2. Remove and plug the intake, outlet, and bypass lines from the pump.
3. Disconnect the electric leads.
4. Unbolt and remove the fuel pump and vibration pads.
5. Install the fuel pump in the reverse order of removal. Be sure that the electric leads are connected to the proper terminals. The negative wire (brown) is connected to the negative terminal (brown plastic plate) and the positive wire (black/red) is connected to the positive terminal (red plastic plate). If the terminals are reversed, the pump will operate in the reverse direction of normal rotation and will deliver no fuel.

TESTING

Fuel Pump Pressure
◆ See Figure 14

Remove the fuel return hose from the fuel distributor. Connect a fuel line and hold the end in a measuring cup. Disconnect the plug for the safety switch on the mixture regulator and turn on the ignition for 30 seconds. If the delivery rate is less than 1 liter in 30 seconds, check the voltage at the fuel pump (11.5) and the fuel lines for kinks.

Disconnect the leak off line between the fuel accumulator and the suction damper. Check the delivery rate again. If it is low replace the accumulator.

Replace the fuel filter and test again. If still low, replace the fuel pump.

Cold Start Valve

1. Disconnect the plugs from the safety switch and mixture control regulator.
2. Remove the cold start valve with fuel line connected.
3. Hold the cold start valve in a container.

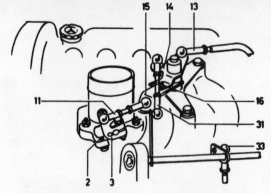

2. Idling speed stop	15. Regulating lever
3. Throttle valve level	16. Stop pin
11. Connecting rod	31. Connecting rod
13. Control pushrod	33. Pushrod
14. Regulating lever	

Fig. 14 View of the regulating linkage used on electronic fuel injected models

4. Turn on the ignition. Connect the valve to battery voltage. It should emit a come shaped spray.
5. Dry the nozzle off. No fuel should leak out.

Hot Start System
◆ See Figure 15

Perform the test at coolant temperature 104°–122°F.
1. Remove the coil wire.
2. Connect a voltmeter to hot-start terminal 3 and ground.
3. Actuate the starter. In approximately 3–4 seconds, the voltmeter should read about 11 volts for 3–4 seconds.
4. If 11 volts are not indicated, check fuse 10. Connect the plug of the 104°F temperature switch and ground and repeat the test. If 11 volts are now indicated, replace the temperature switch. If 11 volts are not indicated, or if the time periods are wrong, replace the hot start relay.

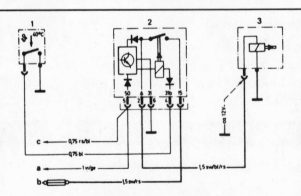

1. Temperature switch 104° F (40° C)
2. Hot-start relay
3. Hot-start solenoid
a. Terminal 50 (starter lock-out switch)
b. Fuse No. 10 (15/54)
c. To thermo-time switch

Fig. 15 Wiring schematic for the hot start system

Fuel Pump Safety Circuit
▶ **See Figure 16**

The pump will only run if the starter motor is actuated or if the engine is running.

1. Remove the air filter.
2. Turn on the ignition and briefly depress the sensor plate.
3. Remove the coil wire from the distributor.
4. Connect a voltmeter to the positive fuel pump terminal and ground.
5. Actuate the starter. Voltmeter should indicate 11 volts.
6. If the fuel pump runs only when the sensor plate is depressed or only when the engine is cranked, replace the fuel pump relay. If the pump is already running when the ignition is turned **ON,** replace the safety switch.

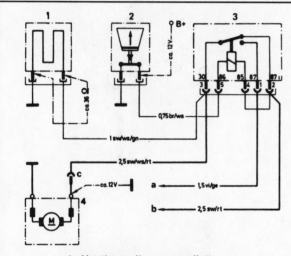

1. Heating coil, warm-up/full-load enrichment compensator
2. Safety switch, sensor plate
3. Relay, fuel pump
4. Fuel pump
   a. To terminal 50 (starter)
   b. To terminal 15/54 (ignition)
   c. To plug connection, tail light harness

Fig. 16 Wiring schematic for the fuel pump safety circuit

DIESEL FUEL SYSTEM

Electric Fuel Pump

➡**Do not confuse the electric fuel pump with the injection pump.**

All Mercedes-Benz fuel injected engines are equipped with electric fuel pumps. The electric fuel pump is located underneath the rear floor panel. The fuel return line was also eliminated and a check ball installed in its place.

Two types of fuel pumps have been used. One, the large pump, has been replaced with a new small design which has a bypass system to prevent vapor lock.

ADJUSTMENTS

Control Linkage
1976–79 MODELS

1. Check the control linkage for ease of operation.
2. Disconnect the control rod. The throttle valve should rest against the idle stop. Reconnect the control rod.
3. Adjust the control rod so that the roller rests tension free in the gate lever slot.

Full Throttle Stop
1976–69 MODELS

1. With the engine stopped, press the accelerator pedal until it rests against the kickdown switch.
2. The throttle valve lever should rest against the full throttle stop. If necessary, adjust the throttle valve lever.
3. If the full throttle stop is not reached, adjust the control rod (bell crank lever to accelerator pedal) to 4.8 in. (from center to center of ball sockets).
4. Adjust the accelerator pedal linkage if necessary with the fastening screw.
5. Adjust the control pressure rod (at idle) by compressing the adjusting clip, and moving the rod completely to the rear against the stop.

Throttle Valve Switch
1980–84 MODELS

1. Set an ohmmeter to 0-infinity.
2. Check the idle speed stop. Push the throttle valve against the idle speed stop. Connect the ohmmeter across terminals 1 and 2. Rotate the throttle valve switch until the ohmmeter reads 0.
3. Advance the throttle valve slightly. The ohmmeter should read 0-infinite ohms.
4. Check the full throttle stop. Push the throttle valve against the full throttle stop and connect an ohmmeter across terminals 2 and 3. The reading should be 0 ohms.
5. Turn the throttle valve back slightly. A reading of infinite ohms should result.

REMOVAL & INSTALLATION

1. Jack the left rear of the car and support it on jackstands. This will provide sufficient working clearance.
2. Remove and plug the intake, outlet, and bypass lines from the pump.
3. Disconnect the electric leads.
4. Unbolt and remove the fuel pump and vibration pads.
5. Install the fuel pump in the reverse order of removal. Be sure that the electric leads are connected to the proper terminals. The negative wire (brown) is connected to the negative terminal

(brown plastic plate) and the positive wire (black/red) is connected to the positive terminal (red plastic plate). If the terminals are reversed, the pump will operate in the reverse direction of normal rotation and will deliver no fuel.

TESTING

Fuel Pump Pressure

1974–75 MODELS

Temporarily reduce the pressure in the ring line by unplugging the connection at the starting valve. Connect the terminals of the starting valve to the battery for approximately 20 seconds. Reconnect the starting valve.

1. Remove the air filter and connect a pressure gauge at the branch connection at the ring line.
2. Run the engine and measure the pressure. It should be 26.5–29.5 psi.
3. Stop the engine. The fuel pressure may drop to 21 psi, after approximately 5 minutes. If the fuel pressure drops uniformly to 0, check the following points for leaks.

Starting valve—Switch on ignition and disconnect hose at starting valve. If there is no drop in pressure, the valve leaks.

Pressure regulator—Switch on the ignition and disconnect the fuel return hose, as soon as the fuel pump stops. If there is no drop in pressure, the regulator leaks.

Ball valve in delivery connection of fuel pump—Switch on the ignition and disconnect the fuel hose in front of the ring line the moment the fuel pump stops. If there is no drop in pressure, replace the fuel pump.

Injection Valves—remove the kick panel and bridge terminals 1 and 3 on the relay shown. This will energize the fuel pump with the engine stopped, and ignition **ON.** Check the valves for leaks.

4. Before removing the gauge, reduce the pressure in the ring line.

The fuel pressure can be adjusted on the regulator with the adjusting screw. Adjust to 28 psi. If a slight turn of the screw shows no change of pressure replace the regulator.

1976—84 MODELS

Remove the fuel return hose from the fuel distributor. Connect a fuel line and hold the end in a measuring cup. Disconnect the plug for the safety switch on the mixture regulator and turn on the ignition for 30 seconds. If the delivery rate is less than 1 liter in 30 seconds, check the voltage at the fuel pump (11.5) and the fuel lines for kinks.

Disconnect the leak off line between the fuel accumulator and the suction damper. Check the delivery rate again. If it is low replace the accumulator.

Replace the fuel filter and test again. If still low, replace the fuel pump.

Fuel Injector

REMOVAL & INSTALLATION

▶ **See Figures 17 and 18**

1. Disconnect the negtive battery cable.
2. Unbolt the fuel lines, then disconnect the overflow tubes.
3. Remove the injectors from the cylinder head.

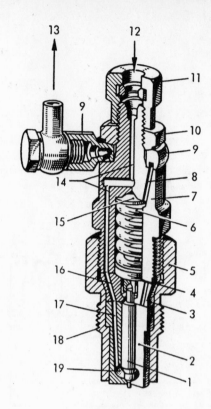

1. Jet needle
2. Nozzle assembly
3. Nozzle element
4. Thrust pin
5. Cap nut for fixing injection nozzle
6. Compression spring
7. Nozzle holder
8. Drain hole in the nozzle holder
9. Through-way jointing piece with annular canal for leak-off oil union
10. Hexagon nut for fixing the through-way jointing piece
11. Cap nut for fixing the injection pipe
12. Fuel feed
13. Leak-off oil drain back to fuel tank
14. Pressure canal in the nozzle holder
15. Special washers belonging to compression spring (machined steel disks)
16. Annular groove and feed bores in nozzle element
17. Annular groove and pressure canal in nozzle assembly
18. Mounting thread
19. Pressure chamber in nozzle assembly

Fig. 17 Cross-sectional view of a nozzle holder/injector assembly

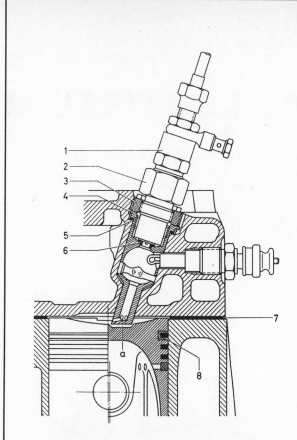

1. Nozzle holder
2. Cap nut of nozzle holder
3. Threaded ring
4. Prechamber
5. Sealing ring
6. Seal
7. Cylinder head gasket
8. Piston ring liner
a. Piston base recess

Fig. 18 Sectional view of an installed nozzle holder/injector assembly

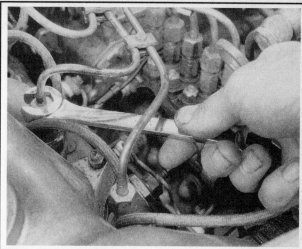

Use a flare nut wrench to loosen and disconnect the fuel line from the injector . . .

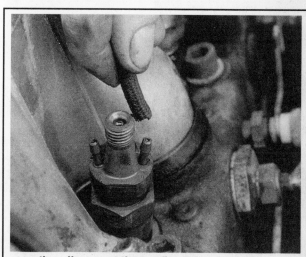

. . . then disconnect the overflow tubes from the injector

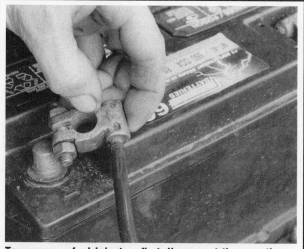

To remove a fuel injector, first disconnect the negative battery cable

Use a ratchet and socket to loosen the fuel injector . . .

1. Fuel injector

. . . then remove the injector from the cylinder head

➡️**If equipped with heat shields (washers), they must be replaced with new ones when reinstalling the fuel injector.**

4. Installation is the reverse of removal.

5. Bleed the system by opening the bleed screw and operating the hand pump to evacuate any air.

Injection Pump

♦ **See Figure 19**

In many cases of poor running, the injection pump itself is at fault. Fuel that is extremely gritty will cause wear of the pump plungers, and plunger springs can break in service. Accurate testing of the pump must be carried out on a test stand. Aside from testing the governor vacuum and control rod, little else other than visual inspection for broken or worn parts can be accomplished.

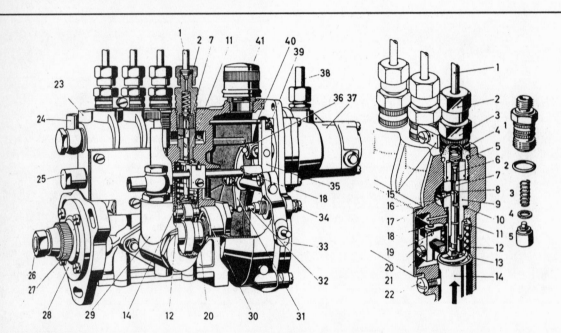

1. Pressure pipe (injection pipe)
2. Cap nut
3. Pipe union
4. Valve spring
5. Seal between pipe union and injection pump housing
6. Pressure valve with pressure valve holder
7. Pressure chamber
8. Plunger ⎫ _ forming pump
9. Cylinder ⎬ = element
10. Seal
11. Governor sleeve with steering arm
12. Tappet spring
13. Plunger vane
14. Roller tappet
15. Clamping jaws (to grip the pipe unions)
16. Suction chamber
17. Control bore (feed and return bore)
18. Control rod
19. Pin on control sleeve rotating lever
20. Adjustable clamping piece with guide groove
21. Clamp screw
22. Tappet guide screw
23. Injection pump housing
24. Fuel feed union
25. Control rod guide bearing and start-metering stop
26. Camshaft (drive side)
27. Link stud
28. Bearing base-plate with gasket and centering
    adjustment
29. Fuel feed pump
30. Journal bearing
31. Rocker arm
32. Stop pin for full load stop
33. Setting lever
34. Setting lever stop, also adjustment screw with full load stop
35. Guide lever
36. Diaphragm pin with pressure pin and compensator spring
37. Diaphragm assembly
38. Vacuum line
39. Diaphragm
40. Guide pin
41. Air cleaner and oil filler bore

Fig. 19 View of a typical diesel fuel injection pump's components

To remove the fuel injection pump, use a flare nut wrench to loosen the fuel lines . . .

1. Injection pump   2. Fuel lines

. . . then separate the fuel lines from their injection pump connections

REMOVAL & INSTALLATION

1. Unscrew all the injection lines, the vacuum line and fuel lines.
2. Plug the lines, then detach the connecting rod for the auxiliary mechanical control and the starting cable at the adjusting lever.
3. Turn the crankshaft, in the normal direction of rotation, to align the 45° BTDC mark with the pointer (No. 1 piston on compression stroke).
4. Matchmark the pump and flange.
5. Unscrew the nut at the bell-shaped support, then the front flange hold-down nuts. Pull the pump from the crankcase, then remove the coupling sleeve from the pump drive collar or driveshaft. New pumps do not come with the splined drive collar, therefore the old one must be removed if the pump is to be exchanged.
6. Using a puller, carefully remove the collar and woodruff key.

To install:

7. Make sure that the crankshaft has not moved from the 45° BTDC position, then insert the woodruff key into its groove in the driveshaft, making sure the shaft is dirt free.

8. Install the drive collar and hex nut, using a pair of pliers wrapped in tape to hold the collar while tightening the nut. It is extremely important that the splines are not damaged in any way during this operation.
9. Try sliding the coupling sleeve onto the drive collar. If it slides on easily, it can be pressed onto the driveshaft. Remove the oil overflow pipe plug at the rear of the injection pump and adjust the start of delivery position by aligning the marks. Apply light finger pressure to the follower in a direction opposite normal direction of rotation (left). This pressure should cause the drive collar to jump two teeth.
10. Grease the paper gaskets with petroleum jelly and install them to the side of crankcase, then install the pump, fingertightening the bolts in the slotted holes.
11. Turn the crankshaft in the direction of rotation to 24° BTDC and check the start of delivery, as outlined previously.

Glow Plugs

♦ **See Figure 20**

The glow plugs provide a means of ignition during starting and perform the same *function* as normal spark plugs, although they do so in a different manner.

TESTING

The light on the dashboard which indicates when the glow plugs are hot enough to fire can also serve as a troubleshooting aid. If the light does not glow, it usually indicates a faulty plug.

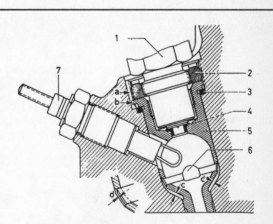

a. Groove in cylinder head
b. Lug securing prechamber
c. Distance between prechamber (5) and cylinder head
d. Max. permissible measure of a retracted ball pin with respect to the outer dia. of the prechamber (.020″)
1. Nozzle holder
2. Threaded ring
3. Seal ring between prechamber and cylinder head
4. Seal ring between prechamber and nozzle holder (nozzle plate)
5. Prechamber (ball pin version)
6. Ball pin in the prechamber
7. Glow plug

Fig. 20 Cross-sectional view of an installed glow plug and its related components

1. Test the plugs by having an assistant hold the starting knob in the preheat position while shorting the plugs to ground, in turn, with a screwdriver. Each plug should produce a spark if working properly. While bridging the connections, the light on the dashboard should light.

2. If, after disconnecting the ground lead of the preheating system, the light still stays lit, a short circuit in the system is indicated. This is usually caused by a carbon-fouled plug electrode or by a lead touching the cylinder head. Check the leads first.

3. If they seem O.K., pull the knob to the preheat position and disconnect one plug power lead at a time, starting from the ground end, until the light goes out, indicating the faulty plug.

4. Glow plugs can be cleaned, but it is better to replace them if they are badly fouled.

REMOVAL & INSTALLATION

5. Loosen the cable, if this has not been done already, by removing the knurled nut.

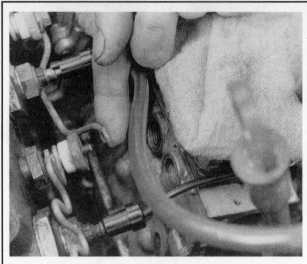

. . . and disconnect the bus bars from the glow plug

To remove a glow plug, disengage the electrical connection and remove the nut on the end of the plug

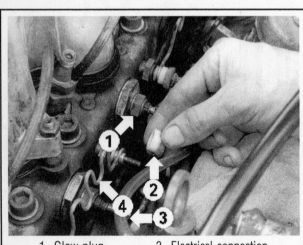

1. Glow plug   3. Electrical connection
2. Ceramic insulator   4. Bus bar
Remove the ceramic insulator . . .

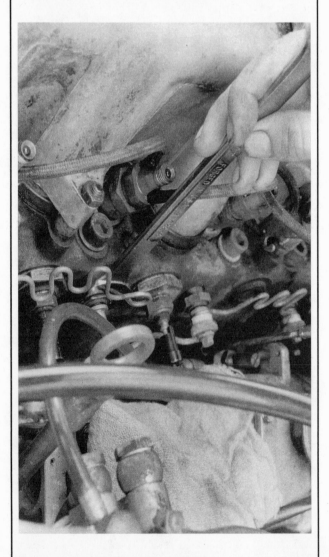

Use a wrench to loosen the glow plug

Remove the glow plug from the cylinder head

6. Unscrew the other nuts and remove the insulators and the bus bars.

7. Using a 21 mm. socket, unscrew and remove the glow plugs.

8. Before installing new plugs, clean the ducts and prechamber bores with a stiff bristle brush or a small scraper. The ball pin in the prechamber is easy to break, so don't go much deeper than 2 in. into the plug hole.

9. Crank the engine a few times to blow out any carbon particles loosened by the scraping, then insert the plugs. Do not exceed 35 ft lbs torque.

10. It might be a good idea to recheck these new plugs to ensure that all connections are tight and not grounded and that the plugs are not faulty.

Fuel Tank

REMOVAL & INSTALLATION

1. Disconnect ground connecting line on battery.

2. Drain fuel tank. Carefully pump off fuel, so that no residual fuel remains in fuel tank.

3. Remove trunk floor and intermediate shelf.

4. Pull off coupler for the fuel gauge.

5. Loosen hose clips on vent lines, pull off hoses, tightly close lines and hoses.

6. Loosen the hose clamps on front and the return line, pull off both hoses on the fuel tank and catch residual fuel in the hose. Tightly close the hoses and the filler neck.

7. Loosen the hose clamp and then pull off vent hose. Close hose and filler neck.

8. Unscrew the fastening nuts and then remove the fuel tank in a downward direction.

To install:

9. Install fuel tank in vice versa sequence and proceed as follows:

a. Glue foam rubber strip on fuel tank at level of filler neck crosswise to driving direction.

➡**Never use felt or similar material, since otherwise corrosion damage may result.**

b. Blow out the filter and check for damage. Renew the sealing ring. Install the fuel filter and tighten the retainers to 35–43 Nm.

c. Be sure to install the fuel tank with specified reinforcing plates and washers. Tighten the self-locking fastening nuts to 26–34 Nm.

d. Install the vent hose between the fuel tank and the filler neck free of kinks and with a continuous slope toward fuel tank.

The slipped-on O-ring serves for sealing at passage to interior.

e. Pay attention to the correct seat of the sleeves on filler neck.

f. Renew any damaged fuel hoses.

g. Check the operation of the fuel gauge (ground the connection line on the battery connected).

h. Check the fuel system for leaks.

Troubleshooting Basic Fuel System Problems

Problem	Cause	Solution
Engine cranks, but won't start (or is hard to start) when cold	• Empty fuel tank • Incorrect starting procedure • Defective fuel pump • No fuel in carburetor • Clogged fuel filter • Engine flooded • Defective choke	• Check for fuel in tank • Follow correct procedure • Check pump output • Check for fuel in the carburetor • Replace fuel filter • Wait 15 minutes; try again • Check choke plate
Engine cranks, but is hard to start (or does not start) when hot— (presence of fuel is assumed)	• Defective choke	• Check choke plate
Rough idle or engine runs rough	• Dirt or moisture in fuel • Clogged air filter • Faulty fuel pump	• Replace fuel filter • Replace air filter • Check fuel pump output
Engine stalls or hesitates on acceleration	• Dirt or moisture in the fuel • Dirty carburetor • Defective fuel pump • Incorrect float level, defective accelerator pump	• Replace fuel filter • Clean the carburetor • Check fuel pump output • Check carburetor
Poor gas mileage	• Clogged air filter • Dirty carburetor • Defective choke, faulty carburetor adjustment	• Replace air filter • Clean carburetor • Check carburetor
Engine is flooded (won't start accompanied by smell of raw fuel)	• Improperly adjusted choke or carburetor	• Wait 15 minutes and try again, without pumping gas pedal • If it won't start, check carburetor

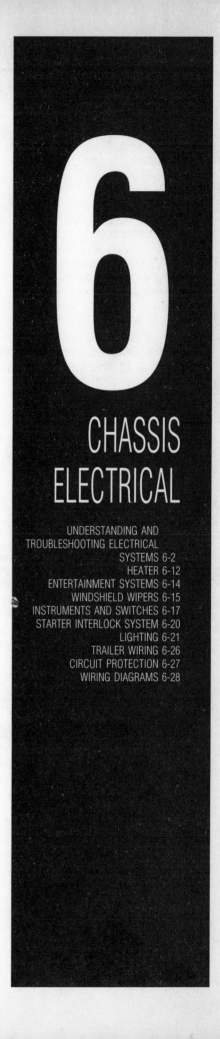

6

CHASSIS ELECTRICAL

UNDERSTANDING AND TROUBLESHOOTING ELECTRICAL SYSTEMS

Over the years import and domestic manufacturers have incorporated electronic control systems into their production lines. In fact, electronic control systems are so prevalent that all new cars and trucks built today are equipped with at least one on-board computer. These electronic components (with no moving parts) should theoretically last the life of the vehicle, provided that nothing external happens to damage the circuits or memory chips.

While it is true that electronic components should never wear out, in the real world malfunctions do occur. It is also true that any computer-based system is extremely sensitive to electrical voltages and cannot tolerate careless or haphazard testing/service procedures. An inexperienced individual can literally cause major damage looking for a minor problem by using the wrong kind of test equipment or connecting test leads/connectors with the ignition switch **ON**. When selecting test equipment, make sure the manufacturer's instructions state that the tester is compatible with whatever type of system is being serviced. Read all instructions carefully and double check all test points before installing probes or making any test connections.

The following section outlines basic diagnosis techniques for dealing with automotive electrical systems. Along with a general explanation of the various types of test equipment available to aid in servicing modern automotive systems, basic repair techniques for wiring harnesses and connectors are also given. Read the basic information before attempting any repairs or testing. This will provide the background of information necessary to avoid the most common and obvious mistakes that can cost both time and money. Although the replacement and testing procedures are simple in themselves, the systems are not, and unless one has a thorough understanding of all components and their function within a particular system, the logical test sequence these systems demand cannot be followed. Minor malfunctions can make a big difference, so it is important to know how each component affects the operation of the overall system in order to find the ultimate cause of a problem without replacing good components unnecessarily. It is not enough to use the correct test equipment; the test equipment must be used correctly.

Safety Precautions

✳✳ CAUTION

Whenever working on or around any electrical or electronic systems, always observe these general precautions to prevent the possibility of personal injury or damage to electronic components.

• Never install or remove battery cables with the key **ON** or the engine running. Jumper cables should be connected with the key **OFF** to avoid power surges that can damage electronic control units. Engines equipped with computer controlled systems should avoid both giving and getting jump starts due to the possibility of serious damage to components from arcing in the engine compartment if connections are made with the ignition **ON**.

• Always remove the battery cables before charging the battery. Never use a high output charger on an installed battery or attempt to use any type of "hot shot" (24 volt) starting aid.

• Exercise care when inserting test probes into connectors to in-sure good contact without damaging the connector or spreading the pins. Always probe connectors from the rear (wire) side, NOT the pin side, to avoid accidental shorting of terminals during test procedures.

• Never remove or attach wiring harness connectors with the ignition switch **ON**, especially to an electronic control unit.

• Do not drop any components during service procedures and never apply 12 volts directly to any component (like a solenoid or relay) unless instructed specifically to do so. Some component electrical windings are designed to safely handle only 4 or 5 volts and can be destroyed in seconds if 12 volts are applied directly to the connector.

• Remove the electronic control unit if the vehicle is to be placed in an environment where temperatures exceed approximately 176°F (80°C), such as a paint spray booth or when arc/gas welding near the control unit location.

Understanding Basic Electricity

Understanding the basic theory of electricity makes electrical troubleshooting much easier. Several gauges are used in electrical troubleshooting to see inside the circuit being tested. Without a basic understanding, it will be difficult to understand testing procedures.

THE WATER ANALOGY

Electricity is the flow of electrons—hypothetical particles thought to constitute the basic stuff of electricity. Many people have been taught electrical theory using an analogy with water. In a comparison with water flowing in a pipe, the electrons would be the water. As the flow of water can be measured, the flow of electricity can be measured. The unit of measurement is amperes, frequently abbreviated amps. An ammeter will measure the actual amount of current flowing in the circuit.

Just as the water pressure is measured in units such as pounds per square inch, electrical pressure is measured in volts. When a voltmeter's two probes are placed on two live portions of an electrical circuit with different electrical pressures, current will flow through the voltmeter and produce a reading which indicates the difference in electrical pressure between the two parts of the circuit.

While increasing the voltage in a circuit will increase the flow of current, the actual flow depends not only on voltage, but on the resistance of the circuit. The standard unit for measuring circuit resistance is an ohm, measured by an ohmmeter. The ohmmeter is somewhat similar to an ammeter, but incorporates its own source of power so that a standard voltage is always present.

CIRCUITS

An actual electric circuit consists of four basic parts. These are: the power source, such as a generator or battery; a hot wire, which conducts the electricity under a relatively high voltage to the component supplied by the circuit; the load, such as a lamp, motor, resistor or relay coil; and the ground wire, which carries the current back to the source under very low voltage. In such a circuit the bulk of the resistance exists between the point where the hot wire is connected to the load, and the point where the load is grounded. In an automobile, the vehicle's frame or body, which is made of steel, is used as a part of the ground circuit for many of the electrical devices.

Remember that, in electrical testing, the voltmeter is connected in parallel with the circuit being tested (without disconnecting any wires) and measures the difference in voltage between the locations of the two probes; that the ammeter is connected in series with the load (the circuit is separated at one point and the ammeter inserted so it becomes a part of the circuit); and the ohmmeter is self-powered, so that all the power in the circuit should be off and the portion of the circuit to be measured contacted at either end by one of the probes of the meter.

For any electrical system to operate, it must make a complete circuit. This simply means that the power flow from the battery must make a complete circle. When an electrical component is operating, power flows from the battery to the component, passes through the component causing it to perform it to function (such as lighting a light bulb) and then returns to the battery through the ground of the circuit. This ground is usually (but not always) the metal part of the vehicle on which the electrical component is mounted.

Perhaps the easiest way to visualize this is to think of connecting a light bulb with two wires attached to it to your vehicle's battery. The battery in your vehicle has two posts (negative and positive). If one of the two wires attached to the light bulb was attached to the negative post of the battery and the other wire was attached to the positive post of the battery, you would have a complete circuit. Current from the battery would flow out one post, through the wire attached to it and then to the light bulb, where it would pass through causing it to light. It would then leave the light bulb, travel through the other wire, and return to the other post of the battery.

AUTOMOTIVE CIRCUITS

The normal automotive circuit differs from this simple example in two ways. First, instead of having a return wire from the bulb to the battery, the light bulb return the current to the battery through the chassis of the vehicle. Since the negative battery cable is attached to the chassis and the chassis is made of electrically conductive metal, the chassis of the vehicle can serve as a ground wire to complete the circuit. Secondly, most automotive circuits contain switches to turn components on and off.

Some electrical components which require a large amount of current to operate also have a relay in their circuit. Since these circuits carry a large amount of current, the thickness of the wire in the circuit (gauge size) is also greater. If this large wire were connected from the component to the control switch on the instrument panel, and then back to the component, a voltage drop would occur in the circuit. To prevent this potential drop in voltage, an electromagnetic switch (relay) is used. The large wires in the circuit are connected from the vehicle battery to one side of the relay, and from the opposite side of the relay to the component. The relay is normally open, preventing current from passing through the circuit. An additional, smaller wire is connected from the relay to the control switch for the circuit. When the control switch is turned on, it grounds the smaller wire from the relay and completes the circuit.

SHORT CIRCUITS

If you were to disconnect the light bulb (from the previous example of a light-bulb being connected to the battery by two wires) from the wires and touch the two wires together (please take our word for this; don't try it), the result will be a shower of sparks. A similar thing happens (on a smaller scale) when the power supply wire to a component or the electrical component itself becomes grounded before the normal ground connection for the circuit. To prevent damage to the system, the fuse for the circuit blows to interrupt the circuit—protecting the components from damage. Because grounding a wire from a power source makes a complete circuit—less the required component to use the power—the phenomenon is called a short circuit. The most common causes of short circuits are: the rubber insulation on a wire breaking or rubbing through to expose the current carrying core of the wire to a metal part of the car, or a shorted switch.

Some electrical systems on the vehicle are protected by a circuit breaker which is, basically, a self-repairing fuse. When either of the described events takes place in a system which is protected by a circuit breaker, the circuit breaker opens the circuit the same way a fuse does. However, when either the short is removed from the circuit or the surge subsides, the circuit breaker resets itself and does not have to be replaced as a fuse does.

Troubleshooting

When diagnosing a specific problem, organized troubleshooting is a must. The complexity of a modern automobile demands that you approach any problem in a logical, organized manner. There are certain troubleshooting techniques that are standard:

1. Establish when the problem occurs. Does the problem appear only under certain conditions? Were there any noises, odors, or other unusual symptoms?

2. Isolate the problem area. To do this, make some simple tests and observations; then eliminate the systems that are working properly. Check for obvious problems such as broken wires, dirty connections or split/disconnected vacuum hoses. Always check the obvious before assuming something complicated is the cause.

3. Test for problems systematically to determine the cause once the problem area is isolated. Are all the components functioning properly? Is there power going to electrical switches and motors? Is there vacuum at vacuum switches and/or actuators? Is there a mechanical problem such as bent linkage or loose mounting screws? Performing careful, systematic checks will often turn up most causes on the first inspection without wasting time checking components that have little or no relationship to the problem.

4. Test all repairs after the work is done to make sure that the problem is fixed. Some causes can be traced to more than one component, so a careful verification of repair work is important in order to pick up additional malfunctions that may cause a problem to reappear or a different problem to arise. A blown fuse, for example, is a simple problem that may require more than another fuse to repair. If you don't look for a problem that caused a fuse to blow, a shorted wire (for example) may go undetected.

Experience has shown that most problems tend to be the result of a fairly simple and obvious cause, such as loose or corroded connectors or air leaks in the intake system. This makes careful inspection of components during testing essential to quick and accurate troubleshooting.

BASIC TROUBLESHOOTING THEORY

Electrical problems generally fall into one of three areas:
• The component that is not functioning is not receiving current.
• The component itself is not functioning.
• The component is not properly grounded.

Problems that fall into the first category are by far the most complicated. It is the current supply system to the component which contains all the switches, relay, fuses, etc.

The electrical system can be checked with a test light and a jumper wire. A test light is a device that looks like a pointed screwdriver with a wire attached to it. It has a light bulb in its handle. A jumper wire is a piece of insulated wire with an alligator clip attached to each end.

If a light bulb is not working, you must follow a systematic plan to determine which of the three causes is the villain.

1. Turn on the switch that controls the inoperable bulb.
2. Disconnect the power supply wire from the bulb.
3. Attach the ground wire to the test light to a good metal ground.
4. Touch the probe end of the test light to the end of the power supply wire that was disconnected from the bulb. If the bulb is receiving current, the test light will go on.

➡ **If the bulb is one which works only when the ignition key is turned on (turn signal), make sure the key is turned on.**

If the test light does not go on, then the problem is in the circuit between the battery and the bulb. As mentioned before, this includes all the switches, fuses, and relays in the system. Turn to a wiring diagram and find the bulb on the diagram. Follow the wire that runs back to the battery. The problem is an open circuit between the battery and the bulb. If the fuse is blown and, when replaced, immediately blows again, there is a short circuit in the system which must be located and repaired. If there is a switch in the system, bypass it with a jumper wire. This is done by connecting one end of the jumper wire to the power supply wire into the switch and the other end of the jumper wire to the wire coming out of the switch. If the test light illuminates with the jumper wire installed, the switch or whatever was bypassed is defective.

➡ **Never substitute the jumper wire for the bulb, as the bulb is the component required to use the power from the power source.**

5. If the bulb in the test light goes on, then the current is getting to the bulb that is not working in the car. This eliminates the first of the three possible causes. Connect the power supply wire and connect a jumper wire from the bulb to a good metal ground. Do this with the switch which controls the bulb works with jumper wire installed, then it has a bad ground. This is usually caused by the metal area on which the bulb mounts to the vehicle being coated with some type of foreign matter.

6. If neither test located the source of the trouble, then the light bulb itself is defective.

The above test procedure can be applied to any of the components of the chassis electrical system by substituting the component that is not working for the light bulb. Remember that for any electrical system to work, all connections must be clean and tight.

TEST EQUIPMENT

➡ **Pinpointing the exact cause of trouble in an electrical system can sometimes only be accomplished by the use of special test equipment. The following describes different types of commonly used test equipment and explains how to use them in diagnosis. In addition to the information covered below, the tool manufacturer's instructions booklet (provided with the tester) should be read and clearly understood before attempting any test procedures.**

Jumper Wires

Jumper wires are simple, yet extremely valuable, pieces of test equipment. They are basically test wires which are used to bypass sections of a circuit. The simplest type of jumper wire is a length of multi-strand wire with an alligator clip at each end. Jumper wires are usually fabricated from lengths of standard automotive wire and whatever type of connector (alligator clip, spade connec-

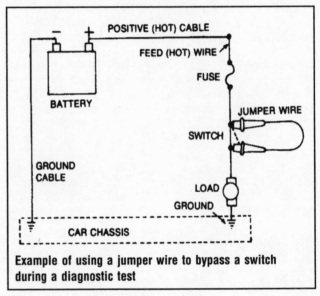

Example of using a jumper wire to bypass a switch during a diagnostic test

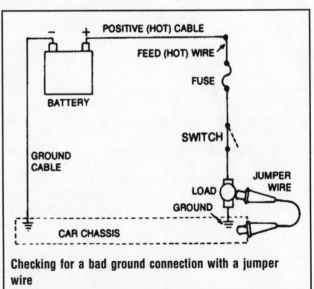

Checking for a bad ground connection with a jumper wire

tor or pin connector) that is required for the particular vehicle being tested. The well equipped tool box will have several different styles of jumper wires in several different lengths. Some jumper wires are made with three or more terminals coming from a common splice for special purpose testing. In cramped, hard-to-reach areas it is advisable to have insulated boots over the jumper wire terminals in order to prevent accidental grounding, sparks, and possible fire, especially when testing fuel system components.

Jumper wires are used primarily to locate open electrical circuits, on either the ground (−) side of the circuit or on the hot (+) side. If an electrical component fails to operate, connect the jumper wire between the component and a good ground. If the component operates only with the jumper installed, the ground circuit is open. If the ground circuit is good, but the component does not operate, the circuit between the power feed and component may be open. By moving the jumper wire successively back from the lamp toward the power source, you can isolate the area of the circuit where the open is located. When the component stops functioning, or the power is cut off, the open is in the segment of wire between the jumper and the point previously tested.

You can sometimes connect the jumper wire directly from the battery to the hot terminal of the component, but first make sure the component uses 12 volts in operation. Some electrical components, such as fuel injectors, are designed to operate on about 4 volts and running 12 volts directly to the injector terminals can cause damage.

By inserting an in-line fuse holder between a set of test leads, a fused jumper wire can be used for bypassing open circuits. Use a 5 amp fuse to provide protection against voltage spikes. When in doubt, use a voltmeter to check the voltage input to the component and measure how much voltage is normally being applied.

✳✳ CAUTION

Never use jumpers made from wire that is of lighter gauge than that which is used in the circuit under test. If the jumper wire is of too small a gauge, it may overheat and possibly melt. Never use jumpers to bypass high resistance loads in a circuit. Bypassing resistances, in effect, creates a short circuit. This may, in turn, cause damage and fire. Jumper wires should only be used to bypass lengths of wire.

Unpowered Test Lights

The 12 volt test light is used to check circuits and components while electrical current is flowing through them. It is used for voltage and ground tests. Twelve volt test lights come in different styles but all have three main parts; a ground clip, a probe, and a light. The most commonly used 12 volt test lights have pick-type probes. To use a 12 volt test light, connect the ground clip to a good ground and probe wherever necessary with the pick. The pick should be sharp so that it can be probed into tight spaces.

✳✳ CAUTION

Do not use a test light to probe electronic ignition spark plug or coil wires. Never use a pick-type test light to probe wiring on computer controlled systems unless specifically instructed to do so. Any wire insulation that is pierced by the test light probe should be taped and sealed with silicone after testing.

Like the jumper wire, the 12 volt test light is used to isolate opens in circuits. But, whereas the jumper wire is used to bypass the open to operate the load, the 12 volt test light is used to locate the presence of voltage in a circuit. If the test light glows, you know that there is power up to that point; if the 12 volt test light does not glow when its probe is inserted into the wire or connector, you know that there is an open circuit (no power). Move the test light in successive steps back toward the power source until the light in the handle does glow. When it glows, the open is between the probe and point which was probed previously.

➡**The test light does not detect that 12 volts (or any particular amount of voltage) is present; it only detects that some voltage is present. It is advisable before using the test light to touch its terminals across the battery posts to make sure the light is operating properly.**

Self-Powered Test Lights

The self-powered test light usually contains a 1.5 volt penlight battery. One type of self-powered test light is similar in design to the 12 volt unit. This type has both the battery and the light in the handle, along with a pick-type probe tip. The second type has the light toward the open tip, so that the light illuminates the contact point. The self-powered test light is a dual purpose piece of test equipment. It can be used to test for either open or short circuits when power is isolated from the circuit (continuity test). A powered test light should not be used on any computer controlled system or component unless specifically instructed to do so. Many engine sensors can be destroyed by even this small amount of voltage applied directly to the terminals.

Voltmeters

A voltmeter is used to measure voltage at any point in a circuit, or to measure the voltage drop across any part of a circuit. It can also be used to check continuity in a wire or circuit by indicating current flow from one end to the other. Analog voltmeters usually have various scales on the meter dial and a selector switch to allow the selection of different voltages. The voltmeter has a positive and a negative lead. To avoid damage to the meter, always connect the negative lead to the negative (−) side of the circuit (to ground or nearest the ground side of the circuit) and connect the positive lead to the positive (+) side of the circuit (to the power source or the nearest power source). Note that the negative voltmeter lead will always be black and that the positive voltmeter will always be some color other than black (usually red).

Depending on how the voltmeter is connected into the circuit, it has several uses. A voltmeter can be connected either in parallel or in series with a circuit and it has a very high resistance to current flow. When connected in parallel, only a small amount of current will flow through the voltmeter current path; the rest will flow through the normal circuit current path and the circuit will work normally. When the voltmeter is connected in series with a circuit, only a small amount of current can flow through the circuit. The circuit will not work properly, but the voltmeter reading will show if the circuit is complete or not.

Ohmmeters

The ohmmeter is designed to read resistance (which is measured in ohms or Ω) in a circuit or component. Although there are several different styles of ohmmeters, all analog meters will usually have a selector switch which permits the measurement of different ranges of resistance (usually the selector switch allows the multiplication of the meter reading by 10, 100, 1000, and 10,000). A calibration knob allows the meter to be set at zero for accurate measurement. Since all ohmmeters are powered by an internal battery, the ohmmeter can be used as a self-powered test light. When the ohmmeter is connected, current from the ohmmeter flows through the circuit or component being tested. Since the ohmmeter's internal resistance and voltage are known values, the amount of current flow through the meter depends on the resistance of the circuit or component being tested.

The ohmmeter can be used to perform a continuity test for opens or shorts (either by observation of the meter needle or as a self-powered test light), and to read actual resistance in a circuit. It should be noted that the ohmmeter is used to check the resistance of a component or wire while there is no voltage applied to the circuit. Current flow from an outside voltage source (such as the vehicle battery) can damage the ohmmeter, so the circuit or component should be isolated from the vehicle electrical system before any testing is done. Since the ohmmeter uses its own voltage source, either lead can be connected to any test point.

➡**When checking diodes or other solid state components, the ohmmeter leads can only be connected one way in order to measure current flow in a single direction. Make sure the positive (+) and negative (−) terminal connections are as described in the test procedures to verify the one-way diode operation.**

In using the meter for making continuity checks, do not be concerned with the actual resistance readings. Zero resistance, or any ohm reading, indicates continuity in the circuit. Infinite resistance indicates an open in the circuit. A high resistance reading where there should be none indicates a problem in the circuit. Checks for short circuits are made in the same manner as checks for open circuits except that the circuit must be isolated from both power and normal ground. Infinite resistance indicates no continuity to ground, while zero resistance indicates a dead short to ground.

Ammeters

An ammeter measures the amount of current flowing through a circuit in units called amperes or amps. Amperes are units of electron flow which indicate how fast the electrons are flowing through the circuit. Since Ohms Law dictates that current flow in a circuit is equal to the circuit voltage divided by the total circuit resistance, increasing voltage also increases the current level (amps). Likewise, any decrease in resistance will increase the amount of amps in a circuit. At normal operating voltage, most circuits have a characteristic amount of amperes, called "current draw" which can be measured using an ammeter. By referring to a specified current draw rating, measuring the amperes, and comparing the two values, one can determine what is happening within the circuit to aid in diagnosis. An open circuit, for example, will not allow any current to flow so the ammeter reading will be zero. More current flows through a heavily loaded circuit or when the charging system is operating.

An ammeter is always connected in series with the circuit being tested. All of the current that normally flows through the circuit must also flow through the ammeter; if there is any other path for the current to follow, the ammeter reading will not be accurate. The ammeter itself has very little resistance to current flow and therefore will not affect the circuit, but it will measure current

draw only when the circuit is closed and electricity is flowing. Excessive current draw can blow fuses and drain the battery, while a reduced current draw can cause motors to run slowly, lights to dim and other components to not operate properly. The ammeter can help diagnose these conditions by locating the cause of the high or low reading.

Multimeters

Different combinations of test meters can be built into a single unit designed for specific tests. Some of the more common combination test devices are known as Volt/Amp testers, Tach/Dwell meters, or Digital Multimeters. The Volt/Amp tester is used for charging system, starting system or battery tests and consists of a voltmeter, an ammeter and a variable resistance carbon pile. The voltmeter will usually have at least two ranges for use with 6, 12 and/or 24 volt systems. The ammeter also has more than one range for testing various levels of battery loads and starter current draw. The carbon pile can be adjusted to offer different amounts of resistance. The Volt/Amp tester has heavy leads to carry large amounts of current and many later models have an inductive ammeter pickup that clamps around the wire to simplify test connections. On some models, the ammeter also has a zero-center scale to allow testing of charging and starting systems without switching leads or polarity. A digital multimeter is a voltmeter, ammeter and ohmmeter combined in an instrument which gives a digital readout. These are often used when testing solid state circuits because of their high input impedance (usually 10 megohms or more).

The tach/dwell meter that combines a tachometer and a dwell (cam angle) meter is a specialized kind of voltmeter. The tachometer scale is marked to show engine speed in rpm and the dwell scale is marked to show degrees of distributor shaft rotation. In most electronic ignition systems, dwell is determined by the control unit, but the dwell meter can also be used to check the duty cycle (operation) of some electronic engine control systems. Some tach/dwell meters are powered by an internal battery, while others take their power from the vehicle battery in use. The battery powered testers usually require calibration (much like an ohmmeter) before testing.

TESTING

Open Circuits

To use the self-powered test light or a multimeter to check for open circuits, first isolate the circuit from the vehicle's 12 volt power source by disconnecting the battery or wiring harness connector. Connect the test light or ohmmeter ground clip to a good ground and probe sections of the circuit sequentially with the test light. (start from either end of the circuit). If the light is out/or there is infinite resistance, the open is between the probe and the circuit ground. If the light is on/or the meter shows continuity, the open is between the probe and end of the circuit toward the power source.

Short Circuits

By isolating the circuit both from power and from ground, and using a self-powered test light or multimeter, you can check for shorts to ground in the circuit. Isolate the circuit from power and ground. Connect the test light or ohmmeter ground clip to a good ground and probe any easy-to-reach test point in the circuit. If the light comes on or there is continuity, there is a short somewhere in the circuit. To isolate the short, probe a test point at either end of the isolated circuit (the light should be on/there should be continuity). Leave the test light probe engaged and open connectors, switches, remove parts, etc., sequentially, until the light goes out/continuity is broken. When the light goes out, the short is between the last circuit component opened and the previous circuit opened.

➡**The battery in the test light and does not provide much current. A weak battery may not provide enough power to illuminate the test light even when a complete circuit is made (especially if there are high resistances in the circuit). Always make sure that the test battery is strong. To check the battery, briefly touch the ground clip to the probe; if the light glows brightly the battery is strong enough for testing. Never use a self-powered test light to perform checks for opens or shorts when power is applied to the electrical system under test. The 12 volt vehicle power will quickly burn out the light bulb in the test light.**

Available Voltage Measurement

Set the voltmeter selector switch to the 20V position and connect the meter negative lead to the negative post of the battery. Connect the positive meter lead to the positive post of the battery and turn the ignition switch **ON** to provide a load. Read the voltage on the meter or digital display. A well charged battery should register over 12 volts. If the meter reads below 11.5 volts, the battery power may be insufficient to operate the electrical system properly. This test determines voltage available from the battery and should be the first step in any electrical trouble diagnosis procedure. Many electrical problems, especially on computer controlled systems, can be caused by a low state of charge in the battery. Excessive corrosion at the battery cable terminals can cause a poor contact that will prevent proper charging and full battery current flow.

Normal battery voltage is 12 volts when fully charged. When the battery is supplying current to one or more circuits it is said to be "under load." When everything is off the electrical system is under a "no-load" condition. A fully charged battery may show about 12.5 volts at no load; will drop to 12 volts under medium load; and will drop even lower under heavy load. If the battery is partially discharged the voltage decrease under heavy load may be excessive, even though the battery shows 12 volts or more at no load. When allowed to discharge further, the battery's available voltage under load will decrease more severely. For this reason, it is important that the battery be fully charged during all testing procedures to avoid errors in diagnosis and incorrect test results.

Voltage Drop

When current flows through a resistance, the voltage beyond the resistance is reduced (the larger the current, the greater the reduction in voltage). When no current is flowing, there is no voltage drop because there is no current flow. All points in the circuit which are connected to the power source are at the same voltage as the power source. The total voltage drop always equals the total source voltage. In a long circuit with many connectors, a series of small, unwanted voltage drops due to corrosion at the connectors can add up to a total loss of voltage which impairs the operation of the normal loads in the circuit. The maximum allowable voltage drop under load is critical, especially if there is more than one high resistance problem in a circuit because all voltage

drops are cumulative. A small drop is normal due to the resistance of the conductors.

INDIRECT COMPUTATION OF VOLTAGE DROPS

1. Set the voltmeter selector switch to the 20 volt position.
2. Connect the meter negative lead to a good ground.
3. While operating the circuit, probe all loads in the circuit with the positive meter lead and observe the voltage readings. A drop should be noticed after the first load. But, there should be little or no voltage drop before the first load.

DIRECT MEASUREMENT OF VOLTAGE DROPS

1. Set the voltmeter switch to the 20 volt position.
2. Connect the voltmeter negative lead to the ground side of the load to be measured.
3. Connect the positive lead to the positive side of the resistance or load to be measured.
4. Read the voltage drop directly on the 20 volt scale.

Too high a voltage indicates too high a resistance. If, for example, a blower motor runs too slowly, you can determine if perhaps there is too high a resistance in the resistor pack. By taking voltage drop readings in all parts of the circuit, you can isolate the problem. Too low a voltage drop indicates too low a resistance. Take the blower motor for example again. If a blower motor runs too fast in the MED and/or LOW position, the problem might be isolated in the resistor pack by taking voltage drop readings in all parts of the circuit to locate a possibly shorted resistor.

HIGH RESISTANCE TESTING

1. Set the voltmeter selector switch to the 4 volt position.
2. Connect the voltmeter positive lead to the positive post of the battery.
3. Turn on the headlights and heater blower to provide a load.
4. Probe various points in the circuit with the negative voltmeter lead.
5. Read the voltage drop on the 4 volt scale. Some average maximum allowable voltage drops are:
- FUSE PANEL: 0.7 volts
- IGNITION SWITCH: 0.5 volts
- HEADLIGHT SWITCH: 0.7 volts
- IGNITION COIL (+): 0.5 volts
- ANY OTHER LOAD: 1.3 volts

➡**Voltage drops are all measured while a load is operating; without current flow, there will be no voltage drop.**

Resistance Measurement

The batteries in an ohmmeter will weaken with age and temperature, so the ohmmeter must be calibrated or "zeroed" before taking measurements. To zero the meter, place the selector switch in its lowest range and touch the two ohmmeter leads together. Turn the calibration knob until the meter needle is exactly on zero.

➡**All analog (needle) type ohmmeters must be zeroed before use, but some digital ohmmeter models are automatically calibrated when the switch is turned on. Self-calibrating digital ohmmeters do not have an adjusting knob, but its a good idea to check for a zero readout before use by touching the leads together. All computer controlled systems require the use of a digital ohmmeter with at least 10 megohms impedance for testing. Before any test procedures are attempted, make sure the ohmmeter used is compatible with the electrical system or damage to the on-board computer could result.**

To measure resistance, first isolate the circuit from the vehicle power source by disconnecting the battery cables or the harness connector. Make sure the key is **OFF** when disconnecting any components or the battery. Where necessary, also isolate at least one side of the circuit to be checked in order to avoid reading parallel resistances. Parallel circuit resistances will always give a lower reading than the actual resistance of either of the branches. When measuring the resistance of parallel circuits, the total resistance will always be lower than the smallest resistance in the circuit. Connect the meter leads to both sides of the circuit (wire or component) and read the actual measured ohms on the meter scale. Make sure the selector switch is set to the proper ohm scale for the circuit being tested to avoid misreading the ohmmeter test value.

✳✳ WARNING

Never use an ohmmeter with power applied to the circuit. Like the self-powered test light, the ohmmeter is designed to operate on its own power supply. The normal 12 volt automotive electrical system current could damage the meter!

Wiring Harnesses

The average automobile contains about ½ mile of wiring, with hundreds of individual connections. To protect the many wires from damage and to keep them from becoming a confusing tangle, they are organized into bundles, enclosed in plastic or taped together and called wiring harnesses. Different harnesses serve different parts of the vehicle. Individual wires are color coded to help trace them through a harness where sections are hidden from view.

Automotive wiring or circuit conductors can be in any one of three forms:

1. Single strand wire
2. Multi-strand wire
3. Printed circuitry

Single strand wire has a solid metal core and is usually used inside such components as alternators, motors, relays and other devices. Multi-strand wire has a core made of many small strands of wire twisted together into a single conductor. Most of the wiring in an automotive electrical system is made up of multi-strand wire, either as a single conductor or grouped together in a harness. All wiring is color coded on the insulator, either as a solid color or as a colored wire with an identification stripe. A printed circuit is a thin film of copper or other conductor that is printed on an insulator backing. Occasionally, a printed circuit is sandwiched between two sheets of plastic for more protection and flexibility. A complete printed circuit, consisting of conductors, insulating material and connectors for lamps or other components is called a printed circuit board. Printed circuitry is used in place of individual wires or harnesses in places where space is limited, such as behind instrument panels.

Since automotive electrical systems are very sensitive to changes in resistance, the selection of properly sized wires is critical when systems are repaired. A loose or corroded connection or a replacement wire that is too small for the circuit will add extra resistance and an additional voltage drop to the circuit. A ten percent voltage drop can result in slow or erratic motor operation, for

example, even though the circuit is complete. The wire gauge number is an expression of the cross-section area of the conductor. The most common system for expressing wire size is the American Wire Gauge (AWG) system.

Gauge numbers are assigned to conductors of various cross-section areas. As gauge number increases, area decreases and the conductor becomes smaller. A 5 gauge conductor is smaller than a 1 gauge conductor and a 10 gauge is smaller than a 5 gauge. As the cross-section area of a conductor decreases, resistance increases and so does the gauge number. A conductor with a higher gauge number will carry less current than a conductor with a lower gauge number.

➡**Gauge wire size refers to the size of the conductor, not the size of the complete wire. It is possible to have two wires of the same gauge with different diameters because one may have thicker insulation than the other.**

12 volt automotive electrical systems generally use 10, 12, 14, 16 and 18 gauge wire. Main power distribution circuits and larger accessories usually use 10 and 12 gauge wire. Battery cables are usually 4 or 6 gauge, although 1 and 2 gauge wires are occasionally used. Wire length must also be considered when making repairs to a circuit. As conductor length increases, so does resistance. An 18 gauge wire, for example, can carry a 10 amp load for 10 feet without excessive voltage drop; however if a 15 foot wire is required for the same 10 amp load, it must be a 16 gauge wire.

An electrical schematic shows the electrical current paths when a circuit is operating properly. It is essential to understand how a circuit works before trying to figure out why it doesn't. Schematics break the entire electrical system down into individual circuits and show only one particular circuit. In a schematic, no attempt is made to represent wiring and components as they physically appear on the vehicle; switches and other components are shown as simply as possible. Face views of harness connectors show the cavity or terminal locations in all multi-pin connectors to help locate test points.

If you need to backprobe a connector while it is on the component, the order of the terminals must be mentally reversed. The wire color code can help in this situation, as well as a keyway, lock tab or other reference mark.

WIRING REPAIR

Soldering is a quick, efficient method of joining metals permanently. Everyone who has the occasion to make wiring repairs should know how to solder. Electrical connections that are soldered are far less likely to come apart and will conduct electricity much better than connections that are only "pig-tailed" together. The most popular (and preferred) method of soldering is with an electrical soldering gun. Soldering irons are available in many sizes and wattage ratings. Irons with higher wattage ratings deliver higher temperatures and recover lost heat faster. A small soldering iron rated for no more than 50 watts is recommended, especially on electrical systems where excess heat can damage the components being soldered.

There are three ingredients necessary for successful soldering; proper flux, good solder and sufficient heat. A soldering flux is necessary to clean the metal of tarnish, prepare it for soldering and to enable the solder to spread into tiny crevices. When soldering, always use a rosin core solder which is non-corrosive and will not attract moisture once the job is finished. Other types of flux (acid core) will leave a residue that will attract moisture and cause the wires to corrode. Tin is a unique metal with a low melting point. In a molten state, it dissolves and alloys easily with many metals. Solder is made by mixing tin with lead. The most common proportions are 40/60, 50/50 and 60/40, with the percentage of tin listed first. Low priced solders usually contain less tin, making them very difficult for a beginner to use because more heat is required to melt the solder. A common solder is 40/60 which is well suited for all-around general use, but 60/40 melts easier and is preferred for electrical work.

Soldering Techniques

Successful soldering requires that the metals to be joined be heated to a temperature that will melt the solder, usually 360–460°F (182–238°C). Contrary to popular belief, the purpose of the soldering iron is not to melt the solder itself, but to heat the parts being soldered to a temperature high enough to melt the solder when it is touched to the work. Melting flux-cored solder on the soldering iron will usually destroy the effectiveness of the flux.

➡**Soldering tips are made of copper for good heat conductivity, but must be "tinned" regularly for quick transference of heat to the project and to prevent the solder from sticking to the iron. To "tin" the iron, simply heat it and touch the flux-cored solder to the tip; the solder will flow over the hot tip. Wipe the excess off with a clean rag, but be careful as the iron will be hot.**

After some use, the tip may become pitted. If so, simply dress the tip smooth with a smooth file and "tin" the tip again. Flux-cored solder will remove oxides but rust, bits of insulation and oil or grease must be removed with a wire brush or emery cloth. For maximum strength in soldered parts, the joint must start off clean and tight. Weak joints will result in gaps too wide for the solder to bridge.

If a separate soldering flux is used, it should be brushed or swabbed on only those areas that are to be soldered. Most solders contain a core of flux and separate fluxing is unnecessary. Hold the work to be soldered firmly. It is best to solder on a wooden board, because a metal vise will only rob the piece to be soldered of heat and make it difficult to melt the solder. Hold the soldering tip with the broadest face against the work to be soldered. Apply solder under the tip close to the work, using enough solder to give a heavy film between the iron and the piece being soldered, while moving slowly and making sure the solder melts properly. Keep the work level or the solder will run to the lowest part and favor the thicker parts, because these require more heat to melt the solder. If the soldering tip overheats (the solder coating on the face of the tip burns up), it should be retinned. Once the soldering is completed, let the soldered joint stand until cool. Tape and seal all soldered wire splices after the repair has cooled.

Wire Harness Connectors

Most connectors in the engine compartment or that are otherwise exposed to the elements are protected against moisture and dirt which could create oxidation and deposits on the terminals.

These special connectors are weather-proof. All repairs require the use of a special terminal and the tool required to service it. This tool is used to remove the pin and sleeve terminals. If removal is attempted with an ordinary pick, there is a good chance that the terminal will be bent or deformed. Unlike standard blade type terminals, these weather-proof terminals cannot be straightened once they are bent. Make certain that the connectors are properly seated and all of the sealing rings are in place when connecting leads. On some models, a hinge-type flap provides a backup or secondary locking feature for the terminals. Most secondary locks are used to improve connector reliability by retaining the terminals if the small terminal lock tangs are not positioned properly.

Molded-on connectors require complete replacement of the connection. This means splicing a new connector assembly into the harness. All splices should be soldered to insure proper contact. Use care when probing the connections or replacing terminals in them as it is possible to short between opposite terminals. If this happens to the wrong terminal pair, it is possible to damage certain components. Always use jumper wires between connectors for circuit checking and never probe through weatherproof seals.

Open circuits are often difficult to locate by sight because corrosion or terminal misalignment are hidden by the connectors. Merely wiggling a connector on a sensor or in the wiring harness may correct the open circuit condition. This should always be considered when an open circuit or a failed sensor is indicated. Intermittent problems may also be caused by oxidized or loose connections. When using a circuit tester for diagnosis, always probe connections from the wire side. Be careful not to damage sealed connectors with test probes.

All wiring harnesses should be replaced with identical parts, using the same gauge wire and connectors. When signal wires are spliced into a harness, use wire with high temperature insulation only. It is seldom necessary to replace a complete harness. If replacement is necessary, pay close attention to insure proper harness routing. Secure the harness with suitable plastic wire clamps to prevent vibrations from causing the harness to wear in spots or contact any hot components.

➡**Weatherproof connectors cannot be replaced with standard connectors. Instructions are provided with replacement connector and terminal packages. Some wire harnesses have mounting indicators (usually pieces of colored tape) to mark where the harness is to be secured.**

In making wiring repairs, its important that you always replace damaged wires with wiring of the same gauge as the wire being replaced. The heavier the wire, the smaller the gauge number. Wires are color-coded to aid in identification and whenever possible the same color coded wire should be used for replacement. A wire stripping and crimping tool is necessary to install solderless terminal connectors. Test all crimps by pulling on the wires; it should not be possible to pull the wires out of a good crimp.

Wires which are open, exposed or otherwise damaged are repaired by simple splicing. Where possible, if the wiring harness is accessible and the damaged place in the wire can be located, it is best to open the harness and check for all possible damage. In an inaccessible harness, the wire must be bypassed with a new insert, usually taped to the outside of the old harness.

When replacing fusible links, be sure to use fusible link wire,

NOT ordinary automotive wire. Make sure the fusible segment is of the same gauge and construction as the one being replaced and double the stripped end when crimping the terminal connector for a good contact. The melted (open) fusible link segment of the wiring harness should be cut off as close to the harness as possible, then a new segment spliced in as described. In the case of a damaged fusible link that feeds two harness wires, the harness connections should be replaced with two fusible link wires so that each circuit will have its own separate protection.

➡**Most of the problems caused in the wiring harness are due to bad ground connections. Always check all vehicle ground connections for corrosion or looseness before performing any power feed checks to eliminate the chance of a bad ground affecting the circuit.**

Hard-Shell Connectors

Unlike molded connectors, the terminal contacts in hard-shell connectors can be replaced. Weatherproof hard-shell connectors with the leads molded into the shell have non-replaceable terminal ends. Replacement usually involves the use of a special terminal removal tool that depresses the locking tangs (barbs) on the connector terminal and allows the connector to be removed from the rear of the shell. The connector shell should be replaced if it shows any evidence of burning, melting, cracks, or breaks. Replace individual terminals that are burnt, corroded, distorted or loose.

➡**The insulation crimp must be tight to prevent the insulation from sliding back on the wire when the wire is pulled. The insulation must be visibly compressed under the crimp tabs, and the ends of the crimp should be turned in for a firm grip on the insulation.**

The wire crimp must be made with all wire strands inside the crimp. The terminal must be fully compressed on the wire strands with the ends of the crimp tabs turned in to make a firm grip on the wire. Check all connections with an ohmmeter to insure a good contact. There should be no measurable resistance between the wire and the terminal when connected.

Fusible Links

The fuse link is a short length of special, Hypalon (high temperature) insulated wire, integral with the engine compartment wiring harness and should not be confused with standard wire. It is several wire gauges smaller than the circuit which it protects. Under no circumstances should a fuse link replacement repair be made using a length of standard wire cut from bulk stock or from another wiring harness.

To repair any blown fuse link use the following procedure:

1. Determine which circuit is damaged, its location and the cause of the open fuse link. If the damaged fuse link is one of three fed by a common No. 10 or 12 gauge feed wire, determine the specific affected circuit.

2. Disconnect the negative battery cable.

3. Cut the damaged fuse link from the wiring harness and discard it. If the fuse link is one of three circuits fed by a single feed wire, cut it out of the harness at each splice end and discard it.

4. Identify and procure the proper fuse link with butt connectors for attaching the fuse link to the harness.

➡**Heat shrink tubing must be slipped over the wire before crimping and soldering the connection.**

5. To repair any fuse link in a 3-link group with one feed:

   a. After cutting the open link out of the harness, cut each of the remaining undamaged fuse links close to the feed wire weld.

   b. Strip approximately ½ in. (13mm) of insulation from the detached ends of the two good fuse links. Insert two wire ends into one end of a butt connector, then carefully push one stripped end of the replacement fuse link into the same end of the butt connector and crimp all three firmly together.

➡**Care must be taken when fitting the three fuse links into the butt connector as the internal diameter is a snug fit for three wires. Make sure to use a proper crimping tool. Pliers, side cutters, etc. will not apply the proper crimp to retain the wires and withstand a pull test.**

   c. After crimping the butt connector to the three fuse links, cut the weld portion from the feed wire and strip approximately ½ in. (13mm) of insulation from the cut end. Insert the stripped end into the open end of the butt connector and crimp very firmly.

   d. To attach the remaining end of the replacement fuse link, strip approximately ½ in. (13mm) of insulation from the wire end of the circuit from which the blown fuse link was removed, and firmly crimp a butt connector or equivalent to the stripped wire. Then, insert the end of the replacement link into the other end of the butt connector and crimp firmly.

   e. Using rosin core solder with a consistency of 60 percent tin and 40 percent lead, solder the connectors and the wires at the repairs then insulate with electrical tape or heat shrink tubing.

6. To replace any fuse link on a single circuit in a harness, cut out the damaged portion, strip approximately ½ in. (13mm) of insulation from the two wire ends and attach the appropriate replacement fuse link to the stripped wire ends with two proper size butt connectors. Solder the connectors and wires, then insulate.

7. To repair any fuse link which has an eyelet terminal on one end such as the charging circuit, cut off the open fuse link behind the weld, strip approximately ½ in. (13mm) of insulation from the cut end and attach the appropriate new eyelet fuse link to the cut stripped wire with an appropriate size butt connector. Solder the connectors and wires at the repair, then insulate.

8. Connect the negative battery cable to the battery and test the system for proper operation.

➡**Do not mistake a resistor wire for a fuse link. The resistor wire is generally longer and has print stating, "Resistor—don't cut or splice."**

When attaching a single No. 16, 17, 18 or 20 gauge fuse link to a heavy gauge wire, always double the stripped wire end of the fuse link before inserting and crimping it into the butt connector for positive wire retention.

Add-On Electrical Equipment

The electrical system in your vehicle is designed to perform under reasonable operating conditions without interference between components. Before any additional electrical equipment is installed, it is recommended that you consult your dealer or a reputable repair facility that is familiar with the vehicle and its systems.

If the vehicle is equipped with mobile radio equipment and/or

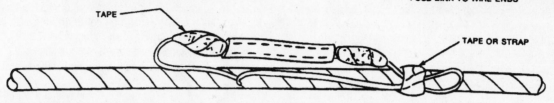

REMOVE EXISTING VINYL TUBE SHIELDING
REINSTALL OVER FUSE LINK BEFORE CRIMPING
FUSE LINK TO WIRE ENDS

TAPE

TAPE OR STRAP

TYPICAL REPAIR USING THE SPECIAL #17 GA. (9.00" LONG-YELLOW) FUSE LINK REQUIRED FOR THE AIR/COND.
CIRCUITS (2) #687E and #261A LOCATED IN THE ENGINE COMPARTMENT

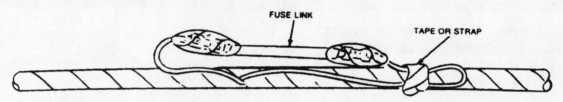

FUSE LINK

TAPE OR STRAP

TYPICAL REPAIR FOR ANY IN-LINE FUSE LINK USING THE SPECIFIED GAUGE FUSE LINK FOR THE SPECIFIC CIRCUIT

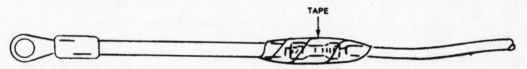

TAPE

TYPICAL REPAIR USING THE EYELET TERMINAL FUSE LINK OF THE SPECIFIED GAUGE FOR ATTACHMENT TO A CIRCUIT WIRE END

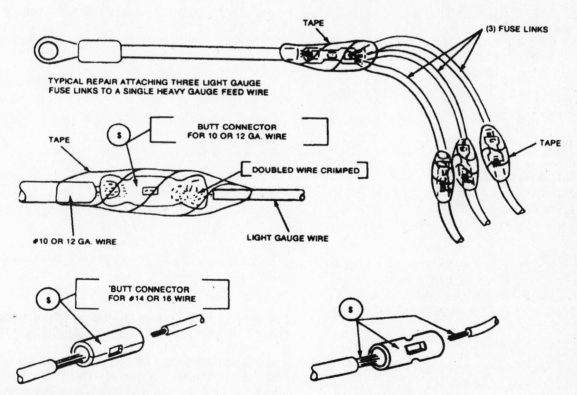

TAPE

(3) FUSE LINKS

TYPICAL REPAIR ATTACHING THREE LIGHT GAUGE
FUSE LINKS TO A SINGLE HEAVY GAUGE FEED WIRE

TAPE

BUTT CONNECTOR
FOR 10 OR 12 GA. WIRE

DOUBLED WIRE CRIMPED

TAPE

#10 OR 12 GA. WIRE

LIGHT GAUGE WIRE

'BUTT CONNECTOR
FOR #14 OR 16 WIRE

FUSIBLE LINK REPAIR PROCEDURE

General fusible link repair—never replace a fusible link with regular wire or a fusible link rated at a higher amperage than the one being replaced

mobile telephone, it may have an effect upon the operation of any on-board computer control modules. Radio Frequency Interference (RFI) from the communications system can be picked up by the vehicle's wiring harnesses and conducted into the control module, giving it the wrong messages at the wrong time. Although well shielded against RFI, the computer should be further protected by taking the following measures:

• Install the antenna as far as possible from the control module. For instance, if the module is located behind the center console area, then the antenna should be mounted at the rear of the vehicle.

• Keep the antenna wiring a minimum of eight inches away from any wiring running to control modules and from the module itself. NEVER wind the antenna wire around any other wiring.

• Mount the equipment as far from the control module as possible. Be very careful during installation not to drill through any wires or short a wire harness with a mounting screw.

• Insure that the electrical feed wire(s) to the equipment are properly and tightly connected. Loose connectors can cause interference.

• Make certain that the equipment is properly grounded to the vehicle. Poor grounding can damage expensive equipment.

HEATER

Blower Motor

REMOVAL & INSTALLATION

1974–76 240D, 230, 280, 280C and 300D Models

1. Remove the heater box.
2. Back out the three retaining screws.
3. Slightly pull out the blower and remove the electrical plug and the blower.
4. Installation is the reverse of removal. To prevent leaks, install the three screws with three new special washers exactly like those removed.

1977–78 230; 1977–83 240D, 280E, 280CE, 300D; 1977–84 300CD and 300TD Models

1. Remove the cover from under the right side of the instrument panel.
2. Disconnect the plug from the blower motor.
3. Unscrew the contact plate screw, lift the contact plate and disconnect both wires to the series resistor.
4. Loosen the blower motor flange screws and lift out the blower motor.
5. Installation is in the reverse order of removal.

1978–80 280S, 280SE, 300SD, 450SE, 450SEL and 6.9 Models

1. Disconnect the series resistor plug at the fire wall.
2. Unscrew both mounting bolts and remove the series resistor.
3. Remove the air inlet grille.
4. Remove the glove box.
5. Remove the cover from under the right side of the instrument panel.
6. Remove the hose between the center air duct and the right side ring nozzle.
7. Remove the clamp and then disconnect the cable control at the lever.
8. Unscrew both mounting nuts and remove the blower motor.

➡**On installation, make sure that the rubber seal between the blower motor and the firewall is not damaged and that the rubber grommet for the connecting cable is correctly seated.**

9. Guide the connecting cable through the air duct on the firewall and into the water box.
10. Insert the blower motor into the housing, position the mounting nuts and then push the blower motor to the left (as far as possible) while tightening.
11. Installation of the remaining components is in the reverse order of installation.

380SL, 380SLC, 450SL and 450SLC Models

1. Working in the engine compartment, unscrew the eight (8) mounting screws and remove the panel which covers the blower motor.
2. Disconnect the plug from the series resistor at the firewall.
3. Remove the mounting bolts and then remove the series resistor.
4. Unscrew the four (4) blower motor retaining nuts and lift out the motor.
5. Installation is in the reverse order of removal. Be sure that the rubber sealing strip is not damaged.

1981–84 300SD, 380SE, 380SEL, 380SEC, 500SEL and 500SEC Models

1. Remove the cover from under the right side of the instrument panel.
2. Remove the cover for the blower motor and disconnect the two-prong plug.
3. Remove the retaining bolts on the blower motor flange and then remove the blower motor.
4. Installation is in the reverse order of removal.

190D and 190E Models

1. Open the hood to a 90° position and then remove the wiper arms.
2. Disconnect the retaining clips for the air intake cover at the firewall.
3. Remove the rubber sealing strip from the cover and then remove the retaining screws. Slide the cover out of the lower windshield trim strip and remove it.
4. Disconnect the vacuum line from the heater valve.
5. Remove the heater cover retaining screws.
6. Pull up the rubber sealing strip from the engine side of the defroster plenum (firewall), unscrew the retaining screws and pull up and out on the blower motor cover.
7. Loosen the cable straps on the connecting cable and then disconnect the plug.

8. Unscrew the mounting bolts and then remove the blower motor.

9. Installation is in the reverse order of removal.

Control Panel

REMOVAL & INSTALLATION

1. Use a prytool to unclip the cover plate.
2. Remove the cover plate.
3. Remove the control panel bezel retaining screws, then remove the bezel.
4. Use a prytool to separate the panel from its mounting.
5. Slide the panel forward, disengage the electrical connections and remove the panel.
6. Installation is the reverse of removal.

Remove the panel bezel retaining screws . . .

To remove the control panel, gently pry the cover to disengage the retaining clips

Remove the panel cover

. . . then remove the bezel

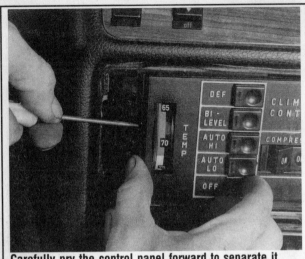

Carefully pry the control panel forward to separate it from its mounting

Slide the unit forward and disengage all the connections at the rear

ENTERTAINMENT SYSTEMS

Radio

REMOVAL & INSTALLATION

1. Pull the control knobs off the radio.
2. Remove the retaining nuts and washers.

3. Slide the radio forward and disengage the electrical connections and the antenna.
4. Remove the radio assembly.
5. Installation is the reverse of removal.

To remove the radio, first pull the knobs off the shafts . . .

. . . then unfasten the retaining nuts from the shafts . . .

. . . and remove the retaining plates

Slide the radio forward and disengage the electrical connections and antenna

WINDSHIELD WIPERS

Windshield Wiper Blade and Arm

REMOVAL & INSTALLATION

1974–76 230, 240D, 280, 280C and 300D Models

1. Unscrew the cap nut at the base of the wiper arm and remove it. Make sure that you get the spring washer.
2. Remove the wiper arm.
3. Installation is in the reverse order of removal.

➡The wiper shaft has a cone end with serrations on which the wiper arm is mounted. New wiper arms have no serrations on the inside cone. When the cap nut is tightened, the shaft serrations dig into the smooth surface of the inside of the wiper arm cone. If the serrations on the inside cone of an old wiper arm are chewed up, loosely install the wiper arm on the shaft and wiggle it back and forth until the old serrations are gone. Adjust the arm and then tighten it down; this will form new serrations.

Other Models

➡On the 190D and 190E, the wiper arm is removed by lifting the cover at the bottom of the arm and removing the retaining nut.

1. Lift the wiper arm so that it is at a 90° angle to the windshield.
2. Disengage the lock on the mounting nut covering cap by lifting the cap slightly upward.
3. Continue to hold the cap in a slightly raised position and then lower the wiper arm to the windshield. This should allow the cap to pivot all the way open.

To remove the wiper arm, first remove the cover to gain access to the cap nut

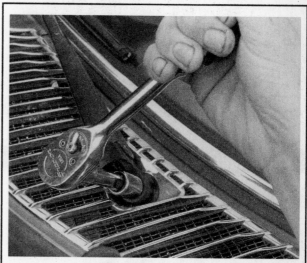

Use a ratchet and socket to loosen the retaining nut

Remove the wiper arm from the mounting stud

4. Unscrew the mounting nut and remove the wiper arm.
5. Installation is in the reverse order of removal.

Wiper Linkage

REMOVAL & INSTALLATION

1974–76 230, 240D, 280, 280C and 300D Models

LEFT SIDE

1. Remove the wiper arm. Remove the grommet, nut, washer and seal from the wiper shaft.
2. Pop both linkage arms off of the ball joints on the wiper shaft.
3. Unscrew the mounting bolts for the wiper shaft and remove along with the linkage.
4. Installation is in the reverse order of removal.

RIGHT SIDE

1. Remove the wiper arm. Remove the grommet, nut, washer and seal from the wiper shaft.
2. Remove the covers underneath both sides of the instrument panel.
3. Remove the glove box.
4. Pop both linkage arms off of the ball joints on the wiper shaft.
5. Unscrew the mounting bolts on the wiper shaft and remove down and to the right along with the linkage.
6. Installation is in the reverse order of removal.

Windshield Wiper Motor

REMOVAL & INSTALLATION

1974–76 230, 240D, 280, 280C and 300D Models

➡ If only the motor is to be removed, DON'T loosen the adjusting nut on the linkage arm.

1. Remove the cover underneath the left side of the instrument panel.
2. Disconnect the ball joint at the linkage connecting rod (it should pop right off).
3. Unscrew the three mounting nuts.
4. From the engine compartment, pull off the cable on the wiper motor and then remove the motor.
5. Installation is in the reverse order of removal. Always use new sealing rings on the wiper motor mounting nuts.

1977–78 230, 240D; 1977–83 280E, 280CE, 300D; 1977–84 300CD and 300TD Models

1. Remove the wiper arms.
2. Remove the air intake grille on the right side.
3. Remove the covering cap and nut on the left and right side bearing shafts.
4. Remove the four expanding rivets and then remove the left side air intake grille.
5. Remove the center air plenum cover (four expanding rivets and a Phillips screw).
6. Carefully pull the left and right side connecting rods off of the wiper motor crank.
7. Remove the water drain tube from the right side bearing shaft.
8. Disconnect the coupler plug in the engine compartment. Unclip the plug from the firewall and pull it all the way through.
9. Unbolt the wiper motor and remove it toward the right side.
10. Installation is in the reverse order of removal.

1978–80 280S, 280SE, 300SD, 450SE, 450SEL and 6.9 Models

1. Remove the wiper arms.
2. Remove the covering caps and nuts on both wiper shafts.
3. Remove the air intake grille.
4. Unscrew the mounting bolts.
5. Disconnect the wiper motor plug under the left side of the instrument panel and then pull it into the engine compartment along with the rubber grommet in the firewall.
6. Pull off the linkage drive rod and then unscrew the crank on the wiper motor.
7. Unscrew the mounting bolts and remove the wiper motor.
8. Installation is in the reverse order of removal.

➡Remove the rubber seal around the motor housing during installation or leave it off.

1981–84 300SD, 380SE, 380SEC, 380SEL, 500SEC and 500SEL Models

1. Remove the wiper arms.
2. Remove the air intake cover. Unscrew the fastening screws and then disconnect the front plug connector.
3. Compress the mounting flange on the rear plug connector. Push the plug out of the firewall toward the front of the car, twist it and then insert it toward the rear of the car.
4. Remove the wiper motor and linkage.
5. Unscrew the nut on the wiper motor shaft.
6. Swivel the wiper linkage and then unscrew the bolts for the wiper motor underneath.
7. Remove the wiper motor.

To install:

8. Mount the wiper motor in the base plate.

9. Push the crank arm on the wiper motor shaft and position the nut. Make sure that the lever on the right-hand wiper shaft is pointing down.

10. Align the crank arm so that the upper edge is parallel with the wiper motor shaft.

11. Tighten the nut on the wiper motor shaft.

12. Attach the wiper motor and linkage assembly to the vehicle.

13. Installation of the remaining components is in the reverse order of removal.

190D and 190E Models

1. Open the hood all the way and disconnect the battery.
2. Remove the wiper arm.
3. Remove the round cover from the wiper shaft.
4. Remove the two clips, the rubber seal and the two screws and then remove the air intake cover.

INSTRUMENTS AND SWITCHES

Instrument Cluster

REMOVAL & INSTALLATION

1974–76 230, 240D, 280, 280C and 300D Models

1. Remove the cover plate from the left side underneath the dashboard.

2. On vehicles with automatic transmission, disconnect the Bowden cable for the gear selector lever, after engaging Park.

3. Remove the bracket holding the handbrake.

4. Unscrew the knurled nut and pull the instrument cluster slightly forward.

5. Disconnect the tachometer drive.

6. Cover the steering column to prevent scratches.

7. If only bulb replacement is desired, this is sufficient. To remove the entire cluster, continue with the remaining steps.

8. Disconnect the oil pressure line.

9. Remove the electrical plug connections.

10. Release the excess pressure in the cooling system and install the cap afterward.

11. Remove the temperature sensor from the cylinder head and plug the hole.

12. Carefully remove the instrument cluster with the capillary tube and temperature sensor.

✷✷ WARNING

Do not bend the capillary tube.

13. Installation is the reverse of removal.

1978–80 280S, 280SE, 300SD, 380SL, 380SLC, 450SE, 450SEL, 450SL, 450SLC and 6.9 Models

1. Remove the steering wheel.

➡The instrument cluster is held in the instrument panel by means of a molded rubber strip. When pulling out the clus-ter, the panel can be slightly raised above the cluster. NEVER force the cluster with a screwdriver or the like.

2. Remove the tachometer shaft from the cable strap underneath the left-hand floor mat, near the jacket tube (except 380SL, SLC and 450SL, SLC).

3. Pull the instrument cluster out as much as possible and loosen or remove the tachometer shaft, all electrical connections and the oil pressure line.

4. Remove the instrument cluster to the left.

✷✷ WARNING

Do not bend the oil pressure line.

5. Installation is in the reverse order of removal. Make sure that the speedometer cable is not bent excessively or it will vibrate when running.

190D and 190E Models

1. Remove the cover under the left side of the instrument panel.

2. Disconnect the defroster ducting which runs behind the instrument cluster.

3. Unscrew the speedometer cable from below and then push the cluster out far enough to disconnect all connections on the back of the instrument cluster.

4. Remove the five clips which secure the instrument cluster and then remove it.

5. Installation is in the reverse order of removal.

1977–78 230, 240D; 1977–83 280E, 280CE, 300D; 1977–84 300CD, 300SD; 1981–84 300TD, 380SE, 380SEC, 380SEL, 500SEC and 500SEL Models

♦ See Figure 1

1. Remove the steering wheel (300SD, 380SE, 380SEC, 380SEL, 500SEC and 500SEL only).

2. Remove the instrument cluster slightly by hand. Don't pull on the edge of the glass.

---

5. Pull the three-piece air intake pan from the windshield and remove it.

6. Unscrew the wiper motor/linkage assembly.

7. Remove the cover and unscrew the four mounting bolts for the fuse box. Pull the fuse box slightly forward and up and then unplug the wiper motor connection.

8. Remove the wiper motor/linkage assembly.

9. Remove the nut on the wiper motor shaft and then pull off the crank arm and linkage.

10. Unscrew and remove the wiper motor.

To install:

11. Attach the wiper motor to the base plate.

12. Press the crank arm onto the wiper motor shaft. Make sure that the crank arm and the pushrod are parallel.

13. Attach the crank arm to the wiper motor and then install the wiper motor/linkage assembly.

14. Installation of the remaining components is in the reverse order of removal.

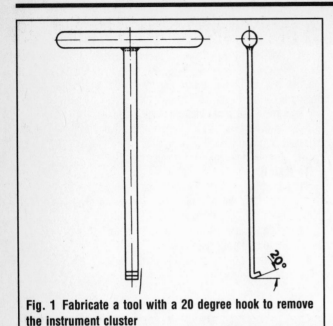

Fig. 1 Fabricate a tool with a 20 degree hook to remove the instrument cluster

3. A removal hook can be fabricated and inserted between the instrument cluster and the dashboard.

4. Guide the removal hook up to the right to the recess (arrow) and pull the instrument cluster out.

5. Pull it out as far as possible and disconnect the speedometer cable, electrical connections and oil pressure line.

➡**The 1981 and later 300SD, 380SE, 380SEC, 380SEL, 500SEC and 500SEL models utilize 5 clips to secure the instrument cluster in place.**

6. To install, reconnect the electrical connections, oil pressure line and speedometer cable. To avoid speedometer cable noise, guide it into the largest radius possible.

7. Push the instrument cluster firmly into the dashboard.

Combination Switch

REMOVAL & INSTALLATION

190D, 190E, 230, 240D, 280, 300D, 300CD, 300SD; 1978–80 300TD, 380SL, 380SLC, 450 and 6.9 Models

1. Remove the rubber sleeve on the switch and then unscrew the retaining screws.

2. Pull the switch out slightly, loosen the screws for the cable connection of the twin carbon contacts and pull out the cable.

3. Remove the cover underneath the left side of the instrument panel.

4. Disconnect the plug and then remove the switch.

5. Installation is in the reverse order of removal.

1981–84 300SD, 380SE, 380SEC, 380SEL, 500SEC and 500SEL Models

1. Remove the steering wheel.

2. Remove the cover underneath the left side of the instrument panel.

3. Unscrew the switch retaining screws.

4. Disconnect the 14-prong plug underneath the instrument panel.

5. Remove the switch.

6. Installation is in the reverse order of removal.

Ignition Switch

REMOVAL & INSTALLATION

Except 190D and 190E Models

➡**The following procedure only applies to models with a dashboard mounted ignition switch.**

1. Remove the instrument cluster.

2. Remove the right-hand cover plate under the dashboard.

3. Remove the plug connection from the ignition switch.

4. Remove the screws which hold the ignition switch to the rear of the lock cylinder and remove the ignition switch.

5. To install the ignition switch, attach the plug connection, after fastening the switch to the steering lock.

6. Install the instrument cluster.

7. Check the switch for proper function and install the lower cover.

190D and 190E Models

1. Remove the cover plate under the left side of the instrument panel.

2. Remove the steering wheel. Remove the instrument cluster.

3. Pry the cylinder rosette (trim ring) upwards and then remove it.

4. Insert the ignition key and turn it to position 1.

5. Disconnect the plug at the rear of the ignition switch.

➡**The plug can only be disconnected when the key is in position 1.**

6. Loosen the screws and then remove the steering column jacket (upper and lower halves).

7. Release the clamp on the jacket tube. Press in the lock-pin in position 1 and then pull the steering lock out slightly from the jacket tube holder.

8. Pull off the ignition key at the right bottom section, slightly to the rear. Swivel the steering lock so that the lock cylinder clears its hole in the instrument panel.

9. Unscrew the retaining screws and remove the ignition switch from the back of the steering lock.

10. Installation is in the reverse order of removal. Remember to reconnect the switch to the steering lock.

Lock Cylinder

REMOVAL & INSTALLATION

Key Removable in Position 1

1. Turn the key to position 1 and remove the key.

2. Pry the cover sleeve from the lock cylinder with a small screwdriver.

3. Using a bent paper clip, hook onto the cover sleeve and remove the sleeve. Be sure that you do not remove the rosette in the dashboard also.

4. Insert the paper clip between the rosette and the steering lock and push in the lock pin. Remove the lock cylinder slightly with the key.

5. Insert the paper clip into the locking hole and pull the lock cylinder completely out.

6. Installation is the reverse of removal. Turn the lock cylinder to position 1 and insert it into the steering lock, making sure that the lock pin engages. Push the cover sleeve into position 1.

7. Make sure the cylinder operates properly.

Key Unremovable in Position 1

EXCEPT 190D AND 190E MODELS

Because of legal requirements, the lock was changed from the previous version, so that the key can only be removed in position 0.

1. Turn the key to position 1.

2. Lift the cover sleeve to the edge of the key and turn the key to position 0.

3. Remove the key and cover sleeve.

4. Insert the key into the lock cylinder and turn to position 1 (90° to the right), push in the lock pin and remove the lock cylinder.

5. To install the lock cylinder, turn the lock cylinder to position 1 and insert the lock cylinder, making sure that the locking pin engages.

6. Turn the key to position 0 and remove the key.

7. Place the cover sleeve on the steering lock, insert and turn the key, and push in the cover sleeve at position 1.

8. Check the locking cylinder for proper function.

190D AND 190E MODELS

1. Pry the cylinder rosette (trim ring) upwards and then remove it.

2. Insert the ignition key and turn it to position 1.

3. Using a bent paper clip, insert each end into the holes on either side of the lock cylinder. Press the clip ends inward; the pressure will unlock the cylinder from the steering lock.

4. Grasp the key and with pressure still on the paper clip, pull the ignition key/lock cylinder assembly out of the steering lock.

5. Remove the paper clip, turn the key to position 0 and remove it. Slide the lock cylinder out of the cover.

To install:

6. Insert the lock cylinder just enough so that the ridge on the cylinder body engages the groove in the steering lock.

7. Slide the cover onto the lock cylinder so that the detent is on the left side.

8. Insert the ignition key, turn it to position 1 and then push the lock cylinder and its cover into the steering lock.

➡**When the ignition key is in position 1 and is aligned with the mark on the cover, the detent on the cover is also aligned with the ridge on the steering lock. This is the only manner in which the lock cylinder/cover can be installed in the steering lock.**

9. Check that the lock cylinder functions properly, if so, install the rosette.

Steering Lock

REMOVAL & INSTALLATION

Except 190D and 190E Models

▸ **See Figure 2**

1. Disconnect the ground cable from the battery.

2. Remove the instrument cluster.

3. Remove the plug connection from the ignition switch behind the dashboard.

4. Pull the ignition key to position 1.

5. Loosen the attaching screw for the steering lock.

6. Remove the cover sleeve from the steering lock.

7. On vehicles with the latest version of the steering lock, pull the connection for the warning buzzer.

8. Push in the lock pin with a small punch.

9. Turn the steering lock and remove it from the holder in the column jacket. Be sure that the rosette is not damaged.

➡**The lock pin can only be pushed in when the cylinder is in position 1.**

10. To install the steering lock, connect the warning buzzer if so equipped.

11. Place the steering lock in position 1 and insert the lock into the steering column while pushing the lockpin in. Be sure that the lockpin engages.

12. Tighten the attaching clamp screw.

13. Attach the plug connection to the ignition switch.

14. Push the cover sleeve onto the lock in position 1.

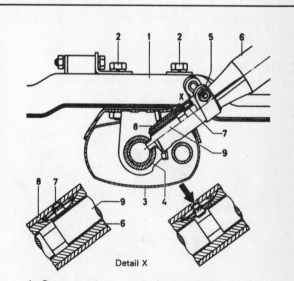

Detail X

1. Cross member
2. Bolt
3. Jacket tube
4. Steering spindle
5. Fastening clip
6. Steering lock
7. Locking pin
8. Holder for steering lock
9. Locking bolt

Fig. 2 Exploded view of the steering lock assembly on all models except 190D and 190E

15. Install the instrument cluster.
16. Check to be sure that the steering lock works properly.

190D and 190E Models

1. Follow Steps 1–8 of the "Ignition Switch Removal and Installation" procedure.
2. Unplug the switch and remove the steering lock.
3. Installation is in the reverse order of removal.

STARTER INTERLOCK SYSTEM

System Description

♦ **See Figures 3, 4, 5 and 6**

Beginning in August of 1973 (1974 models), all Mercedes-Benz cars conformed to the regulation requiring a starter interlock

Ignition interlock over-ride switch location—1975 230

Fig. 3 Location of the ignition interlock over-ride switch—1975 230 models

Fig. 4 Location of the ignition interlock over-ride switch—1975 280 and 280C models

Catalyst Replacement Warning Indicator

A warning light in the instrument cluster comes on at 37,500 mile intervals, indicating that the catalyst should be replaced. The catalyst mileage counter is located under the dash and is driven by the speedometer cable. To reset the mileage counter, push the reset pin on the counter.

Fig. 5 Location of the ignition interlock over-ride switch—1975 450SL and SLC models

Fig. 6 Location of the ignition interlock over-ride switch—1975 450SE and SEL models

system that prevented starting the engine if the seat belts were not buckled. To eliminate the possibility of defeating the system by permanently buckling the seatbelts, the system required that buckling the belts and starting the car take place in a preset sequence. Each front seat contains a contact switch that closes when the seat is occupied. The buckle on the front seat belts also contains a switch that closes if the belt is unbuckled. 1974 cars can be started by reaching in through the open window and starting the car with the key.

1975 models are equipped with the same basic system, but with an additional override switch, located in the engine compartment. In case the engine cannot be started due to a malfunction in the seat belt warning system, the starter interlock can be bypassed for ONE starting attempt, by pushing on the button on the switch with the ignition **ON** and the transmission in N or P. As soon as the transmission is shifted out of N or P, or the ignition is turned **OFF,** the relay in the over-ride switch is opened. To repeat the process, the switch must be depressed again.

DISABLING THE INTERLOCK SYSTEM

As a result of Federal legislation, the starter interlock system used on 1974–75 cars was replaced with a light and buzzer re-minder system. The new law, which took effect 12/26/74, permitted the disconnection of the starter interlock system (but not the warning light) and Mercedes-Benz does not advocate that this be done.

To bypass the interlock feature on all models so equipped (with or without an over-ride switch), replace the seatbelt logic relay (Part No. 000 545 69 32 or 000 545 68 32) with a new relay (Part No. 001 545 00 32). This will disable the interlock feature, but still allow the warning buzzer and buckle-up sequence to remain in effect.

➡**Under no circumstances should the interlock system be bypassed by bridging either the over-ride switch relay or the logic relay, since this could allow the car to be started in gear.**

LIGHTING

Headlights

REMOVAL & INSTALLATION

1974–76 230, 240D, 280 and 280C Models
◗ **See Figure 7**

1. Loosen the screw on the lower portion of the unit.
2. Remove the trim ring together with the lower part of the unit.

A. Sealed beam
B. Clearance lights housing
1. Vertical adjustment screws
2. Horizontal adjustment screws
3. Trim ring
4. Contact plug

Fig. 7 View of the headlight components—1974–76 230, 240D, 280 and 280C models

3. Push the retaining ring in and, at the same time, turn the ring left to the stop.
4. Remove the ring, sealed beam lamp, and disconnect the plug.
5. Installation is the reverse of removal. If installing a Mercedes-Benz replacement sealed beam, be sure that the number "2" is at the top in the center. Be sure to have the headlights adjusted.

1981–84 300SD, 380SE, 380SEC, 380SEL, 500 SEC and 500 SEL Models

1. Open the hood and unscrew the 5 plastic knurled nuts.
2. Remove the assembly from the front of the car. Unplug the electrical connector.
3. Remove the headlight attaching screws.
4. Disconnect the electrical connector and remove the headlight.
5. Installation is the reverse of removal.

All Other Models
◗ **See Figure 8**

1. Loosen the attaching screws and remove the cover.
2. Remove the headlight attaching screws and remove the retaining ring and light as a unit.

➡**Do not disturb the headlight aiming screws.**

3. Pull the retaining ring and light slightly forward and disconnect the plug.
4. Remove the headlight and retaining ring.
5. Installation is the reverse of removal. Be sure that the plug and socket on the rear of the light are tight.

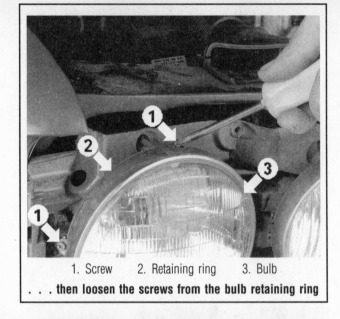

1. Screw 2. Retaining ring 3. Bulb

. . . then loosen the screws from the bulb retaining ring

1. Cover
2. Cover attaching screws
3. Horizontal aiming screws
4. Vertical aiming screws
5. High and low sealed beam
6. High sealed beam
7. Connector
8, 9. Trim ring attaching screws
10. Headlight housing

Fig. 8 View of the headlight components—1974–76 models except 230, 240D, 280 and 280C

Slide the ring and lamp forward to gain access to the bulb electrical connection at the rear

To remove the headlight bulb assembly, unfasten and remove the bezel . . .

Disengage the electrical connection and remove the bulb from the vehicle

Front Turn Signal and Marker Lights

REMOVAL & INSTALLATION

1. Open the hood and remove the lens retaining nuts.
2. Slide the lens forward to gain access to the bulb assembly housing.

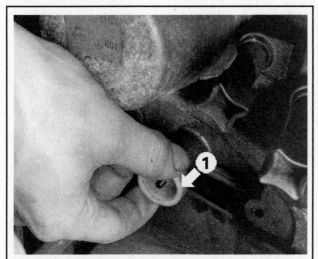

1. Lens retaining nut

To remove the turn signal bulb, open the hood and loosen the lens retaining nuts

Slide the lens forward so that you can reach the bulb housing . . .

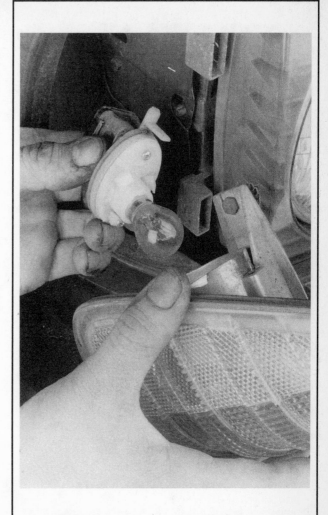

. . . then remove the bulb housing assembly from the rear of the lens

3. Remove the bulb housing from the rear of the lens.
4. Put a slight inward pressure on the bulb and turn it counterclockwise to remove it.

To install:

5. Install the new bulb by turning it clockwise with the same amount of inward pressure that was required for removal.
6. Install the bulb housing onto the rear of the lens.
7. Install the lens cover and fasten the retaining nuts.

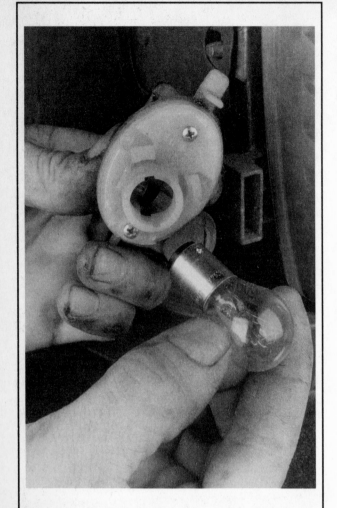

Depress and twist the bulb 1/8 turn counterclockwise to remove it from the socket

Side Marker Lights

REMOVAL & INSTALLATION

1. Unfasten the headlight bezel retaining screws and remove the bezel.
2. Unfasten the headlight bulb retaining ring screws and remove the ring.

➡**Do not loosen or remove the headlight adjustment screws.**

3. Move the headlight to one side so that you can access the side marker lens.
4. Unfasten the side marker bulb socket retaining screw and disengage the socket from the lens.
5. Remove the bulb from the socket by turning it counterclockwise with a slight inward pressure.
6. Install the new bulb, reattach the socket to the lens and fasten the screw.

7. Install the headlight, the retaining ring and fasten the screws.
8. Install the headlight bezel and fasten the retaining screws.

Rear Turn Signal, Brake and Parking Lights

REMOVAL & INSTALLATION

Light Bulbs

1. Open the trunk and loosen the tail light housing nuts.
2. Pull the housing away from the body to gain access to the bulb assembly housing.
3. Remove and replace the defective bulb by putting a slight inward pressure on the bulb and turn it counterclockwise.
4. After replacing the necessary bulbs, install the housing and tighten the retaining nuts.

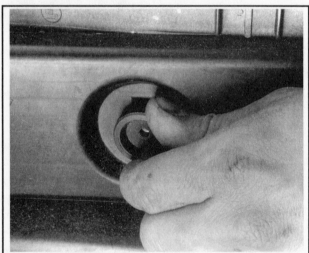

To remove the rear turn signal, brake and parking light bulbs, loosen the bulb housing retaining nuts

Pull the lens housing assembly off the mounting studs

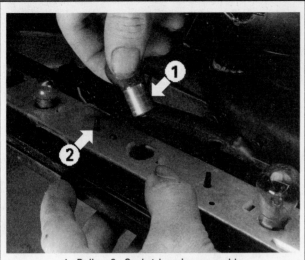

1. Bulb   2. Socket housing assembly

Remove the bulb from the housing by depressing and twisting it 1/8 turn counterclockwise

Lens Assembly

1. Open the trunk and loosen the tail light housing nuts.
2. Pull the housing away from the body to gain access to the lens assembly.
3. Remove the lens retaining nuts.
4. Remove the lens assembly from the trunk.
5. Installation is the reverse of removal.

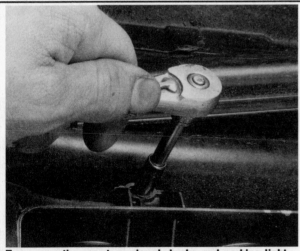

To remove the rear turn signal, brake and parking light lens, loosen the retaining bolts

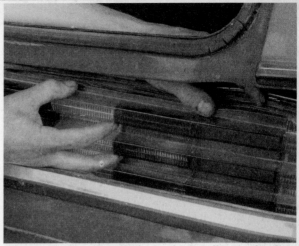

Remove the lens through the trunk after disengaging it from the rubber weatherstrip

Dome Light

REMOVAL & INSTALLATION

1. Unclip the dome light lens from its mounting.
2. Remove the bulb by pulling it from its socket.
3. Installation is the reverse of removal.

To remove the dome light bulb, carefully unclip the lens from its mounting

License Plate Light

REMOVAL & INSTALLATION

1. Remove the lens retaining screws.
2. Pull the lens forward to access the housing assembly.
3. Pull the bulb from the housing assembly.
4. Installation is the reverse of removal.

Pull the lens assembly away from the vehicle to gain access to the bulb

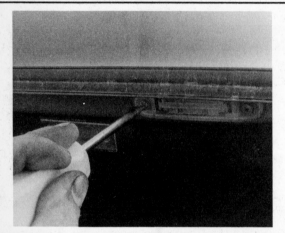

To remove the license plate light bulb, unscrew the lens retainers

Unclip and remove the bulb from the housing assembly

TRAILER WIRING

Wiring the vehicle for towing is fairly easy. There are a number of good wiring kits available and these should be used, rather than trying to design your own.

All trailers will need brake lights and turn signals as well as tail lights and side marker lights. Most areas require extra marker lights for overwide trailers. Also, most areas have recently required back-up lights for trailers, and most trailer manufacturers have been building trailers with back-up lights for several years.

Additionally, some Class I, most Class II and just about all Class III trailers will have electric brakes. Add to this number an accessories wire, to operate trailer internal equipment or to charge the trailer's battery, and you can have as many as seven wires in the harness.

Determine the equipment on your trailer and buy the wiring kit necessary. The kit will contain all the wires needed, plus a plug adapter set which includes the female plug, mounted on the bumper or hitch, and the male plug, wired into, or plugged into the trailer harness.

When installing the kit, follow the manufacturer's instructions.

The color coding of the wires is usually standard throughout the industry. One point to note: some domestic vehicles, and most imported vehicles, have separate turn signals. On most domestic vehicles, the brake lights and rear turn signals operate with the same bulb. For those vehicles without separate turn signals, you can purchase an isolation unit so that the brake lights won't blink whenever the turn signals are operated, or, you can go to your local electronics supply house and buy four diodes to wire in series with the brake and turn signal bulbs. Diodes will isolate the brake and turn signals. The choice is yours. The isolation units are simple and quick to install, but far more expensive than the diodes. The diodes, however, require more work to install properly, since they require the cutting of each bulb's wire and soldering in place of the diode.

One, final point, the best kits are those with a spring loaded cover on the vehicle mounted socket. This cover prevents dirt and moisture from corroding the terminals. Never let the vehicle socket hang loosely; always mount it securely to the bumper or hitch.

CIRCUIT PROTECTION

Fuses

A listing of the protected equipment and the amperage of the fuse is printed in the lid of the fuse box. Spare fuses and a tool for removing and installing fuses are contained in the vehicle tool kit.

Fuses cannot be repaired—they must be replaced. Always determine the cause of the blown fuse before replacing it with a new one.

FUSE BOX LOCATION

230, 240D, 300D, 300TD, 280, 280C, 280E, 280CE and 300CD Models

On early models, the fuse box may be found in the kick panel on the driver's side. On later models, the fuse box is located in the engine compartment on the driver's side, next to the brake master cylinder. Some models have separate fuse boxes or inline fuses for additional equipment. The radio is usually fused with a separate inline glass fuse behind the radio and the ignition is unfused.

190D, 190E, 280S, 280SE, 300SD, 380SE, 380SEC, 380SEL, 450SE, 450SEL, 500SEC, 500SEL and 6.9 Models

The fuse box is located in the engine compartment, on the driver's side, next to the brake master cylinder. Some models may have separate fuse boxes or inline fuses in the engine compartment for additional equipment. The radio is usually fused with a separate inline glass fuse behind the radio and the ignition is unfused. The fuse box also contains various relays.

380SL, 380SLC, 450SL and 450SLC Models

The fuse box is located in the right-hand (passenger's side) kick panel, behind a cover plate. There may also be separate fuse boxes or inline fuses in the engine compartment for additional equipment. The radio is usually fused with a separate inline glass

fuse behind the radio and the ignition is unfused. The kick panel area also contains various relays and switches.

REMOVAL & INSTALLATION

1. Loosen the fuse panel cover nuts, then remove the cover.
2. Remove the defective fuse from the panel and replace it with one of the same amperage.
3. Replace the cover and tighten the nuts.

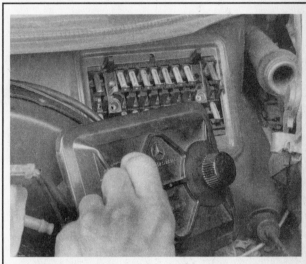

. . . then remove the cover and set it aside

Remove the damaged fuse by pulling it from its housing

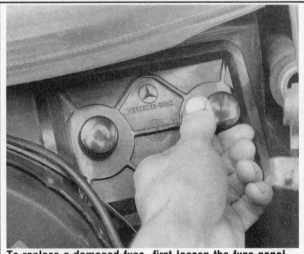

To replace a damaged fuse, first loosen the fuse panel cover retaining nuts . . .

WIRING DIAGRAMS

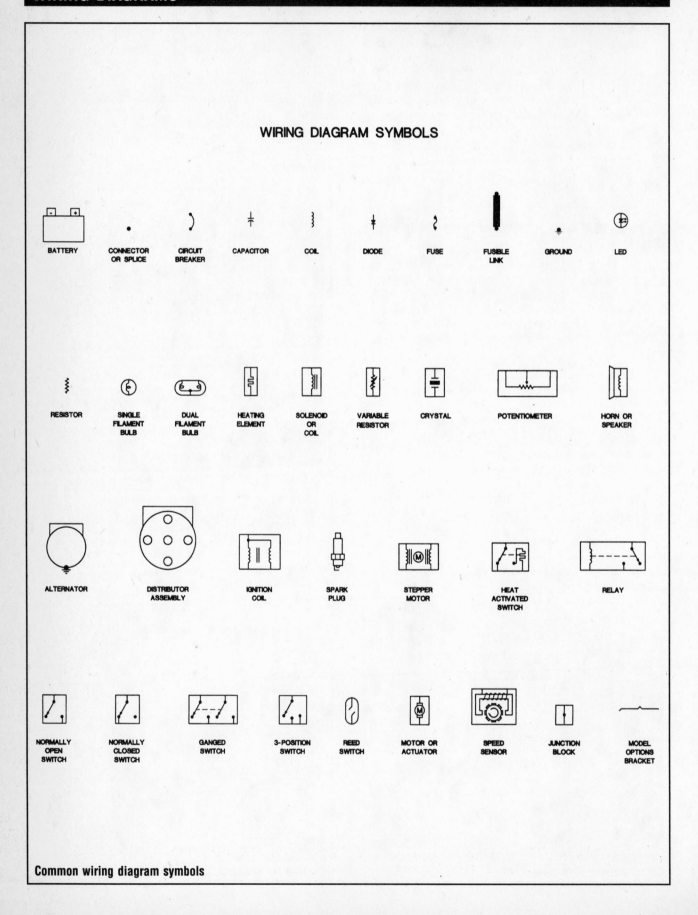

WIRING DIAGRAM SYMBOLS

Common wiring diagram symbols

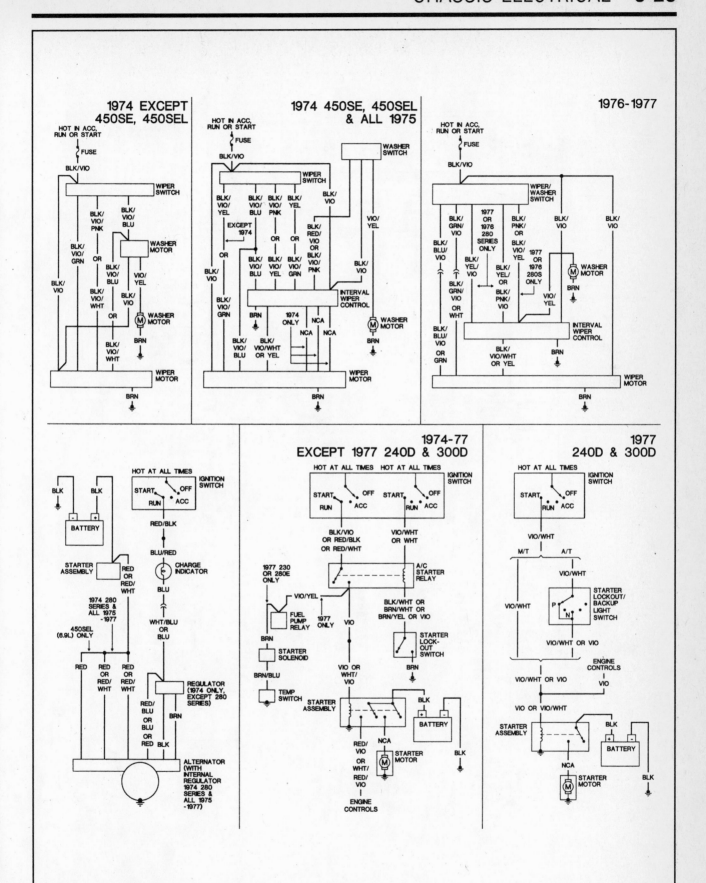

Fig. 9 Chassis wiring—1974–77 230 and 240D; 1974–76 280, 280C and 280S; 1977 280E and 280SE; 1975–77 300D; 1974–75 450SE, 450SEL, 450SL and 450SLC models

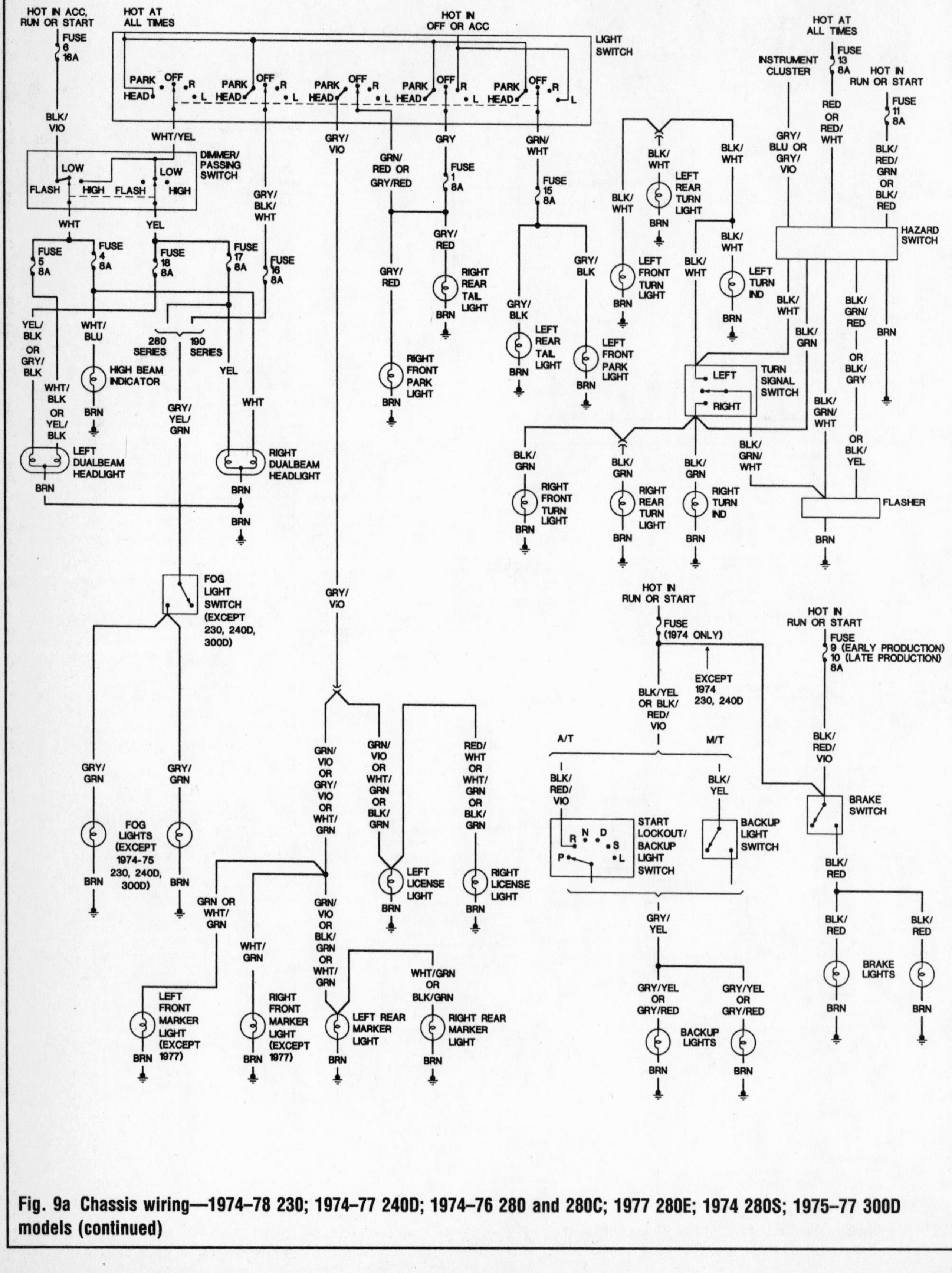

Fig. 9a Chassis wiring—1974–78 230; 1974–77 240D; 1974–76 280 and 280C; 1977 280E; 1974 280S; 1975–77 300D models (continued)

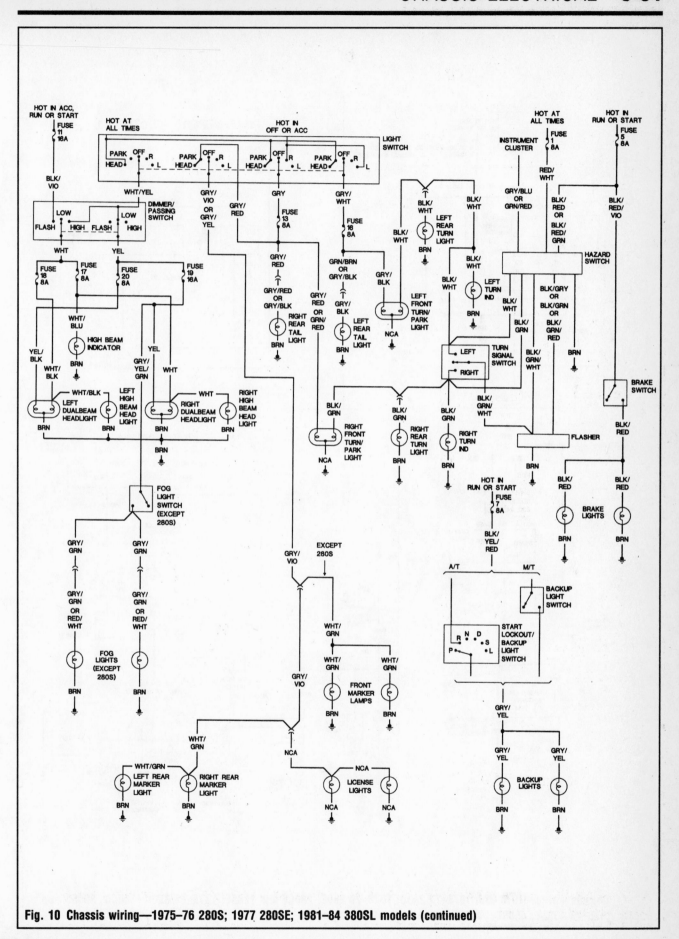

Fig. 10 Chassis wiring—1975–76 280S; 1977 280SE; 1981–84 380SL models (continued)

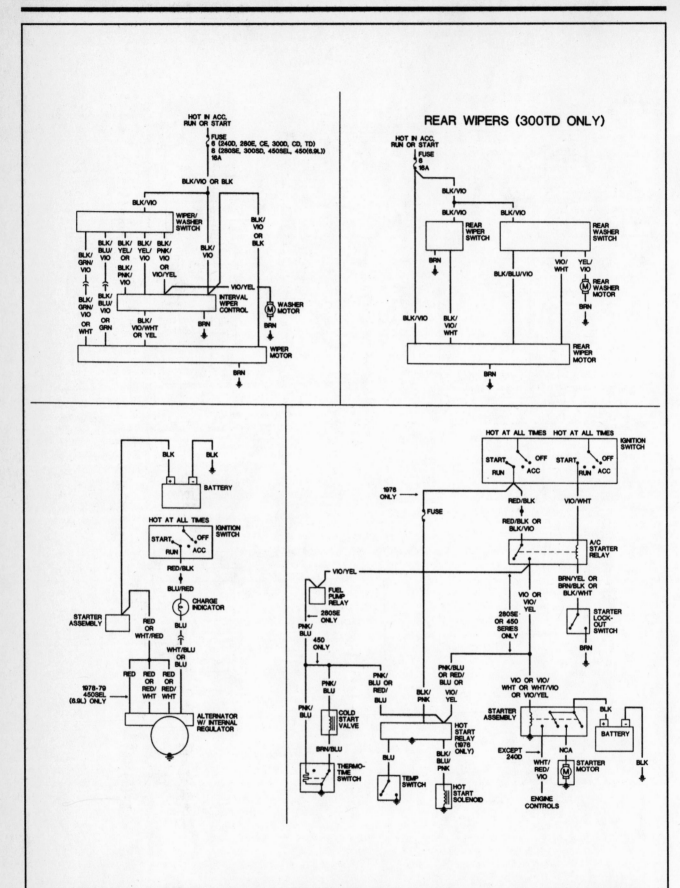

Fig. 11 Chassis wiring—1978 230; 1978–79 240D; 1978–79 280E, 280CE and 280SE; 1978–79 300D, 300CD, 300SD and 300TD; 1976–79 450SE, 450SEL, 450SL, 450SLC and 450 (6.9) models

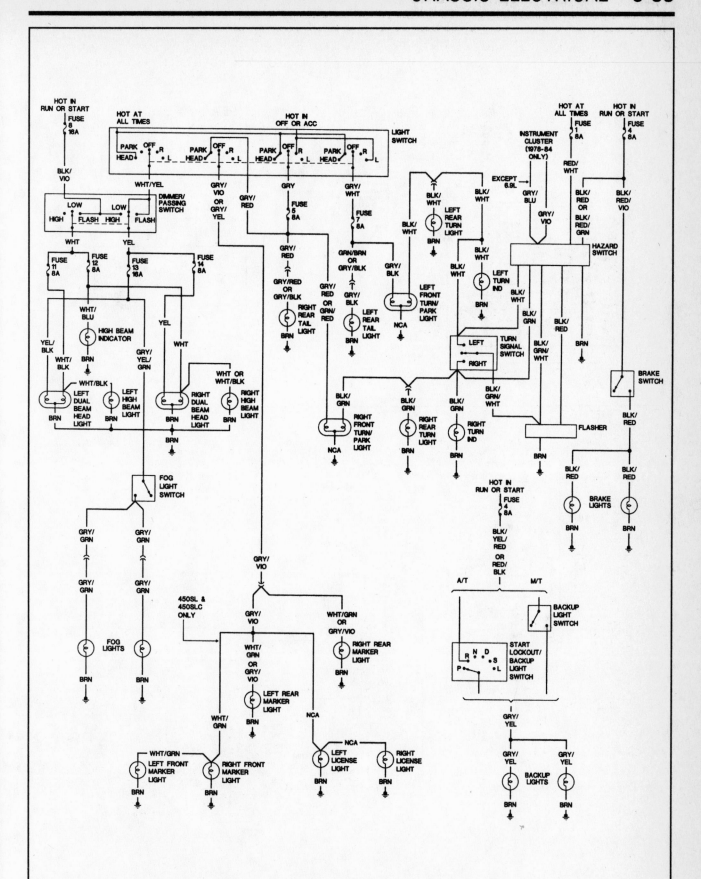

Fig. 12 Chassis wiring—1978–80 280SE; 1978–79 300SD; 1974–77 450SE and 450SEL; 1978–80 450SEL and 450 (6.9); 1974–80 450SL and 450SLC models (continued)

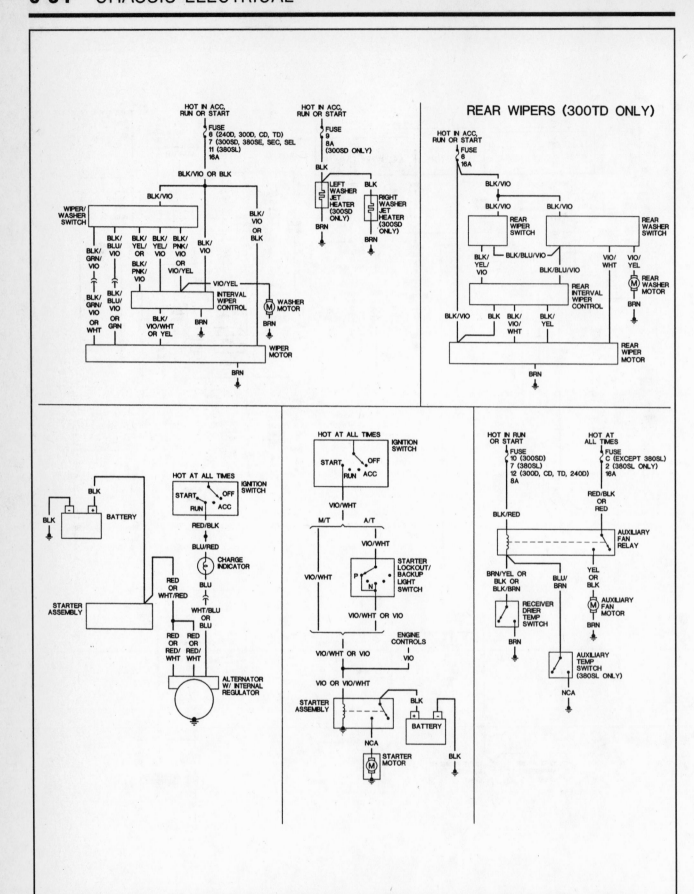

Fig. 13 Chassis wiring—1980–83 240D; 1980–81 280E, 280CE and 280SE; 1980–84 300D, 300CD, 300SD and 300TD; 1981–84 380SL; 1980 450SEL, 450SL and 450SLC models

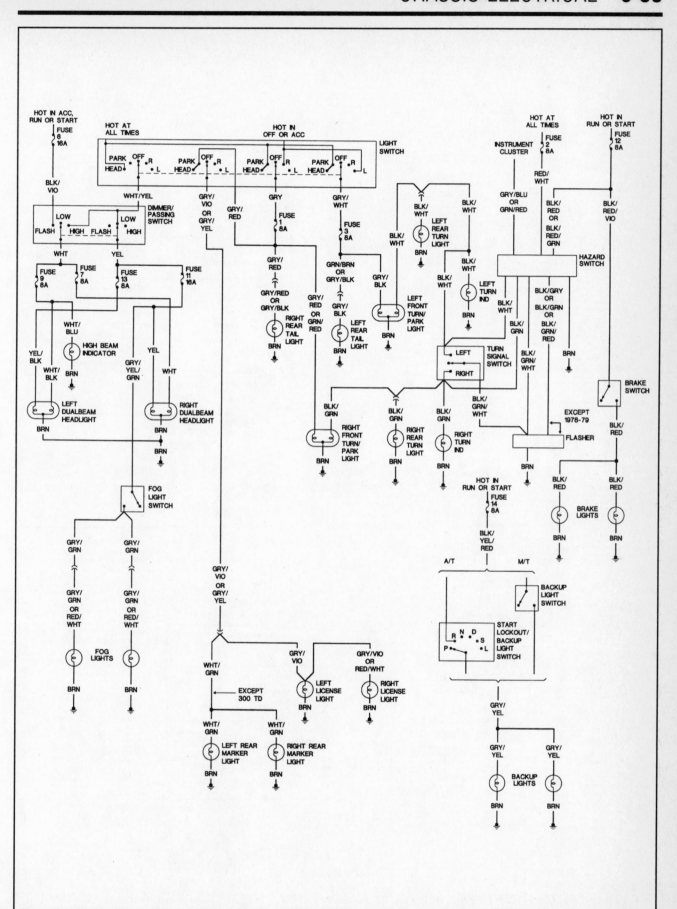

Fig. 14 Chassis wiring—1978-83 240D; 1978-81 280E and 280CE; 1978-84 300D, 300CD and 300TD models (continued)

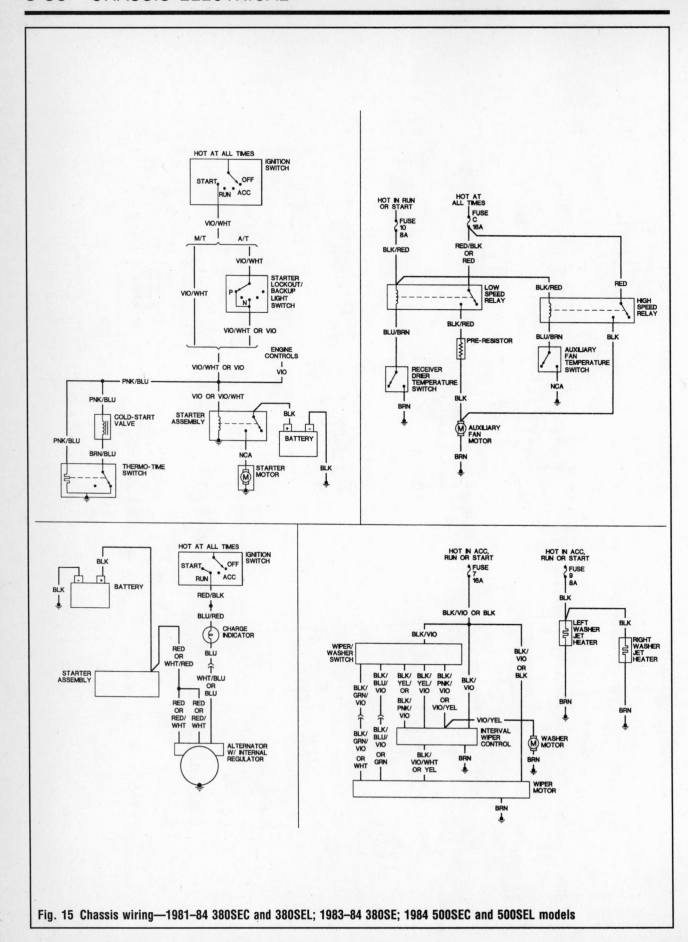

Fig. 15 Chassis wiring—1981–84 380SEC and 380SEL; 1983–84 380SE; 1984 500SEC and 500SEL models

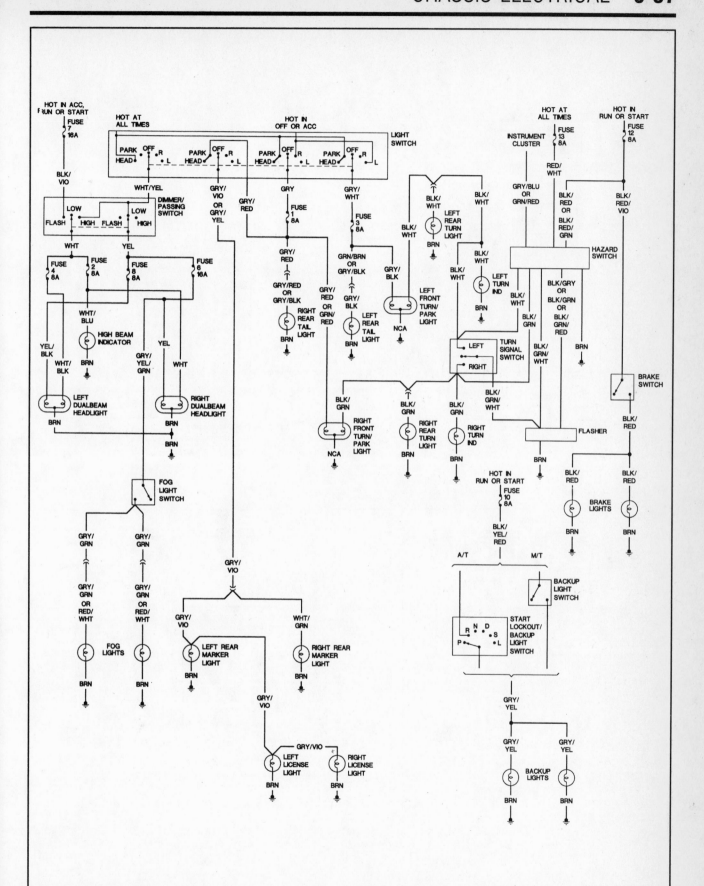

Fig. 16 Chassis wiring—1980–84 300SD; 1981–84 380SE, 380SEC and 380SEL; 1984 500SEC and 500SEL models (continued)

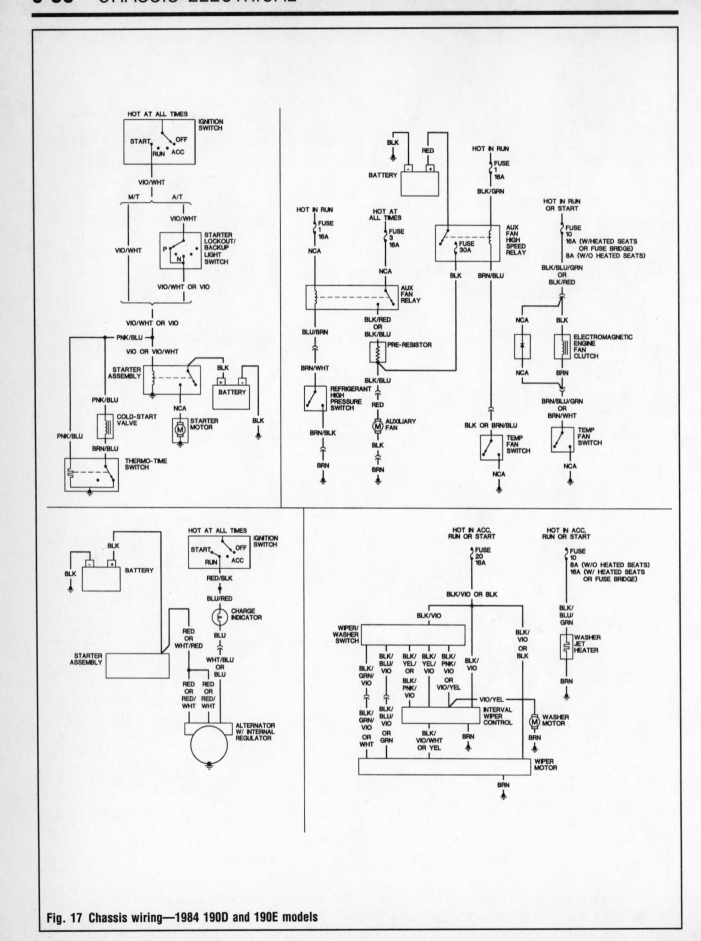

Fig. 17 Chassis wiring—1984 190D and 190E models

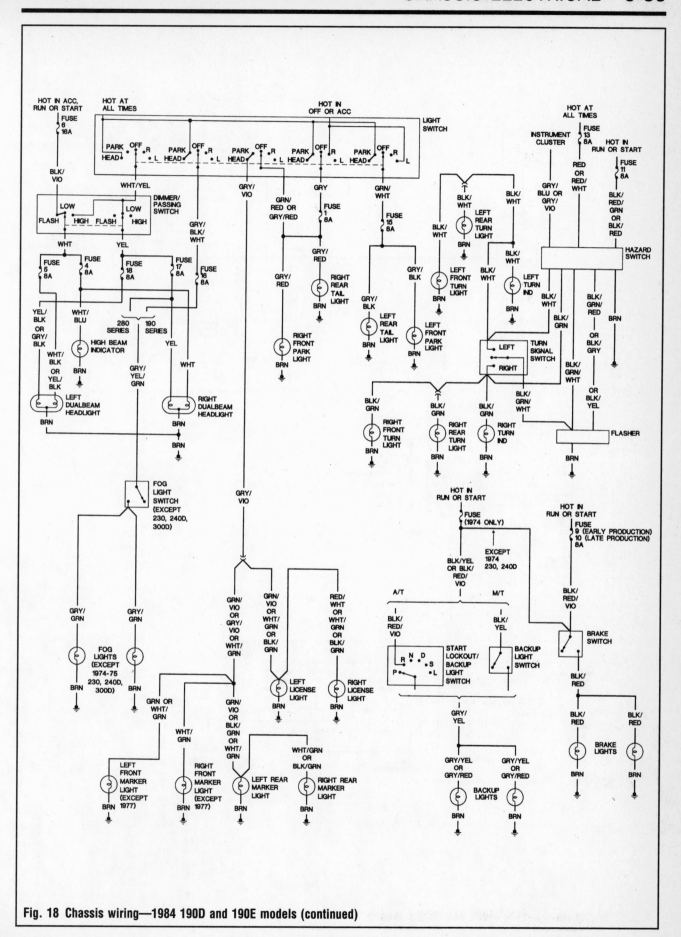

Fig. 18 Chassis wiring—1984 190D and 190E models (continued)

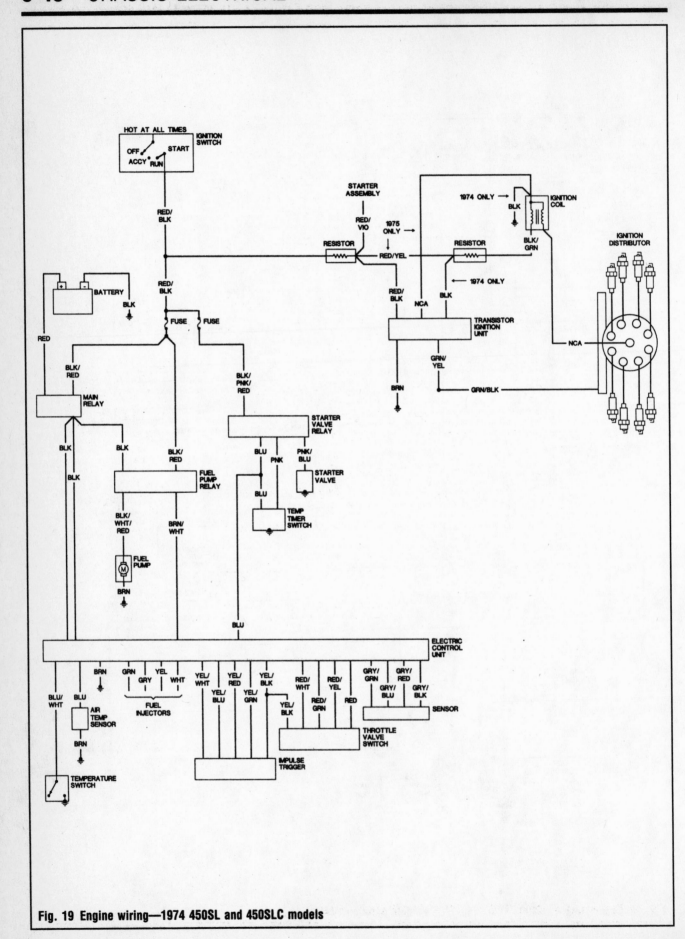

Fig. 19 Engine wiring—1974 450SL and 450SLC models

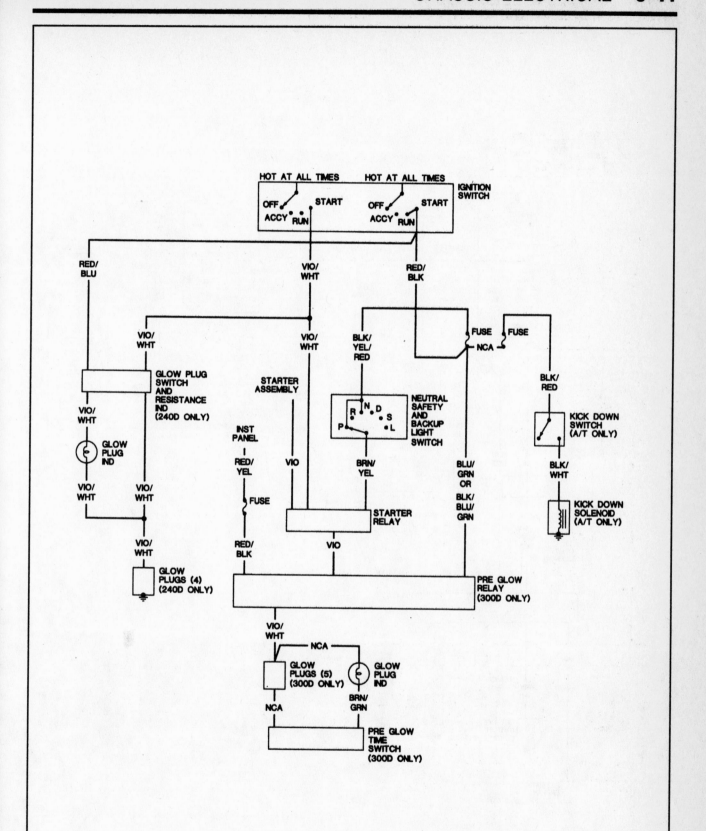

Fig. 20 Engine wiring—1975 300D and 1974–76 240D diesel engines

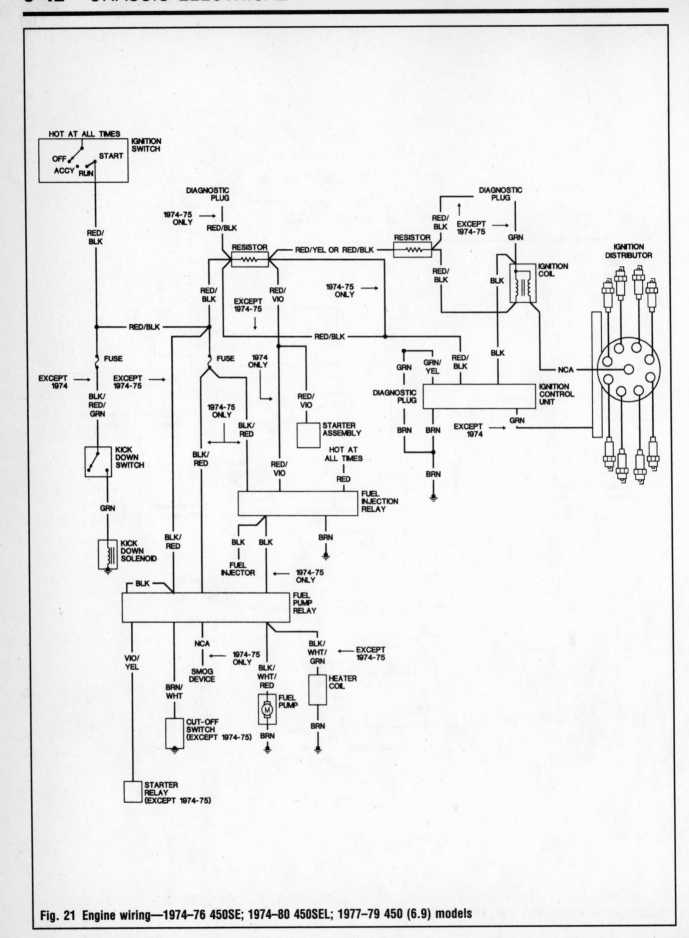

Fig. 21 Engine wiring—1974–76 450SE; 1974–80 450SEL; 1977–79 450 (6.9) models

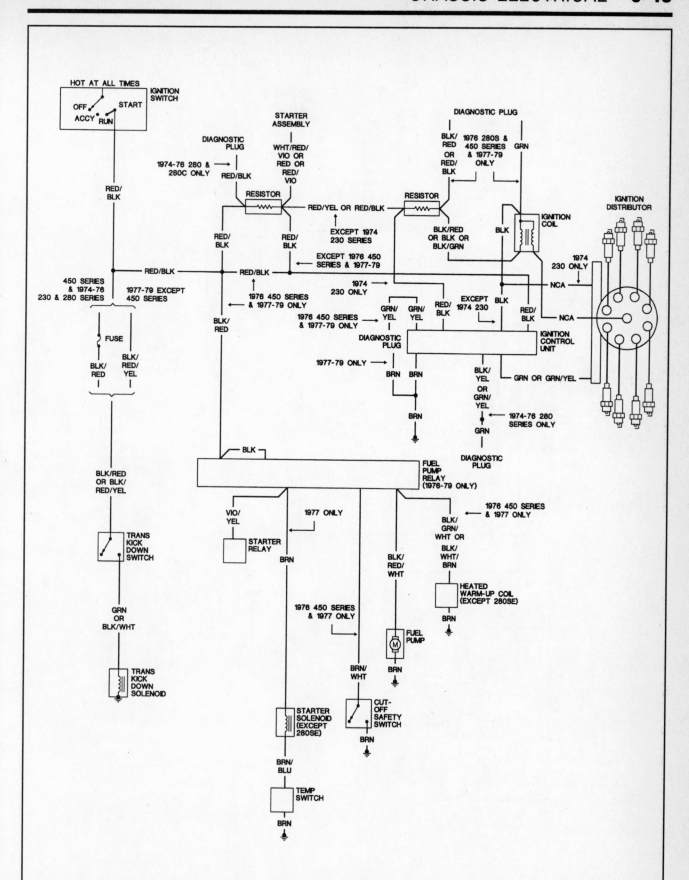

Fig. 22 Engine wiring—1974–78 230; 1974–76 280, 280C and 280S; 1977–79 280E and 280SE; 1978–79 280CE; 1976–80 450SL and 450SLC models

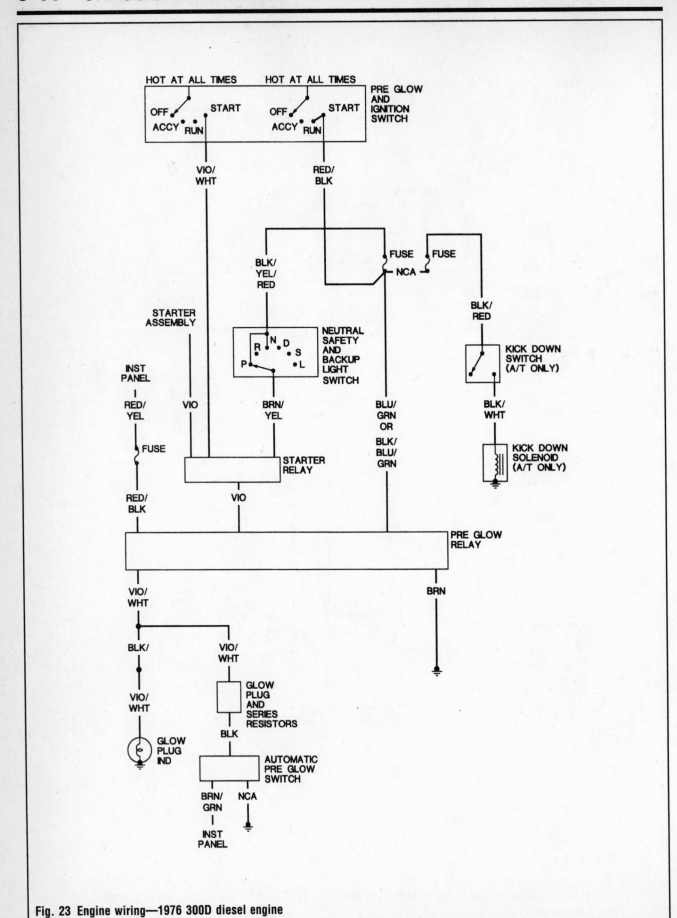

Fig. 23 Engine wiring—1976 300D diesel engine

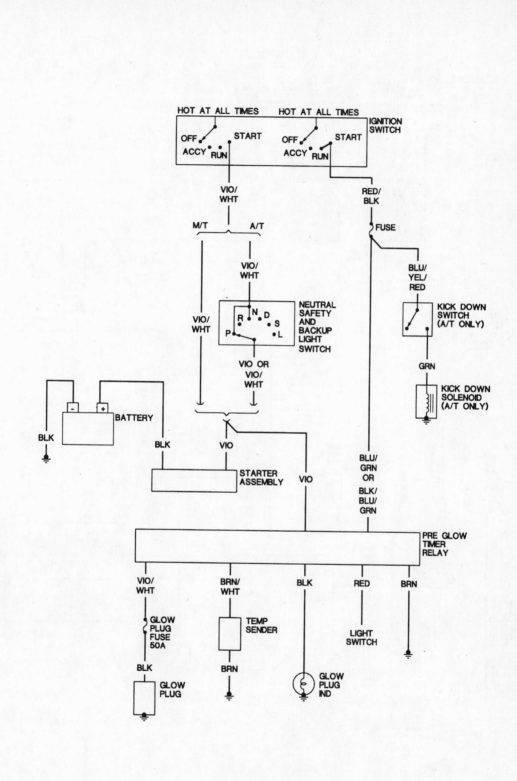

Fig. 24 Engine wiring—1977 300D and 240D diesel engines

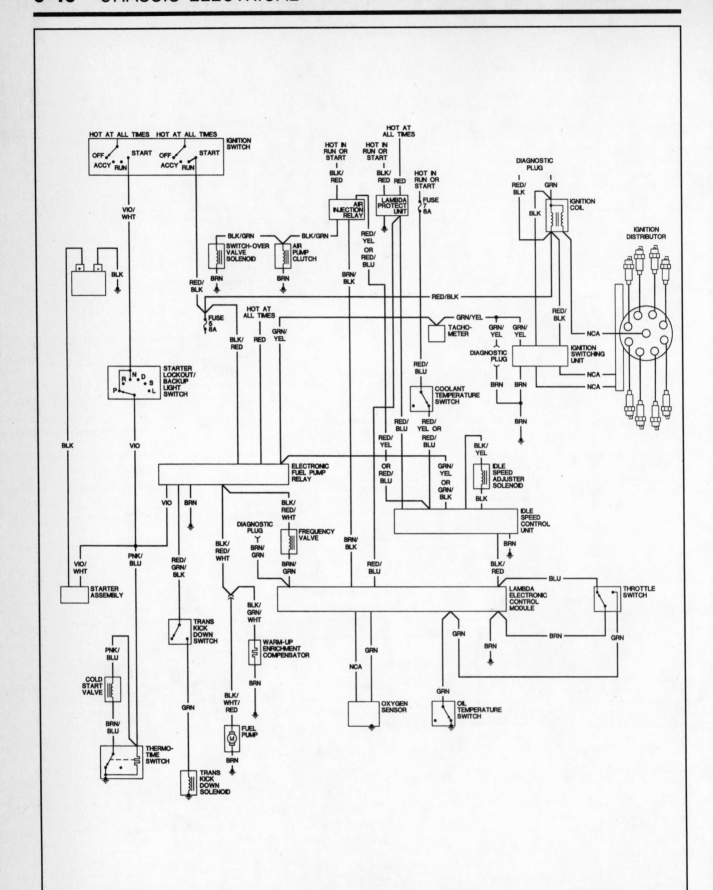

Fig. 25 Engine wiring—1980–81 280E, 280CE and 280SE; 1981–84 380SL, 380SEC and 380SEL; 1983–84 380SE; 1984 500SEC and 500SEL models

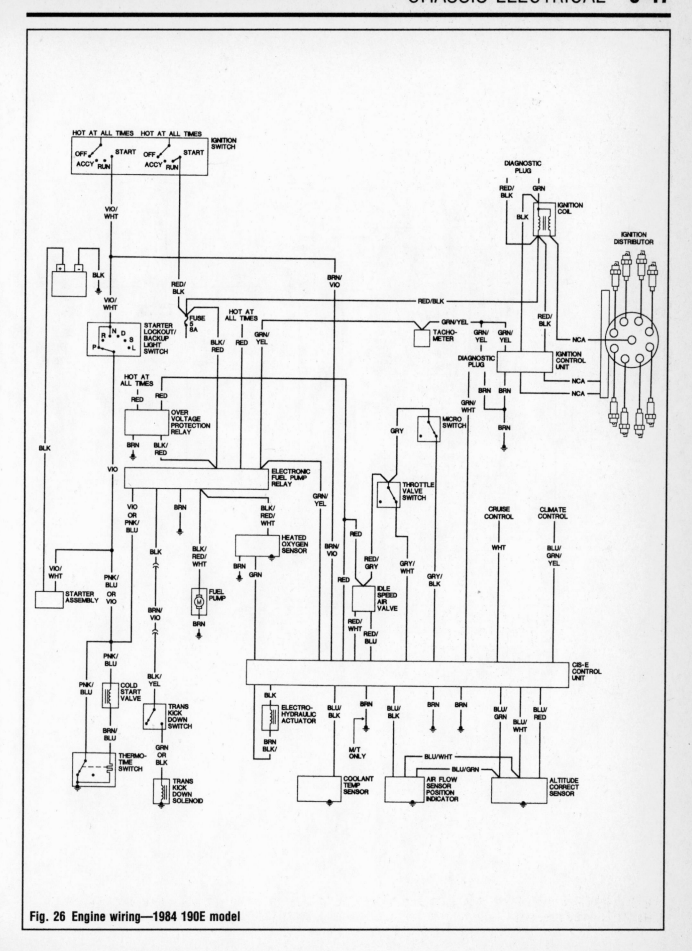

Fig. 26 Engine wiring—1984 190E model

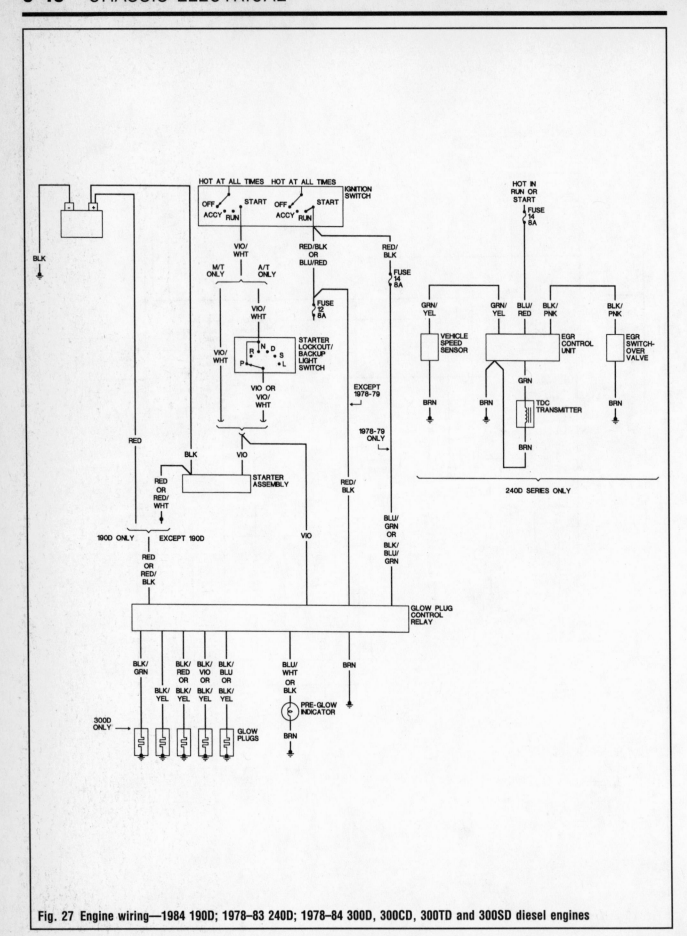

Fig. 27 Engine wiring—1984 190D; 1978-83 240D; 1978-84 300D, 300CD, 300TD and 300SD diesel engines

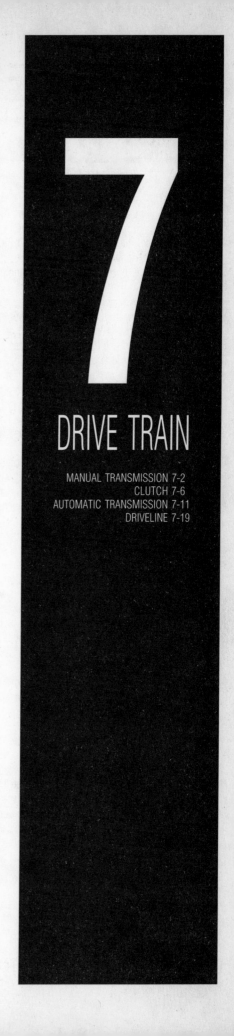

7

DRIVE TRAIN

MANUAL TRANSMISSION

Understanding the Manual Transmission

Because of the way an internal combustion engine breathes, it can produce torque (or twisting force) only within a narrow speed range. Most overhead valve pushrod engines must turn at about 2500 rpm to produce their peak torque. Often by 4500 rpm, they are producing so little torque that continued increases in engine speed produce no power increases.

The torque peak on overhead camshaft engines is, generally, much higher, but much narrower.

The manual transmission and clutch are employed to vary the relationship between engine RPM and the speed of the wheels so that adequate power can be produced under all circumstances. The clutch allows engine torque to be applied to the transmission input shaft gradually, due to mechanical slippage. The vehicle can, consequently, be started smoothly from a full stop.

The transmission changes the ratio between the rotating speeds of the engine and the wheels by the use of gears. 4-speed or 5-speed transmissions are most common. The lower gears allow full engine power to be applied to the rear wheels during acceleration at low speeds.

The clutch driveplate is a thin disc, the center of which is splined to the transmission input shaft. Both sides of the disc are covered with a layer of material which is similar to brake lining and which is capable of allowing slippage without roughness or excessive noise.

The clutch cover is bolted to the engine flywheel and incorporates a diaphragm spring which provides the pressure to engage the clutch. The cover also houses the pressure plate. When the clutch pedal is released, the driven disc is sandwiched between the pressure plate and the smooth surface of the flywheel, thus forcing the disc to turn at the same speed as the engine crankshaft.

The transmission contains a mainshaft which passes all the way through the transmission, from the clutch to the driveshaft. This shaft is separated at one point, so that front and rear portions can turn at different speeds.

Power is transmitted by a countershaft in the lower gears and reverse. The gears of the countershaft mesh with gears on the mainshaft, allowing power to be carried from one to the other. Countershaft gears are often integral with that shaft, while several of the mainshaft gears can either rotate independently of the shaft or be locked to it. Shifting from one gear to the next causes one of the gears to be freed from rotating with the shaft and locks another to it. Gears are locked and unlocked by internal dog clutches which slide between the center of the gear and the shaft. The forward gears usually employ synchronizers; friction members which smoothly bring gear and shaft to the same speed before the toothed dog clutches are engaged.

Identification

Only three models covered by this manual use a manual transmission; the 190D, 190E and 240D. The 1974–81 240D uses a four speed, model G76/18C, the 1982–83 240D uses a four speed, model GL68/20A. The 190 series both are equipped with five speed transmissions, models GL68/20A(B)-5. All four transmissions are similar in design, operation and service.

Transmission Assembly

REMOVAL & INSTALLATION

The transmission should only be removed with the engine as a unit. The transmission-to-bell housing bolts can only be reached from inside. Once the engine/transmission unit has been removed from the vehicle, the transmission and bell housing must be separated from the engine, as follows:

With Engine

ALL MODELS

1. Refer to Section 3 to remove the engine/transmission.
2. After removing the engine/transmission unit, unbolt the bellhousing from the engine. The bolts which hold the transmission to the bellhousing cannot be reached except from inside the bell housing.
3. Remove the starter. Pull the transmission and bellhousing from the engine.
4. The bolts which secure the bellhousing to the transmission are now visible and can be removed to separate the bellhousing and transmission.
   To install:
5. Connect the engine, bellhousing, and transmission, after coating the splines of the mainshaft with grease.
6. Install the starter.
7. Further installation is the reverse of removal.

Without Engine

1974–81 240D MODELS

1. Support the car on jackstands.
2. Disconnect the battery.
3. Disconnect the exhaust pipe and/or muffler to provide clearance around the bellhousing.
4. Unhook the slave cylinder hydraulic line at the connection and plug both openings.
5. Unbolt the rear engine mount.
6. Slightly raise the transmission with a jack and remove the lower plate covering the transmission tunnel.
7. Disconnect the speedometer cable from the rear of the transmission.
8. Disconnect the shift rods from the transmission shift levers.
9. Loosen, but do not remove, the intermediate bearing bolts.
10. Matchmark the U-joint and driveshaft coupling and loosen the U-joint.
11. Matchmark the driveshaft flange and adaptor. Loosen the 3 driveshaft bolts. Remove 2 of the bolts and pivot the driveshaft around enough to reinstall the 2 bolts. Remove the 3rd bolt and position the driveshaft rearward as far as the center bearing permits. Use a piece of wood to block the driveshaft up in the driveshaft tunnel. Reinstall the 3rd bolt. The adaptor plate should remain on the 3-legged transmission flange.
12. Remove the starter.
13. Remove all bolts attaching the transmission to the intermediate flange, but remove the upper 2 bolts last.

➡The clutch housing is heavily ribbed. Because of this, most of the bolts can only be reached with a 17 or 19 mm insert and extension.

14. Turn the transmission 45° to the left so that the starter domes on both sides of the clutch housing do not scrape the transmission tunnel.

15. Keep the transmission level and slide it out.

16. The clutch housing bolts can only be reached from inside. Unbolt the housing and remove it.

17. Installation is the reverse of removal.

1982–83 240D MODELS

1. Disconnect the battery.
2. Disconnect the regulating shaft in the engine compartment.
3. Support the transmission with a floor jack.
4. Unbolt the rear engine mount.
5. Unbolt each side of the engine carrier on the floor frame.
6. Unscrew the exhaust mounting bracket on the transmission. *Note the number and positioning of all washers.*
7. Unbolt the retaining strap and remove the exhaust pipe bracket.
8. Loosen the clamp nut on the driveshaft.
9. Loosen, but do not remove, the intermediate bearing bolts.
10. Unbolt the driveshaft on the transmission so that the companion plate remains with the driveshaft.
11. Carefully push the driveshaft as far to the rear as permitted.
12. Loosen and remove the tachometer drive shaft on the rear transmission case cover. Unclip the clip for the tachometer drive shaft from its holder.
13. Unscrew the holder for the line to the clutch housing. Unscrew the clutch slave cylinder and move it toward the rear until the pushrod is clear of the housing.
14. Push off the clip locks and then remove the shift rods from the intermediate levers on the shift bracket. *Note the position of the disc springs.*

✳✳ WARNING

When the shift rods are disconnected, do not move the shift lever into reverse or you risk damaging the back-up light switch.

15. Unbolt the starter and remove it.
16. Remove all transmission-to-intermediate flange screws. Remove the upper two last.
17. Carefully pull the transmission toward the rear of the vehicle and then remove it downward.

➡**Make sure that the input shaft has cleared the clutch plate before tilting the transmission.**

To install:

18. Lightly grease the centering lug and splines on the transmission input shaft.

➡**Position the clutch slave cylinder and line above the transmission before beginning installation.**

19. Move the transmission into the clutch so that one gear step engages. Rotate the mainshaft back and forth until the splines on the input shaft and clutch plate are aligned.

20. Move the transmission all the way in and then tighten the transmission-to-intermediate flange screws.

21. Install the starter.
22. Install the clutch slave cylinder with the proper plastic shims.
23. Installation of the remaining components is in the reverse order of removal. Please note the following:

a. After installing the driveshaft, roll the car back and forth and then tighten the intermediate bearing free of tension.

b. Tighten the driveshaft clamp nut to 22–29 ft. lbs. (30–40 Nm).

c. Make sure of the proper positioning of all washers, spacers and shims.

190D AND 190E MODELS

1. Disconnect the battery.
2. Cover the insulation mat in the engine compartment to prevent damage.
3. On vehicles equipped with a auxiliary heater, be sure that the water hose is out of the way.
4. Support the transmission with a floor jack.
5. Unbolt the engine mounts at the rear transmission cover.
6. Unbolt the engine carrier on the floor frame.
7. Unscrew the exhaust holder at the transmission. *Note the number and positioning of all washers.*
8. Unscrew the clamping strap and remove the exhaust pipe holder.
9. Remove the intermediate bearing shield plate.
10. Repeat Steps 8–11 of the 1982–83 240D procedure.

➡**On the 190E, the fitted sleeves on the universal flange must be loosened before separating the flange from the companion plate. This will require a cylindrical mandrel.**

11. Disconnect the exhaust system at the rear suspension and suspend it with wire.
12. Loosen and remove the input shaft for the tachometer.
13. Repeat Steps 12–16 of the 1982–83 240D procedure.
14. Rotate the transmission approximately 45° to the left, slide it out of the clutch plate and then remove it downward.

➡**Make sure that the input shaft has cleared the clutch plate before tilting the transmission.**

15. To install, repeat Steps 18–23 of the 1982–83 240D procedure. Remember that the transmission must be tilted approximately 45° to the left when installing.

Adjustment

LINKAGE

◆ See Figures 1, 2, 3 and 4 (p. 3–5)

The only type of shifter used is a floor mounted type.

✳✳ WARNING

On all types of transmissions, never hammer or force a new shift knob on with the shifter installed, as the plastic bushing connected to the lever will be damaged and cause hard shifting.

Proper adjustment of the shaft linkage is dependent on both the position of the shift levers at the transmission and the length

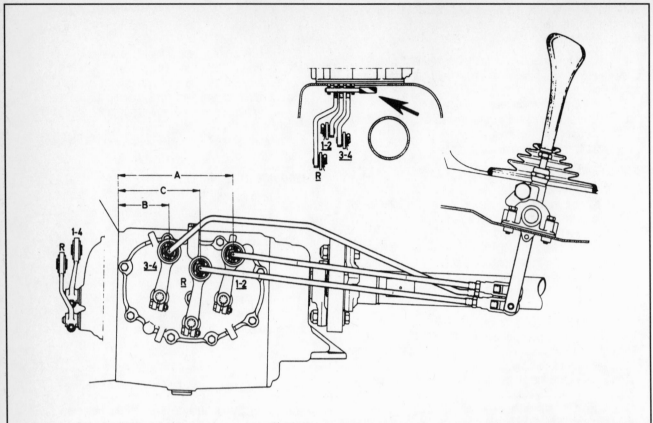

Fig. 1 Transmission linkage used on 1974–81 240D models. The arrow indicates a locking pin installed before adjustment

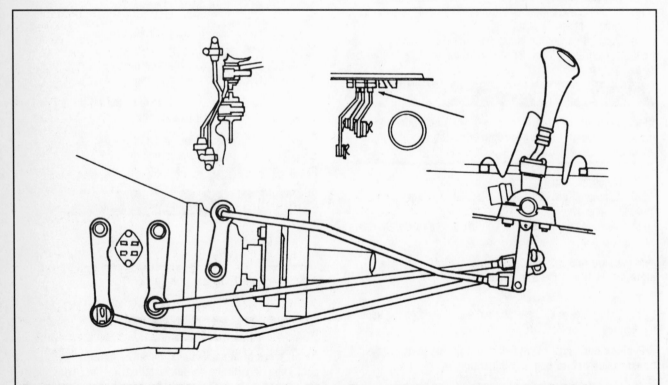

Fig. 2 View of the 1982–83 240D models transmission linkage. The arrow indicates a locking rod installed before adjustment

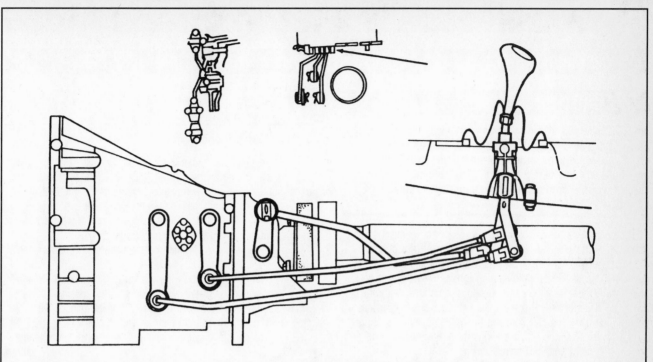

Fig. 3 View of the 4 and 5-speed 190 model's transmission linkage. The arrow indicates a locking rod installed before adjustment

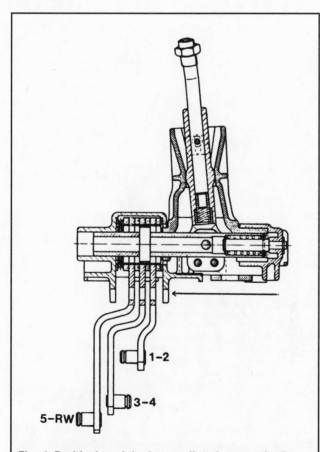

1-2

3-4

5-RW

Fig. 4 Positioning of the intermediate lever on the 5-speed 190 model. The arrow indicates where the locking rod goes

of the shift rods. The shift levers, rods and bearing block are all located underneath the floor tunnel; the driveshaft shield may have to be removed to gain access to them.

1. With the transmission in neutral and the driveshaft shield removed (if so equipped), remove the clip locks and disconnect the shift rods from the intermediate shift levers under the floor shift bearing bracket.

2. With the shifter still in the neutral position, lock the three intermediate shift levers by inserting a 0.2156 in. rod (a No. 3 drill bit will do, or any other tool of approximately the same diameter) through the levers and the holes in the bearing bracket.

3. Check the positioning of the shift levers at the transmission (see illustrations). Adjust by loosening the clamp bolts and moving the levers.

4. With the intermediate levers locked and the shift levers adjusted properly, try hooking the shift rods back onto their respective intermediate levers. The shift rods may be adjusted by loosening the locknut and turning the ball socket on the end until they are the proper length.

➡**When hooking up the shift rods to the intermediate levers, be very careful not to move the transmission shift levers out of their adjusted position.**

➡**When reattaching the shift rods on 190 models, use only clip locks which have a radiused edge. If the old style clip locks with a square edge are used, there is a possibility that the locks will pop out and the shift rods will drop down.**

5. Remove the locking rod from the bearing bracket, start the engine and then shift through the gears a few times. Occasionally slight binding may call for VERY slight further adjustments.

CLUTCH

Understanding the Clutch

✳✳ CAUTION

The clutch driven disc may contain asbestos, which has been determined to be a cancer causing agent. Never clean clutch surfaces with compressed air! Avoid inhaling any dust from any clutch surface! When cleaning clutch surfaces, use a commercially available brake cleaning fluid.

The purpose of the clutch is to disconnect and connect engine power at the transaxle. A vehicle at rest requires a lot of engine torque to get all that weight moving. An internal combustion engine does not develop a high starting torque (unlike steam engines) so it must be allowed to operate without any load until it builds up enough torque to move the vehicle. Torque increases with engine rpm. The clutch allows the engine to build up torque by physically disconnecting the engine from the transaxle, relieving the engine of any load or resistance.

The transfer of engine power to the transaxle (the load) must be smooth and gradual; if it weren't, drive line components would wear out or break quickly. This gradual power transfer is made possible by gradually releasing the clutch pedal. The clutch disc and pressure plate are the connecting link between the engine and transaxle. When the clutch pedal is released, the disc and plate contact each other (the clutch is engaged) physically joining the engine and transaxle. When the pedal is pushed inward, the disc and plate separate (the clutch is disengaged) disconnecting the engine from the transaxle.

Most clutches utilize a single plate, dry friction disc with a diaphragm-style spring pressure plate. The clutch disc has a splined hub which attaches the disc to the input shaft. The disc has friction material where it contacts the flywheel and pressure plate. Torsion springs on the disc help absorb engine torque pulses. The pressure plate applies pressure to the clutch disc, holding it tight against the surface of the flywheel. The clutch operating mechanism consists of a release bearing, fork and cylinder assembly.

The release fork and actuating linkage transfer pedal motion to the release bearing. In the engaged position (pedal released) the diaphragm spring holds the pressure plate against the clutch disc, so engine torque is transmitted to the input shaft. When the clutch pedal is depressed, the release bearing pushes the diaphragm spring center toward the flywheel. The diaphragm spring pivots the fulcrum, relieving the load on the pressure plate. Steel spring straps riveted to the clutch cover lift the pressure plate from the clutch disc, disengaging the engine drive from the transaxle and enabling the gears to be changed.

The clutch is operating properly if:

1. It will stall the engine when released with the vehicle held stationary.

2. The shift lever can be moved freely between 1st and reverse gears when the vehicle is stationary and the clutch disengaged.

Driven Disc and Pressure Plate

INSPECTION

◗ See Figures 5 and 6

A spring plate clutch that automatically compensates for wear is used, so no periodic adjustments are required. Apart from the usual slippage which accompanies severe wear of the clutch plate or disc, Mercedes-Benz has a simple tool, which can be purchased from a dealer that measures the amount of wear on the clutch plate. Actually, it is a simple "go-no go" gauge.

1. A plastic shim is installed between the slave cylinder and the bellhousing.

2. The shim is provided with two flat grooves running diagonally from bottom to center. When the shim is installed, these grooves appear as slots. Use groove (a) for left-hand drive vehicles and groove (b) for right-hand drive vehicles.

3. The clutch slave cylinder pushrod has two different diameters. The jaw width of the test device corresponds to the smaller diameter of the pushrod. If the notches on the test device disappear when the test device is inserted as far as it will go, the clutch plate is still operational.

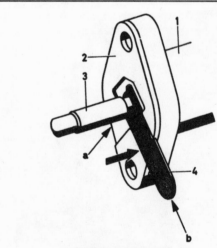

1. Clutch slave cylinder
2. Plastic shim
3. Thrust rod
4. Measuring gauge
(a)—Direction of measuring on lefthand drive vehicle with steering wheel and center shift, as well as on righthand drive vehicles with center shift
(b)—Direction of measuring on righthand drive vehicles with steering wheel shift

Fig. 5 A fully seated measuring gauge indicates that the clutch plate has reached its wear limit

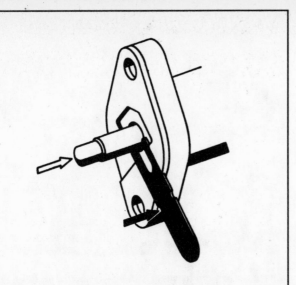

Fig. 6 A partially seated measuring gauge indicates that the clutch plate has not yet reached its wear limit

4. If, however, the notches on the test device remain visible, this is an indication that the clutch plate is worn severely and should be replaced.

REMOVAL & INSTALLATION

✳✳ CAUTION

The clutch driven disc may contain asbestos, which has been determined to be a cancer causing agent. Never clean clutch surfaces with compressed air! Avoid inhaling any dust from any clutch surface! When cleaning clutch surfaces, use a commercially available brake cleaning fluid.

◆ **See Figure 7**

1. To remove the clutch, first remove the transmission and bell-housing.
2. Loosen the clutch pressure plate hold-down bolts evenly, 1–1½ turns at a time, until tension is relieved. Never remove one bolt at a time, as damage to the pressure plate is possible.

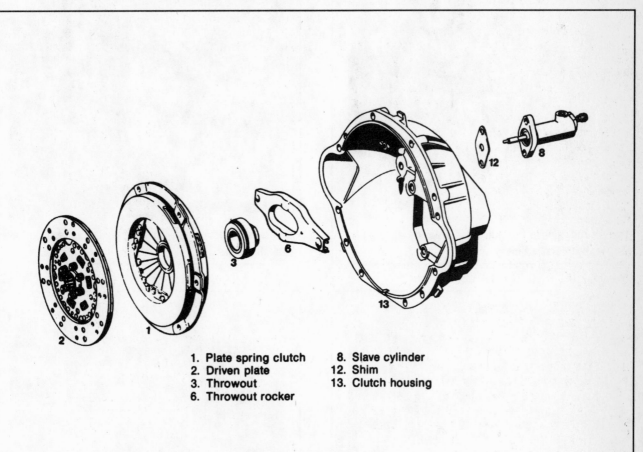

1. Plate spring clutch
2. Driven plate
3. Throwout
6. Throwout rocker
8. Slave cylinder
12. Shim
13. Clutch housing

Fig. 7 Exploded view of a typical clutch assembly's components

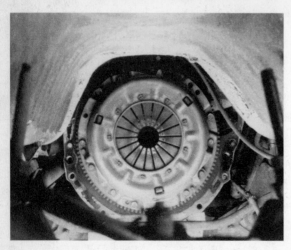

View of the clutch and pressure plate assembly

Check across the flywheel surface, it should be flat

Loosen and remove the clutch and pressure plate bolts evenly, a little at a time . . .

If necessary, lock the flywheel in place and remove the retaining bolts . . .

. . . then carefully remove the clutch and pressure plate assembly from the flywheel

. . . then remove the flywheel from the crankshaft in order replace it or have it machined

Upon installation, it is usually a good idea to apply a thread-locking compound to the flywheel bolts

Typical clutch alignment tool, note how the splines match the transmission's input shaft

Check the pressure plate for excessive wear

Install a clutch alignment arbor, to align the clutch assembly during installation

Be sure that the flywheel surface is clean, before installing the clutch

Clutch plate installed with the arbor in place

Clutch plate and pressure plate installed with the alignment arbor in place

Install the clutch assembly bolts and tighten in steps, using an X pattern

Pressure plate-to-flywheel bolt holes should align

Be sure to use a torque wrench to tighten all bolts

You may want to use a thread locking compound on the clutch assembly bolts

3. Examine the flywheel surface for blue heat marks, scoring, or cracks. If the flywheel is to be machined, always machine both sides.

To install:

4. Coat the splines with high temperature grease and place the clutch disc against the flywheel, centering it with a clutch pilot shaft. A wooden shaft, available at automotive jobbers, is satisfactory, but an old transmission mainshaft works best.

5. Tighten the pressure plate hold-down bolts evenly 1–1½ turns at a time until tight, then remove the pilot shaft.

➡**Most clutch plates have the flywheel side marked as such (Kupplungsseite). Do not assume that the pressure springs always face the transmission.**

Slave Cylinder

REMOVAL & INSTALLATION

1. Detach and plug the pressure line from the slave cylinder.
2. Remove the attaching screws from the slave cylinder.
3. Remove the slave cylinder, pushrod, and spacer.
To install:
4. Place the grooved side of the spacer in contact with the housing and hold it in position.
5. Install the slave cylinder and pushrod into the housing. Be sure that the dust cap is properly seated.
6. Install the attaching screws.
7. Connect the pressure line to the slave cylinder.
8. Bleed the slave cylinder.

BLEEDING THE SLAVE CYLINDER

1. Check the brake fluid level in the compensating tank and fill to maximum level.
2. Put a hose on the bleeder screw of the right front caliper and open the bleeder screw.
3. Have a helper depress the brake pedal until the hose is full and there are no air bubbles. Be sure the bleeder screw is closed each time the pedal is released.
4. Put the free end of the hose on the bleeder screw of the slave cylinder and open the bleeder screw.
5. Keep stepping on the brake pedal. Close the bleeder screw on the caliper and release the brake pedal. Open the bleeder screw and repeat the process until no air bubbles show up at the mouth of the inlet line on the compensating tank.
Between operations, check, and, if necessary, refill the compensating tank.
6. Close the bleeder screws on the caliper and slave cylinder and remove the hose.
7. Check the clutch operation and the fluid level.

AUTOMATIC TRANSMISSION

Understanding Automatic Transmissions

The automatic transmission allows engine torque and power to be transmitted to the rear wheels within a narrow range of engine operating speeds. It will allow the engine to turn fast enough to produce plenty of power and torque at very low speeds, while keeping it at a sensible rpm at high vehicle speeds (and it does this job without driver assistance). The transmission uses a light fluid as the medium for the transmission of power. This fluid also works in the operation of various hydraulic control circuits and as a lubricant. Because the transmission fluid performs all of these functions, trouble within the unit can easily travel from one part to another. For this reason, and because of the complexity and unusual operating principles of the transmission, a very sound understanding of the basic principles of operation will simplify troubleshooting.

TORQUE CONVERTER

The torque converter replaces the conventional clutch. It has three functions:
1. It allows the engine to idle with the vehicle at a standstill, even with the transmission in gear.
2. It allows the transmission to shift from range-to-range smoothly, without requiring that the driver close the throttle during the shift.
3. It multiplies engine torque to an increasing extent as vehicle speed drops and throttle opening is increased. This has the effect of making the transmission more responsive and reduces the amount of shifting required.
The torque converter is a metal case which is shaped like a sphere that has been flattened on opposite sides. It is bolted to the rear end of the engine's crankshaft. Generally, the entire metal case rotates at engine speed and serves as the engine's flywheel.
The case contains three sets of blades. One set is attached directly to the case. This set forms the torus or pump. Another set is directly connected to the output shaft, and forms the turbine. The third set is mounted on a hub which, in turn, is mounted on a stationary shaft through a one-way clutch. This third set is known as the stator.
A pump, which is driven by the converter hub at engine speed, keeps the torque converter full of transmission fluid at all times. Fluid flows continuously through the unit to provide cooling.
Under low speed acceleration, the torque converter functions as follows:
The torus is turning faster than the turbine. It picks up fluid at the center of the converter and, through centrifugal force, slings it outward. Since the outer edge of the converter moves faster than the portions at the center, the fluid picks up speed.
The fluid then enters the outer edge of the turbine blades. It then travels back toward the center of the converter case along the turbine blades. In impinging upon the turbine blades, the fluid loses the energy picked up in the torus.
If the fluid was now returned directly into the torus, both halves of the converter would have to turn at approximately the same speed at all times, and torque input and output would both be the same.
In flowing through the torus and turbine, the fluid picks up two types of flow, or flow in two separate directions. It flows through the turbine blades, and it spins with the engine. The stator, whose blades are stationary when the vehicle is being accelerated at low speeds, converts one type of flow into another. Instead of allowing the fluid to flow straight back into the torus, the stator's curved blades turn the fluid almost 90° toward the direction of rotation of the engine. Thus the fluid does not flow as fast toward the torus,

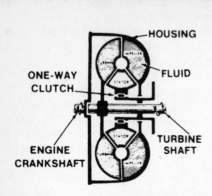

The torque converter housing is rotated by the engine's crankshaft, and turns the impeller—The impeller then spins the turbine, which gives motion to the turbine shaft, driving the gears

but is already spinning when the torus picks it up. This has the effect of allowing the torus to turn much faster than the turbine. This difference in speed may be compared to the difference in speed between the smaller and larger gears in any gear train. The result is that engine power output is higher, and engine torque is multiplied.

As the speed of the turbine increases, the fluid spins faster and faster in the direction of engine rotation. As a result, the ability of the stator to redirect the fluid flow is reduced. Under cruising conditions, the stator is eventually forced to rotate on its one-way clutch in the direction of engine rotation. Under these conditions, the torque converter begins to behave almost like a solid shaft, with the torus and turbine speeds being almost equal.

PLANETARY GEARBOX

The ability of the torque converter to multiply engine torque is limited. Also, the unit tends to be more efficient when the turbine is rotating at relatively high speeds. Therefore, a planetary gearbox is used to carry the power output of the turbine to the driveshaft.

Planetary gears function very similarly to conventional transmission gears. However, their construction is different in that three elements make up one gear system, and, in that all three elements are different from one another. The three elements are: an outer gear that is shaped like a hoop, with teeth cut into the inner surface; a sun gear, mounted on a shaft and located at the very center of the outer gear; and a set of three planet gears, held by pins in a ring-like planet carrier, meshing with both the sun gear and the outer gear. Either the outer gear or the sun gear may be held stationary, providing more than one possible torque multiplication factor for each set of gears. Also, if all three gears are forced to rotate at the same speed, the gearset forms, in effect, a solid shaft.

Most automatics use the planetary gears to provide various reductions ratios. Bands and clutches are used to hold various portions of the gearsets to the transmission case or to the shaft on

which they are mounted. Shifting is accomplished, then, by changing the portion of each planetary gearset which is held to the transmission case or to the shaft.

SERVOS & ACCUMULATORS

The servos are hydraulic pistons and cylinders. They resemble the hydraulic actuators used on many other machines, such as bulldozers. Hydraulic fluid enters the cylinder, under pressure, and forces the piston to move to engage the band or clutches.

The accumulators are used to cushion the engagement of the servos. The transmission fluid must pass through the accumulator on the way to the servo. The accumulator housing contains a thin piston which is sprung away from the discharge passage of the accumulator. When fluid passes through the accumulator on the way to the servo, it must move the piston against spring pressure, and this action smooths out the action of the servo.

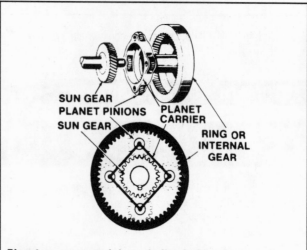

Planetary gears work in a similar fashion to manual transmission gears, but are composed of three parts

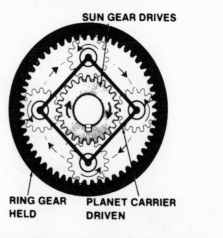

Planetary gears in the maximum reduction (low) range. The ring gear is held and a lower gear ratio is obtained

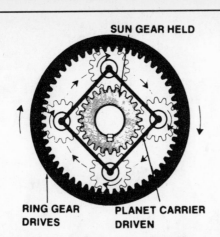

SUN GEAR HELD

RING GEAR DRIVES   **PLANET CARRIER DRIVEN**

Planetary gears in the minimum reduction (drive) range. The ring gear is allowed to revolve, providing a higher gear ratio

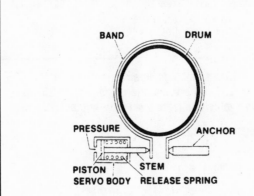

BAND   DRUM

PRESSURE   ANCHOR

PISTON   STEM
SERVO BODY   RELEASE SPRING

Servos, operated by pressure, are used to apply or release the bands, to either hold the ring gear or allow it to rotate

HYDRAULIC CONTROL SYSTEM

The hydraulic pressure used to operate the servos comes from the main transmission oil pump. This fluid is channeled to the various servos through the shift valves. There is generally a manual shift valve which is operated by the transmission selector lever and an automatic shift valve for each automatic upshift the transmission provides.

➡**Many new transmissions are electronically controlled. On these models, electrical solenoids are used to better control the hydraulic fluid. Usually, the solenoids are regulated by an electronic control module.**

There are two pressures which affect the operation of these valves. One is the governor pressure which is effected by vehicle speed. The other is the modulator pressure which is effected by intake manifold vacuum or throttle position. Governor pressure rises with an increase in vehicle speed, and modulator pressure rises as the throttle is opened wider. By responding to these two pressures, the shift valves cause the upshift points to be delayed with increased throttle opening to make the best use of the engine's power output.

Most transmissions also make use of an auxiliary circuit for downshifting. This circuit may be actuated by the throttle linkage the vacuum line which actuates the modulator, by a cable or by a solenoid. It applies pressure to a special downshift surface on the shift valve or valves.

The transmission modulator also governs the line pressure, used to actuate the servos. In this way, the clutches and bands will be actuated with a force matching the torque output of the engine.

Identification

Automatic transmission serial numbers are located on a plate attached to the driver's side of the transmission.

Fluid Pan

FILTER SERVICE

1. Drain the transmission of all fluid by loosening the dipstick tube.
2. Remove the transmission pan.
3. Remove the bolt or bolts which retain the filter to the transmission.
4. Remove the filter and replace it with a new one.
5. Install the transmission pan, using a new gasket.
6. Refill the transmission to the proper level with the specified brand of fluid.

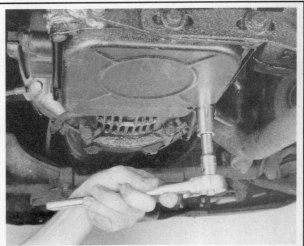

To drain the pan and remove the filter, first loosen the drain plug . . .

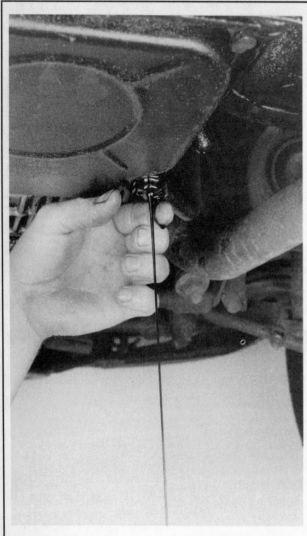

. . . and let the transmission fluid drain into a suitable container

Remove the transmission filter retaining screws

Adjustments

SELECTOR ROD LINKAGE

➡Before performing this adjustment on any Mercedes-Benz vehicle, be sure that the vehicle is resting on its wheels. No part of the vehicle may be jacked for this adjustment.

Column Mounted Linkage

See the "Transmission Application" chart in the specifications for Transmission Application.

W3A 040 (EXCEPT 380SEL, 450SE AND 450SEL)
▶ **See Figure 8**

1. Loosen the counternut on the ball socket.
2. Disconnect the selector rod from the shift lever bracket.

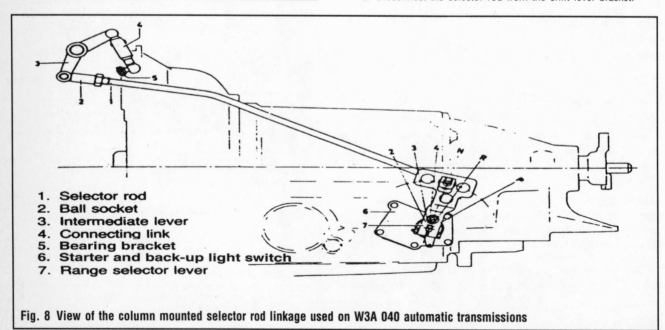

1. Selector rod
2. Ball socket
3. Intermediate lever
4. Connecting link
5. Bearing bracket
6. Starter and back-up light switch
7. Range selector lever

Fig. 8 View of the column mounted selector rod linkage used on W3A 040 automatic transmissions

Transmission Applications

Model	Automatic Transmission	Manual Transmission
190D	W4A 020	GL68/20A-5
190E	W4A 020	GL68/20B-5
230	W4B 025	—
240D (thru '80)	W4B 025	G-76/18C(4-spd.)
240D ('81 and later)	W4B 025	GL68/20A(4-spd.)
280, 280C, 280E, 280CE	W4B 025	—
280S, 280SE	W4B 025	—
300D, 300CD, 300TD	W4B 025	—
300D Turbo. 300CD Turbo	W4A 040	—
300TD Turbo 1981–83	W4A 040	—
300SD 1978–80	W4B 025	—
300SD 1981–84	W4A 040	—
280SL, 380SLC, 380SEL, 380SEC, 380SE	W4A 040	—
450SE, 450SEL, 450SL, 450SLC	W3A 040	—
500SEL, 500SEC	W4A 040	—
6.9	W3B 050	—

3. Set the transmission selector lever and the selector rod in Neutral.

4. Adjust the length of the selector rod until the ball socket aligns with the end of the ball on the intermediate lever.

5. Attach the ball socket to the intermediate lever, making sure that the play in the selector lever in position Three (D) and Four (S) is about equal.

6. Tighten the counternut on the ball socket.

W3A 040 (380SEL, 450SE AND 450SEL ONLY), W4B 025 AND W4A 040

♦ See Figure 9

1. Loosen the counternut on the rear selector rod while holding both recesses of the front selector rod with an open end wrench.

2. Disconnect the selector rod from the selector lever.

3. Set the selector lever on the transmission and on the column to Neutral.

4. Adjust the selector rod until the bearing pin is aligned with the bearing bushing in the selector lever.

5. Connect the rear selector lever to the selector rod and secure it with the lock. Be sure that the clearance of the selector lever in D and S is equal.

6. Tighten the locknut on the rear selector rod while holding the front selector rod as in Step 1.

Floor Mounted Linkage
♦ See Figure 10

➡The vehicle must be standing with the weight normally distributed on all four wheels. No jacks may be used.

1. Disconnect the selector rod from the selector lever.

2. Set the selector lever in Neutral and make sure that there is approximately 1 mm clearance between the selector lever and the N stop of the selector gate.

3. Adjust the length of the selector rod so that it can be attached free of tension.

4. Retighten the counternut.

STARTER LOCKOUT & BACK-UP LIGHT SWITCH

♦ See Figure 11 (p. 17)

1. Disconnect the selector rod and move the selector lever on the transmission to position Neutral.

2. Tighten the clamping screw prior to making adjustments.

3. Loosen the adjusting screw and insert the locating pin through the driver into the locating hole in the shift housing.

4. Tighten the adjusting screw and remove the locating pin.

5. Move the selector lever to position N and connect the selector rod so that there is no tension.

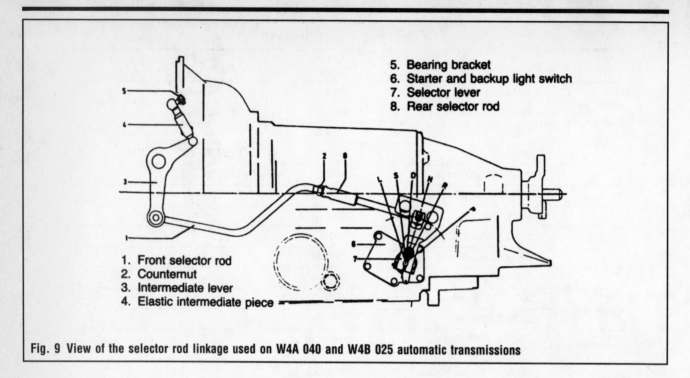

5. Bearing bracket
6. Starter and backup light switch
7. Selector lever
8. Rear selector rod

1. Front selector rod
2. Counternut
3. Intermediate lever
4. Elastic intermediate piece

Fig. 9 View of the selector rod linkage used on W4A 040 and W4B 025 automatic transmissions

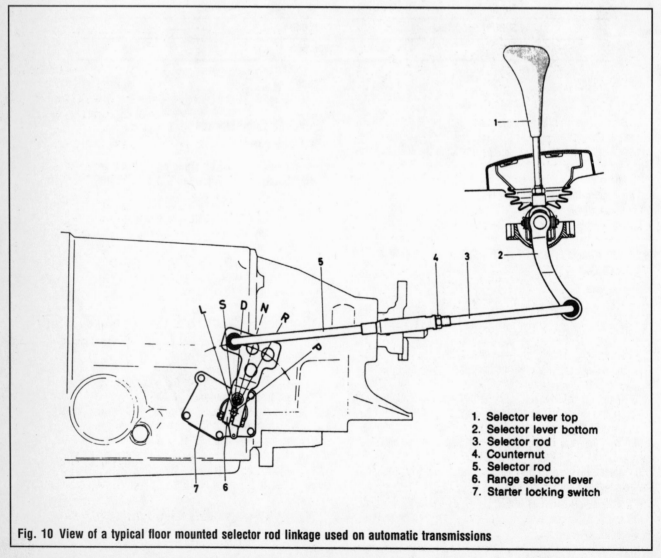

1. Selector lever top
2. Selector lever bottom
3. Selector rod
4. Counternut
5. Selector rod
6. Range selector lever
7. Starter locking switch

Fig. 10 View of a typical floor mounted selector rod linkage used on automatic transmissions

1. Selector range lever
2. Washer
3. Adjusting screw
4. Shaft
5. Locating pin
6. Clamping screw

(a)—Column shift for left-hand and right-hand drive vehicles 200/8, 220 D/8, 230/8, 280 S/8, 280 SE/8 and 300 SEL/8.

(b)—Steering wheel shift for left-hand drive vehicles (220/8, 220 D/8, 230/8, 250/8)

(c)—Steering wheel shift for right-hand drive vehicles (220/8, 220 D/8, 230/8, 250/8)

(d)—Steering wheel shift for left-hand drive vehicles (280S/8, 280 SE/8, 300 SEL/8, 280 SE/3.5 and 300 SEL/3.5)

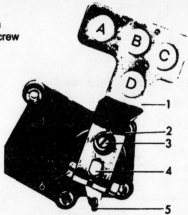

Fig. 11 Location of the starter lockout and back-up light switch adjustment points

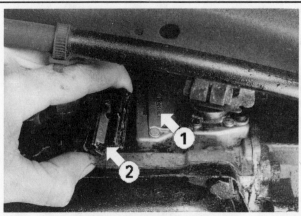

1. Starter lockout and back-up light switch
2. Electrical connection

To remove the starter lockout and back-up light switch, disengage the electrical connection

The starter lockout and back-up light switch is located behind the shift linkage

6. Check to be sure that the engine cannot be started in Neutral or Park.

KICKDOWN SWITCH

◆ **See Figure 12**

1. The kickdown position of the solenoid valve is controlled by the accelerator pedal.
2. Push the accelerator pedal against the kickdown limit stop. In this position the throttle lever should rest against the full load stop of the venturi control unit.
3. Adjustments are made by loosening the clamping screw on

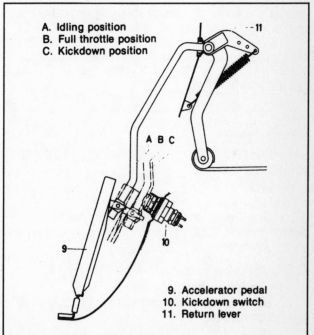

A. Idling position
B. Full throttle position
C. Kickdown position

9. Accelerator pedal
10. Kickdown switch
11. Return lever

Fig. 12 Kickdown switch location and adjustment positions

the return lever on the accelerator pedal shaft and turning the shaft. Tighten the clamping screw again.

CONTROL PRESSURE ROD

Except 190 and 1981–84 300, 380 and 500 Models

4-CYLINDER ENGINES

1. Remove the vacuum control unit from the carburetor.
2. Disconnect the automatic choke connecting rod so the throttle valve rests against the idle stop.
3. Loosen the screw and turn the levers against each other so the control rod rests against the idle stop.
4. Tighten the screw and depress the accelerator to the kickdown position. The throttle valve must rest against the full throttle stop.
5. Install the vacuum control unit on the distributor and connect the automatic choke rod.

DIESEL ENGINES

The control pressure rod can only be adjusted with a special gauge available only from Mercedes-Benz dealers.

6-CYLINDER ENGINES

1. Disconnect the control pressure rod.
2. Push the angle lever in the direction of the arrow.
3. Push the control pressure rod rearward against the stop and adjust its length so there is no binding.
4. Tighten the counter nut after adjustment.

V8 ENGINES

1. Remove the air filter and disconnect the control pressure linkage.
2. The throttle valve should rest against the idle speed stop.
3. Push the regulating lever and angle lever to the idle position.
4. Push the control pressure rod completely rearward against the stop and adjust the length of the rod so there is no tension.
5. When checking the rod for length, hold it to the left of the socket, not above to compensate for rotary motion of the linkage.

CONTROL PRESSURE CABLE

1981–84 Vehicles

380SE, 380SEC, 380SEL, 380SL, 380SLC, 500SEC AND 500SEL MODELS

1. Remove the air cleaner.
2. Loosen the clamping screw.
3. Push the ball socket back, then carefully forward until a slight resistance is felt. At this point, tighten the clamp screw.
4. Install the air cleaner.

TURBODIESELS

1. Pry off the ball socket.
2. Push the ball socket back, then pull carefully forward until a slight resistance is felt.

3. Hold the ball socket above the ball head. The drag lever should rest against the stop.
4. Adjust the cable at the adjusting screw so that the ball socket can be attached with no strain.

190D MODEL

1. Remove the ball socket (19) and extend the telescoping rod (8) to its full length.
2. Pull the control cable forward until a slight resistance is felt. Hold the ball socket over the ball head and engage tension free.
3. Adjust by using the telescoping rod if so required.

190E MODEL

◆ **See Figure 13**

1. Turn the adjusting screw (15) inward until the compression nipple on the spacing sleeve (17) has approximately 1mm of play left.
2. Unscrew the adjusting screw until the tip of the pointer rests directly above the groove on the adjusting screw.

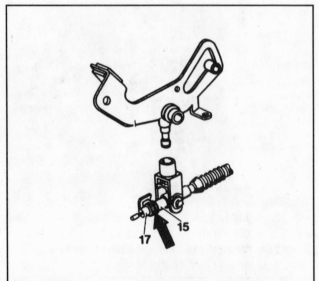

Fig. 13 Control pressure cable adjustment—190E models

Transmission Assembly

REMOVAL & INSTALLATION

Mercedes-Benz automatic transmissions are removed as a unit with the engine. Consult the "Engine Mechanical" portion of Section 3 for removal and installation procedures concerning a given engine.

DRIVELINE

Mercedes-Benz automobiles use either two or three piece driveshafts to connect the transmission to a hypoid independent rear axle. All models covered in this book use independent rear suspension.

Understanding Rear Axles

The rear axle is a special type of transmission that reduces the speed of the drive from the engine and transmission and drives the power to the rear wheels. Power enters the rear axle from the driveshaft via the companion flange. The flange is mounted on the drive pinion shaft. The drive pinion shaft and gear which carry the power into the differential turn at engine speed. The gear on the end of the pinion shaft drives a large ring gear the axis of rotation of which is 90° away from that of the pinion. The pinion and ring gear reduce the speed and multiply the power by the gear ratio of the axle, and change the direction of rotation to turn the axle shafts which drive both wheels. The rear axle gear ratio is found by dividing the number of pinion gear teeth into the number of ring gear teeth.

The ring gear drives the differential case. The case provides the two mounting points for the ends of a pinion shaft on which are mounted two pinion gears. The pinion gears drive the two side gears, one of which is located on the inner end of each axle shaft.

By driving the axle shafts through this arrangement, the differential allows the outer drive wheel to turn faster than the inner drive wheel in a turn.

The main drive pinion and the side bearings, which bear the weight of the differential case, are shimmed to provide proper bearing preload, and to position and the pinion and ring gears properly.

➡ **The proper adjustment of the relationship of the ring and pinion gears is critical. It should be attempted only by those with extensive equipment and/or experience.**

Limited-slip differentials include clutches which tend to link each axle shaft to the differential case. Clutches may be engaged either by spring action or by pressure produced by the torque on the axles during a turn. During turning on a dry pavement, the effects of the clutch are overcome, and each wheel turns at the required speed. When slippage occurs at either wheel, however, the clutches will transmit some of the power to the wheel which has the greater amount of traction. Because of the presence of clutches, limited-slip units require a special lubricant.

BASIC REAR AXLE PROBLEMS

First, determine when the noise is most noticeable.
• Drive Noise: Produced under vehicle acceleration.
• Coast Noise: Produced while the car coasts with a closed throttle.
• Float Noise: Occurs while maintaining constant car speed (just enough to keep speed constant) on a level road.

Road Noise

Brick or rough surfaced concrete roads produce noises that seem to come from the rear axle. Road noise is usually identical in Drive or Coast and driving on a different type of road will tell whether the road is the problem.

Tire Noise

Tire noises are often mistaken for rear axle problems. Snow treads or unevenly worn tires produce vibrations seeming to originate elsewhere. Temporarily inflating the tires to 40 lbs will significantly alter tire noise, but will have no effect on rear axle noises (which normally cease below about 30 mph).

Engine/Transmission Noise

Determine at what speed the noise is most pronounced, then stop the car in a quiet place. With the transmission in Neutral, run the engine through speeds corresponding to road speeds where the noise was noticed. Noises produced with the car standing still are coming from the engine or transmission.

Front Wheel Bearing Noise

While holding the car speed steady; lightly apply the footbrake; this will often decrease bearing noise, as some of the load is taken from the bearing.

Noise Diagnosis

The Noise Is:	Most Probably Produced By
1. Identical under Drive or Coast	Road surface, tires or front wheel bearings
2. Different depending on road surface	Road surface or tires
3. Lower as the car speed is lowered	Tires
4. Similar with car standing or moving	Engine or transmission
5. A vibration	Unbalanced tires, rear wheel bearing, unbalanced driveshaft or worn U-joint
6. A knock or click about every 2 tire revolutions	Rear wheel bearing
7. Most pronounced on turns	Damaged differential gears
8. A steady low-pitched whirring or scraping, started at low speeds	Damaged or worn pinion bearing
9. A chattering vibration on turns	Wrong differential lubricant or worn clutch plates (limited slip rear axle)
10. Noticed only in Drive, Coast or Float conditions	Worn ring gear and/or pinion gear

Rear Axle Noises

Eliminating other possible sources can narrow the cause to the rear axle, which normally produces noise from worn gears or bearings. Gear noises tend to peak in a narrow speed range, while bearing noises will usually vary in pitch with engine speeds.

Driveshaft and U-Joints

REMOVAL & INSTALLATION

230, 240D, 280, 280C, 280E, 280CE, 300D, 300CD, 300TD Models

➡**Matchmark all driveshaft connections prior to removal.**

1. Remove the equalizer and disconnect the parking brake cables.

To remove the driveshaft, loosen the clamp retaining bolts

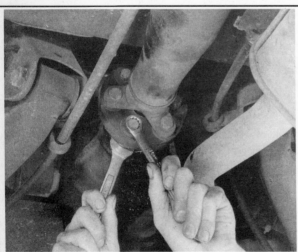
Using a back-up wrench, loosen the driveshaft-to-differential bolts . . .

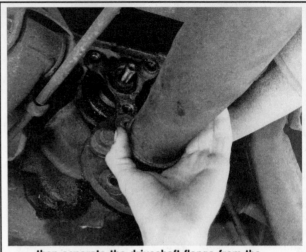
. . . then separate the driveshaft flange from the differential

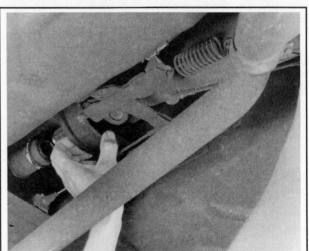
Slide the driveshaft rearward, disengage it from the transmission and remove it from the vehicle

2. Remove the bolts which secure the two brackets to the chassis at the front and rear and remove the brackets. It may be necessary to lower the exhaust system slightly to allow access to the left-hand bolts on the rear bracket.

3. Loosen the nut on the driveshaft about 2 turns without pushing the rubber sleeve back (it slides along). On a two-piece shaft, only loosen the front clamp nut.

4. Remove the nuts which secure the attaching plate to the transmission flange and rear axle.

5. Remove the bolts which secure the intermediate bearing(s) to the chassis. Push the driveshaft together and slightly down, and remove the driveshaft from the vehicle.

➡**If possible, do not separate the parts of the driveshaft since each driveshaft is balanced at the factory. If separation is necessary, all parts must be marked and reassembled in the same relative positions to assure that the driveshafts will remain reasonably well balanced.**

To install:

6. Installation is the reverse of removal.

7. Pack the cavities of the two centering sleeves with special Mercedes-Benz grease.

8. Install the driveshaft and attach the intermediate bearing(s) to the chassis.

9. Rock the car backward and forward several times to be sure that the driveshaft is properly centered without forcing.

10. Prior to tightening the clamp nuts on a three piece driveshaft, be sure that the intermediate shaft does not contact either the front or rear intermediate bearing. The clearance between the intermediate shaft and the bearing should be the same at both ends.

Other Models

➡**Steps 1–3 apply to 4-cylinder and V8 models. Matchmark all driveshaft connections prior to removal.**

1. Fold the torsion bar down after disconnecting the level control linkage (if equipped).

2. Remove the exhaust system.

3. Remove the heat shield from the frame.

4. Support the transmission with a jack and completely remove the rear engine mount crossmember.

5. Without sliding the rubber sleeve back loosen the clamp nut approximately two turns (the rubber sleeve will slide along).

➡**On 3-piece driveshafts, only the front clamp nut need be loosened.**

6. Unscrew the U-joint mounting flange from the U-joint plate.

7. Bend back the locktabs and remove the bolts that attach the driveshaft to the rear axle pinion yoke.

8. Remove the bolts which attach the intermediate bearing(s) to the frame. Push the driveshaft together slightly and remove it from the vehicle.

9. Try not to separate the driveshafts. If it is absolutely necessary, matchmark all components so that they can be reassembled in the same order.

10. Installation is the reverse of removal. Always use new self-locking nuts. After the driveshaft is installed, rock the car back and forth several times to settle the driveshaft. Make sure that neither intermediate shaft is binding against either intermediate bearing, and that the clearance between the intermediate bearing and the driveshaft is the same at both ends.

Axle Shaft

➡**The rubber covered joints are filled with special oil. If they are disassembled for any reason, they must be refilled with the special oil.**

REMOVAL & INSTALLATION

Except 190D, 190E, 380SEC and 500SEC Models

MODELS WITHOUT TORQUE COMPENSATOR (TORSION BAR)

◆ **See Figure 14**

Most models do not use a torque compensator (torsion bar) which is actually a steel bar used to locate the rear axle under acceleration. In general only the 450 series cars and the 300SD use a torque compensator, but it is wise to check for one before servicing the axle shaft. The illustrations apply to either type.

Fig. 14 Most models do not come equipped with a torque compensator (torsion bar), indicated here by the arrow

Troubleshooting the Driveline

The Problem	Is Caused By	What to Do
Shudder as car accelerates from stop or low speed	• Loose U-joint • Defective center bearing	• Tighten or replace U-joint • Replace center bearing
Loud clunk in driveshaft when shifting gears	• Worn U-joints	• Replace U-joints
Roughness or vibration at any speed	• Out-of-balance, bent or dented driveshaft • Worn U-joints • U-joint clamp bolts loose	• Have driveshaft serviced • Service U-joints • Tighten U-joint clamp bolts
Squeaking noise at low speeds	• Lack of U-joint lubrication	• Lubricate U-joints if problem persists, service U-joint
Knock or clicking noise	• U-joint or driveshaft hitting frame tunnel • Worn U-joint	• Correct overloaded condition • Replace U-joint

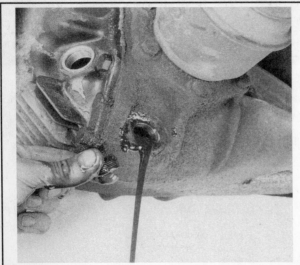

To remove the rear axle shaft, drain the differential fluid

Loosen the rubber mount-to-differential cover bolts . . .

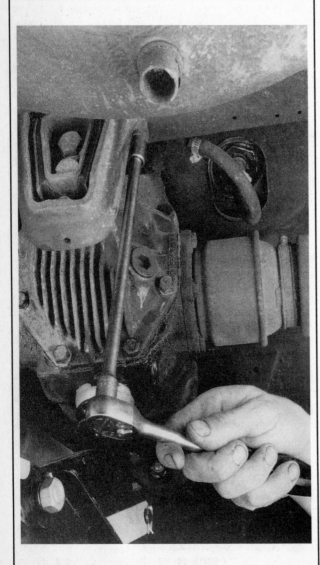

Loosen the rubber mount-to frame bolts

. . . then remove the rubber mount

Loosen the differential cover bolts

Remove the differential cover and set it aside

Use a prytool to disengage the axle lock ring, then remove it from the differential

After the axle has been pressed from the flange, remove it from the differential

➡On the 280, 280C, and 280E only axle shafts identified with a yellow paint dot or part no. 107 350 07 10 (left) or part no. 107 350 0810 (right) can be installed.

1. Jack up the rear of the car and remove the wheel and center axle hold-down bolt (in hub).

2. Remove the brake caliper and suspend it from a hook.

3. Drain the differential oil and place a jack under the differential housing.

4. Unbolt the rubber mount from the chassis and the differential housing, then remove the differential housing cover to expose the ring and pinion gears.

5. Press the shaft from the axle flange. If necessary, loosen the shock absorber.

6. Using a screwdriver, remove the axle lock ring inside the differential case.

7. Pull the axle from the housing by pulling the splined end from the side gears, with the spacer.

➡Axle shafts are stamped R and L for right and left units. Always use new lockrings.

8. Installation is the reverse of removal. Fill the rear axle.

✴✴ WARNING

Check end-play of the lock ring in the groove. If necessary, install a thicker lock ring or spacer to eliminate all end-play, while still allowing the lock ring to rotate. Do not allow the joints in the axle shaft to hang free or the joint bearing may be damaged and leak.

MODELS WITH TORQUE COMPENSATOR (TORSION BAR)

1. Drain the oil from the rear axle.

2. Disconnect and plug the brake lines.

3. Loosen the connecting rod and unscrew the torsion bar bearing bracket. Lower the exhaust system slightly and remove the torsion bar.

4. Lower the shock absorber.

5. Remove the bolt which attaches the rear axle shaft to the rear axle shaft flange.

6. Disconnect the brake cable control. Remove the bracket from the wheel carrier, remove the rubber sleeve, and push back the cover.

7. Press the rear axle shaft out of the flange with a suitable tool.

8. Support the rear axle with a jack.

9. Remove the rear rubber mount.

10. Clean the axle housing and remove the cover from the housing.

➡The axle shafts are the floating type and can be compressed in the constant velocity joints.

11. Remove the locking ring from the end of the axle shafts which engage the side gears in the differential.

12. Disengage the axle shaft from the side gear and remove the axle shaft together with the spacer.

✴✴ WARNING

Do not hang the outer constant velocity joint in a free position (without any support), as the shaft may be damaged and the constant velocity joint housing may leak.

13. Installation is the reverse of removal.

14. If either axle shaft is replaced, be sure that the proper replacement shaft is installed. Axle shafts are marked L and R for left and right.

15. Check the end-play between the lockring on the axle shaft and the side gear. There should be no noticeable end-play, but the lockring should be able to turn in the groove.

16. Be sure to bleed the brakes and fill the rear axle with the proper quantity and type of lubricant.

190D, 190E, 380SEC and 500SEC Models

1. Loosen, but do not remove, the axle shaft collar nut.

2. Raise the rear of the vehicle and support it on jackstands.

3. Disconnect the axle shaft from the hub assembly. On the 190, make sure that while loosening the locking screws, the bit is seated properly in the multi-tooth profile of the screws.

4. Remove the self-locking screws that attach the inner CV-joint to the connecting flange on the differential. Always loosen the screws in a crosswise manner.

➡**Make sure that the end cover on the inner CV-joint is not damaged when separated from the connecting flange.**

5. While supporting the axle shaft, use a slide hammer or the like and press the axle shaft out of the hub assembly.

6. Tilt the axle shaft down and remove it.

✳✳ WARNING

Make sure that the CV-joint boots are not damaged during the removal process.

7. Installation is in the reverse order of removal. Please note the following:

a. Always clean the connecting flanges before installation.

b. Always use new self-locking screws. On the 190, moisten the screw threads and contact faces with oil before installing. Tighten the screws to 51 ft. lbs. (70 Nm) on the 190 and 90–105 ft. lbs. (125–145 Nm) on the others. Always tighten the screws in a crosswise pattern.

c. Tighten the axle shaft collar nut to 203–230 ft. lbs. (280–320 Nm) on the 190 and 22 ft. lbs. (30 Nm) on the others. On the 190, lock the collar nut at the crush flange (see illustration).

Differential

REMOVAL & INSTALLATION

Except 190D and 190E Models

1. Drain the oil from the differential.

2. On cars without torque compensators, remove the brake caliper and suspend it on a hook.

3. On cars with torque compensation, (see previous procedure) disconnect the brake cable control, unbolt the holding bracket on the wheel carrier, remove the rubber sleeve and push the cover back.

4. Remove the bolt from both sides that holds the rear axle shaft to the flange.

5. Press the rear axle shaft out of the flange.

6. If required, loosen the right-hand rear shock absorber and lower the trailing arm to the stop.

7. Remove the exhaust system, if necessary.

8. Remove the heat shield if equipped.

9. Loosen the clamp nut and remove the intermediate bearing from the floor pan. On 3-piece driveshafts, only remove the front nut.

10. Unbolt the driveshaft and remove it.

11. Support the rear axle housing.

12. Unbolt the rear rubber mount from the frame floor.

13. On the 500 series, 450, 380, 280S, 280SE and 300SD, lower the jack until the self-locking nuts are accessible.

14. Unbolt the rear axle center housing from the rear axle carrier.

15. On all other models, remove the bolt from the rubber mount on the cover of the rear axle housing. Fold back the rubber mat in the trunk and remove the rubber plugs; unbolt the rear axle center housing from the rear axle carrier.

16. Lower the rear axle center housing and remove it with the axle shafts. Do not allow the axle shafts to hang free, or the seals will be damaged, resulting in leaks.

17. Installation is the reverse of removal. Install new self-locking nuts, adjust the parking brake and fill the rear axle with the correct fluid.

190D and 190E Models

1. Drain the oil from the differential.

2. Remove the exhaust shielding plate.

3. Loosen the clamp nut on the driveshaft. Unscrew the intermediate bearing screws at the floor pan and remove.

4. Disconnect the driveshaft from the universal flange of the drive pinion and push it forward to remove. Position the driveshaft out of the way and support it with wire.

5. Disconnect the inner CV-joints from the differential connecting flange and wire them out of the way.

6. Support the differential with a floor jack.

7. Remove the four bolts and two locking plates at the rear differential mount.

8. Loosen and remove the screw from the front mount where it connects to the rear axle carrier.

9. Lower the jack and remove the differential.

To install:

1. Raise the differential into position.

2. Position the screw in the front mount but do not tighten it.

3. Install the rear mount screws and plates. Tighten to 29–33 ft. lbs. (40–45 Nm). Now tighten the front mount screw to 33 ft. lbs. (45 Nm).

➡**Always use new self-locking screws and plates.**

4. Position the driveshaft and install the intermediate bearing. Do not tighten it yet.

5. Tighten the driveshaft clamp nut to 25–29 ft. lbs. (35–40 Nm). Now tighten the intermediate bearing screws to 19 ft. lbs. (25 Nm).

6. Installation of the remaining components is in the reverse order of removal.

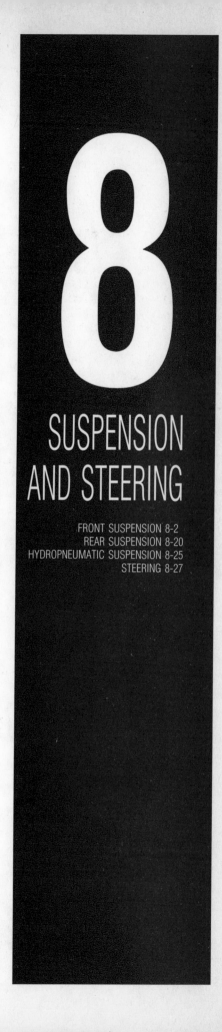

8

SUSPENSION
AND STEERING

FRONT SUSPENSION

TYPICAL FRONT SUSPENSION COMPONENTS

1. Coil springs
2. Track rod ends
3. Steering damper strut
4. Center link
5. Drag link
6. Strut rods
7. Track rods
8. Pitman arm
9. Lower control arms
10. Steering knuckles

Springs

REMOVAL & INSTALLATION

Except 190, 1974–76 230, 240D, 280, 280C, 1975–76 300D, 380SL, 380SLC, 450SL and 450SLC Models

♦ **See Figures 1, 2 and 3**

1. Jack and support the front of the car and support the lower control arm.
2. Remove the wheel. Unbolt the upper shock absorber mount.
3. Install a spring compressor and compress the spring.
4. Remove the front spring with the lower mount.
5. Installation is the reverse of removal. Tighten the upper shock absorber suspension.

➡**Tighten the eccentric bolt on the lower control arm only with the car resting on its wheels.**

1974–75 230 and 240D, 280, 280C, 1975–76 300D, 380SL, 380SLC, 450SL and 450SLC Models

✳✳ WARNING

Be extremely careful when attempting to remove front springs, as they are compressed and under considerable load.

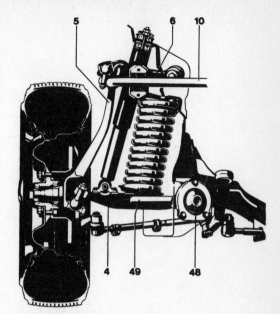

4. Lower control arm	10. Torsion bar
5. Steering knuckle	48. Supporting joint
6. Upper control arm	49. Supporting tube

Fig. 2 Cross-sectional view of the "Zero Offset" type front suspension

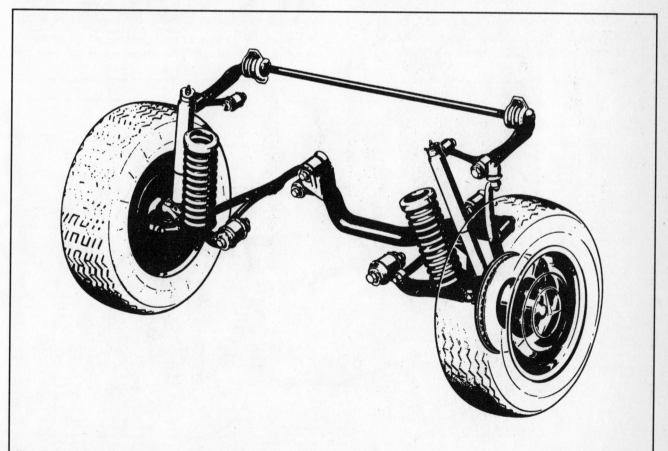

Fig. 1 Typical components of the "Zero Offset" type front suspension

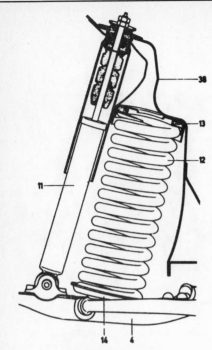

4. Lower control arm
11. Front shock absorber
12. Front spring
13. Rubber mount for front spring
14. Retainer for front spring
38. Front end

Fig. 3 Front spring components on all models except 190D and 190E; 1974–76 230 and 240D, 280 and 280C; 1975–76 300D, 380SL, 380SLC, 450SL and 450SLC models

1. Jack up the front of the car, put up jackstands and remove the front wheels.

2. Support the control arm and remove the lower shock absorber and disconnect the sway bar.

3. First punchmark the position of the eccentric adjusters, then loosen the hex bolts.

4. Support the lower control arm with a jack.

5. Knock out the eccentric pins and gradually lower the arm until spring tension is relieved.

6. The spring can now be removed.

➡ **Check caster and camber after installing a new spring.**

7. Installation is the reverse of removal.

8. For ease of installation, tape the rubber mounts to the springs.

9. If the eccentric adjusters were not matchmarked, install the eccentric bolts as illustrated under "Front End Alignment."

190D and 190E Models
▶ **See Figures 4 and 5**

1. Raise the front of the vehicle and support it with jackstands. Remove the wheel.

2. Remove the engine compartment lining underneath the vehicle (if so equipped).

3. Install a spring compressor so that at least 7½ coils are engaged.

4. Support the lower control arm with a floor jack and then loosen the retaining nut at the upper end of the damper strut.

✳✳ CAUTION

NEVER loosen the damper strut retaining nut unless the wheels are on the ground, the control arm is supported or the springs have been removed.

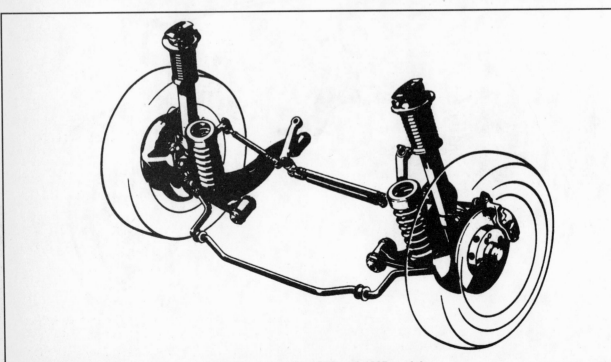

Fig. 4 Common front suspension components used on the 190D and 190E models

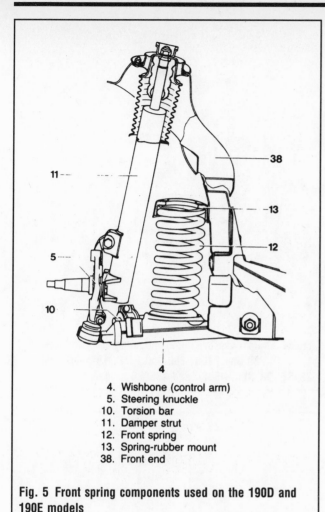

4. Wishbone (control arm)
5. Steering knuckle
10. Torsion bar
11. Damper strut
12. Front spring
13. Spring-rubber mount
38. Front end

Fig. 5 Front spring components used on the 190D and 190E models

5. Lower the jack under the control arm slightly and then remove the spring toward the front.

6. On installation, position the spring between the control arm and the upper mount so that when the control arm is raised, the end of the lower coil will be seated in the impression in the control arm.

7. Use the jack and raise the control arm until the spring is held securely.

8. Using a new nut, tighten the upper end of the damper strut to 44 ft. lbs. (60 Nm).

9. Slowly ease the tension on the spring compressor until the spring is seated properly and then remove the compressor.

10. Installation of the remaining components is in the reverse order of removal.

Shock Absorbers

TESTING

Shock absorbers are normally replaced only if they are leaking excessively (oil visible on the outside cover) or if they are internally worn to a point that the car no longer rides smoothly and rebounds excessively after hitting a bump. A good general test of shock absorber condition is to bounce the front of the car rapidly.

Let go. If the car bounces more than twice (or three times, at the utmost), you can assume the shocks need replacing.

You can also examine the shocks for a bent piston rod, which will bind during travel. These shocks should also be replaced.

REMOVAL & INSTALLATION

Except 190D, 190E, 1974–76 230, 240D, 280, 280C, 1975–76 300D, 380SL, 380SLC, 450SL and 450SLC Models

▶ See Figures 6 and 7

1. Jack and support the front of the car. Support the lower control arm.

2. Loosen the nuts on the upper shock absorber mount. Remove the plate and ring.

3. Place the shock absorber vertical to the lower control arm and remove the lower mounting bolts.

4. Remove the shock absorber.

5. Installation is the reverse of removal. On Bilstein shocks, do not confuse the upper and lower plates.

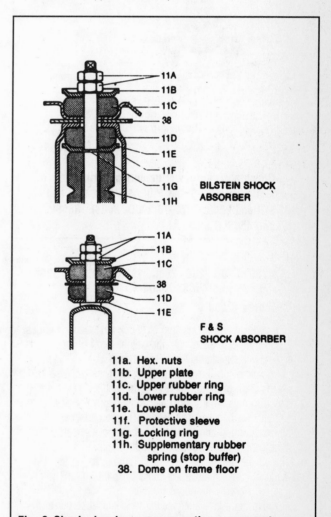

BILSTEIN SHOCK ABSORBER

F & S SHOCK ABSORBER

11a. Hex. nuts
11b. Upper plate
11c. Upper rubber ring
11d. Lower rubber ring
11e. Lower plate
11f. Protective sleeve
11g. Locking ring
11h. Supplementary rubber spring (stop buffer)
38. Dome on frame floor

Fig. 6 Shock absorber upper mounting components on all models except 190D and 190E; 1974–76 230 and 240D, 280 and 280C; 1975–76 300D, 380SL, 380SLC, 450SL and 450SLC models

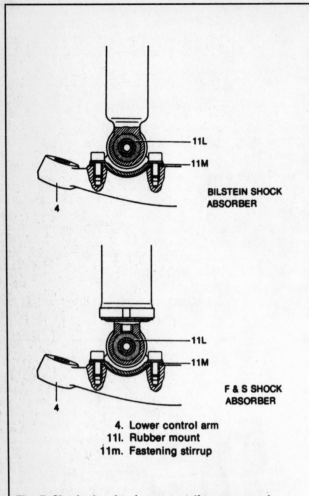

4. Lower control arm
11l. Rubber mount
11m. Fastening stirrup

Fig. 7 Shock absorber lower mounting components on all models except 190D and 190E; 1974–76 230 and 240D, 280 and 280C; 1975–76 300D, 380SL, 380SLC, 450SL and 450SLC models

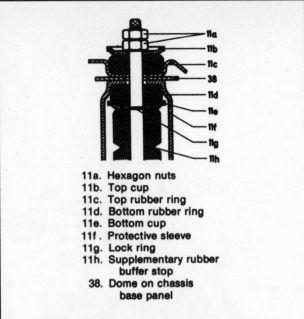

11a. Hexagon nuts
11b. Top cup
11c. Top rubber ring
11d. Bottom rubber ring
11e. Bottom cup
11f. Protective sleeve
11g. Lock ring
11h. Supplementary rubber buffer stop
38. Dome on chassis base panel

Fig. 8 Shock absorber upper mounting components— 1974–76 230 and 240D, 280 and 280C; 1975–76 300D, 380SL, 380SLC, 450SL and 450SLC models

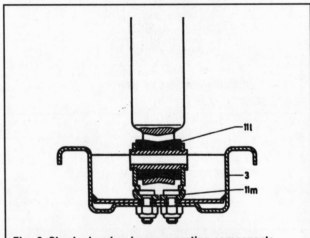

Fig. 9 Shock absorber lower mounting components— 1974–76 230 and 240D, 280 and 280C; 1975–76 300D, 380SL, 380SLC, 450SL and 450SLC models

1974–76 230, 240D, 280, 280C, 1975–75 300D, 380SL, 380SLC, 450SL and 450SLC Models

◆ **See Figures 8 and 9**

1. For removal and installation of shock absorbers, it is best to jack up the front of the car until the weight is off of the wheels and support the car securely on jackstands.

2. When removing the shock absorbers, it is also wise to draw a simple diagram of the location of parts such as lock-rings, rubber stops, locknuts, and steel plates, since many shock absorbers require their own peculiar installation of these parts.

3. Raise the hood and locate the upper shock absorber mount.

4. Support the lower control arm with a jack.

5. Unbolt the mount for the shock absorber at the top. On 450SL and 450SLC, remove the coolant expansion tank to allow access to the right front shock absorber.

6. Remove the nuts which secure the shock absorber to the lower control arm.

7. Push the shock absorber piston rod in, install the stirrup, and remove the shock absorber.

8. Remove the stirrup, since this must be installed on replacement shock absorbers.

➡**Most models use both Bilstein and F&S shock absorbers. On Bilstein shock absorbers, never re-use the upper or lower cups.**

9. Installation is the reverse of removal. Always use new bushings when installing replacement shock absorbers.

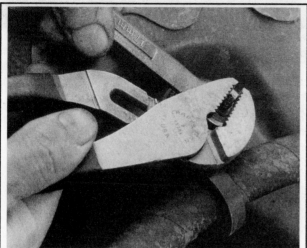

To remove the front shock absorber, hold the tip of the piston rod with pliers and loosen the hex nuts

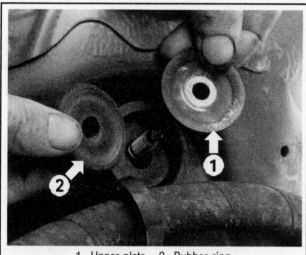

1. Upper plate   2. Rubber ring
Remove the upper plate and the rubber ring

. . . and remove the shock absorber from the vehicle

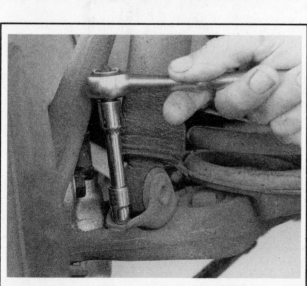

Loosen the shock absorber's lower mounting bolts . . .

Damper Strut

REMOVAL & INSTALLATION

190D and 190E Models
▶ **See Figure 10**

1. Raise the front of the vehicle and support it with jackstands. Remove the wheel.

2. Using a spring compressor, compress the spring until any load is removed from the lower control arm.

➡ **When using a spring compressor, be sure that at least 7½ coils are engaged before applying tension.**

3. Support the lower control arm with a floor jack. Loosen the retaining bolt for the upper end of the damper strut by holding the inner piston rod with an Allen wrench and then un-

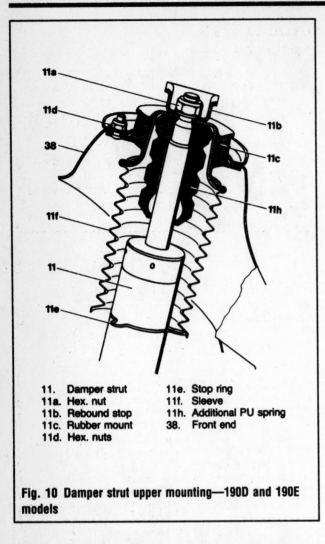

11.	Damper strut	11e.	Stop ring
11a.	Hex. nut	11f.	Sleeve
11b.	Rebound stop	11h.	Additional PU spring
11c.	Rubber mount	38.	Front end
11d.	Hex. nuts		

Fig. 10 Damper strut upper mounting—190D and 190E models

screwing the nut. NEVER use an impact wrench on the retaining nut.

✳✳ CAUTION

Never unscrew the nut with the axle half at full rebound— the spring may fly out with considerable force, causing personal injury.

4. Unbolt the two screws and one nut and then disconnect the lower damper strut from the steering knuckle.

5. Remove the strut down and forward. Secure the steering knuckle in position so that it won't tilt.

6. Installation is in the reverse order of removal. Please note the following:

a. When attaching the lower end of the damper strut to the steering knuckle, first position all three screws; next tighten the two lower screws to 72 ft. lbs. (100 Nm); finally, tighten the nut on the upper clamping connection screw to 54 ft. lbs. (75 Nm).

b. Tighten the retaining nut on the upper end of the damper strut to 44 ft. lbs. (60 Nm).

Steering Knuckle/Ball Joints

BALL JOINT INSPECTION

◗ **See Figures 11 and 12**

All models of Mercedes-Benz covered in this book use steering knuckles with ball joints. Most models use a type of ball joint that is maintenance free.

To check the steering knuckles or ball joints, jack up the car, placing a jack directly under the front spring plate. This unloads the front suspension to allow the maximum play to be observed. Late model ball joints need be replaced only if dried out with plainly visible wear and/or play.

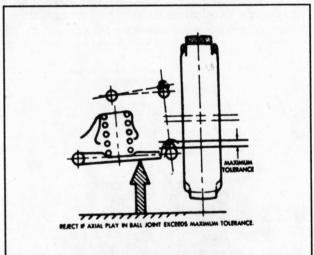

Fig. 11 Check ball joint axial play; if it exceeds maximum tolerance, it must be replaced

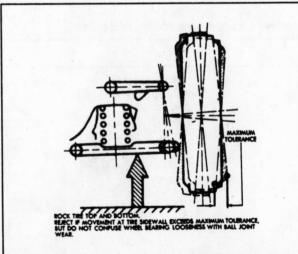

Fig. 12 Rock the tire at its top and bottom to check the ball joint radial play

REMOVAL & INSTALLATION

1974–76 230, 240D, 280, 280C, 1975–76 300D, 380SL, 380SLC, 450SL and 450SLC Models

◆ See Figure 13

1. This should only be done with the front shock absorber installed. If, however, the front shock absorber has been removed, the lower control arm should be supported with a jack and the spring should be clamped with a spring tensioner. In this case, the hex nut on the guide joint should not be loosened without the spring tensioner installed.

2. Jack up the front of the car and support it on jackstands.

3. Remove the wheel.

4. Remove the brake caliper.

5. Unbolt the steering relay lever from the steering knuckle. For safety, install spring clamps on the front springs.

6. Remove the hex nuts from the upper and lower ball joints.

7. Remove the ball joints from the steering knuckle with the aid of a puller.

8. Remove the steering knuckle.

9. Installation is the reverse of removal. Be sure that the seats for the pins of the ball joints are free of grease.

10. Bleed the brakes.

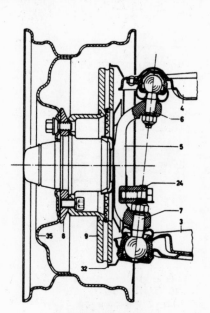

3. Lower control arm
4. Upper control arm
5. Steering knuckle
6. Guide joint
7. Supporting joint
8. Front wheel hub
9. Brake disc
24. Steering knuckle arm
32. Cover plate
35. Wheel

Fig. 13 Cross-sectional view of the steering knuckle/ball joint—1974–76 230 and 240D, 280 and 280C; 1975–76 300D, 380SL, 380SLC, 450SL and 450SLC models

190D and 190E Models

◆ See Figure 14

1. Raise the front of the vehicle and support it with jackstands. Remove the wheel.

2. Install a spring compressor on the spring.

3. Remove the brake caliper and then wire it out of the way. Be careful not to damage the brake line.

4. Remove the brake disc and wheel hub.

5. Unscrew the three socket-head bolts and then remove the brake backing plate from the steering knuckle.

6. Tighten the spring compressor until all tension and/or load has been removed from the lower control arm.

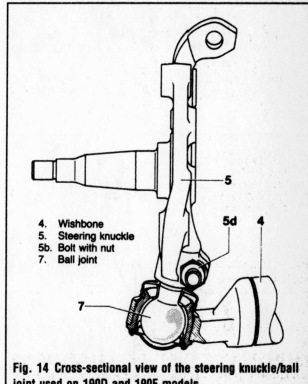

4. Wishbone
5. Steering knuckle
5b. Bolt with nut
7. Ball joint

Fig. 14 Cross-sectional view of the steering knuckle/ball joint used on 190D and 190E models

7. Disconnect the steering knuckle arm from the steering knuckle (this is the arm attached to the tie rod).

✳✳ CAUTION

There must be no tension on the lower control arm.

8. Unscrew the three bolts and disconnect the lower end of the damper strut from the steering knuckle.

9. Remove the hex-head clamp nut at the supporting joint (lower ball joint).

10. Remove the steering knuckle.

11. Installation is in the reverse order of removal. Please note the following:

   a. Tighten the supporting joint clamp nut to 70 ft. lbs. (125 Nm).

   b. Refer to the "Damper Strut Removal and Installation" procedure when connecting the lower end of the damper strut to the steering knuckle.

Except 190D, 190E, 1974–76 230, 240D, 280, 280C, 1975–76 300D, 380SL, 380SLC, 450SL and 450SLC Models

♦ **See Figure 15**

1. Jack and support the car. For safety, it's a good idea to install some type of clamp on the frontspring. Position jackstands at the outside front against the lower control arms.
2. Remove the wheel.
3. Remove the steering knuckle arm from the steering knuckle.
4. Remove and suspend the brake caliper.
5. Remove the front wheel hub.
6. Loosen the brake hose holder on the cover plate.
7. Loosen the nut on the guide joint and remove the joint from the steering knuckle.
8. Loosen the nut on the support joint.
9. Swivel the steering knuckle outward and force the ball joint from the lower control arm.
10. Remove the steering knuckle.
11. If necessary, remove the cover plate from the steering knuckle.

12. Installation is the reverse of removal. Use self-locking nuts and adjust the wheel bearings.

Upper Control Arm

➡ **The 190D and 190E have no upper control arm.**

REMOVAL & INSTALLATION

Except 190D, 190E, 1974–76 230, 240D, 280, 280C, 1975–76 300D, 380SL, 380SLC, 450SL and 450SLC Models

♦ **See Figure 16**

1. Jack and support the car. Position jackstands at the outside front against the lower control arms.
2. Remove the wheel.
3. Loosen the nut on the guide joint.
4. Remove the guide joint from the steering knuckle.
5. Secure the steering knuckle with a hook on the upper control arm stop to prevent it from tilting.
6. Loosen the clamp screw and separate the upper control arm from the torsion bar.
7. Loosen the upper control arm bearing at the front and remove the upper control arm.
8. Installation is the reverse of removal. Use new self-locking nuts and check the front wheel alignment.

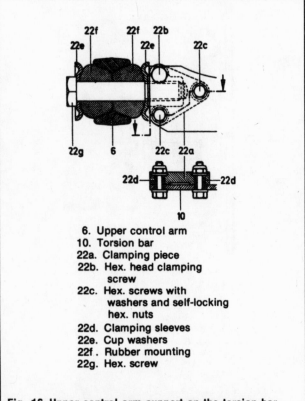

6. **Upper control arm**
10. **Torsion bar**
22a. **Clamping piece**
22b. **Hex. head clamping screw**
22c. **Hex. screws with washers and self-locking hex. nuts**
22d. **Clamping sleeves**
22e. **Cup washers**
22f. **Rubber mounting**
22g. **Hex. screw**

Fig. 16 Upper control arm support on the torsion bar mounting components—all models except 190D and 190E; 1974–76 230 and 240D, 280 and 280C; 1975–76 300D, 380SL, 380SLC, 450SL and 450SLC models

4. **Lower control arm**
5. **Steering knuckle**
6. **Upper control arm**
7. **Support joint**
8. **Guide joint**
9. **Front wheel hub**
29. **Steering knuckle arm**
34. **Brake disc**
43. **Wheel**

Fig. 15 Cross-sectional view of the steering knuckle/ball joint components—all models except 190D and 190E; 1974–76 230 and 240D, 280 and 280C; 1975–76 300D, 380SL, 380SLC, 450SL and 450SLC models

1974–76 230, 240D, 280, 280C, 1975–76 300D, 380SL, 380SLC, 450SL and 450SLC Models

♦ **See Figures 17 and 18 (p. 12–13)**

1. The front shock absorbers should remain installed. Never loosen the hex nuts of the ball joints with the shock absorber removed, unless a spring clamp is installed.
2. Jack the front of the car and remove the wheel.
3. Support the front end on jackstands.
4. Remove the steering arm from the steering knuckle.
5. Separate the brake line and brake hose from each other and plug the openings.
6. Support the lower control arm and unscrew the nuts from the ball joints.
7. Remove the ball joints from the steering knuckle.
8. Loosen the bolts on the upper control arm and remove the upper control arm.
9. Installation is the reverse of removal.

➡**Mount the front hex bolt from the rear in a forward direction, and the rear hex bolt from the front in a rearward direction.**

10. Bleed the brakes.

Lower Control Arm

REMOVAL & INSTALLATION

Except 190D, 190E, 1974–76 230, 240D, 280, 280C, 1975–76 300D, 380SL, 380SLC, 450SL and 450SLC Models

The lower control arm is the same as the front axle half. For safety install a spring compressor on the coil spring.
1. Jack and support the front of the car and remove the wheels.
2. Remove the front shock absorber. Loosen the top mount first.
3. Remove the front springs.
4. Separate and plug the brake lines.
5. Remove the track rod from the steering knuckle arm.
6. Matchmark the position of the eccentric bolts on the bearing of the lower control arm in relation to the frame crossmember.
7. Remove the shield from the cross yoke.
8. Support the front axle half.
9. Loosen the eccentric bolt on the front and rear bearing of the lower control arm and knock them out.
10. Remove the bolt from the cross-yoke bearing.
11. Loosen the screw at the opposite end of the cross-yoke bearing.
12. Pull the cross-yoke bearing down slightly.
13. Loosen the support of the upper control arm on the torsion bar. Remove the clamp screw from the clamp.
14. Remove the upper control arm bearing on the front end.
15. Remove the front axle half.
16. Installation is the reverse of removal. Tighten the eccentric bolts of the lower control arm bearing with the car resting on the wheels. Bleed the brakes and check the front end alignment.

190D and 190E Models

♦ **See Figures 19 and 20 (p. 13)**

1. Remove the engine compartment lining at the bottom of the vehicle (if so equipped).
2. Raise the front of the vehicle and support it with jackstands. Remove the wheel.
3. Support the lower control arm with jackstands and then disconnect the torsion bar bearing at the control arm.
4. Remove the spring as detailed earlier in this chapter.
5. Disconnect the tie rod at the steering knuckle and then press out the ball joint with the proper tool.
6. Remove the brake caliper and position it out of the way. Be sure that you do not damage the brake line.
7. Remove the brake disc/wheel hub assembly.
8. Disconnect the lower end of the damper strut from the steering knuckle and then remove the knuckle.
9. Mark the position of the inner eccentric pins, relative to the frame, on the bearing of the control arm.
10. Unscrew and remove the pins.
11. Remove the jackstands and remove the lower control arm.
12. Installation is in the reverse order of removal. Please note the following:
    a. Tighten the eccentric bolts on the inner arm to 130 ft. lbs. (180 Nm).
    b. To facilitate torsion bar installation, raise the opposite side of the lower control arm with a jack.
    c. Tighten the clamp nut on the tie rod ball joint to 25 ft. lbs. (35 Nm).

1974–76 230, 240D, 280, 280C, 1975–76 300D, 380SL, 380SLC, 450SL and 450SLC Models

1. Since the front shock absorber acts as a deflection stop for the front wheels, the lower shock absorber attaching point should not be loosened unless the vehicle is resting on the wheels or unless the lower control arm is supported.
2. Jack up the front of the vehicle and support it on jackstands.
3. Support the lower control arm.
4. Loosen the lower shock absorber attachment.
5. Unscrew the steering arm from the steering knuckle.
6. Separate the brake line and brake hose and plug the openings.
7. Remove the front spring.
8. Unscrew the hex nuts on the ball joints.
9. Remove the lower ball joint and remove the lower control arm.
10. Installation is the reverse of removal. Bleed the brakes and check the front end alignment.

Front End Alignment

CASTER & CAMBER

Caster and camber are critical to proper handling and tire wear. Neither adjustment should be attempted without the specialized equipment to accurately measure the geometry of the front end.

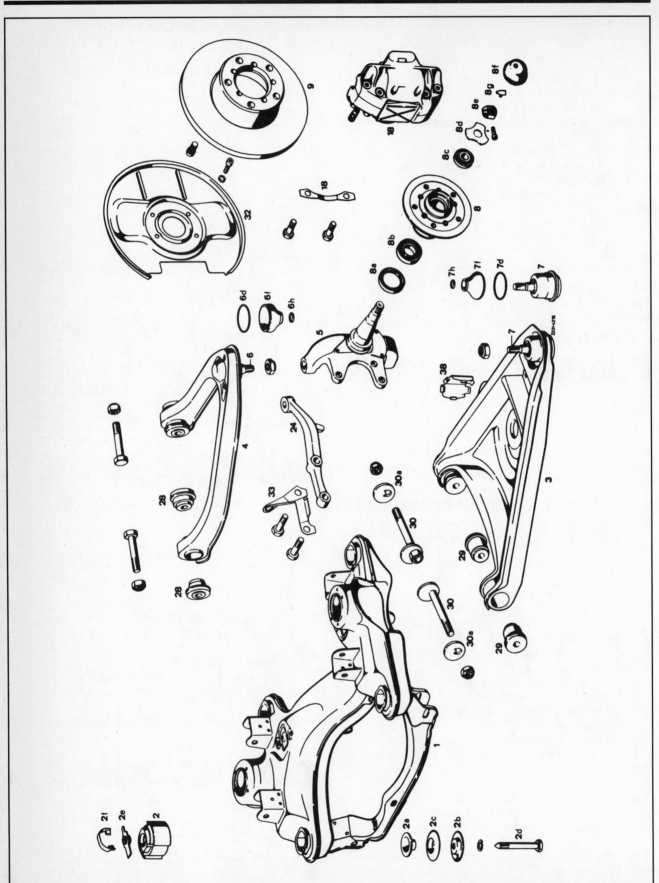

Fig. 17 Front suspension components—1974–76 230 and 240D, 280 and 280C; 1975–76 300D, 380SL, 380SLC, 450SL and 450SLC models

1. Front axle carrier
2. Rubber mount for suspension of front axle
2a. Stop buffer for inward deflection
2b. Stop plate
2c. Stop buffer for outward deflections
2d. Hex. bolt with snap ring
2e. Fastening nut
2f. Nut holder
3. Lower control arm
4. Upper control arm
5. Steering knuckle
6. Guide joint
6d. Circlip
6f. Sleeve
6h. Clamping ring
7. Supporting joint
7d. Circlip
7f. Sleeve
7h. Clamping ring
8. Front wheel hub
8a. Radial sealing ring
8b. Inside tapered roller bearing
8c. Outside tapered roller bearing
8d. Washer
8e. Clamp nut
8f. Wheel cap
8g. Contact spring
9. Brake disc
18. Brake caliper
18a. Lockwasher
24. Steering knuckle arm
28. Rubber slide bearing
29. Rubber bearing (torsion bearing)
30. Cam bolt
30a. Cam washer
32. Cover plate
33. Holder for brake hose
38. Protective cap for steering lock

Fig. 18 Front suspension component list—1974–76 230 and 240D, 280 and 280C; 1975–76 300D, 380SL, 380SLC, 450SL and 450SLC models

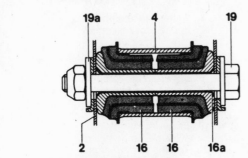

2. Frame cross member
4. Wishbone
16. Torsion rubber bushing
16a. Clamping sleeve
19. Eccentric bolt (camber adjustment)
19a. Eccentric washer

Fig. 19 Cross-sectional view of the front lower control arm bushing—190 models

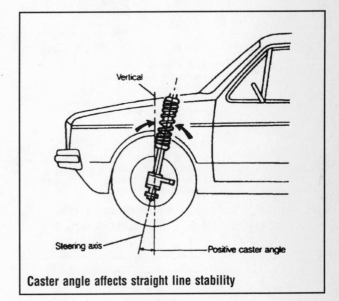

Caster angle affects straight line stability

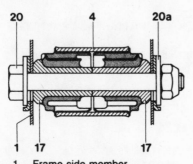

1. Frame side member
4. Wishbone
17. Torsion rubber bushing
20. Eccentric bolt (caster adjustment)
20a. Eccentric washer

Fig. 20 Cross-sectional view of the rear lower control arm bushing—190 models

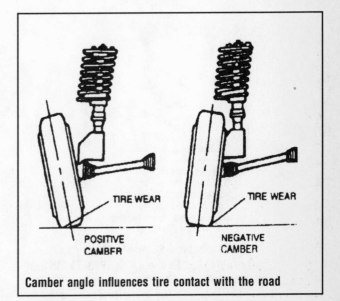

Camber angle influences tire contact with the road

Except 1974–76 230, 240D, 280, 280C, 1975–76 300D, 380SL, 380SLC, 450SL and 450SLC Models

▶ **See Figures 21, 22, and 23**

The front axle provides for caster and camber adjustment, but both wheel adjustments can only be made together. Adjust-

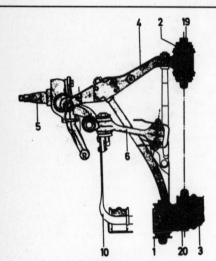

1. Frame side member
2. Frame cross member for front axle
3. Cross yoke
4. Lower control arm
5. Steering knuckle
6. Upper control arm
10. Torsion bar
19. Cam bolt of front bearing (camber adjustment)
20. Cam bolt of rear bearing (caster adjustment)

Fig. 21 Caster and camber adjustment points on the 280S and 280SE; 1978–80 300SD, 450SE, 450SEL and 6.9 models

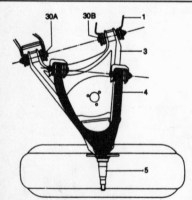

1. Front axle carrier
3. Lower control arm
4. Upper control arm
5. Steering knuckle
30a. Cam bolt front (caster)
30b. Cam bolt rear (camber)

Fig. 22 Caster and camber adjustment points on the 1974–76 230 and 240D, 280 and 280C; 1975–76 300D, 380SL, 380SLC, 450SL and 450SLC models

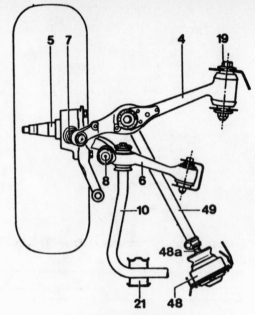

1. Frame side member
2. Frame cross member for front axle
4. Lower control arm
5. Steering knuckle
6. Upper control arm
7. Supporting joint
8. Guide joint
10. Torsion bar
19. Eccentric bolt (camber adjustment)
21. Torsion bar mounting on front end
48. Supporting joint
48a. Ball pin (caster adjustment)
49. Supporting tube

Fig. 23 Caster and camber adjustment points on all models except 280S and 280SE; 1978–80 300SD, 450SE, 450SEL and 6.9; 1974–76 230 and 240D, 280 and 280C; 1975–76 300D, 380SL, 380SLC, 450SL and 450SLC models

ments are made with cam bolts on the lower control arm bearings.

The front bearing cam bolt is used to set caster, while the rear bearing cam bolt is used for camber.

1974–76 230, 240D, 280, 280C, 1975–76 300D, 380SL, 380SLC, 450SL and 450SLC Models

▶ **See Figures 24, 25 and 26**

Caster and camber are dependent upon each other and cannot be adjusted independently. They can only be adjusted simultaneously.

Camber is adjusted by turning the lower control arm about the rear mounting, using the eccentric bolt. Bear in mind that caster will be changed accordingly.

When camber is adjusted in a positive direction, caster is changed in a negative direction, and vice versa. Adjustment of camber by 0° 15' results in a caster change of approximately 0°

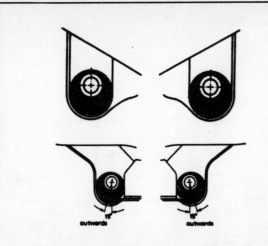

Fig. 24 Caster and camber settings—380SL, 380SLC, 450SL and 450SLC models

CAMBER ECCENTRIC (REAR SEATING)

CASTER ECCENTRIC (FRONT SEATING)
MECHANICAL STEERING

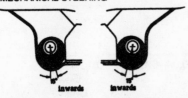

CASTER ECCENTRIC (FRONT SEATING)
POWER STEERING

Fig. 25 Caster and camber settings—1974–76 230 and 240D, 280 and 280C; 1975–76 300D models

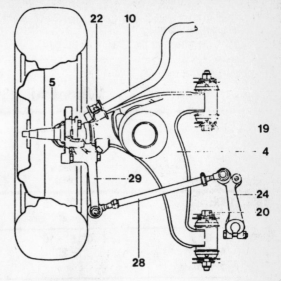

4. Wishbone
5. Steering knuckle
10. Torsion bar
19. Eccentric bolt of front bushing (camber adjustment)
20. Eccentric bolt of rear bushing (caster adjustment)
22. Torsion bar bushing on wishbone
24. Pitman arm
28. Tie rod
29. Steering knuckle arm

Fig. 26 Caster and camber adjustment points—190D and 190E models

20'. Adjustment of caster by 1° results in a camber change of approximately 0° 7'.

TOE-IN

Toe-in is the difference of the distance between the front edges of the wheel rims and the rear edges of the wheel rims.

To measure toe-in, the steering should be in the straight ahead

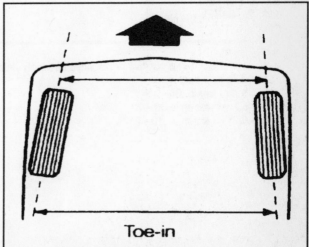

Toe-in

Toe-in means the distance between the wheels is closer at the front than at the rear of the wheels

position and the marks on the pitman arm and pitman shaft should be aligned.

Toe-in is adjusted by changing the length of the two tie-rods or track rods with the wheels in the straight ahead position.

➡Install new tie-rods so that the left-hand thread points toward the left-hand side of the car.

Wheel Alignment Specifications

Car Model	Front Wheels			Rear Wheels	
	Camber (deg)	Caster (deg) Power Steering	Toe-In (in.)	Camber (deg)	Toe-In (mm)
190D, 190E	0°20' + 15' − 25'	10°10' ± 30'	0.06–0.14	See Chart 8	3 + 1 − 0.5
230 ('74–'76) 240D ('74–'76) 300D ('75–'76)	0°15' + 10' − 20'	3°40' ± 20'	0.08–0.16	See Chart 1	See Chart 2
230 ('77–'78) 240D ('77–'83) 280CE ('78–'81) 280E ('77–'81) 300D ('77 and later) 300CD ('78 and later) 300TD ('79 and later)	0° + 10' − 20'	8°45' ± 30'	0.08–0.16	See Chart 3	See Chart 4
280, 280C	0°15' + 10' − 20'	3°40' ± 15'	0.04–0.12	See Chart 1	0 ± 2
280S	20'N ①	9°30' − 10°30'	0.08–0.16	See Chart 5	See Chart 4
300SD ('81 and later) 380SE, 380SEC, 380SEL 500SEC, 500SEL	0° ± 10'	9°15'–10°15'	0.13–0.21	See Chart 6	②
380SL, 380SLC	0° + 10' − 20'	3°40 ± 20'	0.04–0.12	0°10' to 0°40' See Chart 7	0 − 35
450SL, 450SLC	0° + 10' − 20'	3°40' ± 20'	0.04–0.12	See Chart 1	See Chart 2
280SE 300SD ('78–'80) 450SE, 450SEL 6.9	20'N	9°30' − 10°30'	0.08–0.16	See Chart 5	See Chart 4

N Negative
① A 0°10' change in a positive or negative direction yields a 0°10' change in caster in the corresponding direction
② If trailing arm position is
   0–35 mm toe-in .06–.18
   35–50 mm toe-in is .08–.19
   50–60 mm toe-in is .10–.21

Wheel Alignment Chart 1

Control Arm Position mm (in.)	Corresponds to Rear Wheel Camber on:	
	230, 240D, 300D 280, 280C	450SL, 450SLC
+80 (3.17″)	+2°30′ ±30′	—
+75 (2.98″)	+2°15′ ±30′	—
+70 (2.78″)	+2° ±30′	—
+65 (2.58″)	+1°45′ ±30′	—
+60 (2.38″)	+1°30′ ±30′	—
+55 (2.18″)	+1°15′ ±30′	—
+50 (1.99″)	+1° ±30′	+0°50′ ±30′
+45 (1.79″)	+0°45′ ±30′	+0°35′ ±30′
+40 (1.59″)	+0°30′ ±30′	+0°20′ ±30′
+35 (1.39″)	+0°15′ ±30′	+0°05′ ±30′
+30 (1.12″)	0° ±30′	−0°10′ ±30′
+25 (0.99″)	−0°15′ ±30′	−0°25′ ±30′
+20 (0.79″)	−0°30′ ±30′	−0°40′ ±30′
+15 (0.60″)	−0°45′ ±30′	−0°55′ ±30′
+10 (0.40″)	−1° ±30′	−1°10′ ±30′
+5 (0.20″)	−1°15′ ±30′	−1°25′ ±30′
rf0	−1°30′ ±30′	−1°40′ ±30′
−5 (0.20″)	−1°45′ ±30′	−1°55′ ±30°
−10 (0.40″)	−2° ±30′	−2°10′ ±30′
−15 (0.60″)	−2°15′ ±30′	−2°25′ ±30′
−20 (0.79″)	−2°30′ ±30′	−2°40′ ±30′

Wheel Alignment Chart 2
1974–76, 230, 240D, 300D

Rear Wheel Control Arm Position	Corresponds to Rear Wheel Toe-in of:
0 to +35 mm (0–1.39″)	1 +2 mm or 0°10′ +20′ −1 −10′
+35 to +50 mm (1.39″–1.99″)	1.5 +2 mm or 0°15′ +20′ −1 −10′
+50 to +60 mm (1.99″–2.38″)	2 +2 mm or 0°20′ +20′ −1 −10′
+60 to +70 mm (2.38″–2.78″)	2.5 +2 mm or 0°25′ +20′ −1 −10′
+70 to +80 mm (2.78″–3.17″)	3.0 +2 mm or 0°30′ +20′ −1 −10′

Wheel Alignment Chart 3
Rear Wheel Camber 1977 and later
230, 240D, 280E, 280CE, 300D, 300CD, 300TD

Semi-trailing Arm Position mm (in.)	Corresponds to Rear Wheel Camber
+70 (+2.76)	+1°45′ ±30′
+65 (+2.56)	+1°30′ ±30′
+60 (+2.36)	+1°15′ ±30′
+55 (+2.17)	+1° ±30′
+50 (+1.97)	+0°45′ ±30′
+45 (+1.77)	+0°30′ ±30′
+40 (+1.58)	+0°15′ ±30′
+35 (+1.37)	0° ±30′
+30 (+1.18)	−0°15′ ±30′
+25 (+0.98)	−0°30′ ±30′
+20 (+0.79)	−0°45′ ±30′
+15 (+0.59)	−1° ±30′
+10 (+0.39)	−1°15′ ±30′
+5 (+0.20)	−1°30′ ±30′
+0 (0)	−1°45′ ±30′
−5 (−0.20)	−2° ±30′
−10 (−0.39)	−2°15′ ±30′
−15 (−0.59)	−2°30′ ±30′

Wheel Alignment Chart 4
All Models Except 1974–76
230, 240D, 300D

Rear Wheel Control Arm Position	Corresponds to Rear Wheel Toe-in of:
0 to +35 mm (0 to +1.38")	0°10' +20' or 1 +2 mm (0.04" +0.08") −10' −1 −0.04")
+35 to +50 mm (+1.38" to +1.97")	0°15' +20' or 1.5 +2 mm (0.06" +0.08") −10' −1 −0.04")
+50 to +60 mm (+1.97" to +2.36")	0°20' +20' or 2 +2 mm (0.08" +0.08") −10' −1 −0.04")
+60 to +70 mm (+2.36" to +2.76")	0°25' +20' or 2.5 +2 mm (0.10" +0.08") −10' −1 −0.04")
+70 to +80 mm (+2.76" to +3.15")	0°30' +20' or 3 +2 mm (0.12" +0.08") −10' −1 −0.04")

Chart 5 Rear Wheel Camber
450SE, 450SEL, 300SD,
280S, 280SE, 6.9

Semi-trailing Arm Position mm (in.)	Corresponds to Rear Wheel Camber
+65 (2.58")	+1°45' ±30'
+60 (2.38")	+1°30' ±30'
+55 (2.18")	+1°15' ±30'
+50 (1.99")	+1° ±30'
+45 (1.79")	+0°45' ±30'
+40 (1.59")	+0°30' ±30'
+35 (1.39")	+0°15' ±30'
+30 (1.12")	0° ±30'
+25 (0.99")	−0°15' ±30'
+20 (0.79")	−0°30' ±30'
+15 (0.60")	−0°45' ±30'
+10 (0.40")	−1° ±30'
+5 (0.20")	−1°15' ±30'
0	−1°30' ±30'
−5 (0.20")	−1°45' ±30'
−10 (0.40")	−2° ±30'
−15 (0.60")	−2°15' ±30'
−20 (0.79")	−2°30' ±30'

Wheel Alignment Chart 6
('81 and Later 300SD, 380SEL, 380SEC, 500SEC, 500SEL)

Semi-trailing Arm Position mm	Corresponds to Rear Wheel Camber
+65	+1°30′ ± 30′
+60	+1°15′ ± 30′
+55	+1° ± 30′
+50	+0°45′ ± 30′
+45	+0°30′ ± 30′
+40	+0°15′ ± 30′
+35	0° ± 30′
+30	−0°15′ ± 30′
+25	−0°30′ ± 30′
+20	−0°45′ ± 30′
+15	−1° ± 30′
+10	−1°15′ ± 30′
+5	−1°30′ ± 30′
0	−1°45′ ± 30′
−5	−2° ± 30′
−10	−2°15′ ± 30′
−15	−2°30′ ± 30′
−20	−2°45′ ± 30′

Rear Wheel Alignment Chart 7
(380SL, 380SLC)

Semi-trailing Arm Position mm	Corresponds to Rear Wheel Camber
35	0° ± 30′
30	−0°15′ ± 30′
25	−0°30′ ± 30′
20	−0°45′ ± 30′
15	−1° ± 30′
10	−1°15′ ± 30′
5	−1°30′ ± 30′
0	−1°45′ ± 30′
−5	−2° ± 30′
−10	−2°15′ ± 30′
−15	−2°30′ ± 30′
−20	−2°45′ ± 30′

Rear Wheel Alignment Chart 8

Spring Link Position mm	Corresponds to Rear Wheel Camber
+50	−0°15′ ± 30′
+40	−0°30′ ± 30′
+30	−0°45′ ± 30′
+20	−1° ± 30′
+10	−1°15′ ± 30′
0	−1°30′ ± 30′
−10	−1°45′ ± 30′
−20	−2° ± 30′

REAR SUSPENSION

TYPICAL REAR SUSPENSION & DRIVE TRAIN COMPONENTS

1. Differential
2. Axles
3. Shock absorbers' lower mounts
4. Coil springs
5. Control arms
6. Driveshaft

All Mercedes-Benz cars covered in this book use independent rear suspension, known as the diagonal swing arm type.

Springs

REMOVAL & INSTALLATION

190D and 190E Models

1. Raise the rear of the vehicle and support it with jackstands. Remove the wheel.

2. Disconnect the holding clamps for the spring link cover and then remove the cover.

3. Install a spring compressor and compress the spring until the spring link is free of all load.

4. Disconnect the lower end of the shock absorber.

5. Increase the tension on the spring compressor and remove the spring.

6. Installation is in the reverse order of removal. Please note the following:

   a. Position the spring so that the end of the lower coil is seated in the impression of the spring seat and the upper coil seats properly in the rubber mount in the frame floor.

   b. Do not release tension on the spring compressor until the lower end of the shock absorber is connected and tightened to 47 ft. lbs. (65 Nm).

1974–76 230, 240D, 280, 280C, 1975–76 300D, 380SL, 380SLC, 450SL and 450SLC Models

♦ **See Figure 28**

1. Jack up the rear of the car.
2. Remove the rear shock absorber.
3. With a floor jack, raise the control arm to approximately a

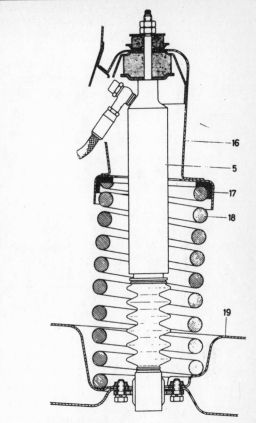

5. Spring strut
16. Dome on frame floor
17. Rubber mount
18. Rear spring
19. Semi-trailing arm

Fig. 28 Cross-sectional view of the rear spring components—1974–76 230 and 240D, 280 and 280C; 1975–76 300D, 380SL, 380SLC, 450SL and 450SLC models

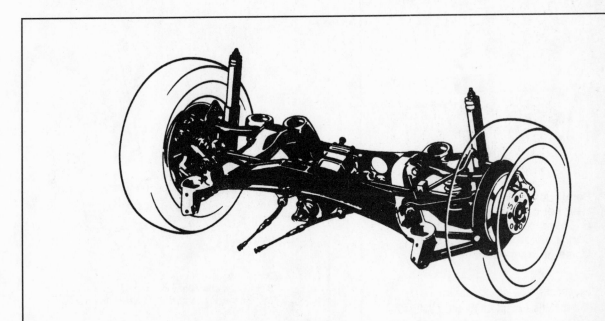

Fig. 27 Typical rear suspension used on 190D and 190E models

horizontal position. Install a spring compressor to aid in this operation.

4. Carefully lower the jack until the control arm contacts the stop on the rear axle support.

5. Remove the spring and spring compressor with great care.

6. Installation is the reverse of removal. For ease of installation, attach the rubber seats to the springs with masking tape.

All Other Models
▶ **See Figure 29**

1. Jack and support the rear of the car and the trailing arm.
2. Remove the rear shock absorber.
3. Be sure that the upper shock absorber attachment is released first.
4. Compress the spring with a spring compressor.
5. Remove the rear spring with the rubber mount.
6. Installation is the reverse of removal. When installing the shock absorber, tighten the lower mount first.

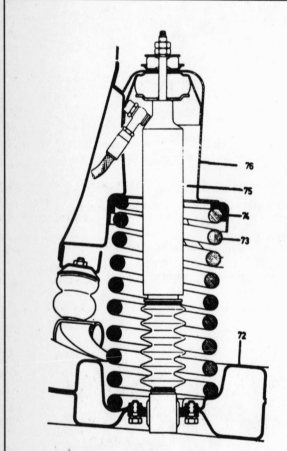

72. Semi-trailing arm
73. Rear spring
74. Rubber mounting
75. Shock absorber or spring strut
76. Dome on frame floor

Fig. 29 Cross-sectional view of the rear spring components—all models except 190D and 190E; 1974–76 230 and 240D, 280 and 280C; 1975–76 300D, 380SL, 380SLC, 450SL and 450SLC models

Shock Absorbers

REMOVAL & INSTALLATION

190D, 190E, 1974–76 230, 240D, 280, 280C, 1975–76 300D, 380SL, 380SLC, 450SL and 450SLC Models
▶ **See Figures 30, 31 and 32**

1. Jack up the rear of the car and support the control arm.
2. From inside the trunk (sedans), remove the rubber cap, locknut, and hex nut from the upper mount of the shock absorber. On

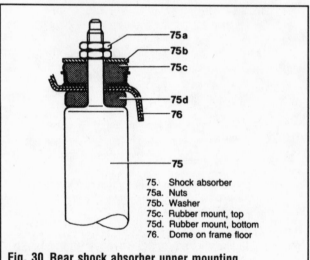

75. Shock absorber
75a. Nuts
75b. Washer
75c. Rubber mount, top
75d. Rubber mount, bottom
76. Dome on frame floor

Fig. 30 Rear shock absorber upper mounting components—190D and 190E models

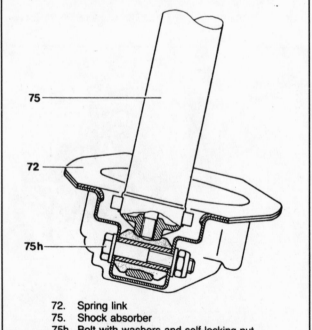

72. Spring link
75. Shock absorber
75h. Bolt with washers and self-locking nut

Fig. 31 Rear shock absorber lower mounting components—190D and 190E models

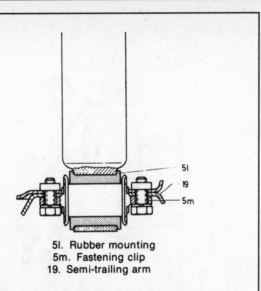

5l. Rubber mounting
5m. Fastening clip
19. Semi-trailing arm

Fig. 32 Rear shock absorber lower mounting assembly—1974–76 230 and 240D, 280 and 280C; 1975–76 300D, all 380 models, 450SL, 450SLC, 500SEC and 500SEL models

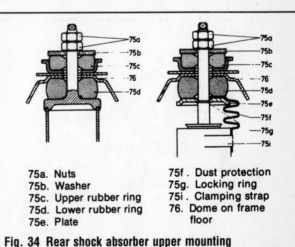

After unfastening the rear shock absorber's upper mount, remove the lower mounting bolts

the 280SL and 450SL, the upper mount of the rear shock absorber is accessible after removing the top, top flap, rear seat, backrest, and lining. On the 380SLC and 450SLC, remove the rear seat, backrest and cover plate.

3. Unbolt the mounting for the rear shock absorber at the bottom and remove the shock absorber.

4. Installation is the reverse of removal.

All Other Models

◆ **See Figures 33, 34, 35, 36 and 37**

1. Remove the rear seat and backrest.
2. Remove the cover from the rear wall.
3. Jack and support the car and the trailing arm.
4. Loosen the nuts on the upper mount. Remove the washer and rubber ring.
5. Loosen the lower mount and remove the shock absorber downward.
6. Installation is the reverse of removal. Tighten the upper mounting nut to the end of the threads.

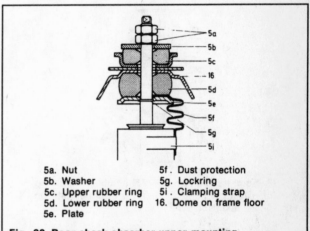

5a. Nut	5f. Dust protection
5b. Washer	5g. Lockring
5c. Upper rubber ring	5i. Clamping strap
5d. Lower rubber ring	16. Dome on frame floor
5e. Plate	

Fig. 33 Rear shock absorber upper mounting assembly—1981–84 300SD, 380SE, 380SEC, 380SEL, 380SL, 380SLC, 450SL, 450SLC, 500SEC and 500SEL models

75a. Nuts	75f. Dust protection
75b. Washer	75g. Locking ring
75c. Upper rubber ring	75i. Clamping strap
75d. Lower rubber ring	76. Dome on frame floor
75e. Plate	

Fig. 34 Rear shock absorber upper mounting assembly—1977–83 230 and 240D, 280CE, 280E, 280S and 280SE; 1978–80 300SD; 1977–84 300D and 300CD; 1979–80 300TD, 450SE, 450SEL and 6.9 models

Bilstein

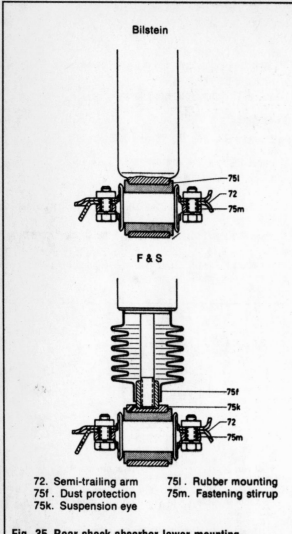

F & S

75l. 72. 75m.

75f. 75k. 72. 75m.

72. Semi-trailing arm
75f. Dust protection
75k. Suspension eye

75l. Rubber mounting
75m. Fastening stirrup

Fig. 35 Rear shock absorber lower mounting assembly—1977–83 230 and 240D, 280CE, 280E, 280S and 280SE; 1978–80 300SD; 1977–84 300D and 300CD; 1979–80 300TD, 450SE, 450SEL and 6.9 models

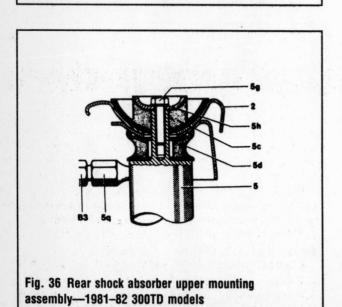

5g
2
5h
5c
5d
5

B3 5q

Fig. 36 Rear shock absorber upper mounting assembly—1981–82 300TD models

5i 5g 5c
2
5d
5

B3 5q

2. Frame—transverse
   member
5. Suspension strut
5c. Upper rubber mount
5d. Lower rubber mount
5g. Special screw

5i. Plate
5q. Stud
B3. Pressure line (pres-
   sure hose),
   pressure reservoir—
   suspension strut

Fig. 37 Rear shock absorber upper mounting assembly—1983–84 300TD models. Retrofitting is not possible

Rear End Alignment

Suspension adjustments should only be checked when the vehicle is resting on a level surface and is carrying the required fluids (full tank of gas, engine oil, etc.).

CAMBER

♦ **See Figures 38 and 39**

Rear wheel camber is determined by the position of the control arm. The difference in height (a) between the axis of the control arm mounting point on the rear axle subframe and the lower edge of the cup on the constant velocity joint is directly translated in degrees of camber.

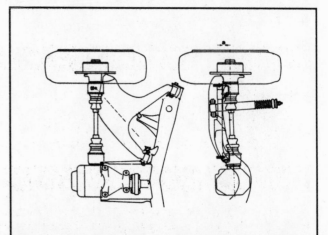

Fig. 38 Rear wheel camber measurement on all 1974–76 230 and 240D, 280 and 280C; 1975–76 300D, 380SL, 380SLC, 450SL and 450SLC models

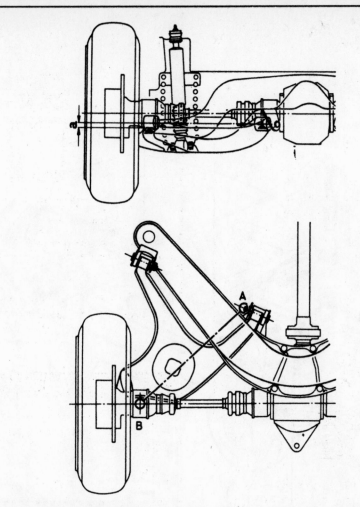

Fig. 39 Rear wheel camber measurement on all models except 190D and 190E; 1974–76 230 and 240D, 280 and 280C; 1975–76 300D, 380SL, 380SLC, 450SL and 450SLC models

TOE-IN

Toe-in, on the rear wheels, is dependent on the camber of the rear wheels.

HYDROPNEUMATIC SUSPENSION

♦ **See Figure 40**

The hydropneumatic suspension is used on the 380SEL, 500SEL and the 6.9. Service of this system should be left to a Mercedes-Benz dealer or other qualified service establishment.

Operation

The system is a gas pressure system with a hydraulic level control. The car is supported by 4 suspension struts that also serve as shock absorbers. The suspension consists of a strut and pressure reservoir, connected by a line. The load is transmitted to the pressure reservoirs via the struts, resulting in an adjustment of the gas cushion in each pressure reservoir.

To regulate the level of the car, the oil level in the struts is increased or reduced by the hydraulic system, composed of an oil pump, pressure regulator, main pressure reservoir, and oil reservoir. The pressure regulator also contains a level selector valve as part of the unit.

The oil volume is controlled by a levelling valve at the front and rear axle and by the level selector valve. This allows adjustment of the vehicle level by using the level selector switch on the dashboard. When the engine is not running, the main pressure reservoir supplies the system.

A hydraulic oil pump, driven by the engine, pumps oil from the oil reservoir to the main pressure reservoir. When the maximum oil pressure in the main reservoir is reached, the pressure regulator in the reservoir valve unit reverses the flow of oil. If the pres-

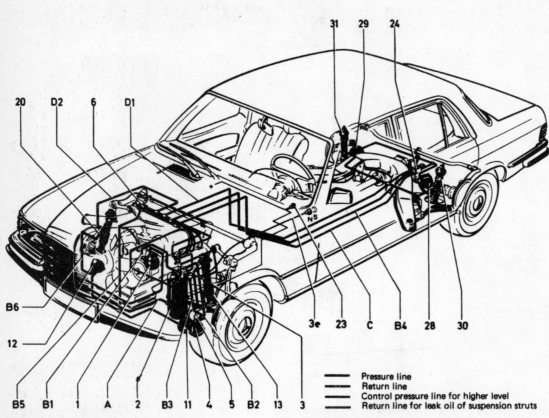

	Pressure line
	Return line
	Control pressure line for higher level
	Return line for leak oil of suspension struts

1. Hydraulic oil pump
2. Hydraulic oil reservoir
3. Valve unit (pressure regulator and level selector valve)
3a. Pressure regulator of valve unit
3b. Level selector valve of valve unit
3e. Control knob for level selector valve of valve unit
4. Main pressure reservoir
5. Electric pressure switch for warning light
6. Levelling valve, front axle
11. Pressure reservoir, front axle left
12. Pressure reservoir, front axle right
13. Suspension strut, front axle left
20. Suspension strut, front axle right
23. Warning light
24. Levelling valve, rear axle
28. Pressure reservoir, rear axle left
29. Pressure reservoir, rear axle right
30. Suspension strut, rear axle left
31. Suspension strut, rear axle right

A. Suction line, oil reservoir to hydraulic oil pump
B1. Pressure line, oil pump to pressure regulator of valve unit
B2. Pressure line, pressure regulator of valve unit to main pressure reservoir
B3. Pressure, main pressure reservoir to level selector valve
B4. Pressure line, level selector valve of valve unit to levelling valve on front and rear axle
B5. Pressure line, levelling valves to pressure reservoirs
B6. Pressure line, pressure reservoirs to suspension struts
C. Control pressure line for "higher level" level selector valve to levelling valves
D1. Return line, levelling valve to pressure regulator
D2. Return line, leak oil of suspension struts

Fig. 40 View of the Hydropneumatic suspension components

sure in the reservoir drops to a pre-set minimum (as a result of operation of the system) the pressure regulator again reverses the flow of oil, pumping oil into the pressure reservoir until maximum pressure is reached, when the flow will be reversed once more.

The oil in the pressure reservoir is connected to level selector valve and to the individual levelling valves by pressure lines. If the car level drops, due to an increased load, the levelling valve opens the passage to the suspension struts, allowing the passage of oil until normal vehicle attitude is reached. If the level rises, due to a decreased load, the levelling valve opens and allows oil to flow from the suspension struts back to the oil reservoir, until the car resumes its normal level.

STEERING

Steering Wheel

REMOVAL & INSTALLATION

1. Remove the padded plate. It is best to pull at one corner near the wheel spokes.
2. Unscrew the hex nut from the steering shaft and remove the spring washer and the steering wheel.

To remove the steering wheel, first remove the horn pad by pulling it off

Loosen the steering wheel-to-steering shaft retaining nut and remove the spring washer

1. Matchmarks (steering wheel-to-shaft)
2. Horn electrical connection

Disengage the horn electrical connection and matchmark the position of the wheel-to-shaft relationship

Remove the steering wheel from the shaft

3. Installation is the reverse of removal. Be sure that the alignment mark on the steering shaft is pointing upward and be sure that the slightly curved spoke of the steering wheel is down.

Ignition Switch and Lock Cylinder

Refer to Section 6.

Track Rod

REMOVAL & INSTALLATION

1. Remove the cotter pins and castellated nuts from the track rod joints. The 190D and 190E use only a self-locking hex nut.

2. Remove the track rod from the steering arms with a puller.

3. Check the track rod ends. The rods use 22 mm ball joints and should be replaced if either ball joints is defective.

4. Check the rubber sleeves. The ball joint should be replaced if the sleeve is defective.

5. Installation is the reverse of removal. Install the track rods so that the end with the left-hand threads is on the left side. Use new locknuts on the 190D and 190E.

Track Rod End

REMOVAL & INSTALLATION

1. Remove the cotter pins and nuts from the track rod end studs.

2. Mark the track rod adjustment sleeve at both ends with tape.

3. Using a track rod end removing tool, remove the rod end from the steering knuckle.

4. Remove the inner stud in the same manner as the outer.

5. Loosen the clamp bolts and unscrew the ends if they are being replaced.

To install:

6. Lubricate the track rod end threads with chassis grease if they were removed. Install each end assembly an equal distance from the sleeve.

7. Ensure that the track rod end stud threads and nut are clean. Install new seals and install the studs into the steering arms and relay rod.

Use a pair of pliers to remove the cotter pin

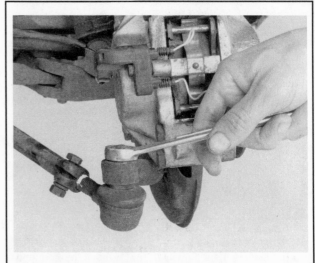

Use a wrench to loosen the castellated nut . . .

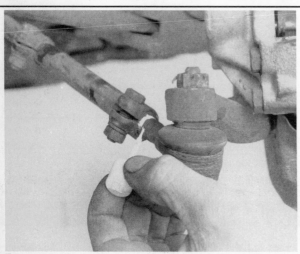

To remove the track rod end, matchmark its position to the adjuster rod

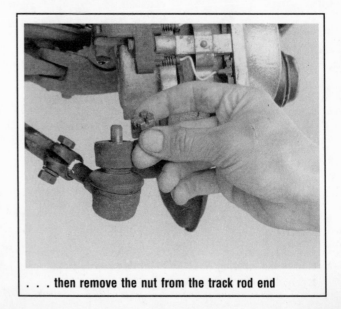

. . . then remove the nut from the track rod end

Install a suitable puller on the track rod end . . .

Unscrew the track rod from the adjusting sleeve . . .

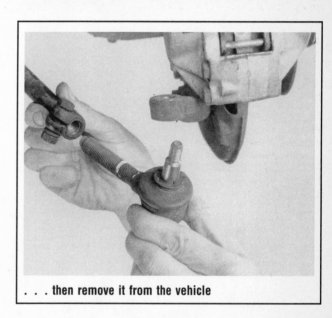

. . . and separate the track rod end from the steering knuckle

. . . then remove it from the vehicle

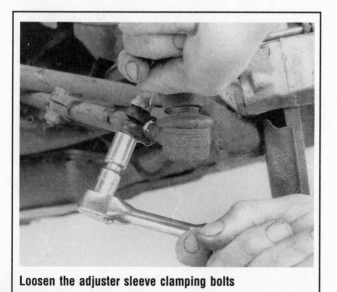

Loosen the adjuster sleeve clamping bolts

8. Install the stud nuts. Tighten the inner and outer end nuts. Install new cotter pins.

9. Have a qualified alignment mechanic adjust the toe-in to specifications.

➡**Before tightening the sleeve clamps, ensure that the clamps are positioned so that adjusting sleeve slot is covered by the clamp. Never back the nut off to insert cotter pin, always tighten it until the pin can fit through castellations.**

Drag Link

REMOVAL & INSTALLATION

1. Remove the castle nuts from the drag link joints.
2. Unbolt the steering damper and force it from the bracket.

3. Remove the drag link with a puller.
4. Installation is the reverse of removal.
5. Check the front wheel alignment.

Power Steering Pump

REMOVAL & INSTALLATION

Many types of power steering pumps are used on Mercedes-Benz vehicles. Use only the instructions that apply to your vehicle. See Chapter 1 for procedures to loosen or adjust power steering pump drive belt.

1974–76 230, 240D and 300D Models

1. Remove the wing nut on the reservoir and remove the cover, spring, and damping plate.
2. Suck the fluid from the reservoir with a syringe.
3. Loosen the hose on the pump and plug both pump and hose.
4. On pumps with the reservoir attached, loosen the return hose and plug it.
5. On other types, loosen the connecting hose from the reservoir to the pump.
6. Remove the radiator.
7. Remove the nut from the pulley shaft. On pumps with cylindrical shafts, remove the pulley.

8. On pumps with tapered shafts, pull the pulley from the shaft with a jaw type puller.
9. Unscrew both front mounting bolts.
10. Remove the rear mounting bolt with spacer.
11. Remove the pump from the mounting bracket.
12. On all 4 cylinder models, remove the screws between the pump housing and the bracket. Remove the pump and pulley.
13. Installation, in all cases, is the reverse of removal.

Except 1974–76 230, 240D and 300D Models

1. Remove the nut from the supply tank.
2. Remove the spring and damping plate.
3. Drain the oil from the tank with a syringe.
4. Loosen and remove the expanding and return hoses from the pump. Plug all connections and pump openings.
5. If necessary for clearance, loosen the radiator shell. Loosen the mounting bolts, and move the pump toward the engine by using the toothed wheel. Remove the belt. Remove the pulley, and then remove the pump.
6. Loosen the nut on the attaching plate and the bolt on the support.
7. Push the pump toward the engine and remove the belts from the pulley.
8. Unscrew the mounting bolts and remove the pump and carrier.
9. Installation is the reverse of removal.

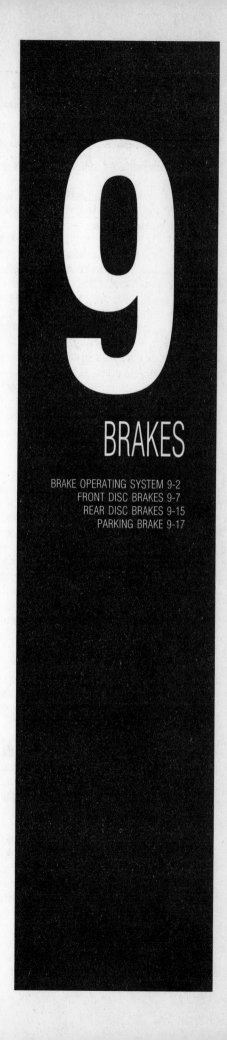

9

BRAKES

BRAKE OPERATING SYSTEM

Basic Operating Principles

Hydraulic systems are used to actuate the brakes of all modern automobiles. The system transports the power required to force the frictional surfaces of the braking system together from the pedal to the individual brake units at each wheel. A hydraulic system is used for two reasons.

First, fluid under pressure can be carried to all parts of an automobile by small pipes and flexible hoses without taking up a significant amount of room or posing routing problems.

Second, a great mechanical advantage can be given to the brake pedal end of the system, and the foot pressure required to actuate the brakes can be reduced by making the surface area of the master cylinder pistons smaller than that of any of the pistons in the wheel cylinders or calipers.

The master cylinder consists of a fluid reservoir along with a double cylinder and piston assembly. Double type master cylinders are designed to separate the front and rear braking systems hydraulically in case of a leak. The master cylinder coverts mechanical motion from the pedal into hydraulic pressure within the lines. This pressure is translated back into mechanical motion at the wheels by either the wheel cylinder (drum brakes) or the caliper (disc brakes).

Steel lines carry the brake fluid to a point on the vehicle's frame near each of the vehicle's wheels. The fluid is then carried to the calipers and wheel cylinders by flexible tubes in order to allow for suspension and steering movements.

In drum brake systems, each wheel cylinder contains two pistons, one at either end, which push outward in opposite directions and force the brake shoe into contact with the drum.

In disc brake systems, the cylinders are part of the calipers. At least one cylinder in each caliper is used to force the brake pads against the disc.

All pistons employ some type of seal, usually made of rubber, to minimize fluid leakage. A rubber dust boot seals the outer end of the cylinder against dust and dirt. The boot fits around the outer end of the piston on disc brake calipers, and around the brake actuating rod on wheel cylinders.

The hydraulic system operates as follows: When at rest, the entire system, from the piston(s) in the master cylinder to those in the wheel cylinders or calipers, is full of brake fluid. Upon application of the brake pedal, fluid trapped in front of the master cylinder piston(s) is forced through the lines to the wheel cylinders. Here, it forces the pistons outward, in the case of drum brakes, and inward toward the disc, in the case of disc brakes. The motion of the pistons is opposed by return springs mounted outside the cylinders in drum brakes, and by spring seals, in disc brakes.

Upon release of the brake pedal, a spring located inside the master cylinder immediately returns the master cylinder pistons to the normal position. The pistons contain check valves and the master cylinder has compensating ports drilled in it. These are uncovered as the pistons reach their normal position. The piston check valves allow fluid to flow toward the wheel cylinders or calipers as the pistons withdraw. Then, as the return springs force the brake pads or shoes into the released position, the excess fluid reservoir through the compensating ports. It is during the time the pedal is in the released position that any fluid that has leaked out of the system will be replaced through the compensating ports.

Dual circuit master cylinders employ two pistons, located one behind the other, in the same cylinder. The primary piston is actuated directly by mechanical linkage from the brake pedal through the power booster. The secondary piston is actuated by fluid trapped between the two pistons. If a leak develops in front of the secondary piston, it moves forward until it bottoms against the front of the master cylinder, and the fluid trapped between the pistons will operate the rear brakes. If the rear brakes develop a leak, the primary piston will move forward until direct contact with the secondary piston takes place, and it will force the secondary piston to actuate the front brakes. In either case, the brake pedal moves farther when the brakes are applied, and less braking power is available.

All dual circuit systems use a switch to warn the driver when only half of the brake system is operational. This switch is usually located in a valve body which is mounted on the firewall or the frame below the master cylinder. A hydraulic piston receives pressure from both circuits, each circuit's pressure being applied to one end of the piston. When the pressures are in balance, the piston remains stationary. When one circuit has a leak, however, the greater pressure in that circuit during application of the brakes will push the piston to one side, closing the switch and activating the brake warning light.

In disc brake systems, this valve body also contains a metering valve and, in some cases, a proportioning valve. The metering valve keeps pressure from traveling to the disc brakes on the front wheels until the brake shoes on the rear wheels have contacted the drums, ensuring that the front brakes will never be used alone. The proportioning valve controls the pressure to the rear brakes to lessen the chance of rear wheel lock-up during very hard braking.

Warning lights may be tested by depressing the brake pedal and holding it while opening one of the wheel cylinder bleeder screws. If this does not cause the light to go on, substitute a new lamp, make continuity checks, and, finally, replace the switch as necessary.

The hydraulic system may be checked for leaks by applying pressure to the pedal gradually and steadily. If the pedal sinks very slowly to the floor, the system has a leak. This is not to be confused with a springy or spongy feel due to the compression of air within the lines. If the system leaks, there will be a gradual change in the position of the pedal with a constant pressure.

Check for leaks along all lines and at wheel cylinders. If no external leaks are apparent, the problem is inside the master cylinder.

DISC BRAKES

Instead of the traditional expanding brakes that press outward against a circular drum, disc brake systems utilize a disc (rotor) with brake pads positioned on either side of it. An easily-seen analogy is the hand brake arrangement on a bicycle. The pads squeeze onto the rim of the bike wheel, slowing its motion. Automobile disc brakes use the identical principle but apply the braking effort to a separate disc instead of the wheel.

The disc (rotor) is a casting, usually equipped with cooling fins between the two braking surfaces. This enables air to circulate between the braking surfaces making them less sensitive to heat buildup and more resistant to fade. Dirt and water do not drastically affect braking action since contaminants are thrown off by the centrifugal action of the rotor or scraped off the by the pads. Also, the equal clamping action of the two brake pads tends to ensure uniform, straight line stops. Disc brakes are inherently self-adjusting. There are three general types of disc brake:

1. A fixed caliper.
2. A floating caliper.
3. A sliding caliper.

The fixed caliper design uses two pistons mounted on either side of the rotor (in each side of the caliper). The caliper is mounted rigidly and does not move.

The sliding and floating designs are quite similar. In fact, these two types are often lumped together. In both designs, the pad on the inside of the rotor is moved into contact with the rotor by hydraulic force. The caliper, which is not held in a fixed position, moves slightly, bringing the outside pad into contact with the rotor. There are various methods of attaching floating calipers. Some pivot at the bottom or top, and some slide on mounting bolts. In any event, the end result is the same.

DRUM BRAKES

Drum brakes employ two brake shoes mounted on a stationary backing plate. These shoes are positioned inside a circular drum which rotates with the wheel assembly. The shoes are held in place by springs. This allows them to slide toward the drums (when they are applied) while keeping the linings and drums in alignment. The shoes are actuated by a wheel cylinder which is mounted at the top of the backing plate. When the brakes are applied, hydraulic pressure forces the wheel cylinder's actuating links outward. Since these links bear directly against the top of the brake shoes, the tops of the shoes are then forced against the inner side of the drum. This action forces the bottoms of the two shoes to contact the brake drum by rotating the entire assembly slightly (known as servo action). When pressure within the wheel cylinder is relaxed, return springs pull the shoes back away from the drum.

Most modern drum brakes are designed to self-adjust themselves during application when the vehicle is moving in reverse. This motion causes both shoes to rotate very slightly with the drum, rocking an adjusting lever, thereby causing rotation of the adjusting screw. Some drum brake systems are designed to self-adjust during application whenever the brakes are applied. This on-board adjustment system reduces the need for maintenance adjustments and keeps both the brake function and pedal feel satisfactory.

POWER BOOSTERS

Virtually all modern vehicles use a vacuum assisted power brake system to multiply the braking force and reduce pedal effort. Since vacuum is always available when the engine is operating, the system is simple and efficient. A vacuum diaphragm is located on the front of the master cylinder and assists the driver in applying the brakes, reducing both the effort and travel he must put into moving the brake pedal.

The vacuum diaphragm housing is normally connected to the intake manifold by a vacuum hose. A check valve is placed at the point where the hose enters the diaphragm housing, so that during periods of low manifold vacuum brakes assist will not be lost.

Depressing the brake pedal closes off the vacuum source and allows atmospheric pressure to enter on one side of the diaphragm. This causes the master cylinder pistons to move and apply the brakes. When the brake pedal is released, vacuum is applied to both sides of the diaphragm and springs return the diaphragm and master cylinder pistons to the released position.

If the vacuum supply fails, the brake pedal rod will contact the end of the master cylinder actuator rod and the system will apply the brakes without any power assistance. The driver will notice that much higher pedal effort is needed to stop the car and that the pedal feels harder than usual.

Vacuum Leak Test

1. Operate the engine at idle without touching the brake pedal for at least one minute.
2. Turn off the engine and wait one minute.
3. Test for the presence of assist vacuum by depressing the brake pedal and releasing it several times. If vacuum is present in the system, light application will produce less and less pedal travel. If there is no vacuum, air is leaking into the system.

System Operation Test

1. With the engine **OFF**, pump the brake pedal until the supply vacuum is entirely gone.
2. Put light, steady pressure on the brake pedal.
3. Start the engine and let it idle. If the system is operating correctly, the brake pedal should fall toward the floor if the constant pressure is maintained.

Power brake systems may be tested for hydraulic leaks just as ordinary systems are tested.

Description

◆ See Figure 1

All Mercedes-Benz cars imported into the U.S. are equipped with 4-wheel disc brakes. The disc brakes are basically similar on all models, though there may be slight differences in design from model to model. The caliper bore sizes, for instance, differ de-

Fig. 1 The arrow indicates the location of the reset pin on a master cylinder equipped with a pressure differential warning valve

pending upon application. The bore size (in mm) is usually stamped on the outside of the caliper, but occasionally, a code is used. For instance, the 14 on a Teves (ATE) caliper is really a 57 mm bore (obviously, it isn't a 14mm bore).

Three different manufacturers make calipers for Mercedes-Benz production—Teves (ATE), Bendix or Girling—but calipers of the same manufacturer are installed on the same axle. For service, install calipers of the same manufacturer on the front axle; on the rear axle, calipers of any manufacturer can be installed.

Most models are equipped with brake pad wear indicators to indicate when the pad lining requires replacement. Beginning in 1976, a new design, step-type master cylinder is used which eliminates the need for the vacuum pump previously used on 230, 280, 280C and 280S. The brake circuits are reversed from 1974 and 1975 models; the front brakes are connected to the primary side of the master cylinder and the rear brakes to the secondary side. A pressure differential warning indicator is also used, which will immediately indicate the total loss of one part of the braking system by lighting the brake warning light on the dash. Once the warning light has come on, it will remain on until the system is repaired and the switch on the master cylinder reset. The warning light will only go out after pushing the reset pin in the switch.

Beginning with 1978 models, the pressure differential warning indicator has been eliminated from models with the step-type master cylinder. The master cylinder reservoir has 2 chambers with 2 sets of electrical contacts. Loss of brake fluid in either reservoir will light the warning light on the dash.

Since disc brakes are used at all four wheels, no adjustments are necessary. Disc brakes are inherently self-adjusting. The only adjustment possible is to the handbrake, which is covered at the end of this section.

Master Cylinder

The dual master cylinder has a safety feature which the single unit lacks—if a leak develops in one brake circuit (rear wheels, for example), the other circuit will still operate.

Failure of one system is immediately obvious—the pedal travel increases appreciably and a warning light is activated. When the fluid falls below a certain level, a switch activates the circuit.

❊❊ CAUTION

This design was not intended to allow driving the car for any distance with, in effect, a two-wheel brake system. If one brake circuit fails, braking action is correspondingly lower. Front circuit failure is the more serious, however, since the front brakes contribute up to 75% of the braking force required to stop the car.

REMOVAL & INSTALLATION

1. To remove the master cylinder, use a tool such as a turkey baster to remove the brake fluid from the reservoir.
2. Disconnect the switch connectors using a small screwdriver. Disconnect the brake lines at the master cylinder. Plug the ends with bleed screw caps or the equivalent.
3. Unbolt the master cylinder from the power brake unit and re-

To remove the brake master cylinder, use a turkey baster or similar implement to remove the fluid . . .

. . . and place the old brake fluid into a suitable container

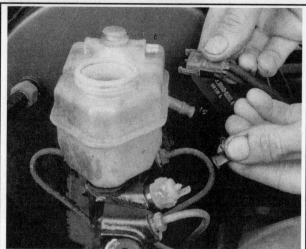

Disengage any electrical connections from the master cylinder

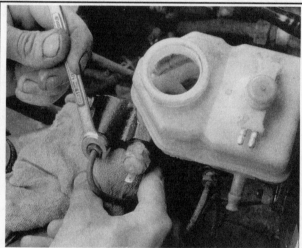

Using a rag to catch any spilled fluid and a flare nut wrench, disengage the fluid lines

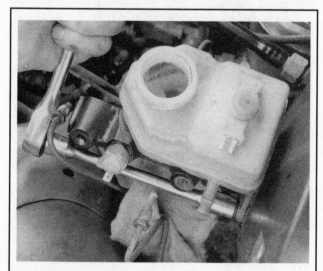

Loosen the master cylinder-to-brake booster nuts . . .

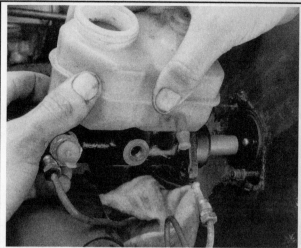

. . . then remove the master cylinder from the engine compartment

move. Be careful you do not lose the O-ring in the flange groove of the master cylinder.

4. Installation is the reverse of removal. Be sure to replace the O-ring between the master cylinder and the power brake unit, since this must be absolutely tight. Torque the nuts to 12–15 ft. lbs. Be sure that both chambers are completely filled with brake fluid and bleed the brakes.

✳✳ WARNING

Clean, high quality brake fluid is essential to the safe and proper operation of the brake system. You should always buy the highest quality brake fluid that is available. If the brake fluid becomes contaminated, drain and flush the system, then refill the master cylinder with new fluid. Never re-use any brake fluid. Any brake fluid that is removed from the system should be discarded.

OVERHAUL

♦ See Figures 2 and 3

1. To disassemble pull the reservoir out of the top of the cylinder.
2. Remove the screw cap, strainer, and splash shield.
3. Unscrew the cover caps and take out the inserts and O-rings.
4. Push the piston inward slightly and remove the stop screws.
5. Remove the piston stop-ring in the same manner, then pull out the piston and other components.
6. The spring must be unscrewed from the piston.
7. Clean all parts in clean brake fluid.
8. Check the housing bore for score marks and rust. Do not hone the cylinder bore. If slight rust marks do not come out with crocus cloth, replace the housing.
9. Assembly is the reverse of disassembly. Before installing the pistons, coat the sleeves of both pistons with brake fluid.

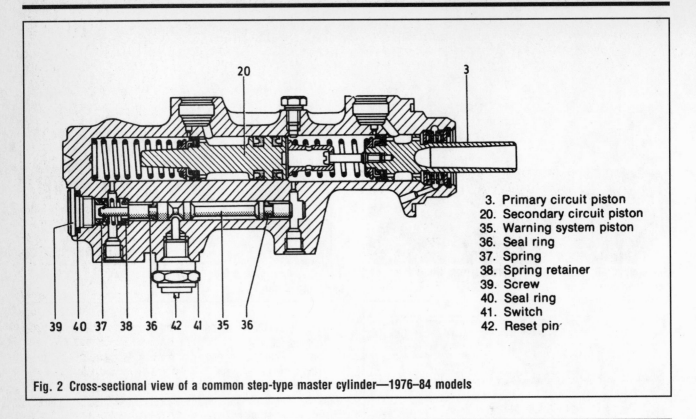

3. Primary circuit piston
20. Secondary circuit piston
35. Warning system piston
36. Seal ring
37. Spring
38. Spring retainer
39. Screw
40. Seal ring
41. Switch
42. Reset pin

Fig. 2 Cross-sectional view of a common step-type master cylinder—1976–84 models

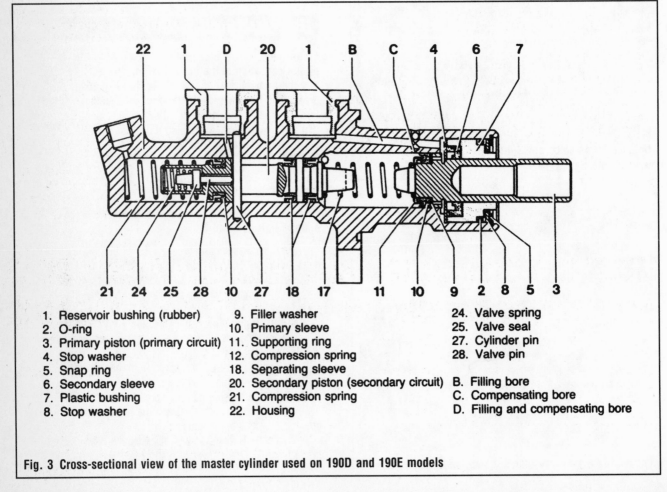

1. Reservoir bushing (rubber)
2. O-ring
3. Primary piston (primary circuit)
4. Stop washer
5. Snap ring
6. Secondary sleeve
7. Plastic bushing
8. Stop washer
9. Filler washer
10. Primary sleeve
11. Supporting ring
12. Compression spring
18. Separating sleeve
20. Secondary piston (secondary circuit)
21. Compression spring
22. Housing
24. Valve spring
25. Valve seal
27. Cylinder pin
28. Valve pin

B. Filling bore
C. Compensating bore
D. Filling and compensating bore

Fig. 3 Cross-sectional view of the master cylinder used on 190D and 190E models

➡Do not force the pistons into the housings. A special tool is available to install the pistons, but if it is not available, install the pistons very carefully with a slight twisting motion. The special assembly tools can be fabricated in the shop from light metal alloy, according to the dimensions given.

BRAKE BLEEDING

1. Cap 2. Bleeder screw

To bleed the brake system, first remove the bleeder screw cap (if equipped)

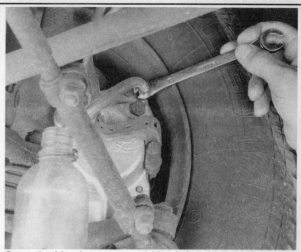

Open the bleeder screw and bleed the old fluid through a hose into a container partially filled with clean fluid

Always bleed the brakes after performing any service, or if the pedal seems spongy (soft). The location of the bleed screws can be seen by consulting the illustrations throughout this section. Prior to bleeding each wheel, connect a hose to the bleed screw and insert the hose into a jar of clean brake fluid.

➡On dual master cylinders, bleed only the circuit that has been opened. If both circuits have been opened, first bleed the circuit connected to the pushrod bore starting with the wheel farthest from the master cylinder, then bleed the other circuit.

1. First have an assistant pump the brakes and hold the pedal.
2. Then, starting at the point farthest from the master cylinder, slightly open the bleed screw.
3. When the pedal hits the floor, close the bleed screw before allowing the pedal to return (to prevent air from being sucked into the system).
4. Continue this procedure until no more air bubbles exit from the bleed screw hole, then go to the next wheel. Fluid, which has been bled from the system, is filled with microscopic air bubbles after the bleeding process is completed, therefore it should be discarded.

FRONT DISC BRAKES

Brake Pads

REMOVAL & INSTALLATION

Fixed Caliper
♦ See Figure 4

➡These procedures apply to front or rear brake pads on all models, but the 190D, 190E, 300SD, 380SE, 380SEC, 380SEL, 500SEC and 500SEL which utilize floating calipers on the front wheels.

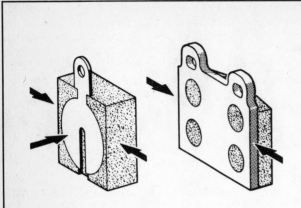

Fig. 4 Apply an anti-squeal compound or heat resistant lubricant to the brake pad backing plates, where indicated by the arrows

1. Remove the cover plate. The cover plate is only installed on front brakes of cars with solid brake discs (not ventilated) and 57mm calipers.

2. On models with the brake pad lining wear indicator, pull the cable sensors from the plug connections at the inside edge of the caliper.

Typical front disc brake system

1. Brake pad   3. Caliper
2. Wear indicator electrical connection

To remove the brake pads, first disengage the brake pad lining wear indicator's electrical connector

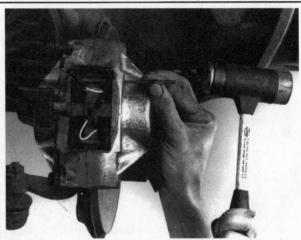

Use a punch to drive out the retaining pin from the caliper . . .

. . . and remove the pin from the rear of the caliper

Remove the cross spring from the caliper

Pull the brake pads from the caliper and check the lining for excessive wear or damage

3. Remove the sensors from the brake lining or backing plate.

➡**If the contact pin insulation is worn, the clip sensor should be replaced.**

4. On models with Teves (ATE) brake calipers, use a punch to knock the retaining pins out of the caliper. Remove the cross-spring.

5. On models with the Bendix (BX) caliper, remove the locking eyes, retaining pins and pad retaining springs.

6. On models with Girling calipers (usually only at rear axle), remove the locking eyes, the retaining pins and the pad retaining plates.

7. Pull the brake shoes out of the caliper. Mercedes-Benz recommends a special tool, an impact puller for this, but you can carefully grab the pad backing plate ears with pliers or a piece of bent welding rod and wiggle them out. It's best to leave one pad in the caliper always.

8. Use a small brush to clean the pad guides on the inside of

the brake caliper. Check the dust boots for cracks or damage. If necessary, remove and overhaul the caliper.

9. When the pads are removed, the pistons will move forward slightly, due to hydraulic pressure in the system. To install the pads, the pistons must be pushed back slightly. Mercedes-Benz recommends a special tool to do this, but a flat piece of hardwood will do if used carefully. Other tools will increase the chances of damaging the piston or dust boots.

➡**It should be relatively easy to push the pistons back.**

10. Check the thickness of the brake disc. Refer to the brake specifications for tolerances.

11. Check the brake discs for scoring or cracks. Score marks up to 0.02 in. deep can be accepted as normal scoring.

12. Clean the air passages of ventilated discs with a thin piece of wire. Blow out all loose dirt. Do not clean with solvent unless the disc is removed from the car.

13. Clean the rain groove in the backing plate and measure the thickness of the lining. See the Brake Specifications for minimum lining thickness.

To install:

14. Apply a heat resistant, long-term lubricant to the backing plate as shown. Install the brake pad.

15. Depending on the type of caliper, install the cross-spring, retaining plate, retaining pins and locking eyes.

16. On cars with a brake pad wear indicator, connect the sensors into the brake lining and the cable to the plug connection.

17. If equipped, install the cover plate.

18. On vehicles with a pressure differential warning system (1976 and 1977), the warning indicator may light when pads are replaced. To extinguish the light, push the reset pin on the switch after replacing the lining. The switch is located on the outboard side of the master cylinder.

Floating Caliper

➡**This procedure applies only to the front brake pads on the 190D, 190E, 300SD, 380SE, 380SEC, 380SEL, 500SEC and 500SEL.**

1. Use a small prybar to lift the two holding lugs on the sides of the plug connection (on the caliper) and then open the cover.

2. Disconnect the clip sensor cable from the plug. Do not pull on the cable.

3. Hold the sliding caliper pin and unscrew the upper hex screw.

4. Swing the cylinder housing (top of the caliper assembly) out and down. Remove the brake pads.

5. Disconnect the clip sensor from the brake pad backing plate.

6. To install, follow Steps 8–14 of the "Fixed Caliper Removal and Installation" procedure.

➡**When inserting the brake pads, the spring clamp must be parallel to the upper edge of the brake pad.**

7. Connect the clip sensor to the inner pad.

8. Swing the cylinder housing up into position and tighten the sliding bolt to 25 ft. lbs. (35 Nm) using a new self-locking nut.

Brake Caliper

REMOVAL & INSTALLATION

Fixed Caliper

◆ **See Figures 5 and 6**

1. Drain brake fluid from the front brake circuit through an open bleeder screw.

2. Disconnect the brake hose from the brake line (or, on some models, disconnect the brake line from the caliper).

3. Immediately plug the lines and openings to prevent loss of fluid.

4. On models where the brake line does not connect directly to the caliper, remove the hose from the caliper.

5. Remove the brake hose from the bracket.

6. Plug the connection at the brake caliper.

7. Unlock the lockwasher and remove the hex mounting bolts.

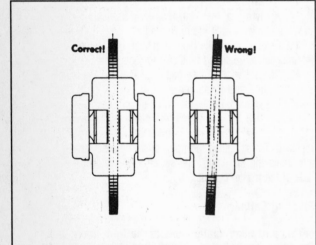

Fig. 5 Uneven brake pad wear will occur if the caliper and rotor are misaligned on fixed caliper systems

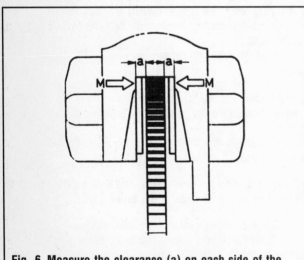

Fig. 6 Measure the clearance (a) on each side of the rotor at point M on fixed caliper systems

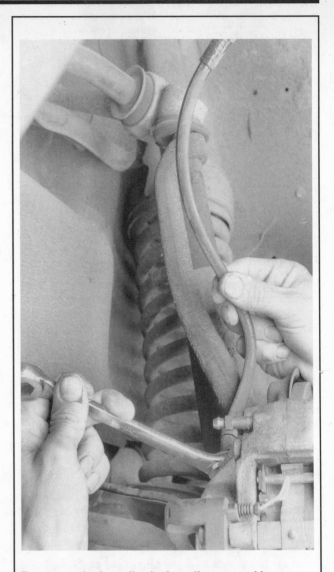

To remove the front disc brake caliper assembly, use a flare nut wrench to disconnect the brake hose

Loosen the brake caliper mounting bolts . . .

. . . and remove the caliper assembly from the rotor

✳✳ WARNING

The caliper mounting bolts should not be removed unless the calipers are at approximately room temperature.

8. Remove the calipers from the steering knuckle. As the caliper is removed, take note of any shim that may be installed and tape these (if any) in their original positions.

To install:

9. Use a new lockplate and attach the brake caliper to the steering knuckle. The proper torque for the mounting bolts is 82 ft. lbs.

It is extremely important that the brake disc be parallel to the caliper. Using a feeler gauge, measure the clearance at the top and bottom of the caliper (between disc and caliper) and on both sides of the disc. The clearance should not vary more than 0.15 mm. If the clearance varies, position the brake caliper by adding or subtracting shims as required. This procedure only applies to models equipped with shims, usually on the rear brake calipers.

10. Insert the brake hose into the bracket, making sure that the grommet is not damaged, or connect the brake line to the calipers. If applicable, connect the brake hose to the brake line. Make sure that the hose is not twisted.

11. On some models a locking disc is attached to the brake line bracket. Install the brake hose into the disc so that the disc or hose does not bind.

12. Turn the steering lock-to-lock to make sure that the brake hose or lines do not bind.

13. Fill the master cylinder and bleed the brake system.

14. Before driving the car, depress the brake pedal hard, several times, to seat the pads.

Floating Caliper

1. Drain the brake fluid from the front brake circuit through an open bleeder screw.

2. Disconnect the brake hose from the brake line and plug each end; a golf tee usually works well for this purpose.

3. Use a small prybar to lift the two holding lugs on the sides of the plug connection (on the caliper) and then open the cover.

4. Disconnect the brake pad wear indicator and the brake hose

from the cylinder housing. Plug the open holes in the end of the brake hose and cylinder housing.

5. Unbolt the brake carrier from the steering knuckle and remove the caliper assembly.

6. On installation, use new mounting bolts and tighten them to 83 ft. lbs. (115 Nm).

7. Installation of the remaining components is in the reverse order of removal.

8. Bleed the brake system.

Caliper Piston Seal

REMOVAL & INSTALLATION

◆ **See Figure 7**

✳✳ WARNING

Do not unbolt the two caliper halves for any reason. Remove the brake caliper for easier service.

1. Remove the friction pads, brake line, and dust cap, then pry the clamp ring from the housing.

2. Using a rubber-backed piece of flat steel, hold one piston in place while blowing the other one out with compressed air (7–8 psi).

3. Remove the piston seals from the cylinder bores and examine the bores. Scored bores necessitate replacement of the entire caliper, since the inner surface is chrome plated and cannot be honed.

4. Clean the bores with crocus cloth only, never use emery paper.

5. Install the new seals, coating them with brake fluid beforehand, then install the (front) piston so that the projection points downward. The rear caliper pistons must be installed with the projection facing downward.

➡ **If the projection is in any other position, the brakes may squeal badly.**

➡ **Floating calipers have only one piston.**

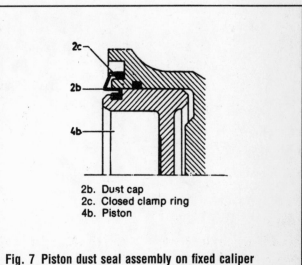

2b. Dust cap
2c. Closed clamp ring
4b. Piston

Fig. 7 Piston dust seal assembly on fixed caliper systems

6. Install the dust cap, clamp ring and heat shield.

7. The recess in the heat shield must fit the piston projection, but be above the shield level by about 0.004 in.

➡ **The heat shields differ for inner and outer pistons.**

8. Install the friction pads and the caliper assembly, then bleed the brakes.

Brake Disc (Rotor)

REMOVAL & INSTALLATION

1. Removal for the various types is similar.

2. On all models, remove the brake caliper. On 1974–76 230, 240D, 300D, 280 and 280C models and on 380SL, SLC, 450SL and SLC models, the hub and disc can be removed by prying off the dust cap, removing the socket screw and clamp nut, and pull-

. . . then remove the clamp nut from the spindle

To remove the front disc brake rotor, use a pair of channel lock pliers to pull off the dust cap

Remove the outer wheel bearing from the rotor hub

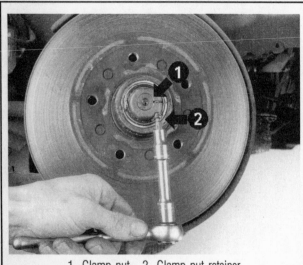

1. Clamp nut   2. Clamp nut retainer

Loosen the clamp nut retainer . . .

Remove the front brake rotor from the spindle

ing off the wheel hub. Fasten the hub in a vise or holding fixture (be careful not to distort the housing), matchmark the disc and hub, then unbolt the brake disc.

3. On all other models the disc can be unbolted from the hub.

4. Inspect the disc for burning (blue color), cracks and scoring. The disc becomes scored slightly in normal service; therefore, replace it only if the depth of individual scores exceeds 0.020 in.

5. To ensure proper alignment, clean the hub and disc with emery paper to remove all rust and/or burrs, then bolt the disc to the hub.

6. It is a wise precaution to use new lockwashers under the bolts.

7. Install the hub and disc, then check the disc for runout (wobble), using a dial indicator as illustrated.

8. If runout is excessive, it sometimes helps to remove the disc and reseat it on the hub. Install the caliper assembly and bleed the brakes.

➡ **If new brake discs are being installed, remove the anti-corrosion paint before installing it.**

Wheel Bearings

REMOVAL & INSTALLATION

◆ **See Figures 8, 9, 10 and 11**

If the wheel bearing play is being checked for correct setting only, it is not necessary to remove the caliper. It is only necessary to remove the brake pads.

1. Remove the brake caliper.

2. Pull the cap from the hub with a pair of channel-lock pliers. Remove the radio suppression spring, if equipped.

3. Loosen the socket screw of the clamp nut on the wheel spindle. Remove the clamp nut and washer.

4. Remove the front wheel hub and brake disc.

5. Remove the inner race with the roller cage of the outer bearing.

6. Using a brass or aluminum drift, carefully tap the outer race of the inner bearing until it can be removed with the inner race, bearing cage, and seal.

7. In the same manner, tap the outer race of the bearing out of the hub.

8. Separate the front hub from the brake disc.

9. To assemble, press the outer races into the front wheel hub.

10. Pack the bearing cage with bearing grease and insert the inner race with the bearing into the wheel hub.

11. Coat the sealing ring with sealant and press it into the hub.

12. Pack the front wheel hub with 45–55 grams of wheel bearing grease. The races of the tapered bearing should be well packed, also apply grease to the front faces of the rollers. Pack the front bearings with the specified amount of grease. Too much grease will cause overheating of the lubricant and it may lose its lubricity. Too little grease will not lubricate properly.

13. Coat the contact surface of the sealing ring on the wheel spindle with Molykote® paste.

14. Press the wheel hub onto the wheel spindle.

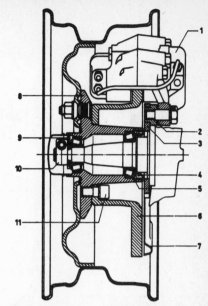

1. Brake caliper
2. Shim
3. Caliper bracket
4. Seal
5. Puller ring
6. Brake disc
7. Cover plate
8. Wheel hub
9. Washer
10. Clamp nut
11. Screw and lockwasher

Fig. 8 Cross-sectional view of the wheel bearing assembly—1974–76 230, 240D, 280, 280C and 300D models

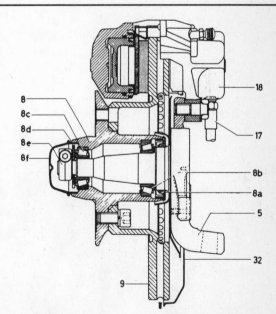

5. Steering knuckle
8. Wheel hub
8a. Radial sealing ring
8b. Tapered roller bearing, outside
8c. Tapered roller bearing, inside
8d. Washer
8e. Clamping nut
8 . Wheel cap
9. Brake disc
17. Brake hose
18. Brake caliper
32. Cover plate

Fig. 9 Cross-sectional view of the wheel bearing assembly—380SL, 380SLC, 450SL and 450SLC models

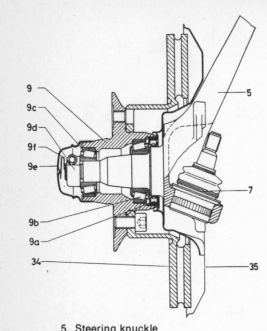

5. Steering knuckle
7. Supporting joint
9. Front wheel hub
9a. Radial sealing ring
9b. Tapered roller bearing, inside
9c. Tapered roller bearing, outside
9d. Clamping nut
9e. Wheel cap
9f . Contact spring
34. Brake disc
35. Cover plate

Fig. 10 Cross-sectional view of the wheel bearing assembly—230, 240D, 280, 280C, 280CE, 280E, 280S, 280SE, 300D, 300CD, 300SD, 300TD, 300SE, 300SEC, 380SEL, 450SE, 450SEL, 500SEC, 500SEL and 6.9 models

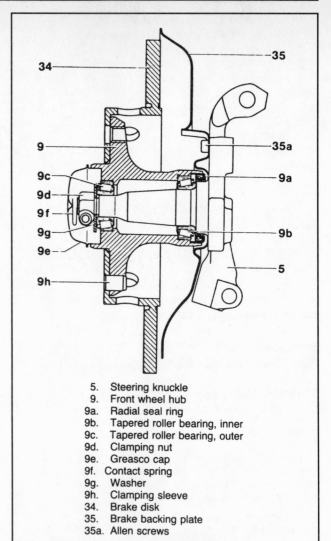

5. Steering knuckle
9. Front wheel hub
9a. Radial seal ring
9b. Tapered roller bearing, inner
9c. Tapered roller bearing, outer
9d. Clamping nut
9e. Greasco cap
9f. Contact spring
9g. Washer
9h. Clamping sleeve
34. Brake disk
35. Brake backing plate
35a. Allen screws

Fig. 11 Cross-sectional view of the wheel bearing assembly—190D and 190E models

To remove the inner bearing seal, use a seal removal tool to pry it out

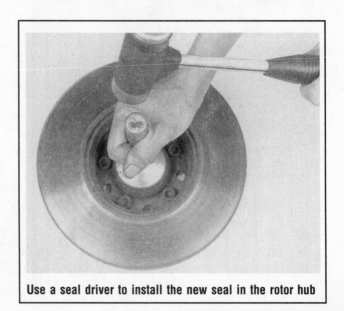

Use a seal driver to install the new seal in the rotor hub

15. Install the inner race and cage of the outer bearing.
16. Install the steel washer and the clamp nut.

ADJUSTMENT

1. Tighten the clamp nut until the hub can just be turned.
2. Slacken the clamp nut and seat the bearings on the spindle by rapping the spindle sharply with a hammer.
3. Attach a dial indicator, with the pointer indexed, onto the wheel hub.

4. Check the end-play of the hub by pushing and pulling on the flange. The end-play should be approximately 0.0004–0.0008 in.
5. Make an additional check by rotating the washer between the inner race of the outer bearing and the clamp nut. It should be able to be turned by hand.
6. Check the position of the suppressor pin in the wheel spindle and the contact spring in the dust cap.
7. Pack the dust cap with 20–25 grams of wheel bearing grease and install the cap.
8. Install the brake caliper and bleed the brakes.

REAR DISC BRAKES

✳✳ CAUTION

Brake pads may contain asbestos, which has been determined to be a cancer causing agent. Wear an approved filter mask or respirator whenever working around brakes, to avoid inhaling dust from any brake surface. Never clean brake components with compressed air! instead, use a commercially available brake cleaning fluid.

Brake Pads

REMOVAL & INSTALLATION

➡Floating calipers are used only on the front brakes of certain models. All models use fixed calipers on the rear brakes.

The procedure for removing the rear disc brake pads is the same as for front disc brake pads. Use the instructions given under "Front Disc Brake Pad Removal and Installation," with the accompanying illustrations.

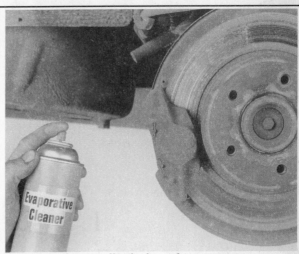
To remove the rear disc brake pads, spray an evaporative cleaner on the parts before disassembly

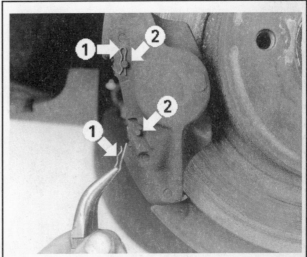
1. Locking eye   2. Retaining pin

Remove the locking eyes from the end of the retaining pins . . .

Typical rear disc brake system

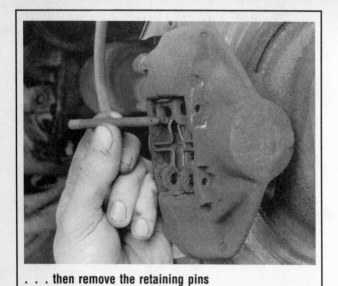

. . . then remove the retaining pins

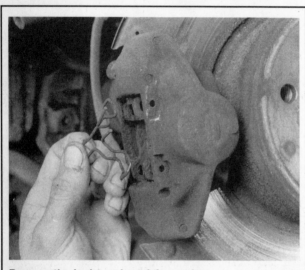

Remove the brake pad retaining spring

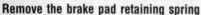

Pull the brake pads from the caliper and inspect them for wear or damage

Brake Caliper

REMOVAL & INSTALLATION

➤**Floating calipers are used only on the front brakes of certain models. All models use fixed calipers on the rear brakes.**

Use the procedure given under "Front Brake Caliper Removal and Installation." Some rear brake calipers have no disc run-out compensating feature. These calipers can only be installed on vehicles where the rear axle shaft is supported on grooved ball bearings. Calipers with a compensating feature may be installed on axles with grooved ball bearings or self-aligning bearings.

To remove the rear brake caliper, pull it off the rotor after loosening the caliper mounting bolts

After removing the caliper, support it with a piece of mechanic's wire. Dont let it hang by the hose

OVERHAUL

➡**Floating calipers are used only on the front brakes of certain models. All models use fixed calipers on the rear brakes.**

Rear disc brake caliper overhaul procedures are the same as those given for front disc brake caliper overhaul.

Brake Disc (Rotor)

REMOVAL & INSTALLATION

1. Remove the brake caliper.
2. Remove the brake disc from the rear axle shaft flange. Jammed brake discs can be loosened from the axle shaft flanges by light taps with a plastic hammer. Be sure that the parking brake is fully released.
3. Installation is the reverse of removal.
4. Inspection procedures are the same as those for front brake discs.

Lift the rotor from the rear axle to remove it from the vehicle

PARKING BRAKE

Front Cable

REMOVAL & INSTALLATION

190D and 190E Models

1. Disconnect the return spring at the cable control compensator.
2. Unbolt the brake cable from the intermediate lever and pull the cable away.
3. Remove the parking brake lever.
4. Loosen the brake cable at the lever and then pull it out toward the rear, through the floor.
5. Installation is in the reverse order of removal.

230, 240D, 280, 280C, 280CE, 300D, 300CD and 300TD Models

1. Remove the spring from the equalizer.
2. Back off the adjusting screw completely.
3. Detach the relay lever from the bracket on the frame and from the adjusting shackle.
4. Detach the cable from the relay lever by pulling the cotter pin out of the bolt.
5. Remove the clip from the cable guide. Remove the clips from the chassis.
6. Detach the brake cable from the parking brake link. Remove the clip from the cable guide and detach the brake cable from the parking brake.
7. Pull the cable downward from the chassis.
8. Installation is the reverse of removal.

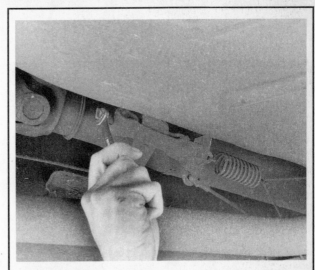

To remove the front parking brake cable, back off the adjusting screw completely

380SL, 380SLC, 450SL and 450SLC Models

1. Remove the exhaust system.
2. Disconnect the return spring.
3. Remove the bolts which attach the guide to the intermediate lever.
4. Remove the adjusting screw from the adjusting bracket.
5. Loosen the brake control cables on the intermediate lever and pull the cotter pin from the flange bolt. Remove the flange bolt.
6. Remove the spring clamp from the cable guide and remove the cable control from the bracket.

7. Remove the tunnel cover.

8. Disconnect the brake control from the parking brake and remove the spring clamp from the cable guide. Remove the cable control from the parking brake.

9. Remove the brake control cable out of the frame toward the rear.

10. Installation is the reverse of removal.

All Other Models

1. Remove the floor mat.
2. Remove the legroom cover (upper and lower).
3. Remove the air duct.
4. Disconnect the 4 rubber rings and lower and support the exhaust system.
5. Remove the shield above the exhaust pipes.
6. Disconnect the return spring from the bracket.
7. Back off the adjusting screw on the bracket.
8. Disconnect the intermediate lever from the adjusting bracket.
9. Loosen the brake cable controls on the intermediate lever while pulling the cotter pin from the flange bolt. Remove the flange bolt.
10. Remove the spring clip from the cable guide on the floor pan.
11. Disconnect the brake cable control from the parking brake bracket.
12. Remove the spring clip from the cable guide and remove the cable control from the parking brake.
13. Pull the cable away upward.
14. Installation is the reverse of removal. Adjust the parking brake.

Rear Cable

REMOVAL & INSTALLATION

230, 240D, 280, 280C, 280CE, 280E, 300D, 300CD and 300TD Models

1. Remove the parking brake shoes after removing the wheel.
2. Remove the screw from the wheel support and detach the brake cable.
3. Back off the adjusting screw from the adjusting shackle.
4. Remove the spring clips, detach the cable, and remove the equalizer.
5. Installation is the reverse of removal.

All Other Models

1. Remove the parking brake shoes.
2. Remove the bolt from the wheel carrier and remove the cable.
3. Remove the exhaust system. On some models the exhaust

system can be lowered and supported after removing the rubber rings. If equipped, remove the heat shield from above the exhaust pipes.

4. Disconnect the draw spring from the holder.
5. Detach the guide from the intermediate lever.
6. Remove the adjusting screw from the bracket.
7. Disconnect the intermediate lever on the bearing and remove it from the adjusting bracket.
8. Remove the holder, compensating lever, cable control plates, and intermediate lever from the tunnel.
9. Remove the spring clamps and disconnect the cable from the plate.
10. Installation is the reverse of removal.

ADJUSTMENT

1. If the floor pedal can be depressed more than two notches before actuating the brakes, adjust by jacking up the rear of the car, then removing one lug bolt and adjusting the star wheel with a screwdriver.
2. Move the screwdriver upward on the left (driver's) side, downward on the right (passenger's) side to tighten the shoes.
3. When the wheel is locked, back off about 2–4 clicks.
4. With this type system, the adjusting bolt on the cable relay lever only serves to equalize cable length; therefore, do not attempt to adjust the brakes by turning this bolt.

Brake Shoes

REMOVAL & INSTALLATION

1. Remove the brake caliper.
2. Remove the brake disc.
3. Disconnect the lower spring with brake pliers.
4. Turn the rear axle shaft flange so that one hole faces the spring. With brake spring removal pliers, disconnect and remove the spring from the cover plate.
5. Remove the spring on the other brake shoe in a similar manner.
6. Pull both brake shoes apart so that they can be removed past the rear axle shaft flange.
7. Disconnect the upper return spring from the brake shoes and remove the adjuster.
8. Force the pin out of the expanding lock and remove the expanding lock from the brake cable.
9. Remove the brake shoes.
10. Installation is the reverse of removal. Coat all bearing and sliding surfaces with Molykote® prior to installation. Attach the lower spring with the small eye to the brake shoes.
11. Adjust the parking brakes.

To gain access to the parking brake shoes, remove the rear brake rotor

1. Parking brake shoes

The parking brake shoes are located behind the axle flange

Brake Specifications

Year	Model	Lug Nut Torque (ft/lb)	Master Cylinder Bore (in.)	Front Brake Disc		Rear Brake Disc		Thickness Minimum Lining	
				Minimum Thickness (in.)	Maximum Run-Out (in.)	Minimum Thickness (in.)	Maximum Run-Out (in.)	Front ▲ (in.)	Rear ▲ (in.)
1974–75	230 240D 280 280C 300D	75	¹⁵⁄₁₆	①	0.0047 (max.)	0.33	0.0047 (max.)	0.08 ②	0.08 ②
1976–84	230 240D 280 280C 280CE 280E 300D 300CD 300TD	75	③	①	0.0047 (max.)	0.33	0.0047 (max.)	0.08 ②	0.08 ②
1974–84	280S 280SE 300SD 380SE 380SEC 380SEL 380SL 380SLC 450SE 450SEL 450SL 450SLC 500SEC 500SEL 6.9	75	③	④ ⑤	0.0047 (max.)	0.33	0.0047 (max.)	0.08 ②	0.08 ②
1984	190D 190E	75	⑥	0.35	0.0047 (max.)	0.30	0.0059 (max.)	0.08 ②	0.08 ②

▲ New thickness of brake lining and back-up plate—0.59 in.
New thickness of backing plate—0.20 in.
New thickness of brake lining—0.39 in.
—Not Applicable
NOTE: *Minimum lining thickness is as recommended by the manufacturer. Due to variations in state inspection regulations, the minimum allowable thickness may be different than recommended by the manufacturer.*
① Caliper w/57 mm piston diameter: 0.44 in.
Caliper w/60 mm piston diameter: 0.42 in.
② 1976 and later brake pads are equipped with electric pad wear indicators
③ Pushrod circuit: ¹⁵⁄₁₆ in.
Floating circuit: ¾ in.
④ Caliper w/57 mm piston diameter: 0.81 in.
Caliper w/60 mm piston diameter: 0.79 in.
⑤ March, 1980 and later: 0.76 in.
⑥ Pushrod circuit: ⅞ in.
Floating circuit: ¹¹⁄₁₆ in.

Troubleshooting the Brake System

Problem	Cause	Solution
Low brake pedal (excessive pedal travel required for braking action.)	• Excessive clearance between rear linings and drums caused by inoperative automatic adjusters	• Make 10 to 15 alternate forward and reverse brake stops to adjust brakes. If brake pedal does not come up, repair or replace adjuster parts as necessary.
	• Worn rear brakelining	• Inspect and replace lining if worn beyond minimum thickness specification
	• Bent, distorted brakeshoes, front or rear	• Replace brakeshoes in axle sets
	• Air in hydraulic system	• Remove air from system. Refer to Brake Bleeding.
Low brake pedal (pedal may go to floor with steady pressure applied.)	• Fluid leak in hydraulic system	• Fill master cylinder to fill line; have helper apply brakes and check calipers, wheel cylinders, differential valve tubes, hoses and fittings for leaks. Repair or replace as necessary.
	• Air in hydraulic system	• Remove air from system. Refer to Brake Bleeding.
	• Incorrect or non-recommended brake fluid (fluid evaporates at below normal temp).	• Flush hydraulic system with clean brake fluid. Refill with correct-type fluid.
	• Master cylinder piston seals worn, or master cylinder bore is scored, worn or corroded	• Repair or replace master cylinder
Low brake pedal (pedal goes to floor on first application—o.k. on subsequent applications.)	• Disc brake pads sticking on abutment surfaces of anchor plate. Caused by a build-up of dirt, rust, or corrosion on abutment surfaces	• Clean abutment surfaces
Fading brake pedal (pedal height decreases with steady pressure applied.)	• Fluid leak in hydraulic system	• Fill master cylinder reservoirs to fill mark, have helper apply brakes, check calipers, wheel cylinders, differential valve, tubes, hoses, and fittings for fluid leaks. Repair or replace parts as necessary.
	• Master cylinder piston seals worn, or master cylinder bore is scored, worn or corroded	• Repair or replace master cylinder
Decreasing brake pedal travel (pedal travel required for braking action decreases and may be accompanied by a hard pedal.)	• Caliper or wheel cylinder pistons sticking or seized	• Repair or replace the calipers, or wheel cylinders
	• Master cylinder compensator ports blocked (preventing fluid return to reservoirs) or pistons sticking or seized in master cylinder bore	• Repair or replace the master cylinder
	• Power brake unit binding internally	• Test unit according to the following procedure: (a) Shift transmission into neutral and start engine (b) Increase engine speed to 1500 rpm, close throttle and fully depress brake pedal (c) Slow release brake pedal and stop engine (d) Have helper remove vacuum check valve and hose from power unit. Observe for backward movement of brake pedal. (e) If the pedal moves backward, the power unit has an internal bind—replace power unit

Troubleshooting the Brake System (cont.)

Problem	Cause	Solution
Spongy brake pedal (pedal has abnormally soft, springy, spongy feel when depressed.)	• Air in hydraulic system • Brakeshoes bent or distorted • Brakelining not yet seated with drums and rotors • Rear drum brakes not properly adjusted	• Remove air from system. Refer to Brake Bleeding. • Replace brakeshoes • Burnish brakes • Adjust brakes
Hard brake pedal (excessive pedal pressure required to stop vehicle. May be accompanied by brake fade.)	• Loose or leaking power brake unit vacuum hose • Incorrect or poor quality brakelining • Bent, broken, distorted brakeshoes • Calipers binding or dragging on mounting pins. Rear brakeshoes dragging on support plate. • Caliper, wheel cylinder, or master cylinder pistons sticking or seized • Power brake unit vacuum check valve malfunction • Power brake unit has internal bind • Master cylinder compensator ports (at bottom of reservoirs) blocked by dirt, scale, rust, or have small burrs (blocked ports prevent fluid return to reservoirs). • Brake hoses, tubes, fittings clogged or restricted • Brake fluid contaminated with improper fluids (motor oil, transmission fluid, causing rubber components to swell and stick in bores • Low engine vacuum	• Tighten connections or replace leaking hose • Replace with lining in axle sets • Replace brakeshoes • Replace mounting pins and bushings. Clean rust or burrs from rear brake support plate ledges and lubricate ledges with molydisulfide grease. **NOTE:** If ledges are deeply grooved or scored, do not attempt to sand or grind them smooth—replace support plate. • Repair or replace parts as necessary • Test valve according to the following procedure: (a) Start engine, increase engine speed to 1500 rpm, close throttle and immediately stop engine (b) Wait at least 90 seconds then depress brake pedal (c) If brakes are not vacuum assisted for 2 or more applications, check valve is faulty • Test unit according to the following procedure: (a) With engine stopped, apply brakes several times to exhaust all vacuum in system (b) Shift transmission into neutral, depress brake pedal and start engine (c) If pedal height decreases with foot pressure and less pressure is required to hold pedal in applied position, power unit vacuum system is operating normally. Test power unit. If power unit exhibits a bind condition, replace the power unit. • Repair or replace master cylinder **CAUTION:** Do not attempt to clean blocked ports with wire, pencils, or similar implements. Use compressed air only. • Use compressed air to check or unclog parts. Replace any damaged parts. • Replace all rubber components, combination valve and hoses. Flush entire brake system with DOT 3 brake fluid or equivalent. • Adjust or repair engine

Troubleshooting the Brake System (cont.)

Problem	Cause	Solution
Grabbing brakes (severe reaction to brake pedal pressure.)	• Brakelining(s) contaminated by grease or brake fluid	• Determine and correct cause of contamination and replace brakeshoes in axle sets
	• Parking brake cables incorrectly adjusted or seized	• Adjust cables. Replace seized cables.
	• Incorrect brakelining or lining loose on brakeshoes	• Replace brakeshoes in axle sets
	• Caliper anchor plate bolts loose	• Tighten bolts
	• Rear brakeshoes binding on support plate ledges	• Clean and lubricate ledges. Replace support plate(s) if ledges are deeply grooved. Do not attempt to smooth ledges by grinding.
	• Incorrect or missing power brake reaction disc	• Install correct disc
	• Rear brake support plates loose	• Tighten mounting bolts
Dragging brakes (slow or incomplete release of brakes)	• Brake pedal binding at pivot	• Loosen and lubricate
	• Power brake unit has internal bind	• Inspect for internal bind. Replace unit if internal bind exists.
	• Parking brake cables incorrrectly adjusted or seized	• Adjust cables. Replace seized cables.
	• Rear brakeshoe return springs weak or broken	• Replace return springs. Replace brakeshoe if necessary in axle sets.
	• Automatic adjusters malfunctioning	• Repair or replace adjuster parts as required
	• Caliper, wheel cylinder or master cylinder pistons sticking or seized	• Repair or replace parts as necessary
	• Master cylinder compensating ports blocked (fluid does not return to reservoirs).	• Use compressed air to clear ports. Do not use wire, pencils, or similar objects to open blocked ports.
Vehicle moves to one side when brakes are applied	• Incorrect front tire pressure	• Inflate to recommended cold (reduced load) inflation pressure
	• Worn or damaged wheel bearings	• Replace worn or damaged bearings
	• Brakelining on one side contaminated	• Determine and correct cause of contamination and replace brakelining in axle sets
	• Brakeshoes on one side bent, distorted, or lining loose on shoe	• Replace brakeshoes in axle sets
	• Support plate bent or loose on one side	• Tighten or replace support plate
	• Brakelining not yet seated with drums or rotors	• Burnish brakelining
	• Caliper anchor plate loose on one side	• Tighten anchor plate bolts
	• Caliper piston sticking or seized	• Repair or replace caliper
	• Brakelinings water soaked	• Drive vehicle with brakes lightly applied to dry linings
	• Loose suspension component attaching or mounting bolts	• Tighten suspension bolts. Replace worn suspension components.
	• Brake combination valve failure	• Replace combination valve
Chatter or shudder when brakes are applied (pedal pulsation and roughness may also occur.)	• Brakeshoes distorted, bent, contaminated, or worn	• Replace brakeshoes in axle sets
	• Caliper anchor plate or support plate loose	• Tighten mounting bolts
	• Excessive thickness variation of rotor(s)	• Refinish or replace rotors in axle sets

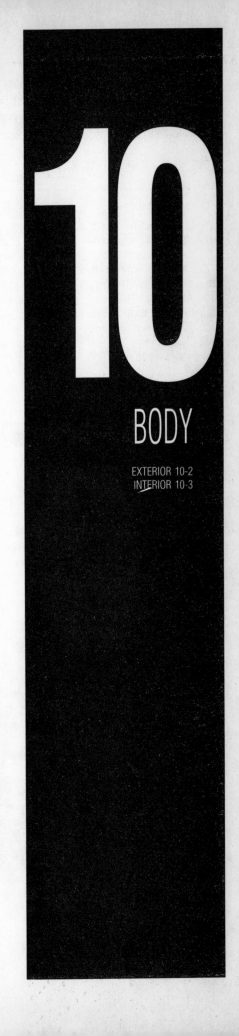

10

BODY

EXTERIOR

Doors

REMOVAL & INSTALLATION

When removing the door, it is easier to remove the hinges with the door because the door side hinges are very accessible.

1. Disconnect the negative battery cable. Mark the position of the door hinges-to-body to make the installation easier.

2. If equipped with power operated components, remove the trim panel and detach the inner panel water deflector enough to disconnect the wiring harness from the components. Separate and remove the rubber conduit and the wiring harness from the door.

3. Using an assistant (to support the door), remove the upper and lower hinge-to-body bolts. Remove the door from the vehicle.

4. To install, reverse the removal procedures.

Hood

REMOVAL & INSTALLATION

1. Disconnect the negative battery cable. Using a scratch awl, scribe the hinge onto the hood. If equipped with a hood light, disconnect the electrical connector.

2. Using an assistant to support the hood, remove the hinge-to-hood bolts. Remove the hood.

3. To install, reverse the removal procedures. Check the hood alignment with the hood latch.

To remove the hood, first matchmark the position of the hinges

Loosen the hinge bolts and remove the hood

ALIGNMENT

➡**When aligning the hood and the latch, align the hood (first), then the latch (second).**

Hood

The hood hinge-to-body mount is slotted to provide forward and rearward movement. Adjust the hood so that it is flush with the body sheet metal.

1. Using a scratch awl, scribe the hinge outline onto the hood.

2. Loosen the appropriate screws and shift the hood into proper alignment with the vehicle's sheet metal.

3. After adjustment, tighten the appropriate retainers.

Striker

The striker, on the hood, adjusts laterally to align with the hood latch assembly.

Trunk Lid

REMOVAL & INSTALLATION

1. Disconnect the negative battery cable. Open the trunk lid and place protective coverings over the rear fenders to protect the paint from damage.

2. Mark the location of the hinge-to-trunk lid bolts and disconnect the electrical connections and wiring from the lid, if equipped.

3. Using an assistant to support the lid, remove the hinge-to-lid bolts and the lid from the vehicle.

To install:

4. Reverse the removal procedures. Adjust the position of the trunk lid to the body.

Bumpers

REMOVAL & INSTALLATION

Front

1. Disconnect the negative battery cable. Raise and support the vehicle safely.
2. Properly support the bumper.
3. Remove the bolts from the frame and remove the bumper.
4. Installation is the reverse of the removal procedure.

Rear

1. Disconnect the negative battery cable. Raise and support the vehicle safely.
2. Properly support the bumper.
3. Remove the bolts from the frame and remove the bumper.
4. Installation is the reverse of the removal procedure.

Grille

REMOVAL & INSTALLATION

1. Disconnect the negative battery cable. Open the hood.
2. Remove the sheet metal screws that retain the grille assembly to its mounting.

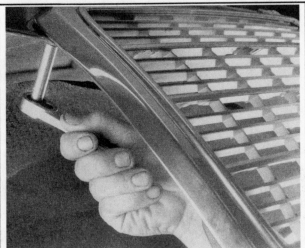

To remove the grille, first open the hood and loosen the retaining bolts

Remove the grille from the vehicle

3. Remove the grille assembly from the vehicle.
4. Installation is the reverse of the removal procedure.

Outside Mirrors

REMOVAL & INSTALLATION

1. Remove the door trim panel.
2. Remove the mirror base to door outer panel stud nuts and remove the mirror from the door.
3. Install the base gasket and reverse the above to install.

INTERIOR

Front Door Panels

REMOVAL & INSTALLATION

1. Disconnect the negative battery cable. Remove the door handles and the locking knob from the inside of the doors.

➡️**If equipped with door pull handles, remove the screws through the handle into the door inner panel.**

2. If equipped with a switch cover plate in the door armrest, remove the cover plate screws, then disconnect the switches and the cigar lighter, if equipped from the electrical harness.
3. If equipped with an integral armrest, remove the screws inserted through the pull cup into the armrest hanger support. If

1. Retaining screws   2. Trim piece

To remove the door panel, first unfasten the door lock trim piece retaining screws . . .

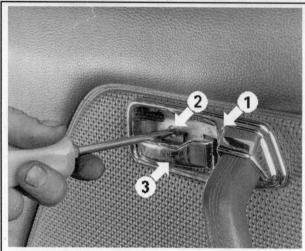

1. Trim piece   2. Retaining screw   3. Door handle

Loosen the door handle interior trim retaining screw

. . . and remove the trim piece

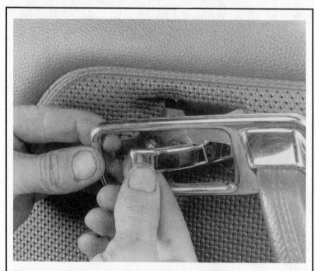

Remove the door handle interior trim piece

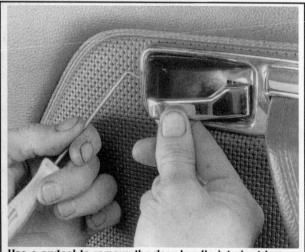

Use a prytool to remove the door handle interior trim piece to gain access to the retaining screw

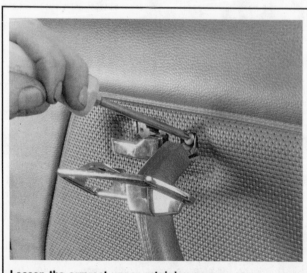

Loosen the armrest upper retaining screw . . .

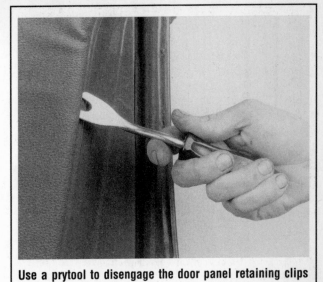

Use a prytool to disengage the door panel retaining clips

. . . then remove the lower retaining screws

Remove the armrest from the door panel

Unscrew the door lock button

After all the clips are disengaged, remove the door panel from the vehicle equipped with an armrest applied after the door trim installation, remove the armrest-to-inner panel screws.

4. Along the upper edge of the trim panel, remove the mounting screws. At the lower edge of the panel, insert a removal tool between the inner panel and the trim panel, then disengage the retaining clips from around the outer perimeter.

5. If equipped with an insulator pad glued to the door inner panel, remove the pad with a putty knife by separating it from the inner panel.

6. To install, reverse the removal procedures.

Rear Door Panels

REMOVAL AND INSTALLATION

1. If equipped with a switch cover plate in the door armrest, remove the cover plate screws, then disconnect the switch from the electrical harness.

➡**If equipped with door pull handles, remove the screws through the handle into the door inner panel.**

2. If equipped with an integral armrest, remove the screws inserted through the pull cup into the armrest hanger support. If equipped with an armrest applied after the door trim installation, remove the armrest-to-inner panel screws.

3. Use a prytool to unsnap the door panel retaining clips and remove the panel.

4. To install, reverse the service removal procedures.

GLOSSARY

AIR/FUEL RATIO: The ratio of air-to-gasoline by weight in the fuel mixture drawn into the engine.

AIR INJECTION: One method of reducing harmful exhaust emissions by injecting air into each of the exhaust ports of an engine. The fresh air entering the hot exhaust manifold causes any remaining fuel to be burned before it can exit the tailpipe.

ALTERNATOR: A device used for converting mechanical energy into electrical energy.

AMMETER: An instrument, calibrated in amperes, used to measure the flow of an electrical current in a circuit. Ammeters are always connected in series with the circuit being tested.

AMPERE: The rate of flow of electrical current present when one volt of electrical pressure is applied against one ohm of electrical resistance.

ANALOG COMPUTER: Any microprocessor that uses similar (analogous) electrical signals to make its calculations.

ARMATURE: A laminated, soft iron core wrapped by a wire that converts electrical energy to mechanical energy as in a motor or relay. When rotated in a magnetic field, it changes mechanical energy into electrical energy as in a generator.

ATMOSPHERIC PRESSURE: The pressure on the Earth's surface caused by the weight of the air in the atmosphere. At sea level, this pressure is 14.7 psi at 32°F (101 kPa at 0°C).

ATOMIZATION: The breaking down of a liquid into a fine mist that can be suspended in air.

AXIAL PLAY: Movement parallel to a shaft or bearing bore.

BACKFIRE: The sudden combustion of gases in the intake or exhaust system that results in a loud explosion.

BACKLASH: The clearance or play between two parts, such as meshed gears.

BACKPRESSURE: Restrictions in the exhaust system that slow the exit of exhaust gases from the combustion chamber.

BAKELITE: A heat resistant, plastic insulator material commonly used in printed circuit boards and transistorized components.

BALL BEARING: A bearing made up of hardened inner and outer races between which hardened steel balls roll.

BALLAST RESISTOR: A resistor in the primary ignition circuit that lowers voltage after the engine is started to reduce wear on ignition components.

BEARING: A friction reducing, supportive device usually located between a stationary part and a moving part.

BIMETAL TEMPERATURE SENSOR: Any sensor or switch made of two dissimilar types of metal that bend when heated or cooled due to the different expansion rates of the alloys. These types of sensors usually function as an on/off switch.

BLOWBY: Combustion gases, composed of water vapor and unburned fuel, that leak past the piston rings into the crankcase during normal engine operation. These gases are removed by the PCV system to prevent the buildup of harmful acids in the crankcase.

BRAKE PAD: A brake shoe and lining assembly used with disc brakes.

BRAKE SHOE: The backing for the brake lining. The term is, however, usually applied to the assembly of the brake backing and lining.

BUSHING: A liner, usually removable, for a bearing; an anti-friction liner used in place of a bearing.

CALIPER: A hydraulically activated device in a disc brake system, which is mounted straddling the brake rotor (disc). The caliper contains at least one piston and two brake pads. Hydraulic pressure on the piston(s) forces the pads against the rotor.

CAMSHAFT: A shaft in the engine on which are the lobes (cams) which operate the valves. The camshaft is driven by the crankshaft, via a belt, chain or gears, at one half the crankshaft speed.

CAPACITOR: A device which stores an electrical charge.

CARBON MONOXIDE (CO): A colorless, odorless gas given off as a normal byproduct of combustion. It is poisonous and extremely dangerous in confined areas, building up slowly to toxic levels without warning if adequate ventilation is not available.

CARBURETOR: A device, usually mounted on the intake manifold of an engine, which mixes the air and fuel in the proper proportion to allow even combustion.

CATALYTIC CONVERTER: A device installed in the exhaust system, like a muffler, that converts harmful byproducts of combustion into carbon dioxide and water vapor by means of a heat-producing chemical reaction.

CENTRIFUGAL ADVANCE: A mechanical method of advancing the spark timing by using flyweights in the distributor that react to centrifugal force generated by the distributor shaft rotation.

CHECK VALVE: Any one-way valve installed to permit the flow of air, fuel or vacuum in one direction only.

CHOKE: A device, usually a moveable valve, placed in the intake path of a carburetor to restrict the flow of air.

CIRCUIT: Any unbroken path through which an electrical current can flow. Also used to describe fuel flow in some instances.

CIRCUIT BREAKER: A switch which protects an electrical circuit from overload by opening the circuit when the current flow exceeds a predetermined level. Some circuit breakers must be reset manually, while most reset automatically.

COIL (IGNITION): A transformer in the ignition circuit which steps up the voltage provided to the spark plugs.

COMBINATION MANIFOLD: An assembly which includes both the intake and exhaust manifolds in one casting.

COMBINATION VALVE: A device used in some fuel systems that routes fuel vapors to a charcoal storage canister instead of venting them into the atmosphere. The valve relieves fuel tank pressure and allows fresh air into the tank as the fuel level drops to prevent a vapor lock situation.

COMPRESSION RATIO: The comparison of the total volume of the cylinder and combustion chamber with the piston at BDC and the piston at TDC.

CONDENSER: 1. An electrical device which acts to store an electrical charge, preventing voltage surges. 2. A radiator-like device in the air conditioning system in which refrigerant gas condenses into a liquid, giving off heat.

CONDUCTOR: Any material through which an electrical current can be transmitted easily.

CONTINUITY: Continuous or complete circuit. Can be checked with an ohmmeter.

COUNTERSHAFT: An intermediate shaft which is rotated by a mainshaft and transmits, in turn, that rotation to a working part.

CRANKCASE: The lower part of an engine in which the crankshaft and related parts operate.

CRANKSHAFT: The main driving shaft of an engine which receives reciprocating motion from the pistons and converts it to rotary motion.

CYLINDER: In an engine, the round hole in the engine block in which the piston(s) ride.

CYLINDER BLOCK: The main structural member of an engine in which is found the cylinders, crankshaft and other principal parts.

CYLINDER HEAD: The detachable portion of the engine, usually fastened to the top of the cylinder block and containing all or most of the combustion chambers. On overhead valve engines, it contains the valves and their operating parts. On overhead cam engines, it contains the camshaft as well.

DEAD CENTER: The extreme top or bottom of the piston stroke.

DETONATION: An unwanted explosion of the air/fuel mixture in the combustion chamber caused by excess heat and compression, advanced timing, or an overly lean mixture. Also referred to as "ping".

DIAPHRAGM: A thin, flexible wall separating two cavities, such as in a vacuum advance unit.

DIESELING: A condition in which hot spots in the combustion chamber cause the engine to run on after the key is turned off.

DIFFERENTIAL: A geared assembly which allows the transmission of motion between drive axles, giving one axle the ability to turn faster than the other.

DIODE: An electrical device that will allow current to flow in one direction only.

DISC BRAKE: A hydraulic braking assembly consisting of a brake disc, or rotor, mounted on an axle, and a caliper assembly containing, usually two brake pads which are activated by hydraulic pressure. The pads are forced against the sides of the disc, creating friction which slows the vehicle.

DISTRIBUTOR: A mechanically driven device on an engine which is responsible for electrically firing the spark plug at a predetermined point of the piston stroke.

DOWEL PIN: A pin, inserted in mating holes in two different parts allowing those parts to maintain a fixed relationship.

DRUM BRAKE: A braking system which consists of two brake shoes and one or two wheel cylinders, mounted on a fixed backing plate, and a brake drum, mounted on an axle, which revolves around the assembly.

DWELL: The rate, measured in degrees of shaft rotation, at which an electrical circuit cycles on and off.

ELECTRONIC CONTROL UNIT (ECU): Ignition module, module, amplifier or igniter. See Module for definition.

ELECTRONIC IGNITION: A system in which the timing and firing of the spark plugs is controlled by an electronic control unit, usually called a module. These systems have no points or condenser.

END-PLAY: The measured amount of axial movement in a shaft.

ENGINE: A device that converts heat into mechanical energy.

EXHAUST MANIFOLD: A set of cast passages or pipes which conduct exhaust gases from the engine.

FEELER GAUGE: A blade, usually metal, of precisely predetermined thickness, used to measure the clearance between two parts.

FIRING ORDER: The order in which combustion occurs in the cylinders of an engine. Also the order in which spark is distributed to the plugs by the distributor.

FLOODING: The presence of too much fuel in the intake manifold and combustion chamber which prevents the air/fuel mixture from firing, thereby causing a no-start situation.

FLYWHEEL: A disc shaped part bolted to the rear end of the crankshaft. Around the outer perimeter is affixed the ring gear. The starter drive engages the ring gear, turning the flywheel, which rotates the crankshaft, imparting the initial starting motion to the engine.

FOOT POUND (ft. lbs. or sometimes, ft.lb.): The amount of energy or work needed to raise an item weighing one pound, a distance of one foot.

FUSE: A protective device in a circuit which prevents circuit overload by breaking the circuit when a specific amperage is present. The device is constructed around a strip or wire of a lower amperage rating than the circuit it is designed to protect. When an amperage higher than that stamped on the fuse is present in the circuit, the strip or wire melts, opening the circuit.

GEAR RATIO: The ratio between the number of teeth on meshing gears.

GENERATOR: A device which converts mechanical energy into electrical energy.

HEAT RANGE: The measure of a spark plug's ability to dissipate heat from its firing end. The higher the heat range, the hotter the plug fires.

HUB: The center part of a wheel or gear.

HYDROCARBON (HC): Any chemical compound made up of hydrogen and carbon. A major pollutant formed by the engine as a byproduct of combustion.

HYDROMETER: An instrument used to measure the specific gravity of a solution.

INCH POUND (inch lbs.; sometimes in.lb. or in. lbs.): One twelfth of a foot pound.

INDUCTION: A means of transferring electrical energy in the form of a magnetic field. Principle used in the ignition coil to increase voltage.

INJECTOR: A device which receives metered fuel under relatively low pressure and is activated to inject the fuel into the engine under relatively high pressure at a predetermined time.

INPUT SHAFT: The shaft to which torque is applied, usually carrying the driving gear or gears.

INTAKE MANIFOLD: A casting of passages or pipes used to conduct air or a fuel/air mixture to the cylinders.

JOURNAL: The bearing surface within which a shaft operates.

KEY: A small block usually fitted in a notch between a shaft and a hub to prevent slippage of the two parts.

MANIFOLD: A casting of passages or set of pipes which connect the cylinders to an inlet or outlet source.

MANIFOLD VACUUM: Low pressure in an engine intake manifold formed just below the throttle plates. Manifold vacuum is highest at idle and drops under acceleration.

MASTER CYLINDER: The primary fluid pressurizing device in a hydraulic system. In automotive use, it is found in brake and hydraulic clutch systems and is pedal activated, either directly or, in a power brake system, through the power booster.

MODULE: Electronic control unit, amplifier or igniter of solid state or integrated design which controls the current flow in the ignition

primary circuit based on input from the pick-up coil. When the module opens the primary circuit, high secondary voltage is induced in the coil.

NEEDLE BEARING: A bearing which consists of a number (usually a large number) of long, thin rollers.

OHM: (Ω) The unit used to measure the resistance of conductor-to-electrical flow. One ohm is the amount of resistance that limits current flow to one ampere in a circuit with one volt of pressure.

OHMMETER: An instrument used for measuring the resistance, in ohms, in an electrical circuit.

OUTPUT SHAFT: The shaft which transmits torque from a device, such as a transmission.

OVERDRIVE: A gear assembly which produces more shaft revolutions than that transmitted to it.

OVERHEAD CAMSHAFT (OHC): An engine configuration in which the camshaft is mounted on top of the cylinder head and operates the valve either directly or by means of rocker arms.

OVERHEAD VALVE (OHV): An engine configuration in which all of the valves are located in the cylinder head and the camshaft is located in the cylinder block. The camshaft operates the valves via lifters and pushrods.

OXIDES OF NITROGEN (NOx): Chemical compounds of nitrogen produced as a byproduct of combustion. They combine with hydrocarbons to produce smog.

OXYGEN SENSOR: Used with the feedback system to sense the presence of oxygen in the exhaust gas and signal the computer which can reference the voltage signal to an air/fuel ratio.

PINION: The smaller of two meshing gears.

PISTON RING: An open-ended ring which fits into a groove on the outer diameter of the piston. Its chief function is to form a seal between the piston and cylinder wall. Most automotive pistons have three rings: two for compression sealing; one for oil sealing.

PRELOAD: A predetermined load placed on a bearing during assembly or by adjustment.

PRIMARY CIRCUIT: The low voltage side of the ignition system which consists of the ignition switch, ballast resistor or resistance wire, bypass, coil, electronic control unit and pick-up coil as well as the connecting wires and harnesses.

PRESS FIT: The mating of two parts under pressure, due to the inner diameter of one being smaller than the outer diameter of the other, or vice versa; an interference fit.

RACE: The surface on the inner or outer ring of a bearing on which the balls, needles or rollers move.

REGULATOR: A device which maintains the amperage and/or voltage levels of a circuit at predetermined values.

RELAY: A switch which automatically opens and/or closes a circuit.

RESISTANCE: The opposition to the flow of current through a circuit or electrical device, and is measured in ohms. Resistance is equal to the voltage divided by the amperage.

RESISTOR: A device, usually made of wire, which offers a preset amount of resistance in an electrical circuit.

RING GEAR: The name given to a ring-shaped gear attached to a differential case, or affixed to a flywheel or as part of a planetary gear set.

ROLLER BEARING: A bearing made up of hardened inner and outer races between which hardened steel rollers move.

ROTOR: 1. The disc-shaped part of a disc brake assembly, upon which the brake pads bear; also called, brake disc. 2. The device mounted atop the distributor shaft, which passes current to the distributor cap tower contacts.

SECONDARY CIRCUIT: The high voltage side of the ignition system, usually above 20,000 volts. The secondary includes the ignition coil, coil wire, distributor cap and rotor, spark plug wires and spark plugs.

SENDING UNIT: A mechanical, electrical, hydraulic or electromagnetic device which transmits information to a gauge.

SENSOR: Any device designed to measure engine operating conditions or ambient pressures and temperatures. Usually electronic in nature and designed to send a voltage signal to an on-board computer, some sensors may operate as a simple on/off switch or they may provide a variable voltage signal (like a potentiometer) as conditions or measured parameters change.

SHIM: Spacers of precise, predetermined thickness used between parts to establish a proper working relationship.

SLAVE CYLINDER: In automotive use, a device in the hydraulic clutch system which is activated by hydraulic force, disengaging the clutch.

SOLENOID: A coil used to produce a magnetic field, the effect of which is to produce work.

SPARK PLUG: A device screwed into the combustion chamber of a spark ignition engine. The basic construction is a conductive core inside of a ceramic insulator, mounted in an outer conductive base. An electrical charge from the spark plug wire travels along the conductive core and jumps a preset air gap to a grounding point or points at the end of the conductive base. The resultant spark ignites the fuel/air mixture in the combustion chamber.

SPLINES: Ridges machined or cast onto the outer diameter of a shaft or inner diameter of a bore to enable parts to mate without rotation.

TACHOMETER: A device used to measure the rotary speed of an engine, shaft, gear, etc., usually in rotations per minute.

THERMOSTAT: A valve, located in the cooling system of an engine, which is closed when cold and opens gradually in response to engine heating, controlling the temperature of the coolant and rate of coolant flow.

TOP DEAD CENTER (TDC): The point at which the piston reaches the top of its travel on the compression stroke.

TORQUE: The twisting force applied to an object.

TORQUE CONVERTER: A turbine used to transmit power from a driving member to a driven member via hydraulic action, providing changes in drive ratio and torque. In automotive use, it links the driveplate at the rear of the engine to the automatic transmission.

TRANSDUCER: A device used to change a force into an electrical signal.

TRANSISTOR: A semi-conductor component which can be actuated by a small voltage to perform an electrical switching function.

TUNE-UP: A regular maintenance function, usually associated with the replacement and adjustment of parts and components in the electrical and fuel systems of a vehicle for the purpose of attaining optimum performance.

TURBOCHARGER: An exhaust driven pump which compresses intake air and forces it into the combustion chambers at higher than atmospheric pressures. The increased air pressure allows more fuel to be burned and results in increased horsepower being produced.

VACUUM ADVANCE: A device which advances the ignition timing in response to increased engine vacuum.

VACUUM GAUGE: An instrument used to measure the presence of vacuum in a chamber.

VALVE: A device which control the pressure, direction of flow or rate of flow of a liquid or gas.

VALVE CLEARANCE: The measured gap between the end of the valve stem and the rocker arm, cam lobe or follower that activates the valve.

VISCOSITY: The rating of a liquid's internal resistance to flow.

VOLTMETER: An instrument used for measuring electrical force in units called volts. Voltmeters are always connected parallel with the circuit being tested.

WHEEL CYLINDER: Found in the automotive drum brake assembly, it is a device, actuated by hydraulic pressure, which, through internal pistons, pushes the brake shoes outward against the drums.

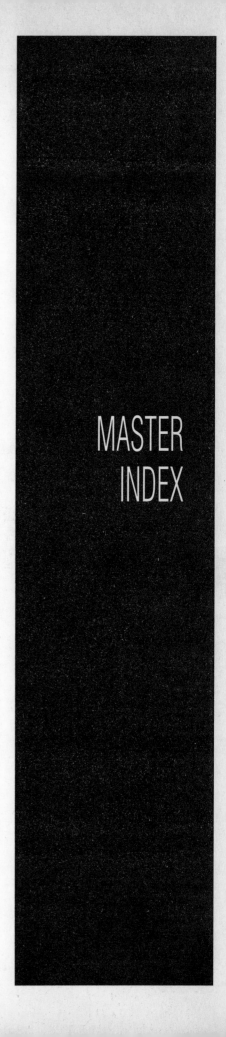

MASTER
INDEX